THE
PEOPLE'S
WAR

"The manner in which the American colonies declared themselves independent of the King of England, throughout the different provinces, on July 4, 1776."
—From The New, Comprehensive and Complete History of England *by Edward Barnard, London, ca. 1783.*

THE
PEOPLE'S
WAR

Original Voices of the American Revolution

Noel Rae

LYONS PRESS
Guilford, Connecticut

An imprint of Globe Pequot Presss

Lyons Press is an imprint of Globe Pequot Press.

All images courtesy of the Library of Congress.

Text design: Sheryl P. Kober
Layout artist: Justin Marciano
Project editor: Kristen Mellitt

Library of Congress Cataloging-in-Publication Data is available on file.

ISBN 978-0-7627-7070-0

Printed in the United States of America

10 9 8 7 6 5 4 3 2 1

Contents

Introduction

Late in 1780, while languishing fretfully in Amsterdam, where he hoped to raise a large loan that would help finance America's war for independence, now in its sixth year and going badly, John Adams addressed a series of letters to Holland's leading bankers, explaining his country and its cause and hoping to persuade them that such a loan could not fail to be an excellent investment since they would be backing a winner.

Basically, Adams claimed, America was unconquerable. "Such is the Nature of that Country and such the Character of the People, that if the English were to send ever so many Ships, and ever so many Troops, they never would subdue all the Americans." So true was this that any "Victories gained by the English will conquer themselves sooner than the Americans." Despite the war, the American population continued to grow at a rate that doubled it every eighteen years, so that there were now "seventy thousands of Fighting Men in America more than We had on the day that Hostilities were first commenced on the 19 of April, 1775." France and Spain were powerful allies, whose combined fleets and armies outmatched those of Great Britain. Americans were solidly united: "We are all equal in America, in a political view," while "the Tories are in so small a Number, and of such little Force, that they are counted as Nothing." Above all, the American cause did not depend upon a few outstanding leaders but "upon the essential unalterable character of the whole body of the people." Indeed, "if there ever was a war that could be called *the People's War,* it is this of America against Great Britain, it having been determined on by the People, and pursued by the People, in every step of its Progress."

As usual, Adams was wrong as well as right. With women, blacks, and many poor whites disenfranchised, Americans were far from being equal "in a political view." (He also predicted that "Peace will not be made these twenty Years" and that "if there is ever any affection again between Americans and Britons it will be miraculous indeed.") But it is the thesis of this book that he was absolutely right when he claimed that the outcome of the war depended on the people them-selves, on their "essential, unalterable character," rather than on the quality of their leaders—a point especially worth making in light of the recent loss of Charleston, the humiliating defeat of General Gates at the Battle of Camden, and the stunning treason of General Bene-dict Arnold. But Adams's assessment of the country's basic strength seems not to have been shared by most historians, perhaps because so many of them write from a top-down perspective that focuses on the prominent players and largely ignores everyone else; or because they prefer studies of the theoretical kind where impersonal forces are seen at work and individuals are all but superfluous.

This book, by contrast, is based on the belief that it is individu-als, and not just the famous ones, who have made history, and that it is individuals and their stories that make for the most informative, illuminating, and enjoyable reading. It is organized as a straightfor-ward narrative that takes the reader from the run-up to the Stamp Act, through the decisive British defeat at Yorktown, and then con-cludes with an account of what happened after the war to many of the participants we have come to know. Apart from necessary edito-rial introductions and bridges, this version of events is told in the voices of those men and women who did most of the fighting and suffering, ordinary people, little known to history, but here emerging briefly from obscurity to tell us of their experiences: the farm boy who ran away to sea at the age of twelve and whose many adventures included a stint on the dreaded prison hulk *Jersey*; the militiaman who kept volunteering for further service, to the dismay of his wife who wanted him home; the slave girl laboring over an ode to General Washington and the Quaker girl flirting with young officers billeted at her home outside Philadelphia; the infantryman taking careful aim at the back of a retreating redcoat and the backcountry virago who gunned down a group of Tories who made the mistake of invading her cabin; the Patriot clergyman convinced that Mother Ann Lee, founder of the Shakers, was a British spy; the Boston merchant ruined by the depredations of the British; the sergeant's wife who regularly brought hot meals up to her husband in the lines at Yorktown—these and many others like them are the people whose stories make up the bulk of the book. And these stories, though sometimes edited for grammar, length, spelling, and sequence, are told in their own words, drawn from what they themselves wrote or, if illiterate, dictated: letters, diaries, petitions, sworn statements, memoirs, pension applications, many of them poorly spelled and clumsily penned but all telling with living immediacy just what it was like in those exciting and important times.

Adams was also wrong when he claimed that Americans were united in the cause of independence. With perhaps one third of the population in opposition, the Revolutionary War was also a civil war, or rather a series of civil wars: British-British against British-Americans (as the Americans at first thought of themselves), Loyalists against Patriots, American Indians against white Americans, white Americans against black Americans. To bring this home, events are often presented from different perspectives—Bunker Hill, for example, as experienced by the militiamen in their earth fort and also by the redcoats heading uphill toward them with fixed bayonets, or the murder of Mrs. Caldwell in New Jersey, notorious at the time, as reported in complete contradiction by the Whig and the Tory presses. Incidents in the bitter guerilla war between Patriots and Loyalists in the South are also presented from opposing points of view, while the little-known story of General John Sullivan's scorched-earth campaign against the Indians of upper New York is witnessed by a Seneca warrior, the Irish-born widow of another warrior, and a junior American officer. As for slaves, although only a few were lured into active participation by the promises made by both sides, they too were involved in a civil war, unacknowledged as such and undeclared, but a war nonetheless.

And because this was also an international war, the first-person stories of many non-Americans have also been included: French officers with their elegant uniforms and gallant manners, determined to like everything they saw; the despised Hessians, for whom no one—not even their own commanders—had a good word but who, when given a chance to tell their side of things, for the most part turn out to have been the hapless victims of greedy German princes, forcibly conscripted and brutally treated, and consequently quick to desert; and of course the British—proud, sometimes aggressive, more often halfhearted, and nearly always hopelessly out of touch, some of them, such as George III and his ministers, vainly trying to control events from the Mother Country, others in the colonies fighting a war they could not win but could most certainly lose.

"Who shall write the history of the American Revolution?" asked John Adams in a letter to Thomas Jefferson many years after the war when they were both old men. "Who can write it? Who will ever be able to write it?" Despite his implication that no one was up to the task, many thousands of books on the subject have appeared. Here is yet another. It tells a familiar story, but for the most part tells it in the words of those best qualified to do so: the men and women who were there.

Sons of Liberty burning stamps in Boston, 1765.

CHAPTER ONE

The Mother Country

THE SEAT OF EMPIRE

February 19, 1758. A dreary winter's day in London, foggy and damp, the light dim, the sulfurous air "full of floating Sea-Coal Soot," the worn cobblestoned streets wet and slippery, the gutters brimming with a foul brew of mud, dung, rotten garbage, ashes, offal, and strong-smelling horse urine—a good day for staying indoors, especially if, like Benjamin Franklin, you are ensconced in a suite of comfortable rooms in a neat, well-kept house on Craven Street, near Charing Cross. They are the best rooms in the house, wood-paneled and carpeted; the chairs are cushioned, and there is a glowing fire in the grate. Wax candles give off a soft light to read and write by. Should he want anything—a bowl of rum punch perhaps, or a hot buttered muffin—all he has to do is ring the bell and either Peter or King, servants he has brought with him from America, will answer his summons.

Now aged fifty-one and in his own words "a fat old fellow," Franklin is also under doctor's orders not to go out until he has completed his recovery from a "violent Cold and something of a Fever." Among his symptoms are "a Giddiness and Swimming in my Head which, every time I rise up, or turn suddenly, makes me stagger a little. I hear a humming Noise in my Head, and seem now and then to see little faint twinkling Lights." This has been his third bout of the fever because "too soon thinking myself well, I ventured out twice to do a little Business and . . . both times got fresh cold and fell down again. My good Doctor grew very angry with me for acting contrary to his Cautions and Directions, and obliged me to promise more Observance for the Future." Among the remedies prescribed by Dr.

Fothergill are powder of contrayerva (a tropical aromatic root), harts-horn drops (ammonia water made from the shavings of the horn of a stag), and cupping (drawing blood by cutting a vein and then apply-ing a glass that had been heated to produce a vacuum). Also help-ing him recover are his strong constitution and the attentions of his landlady, the handsome and "very obliging" widow Mrs. Stevenson, who "takes great care of my Health, and is very diligent when I am any way indisposed."

Though still convalescing, Franklin keeps as busy as ever, and is now writing to his "good old Wife" Deborah, who, rather than face the hardships of an Atlantic crossing, had chosen to remain in Philadelphia. Franklin had urged her to come with him, but he does not seem to have urged very hard. In a drinking song written several years earlier, he had celebrated her as "My Plain Country Joan" and it may have been tacitly understood that the homely, stocky, and uneducated daughter of the Widow Read, purveyor of a "well-known Ointment for the Itch" that sold for "two shillings a Gallypot," would feel uncomfortable mingling with polite London society.

After complaining about the sooty, foggy air of London—the whole city "one great smoaky House, and every Street a Chimney .... You never get a sweet Breath of what is pure without riding some Miles for it into the Country"—Franklin devotes much of his letter to a description of the large consignment of expensive goods that he is shipping back to Philadelphia, many of them to furnish their new house: "Some Carpeting for a best Room Floor . . . two large fine Flanders Bed Ticks and two pair large superfine Blankets . . . two fine Damask Table Cloths and Napkins . . . fifty-six Yards of Cotton, printed curiously from Copper Plates." As yet he has not been able to find a harpsichord for their daughter, Sally, though willing to pay as much as forty guineas. For Deborah he is sending "seven Yards of printed Cotton, blue Ground, to make you a Gown. I bought it by Candlelight and lik'd it then, but not so well afterwards. If you do not fancy it, send it as a Present from me to Sister Jenny. There is a better Gown for you, of flower'd Tissue, sixteen Yards, of Mrs.

Stevenson's Fancy, cost nine Guineas, and I think it a great Beauty." Also for Deborah is "a large fine Jugg for Beer, to stand in the Cooler. I fell in Love with it at first sight; for I thought it looked like a fat jolly Dame, clean and tidy, with a neat blue and white Calico Gown on, good natur'd and lovely, and put me in mind of—Somebody."

Despite the weather, Franklin liked being in London with its "bustling, crowded Streets" and sense of being at the center of things. "When a man is tired of London, he is tired of life; for there is in London all that life can afford," wrote Dr. Johnson, England's leading man of letters. For a politician it was "the seat of government"; for a farmer "a vast market for cattle"; for a merchant "a place where a prodigious deal of business is done on 'Change"; for a play-goer "the grand scene of theatrical entertainments"; for "a man of pleasure" it was "an assemblage of taverns, and the great emporium for ladies of easy virtue." And finally "the intellectual man . . . is struck with it as comprehending the whole of human life in all its variety."

From his lodgings in Craven Street, Franklin was well placed to enjoy and observe all that London had to offer. On a fine day he could pick his way down the dirt-strewn street to the brimming waters of the unembanked River Thames—or to the smelly mud flats that appeared when the tide was low—and walk out onto the wharf where collier-barges with red sails unloaded their cargoes of sea-coal and small ships delivered vegetables and fruit from market gardens upriver. To his right and left were many other wharves and landings, and sets of stairs leading down to the water's edge where boats that ferried people up, down, or across the river could pick up and deliver their passengers.

Standing on the wharf and looking upstream to his right, Franklin would have seen the massive gray roof, flying buttresses, and twin towers of Westminster Abbey, where kings were crowned and heroes buried. Between the Abbey and the river stood Westminster Palace, home to several law courts, the House of Commons, and the House of Lords, buildings that were destined to be largely destroyed by fire in 1834 and replaced with the familiar gothic structures. At the moment (that is, in 1758), Britain was once again at war with France—the Seven Years' War to the British, the French and Indian War to the Americans, and to some historians the first World War. Under the government of the influential but inept Duke of Newcastle, the war had gotten off to a bad start: A surprise attack on the Philippines had failed; in India the French had captured Pondicherry and their ally, the Nawab of Bengal, after taking Calcutta, had confined his British prisoners in a small, stuffy cell—the notorious Black Hole—where 123 were reported to have died of asphyxiation. The French had also taken Minorca in the Mediterranean and Goree off the West African coast, thus threatening Britain's virtual monopoly of the lucrative slave trade. Worst of all, General Braddock and his army of 2,000 redcoats and militiamen had been ambushed while crossing the Monongahela River in Ohio by a small force of Indians and Frenchmen, with a loss in killed and wounded of almost half his force. But now in 1758, things were looking brighter, thanks to the leadership of William Pitt the Elder, the great statesman of his age.

Spanning the River Thames was the brand-new and very expensive Westminster Bridge, "the finest bridge in Europe." Because of an acoustical phenomenon, music played under its arches resonated wonderfully. "The surprising echo in the arches," wrote *The Gentleman's Magazine,* "brings much company with French horns to entertain themselves under it in the summer." At the far end of the bridge was Lambeth Palace, official residence of the Archbishop of Canterbury, currently Thomas Secker, a worldly-wise prelate fond of striking off the kind of epigram that Franklin often included in his annual publication, *Poor Richard's Almanack:* "He enjoys much that is thankful for little," and "If you would not step into the harlot's house, do not go by the harlot's door." The archbishop was not, of course, the head of the Church of England; that distinction belonged to the monarch, currently George II. Responsibility for Anglican churches overseas lay with the Bishop of London. Because new ministers could be ordained only by the laying on of episcopal hands, which for American postulants entailed a round-trip of some six thousand miles, there was talk of sending a bishop out to the colonies, much to the alarm of Puritan New England.

Beyond Lambeth Palace were the Vauxhall pleasure gardens, where for the admission price of one shilling visitors could stroll along formal promenades lit by Chinese lanterns hung in the trees, admire artificial waterfalls and newly built ruins, see and be seen, buy overpriced refreshments, or listen to music played by orchestras, which for some reason were hidden from view behind screens of bushes. The gardens also contained dimly lit alleys with abundant shrubbery suitable for "amorous *rencontres.*" Known whores were barred, but not demi-mondaines such as the French-born Miss Charpillon, whose "blue eyes," according to Casanova, "languished and sparkled alternately," and whose "bosom was small but perfectly formed." Casanova had first met her in Paris and then heard of her again during a visit to London from his friend, Lord Pembroke. "The hussy inspired me with a violent desire once," Pembroke told him. "I met her and her aunt one evening at Vauxhall, and offered her twenty guineas if she would walk down one of the alleys with me. She accepted, on condition that I paid in advance, which I was weak enough to do. As soon as we were in the alley she ran away from me, and I was not able to catch her again the whole of that evening."

Outraged, Casanova told him that he "ought to have boxed her ears in public." But the earl took it in a more philosophic spirit. "I should only have got into trouble and been laughed at for my pains."

The south bank of the river opposite Craven Street was only lightly built up, much of the land still gardens and fields, including the extensive area known as St. George's Fields, suitable for fairs, games, and riots on a large scale. The King's Bench Prison was nearby. On Sundays, wrote a visitor, these open areas were filled with "dirty blackguards and poor parentless children who have not any friends to take care of them, going about the fields and ditches where wild honey-suckles, nettles, and thistles grow."

Looking downstream to his left, Franklin would have had a good view of the city's only other bridge, the famous London Bridge, now some six hundred years old, its arches so narrow that ships of any size could not pass through. The upper part of the bridge was still crowded with houses, but some in the middle had recently been removed, creating a gap through which he could have seen the masts of ships from all over the world crowded into the docking area known as the Pool of London; "a forest of masts" was the term that seems to have occurred to just about every traveler who described it.

The Pool ended at the Tower of London, where traitors were imprisoned and the Crown Jewels kept secure, and which also housed a menagerie. The four turrets of the main keep, the White Tower, would have been just visible from the foot of Craven Street. Then, farther to the left, was the City itself, its skyline dominated by the great dome of St Paul's Cathedral and punctuated by the steeples and towers of hundreds of smaller churches, many of them built since the Great Fire of 1666.

At the top of Craven Street, on the right-hand side, was the large open-air Hungerford Market where fruit and vegetables were sold. Much of this produce was grown in nearby market gardens and often had a strong taste of soot. On the top left-hand side of Craven Street stood Northumberland House, a huge mansion belonging to the rich and powerful Percy family, whose head was the Duke of Northumberland, father to the Lord Percy who was to command the relief column sent out from Boston to assist the red-coats during their retreat from Concord. As a young man recently arrived in town and looking for a patron to advance his career, James Boswell wangled an invitation to a "rout," or party, there and was dazzled by the splendor of the occasion. It was "indeed magnificent. Three large rooms and the gallery (a prodigious one) were full of the best company, between three and four hundred of them . . . . This is indeed a noble family in every respect. They live in the most princely manner, perfectly suitable to their high rank. Yet they are easy and affable. They keep up the true figure of old English nobility." Always alert to the figure he cut, Boswell had been careful not to overdress. "Fain would I have got rich laced clothes, but I commanded my inclination and got just a plain suit of a pink colour, with a gold button."

Just beyond Northumberland House was Charing Cross, with its statue of Charles I, beheaded following his defeat by Oliver Cromwell in the English Civil War—a would-be despot to the Whigs, "St. Charles, the Martyr King," to the true-blue High Church Tories. Near the statue was a pillory, where malefactors could be pelted with clods of dung and fistfuls of garbage picked up from the street.

Charing Cross was the starting point for the Strand, a busy street leading to the City and lined with coffeehouses, book sellers, tobacconists, milliners, stationers, and dozens of other shops, most with brightly painted signs hanging out over the windows that displayed their wares. Living quarters for the shop owners were above or in the back, while apprentices often resided on a sleeping-shelf under the counter. The Strand also had many chop-houses, taverns, and other places to eat and drink. "A beefsteak-house is a most excellent place to dine at," wrote Boswell. "You come in to a warm, comfortable, large room, where a number of people are sitting at table. You take whatever place you find empty; call for what you like. . . . You may either chat or not as you like. Nobody minds you, and you pay very reasonably. My dinner (beef, bread, and beer and waiter) was only a shilling." Another attraction for Boswell was "the civil nymph with white-thread stockings who tramps along the Strand and will resign her engaging person to your honour for a pint of wine and a shilling." For example, April 1763: "I should have mentioned last night that I met with a monstrous big whore in the Strand, whom I had a great curiosity to lubricate, as the saying is . . ." June 1763: "In the Strand I picked up a little profligate wretch and gave her sixpence . . ." August 1763: "On Monday night, coming up the Strand, I was tapped on the shoulder by a fine fresh lass. I went home with her. She was an officer's daughter, and born at Gibraltar. I could not resist indulging myself with the enjoyment of her . . ."

There were also a number of brothels in the Strand. In one of them, the Star Tavern, in an incident that occurred a few years before Franklin's arrival, three sailors were robbed of their money and watches, upon which, according to the formal report, they "demanded a reparation for their loss." But instead of being granted their request, "some bullies belonging to the house pushed them from the door; whereupon they went away, denouncing vengeance; and having collected a number of their companions in the neighbourhood of Wapping, they returned at night, broke open the house, turned the women almost naked into the streets, ripped up the beds, threw the feathers out of the window, broke the furniture in pieces, and made a bonfire of it."

At the end of the Strand was Temple Bar, the gateway to the ancient City of London. Here, in symbolic acknowledgment of the rights and privileges of the City, the monarch always had to stop and ask the Lord Mayor for permission to come any further. Here too were displayed the heads of those who had been executed for treason following the Jacobite Rebellion of 1745; to make them last, the heads had been boiled in salt water and then coated with tar before being stuck high up in the air on pike-staffs. For better viewing, small telescopes called "spy-glasses" could be rented for a half penny.

As Franklin observed with some satisfaction, there was no need for such warning displays in the colonies: "Scotland has had its Rebellions, and England its Plots, against the present Royal Family, but America is untainted with those Crimes." Indeed "there is in it scarce a Man . . . who is not firmly attached to his King by Principle and by Affection."

A tireless and pragmatic civic improver—the Library Company of Philadelphia, the Pennsylvania Hospital, the Public Academy in the City of Philadelphia, the Union Fire Company—Franklin had not been in London long before he drew up a proposal "for the more effectual cleaning and keeping clean the Streets." (Let "the Mud when rak'd up be not left in Heaps to be spread abroad again by the Wheels of Carriages and Trampling of Horses"; instead, let "the Scavengers be provided with Bodies of Carts, not plac'd high upon Wheels, but low upon Sliders; with Lattice Bottoms, which being cover'd with Straw, will retain the Mud thrown into them, and permit the Water to drain from it . . .")

Had London been populated by forward-looking Philadelphians, his plan might have been adopted; but Franklin met with no more success in this scheme than when he tried to introduce his low-cost, smoke-reducing, cast-iron stove, which gave twice the heat for half the fuel. So foul were the streets that to get about town he had to hire his own coach at a cost of twelve guineas a month, the local hackney cabs being "miserable, dirty, broken, shabby things, unfit to go into when dressed clean, and such as one would be ashamed to get out of at any Gentleman's Door." The coach was often in use, for Franklin was a frequent guest—"all jollity and pleasantry" according to Boswell, who ran into him at Sir John Pringle's—and many were the gentlemen's doors at which he alighted: to dine with Lord and Lady Macclesfield, to visit Lord Despencer at Wycombe, or stay with the Bishop of St. Asaph in Hampshire. Though he had started out in life as the youngest of the ten sons of a poor Boston candlemaker and soap boiler, he was now the famous Dr. Franklin, Fellow of the Royal Society, author of *Experiments and Observations on Electricity,* and inventor of the lightning rod, which, as with his stove, he had philanthropically refused to patent. His philanthropy had not, however, made him poor, and thanks to his printing business and shop in Philadelphia, now in the capable hands of his wife, the popularity of *Poor Richard's Almanack,* his thrift ("a penny saved is a penny earned"), his investments, his salary and allowances as agent for the Pennsylvania Assembly, and another salary from the American post office, Franklin was very comfortably off—hence the large consignments of expensive goods that he could afford to ship back to Deborah.

Moreover, he had important business to transact on behalf of the Assembly: persuade the king's ministers to revoke the charter that empowered the selfish Penn family, who refused to pay their fair share of taxes, and get "the Crown to take the Province under its immediate Government and Protection." As well as seeking this major extension of royal power in the colonies, Franklin soon became engaged on behalf of the Grand Ohio Company in its negotiations with the ministry for a grant of several million acres in a region that had been set aside for the Indians. During the summer months, when the political establishment largely closed down, he went on long and enjoyable trips around the country, to Scotland and Ireland, and also to Holland and France; and then, in the fall, he returned to his snug quarters at the house on Craven Street and the ministrations of Mrs. Stevenson.

One of these trips took him to Ecton, in Northamptonshire, "being the village where my father was born, and where his father, grandfather, and great-grandfather had lived, and how many of the family before them we know not." The old family farmhouse was now "a decayed old stone building, but still known by the name of Franklin House." The rector "entertained us very kindly, and showed us the old church register, in which were the births, marriages, and burials of our ancestors for 200 years, as early as his book began. His wife, a good-natured chatty old lady, remembered a great deal about the family; carried us out into the church-yard, and showed us several of their gravestones, which were so covered with moss that we could not read the letters till she ordered a hard brush and basin of water, with which Peter scoured them clean, and then Billy copied them."

Billy was Franklin's son William, currently studying law at the Middle Temple in London and later to become royal governor of New Jersey. Peter was one of the servants Franklin had brought with him from Philadelphia. Surprisingly, Peter, like King, the other servant, was a slave, surprising not because Franklin thought that slavery was wrong—like most of his contemporaries, he regarded it as part of the natural order of things—but because he already knew from experience in Pennsylvania that slaves made bad servants, indolence being "natural to the Man who is not to be benefited by his own Care and Diligence" and "every Slave being by nature a Thief." And in fact, not long after the Ecton visit, Franklin mentioned in a letter to Deborah that King, who had often been "in Mischief," had indeed turned out to be a thief—not of cash or silver spoons, but of himself. In other words, King had run away. (He "was soon found in Suffolk, where he had been taken in the Service of a Lady that was very fond of the Merit of making him a Christian, and contributing to his Education and Improvement." The lady "sent him to School, has him taught to read and write, to play the Violin and French Horn, with some other Accomplishments more useful in a Servant.") Franklin seems to have made no effort to frustrate King's personal bid for independence, and anyway the legal situation was unclear. In his recent *Commentaries on the Laws of England,* Sir William Blackstone had ringingly declared that "the spirit of liberty is so deeply implanted in our constitution and rooted in our very soil, that a slave or Negro, the moment he lands in England, falls under the protection of the laws and so far becomes a free man." But there was a snag: "any right the master may have lawfully acquired to the perpetual service" of a slave would not be affected. Though now free, the slave "will remain exactly in the same state of subjection for life." At any rate, the enterprising and musically talented King disappears from the historical record. Franklin's ideas about slavery, as about so much else, would continue to evolve. As for Peter, "he continues with me, and behaves as well as I can expect. . . . We rub on pretty comfortably."

Seven years after his arrival in London, and again in the month of February, Franklin, who had by now become the colonies' unofficial ambassador to the mother country, was summoned to the House of Commons in the hope that he could help clear away some of the political fog generated by the Stamp Act crisis. For formal occasions such as this, Franklin usually wore a well-cut suit of Manchester velvet, and doubtless made the short journey from Craven Street not on foot but in his twelve-guineas-a-month private coach. After being called to the bar of the House, a total of 174 questions, some friendly and some hostile, were put to him. The session lasted many hours, and as the winter daylight faded, hundreds of candles were lit to illuminate the medieval gloom of Westminster Palace.

Franklin had spent several weeks preparing for the occasion, and in his answers he emphasized several points: Americans were already heavily taxed—in Pennsylvania "there are taxes on all estates real and personal; a poll tax; a tax on all offices, professions, trades, and businesses, according to their profits; an excise tax on all wine, rum, and other spirits; and a duty of ten pounds per head on all Negroes imported, with some other duties." Nor were Americans anywhere near so rich as supposed: "In my opinion there is not gold and silver enough in the colonies to pay the stamp duty for one year." Members should also understand that there was an important difference between *external* taxes such as customs duties, which were acceptable because their purpose was to regulate trade, and *internal* taxes, whose purpose was to raise revenue. Americans, who were entitled "to all the privileges and liberties of Englishmen," had "the utmost respect and veneration" for the British Parliament—"the great bulwark and security of their liberties and privileges"—but denied that it had any right to impose internal taxes because "we are not represented there."

Question number thirty-six was put to him by Grey Cooper, one of the group known as the Rockingham Whigs, who were sympathetic to the American cause: "What was the temper of America towards Great Britain before the year 1763?"—that is, before the Stamp Act was passed.

"The best in the World!" Franklin replied. "They submitted willingly to the Government of the Crown, and paid, in their Courts, Obedience to the Acts of Parliament. . . . They were governed by this Country at the Expense only of a little Pen, Ink, and Paper. They were led by a Thread. They had not only a Respect, but an Affection for Great Britain, for its Laws, its Customs and Manners, and even a Fondness for its Fashions, that greatly increased the Commerce. Natives of Britain were always treated with particular Regard; to be an *Old-England man* was, of itself, a Character of some Respect, and gave a kind of Rank among us."

Three thousand miles to the west, in Plymouth, Massachusetts, where the exiled Pilgrim Fathers had settled and where the winters were colder than in London but the air was clean and bracing, Mercy Otis Warren was to express much the same opinion. A true daughter of New England, the prim and high-minded Mrs. Warren was a contemporary of the events she described in her *History of the Rise, Progress and Termination of the American Revolution*. "All America," she wrote in volume one, "from the first emigrants to the present generation, felt an attachment to the inhabitants, a regard to the interest, and a reverence for the laws and government of England."

To be sure, "all America" did not include the Indians who were steadily receding as the frontier moved west, or the half million slaves of African descent, or the hundred thousand or so Germans who had settled in Pennsylvania and kept to their old language and ways; but setting these exceptions aside, it was true that the sense of attachment was as strong as it was unquestioned. "Nothing can eradicate from the English colonists' hearts their natural, almost mechanical affection to Great Britain," said Governor Thomas Pownall of Massachusetts. To go to England was to "go home." "From my Infancy I have always felt a great inclination to visit the Mother Country," wrote Abigail Adams, and George Washington wrote of "the longing desire which for many years I have had of visiting England." Much later, in his *Autobiography*, Jefferson was to write of the "habitual belief that it was our duty to be subordinate to the mother country."

Unquestioning respect for the monarchy was part of this "habitual belief." "I had been taught to consider them [kings] as nearly as essential to political order as the Sun is to the order of our Solar System," wrote the future revolutionary Benjamin Rush. Regardless of who was actually on the throne, he was always spoken of as "the best of kings." Distance and ignorance helped to sustain this fiction. Few in America knew the inside stories about the Hanoverian royal family—how the boorish George I allowed his blowsy German mistresses to sell titles and promotions while at the same time keeping his wife locked away in a castle in north Germany for thirty-two years as punishment for her suspected adultery, never once allowing any of their children to visit her; or that his son, George II, grew up loathing his father for treating his mother this way, but then came to loathe his own son, Prince Frederick, "a silly puppy and undutiful, insolent rascal" for whom, he said, "he did not care a louse"; or that when "Poor Fred," as he was called, died, probably as the result of being struck by the ball during a game of cricket, the king wrote, "This has been a fatal year to my family. I have lost my eldest son, but I was glad of it." (Poor Fred fared no better with his mother, Queen Caroline, who called him "the lowest stinking coward in the world . . . *canaille* . . . that monster . . . my filthy beast of a son . . .") As for George II's behavior to the rest of his family, the courtier Lord Hervey wrote of one occasion when the king burst in upon his family while at breakfast and in the space of a few minutes "snubbed his Queen, who was drinking chocolate, for being always stuffing, the princess Emily for not hearing him, the princess Caroline for being grown fat, the Duke [of Cumberland] for standing awkwardly . . . and then carried the Queen to walk, and be re-snubbed, in the garden." As to his grandson, the future George III, he was dismissed as being "fit for nothing but to read the Bible to his mother."

Americans of course knew that their king was also the Elector, or ruler, of Hanover, but not that George II was such a Germanophile that "there was nothing English ever commended in his presence that he did not always show, or pretend to show, was surpassed by something of the same kind in Germany." More serious was the comment by Sir Nathaniel Wraxall on the first two Georges that "their policy, their treaties, their wars, and all their measures, were warped by foreign predilections, to which they sacrificed the interests of Great Britain"—and, by extension, the interests of the colonies also.

Those interested in following the day-by-day doings of the court could subscribe to *The Gentleman's Magazine*, where they could read that on Monday, October 20, 1760, "His Majesty, attended by the royal family, &c, reviewed, from a tent in Hyde Park, Col. Burgoyne's regiment of light dragoons. After which a new experiment was tried of a shell charged with fuming combustibles, which threw out a great smoke, and is intended to cover a retreat." (We shall meet Burgoyne again, at Saratoga.) Five days later the magazine reported that His Majesty, who was living at Kensington Palace, rose at his usual hour, "called his page, drank his chocolate, and enquired about the mails. He opened his window, and looking out of it, and seeing it a fine day, said he would walk in the gardens. This passed while the page attended him at breakfast, but on leaving the room he [the page] heard a deep sigh, immediately followed by a noise like the falling of a billet of wood from the fire, and returning hastily found the king dropt from his seat, as if attempting to ring the bell, who said faintly 'Call Amelia' [his youngest daughter] and then expired." This was the tidied-up version of the event; those in the know soon learned that after drinking his chocolate the king had retired to his toilet and that the seat from which he dropped, felled by a heart attack, was what was then known as the "close-stool."

Since he was seventy-seven, his death was not unexpected, nor was he much regretted. On the other hand he was a warrior king who had led his armies into battle, and he died just as the Seven Years' War was coming to a triumphant end, with victories over the French on land and at sea. It was a propitious moment for the old king to die, and for his grandson to succeed him.

"No British monarch had ascended the throne with so many advantages as George the Third," wrote Horace Walpole, the well-placed diarist. "In the flower and bloom of youth, George had a handsome, open, and honest countenance; and . . . none of those vices that fall under the censure of those who are past enjoying them themselves. The moment of his accession was fortunate beyond example. . . . Conquest had crowned our arms with wonderful circumstances of glory and fortune: and the young King seemed to have the option of extending our victories and acquisitions, or of giving peace to the world."

Unlike his two predecessors the new king could fairly claim, in his first speech from the throne, "Born and educated in this country, I glory in the name of Briton"—in some versions the name is "Britain," but the meaning ("I am not a German") is the same—adding that "the peculiar happiness of my life will ever consist in promoting the welfare of a people whose loyalty and warm affection to me I consider as the greatest and most permanent security of my throne." He invoked "the blessing of heaven upon our joint endeavours," announced that it was his "fixed purpose to countenance and encourage the practice of true religion and virtue," and within a week of becoming king issued a *Proclamation for the Encouragement of Piety and Virtue, and for the Preventing and Punishing Vice, Profaneness, and Immorality.* Soon afterward the poet Thomas Gray was writing to a friend about "his Majesty's reproof to his Chaplains: 'I desire those Gentlemen may be told that I come here to praise God, & not to hear my own praises.'"

"His person is tall," wrote Walpole, "his manner is graceful and obliging—the most amiable young man in the world." "A fine pleasant-looking young man," said Lady Susan Fox-Strangways, "a healthy complexion . . . fine teeth, a look of happiness & good humour that pleas'd everyone." According to the Duchess of Northumberland, he had "an unparalleled air of majestic dignity. There was a noble openness in his countenance, blended with a cheerful good-natured affability. He was fair and fresh coloured. . . . His eyes were blue, his teeth extremely fine. His hair a light auburn . . . his voice was strong, melodious, and clear."

His private life was impeccable. Though for a while madly in love with the beautiful Lady Sarah Lennox, who used to dress in a skimpy "peasant" costume and play at haymaking in a field near Holland House where the young king was wont to ride, he never laid a finger on her, settling instead for the plain but much more appropriate Princess Charlotte of Mecklenburg-Strelitz, who soon produced the first of their fifteen children. He was a faithful and attentive husband, sometimes accompanying his wife on the flute when she sang, and a loving father, wheeling the small children around in wicker chariots, reading aloud to the family, and, according to his former wet nurse, Mrs. Scott, "at times would shed the dignity of the monarch and crawl about on the floor on his hands and knees with the children." He got up at six every morning to start work on state papers, lighting the fire himself if it was cold; was abstemious in his eating and drinking, but when he did put on weight had the willpower to lose thirty-one pounds in a self-imposed diet; said his prayers before going to bed; and always observed the Sabbath. He took a great interest in scientific farming, writing letters to the *Annals of Agriculture* under the pen name of Ralph Robinson, acquired large libraries, collected drawings and paintings, loved the music of Handel, was exceptionally well-informed about public affairs, was fluent in French and German, and made such an impression on Dr. Johnson that, after meeting him in the library of the Queen's House (now Buckingham Palace), the great man declared, "Sir, they may talk of the King as they will; but he is the finest gentleman I have ever seen." This opinion was seconded by England's leading bluestocking, Mrs. Montagu: "There hardly passes a day in which one does not hear of something he has said, or done, which raises one's opinions of his understanding and heart."

Reports of the king's virtuous behavior went down well in the American colonies. John Adams, a chubby and ambitious young schoolteacher, wrote in his diary: "His Majesty has declared himself, by his Speech to his Parliament, to be a man of Piety and Candor in Religion, a friend of Liberty and Property in Government, and a Patron of Merit—These are sentiments worthy of a King—a Patriot King." A few years later the Massachusetts firebrand James Otis wrote in one of his political tracts: "We are blessed with a prince who has given abundant demonstrations that in all his actions he studies the good of his people." John Dickinson, author of *Letters from a Farmer in Pennsylvania,* called George "an excellent prince" in whose "good dispositions they could confide." Most Americans seem to have felt the same. True, after a while a note of caution crept in—"even the wisest of kings may be misled," said the *Constitutional Courant*—but the chorus of praise was kept up for fifteen years.

And then, all of a sudden, he was "a Royal Brute . . . a hardened, sullen-tempered Pharaoh" (Thomas Paine); "fierce, cruel, unrelenting, and bloody" (the Rev. Hugh Brackenridge); "a Wretch Callous to every Humane feeling" (Abigail Adams, who added that "our worthy preacher told us that he believed one of our Great Sins for which a righteous God has come out in Judgment against us was our Bigoted attachment to so wicked a Man"). The Declaration of Independence summed it up: George III was "a Tyrant . . . unfit to be the ruler of a free people."

What on earth had gone wrong?

Well, from the beginning there had been signs and portents. Although this was supposed to be the Age of Enlightenment, many people, even the best educated, were intellectually still at least partly in the Dark Ages. Omens, particularly bad omens, were still taken seriously, and it seemed significant that the new king's coronation, though magnificent, had been marred by several mishaps: "The Bishop of Rochester would have drop'd the Crown, if it had not been pinn'd to the Cushion," wrote Thomas Gray. "The Sword of State had been entirely forgot, so Lord Huntingdon was forced to carry the Lord Mayor's great two-handed sword instead of it." Worse yet, it was widely reported that at one point during the ceremony "the great diamond fell from the sceptre" —in an even more fateful version of this story, the diamond was said to have fallen not from the scepter but from the crown itself. (Another unfortunate but perhaps not ominous incident occurred during a call-of-nature break in the very long ceremony. "The Queen," wrote Thomas Gray, "retired while she was in the Abbey to a sort of closet furnish'd with necessary conveniences. One of the ladies, opening the door to see all was right, found the Duke of Newcastle perk'd up & in the very act upon the anointed velvet close-stool.")

There were other warning signs. The *Pennsylvania Packet* reported that "a pious lady of New York, having some years ago been to see the waxworks shown there, among which was the likeness of George the Third, she dreamed the night following that she saw the King in his great chair fast asleep, and his crown lying at his feet. Beyond him stood the devil, and after some time he cried out with a strong and terrifying voice, 'Arouse, O Prince, for thy kingdom is departed from thee.'" An account of this dream was sent to Lord North in London, "but he did not dare show it to his master." There was also the story of what had happened when the king reviewed the fleet. "The weather was so fine that hundreds of small boats were on the sea; and yet, so it was, that at the mast-head of the royal yacht, on board which the King then was, the great union flag was rent from top to bottom, in the sight of twenty thousand people."

Another harbinger of trouble was the way the young king had been brought up, isolated from other young people and under the thumb of his mother and his tutor, the pedantic Lord Bute, both of them ambitious to increase royal power. "Nurtured in all the inflated ideas of kingly prerogative, surrounded by flatterers and dependents . . . dazzled with the acquisition of empire, in the morning of youth, and in the zenith of national prosperity; more obstinate than cruel, rather weak than remarkably wicked"—small wonder, wrote Mercy Otis Warren, that his head had been turned, making him as stubborn as he was self-righteous.

Many others commented on this aspect of the king's character. "He is very obstinate," said Charles Townshend, originator of the Townshend Duties; Samuel Curwen, an exiled American Loyalist, wrote of his "inflexible temper" as something that was well-known; and Lord Waldegrave, another of his tutors, wrote, "I found his Royal Highness uncommonly full of princely prejudice, contracted in the nursery. . . . He did not want resolution, but it is mixed with too much obstinacy." And as the great orator Edmund Burke was to say pointedly, but without mentioning the king, "Obstinacy, Sir, is certainly a great vice; and in the changeful state of political affairs, it is frequently the cause of great mischief."

Although far from being the bullying and narrow-minded dullard sometimes portrayed, there can be little doubt that George lacked the imagination, political sensitivity, flexibility, and sense of proportion needed to run an empire; but, conscious of what he called "the uprightness of my own intentions," that is what he set out to do. "George, be King!" he had been admonished as a boy by his mother, the Dowager Princess of Wales ("a passionate, domineering woman . . . ardently fond of power and all its appanages," according to Walpole). As king, he would root out factionalism and corruption and restore to the monarchy the powers that had fallen into the hands of the Whig oligarchs. "The watchwords of the new government were prerogative and purity," wrote Catharine Macaulay, the radical historian and warm friend to the American cause.

However, political purity was soon abandoned in the pursuit of royal prerogative. Anxious to end the Seven Years' War, and jealous of William Pitt's great popularity, the young king changed ministers and entrusted Henry Fox, later Lord Holland, with the task of pushing the Peace of Paris through Parliament. According to Horace Walpole, Fox, who had accumulated a large fortune while Paymaster General by lending out government money and pocketing the interest, arranged for a shop to be "publicly opened at the Pay Office, whither the members flocked, and received the wages of their venality in bank bills, even to so low a sum as two hundred pounds for their votes for the treaty. Twenty-five thousand pounds . . . were issued in one morning—and in a single fortnight, a vast majority was purchased to approve the peace."

There was nothing new about this way of doing the nation's business. Mr. Roberts, Secretary of the Treasury during the reign of George II, told Sir Nathaniel Wraxall that "there were a number of

Members who regularly received from him their Payment or Stipend, at the end of every Session, in Bank Notes. The Sums, which varied according to the Merits, Ability, and Attendance of the respective Individuals, amounted usually from Five Hundred Pounds to Eight Hundred Pounds, per annum. 'This Largess I distributed,' added Roberts, 'in the Court of Requests, on the day of the Prorogation of Parliament. I took my stand there; and as the Gentlemen passed me, in going to or returning from the House, I conveyed the Money in a squeeze of the hand.'"

Parliamentary elections were run on similar lines. In the counties, only those who owned property to the value of forty shillings could vote, their choice often depending on which of the candidates was most generous with the free food and drink, or issued the direst threats. Many other seats in Parliament represented the so-called rotten boroughs, which had only a handful of voters and were often openly up for sale. "Four thousand Pounds is now the market Price for a Borough," wrote Franklin to his friend Joseph Galloway in Philadelphia at the time of one election. "This whole venal Nation is now at Market, and will be sold for about two Millions and might be bought out of the Hands of the present Bidders (if he would offer Half a Million more) by the Devil himself."

To those who complained that this system did a better job of representing property than people, there were two answers. The first was that this was as it should be; the second was the theory known as "virtual representation." According to this theory, it was acknowledged that a rotten borough such as Old Sarum had a voting population of less than a dozen, and that a city such as Bath with a population of some twenty-five thousand had only thirty-three voters, or that the whole of Scotland, population about two million, had fewer than three thousand voters, and so on; but this did not mean that those who did not vote were not represented. Of course they were, and the same went for the colonists who had no parliamentary votes at all. Lord Mansfield, Chief Justice of the King's Bench, explained why: "A Member of Parliament chosen for any borough represents not only the constituents and inhabitants of that particular place, but he represents all the other commons of this land, and the inhabitants of all the colonies and dominions of Great Britain." In his pamphlet, *Taxation No Tyranny*, Dr. Johnson strongly seconded Lord Mansfield's argument, but William Pitt, "the genius and guardian angel of Britain and British America" in the words of John Adams, dismissed it out of hand: "The idea of a virtual representation of America in this House is the most contemptible idea that ever entered the head of a man. It does not deserve serious consideration."

Once elected, members spent much of their time scrambling for jobs, titles, pensions, honors, and promotions for themselves and their families. Hitherto patronage had been distributed by the Whig oligarchs to build loyalty to their factions—the "Rockingham Whigs," or the group led by the Duke of Bedford and known as the "Bloomsbury Gang"—but soon George was taking over the system to form the voting bloc known as the King's Friends. In 1770, 192 members of Parliament held crown offices of one sort or another, from which they could be—and were—dismissed if they voted the wrong way. Many of these positions were sinecures that had few or no duties but were very well paid. Lords of the Bedchamber received £1,000 a year for one month's attendance. Lord Holland obtained the Writership of Tallies and Counter Tallies, and the Clerkship of the Pells in Ireland, worth £2,500 a year, and held the post not only for his own lifetime but also for those of his two sons. George Grenville, the son of George Grenville of Stamp Act fame, was given a lifetime appointment as Teller of the Exchequer at the ripe old age of ten years and nine months. If a position did have responsibilities, then the practice was for the office-holder to hire someone at a much lower salary—General Irwin, for example, was Commissary-General of stores at Gibraltar at £800 a year and paid a clerk £90 a year to do the work.

The system was not confined to the home country. Following their appointment, colonial governors often stayed at home while lieutenant governors filled in for them: Cadwallader Colden, who was three times lieutenant governor of New York, received half the salary and half the perquisites of his absentee superiors, while the citizens of New York were in effect paying double the tax required to support the office. Anglican clergymen who could not find a good living at home shipped out for the southern colonies, where the Church of England was supported by the taxpayers. The position of postmaster for the colonies was held by an Englishman, while Franklin, who had done the actual work of setting up the system, was only deputy postmaster—but his salary of £300 a year was to have been for life had he not lost it because of a political indiscretion. And like other colonials, Franklin was ready enough to work the patronage system to his advantage: It was through his influence that his son William was made governor of New Jersey, and he also found jobs in the colonial postal service for his brothers Peter and John, John's stepson, his sister Jane Mecom's two sons, and two of his wife's relatives.

Despite his early disapproval, George had little trouble reconciling himself to a corrupt political system: Unlike others, he was using it not for self-advancement but to pursue policies that he knew were right. Since his motives were also of the highest, it followed that there could be no such thing as a loyal opposition: "I have no wish but for the prosperity of my dominions, therefore must look on all who will not heartily assist me as bad men as well as ungrateful subjects." Inevitably, his list of enemies was long: The Duke of Newcastle was "a knave"; Pitt was "a snake in the grass" and "a trumpet of sedition"; Charles James Fox was "as contemptible as he is odious"; Edmund Burke was "a pest"; and the Duke of Devonshire was "impious." Petitions for redress of grievances from the colonies were construed as personal insults.

To be sure, George had no intention of trying to rule directly—that, as he knew from his history books, would have been despotism. Instead he worked through politicians who either thought the way he did (Lord George Germain) or were ready to do his bidding (Lord North). The list of candidates was quite limited, as nearly all the top jobs in government or the services were held by members of aristocratic families—of the generals who were to serve in America, Burgoyne was related by marriage to the Earl of Derby, Sir William Howe was the son of Lord Howe, Gage was the son of Lord Gage, and Clinton was related to Lord Lincoln and by marriage to the Duke of Newcastle, while Cornwallis was an earl in his own right.

Unfortunately for George, most members of the aristocracy were not as biddable as he could have wished; they bowed low, but otherwise acted as if the king were no more than the first among equals. They set their own standards, allowing themselves to do just about anything they pleased, drawing the line only when it came to cheating at cards, fixing a horse race, acting the coward, or committing treason. The ladies also had their standards. Replying to the pious Countess of Huntingdon, who had sent her some tracts on Methodism written by John Wesley, the Duchess of Buckingham wrote that she had found them "most repulsive." By "perpetually endeavouring to level all ranks and do away with all distinctions," Methodists were "strongly tinctured with impertinence and disrespect towards their superiors." It was, said the duchess, "monstrous to be told that you have a heart as sinful as the common wretches that crawl the earth. This is highly offensive and insulting."

It took the king several years to recruit the men through whom he could impose his personal rule and ruin his empire, but in the end he found them. They included Lord George Germain, who replaced Dartmouth as colonial secretary, a domineering and arrogant hard-liner—"haughty, obstinate, and overbearing," according to Walpole; "of a vindictive, implacable disposition," according to Lord Shelburne. Earlier in his career Germain had been disgraced for his conduct at the Battle of Minden when, as commander of the combined British and German cavalry, he had pretended not to understand repeated orders to charge the French enemy in front of him, a charge he would have had to lead in person. For this he was court-martialed. George II was keen to have him shot for cowardice in the face of the enemy, but thanks to the intervention of Germain's father, the Duke of Dorset, he got off with a sentence declaring him "unfit to serve His Majesty in any military capacity whatsoever." But that prohibition did not apply to the new king, who saw eye to eye with him on the need for "smart blows" and "bloody noses" when the time came to bring the rebellious Americans to heel—congenial work for Germain, who despised the colonists for their modest social origins. The king also needed him as a spokesman in the House of Commons; despite his title, Germain was not a peer in his own right, since his father was still alive.

As First Lord of the Admiralty the king appointed the corrupt and duplicitous Lord Sandwich, a founding member of the orgiastic Hell Fire Club and a man who, according to Lord Chesterfield, had from his earliest youth pursued "one uniform, unblushing course of debauchery and dissipation." In May 1776, during a crucial period of the war, the philosopher David Hume had encountered Lord Sandwich by chance at an inn near Newbury, along with some other gentlemen "and two or three ladies of pleasure." They told him that they had already "passed five or six days there, and intended to pass all this week and the next in the same place; that their chief object was to enjoy the trouting season; that they had been very success-ful; that Lord Sandwich in particular had caught trouts near twenty inches long, which gave him incredible satisfaction." Though often neglecting his duties, Sandwich was assiduous at the gaming table, once spending twenty-four hours there at a stretch and making do on slices of bread and beef. He was so disliked and despised by officers in the Royal Navy that many refused to serve under him against the Americans unless, like Admiral Lord Howe, they were more or less ordered to do so by the king himself.

By contrast, Lord North, prime minister in the years up to and during the Revolution, was genial and well-liked, "one of the best companions in the Kingdom," according to Edward Gibbon (who owed him his appointment as one of the Lords Commissioners of Trade and Plantations at a salary of over £700 a year, in return for which "I enjoyed many days and weeks without being called away from my library to the office"). Though he often fell asleep during debates, North was a skilled parliamentarian, but his only policy was to muddle through and his personality was too feeble to control the other members of his ministry, who often bypassed him, as did the king. No one knew better than he that he was not fit to be prime minister in a time of war when, as he wrote, what the country needed was someone "capable of leading, of discerning between opinions, of deciding quickly and confidently, and of connecting all the operations of government, that this nation might act uniformly, and with force," and then concluded, "Lord North is not such a man." As the war went from bad to worse, he kept trying to resign, but the king, who had at last found in North the perfect instrument to execute his wishes, refused to let him go. Only in appearance was North remarkable. "Nothing could be more coarse or clumsy or ungracious than his outside," wrote Horace Walpole. He had a shambling, rolling gait and a tongue that was too large for his mouth; he was so shortsighted that his "large prominent eyes . . . rolled about to no purpose," while his "wide mouth, thick lips, and inflated visage gave him the air of a blind trumpeter."

Although many Americans liked to think of England as home, and of themselves as Englishmen, the differences between the mother country and the colonies were great and growing. While in America, and especially in New England, clergymen were generally looked up to as men of probity and learning, the Church of England had more or less become one huge sinecure. "No man can now be made a bishop for his learning and piety," said Dr. Johnson. "His only chance for promotion is his being connected with somebody who has Parliamentary interest"—for example, Lord North's brother, Brownlow, who was Bishop of Winchester. Lethargic Anglican clergymen also dominated the universities, where many of the students were young gentlemen with time and money on their hands. Recalling his final examination at Oxford, Lord Eldon wrote, "I was examined in Hebrew and

History: 'What is the Hebrew for the Place of the Skull?' said the Examiner. 'Golgotha,' I replied. 'Who founded University College?' I answered, 'King Alfred.' 'Very well, sir,' said the Examiner, 'then you are competent for your degree.'" By contrast, for his master's degree at Harvard, Samuel Adams had to compose and then declaim in public a thesis in Latin in response to the question: "*An supremo Magistratui resistere liceat, si aliter servari Respublica nequit?*—Whether it be lawful to resist the Supreme Magistrate, if the Commonwealth cannot be otherwise preserved." (Being the man he was, Adams answered "on the affirmative side.")

Though the American and English legal systems were largely the same, there was far less crime in the colonies, thanks to widespread prosperity among white people. Labor was always in short supply, so punishments were usually mild—as the saying went, a man had to have a lot of friends to be hanged in New England. But in Old England life was cheap and the application of the laws harsh. There were no fewer than 160 capital crimes, and executions were public and frequent. Some instances from the Newgate Calendar: "Two boys, and small for their years, named John Bunn and Joseph Leach, the former fourteen, and the other fifteen years old, for a street robbery, were hanged at Tyburn. Let children beware of committing crimes, for their youth will not always save them." "Barbara Spencer, Alice Hall, and Elizabeth Bray were indicted at the Old Bailey for high treason, in counterfeiting the current coin of the kingdom; when Hall and Bray were acquitted, as being only agents to the other, and Spencer, being found guilty, was sentenced to be burnt." A footnote adds: "Women convicted of high or petit treason are always thus sentenced, but they are first tied to a stake, and strangled before they are burnt." Wives who murdered their husbands were also strangled and then burned at the stake, this part of the law being "founded on a well-known part of the Christian system of religion which says, 'That wives should be obedient to their husbands in all things.'" One of the few penal reforms of the period was to suspend the death sentences of those convicted of crimes against property and instead transport them to the southern colonies, where they would be sold into virtual slavery.

Members of the British establishment never wearied of congratulating themselves on the glories of their constitution, and it was true that no other European country had a free press or a parliament that controlled the purse strings or the legal protection of habeas corpus. Also unlike the rest of Europe, those who dissented from the established church suffered discrimination, not persecution; aristocrats paid taxes on their landed estates, and their ranks were open to commoners who had recently made large fortunes.

And it was also true that for those with means, the system worked very nicely. Out of his father's allowance of £200 a year, Boswell reckoned that food, lodging, clean linen every day, candles and coals, and "having my shoes wiped at least once a day and sometimes oftener" would come to £157 a year. "By this calculation I have just £43 left for coach-hire, diversion, and the tavern, which I will find a very slight allowance," but "If I get a commission in the Guards, I shall then have about £90 a year more, which will make me pretty easy." Edward Gibbon lived well. "I had now attained the solid comforts of life," he wrote of his time in London as the celebrated author of *The Decline and Fall of the Roman Empire*, inheritor of his father's estate, and beneficiary of a substantial unearned salary as a Lord Commissioner of Trade and Plantations. "A convenient, well-furnished house, a domestic table, half a dozen chosen servants, my own carriage, and all the decent luxuries whose value is the more sensibly felt the longer they are enjoyed." His acquaintance, the wealthy bluestocking Mrs. Montagu, lived even better at "her very elegant house in Hill Street" in Mayfair, where she often entertained the more obsequious members of literary society. "A service of plate, and a table plentifully covered, disposed her guests to admire the splendour of her fortune, not less than the lustre of her talents," wrote Sir Nathaniel Wraxall, adding that although "all the lines of her countenance bespoke intelligence, her manner was more dictatorial and sententious than conciliating or diffident."

To pay for such entertainments, Mrs. Montagu gave close attention to her investments, which included some family-owned coal mines in the north of England. In May 1776, during one of her visits there to ensure that all was well, she wrote to her friend Mrs. Carter: "The people here are little better than savages, and their Countenances bear the marks of hard labour and total ignorance. Our Pitmen are literally as black as a coal; they earn much more than labourers, their children get a shilling a day at 9 or 10 years old, but they are so barbarous and uncultivated they know no use of money but to buy much meat and liquor with it. . . . They are ragged and dirty, and their wives are idle and drunken, so that while they live in plenty they present to your view an air of misery, poverty, and oppression. . . . They are useful persons to the general commonwealth, but considered separately a strange set of barbarians. As the Children are so early sent into the mines, I am afraid it will be impossible ever to civilize them . . ."

Since they had no political voice, the poor and the dispossessed had two choices: stay put and struggle to survive, or go. A 1774 letter addressed to some potential emigrants in Inverness, Scotland, and reprinted in the *South-Carolina Gazette*, gave six good reasons for going:

✳

1. The price of land is so low in some of the British colonies that forty or fifty pounds will purchase as much ground there as one thousand in this country. 2. There are few or no taxes at present in the colonies, most of their public debt being paid off since the last peace. 3. The climate in general is very healthy, and provisions of all kinds are extraordinary good and so cheap that a shilling will go as far in America as four shillings in Scotland. 4. The price of labour . . . is high in the colonies: a day labourer can gain there thrice the wages he can in this country. 5. There are no beggars in North America, the poor, when they appear, are amply provided for. Lastly, there are no titled, proud

lords to tyrannize over the lower sort of people, men there being upon a level and more valued, in proportion to their abilities, than they are in Scotland.

Every year thousands of people, often whole communities, left Britain for a new and more hopeful life. Between 1760 and 1773, the population of Georgia tripled, while that of North Carolina went from 70,000 in 1750 to 180,000 in 1770. Even the onset of war did not stop the flow. "The emigration of people from all parts of England is very amazing indeed," said a letter in the *Virginia Gazette* in 1774, "and if no stop is put to it England will really be drained of multitudes of mechanics of all sorts, also people of considerable property; ships are daily taken up for this purpose and the spirit of emigration daily increases: 'America, that land of promise!' is their cry."

Those who stayed and struggled to survive were by no means always passive. "All Respect to Law and Government seems to be lost among the common People," wrote Franklin to Joseph Galloway, adding that he had "seen Riots in the Country about Corn; Riots about Elections; Riots about Work-houses; Riots of colliers; Riots of weavers; Riots of coal-heavers; Riots of sawyers; Riots of chairmen; Riots of smugglers in which Custom–house Officers and Excisemen have been murdered . . ."

Some riots were overtly political, notably those that had to do with John Wilkes, the radical demagogue who was several times elected Member of Parliament for Middlesex, one of the few constituencies with a large electorate, but not allowed to take his seat on the grounds that he had been convicted of seditious libel for criticizing the king's speech in his pamphlet *The North Briton*. In the summer of 1768, Wilkes was in the King's Bench prison near St. George's Field when a large crowd of sailors mobbed the building, offering to tear it down and free him if he would but give the word. Wilkes declined the offer, but the sailors promised to return the next day, when a huge crowd also appeared to see what would happen. Also present was William Hickey, a young and well-to-do man about town:

As I had been present the whole of the 9th [May] and concluded there would be a renewal of the disturbance on the following day, I was stationed close to the prison gates by nine in the morning of the 10th, where I found already assembled a large party of the Third Regiment of Guards, which consisted principally of Scotchmen, a circumstance that tended to increase the mischief [for various reasons the Scots were at this time very unpopular among the English]. Several Justices of the Peace and an immense body of constables were also in attendance. At ten o'clock full a thousand seamen made their promised visit, again mounting to Mr. Wilkes's window, offering him liberty if he chose it, notwithstanding the presence of the 'lobsters' (as they called the soldiers), Wilkes renewing his entreaties that they would depart quietly. They, as before, cheered and did so, a mere gaping inoffensive mob remaining. A stupid, over-zealous Justice, however, thought proper to read the Riot Act, which not one hundredth part of the crowd knew had been done, after which the same blockhead of a Magistrate (Mr. Gillam) ordered the constables to disperse the mob, which they attempted by seizing several inoffensive persons and delivering them into charge of the military. This ill-timed and unnecessary violence at last raised a general indignation amongst the spectators; loud hisses commenced and abuse of the Scotch soldiers, and some few stones were thrown, one of which hit Gillam, whereupon the Magistrates ordered the Guards to fire, which the infernal scoundrels instantly did, with ball, whereby several persons lost their lives, some of them not being in the mob at all, for the vile assassins fired in all directions, and even across the public high road. One poor woman was killed seated upon a cartload of hay going by at the time.

At the time the firing commenced I was leaning upon the railing that separated the fields from the road, talking to a gentleman who stood near me, and we were mutually reprobating the infamous conduct of the soldiers and Magistrates when we observed several of the Guards running towards us, and soon they were in pursuit of a man in a scarlet waistcoat, who jumped over the rail within a foot of us, four soldiers being about fifty yards behind him in chase. My new acquaintance and I followed. The pursued man ran round a windmill, when finding himself in danger of being overtaken, he made for an inn near the Borough, kept by a Mr. Allen, the yard of which he entered, darting through a barn used as a cow house, having a door at each end, two of the Guards being then close at his heels. At the very instant he passed the second door, the son of Mr. Allen entered by the opposite one, and unluckily having a red waistcoat on, one of the soldiers, upon seeing him, presented his firelock and the young man in a fright dropped on his knees, when the soldier fired, killing him upon the spot. All this was the work of a minute, my companion and myself being witnesses of the whole transaction. The mob, now justly irritated at the brutality of the soldiers, became outrageous, and volleys of stones flew in every direction. The soldiers loaded and fired again and again, by which many lives were wantonly sacrificed. . . . A very large body of Horse Guards having now joined the foot, galloping round the ground, striking everyone they met violently with their broad swords, made the remaining there any longer a service of danger. I therefore proposed leaving the spot, to which my new acquaintance acceded, and we agreed to dine together. . . .

Reports of what soon came to be known as the Massacre of St. George's Fields were printed throughout the colonies, where they confirmed the deep suspicion that the only purpose of a standing army in peacetime was to support arbitrary government. "The experience of all ages, and the observations both of the historian and philosopher agree, that a standing army is the most ready engine in the hand of despotism to debase the powers of the human mind and eradicate the manly spirit of freedom," wrote Mercy Otis Warren.

Before the Seven Years' War there had never been a standing army in the British-American colonies, but following the Peace of Paris the government decided to maintain a force of some ten thousand redcoats there, ostensibly to protect the Americans from a combined French and Indian threat that no longer existed, but clearly also to strengthen the hands of royal governors when enforcing orders received from London. And as Mrs. Warren warned, "The people have certainly everything to fear from a government when the springs of its authority are fortified by a standing military force."

THE STAMP ACT COMES AND GOES

The first shots in the long and bloody Seven Years' War were fired early on a May morning in 1754 in the leafy forests of the Ohio Valley Wilderness, when a force of Virginia militiamen and their Indian allies surrounded and, without warning, opened fire on a small group of Frenchmen who were just rousing themselves from sleep. A few minutes later, ten of the French were dead, including their leader, the Sieur de Jumonville, and twenty-two taken prisoner. After scalping the corpses, the Indian warriors turned their attention to the prisoners, who hastened to put themselves under the protection of the American commander, a young, hot-headed, and over-promoted lieutenant colonel, tall and strong, with reddish hair, broad hands and big feet, named George Washington.

His orders from Governor Dinwiddie of Virginia had been clear. He was to scout the Ohio Valley for French interlopers, who were known to be building a series of forts that would militarily connect Canada and New Orleans, thus hemming in the westward course of the British Empire; but since this was one of those periods when Britain and France were not actually at war, he was "to act on the defensive." Only if the intruders resisted orders to leave the area was he to "make prisoners of, or kill and destroy them." Late in April, as he headed into the contested area, Washington learned that the

American outpost at what is now Pittsburgh had been taken over by a large force of what he routinely called "the treacherous French"— news, he wrote, that "should rouse from the Lethargy we have fallen into the heroic Spirit of every freeborn Englishman to attest the rights and privileges of our King." A month later he was informed that a smaller French force was out in the woods heading in his direction. Then came a message from his Indian ally, called the Half-King, "that he had seen the Tract of two French men crossing the Road and believ'd the whole body were lying not far off." Washington at once set off with forty men through the thick forest and, "having marched in small path & heavy Rain, and a night as dark as it is possible to conceive," joined forces with the Half-King.

"When we came to the Half-King I council'd with him, and got his assent to go hand in hand and strike the French," Washington wrote in his report to Governor Dinwiddie. "Accordingly himself, Monacatoocha, and a few other Indians set out with us, and when we came to the place where the Tracts were, the Half-King sent two Indians to follow their Tract and discover their Lodgement, which they did in about half a mile from the Road in a very obscure place surrounded with Rocks. I thereupon in conjunction with the Half-King & Monacatoocha formed a disposition to attack them on all sides, which we accordingly did, and after an Engagement of about fifteen Minutes we kill'd ten, wounded one, and took 21 Prisoners. Amongst those that were kill'd was Monsieur de Jumonville, the Commander . . ." Since he also stated in his report that "I was the first Man that approach'd them & the first whom they saw," it is also very probable that Washington was the first to open fire.

But that was an honor he was reluctant to claim, for no sooner had the firing ceased than one of the surviving French officers, Monsieur Laforce, angrily protested that they had been attacked without warning or provocation while on a peaceful diplomatic mission; they were an embassy, not a fighting or scouting force, and furthermore they had papers with them to prove it. Faced with the possibility that instead of a small triumph, he was responsible for a major blunder,

Washington took the obvious course: strenuous denial. Monsieur Laforce, he wrote to Dinwiddie, as well as being a Frenchman, was "a person of great subtilty and cunning," and therefore not to be believed. "These Officers pretend they were coming on an Embassy, but the absurdity of this pretext is too glaring." If they were really on a diplomatic mission, why were they "skulking" in such a secluded spot, "fitter for a Deserter than an Ambassador to hide in"? Why had they "sent Spies to Reconnoitre our Camp, as we are told, tho' they deny it"? Moreover "the Sense of the Half-King on this Subject is that they have bad Hearts, and this is a mere pretence, they never design'd to have come to us but in a hostile manner." To conclude, although "in strict Justice they ought to be hang'd for Spyes of the worst sort," he was sending the prisoners under escort to the governor and "I doubt not but they will endeavour to amuse your Honour with many smooth Story's as they did me, but were confuted in them all . . ."

Happily for his and his country's future, Washington was to enjoy throughout his military career what Napoleon would later say was the single most important quality in a commander: good luck. In this case it was to be the target of French revenge—"I shall expect every hour to be attack'd, and by unequal numbers"—so that what might have been a career-ending mistake was blotted out by the smoke and noise of a battle from which he emerged a hero. This took place at the poorly designed and badly sited redoubt he had built in the middle of the Great Meadow. Many years later, Washington recalled the fight: "About 9 o'clock on the third of July the enemy advanced with Shouts, and dismal Indian yells, to our Intrenchments, but was opposed by so warm, spirited, and constant a fire that to force the works in that way was abandoned by them; they then, from every little rising, tree, stump, stone, and bush, kept up a constant galling fire upon us; which was returned in the best manner we could till late in the Afternoon when there fell the most tremendous rain that can be conceived, filling our trenches with Water, wet not only the Ammunition in the Cartouch boxes and firelocks, but that which was in a small temporary Stockade in the middle of the Intrenchments called

Fort Necessity . . ." With their powder wet, their food running low, and one third of their number killed or wounded, the Americans were headed for defeat when, quite unexpectedly, the French offered to parley. The terms they offered were generous: The Americans did not even have to surrender but were allowed to depart and "the next Morning we marched out with the honors of war." Washington estimated French losses at three hundred, but the official French figures were two killed and seventeen wounded.

The following year Washington had another opportunity to learn from failure when, the war having become official, he served as a staff officer in General Braddock's army of redcoats and colonial militia on their way to attack the French at Fort Duquesne. Since there was no road over the mountains and through the forests, the army's engineers had to build their own, often advancing only three or four miles a day. Progress was even more painful for Washington, who came down with acute dysentery and "violent Fevers & Pains." A dose of Dr. James's Powder induced sweating, purging, and vomiting, but "my illness was too violent to suffer me to ride, therefore I was indebted to a cover'd Waggon for some part of my Transport; but even in this I could not continue for the jolting was so great." But he was determined to be in at the kill, "the General giving me his word and honour that I should be brought up before he reach'd the French Fort." In the middle of July, the army reached the Monongahela River, seven miles from Duquesne. Washington, still sick, tied cushions to his saddle and rode up to join Braddock. Just after they had crossed the river, "we were attack'd, (very unexpectedly I must own) by about 300 French and Indians. Our numbers consisted of about 1,300 well arm'd Men, chiefly regulars, who were struck with such a deadly Panick that nothing but confusion and disobedience of orders prevail'd amongst them. The Officers in general behav'd with incomparable bravery, for which they greatly suffer'd. . . . The Virginians behav'd like men, and died like Soldiers," but "the dastardly behaviour of the English Soldiers expos'd all those who were inclin'd to do their duty to almost certain Death; and at length, in despite of every effort to the contrary, broke and run as Sheep before the Hounds . . ." General Braddock was mortally wounded, and sixty other officers were also killed or wounded, but though he had been in the thick of the fighting Washington's luck continued to hold and he "escap'd without a wound, tho' I had four Bullets through my Coat and two Horses shot under me."

Following Braddock's defeat the British army withdrew all the way back to Philadelphia, leaving Washington and the Virginia Regiment to hold the line: "I have been posted for twenty Months past upon our cold and barren Frontiers to perform I think I may say impossibilities, that is, to protect from the cruel incursions of a Crafty Savage enemy a line of Inhabitants of more than 350 Miles extent with a force inadequate to the task." His efforts were acknowledged by his fellow Virginians, whose assembly rewarded the officers with generous grants of land, but his hopes that he and his regiment would be incorporated into the regular British army were disappointed. (This would be the second time that Washington failed to get one of His Majesty's commissions; as a boy he had hoped to enlist as a midshipman in the Royal Navy, but his possessive mother nagged him out of it.) The inferior status foisted on provincial officers sharpened this disappointment; although the motives that had led him to take up arms "were pure and Noble," and he "had no view of acquisition but that of Honour, by serving faithfully my King and Country," he could not help feeling bitter at the fact that while a British lieutenant colonel was paid twenty-two shillings a day he was getting only twelve shillings and six pence. Also, after retirement regular British officers received half pay for life while the pay of provincial officers ended with their service. Worst of all was the rule whereby any regular officer automatically outranked any provincial officer, so that "every Captain bearing the King's commission; every half-pay officer, or other, appearing with such a commission, would rank before me." Clearly, part of the problem was that "our Services . . . have not been properly represented to His Majesty: otherwise the best of Kings would have graciously taken Notice of Us."

As if to confirm this suspicion, an official court of inquiry, composed entirely of British officers, sent home a report that laid most of the blame for Braddock's defeat on the provincial forces. At the same time Washington's conduct during the so-called Jumonville Affair and the fight at Fort Necessity, though making him a hero to Virginians, was proof to the English that as an officer he was incompetent. "Washington and many such may have courage and resolution," wrote General Lord Albermarle to the Duke of Newcastle, "but they have no knowledge or experience in our profession. Consequently, there can be no dependence on them."

And so, while the war spread around the world, Washington decided that he had had enough. Thanks to what he called "the animating prospect of possessing Mrs. Custis," (and her fortune), he was able to resign his command, become a member of the Tidewater aristocracy, and win election to the House of Burgesses. Early in 1759, while still in his late twenties, he was writing to a relative: "I am now I believe fix'd at this Seat [Mount Vernon] with an agreeable Consort for Life and hope to find more happiness in retirement than I ever experienced amidst a wide and bustling World."

As it happened, 1759 was for the British "the Year of Victories," when under the energetic and inspiring leadership of William Pitt the Elder, they defeated the French and Spanish at sea, in India and the Far East, in Africa, Europe, Canada, and America. George II died the next year and, as Horace Walpole said, "the young King seemed to have the option of extending our victories and acquisitions, or of giving peace to the world." Eager to assert himself, and envious of Pitt's great popularity, George III decided to end the war, and before long Henry Fox was at work purchasing the votes needed in the House of Commons to ratify the Peace of Paris.

Like many another peace treaty, this one did little more than patch things over. Indeed, by humiliating the French and forcing them to give up possessions all over the world, the treaty more or less guaranteed that revenge would be high on their agenda, although in their weakened state they would have to resort to indirect means. Among these was the scheme to instigate another Jacobite Rebellion, along the lines of the one that had failed in 1745. To get things started, the Maréchal de Broglie and the Duc de Choiseul, then France's chief minister, invited the Pretender, Prince Charles Edward Stuart, to join them for a secret midnight meeting in Paris; but during his years of exile the handsome young man once known as Bonnie Prince Charlie had become a middle-aged drunkard who turned up for the meeting several hours late and, in the words of Sir Nathaniel Wraxall, "in a state of such intoxication as to be utterly incapable even of ordinary conversation." Or perhaps the loss of Canada could be turned to good advantage. Only when the Indians were reinforced by French regulars did the American colonists need the help of British regulars. So if Canada were British rather than French, what need would the colonists have for the British army and navy? Might they not then wonder why they should remain part of the British Empire? A confidential agent, Baron de Kalb, was dispatched to assess the situation. De Kalb traveled extensively throughout the colonies and wrote detailed reports, most of which were intercepted and read by the British secret service, which then forwarded them to Paris. Choiseul, however, seems to have paid them scant attention, perhaps because they did not contain what he wanted to hear—although a few New Englanders were restive, "they all, from the leaders down to the humblest citizen, seem to be imbued with a heartfelt love of the mother country." In fact, so great was their hostility to the French, wrote de Kalb, that "it would be impossible to get them to accept help from us."

But as events were to prove, there was no need for Choiseul to do anything; France's revenge could safely be left in the hands of the British, who emerged from the war with a serious case of swaggering over-confidence. "John Bull," wrote Franklin, was so "drunk with Victory" that he was likely to "double his Fists and bid all the

World kiss his Arse—till he provokes them to drub him again into his Senses."

The starting point for trouble with the colonies was the national debt, amounting at the end of the war to £122,603,366, on which the interest was some four and a half million pounds a year. The Land Tax, the main source of revenue, was already at four shillings in the pound, or twenty percent, and since it fell largely on the politically influential land-owning class, could not be raised. Revenue from customs was down because of a post-war slump. An attempt to increase excise revenue by a tax on cider had produced such widespread rioting in the west of England that it had to be repealed. Other excise taxes were equally unpopular. "There is a cruel tax going to be lain on cottagers who are to pay the tax if they have seven windows," wrote Mrs. Montagu in 1766, "so these poor wretches must live without light and air; all this to please America." Mrs. Montagu also lamented the fate of the country gentleman who was going to have to pay a wheel tax of ten pounds a year for his coach: "I grieve for the gouty Squires and their fat wives who will not be able to let the coach and old Dobbin and Whiteface tug them to church, or to visit a neighbour, while your American drives his gilded Car [coach] and 6 bays, tho' perhaps his Father was transported for felony."

Mrs. Montagu was not alone in her low opinion of the Americans. Dr. Johnson felt even more strongly. According to Boswell, the doctor was once in the middle of a friendly discussion about religion with "Mrs. Knowles, the ingenious Quaker lady, Miss Seward, the poetess of Lichfield," and two clergymen, when he suddenly exploded: "'I am willing to love all mankind, *except an American.*' And his inflammable corruption bursting into horrid fire, he breathed out threatenings and slaughter, calling them 'Rascals—Robbers—Pirates;' and exclaiming he'd 'burn and destroy them.'" Few others were as extreme, but an attitude of smug superiority was common. Writing of the need for "a fair and equal Representation of all the Parts of this Empire in Parliament" as "the only firm Basis on which political Grandeur and Prosperity can be founded," Franklin complained that "the Pride of this People cannot bear the Thought of it. . . . Every Man in England seems to consider himself as a Piece of a Sovereign over America; seems to jostle himself into the Throne with the King, and talks about *our subjects in the Colonies.*"

Moreover most English people were convinced that not only had the Americans done little to help during the last war but also that they were now expecting to benefit scot-free from the presence of an army of ten thousand redcoats permanently stationed among them for their defense, at a cost of some £400,000 a year. "Must America be defended entirely by us, and be themselves quite excused?" asked prime minister George Grenville, tacitly confirming Washington's suspicion that "our services have not been properly represented."

And so, when Grenville introduced a bill to extend to the colonies a tax that had long been paid by those at home, it seemed so obviously right and fair that the debate in Parliament was, as Burke said, "languid," and the measure passed "unopposed and almost unperceived." Very few in Britain foresaw the trouble the Stamp Act was to cause. Even Franklin, though he had his doubts, was taken unawares, and rather than strongly oppose the measure used his influence to get his friend John Hughes appointed one of the collectors for Pennsylvania (a favor that, but for the intervention of Deborah Franklin, almost resulted in Hughes having his house torn down by the mob).

The Stamp Act required that, to be valid, nearly all legal and commercial documents had to bear a special stamp, printed in England and sold by official agents. A will had to carry a five-shilling stamp and a bill of lading a fourpenny stamp; a college degree cost two pounds and a license to sell liquor one pound. Newspapers and pamphlets were also taxed, the rate varying between a half penny and one shilling, depending on their size and length, with an added tax for advertisements. For almanacs and calendars "which shall be written or printed on one side only" the stamp was two pence. For any document "in any other than the English language, a stamp duty of double the amount" (this was aimed at the unpopular German-speaking Pennsylvanians). Playing cards were taxed at one shilling a pack and dice at ten shillings.

The revenue, estimated at £60,000 a year, was to be used for "defraying the expenses of defending, protecting, and securing the British colonies in America" and was to be paid into a special account, thus forestalling any suspicion that it would be diverted to sinecures and pensions. Commissioners were to be appointed to administer the tax, and offenders were to be tried in admiralty courts, which had no jury.

According to Horace Walpole,

it had been proposed to Sir Robert Walpole [his father, and prime minister for many years] to raise the revenue by imposing taxes on America, but that minister, who could foresee beyond the benefit of the actual moment, declared it must be a bolder man than himself who should venture on such an expedient. That man was found in Grenville, who . . . termed it [the Stamp Act] but an experiment towards further aid—and as such the Americans immediately understood it. Little did he weigh the danger of a contest between the mother country and such distant, extensive, and now powerful subjects.

But in the eyes of Grenville and most M.P.s, the Stamp Act, as well as spreading the burden more fairly, did no more than tighten up and slightly extend a system already in force. For well over a hundred years, Parliament had regulated the economic affairs of the colonies— in theory to the benefit of the empire as a whole, in fact mostly to the benefit of the mother country—and no one had objected. Under the Navigation Acts of the previous century, only British or colonial ships were allowed to carry goods between the two countries. Almost all colonial products, even if they were eventually to be sold elsewhere, had to be routed through Britain, and vice versa: The Virginia tobacco that was so popular in France, and the wine and olive oil imported by the colonists from Portugal, all had to be shipped first to England, unloaded, and then re-shipped, a system ripe with easy commissions, brokerage fees, and opportunities for price-fixing. Nor were colonists permitted to produce goods that might compete with those of the mother country. Under the Wool Act of 1698, they could make but not export woolen goods; under the Hat Act colonial hat makers were not allowed to employ more than two apprentices, or any Negroes, or export hats from one colony to another; under the Iron Acts of 1750 and 1757, no rolling mills or steel furnaces were allowed; under the Currency Act of 1764, the colonies were barred from issuing paper money, even for purely internal use, and even though they were often short of specie since the permanent imbalance of trade with England drained them of gold and silver. Every law made in the colonies was reviewed by the Lords Commissioners for Trade and Plantations (usually known as the Board of Trade), which then recommended to the Privy Council whether it should be approved or rejected.

Americans put up with this one-sided system partly because there wasn't much they could do about it, partly because they did benefit from the protection of the British army and navy, but mostly because many of the laws were dead on arrival. No inspector from the Board of Trade ever came to check on the number and race of a colonial hat-maker's employees. The Molasses Act of 1733 might impose a duty of three pence a gallon on molasses imported from the French and Dutch West Indies, but New England distillers simply ignored it. Like Thomas Paine, who while still in England was fired twice from the customs service for slacking off, colonial customs officers were famously idle, or venal, or both; and if anyone was accused of smuggling, it was almost impossible to get a jury to convict him (hence the non-jury admiralty courts specified by the Stamp Act). This failure to enforce the laws even had a name: Salutary Neglect. "Long had the colonies been neglected, or overlooked," wrote Horace Walpole approvingly. "Sir Robert Walpole, whose maxim was *quieta non movere*, had been content with seeing no troubles arise in America. He had left that province to its proper minister, the Duke of Newcastle, Secretary of State, who had a closet full of dispatches from that quarter unopened for a large number of years. The Board of Trade, whose department it was, had sunk into a perfect sinecure . . ."

Force of habit was another reason the system endured. Not long after his marriage to the wealthy Martha Custis, Washington decided to order a new, prestige-conferring coach "made in the newest taste, handsome, genteel & light. It should have steel springs and be painted green unless any other colour more in vogue & equally lasting is entitled to precedence. . . . A light gilding on the mouldings (that is round the panels) & any other ornaments that may not have a heavy & tawdry look (together with my [coat of] arms agreeable to the Impression here sent) might be added, by way of decoration." There should be room for two postilions, and "on the Harness let my Crest be engraved." At that time no one in America could possibly fulfill such an order. The very finest coaches were made in France, but it probably never even occurred to Washington to order it from that country. He had no agent there, no line of credit, and how could he specify in a foreign language all those details about fashionable colors and having his crest stamped on the leather? Also, since the coach would have had to be shipped first to England, Washington would have had to pay the 75 percent import tax imposed by the protectionist British government on all vehicles made in France. So, as usual, his purchase order was addressed to Messrs Robert Cary & Co. of London, who handled his tobacco sales and who, after a long delay, sent him a coach, whose panels, being made of unseasoned wood, soon cracked and had to be replaced.

As Franklin kept explaining, the colonists made an important distinction between laws to regulate trade and laws to raise a revenue. Regulating trade within the British Empire was acknowledged to be Parliament's right, and so-called "external" taxes paid in the form of customs duties were acceptable; but the right to make "internal" laws for the purpose of raising a revenue belonged solely to their own assemblies. But now Grenville seemed to be trampling on this cherished distinction: The purpose of the "just and necessary" Stamp Act was "for raising a further revenue within your Majesty's dominions in America." But Americans—or at least white Americans—had no intention of being treated as inferiors. "His Majesty's liege subjects in these colonies are entitled to all the inherent rights and liberties of his natural born subjects within the kingdom of Great Britain," ran the second article of the resolves of the Stamp Act Congress. These rights included habeas corpus, free speech, trial by jury, and the right not to be taxed without their consent. English history was their history too, including the story of how Charles I had tried to impose despotic rule by raising money without the consent of Parliament. The cry "Taxation without representation is tyranny" was based on English, not American, precedent; so too was the cry "Resistance to tyranny is obedience to God."

For as long as the obtuseness of the British government allowed him to do so, Franklin remained a warm advocate of the British Empire, but not of the supremacy of the British Parliament. As he wrote to his friend, the Scottish jurist Lord Kames, "All the Colonies acknowledge the King as their Sovereign; his Governors there represent his Person; Laws are made by their Assemblies or little Parliaments, with the Governors' Assent, subject still to the King's Pleasure to confirm or annul them. . . . In this view, they seem to be so many separate little States, subject to the same Prince." In other words, George III was King of England, Elector of Hanover, King of Scotland, King of Ireland, and—though Franklin did not actually spell it out—he was also King of Massachusetts, King of Connecticut, and so on. "The *Sovereignty* of the King is therefore easily understood. But nothing is more common here [in England] than to talk of the *Sovereignty* of Parliament, and the *Sovereignty* of this Nation over the Colonies."

Franklin concluded his letter to Lord Kames by taking the long view: "America, an immense Territory, favoured by Nature with all Advantages of Climate, Soil, great navigable Rivers, and Lakes, &c. must become a great Country, populous and mighty; and will, in less Time than is generally conceived, be able to shake off any Shackles that may be imposed on her . . . for the Seeds of Liberty are universally found there, and nothing can eradicate them."

To the astonishment and indignation of Grenville, the new tax, though meekly accepted in the West Indies, was strongly opposed by the Americans, who boycotted English imports and closed their courts rather than pay it. This caused a good deal of hardship, particularly among lawyers, never a good class to alienate. "So sudden an Interruption in my Career is very unfortunate for me," John Adams, now happily married to Abigail Smith and beginning to prosper in his legal career, wrote in his diary. He had had "Poverty to struggle with—Envy and Jealousy and Malice of Enemies to encounter—no Friends, or but few to assist me, so that I have groped in dark Obscurity till of late, and had just become known, and gained a small degree of Reputation, when this execrable Project was set on foot for my Ruin, as well as that of America in general and of Great Britain."

Others took to the streets. Every port to which the stamps were sent was the scene of mob violence. This account of what happened in New York comes from the diary of Captain John Montresor of the Royal Engineers, who had spent the last ten years in the country and was now on the staff of General Thomas Gage, Washington's former comrade in arms during the Braddock campaign and now commander-in-chief of the British forces in America.

＊

October 22nd, [1765]. The Frigates fired signals of the arrival of the vessel with the Stamps. 23rd. 2000 people (mob) on the Battery expecting the Stamps would be landed, but were disappointed. However they were secretly landed in the night and deposited in the Fort and took charge of by the Governor. Many placards put up threatening the Lives, Houses and properties of any one who shall either issue or receive a stamp. 31st. This night a mob in 3 squads went through

the Streets crying "Liberty!" at the same time breaking the Lamps &
threatening particulars that they would the next night pull down their
Houses. Some thousands of windows broke. Major James of the Royal
Artillery [who had vowed "to cram the stamps down the Americans'
throats"] threatened to be buried alive by the Populace.

[On November 1] the Rabble or rather Rebels assembled again
early in the evening & Continued the Riot till 4 this morning,
their numbers about 2,000, during which time they broke open the
Governor's coach house under the Fort fire & then took out his chariot
& 2 Sleighs & a chair which they burnt in the Bowling Green with
effigies & Gallows. . . . From thence they proceeded to Major James'
House and there after breaking every window, cut down all the window shutters & broke down all the partitions—then they destroyed 9
¼ casks of Wine & destroyed & Stole all his plate, Furniture, apparel,
Books &c to the value of £1500. [On November 3] all the officers in
town were ordered from Head Quarters to attend the Fort every afternoon at 4 o'clock and those for duty continued there 24 hours. Even
the master of the vessel who brought the Stamps, his life being threatened, was obliged to fly. [Next day] the Governor's Family obliged to
seek protection on board His Majesty's Ship the *Coventry*. 5th. By the
advice of the Council, opinion of the Commander in Chief and earnest
request of the Corporation, the Stamps were delivered to the mayor &
Corporation, they to be responsible to the Crown to the amount of
what these Stamps would come to when distributed, also any damages
they shall sustain, losses &c. Seven Boxes of Stamps were delivered and
proceeded to the city Hall in Carts and deposited there attended by
5000 people. 6th. Perfect tranquillity (as to appearances) this day. The
Governor's family returned from on board the Man of war.

But simply locking the stamps away was not enough to restore
calm. In mid-December Montresor noted that "placards seditious
and infamous as ever" were still being posted, and on the 17th effigies of "Mr. Grenville and General Murray were paraded several times

through the streets amidst a large concourse of people" and then "were carried to the Common and there burnt. Their numerous attendants the Mob were furnished all with Candles which they forced from the Houses as they went along, threatening to set them on fire if Refused." Next month (January 1766), "Children nightly trampouze the Streets with lanthorns upon Poles & hallowing. 18th. Advices from Hartford in Connecticut that a large body had assembled there of the Inhabitants for forming a new system of government. Some were for choosing a Protector as in Oliver Cromwell's time. February 4th. Advices from S. Carolina that the Governor of Georgia had gallantly headed some regular troops and militia in opposition to the Mob & enforced the Stamp Act, but not without some trifling slaughter. 6th. The Sons of Liberty (who have the sole regulation of the licentious press here) declare that they will fight up to their knees in blood rather than suffer the Stamp Act to be put in force in this Province."

But while children were trampouzing with lanthorns through the streets of New York, and the governor and his troops were inflicting some trifling slaughter on the mob in Georgia, back in England the Stamp Act had been repealed. In part this was due to the influence of the king, who could not stand the tactless and pontificating Grenville, with his habit of lecturing everyone at great length and who failed to act "with that defference he ow'd Me." (George usually made a point of capitalizing references to himself.) Exercising his prerogative, he had dismissed Grenville and replaced him with the liberal-minded Lord Rockingham, Burke's patron. Soon afterward, news of the Stamp Act riots started coming in. Even less welcome, wrote Horace Walpole, was the colonists' "refusal of paying the debts they owed to our merchants at home for goods and wares exported to the American provinces. These debts involved the merchants of London, Liverpool, Manchester, and other great trading towns in a common cause with the Americans, who forswore all traffic with us, unless the obnoxious Stamp Act were repealed." Since the Rockingham Whigs had opposed the Stamp Act, and since to enforce it "would risk lighting up a rebellion in the colonies," while also causing "insurrections in the trading towns at home," it was not long before one of their leaders, General Conway, brought in a bill to repeal that Act, "and drew an affecting picture of the mischiefs it had occasioned and threatened. All orders for goods from this country were stopped: the North Americans would neither take any more, nor pay for that they had. Eight merchants who had received orders to the amount of four hundred thousand pounds had received counter-orders. The debt to those merchants amounted to £950,000. . . . Nottingham had dismissed a thousand hands: Leicester, Leeds, and other towns in proportion. Three in ten of the labourers of Manchester were discharged. The trade of England was not only stopped, but in danger of being lost. . . . As the colonies would not take our manufactures, they would set up their own. He had a piece of cloth, he said, in his pocket made at Philadelphia, as cheap as in England. Would the House risk the whole for so trifling an object as this Act?"

As the debate in Parliament got under way, William Pitt, who suffered from bouts of melancholia and chronic gout, rose dramatically from his sickbed to defend the colonists: "They are the subjects of this kingdom, equally entitled with yourselves to all the natural rights of mankind and the peculiar privileges of Englishmen. Equally bound by its laws, and equally participating of the constitution of this free country. The Americans are the sons, not the bastards, of England. Taxation is no part of the governing or legislative power." Later in the debate, lashing into Grenville (his brother-in-law), he said: "The gentleman tells us, America is obstinate; America is almost in open rebellion. I rejoice that America has resisted. Three millions of people so dead to all the feelings of liberty as voluntarily to submit to be slaves would have been fit instruments to make slaves of the rest."

This idea that the rights and liberties of the British were inextricably linked with those of Americans was often argued but never made much headway. Franklin was pessimistic about the prospect of repeal because of the "mistaken Opinion that the Honour and Dignity of Government is better supported by persisting in a wrong Measure once entered into, than by rectifying an Error as soon as it is discovered." In general this was surely true enough, but not in this case, an exception largely due to the king. Getting rid of the insufferable Grenville, who according to Franklin was "besotted with his Stamp Scheme," also meant getting rid of his policies. "Repealing infinitely more eligible than Enforcing, which could only tend to widen the breach between this Country & America," the king wrote in one of his memoranda to himself. "On Friday 6th of February Ld. Rockingham said to Me that now the two partys meant to push for Repeal, or Enforce. I immediately answer'd that in that case I was for the former. He ask'd my permission to say so, which I freely gave."

Soon afterward, the king received this note, datelined "Grosvenor House, Saturday Morning, near 5 o'clock, Feb: ye 22d 1766: Lord Rockingham humbly presumes to acquaint his Majesty that . . . after long debate the Question was put upon *Repeal* & upon division the Numbers were for the *Repeal* 275—against it—167 . . . the Joy in the Lobby of the House of Commons which was full of Considerable Merchants both of London & from different Manufacturing Parts of this Country, was extreme."

A month later, when the repeal had been completed, the king wrote: "Ld. R.—I am glad the American Affair has ended this day without any great altercation."

Meanwhile, in New York, Captain Montresor was continuing his diary:

April 3rd. The Sons or Spawns of Liberty and Inquisition here still venting threats and Insulting the Crown & Officers under it. 4th. Accounts by the way of Philadelphia from South Carolina that the Stamp Act was repealed and all American affairs settled by Parliament. 23rd. Upon the news from England by the way of Boston arriving relating to the apparent probability of the Repeal of the Stamp Act and Mr. Pitt's speech, one Swinney, an inflammatory news-carrier and monger, galloped on Horse Back through the Street crying *Pitt and no King* till meeting with an English Butcher, who silenced him. 24th. Came up by the Skiff of a Pilot Boat an account that the Duke of Cumberland, Packet Boat, Captain Goodrich, from Falmouth, was arrived at Sandy Hook and brought advices that the Stamp Act was repealed. Many streets were illuminated and squibs and firing of muskets ensued and Captain Sears, a principal Ringleader of the Sons of Liberty, went to the Rector and the several Ministers of the places of worship here to order them to ring their Bells at 3 o'clock the next morning. Mr. Pitt's speech published at large and highly applauded by the Sons of Liberty. 26th. At 3 o'clock this morning All the Bells of this place rung and having no peal made a most hideous Din. About 8 o'clock a.m. the Captain of the Packet arrived with the mail in his Boat and was demanded by the Sons of Liberty before he came ashore whether the Stamp Act was repealed—he answered in the affirmative, adding Totally. Upon which they fixed him in a chair and carried him and the mail to the Post Office with great acclamations of joy, cheering him all the way. The bells still ringing.

In Massachusetts, John Adams, his legal career now happily back on track, wrote in his diary: "The repeal of the Stamp Act has hushed into silence almost every popular clamor, and composed every wave of popular disorder into a smooth and peaceful calm." Throughout the colonies, the king's official birthday, June 4, was celebrated with parades, illuminations, gunfire salutes, roast oxen, and "Beer and Grog for the Populace." In New York, the Common Council voted to erect an equestrian statue of the king on Bowling Green, the statue to be made of lead but plated with gold, and Lt. Gov. Colden was reimbursed the sum of £195 and 3 shillings, which was "the Loss & value ascertained on Oath" of his coach that the mob had burned. In London, Benjamin Franklin took a rosy view of the future: "We now see that tho' the Parliament may sometimes thro' Misinformation be misled to do a wrong Thing towards America, yet as soon as they are rightly inform'd, they will immediately rectify it, which ought to confirm our Veneration for that most August Body and Confidence in its Justice and Equity."

Soon afterward Franklin was once again writing to Deborah. Another package was on its way home, this one containing "a fine Piece of Pompadour Satin, fourteen Yards, cost eleven Shillings a Yard; a silk Negligee and Petticoat of brocaded Lutestring for my dear Sally, with two dozen Gloves, four Bottles of Lavender Water." With Mrs. Stevenson's help he had also bought three damask tablecloths, some crimson mohair to make curtains, "a large true Turkey Carpet, cost ten Guineas, for the dining Parlour. . . . Also a box with three fine Cheeses. Perhaps a bit of them may be left when I come Home."

But it would be almost ten years before Franklin went home. As agent for the Pennsylvania Assembly and unofficial ambassador for all the American colonies to the mother country, he was constantly busy. The fight with the Penn family went on, and there were promising developments concerning the Grand Ohio Company as it negotiated to buy the land that the Six Nations had been persuaded to hand over at the Treaty of Fort Stanwix in 1768. The deal required complicated maneuvers. Lord Hillsborough, colonial secretary for many years, opposed the scheme: So remote a colony would be hard to control and, even worse, would very likely attract immigrants from Ireland, making it hard to find workers for his vast estates there. To counteract Hillsborough, Franklin cut in several other members of the Privy Council, which had the final say on the project. He also arranged for the new colony to be called Vandalia, in honor of the German-born queen. Then, in 1772, Hillsborough was replaced by Lord Dartmouth, known to favor the scheme. The price offered was £10,460, 7 shillings, and 3 pence—the sum expended by the government for the rum, guns, blankets, knives, and other presents given to the Indians at

Fort Stanwix. Had the deal not collapsed with the onset of the Revolution, the Grand Ohio Company would have been able to buy 20,920,000 acres at a rate of about one penny for eight acres.

There were other benefits to staying on in London. "As to my Situation here, nothing can be more agreeable," Franklin wrote from his comfortable lodgings on Craven Street to a friend in 1772. "A general Respect paid me by the Learned, a Number of Friends and Acquaintances among them, with whom I have a pleasing Intercourse; a Character of so much Weight that it has protected me when some in Power would have done me Injury. . . . My Company so much desired that I seldom dine at Home in Winter, and could spend the whole Summer in the Country-houses of inviting Friends, if I chose it. Learned and ingenious Foreigners that come to England almost all make a Point of visiting me, for my Reputation is still higher abroad than here. Several of the foreign Ambassadors have assiduously cultivated my Acquaintance, treating me as one of their Corps, partly I believe from the Desire they have, from Time to Time, of hearing something of American Affairs, an Object become of Importance in foreign Courts . . . and partly that they may have an Opportunity of introducing me to the Gentlemen of their Country who desire it. The King, too, has lately been heard to speak of me with great Regard."

British redcoats advance up Bunker Hill, June 17, 1775.

CHAPTER TWO

Boston and New England

For the ten years between the end of the Stamp Act crisis and the British evacuation of Boston, resistance to the mother country was led by her eldest and least grateful daughter, New England.

There was an irony to this because by descent and mind-set, New Englanders were the most English of the Americans, having come largely from East Anglia and still holding fast to the traditions they had brought over with them: building houses of wood around village greens like the one at Lexington, regularly convening town meetings, establishing schools, naming their counties and towns after the places they had left behind—Essex, Braintree, Boston—even speaking in accents derived from the so-called Norfolk Whine. But New Englanders held even faster to those traditions that had set their forefathers at odds with the establishment majority in the old country: their Puritan beliefs and practices so inimical to those of the Church of England, their social structure that had no place for a landed aristocracy, the radicalism that had inspired Parliamentary resistance to arbitrary royal power, and the militant spirit that had brought victory to Cromwell's New Model Army in the English Civil War and then sent Charles I to the block.

BOSTON

To young John Adams, born and raised on a farm in Braintree, it was the big city, bewildering in its noise and bustle. "My Eyes are so diverted with Chimney Sweeps, Carriers of Wood, Merchants, Ladies, Priests, Carts, Horses, Oxen, Coaches, Market men and Women, Soldiers, Sailors; and my Ears with the Rattle Gabble of them all that I can't think long enough in the Street upon any one Thing to start and pursue a Thought."

To Anne Hulton, genteel sister of one of the Commissioners of Customs sent over in 1767 to enforce the law, it was "like a large Seaport Town in England, & the People speak as good English as anywhere. It is built on a Peninsula & about two mile Long, joyn'd to the Continent by a piece of Land call'd the Neck, which is a mile Long, & twice as broad as a great Street. This is the only way by Land out of the Town. . . . There are a great number of By Streets & hobbling Pavements. The publick buildings are the Exchange, the Town House, & Fennil Hall. There are two Episcopal churches, besides the King's Chapel, but one Presbyterian (properly call'd) and about 12 Independent Congregationalists. Some of these Ministers are very flaming preachers, that is they take occasion to inflame the People, both by their sermons and prayers against Government, & all belonging to it."

To John Winthrop, first governor of Massachusetts Bay and leader of the great Puritan migration of 1630, "flaming preachers" would have been welcome, for the new settlement was to be nothing less than a shining example to the whole world of a perfect biblical commonwealth. "Wee shall be as a Citty upon a hill," he wrote in *A Modell of Christian Charity.* "The eyes of all people are upon us." The Indians, to whom the place had been known as Shawmut, had neither opposed nor welcomed the newcomers for the good reason that a few years earlier they had been almost wiped out by what Edward Johnson, author of *Wonder-working Providence of Sion's Savior in New England,* called "a sore Consumption, sweeping away whole Families"—probably smallpox or measles, contracted from one of the European fishing ships that often put in on the New England coast. To Johnson, this epidemic was a sure sign that even before they arrived the Puritans' enterprise was looked on with divine favor: "By this meanes Christ not onely made roome for his people to plant [i.e., settle]; but also tamed the hard and cruell hearts of these barbarous Indians." Or as Francis Higginson, another early clergyman, put it: "We doubt not but God will be with us, and if God be with us, who can be against us?"

The belief that New Englanders were of special interest to the Almighty was still widely held at the time of the Revolution, although there had been a sad falling-off in public morality. "There is every Year some new and astonishing scene of Vice, laid open to the Consideration of the Public," wrote John Adams in his diary in December 1760. "Parson Potter's Affair with Mrs. Winchester and other women is hardly forgotten. A Minister, famous for Learning, oratory, orthodoxy, Piety and Gravity, discovered to have the most debauched and polluted of Minds, to have pursued a series of wanton Intrigues with one woman and another, to have got his maid with Child, and all that." Parson Potter was not the only one: "Lately Deacon Savil's Affair has become public," ran another entry in the Adams diary, "An old Man 77 Years of Age, a Deacon, whose chief Ambition has always been Prayer and religious Conversation, and sacerdotal Company, discovered to have been the most salacious, rampant Stallion in the Universe—rambling all the Town over, lodging with this and that Boy and attempting at least the Crime of buggery."

Gluttony was another of the deadly sins corrupting the clergy. According to a letter in the *Boston Gazette*, at the dinner following the installation of the Rev. Alexander Cumming as co-pastor of the Old South Church, "there were six tables that held one with another 18 persons, upon each table a good rich plum pudding, a dish of boil'd pork and fowls, and a corn'd leg of pork with sauce proper for it, a leg of bacon, a piece of alamode beef, a leg of mutton with caper sauce, a piece of roast beef, a roast loin of veal, a roast turkey, a venison pastee, besides chess cakes and tarts, cheese and butter. Half a dozen cooks were employed upon this occasion, upwards of twenty tenders to wait upon the tables; they had the best of old cyder, one barrel of Lisbon wine, punch in plenty before and after dinner made of old Barbados spirit." Answering the charge of extravagance, another letter writer to the *Gazette* claimed "that many poor people were the better for what remained of so plentiful and splendid a Feast."

But despite occasional scandals the clergy still enjoyed great prestige. On Sundays respectable people usually attended a lengthy service in the morning and then another in the afternoon. In her diary for November 18, 1771, Anna Green Winslow, aged twelve and staying in Boston with her aunt, recorded how the Rev. Mr. Beacon had preached on a text from Psalm 149, "For the Lord taketh pleasure in his people; he will beautify the meek with salvation." As well as having to listen to the sermon, Anna was also expected to write a summary of it afterward, but in this she did not get very far ("he said a great deal about it that I can't remember"), although she was able to recall its conclusion: "He said he would lastly address himself to the young people: My dear young friends, you are pleased with beauty, & like to be tho't beautifull—but let me tell ye, you'll never be truly beautifull till you are like the King's daughter, all glorious within, all the orniments you can put on while your souls are unholy make you the more like white sepulchres garnish'd without, but full of deformyty within. You think me very unpolite no doubt to address you in this manner, but I must go a little further and tell you, how course so ever it may sound to your delicacy, that while you are without holiness, your beauty is deformity—you are all over black & defil'd, ugly and loathsome to all holy beings, the wrath of the great God lies upon you, & if you die in this condition you will be turn'd into hell, with ugly devils, to eternity."

If not on this occasion then on many others, another young woman would also have been in church listening to the minister rail on about being "black & defil'd." This was Phillis Wheatley, the "Ethiopian poetess," who had been born in Africa, enslaved at the age of seven, and shipped directly to Boston, where she had the good fortune to be bought by a prosperous and kindly family called Wheatley. "I was a poor little outcast and a stranger when she [Mrs. Wheatley] took me in," wrote Phillis in 1774, when she was not yet twenty, "not only into her house, but I presently became a sharer in her most tender affections. I was treated by her more like her child than her servant; no opportunity was left unimproved in giving me the best advice; but in terms how tender! how engaging! This I hope ever to keep in remembrance." Phillis was very bright; after studying the Bible, she learned Latin, translated Ovid, and soon started writing her own poems. These were skillful rather than inspired. Her most famous was titled *On Being Brought From Africa To America* and, rather oddly, was based on the argument popular among slave-traders that bringing Africans to this country was actually doing them a favor, since only here could they be exposed to the Word of God and given the chance to save their souls by becoming Christians. (The poem starts: "'Twas Mercy brought me from my Pagan land/ Taught my benighted soul to understand/ That there's a God, that there's a Saviour too . . ." and concludes: "Remember, Christians, Negroes black as Cain/ May be refined and join the angelic strain.") Another poem, an ode on the death of the renowned evangelist George Whitefield, whom she had heard preach to a vast crowd on the Common, was forwarded to the Countess of Huntingdon, friend of Lord Dartmouth and patroness of Methodism. As a consequence, when the Wheatleys, thinking that a sea voyage would be good for her fragile health, sent Phillis to England, she was received by that august personage, who also helped to get her poems published. As a phenomenon—a black bluestocking—she was briefly taken up by London society, was presented with a copy of *Paradise Lost* by the Lord Mayor, and escorted by the abolitionist Granville Sharp to see the lions at the Tower of London. There were even plans for her to be presented at court, but then news came that Mrs. Wheatley was sick and needed her help, so Phillis went back to Boston. Although her volume of poems got only mixed reviews in England ("of no astonishing powers of genius," said one), Boston booksellers ordered three hundred copies; but then came the Tea Party followed by the Coercive Acts; the port was closed, and the books had to be sent back—surely one of the worst cases ever of an author's hard luck. On the brighter side, while back in Boston, she was admitted as a member of the Old South Church, although like other slaves—who were not all that numerous in Boston—she had to sit up in the gallery.

As well as excoriating their listeners for their failings, the clergy exercised great influence in politics. "His Majesty has very few subjects whose loyalty he can depend upon on the Continent, besides members of the Church of England. The rest are all downright republicans," wrote the Boston Loyalist Samuel Auchmuty to Dr. Johnson. For their part, Congregationalist and Presbyterian ministers took an equally dim view of Anglicans, with their worldly ways, unscriptural episcopate, and Romish ceremonies. To the Rev. Ezra Stiles, minister at Newport, Rhode Island, and later president of Yale, the Church of England in America, especially in New England, was "an asylum for polite Vice and Irreligion," its members "profane Swearers & abandoned Debauchees" who "had fled from other Communions for Drunkenness, Whoring, Swearing, or other moral Scandal." Great alarm was caused by rumors that an Anglican bishop was to be sent over to reside in America, but Stiles was not worried. "The present Endeavors of Episcopalian and deistical Crown officers to . . . plague and become a Scourge to the New England Puritans will be defeated by the irresistible and overruling Providence of the Most High."

As to Boston itself, by the time of the Revolution, it had a population of about sixteen thousand in an area measuring some 780 acres—since then the land area has increased fourfold as a result of extending the waterfront and filling in the Back Bay and the Mill Pond. There were fewer than two thousand houses, most of them built of wood and crowded close together. Fires were common, but could be "sanctified" as a sign of God's special concern for his people: Like a loving father, he punished his errant children to save them from further sin—"May this Chastisement bring us to unfeigned Repentance and Reformation," ran a typical post-conflagration prayer. Polluted wells brought on attacks of dysentery, known as "the bloody flux." The cobbled streets were often ankle-deep in horse dung, which turned to clouds of dust in the summer. In winter the air was thick with smoke from the thousands of wood burning fires that heated the houses, but wood was becoming scarce and expensive, and many householders turned to burning coal shipped in from England, perhaps including some from Mrs. Montagu's mines near Newcastle. Pigs wandered about, eating the garbage. The gallows stood near the town gate on the Neck; heaps of stones nearby marked the graves of suicides and criminals. Town bulls were kept on the Common. Beacon Hill, much higher then than now, was surmounted by a pole bearing a barrel filled with pitch that could be set on fire to warn the countryside in the event of a sudden attack by pirates, or as they were commonly called, "the cruel Spaniards," or "the treacherous French." There were no police to maintain public order, just a few constables, mostly employed in carrying out court business, a small night watch to make the rounds, and the militia.

As always in Boston, the weather was a trial. "January 23. Sunday. Severe cold," wrote the merchant John Rowe in his diary. "The Ink freezes as I write—very Bad traveling—no Post in—it froze all the way from the South End down to Castle William, also almost the whole harbour." "Since about the middle of December," wrote Anna Green Winslow, in a letter to her parents in February 1772, "we have had till this week, a series of cold and stormy weather—every snow storm (of which we have had abundance) except the first ended with rain, by which means the snow was so hardened that strong gales at N W soon turned it, & all above ground to ice, which this day sevennight was from one to three, four & they say, in some places, five feet thick in the streets of this town. Last Saturday morning we had a snow storm come on, which continued till four o'clock P M when it turned to rain, since which we have had a warm air, with many showers of rain, one this morning attended with thunder. The streets have been very wet, the waters running like rivers all this week, so that I could not possibly go to school . . ." In April there was a complete change, "the ground very dry, & when I came home from meeting in the afternoon the Dust blew so that it almost put my eyes out . . ."

Another feature of town life was recalled many years later by the merchant Samuel Breck, who received much of his later education in France. "The large whipping post painted red stood conspicuously and prominently in the most public street in the town. It was placed in State Street directly under the windows of a great writing school which I frequented, and from them the scholars were indulged in the spectacle of all kinds of punishment suited to harden their hearts and brutalize their feelings. Here women were taken in a huge cage, in which they were dragged on wheels from prison, and tied to the post with bare backs on which thirty or forty lashes were bestowed among the screams of the culprit and the uproar of the mob. A little further in the street was to be seen the pillory with three or four fellows fastened by the head and hands, and standing for an hour in that helpless posture, exposed to gross and cruel jeers from the multitude, who pelted them incessantly with rotten eggs and every repulsive kind of garbage that could be collected."

According to General Howe's *Orderly Book,* among those punished at the whipping post was Winifried McCowen, who during the blockade "stole the Town Bull and caused him to be killed," which crime earned her "100 lashes on her bare back." Others at risk were prostitutes from the area officially known as Mount Vernon but more commonly called Mount Whoredom—"Satan's seat," the Rev. James Davis later called it. "There awful impieties prevail, and all conceivable abominations are practiced." The number of "females wholly devoid of shame and modesty" was in the hundreds. Lt. Williams of the 23rd Regiment of the British army agreed: "No town of its size could turn out more whores than this could."

Dr. Alexander Hamilton, a Scottish-born physician and bachelor from Maryland (and no relation of the future statesman), visited the town in the middle of the century. He found that "the middling people here are to a degree disingenuous and dissembling," but "the better sort are polite, mannerly, and hospitable to strangers. . . . There is abundance of men of learning and parts; so that one is at no loss for agreeable conversation nor for any set of company he pleases. Assemblies of the gayer sort are frequent here, the gentlemen and ladies meeting almost every week at concerts of musick and balls. I was present at two or three such and saw as fine a ring of ladies, as good dancing, and heard musick as elegant as I had been witness to anywhere. I must take notice that this place abounds with pretty women who appear rather more abroad than they do at [New] York and dress elegantly. They are, for the most part, free and affable as well as pretty. I saw not one prude while I was here."

Along with its "middling people" and "better sort," Boston also had its "meaner sort" or, as they preferred to be called, "lusty fellows" and "stout lads"—dock workers, rope makers, laborers, seamen, unruly apprentices, and tavern layabouts—who, like their counterparts in the mother country, were always ready for a riot. November 5, Pope's Day (Guy Fawkes Day in England), had long been a favorite, but since there were virtually no Catholics available to beat up, mobs from the North End and South End fought vicious battles with each other on the principle that any fight was better than no fight. Peter Oliver, a Loyalist and member of Boston's elite, wrote of "the Mob Whistle, as horrid as the Iroquois Yell, which always tingled in the Ears of every one who had once heard it." Along with tarring and feathering, one of the mob's favorite tactics was to besmirch the house of a designated victim with buckets of raw sewage, known as "Hillsborough paint" in derisive honor of the unpopular colonial secretary. "Twice my house was besmeared, the last time with the Vilest filth," wrote Nathaniel Rogers, a merchant who had been unwilling to join the non-importation agreement. Joseph Scott, accused of selling supplies to the British army, was another victim. "Last night they gave Scott a *Hillsborough treat*, and not content with disfiguring the outside of his shop, they by help of a ladder open'd his chamber window and emptied several buckets full into it," wrote another merchant, John Andrews. The fact that some of these activities had a political coloration was largely the result of the machinations of Samuel Adams, by whose influence the mob was at times converted into the Sons of Liberty. During the Stamp Act riots, they destroyed the mansion belonging to Lt. Gov. Hutchinson and so terrorized the custom officials that they had to take refuge in Castle William, a fort on an island in the harbor.

A major difference between the Boston mob and its London counterpart was that in Boston many of the "meaner sort" had a voice in town elections, the magic of the franchise suddenly transforming them into "the Body of the People." To General Gage, such town meetings were nothing but "democraticall despotism," and it was true that voters were subjected to a good deal of manipulation, notably by the Caucus Club.

In February 1763, John Adams described one of its meetings held "in the Garret of Tom Daws, the Adjutant of the Boston Regiment. He has a large House, and he has a moveable Partition in his Garret, which he takes down and the whole Clubb meets in one Room. There they smoke Tobacco till you cannot see from one End of the Garret to the other. There . . . they choose a Moderator, who puts Questions to the Vote regularly, and Selectmen, Assessors, Collectors, Wardens, Fire Wards, and Representatives are Regularly chosen before they are chosen in the Town. . . . They send Committees to wait on the Merchants Clubb and to propose, and join, in the Choice of Men and Measures."

But despite such backroom politics, the spirit of democracy, or at least belief in the importance of consent, ran deep among New Englanders. When he was a boy, Paul Revere and six other youths signed up as bell ringers for Christ's Church, the only church in Boston that had a peal of eight bells. In a move that would have been inconceivable in the English cathedral town of Gloucester, where the bells were cast, the seven boys drew up a compact, still preserved in the church's archives, agreeing to "attend there once a week on Evenings to ring the Bells for two hours Each time from the date hereof to one year: That we will choose a Moderator Every three months whose Business shall be to give out the Changes and other Business as shall be agreed by a Majority of Voices then Present: that None shall be admitted a Member of this Society without Unanimous Vote of the Members then Present. . . . All Differences to be decided by a Majority of Voices."

The militia did things in much the same way. When Captain John Parker, on that fateful day in April 1775, summoned his company to assemble on the green at Lexington, it was in order "to consult what to do." And Abigail Adams, writing to her husband from Braintree a couple of years earlier, told how late in the evening the local militia had passed under her window on their way to secure the town's gunpowder from possible seizure by the British, and on their return brought with them under-sheriff John Vinton, a Tory. As Abigail watched, they called a halt near the Adams house and made Vinton hand over some official warrants. "Upon his producing them, they put it to the vote whether they should burn them, and it pass'd in the affirmative. They then made a circle and burnt them. They then call'd a vote whether they should huzza, but it being Sunday evening it pass'd in the negative."

It had long been a tenet of Puritan thinking that prosperity was an outward and visible sign of divine approval, and that as God's people they had a duty to "increase and multiply." But for some time now the divine countenance seemed to be frowning rather than smiling. In 1743, Boston, with its population of sixteen thousand, had been the largest town in British North America; Philadelphia had thirteen thousand people and New York eleven thousand. Thirty years later the population of Philadelphia had tripled and New York's had more than doubled, but Boston's remained the same. To add to the worry caused by this relative decline in size, Boston had serious economic problems. Some were short-term—the debts run up during the Seven Years' War, the post-war slump that dragged on and on—but others went deeper. Shipbuilding, "this most ancient and almost only Manufacture the Town of Boston ever had," was a fraction of what it had once been. Rum distilling, second only to shipbuilding in economic importance and essential for the slave trade, had also greatly declined as rival distilleries in Halifax and Newport, and in the West Indies themselves, out-produced Boston. In 1760 a huge fire destroyed four hundred buildings, nearly a quarter of the town, the flames soaring so high that their light in the night sky could be seen as far away as Portsmouth, New Hampshire. To be sure, this could be sanctified as yet another example of God's special concern; as a contemporary versifier put it: "Then can we clear ourselves, a'nt we to blame/ Who sin without Remorse and cast off Shame/ And pay no Rev'rence to his holy Name?/ This is the Cause He sent his Judgment down/ This awful desolation! On the town." And then there was the way the present generation of young people misbehaved, ignoring their elders and teachers and having no sense of values—"woeful youth," who in the words of the *New England Primer* "won't obey or mind the truth/ Nor hearken to what preachers say/ But do their parents disobey."

Finally there was the "restive spirit" mentioned by de Kalb in his report to Choiseul, the result in the opinion of many in the British establishment not of legitimate grievances but of "designing men." Of these, Sam Adams was the worst, the master conspirator who was behind it all, a man so duplicitous that he even bore a striking physical resemblance to General Gage. Joseph Galloway of Philadelphia, whose efforts to work out a compromise with Britain were anathema to Adams, described him as a latter-day Caius Cassius, a man who "eats little, drinks little, sleeps little, thinks much, and is most decisive and indefatigable in his objects." Not only did he control the Caucus Club and the Sons of Liberty, he also dominated the vain but immensely rich John Hancock; as the saying went, "Sam Adams writes the letters, and John Hancock pays the postage." Dr. Benjamin Rush, also of Philadelphia, got to know Adams quite well when they were both members of the Continental Congress and later recalled: "He was near sixty years of age when he took his seat in Congress, but possessed all the vigor of mind of a young man of five and twenty. He was a republican in principle and manner. He once acknowledged to me 'that the independence of the United States upon Great Britain had been the first wish of his heart seven years before the war.' About the same time he said to me 'if it were revealed to him that 999 Americans out of 1,000 would perish in a war for liberty, he would vote for that war, rather than see his country enslaved.'"

It was not so much the authoritarianism of the British government that Adams detested, as its corruption. The large amount of other people's blood that he was prepared to shed would not be to establish an enlightened, tolerant, and democratic society. Rather, his model was John Winthrop's "Citty upon a Hill," or what Adams himself called a "Christian Sparta"—not, surely, a place where everyone would have wanted to live. In many ways, Adams was as much a reactionary as he was a revolutionary; but he was also a brilliant propagandist and rabble-rouser, and it was largely thanks to him, and to the flaming preachers, and also of course to George III and his ministers, that New England in general and Boston in particular became, in the words of the Loyalist Peter Oliver, "the Volcano from whence issued all the Smoak, Flame & Lava which hath since enveloped the whole British American Continent."

The Massacre

Meanwhile, back in England there had been yet another change of ministry and Charles Townshend had become Chancellor of the Exchequer. Charming and volatile, "the delight and ornament of this House" in the words of Burke, Townshend had two nicknames: Champagne Charlie, for obvious reasons, and the Weathercock, for the frequency with which he changed his political position. One of his first acts, done without consulting any of his ministerial colleagues, was to promise to cut the land tax from four to three shillings in the pound while also imposing duties on certain goods imported by the colonies—paper, glass, tea, painters' colors, and lead ("for every hundred weight avoirdupois of white lead, two shillings; for every pound weight avoirdupois of tea, three pence"). There was no pretense that these duties were to "regulate trade"; in fact, Townshend "laughed most unmercifully" at the colonists' cherished distinction between internal and external taxation. To be sure, it was a disappointment when he revealed that the new duties would yield a mere £40,000 a year; but never mind, other taxes would be sure to follow. As Townshend explained, the act was not only "for asserting the Superiority of the Crown" but also for laying "a foundation for such taxation as might in time ease this Country of a considerable burden." The act also made provision "for more effectually preventing the clandestine running of goods in the said colonies" by establishing an enlarged and more powerful Board of Customs Commissioners, to be based in Boston. Since no American jury could be relied on to find a smuggler guilty, customs cases were to be tried in admiralty courts. These had arbitrary rules of evidence but no juries, could authorize searches and seizures on mere suspicion and assess triple damages against offenders. Part of all forfeitures went to informers, and another part to the judges.

Led by Henry Hulton, an able and conscientious civil servant, the new commissioners arrived to a chilly welcome in November 1767, just after the Town Board, in protest against the new duties, had approved an agreement not to import goods made in Britain, particularly cloth, and to encourage their local manufacture. The commissioners got through the winter unscathed, but the following May one of them, Joseph Harrison, tried to seize and search John Hancock's sloop, *Liberty*, just arrived from Madeira, whose captain had declared a cargo of twenty-five pipes of wine, suspiciously less than its capacity. Harrison knew that "a Seizure must be attended with the utmost Risque and Danger" but was determined to do his duty and applied to the captain of the *Romney*, a British man-of-war then in the harbor, for assistance if needed. And then, as he wrote in his account to his patron, the Marquis of Rockingham,

I proceeded to execute my Orders; first informing my Brother Officer Mr. Hallowell, the Controller, of the Service I was going upon, who generously declared that I should not singly be exposed to the Fury of the Populace, but that he would share the Danger with me. Accordingly we set out together towards the Wharf where the Vessel lay, and in our way thither my Son (about 18 Years of Age) accidentally joined us in the Street and went along with us. When we got down to the Wharf we found the Sloop lying there and after waiting till we saw the Man of Warr's Boat ready to put off, the Controller and I stepped on board, seized the Vessel, and I put the King's Mark on the Main Mast. By this time the People began to muster together on the Wharf, from all Quarters; and several Men had got on board in order to regain Possession just as the Man of Warr's Boat, well Man'd and Armed, had got alongside. They soon drove the Intruders out and I delivered the Vessel into custody of the commanding Officer. We then went ashore and walked off the Wharf without any Insult or Molestation from the People, who were eagerly engaged in a Scuffle with the Man of Warr's Men and endeavouring to detain the Sloop at the Wharf. But we had scarce got into the Street before we were pursued by the Mob which by this time was increased to a great Multitude. The onset was begun by throwing Dirt at me, which was presently succeeded by Volleys of Stones, Brickbatts, Sticks, or anything that came to hand. In this manner I run the Gauntlet near 200 Yards, my poor Son following behind endeavouring to shelter his Father by receiving the strokes of many of the Stones thrown at him till at length he became equally an Object of their Resentment, was knocked down and then laid hold of by the Legs, Arms, and Hair of his Head, and in that manner dragged along the Kennel [gutter] in a most barbarous and cruel manner till a few compassionate people, happening to see him in that Distress, formed a Resolution of attempting to rescue him out of the Hands of the Mob; which with much difficulty they effected, and got him into a House; tho' this pulling and hauling between Friends and Enemies had like to have been fatal to him. About this time I received a violent Blow on the Breast which had like to have brought me to the Ground, and I verily believe if I had fallen I should never have got up again, the People to all appearance being determined on Blood and Murder. But luckily just at that critical moment a friendly Man came up and supported me; and observed that now was the time for my Escape as the whole Attention of the Mob was engaged in the Scuffle about my Son, who he assured me would be taken out of their Hands by some persons of his Acquaintance. He then bid me follow him, which I accordingly did, and by suddenly turning the corner of a Street was presently out of Sight of the Crowd, and soon after got to a Friend's House, where I was kindly received and on whom I could depend for Safety and Protection. And in about an Hour's time I had the satisfaction of hearing my Son was in Safety, and had been conducted home by the Persons who rescued him from the Mob; but in a miserable Condition, being much bruised and wounded, tho' not danger-ously, and I hope will soon get well again.

After also beating up Controller Hallowell, before he too was res-cued by some of the more respectable citizens, the mob proceeded to smash up the houses of the customs collectors, then hauled Harrison's "fine sailing pleasure boat" through the streets to the Liberty Tree, "where she was formally condemned, and from thence dragged up into the Common and there burned to Ashes. . . . With this Exploit they concluded the mischievous Labour of that Night; and soon after dis-persed." The next day, fearing for their lives, most of the commissioners and their families sought refuge onboard the *Romney*, while Harrison and his family went to Castle William in the harbor; it was from there that he wrote his account to Rockingham.

"How these things will end God only knows," he concluded. "At present affairs here wear a Dark and Gloomy Aspect, and I fear the worst is not over. The People are distracted and Liberty mad, and the Enthusiasm is spreading fast over the other Colonies; and if some prudent, judicious, and effectual Measures are not immediately taken by the Ministry at Home to prevent it, I shall not be surprised if something like a general Rising of the People should take Place."

In fact, the London government had already decided on certain "prudent, judicious, and effectual measures" and orders had been sent to General Gage at British headquarters in New York to dispatch troops to Boston "to be Quartered in that Town, and to give every legal assistance to the Civil Magistrate in the Preservation of the Public Peace, and to the Officers of the Revenue." (There was of course a militia in Boston, but it was not to be expected that they would turn out against their fellow citizens. In his report on the Stamp Act Riots, Governor Bernard had written that when "I sent a written order to the Colonel of the Militia to beat an alarm, he answered that it would signify nothing, for as soon as the drum was heard, the drummer would be knocked down, and the drum broke. He added that probably all the drummers of the Regiment were in the Mob.")

Two of the regiments destined for Boston, the 14th and the 29th, were to be sent from the military base at Halifax, Nova Scotia, and two others, the 64th and 65th from Cork, in Ireland. Many of the rank and file in all four regiments had been recruited in Ireland and were Catholics, a fact hardly likely to endear them to New Englanders, who still tended to think of the Pope as the "Whore of Rome." Stationing these troops in town seemed an added provocation. Families of Huguenot descent, such as the Reveres and Bowdoins, well remembered how their forefathers had come to America from France to escape the notorious *dragonnades*—an attempt to force Protestants to convert to Catholicism by quartering dragoons in their homes, with license to behave as brutally as they pleased. Some of the Stuart

kings had tried the same thing in England, with the result that forcibly quartering troops on civilians was specifically banned by the Bill
of Rights of 1689, to whose protection the colonists felt fully entitled.
And anyway, as members of the governor's council pointed out, there
was no need to keep the troops in town since there were perfectly
adequate barracks out at Fort William on Castle Island. But Gage had
his orders, and although the troops were not to be billeted on individual families but in disused warehouses and newly built barracks,
and for a while in Faneuil Hall and the Town House, he insisted that
they stay in the town. The first two regiments arrived on September
29, 1768. "The American war may be dated from the hostile parade of
this day," wrote Mercy Otis Warren. "A day which marks with infamy
the councils of Britain."

Keenly aware of the importance of putting their own interpreta-
tion on events, a number of anonymous Bostonians, almost certainly
including Samuel Adams, at once began publishing a newspaper,
the *Boston Evening Post,* whose articles were soon reprinted in every
other colony, and sometimes in England too. The editorial policy of
the paper, which ran for nearly a year, was based on certain locally
acceptable axioms: Troops were not needed to keep order since, apart
from the occasional "brush" or "little trifling disturbance" caused by
the "frolicsome" behavior of some wild "lads," calm reigned in Boston, whose good citizens were as loyal, peace-loving, and quietly virtuous as always. Clearly, however, a handful of "designing men" had
"transmitted to the ministry the most exaggerated accounts" of these
minor incidents—which, indeed, they had very probably "contrived
and executed themselves"—and these slanderers were none other than
Governor Bernard and the Commissioners of Customs. The first issue
of the paper came out on September 30, 1768:

At 3 o'clock in the afternoon, the *Launceston* of 40 guns, the *Mermaid*
of 38, *Glasgow* 20, the *Beaver* 14, *Senegal* 14, *Bonetta* 10, several armed
schooners, which together with the *Romney* of 60 guns, and the other

ships of war before in the harbour, all commanded by Capt. Smith, came up to town, bringing with them the 14th Regiment, Col. Dalrymple, and 29th Regiment, Col. Carr; none having been disembarked at Castle Island,—So that we now behold Boston surrounded at a time of profound peace with about 14 ships of war, with springs on their cables, and their broadsides to the town! If the people of England could but look into the town to see the utmost good order and observance of the laws, and that this mighty armament has no other rebellion to subdue than what existed in the brain or letter of the inveterate G – --r B – -d and the detested Comm—s – rs of the Board of C – s!

October 1. At about 1 o'clock, all the troops landed under cover of the cannon of the ships of war, and marched into the Common, with muskets charged, bayonets fixed, colours flying, drums beating and fifes &c. playing.

When the town Selectmen refused to provide quarters for the troops, Governor Bernard arranged for some of them to be temporarily housed in public buildings.

October 3. We now behold the Representatives' Chamber, Court-House, and Faneuil Hall, those seats of freedom and justice, occupied with troops, and guards placed at the doors; the Common covered with tents, and alive with soldiers, marching and counter-marching to relieve the guards. In short the town is now a perfect garrison.

October 14. The troops still keep possession of Faneuil Hall, the Court House, Representatives' Chambers, &c, guards placed at the passage-way into the town, near the Neck. Patrolling companies near the ferry ways, and parties sent into the country to prevent desertions. In the forenoon one Rogers, a New-England man, sentenced to receive 1,000 stripes, and a number of other soldiers, were scourged in the Common by the black drummers in a manner which, however necessary, was shocking to humanity.

October 24. Large quantities of tea have been sent from hence by the merchants to the other colonies, they not being able to make sale of it here.

October 29. The inhabitants of this town have been of late greatly insulted and abused by some of the officers and soldiers, several have been assaulted on frivolous pretences, and put under guard without any lawful warrant for so doing. A physician of the town walking the streets the other evening was jostled by an officer, when a scuffle ensued; he was afterwards met by the same officer in company with another, both as yet unknown, who repeated his blows, and as is supposed gave him a stroke with a pistol, which so wounded him as to endanger his life. A tradesman of this town on going under the rails of the Common in his way home, had a thrust in the breast with a bayonet from a soldier; another person passing the street was struck with a musket; but the most atrocious offence and alarming behaviour was that of a captain, the last evening, who in company with two other officers, endeavoured to persuade some Negro servants to ill-treat and abuse their masters, assuring them that the soldiers were come to procure their freedoms, and that with their help and assistance they should be able to drive all the Liberty Boys to the devil; with discourse of the like import, tending to incite an insurrection.

The editor then added:

Here, Americans, you may behold some of the first fruits springing up from that root of bitterness, a standing army. Troops are quartered upon us in a time of peace, on pretence of preserving order in a town that was as orderly before their arrival as any one large town in the whole extent of his Majesty's dominions.

October 31. All the troops in town marched into the Common this morning, drumming the dead beat; at 8 o'clock, Richard Arnes, a private of the 14th Regiment, dressed in white, having just before had the sacrament administered to him by the Revd. Mr. Palms, chaplain of the regiment, who also accompanied him, was pursuant to the sentence of a General Court Martial, shot for desertion. The regiment then marched round the corpse as it lay on the ground, when it was put into the coffin, which was carried by his side into the Common, and buried in a grave near where he was shot, and the church service read over him.

November 1. An householder at the west part of the town, hearing the cries of two women in the night, who were rudely treated by some soldiers, ventured to expostulate with them for this behaviour, for which boldness he was knocked down with a musket and much wounded; they went off undiscovered; another had a thrust with a bayonet near his eye. The troops still occupy the Town-House, and the main guard is fixed in a house on the south side of the same and two pieces of mounted cannon planted before the door.

November 6. This being Lord's day, the minds of serious people at public worship were greatly disturbed with drums beating and fifes playing, unheard of before in this land.

November 14. The inhabitants of Windham, a considerable town in Connecticut, have lately instructed their representatives to "encourage a spirit of industry and frugality, and the woolen, linen, glass, and paper manufactures," rightly judging that under the difficulties brought upon them by the late Revenue Acts, no step can have a greater tendency to procure them relief.

November 25. The town watch has been lately greatly abused and interrupted in their duty by some officers; two of them came to the Town-House watch with swords under their arms, calling them damned scoundrels, forbidding them to challenge officers as they passed, or to give the time of night in their rounds, as also from keeping in the watch house, threatening that in such case they would have them in irons, and bring four regiments and blow them all to hell; also telling the watchmen they were the King's soldiers and gentlemen, who had orders from his Majesty, and they were above the Selectmen who gave them their orders.

December 12. A married lady of this town was the other evening, when passing from one house to another, taken hold of by a soldier, who otherways behaved to her with great rudeness; a woman near Long Lane was stopped by several soldiers, one of whom cried out "Seize her and carry her off." She was much surprised, but luckily got shelter in a house nearby. Another woman was pursued by a soldier into a house near the north end, who dared to enter the same, and behave with great insolence.

December 19. Last evening after church service, there was a considerable gathering of children and servants, near the Town House, drawn by the music of the fife, &c. which is again heard on the Sabbath, to the great concern of the sober and thoughtful inhabitants; some of the youths having behaved so as to displease the officer, orders were given the guard to clear the parade; they marched up with bayonets presented—one of the lads was pursued by a soldier to some distance, who made a thrust with his bayonet, which passed thro' his coat, and had he not thrown himself on the ground that instant, it's thought he would be run thro' the body.

December 29. The other evening as a journeyman to a silver-smith was going through an alley leading into Ann Street he met a soldier, who took hold of him and ordered him to deliver up his money; a scuffle ensued, when the smith was thrown by the soldier, who clapt his knee upon his breast and a hand upon his mouth, to prevent an alarm, and with the other hand robbed him of the few pence he had in his pocket; a whistling was then made, supposed by some of his comrades, when the soldier ran and made his escape, leaving the journeyman much wounded. This is not the only instance of a street robbery since the arrival of the troops, which before was a crime unknown in this town.

March 20, 1769. Saturday last being the anniversary of the repeal of the Stamp Act, the same was noticed as has been usual. The British flag was displayed on Liberty Tree, and at noon a number of gentlemen met in the hall under the same, where a number of loyal toasts were drank, and the greatest order and decorum observed by the company. The confinement of the soldiery to their barracks upon Saturday, together with a wicked report which was spread among them by our enemies that the Sons of Liberty had intended to expose the effigy of St. Patrick upon the Tree of Liberty on said day, so provoked our military that numbers of the three companies quartering at Murray's sugar-house, determined to sally forth that night and cut down the Tree of Liberty; accordingly, just before 11 o'clock the signal was given by firing a gun, as was intended, over the guard house, when by carelessness they fired a brace of balls through the same, but happily hurt no one; immediately thereupon every man was out with his arms complete; and also axes and saws to demolish the Tree of Liberty; one soldier in his freak fired a ball from one room to another, and shot the tail of a sergeant's shirt off, but did no other damage. The officers were immediately alarmed, and by their intreaties and promises of pardon the soldiery returned to their barracks, and remained quiet through the night.

April 30. The quartering of troops in the body of a town is as ruinous to the soldiery as it is distressing to the inhabitants; every day furnishes out fresh instances of their debaucheries and consequent violences. As an aged woman of the north part of Boston was setting the other evening in a lower room, having no person in the house with her, a soldier came in and seeing her have a Bible on the table before her, he expressed his approbation of her piety and attempted a kind of exposition upon some parts thereof; but soon dropping this discourse, he acquainted her that he had a bad swelling on his hip, and should be glad of her advice; but while the good woman was attending to his relation, this abandoned wretch seized her by the shoulders, threw her upon the floor, and notwithstanding her years, attempted a rape upon her, which was prevented by her resistance and screams occasioned by his brutal behaviour; he thought proper to hurry off, taking with him a bundle of shirts and linen, which had been just before sent into the house for washing and ironing; a business which the person followed to obtain a livelihood.

May 3. Last Lord's day some assemblies in this town were greatly disturbed during divine service by the rattling of drums and play of fifes. A party of soldiers with those noisy instruments passed one of those assemblies twice in the space of half an hour. It has also been noticed by some persons that the sawing of wood at the barracks is more heard on the Sabbath than on week days.

June 14. A worthy old gentleman the other morning discovered a soldier in bed with a favourite grand-daughter. The aged parent, in the height of his astonishment, ordered the soldier immediately to quit the room; but he absolutely refused, saying she was his wife, and he had an undoubted right to her, and that if he went out of the house he was determined to carry her with him. Upon examining further into the matter, it was found that the soldier had found means to ingratiate himself with one of the family, and had by her aid seduced the girl with the promise of marriage; that accordingly, one evening, as the girl informs, he carried her to a house in town where, as she thought, they were married by a person drest as a priest. This discovery has greatly distressed the unhappy parents, and thereby much impaired their healths.

July 4. On Monday last, one T – -z P – -k, an ensign of the 64th Regiment, observing a woman standing near the door of her house, made up to her, and after using a great deal of fulsome language and attempting some indecencies, she made her escape and got inside the door, which she shut against him; he however followed her, and finding the door fastened on the inside, attempted to force it open, but not being able to do it, he went off, swearing he would return again; and on the Wednesday night following he was as good as his word, the said woman being sitting at her chamber window, he accosted her, by calling her his "Sweet angel," and desiring her to come down and let him in; the husband, who is a person of character, being in the same room and hearing one speak in the street, asked his wife who it was; she told him it was the same impudent fellow that had attempted a few days before to break open the door; upon which he immediately ran to the window and asked him what he wanted. "I want," says he, "that angel at the window." The gentleman replied, "She is my wife." "I don't care whose wife she is," returned he, "for by G-d I'll have her in spite of all the men in the country. If you are her husband, by G-d you shan't keep her long, and if you don't put your head into the window immediately, I'll be d—d if I don't blow your brains out." The gentleman tried to keep his temper, and told him unless he retired immediately he would apply to a magistrate and have him punished for his temerity; upon which the brave officer redoubled his threats and curses, swore by G-d such a d—d ugly fellow as he was not fit to have such a wife, and he would take her away from him at all events, for which purpose he would tarry in town till next summer, and would sacrifice him tho' death was the consequence; with abundance of other scurrilous abusive treatment; which at length provok'd the husband so much that he took a loaded pistol which was in the room and attempted to fire at him, but was prevented by the fright and intreaties of his wife. Mr. Ensign at last went off, and the next day the gentleman applied to a magistrate for a warrant, by virtue of which the offender was taken and obliged to give bail in £200 lawful money, to answer for his conduct at the next sessions of the peace.

July 13. We are informed from Ipswich that the young ladies of a parish called Chebacco, to the number of seventy-seven, assembled at the house of the Rev. Mr. John Cleavland, with their spinning wheels; and though the weather that day was extremely hot, and divers of the young ladies were but about thirteen years of age, yet by six o'clock in the afternoon, they spun of linen yarn 440 knots, and carded and spun of cotton 730 knots, and of tow 600. After the music of the wheels was over, Mr. Cleavland entertained them with a sermon, on Proverbs xiv. 1. "Every wise woman buildeth her house; but the foolish plucketh it down with her hands," which he concluded by observing how the women might recover to this country the full and free enjoyment of all our rights, properties, and privileges (which is more than the men have been able to do) and so have the honour of building not only their own, but the houses of many thousands, and perhaps prevent the ruin of the whole British empire, viz. by living upon, as far as possible, only the produce of this country; and to be sure to lay aside the use of all foreign teas, also by wearing, as far as possible, only clothing of this country's manufacture.

After less than a year the *Boston Evening Post* ceased publication, but other papers took up the cause, among them the *Boston Gazette and Country Journal* whose issue of March 12, 1770, ran this story:

On the evening of Monday, being the fifth current, several soldiers of the 29th Regiment were seen parading the streets with their drawn cutlasses and bayonets, abusing and wounding numbers of inhabitants. A few minutes after nine o'clock four youths, named Edward Archbald, William Merchant, Francis Archbald, and John Leech, jun., came down Cornhill together, and separating at Doctor Loring's corner, the two former were passing the narrow alley leading to Murray's barrack in which was a soldier brandishing a broad sword of an uncommon size against the walls, out of which he struck fire plentifully. A person of mean countenance armed with a large cudgel bore him company. Edward Archbald admonished Merchant to take care of the sword, on which the soldier turned round and struck Archbald on the arm, then pushed at Merchant and pierced through his clothes inside the arm close to the armpit and grazed the skin. Merchant then struck the soldier with a short stick he had; and the other person ran to the barrack and brought with him two soldiers, one armed with a pair of tongs, the other with a shovel. He with the tongs pursued Archbald back through the alley, collared and laid him over the head with the tongs. The noise brought people together; and John Hicks, a young lad, coming up, knocked the soldier down but let him get back up again; and more lads gathering, drove them back to the barrack where the boys stood some time, as it were to keep them in. In less than a minute ten or twelve of them came out with drawn cutlasses, clubs, and bayonets and set upon the unarmed boys and young folk who stood them a little while but, finding the inequality of their equipment, dispersed.

On hearing the noise, one Samuel Atwood came up to see what was the matter; and entering the alley from Dock Square, heard the latter part of the combat; and when the boys had dispersed he met the ten or twelve soldiers aforesaid rushing down the alley towards the square and asked them if they intended to murder people? They answered, "Yes, by G-d, root and branch!" With that one of them struck Mr. Atwood with a club which was repeated by another; and being unarmed, he turned to go off and received a wound on the left shoulder which reached the bone and gave him much pain. Retreating a few steps, Mr. Atwood met two officers and said, "Gentlemen, what is the matter?" They answered, "You'll see by and by." Immediately after those heroes appeared in the square, asking, "Where were the boogers? Where were the cowards?"

One of them advanced towards a youth who had a split of a raw stave in his hand and said, "Damn them! Here is one of them!" but the young man seeing a person near him with a drawn sword and good cane ready to support him, held up his stave in defiance, and they quietly passed by him up the little alley by Mr. Silsby's to King Street, where they attacked single and unarmed persons till they raised much clamour, and then turned down Cornhill Street, insulting all they met in like manner and pursuing some to their very doors.

Thirty or forty persons, mostly lads, being by this means gathered in King Street, Capt. Preston with a party of men with charged bayonets, came from the main guard to the commissioner's house, the soldiers pushing their bayonets, crying, "Make way!" They took place by the Custom House and, continuing to push to drive the people off, pricked some in several places, on which they were clamorous and, it is said, threw snow balls. On this, the Captain commanded them to fire; and more snow balls coming, he again said, "Damn you, fire!—be the consequence what it will!" One soldier then fired, and a townsman with a cudgel struck him over the hands with such force that he dropped his firelock; and, rushing forward, aimed a blow at the Captain's head which grazed his hat and fell pretty heavy upon his arm. However, the soldiers continued the fire successively till seven or eight or, as some say, eleven guns were discharged. By this fatal manoeuvre three men were laid dead on the spot and two more struggling for life.

The dead are Mr. Samuel Gray, killed on the spot, the ball entering his head and beating off a large portion of his skull.

A mulatto man named Crispus Attucks, who was born in Framingham, but lately belonged to New-Providence [Bahamas] and was here in order to go to North Carolina, also killed instantly, two balls entering his breast, one of them in special goring the right lobe of the lungs and a great part of the liver most horribly.

Mr. James Caldwell, mate of Capt. Morton's vessel, in like manner killed by two balls entering his back.

Mr. Samuel Maverick, a promising youth of seventeen years of age, son of the widow Maverick, and an apprentice to Mr. Greenwood, ivory-turner, mortally wounded; a ball went through his belly and was cut out at his back. He died the next morning.

A lad named Christopher Monk, about seventeen years of age, an apprentice to Mr. Walker, shipwright, wounded; a ball entered his back about four inches above the left kidney near the spine and was cut out of the breast on the same side. Apprehended he will die.

A lad named John Clark, about seventeen years of age, whose parents live at Medford, and an apprentice to Capt. Samuel Howard of this town, wounded; a ball entered just above his groin and came out at his hip on the opposite side. Apprehended he will die.

After listing the other wounded, the article told how Lieutenant Governor Hutchinson had pacified the outraged citizens by promising that Captain Preston and the soldiers who had fired would be arrested, which was done a few hours later. The *Boston Gazette and Country Journal* continued: "Tuesday morning presented a most shocking scene, the blood of our fellow citizens running like water through King Street and the Merchants' Exchange. . . . Our blood might also be tracked up to the head of Long Lane, and through divers other streets and passages. At eleven o'clock the inhabitants met at Faneuil Hall; and after some animated speeches becoming the occasion, they chose a committee of fifteen respectable gentlemen to wait upon the lieutenant governor in Council to request of him to issue his orders for the immediate removal of the troops."

So much for the "Lads-throw-snowballs, Redcoats-open-fire" version of the Boston Massacre. A different view was provided by the Tory Peter Oliver, who was present at the occasion, in his book, *The Origin & Progress of the American Revolution*. According to him "the Rabble," armed with "massy Clubs," were all set to commit another of their "accustomed Outrages," in this case robbing the Custom House of "the King's Monies":

From several Threatenings being thrown out, those Monies were thought insecure, & a Sentinel was appointed to guard them. According to common Custom, when a Riot was to be brought on, the Factioneers would employ Boys & Negroes to assemble to make Bonfires in the Streets; & when all was ready, the Mob Whistle, already mentioned, with sometimes the Mob Horn in Unison, would echo through the Streets, to the great Terror of the peaceable Inhabitants. Those Boys & Negroes assembled before the Custom House, & abused the Sentinel; he called for Aid, & a Party of eight Soldiers were sent to him. This party was headed by a young Officer; Capt. Preston, an amiable, solid officer, imagining that the other would not behave with that Prudence which the Occasion demanded, took the Command upon his self.

By this time there were 4 or 500 of the Rioters collected; the Rioters pelted the Soldiers with Brickbats, Ice, Oystershells & broken Glass Bottles. Capt. Preston behaved with great Coolness & Prudence. The Rioters calling out, "Damn you, fire! Fire if you dare!" & Capt. Preston desiring them to be quiet, and ordering his men not to fire. But at last a Stout Fellow of the Mob knocked down one of the soldiers; & endeavouring to wrest his Gun from him, the Soldier cried, "Damn you, fire!" pulled Trigger & killed his Man. The other Soldiers, in the midst of the Noise, supposing it was the Captain who gave the order, discharged their Pieces, & five Persons were killed.

The Patriots' version of events stressed the significance of a brawl at a rope maker's a day before the massacre. Relations between town and army, already bad, had been made worse by the practice of off-duty soldiers supplementing their pay of eight pence a day (before deductions) by doing casual labor for wages lower than those paid to civilians. According to *A Short Narrative of the Horrid Massacre in Boston*, compiled by James Bowdoin, Joseph Warren, and Samuel Pemberton, "a soldier of the 29th Regiment accosted a Negro who was employed in one of the rope-walks by inquiring 'whether his master wanted to hire a man?' The Negro answered that his 'master wished to have the vault emptied, and that was a proper work for a Lobster.'" Since "Lobster" was a derisive term for redcoat, and "vault" meant latrine, "this produced a conflict between the soldier and the Negro," which soon turned into a large-scale riot in which the soldiers came off the worse, and departed "looking vengeance on the inhabitants."

The *Short Narrative* included over ninety depositions by eyewitnesses (twenty other depositions, favorable to Captain Preston and the soldiers, were omitted). William Newhall swore that on Thursday night "he met four soldiers of the 29th Regiment, and that he heard them say 'there were a great many that would eat their dinners on Monday next that should not eat any on Tuesday.'" Daniel Calef heard the wife of one of the soldiers of the 29th say that "before Tuesday or Wednesday night they would wet their swords or bayonets in New England people's blood." Caleb Swan declared that on the night of the 5th "he heard a woman's voice, whom he knew to be the supposed wife of one Montgomery, a grenadier of the 29th Regiment, standing at her door, and heard her say, 'The town was too haughty and too proud; and that many of their arses would be laid low before the morning.'" Also "Margaret Swansborough declares that a free woman named Black Peg, who has kept much with the soldiers, on hearing the disturbance on Monday evening the 5th instant, said, 'the soldiers were not to be trod upon by the inhabitants, but would know before morning whether they or the inhabitants were to be masters.'" And so "by the foregoing depositions it appears very clearly there was a general combination among the soldiers of the 29th Regiment at least, to commit some extraordinary act of violence upon the town."

After the shooting Lt. Gov. Hutchinson had done his best to calm things down. He promised the people of the town that justice would be done, and helped persuade Colonel Dalrymple to order the two regiments to the barracks at Castle William. Captain Preston and the eight soldiers were placed under arrest to await trial, which the radicals hoped would take place soon and were certain would result in verdicts of guilty. But to their chagrin, Hutchinson, with the cooperation of the judges and other officials, saw to it that the trials were postponed until the end of the year, when tempers had cooled. Preston and the soldiers were tried separately, but in both trials John Adams appeared for the defense. As he told it in his autobiography, the day after the massacre he was in his office when he was visited by a merchant called James Forrest.

"I had some Acquaintance with him. With tears streaming from his Eyes, he said I am come with a very solemn Message from a very unfortunate man, Captain Preston in Prison. He wishes for Council, and can get no one. I have waited on Mr. Quincy, who says he will engage if you will give him your Assistance: without it positively he will not. Even Mr. Auchmuty declines unless you will engage . . ." Rising to the occasion, Adams accepted the case, doing so at some length: "I had no hesitation in answering that Council ought to be the very last thing that an accused Person should want in a free Country. That the Bar ought in my Opinion to be independent and impartial at all Times . . . that Persons whose lives were at stake ought to have the Council they preferred . . . that every lawyer must hold himself responsible not only to his country, but to the highest and most infallible of all Trybunals . . ." However, Preston must "expect from me no Art or Address, No Sophistry or Prevarication in such a Cause" but "if he thinks he cannot have a fair Tryal of that issue without my Assistance, without hesitation he shall have it."

Adams worked hard on his cases and mounted a defense that was based in part on the line adopted by his cousin Samuel Adams in the *Boston Evening Post*—that the good citizens of Boston, peace-loving and orderly, could not be "supposed answerable for the unjustifiable conduct of a few individuals hastily assembled in the streets." He then buttressed this argument by following the line taken by Peter Oliver. Who were the real villains? Answer: the rabble—"saucy boys, Negroes and mulattoes, Irish teagues and outlandish jack tarrs." (By "outlandish" he meant from out of town, i.e., "outside agitators.") Crispus Attucks was especially to blame, "a stout mulatto fellow . . . whose very looks was enough to terrify any person . . . to whose mad behaviour, in all probability, the dreadful carnage of that night, is chiefly to be ascribed. And it is in this manner this town has been often treated; a Carr from Ireland, and an Attucks from Framingham, happening to be here, shall sally out upon their thoughtless enterprises, at the head of such a rabble of Negroes &c. as they can collect together, and then there are not wanting persons to ascribe all their doings to the good people of the town."

"Carr from Ireland"—Patrick Carr, who worked for a leather-breeches maker in Queen Street—could not speak on his own behalf since one of the musket shots "went through his right hip & tore away part of the backbone & greatly injured the hip bone," and he was now dead. But before he died he answered several questions put to him by his physician, Dr. Jeffries, who described their conversation to the court:

I asked him whether he thought the soldiers were abused a great deal, after they went down there. He said, he thought they were. I asked him whether he thought the soldiers would have been hurt, if they had not fired. He said he really thought they would, for he heard many voices cry out, "Kill them." I asked him then, meaning to close all, whether he thought they fired in self-defense, or on purpose to destroy the people. He said he really thought they did fire to defend themselves; that he did not blame the man, whoever he was, that shot him.

Though dead, Carr was presented as something of an expert witness. "He told me also," said Dr. Jeffries, "he was a native of Ireland, that he had frequently seen mobs, and soldiers called upon to quell them. . . . He had seen soldiers often fire on the people in Ireland, but he had never seen them bear half so much as before they fired in his life." Though this evidence was hearsay, it carried great weight since they were the words of a dying man, and someone about to appear before his Maker would surely not tell a lie.

Also helping Josiah Quincy and John Adams conduct the defense was the skill with which the authorities had packed the juries, eliminating the town radicals and calling only Loyalists and moderates from outside

Boston. Moreover the two lawyers were able to prove that Captain Preston had not given the order to fire, and that the soldiers were so menaced by the mob that they were acting in self-defense. Preston and six of the eight soldiers (five of them with Irish names) were acquitted completely, while Kilroy and Montgomery, whose "supposed wife" had been heard to say that "many of their arses would be laid low before morning," were found "not guilty of murder, but guilty of manslaughter." When they came up for sentencing, both pleaded "benefit of clergy," a relic of English medieval law that exempted members of the clergy from punishment by a king's court. To be entitled to the benefit, a prisoner did not have to prove that he was in holy orders, only that he could read, since in the Middle Ages the clergy were the only literate class. The claim was established by reading aloud (or reciting from memory) a few sentences from the Bible in court. However, the privilege could be claimed only once in a lifetime, and to prevent double-dipping anyone who invoked it was branded on the right thumb, usually after imbibing a large amount of rum. This is what happened to Kilroy and Montgomery, who then rejoined their regiment, which in the meantime had been sent to New Jersey. Before leaving, Montgomery admitted "that being knocked down and rising again, in the agony from the blow he said, 'Damn you, fire!' And immediately he fired himself, and the rest followed him."

For John Adams, the case had been one of his finest hours. A few years later he wrote in his diary that his defense had been "one of the most gallant, generous, manly, and disinterested Actions of my whole Life." Much later, in his autobiography, he responded to certain "Calumnies and Insinuations" concerning his fees by stating that "before or after the Tryal, Preston sent me ten Guineas and at the Tryal of the Soldiers afterwards Eight Guineas more, which were all the fees I ever received or were offered to me . . . for fourteen or fifteen days Labour, in the most exhausting and fatiguing Causes I ever tried: for hazarding a Popularity very general and very hardly earned: and for incurring a Clamour and popular Suspicions and prejudices." There is, however, a discrepancy in this matter of the fees, since it is on record that the king, who took a personal interest in both cases, paid a total of £264 and 7 shillings for the expenses of Preston and the soldiers, of which £140 and 2 shillings went to their lawyers. But perhaps Josiah Quincy took it all? (Captain Preston, by the way, returned to England after his acquittal and was rewarded with a pension of £200 a year.)

In the years that followed, Samuel Adams and the Sons of Liberty did their best to keep the memory of the massacre on the boil by means of an annual commemorative ceremony in the Old South Church. High-flown, lurid rhetoric was expected of the speakers, nor were the audiences disappointed. "The fatal fifth of March, 1770, can never be forgotten," declaimed Dr. Joseph Warren, who spoke at the 1772 service. "The horrors of that dreadful night are but too deeply impressed on our hearts—language is too feeble to paint the emotion of our souls, when our streets were stained with the blood of our brethren— when our ears were wounded by the groans of the dying, and our eyes were tormented with the sight of the mangled bodies of the dead— When our alarmed imagination presented to our view our houses wrapt in flames, our children subjected to the barbarous caprice of the raging soldiery—our beauteous virgins exposed to all the insolence of unbridled passions—our virtuous wives, endeared to us by every tender tie, falling sacrifice to worse than brutal violence . . ."

Despite such efforts, the next three years were fairly calm. The non-importation agreement collapsed, trade with the mother country picked up, and life returned more or less to normal. True, the redcoats were still causing trouble, but of a more routine kind.

"Dear mamma," wrote Anna Green Winslow, now aged thirteen,

I suppose that you would be glad to hear that Betty Smith, who has given you so much trouble, is well & behaves herself well & I should be glad if I could write you so. But the truth is, no sooner was the 29ᵗʰ Regiment encamp'd upon the common but miss Betty took herself among them (as the Irish say) & there she stay'd with Bill Pinchion & awhile. The next news of her was, that she was got into gaol for stealing: from whence she was taken to the publick whipping post. The next adventure was to the Castle, after the soldiers were remov'd there, for the murder of the 5th March last. When they turn'd her away from there, she came up to town again, and soon got into the workhouse for new misdemeanours. She soon ran away from there and sit up her old trade of pilfering again, for which she was put a second time into gaol; there she still remains. About two months agone (as well as I can remember) she & a number of her wretched companions set the gaol on fire, in order to get out, but the fire was timely discovered & extinguished, & there, as I said, she still remains till this day, in order to be tried for her crimes. I heard somebody say that as she has some connections with the army no doubt but she would be cleared, and perhaps have a pension into the bargain. Mr. Henry says the way of sin is downhill, when persons get into that way they are not easily stopped.

THE TEA PARTY

Here, had there been such a list in 1773, were several good reasons not to drink tea:

→ It was bad for your health. Unlike tobacco, which it had long been known was good for you ("it helps digestion," wrote the traveler John Josselyn, "heats the cold and cools them that sweat . . . purgeth the stomach, killeth nits and lice"), tea could harm you. According to Dr. Johnson, writing in the *Literary Magazine* in 1757, tea "when it is made strong, and stands long to draw the grosser particles, will convulse the bowels . . ." and according to Dr. Thomas Young, writing in the *Boston Evening Post*, tea was known to cause "spasms, vapours, dropsies, rheumatisms, consumptions." It was particularly damaging to the teeth. Writing in the 1750s, the visiting Swedish naturalist, Peter Kalm, observed that people of European descent were apt to lose their teeth at an early age, "even girls not above twenty frequently had lost half of them." At first Kalm thought this might be due to the "great quantities of fruit and sweetmeats which are here eaten," but then realized that "I have known many people who never eat any fruit and still have hardly a tooth left." Soon he began to suspect the tea, "which is drunk here in the morning and afternoon, especially by women, and is so common that there is hardly a farmer's wife or a poor woman who does not drink it." Proof that strong tea "entered into and corroded the teeth" came when he observed that Indian women who lived close to the European settlements and had taken up tea-drinking lost their teeth prematurely, but "those who had not used tea preserved their teeth strong and sound to a great age." The harmful effect was compounded by the way the women drank it—"they never poured it out of the cup into the saucer to cool, but drank it as hot as it came from the pot." Men kept their teeth because "they cared very little for tea, and a bowl of punch was more agreeable to them."

→ It was a breeding ground for fleas. This was well-known, especially to the non-importing tea-boycotting Patriots.

→ It was dirty. Another well-known fact was that while being packed into lead-lined casks in Canton before being shipped to London, the tea leaves were compacted by being trodden down by barefoot Chinese peasants who did not wash their feet.

→ It was expensive. A pound of even the cheapest bohea that had been smuggled in duty-free from the Dutch port of St. Eustatia in the West Indies cost about two shillings, almost a day's wages for a laboring man. One anti-tea letter writer cited the case of a poor family whose indulgence in this luxury had caused their children to die of malnutrition. (At-risk children were also mentioned by Dr. Johnson in his 1757 review of James Hanway's *An Essay on Tea:* "The careless spending of time among servants, who are charged with the care of infants, is often fatal: the nurse frequently destroys the child! The poor infant, being left neglected, expires whilst she is sipping her tea!")

→ It encouraged prideful ostentation. Status-conscious tea-drinkers vied to excel each other in the quality of their china, teaspoons, and tea caddies.

→ It also encouraged lawlessness. The Dutch were not the only smugglers. American traders were also experts; so were the British. Smuggling also involved bribing officials, making false statements on oath, and occasional violence.

→ It was ruinous to the economy of the Empire. Because China was at the time the only source for tea, and because apart from "sing-songs" (mechanical toys, musical boxes, fancy clocks) there were very few British manufactures that the Chinese wanted, the only way to pay for the tea was with large amounts of silver. According to contemporary mercantilist thinking, whereby whoever ended up with the most cash was the winner, such an imbalance was disastrous. (Only later would the East India Company come up with the idea of growing large crops of opium in India and then forcing it at gunpoint on the unwilling Chinese.)

→ It enhanced the importance of the East India Company at the expense of the American colonies. Because of the large private fortunes made while in the Company's employment by the so-called nabobs who, on their return to England, often bought seats in Parliament; and because the Company itself had close links with the political establishment, more attention was paid by the London government to the affairs of the Company than to those of the American colonies. (Similarly, Franklin had earlier complained that the lobby representing the West Indies sugar interest also outweighed that of the colonies.) But in 1773 the Company was in deep trouble; because of mismanagement, greed, overproduction, competition by the Dutch, and non-importation in the colonies, it had a surplus of seventeen million pounds of tea in its London warehouses; it also owed more than a million pounds in duties and had defaulted on a £300,000 loan from the Bank of England. Its other main branch of business—collecting taxes in Bengal and other parts of India, handing over part to the rulers, and pocketing the rest (about two-thirds)—wasn't going too well either because this had resulted in a series of expensive wars with Hyder Ali, ruler of Mysore. So when Lord North, hoping to solve some of the Company's problems, introduced the Tea Act in Parliament, there was little debate and no need for a formal vote.

→ And once that act had been passed and shiploads of tea taxable at three pence per pound were on their way, then, in the words of Dr. Benjamin Rush, tea became truly lethal: "The baneful chests contain in them a slow poison, something worse than death—the seeds of SLAVERY!"

Among the few warning voices raised in Parliament had been that of William Dowdeswell. "I tell the Noble Lord now, that if he don't take off the duty they won't take the tea." He also calculated that after deducting the expenses of collection, net revenue from the dutiable tea would be a mere £400—as it turned out, a wildly optimistic forecast. But the good-natured Lord North thought he was doing the colonists as well as the Company a favor. As a matter of principle the Townshend tax of three pence a pound was retained, but the much higher tax of a shilling a pound, payable when the tea was brought into London from China, was entirely remitted; the act would thus bring the price of legally imported tea below that of smuggled Dutch tea. Who could resist such a bargain? Certainly not the penny-pinching colonials. But as Franklin, still in London, wrote to a friend in Boston, the ministers "have no idea that any people can act from any other principle but that of interest; and they believe that three pence in a pound of tea, of which one does not perhaps drink ten pounds in a year, is sufficient to overcome all the patriotism of an American."

Once again the Liberty Boys resorted to direct action. As he put into Philadelphia, Captain Ayres, master of the tea-ship *Polly*, received this message from the Committee for Tarring and Feathering: "What think you, Captain, of a Halter around your neck, then Gallons of liquid Tar decanted on your pate—with the Feathers of a dozen live Geese laid over that to enliven your Appearance?" Ayres took the hint and returned with his cargo to London. In Charleston a compromise was reached whereby the tea was unloaded and stored in a damp cellar where it would rot away. In Annapolis, Maryland, the brig *Peggy Stewart* arrived bearing 2,320 pounds of tea on which the ship's owner, Anthony Stewart, hoping to dodge the issue, had already paid the duties. But this was "deemed a submission to the contested claim of the British Parliament," wrote William Eddis, an English official. "Very severe censures were accordingly passed on the parties concerned, and a general spirit of resentment seemed to predominate." Stewart tried to talk his way out of it, but he and his associates were forced to sign a groveling confession: "We do severally acknowledge that we have committed a most daring insult and act of the most pernicious tendency to the liberties of America . . . and we solemnly declare for the future that we never will infringe any resolution formed by the people for the salvation of their rights." Moreover "to show our desire of living in amity with the friends of America, we request this meeting, or as many as may choose to attend, to be present at any place where the people shall appoint, and we will there commit to the flames, or otherwise destroy, as the people may choose, the detestable article which has been the cause of this our misconduct." But even that wouldn't do, and in the end Stewart was induced "from an anxious desire to ensure his own personal safety" to propose setting fire not only to the cargo but to the ship itself. This offer was accepted, "and in a few hours the brig, with her sails, cordage, and every appurtenance, was effectually burnt."

But once again the hotbed of resistance was Boston, where the rioting started even before the tea arrived. "The Ships laden with Tea from the East India House are hourly expected," wrote Anne Hulton, Commissioner Henry Hulton's sister, to a friend back in England. "The People will not suffer it to be landed at Boston, they demand the

Consignees to promise to send it back. Mr. Clark resolutely refuses to comply, will submit to no other terms than to put it into warehouse till they can hear from England. They threaten to tear him to pieces if it is landed. . . . His Son who is just arrived from England & all the family were got together the first night rejoicing at his Arrival, when the mob surrounded the House, attacking it with Stones and Clubs, did great damage to the House & Furniture. . . . A great number of Stones each so large as to have kill'd any person they had hit were thrown about the Table where the Family were at Supper, but Providence directed 'em so that they did not fall on any person . . ."

On November 29, the merchant John Rowe, a moderate Patriot, found posters stuck up all over town: "Friends! Brethren! Countrymen! That worst of Plagues, the detested Tea, ship'd for this Port by the East India Company, is now arriv'd in this harbour. The Hour of Destruction or manly Opposition to the Machinations of Tyranny stares you in the Face; every Friend to his Country, to Himself, & to Posterity, is now called upon to meet at Faneuil Hall, at nine of Clock this Day, at which time the Bells will begin to ring, to make United & Successful Resistance to this last, worst, and most Destructive Measure of Administration."

The Patriots ordered the three tea ships to dock at Griffin's wharf and posted guards to ensure that no cargo was unloaded. They then tried to force the owners to send the ships back, but the owners refused because without proper clearance from the customs officials their ships would be liable to seizure and confiscation; and the customs officials would not give them clearance unless the tea was landed and declared for duty; and the Liberty Boys would not allow the tea to be landed; and Governor Hutchinson refused to overrule the customs officers. The stand-off continued for two weeks, when it seemed likely that the governor would try to use force to land the tea. A mass meeting was held at the Old South Church, presided over by Samuel Adams. It went on for several hours until, in apparent despair at Hutchinson's obstinacy, Adams finally declared that they could do nothing more to save the country. He can hardly have been surprised when war whoops at once came from the gallery and doorway, along with cries of "The Mohawks are come!" and

"Boston harbor a tea-pot tonight!" What happened next was described many years later by one of the participants, George Hewes:

✳

It was now evening, and I immediately dressed myself in the costume of an Indian, equipped with a small hatchet, which I and my associates denominated the tomahawk, with which, and a club, after having painted my face and hands with coal dust in the shop of a blacksmith, I repaired to Griffin's wharf, where the ships lay that contained the tea. When I first appeared in the street after being thus disguised, I fell in with many who were dressed, equipped, and painted as I was, and who fell in with me and marched in order to the place of our destination.

When we arrived at the wharf, there were three of our number who assumed an authority to direct our operations, to which we gladly submitted. They divided us into three parties, for the purpose of boarding the three ships which contained the tea at the same time. . . . The commander of the division to which I belonged, as soon as we were on board the ship, appointed me boatswain, and ordered me to go to the captain and demand of him the keys to the hatches and a dozen candles. I made the demand accordingly, and the captain promptly replied, and delivered the articles; but requested me at the same time to do no damage to the ship or rigging. We then were ordered by our commander to open the hatches and take out all the chests of tea and throw them overboard, and we immediately proceeded to execute his orders, first cutting and splitting the chests with our tomahawks, so as thoroughly to expose them to the effects of the water.

In about three hours from the time we went on board, we had thus broken and thrown overboard every tea chest to be found in the ship, while those in the other ships were disposing of the tea in the same way, at the same time. We were surrounded by British armed ships, but no attempt was made to resist us. We then quietly retired to our several places of residence, without having any conversation with each other, or taking any measures to discover who were our associates.

The next morning, after we had cleared the ships of the tea, it was discovered that very considerable quantities of it were floating upon the surface of the water; and to prevent the possibility of any of its being saved for use, a number of small boats were manned by sailors and citizens, who rowed them into those parts of the harbor wherever the tea was visible, and by beating it with oars and paddles so thoroughly drenched it as to render its entire destruction inevitable.

Not all Bostonians approved. "I am sincerely sorry for the event," wrote John Rowe. "'Tis a Disastrous Affair & some People are much alarmed." Rowe hoped to fend off the anticipated retaliation by contributing to a fund that would pay for the 340 chests of tea, valued at £9,000, a move also favored by Franklin; but Sam Adams saw to it that this initiative went nowhere.

Viewed from London, the Tea Party was nothing less than an act of rebellion. "My Lord," wrote the Attorney-General to Lord Dartmouth, "having received your Lordship's commands to take into our consideration a case transmitted to us and two questions put thereupon, we have considered the same and humbly submit to your lordship the following answer to the said questions:

"We are of opinion that the acts and proceedings stated in the above-mentioned case do amount to the crime of high treason, namely to the levying of war against His Majesty . . ." The threats made against Mr. Clark and the other consignees were also "an overt act of high treason," and "if it can be established in evidence that they were so employed by the select-men of Boston, town-clerk and members of the House of Representatives, these also are guilty of the same offence." Finally, "The methods of proceeding against them are either by prosecuting them for their treason in the country in the ordinary course of justice; or . . . transmitting them hither to be tried in some county of England to be assigned by the King's commission."

Lord North may have blenched at such drastic measures, but the king approved. "Perseverance," he wrote, "and the meeting of difficulties as they arise with firmness seem the only means." Also "the dye is now cast, the Colonies must either submit or triumph; I do not wish to come to severer measures, but we must not retreat." Appeasement had been tried but didn't work: Repeal of the Stamp Act was now "the fatal compliance in 1766"; repeal of most of the Townshend Duties had been taken by the colonies as a sign of weakness. Writing to Lord North after a conversation with General Gage, who had returned for a visit to London early in 1774, the king quoted him as saying, "They will be Lyons whilst we are Lambs, but if we take the resolute part they will undoubtedly prove very meek." Gage, who had lived in America for nearly twenty years, and whose wife was American, had long advocated strong measures. "Quash this spirit at a blow, without too much regard to the expense, and it will prove economy in the end," he had written at the time of the *Liberty* riots. "I know of nothing that can so effectually quell the spirit of sedition . . . as speedy, vigorous, and unanimous measures taken in England to suppress it." One such measure was to recall Thomas Hutchinson and replace him as governor by General Gage, who would also continue to serve as commander-in-chief.

It was generally assumed in London that the colonies would not stick together, that if one of them were singled out for exemplary punishment, the others would either be intimidated or would sit back and, if not actually gloat, at least watch with indifference. This was not impossible, and it was a tribute to the diplomatic and political skills of the members of the Continental Congress, notably John and Samuel Adams, that it did not happen. Another non-event was the massive outpouring of popular support in Britain for the American cause. To the colonists it was obvious that an attack on their rights would be followed by an attack on those of their fellow-citizens at home, but the English—perhaps because they had fewer rights but more prejudices—did not see it that way. The American cause certainly had its supporters in England, but at the moment they were few and without influence.

And so, once again without much debate, Parliament proceeded to approve by large majorities a series of punitive laws known as the Coercive, or Intolerable, Acts. The first, the Boston Port Act, was passed on March 31, 1774; it declared that because "dangerous commotions and insurrections have been fomented and raised in the town of Boston . . . by divers ill-affected persons, to the subversion of his Majesty's government, and to the utter destruction of the publick peace" the entire port was to be closed. Only army or navy ships were to be allowed to come and go; also ships carrying "fuel or victual brought coastwise from any part of the continent of America, for the necessary use and sustenance of the inhabitants of the town of Boston." (In other words, they were not going to be starved into submission.) The act was to remain in effect until the tea was paid for, and customs officers and others who had suffered in the various riots were compensated.

A few weeks later Lord North introduced the Massachusetts Government Act, whose purpose was to "purge the constitution of all its crudities" by taking "the executive power from the hands of the democratic part of the government." Members of the council would now be appointed by the governor, rather than elected by the House of Representatives; town meetings would be limited to one a year. Also approved was the Administration of Justice Act, authorizing the governor to transfer certain trials to another colony or to Great Britain, as recommended by the Attorney-General. John Hancock and Sam Adams were the prime targets of this act. Equally offensive to New Englanders, though not one of the Coercive Acts, was the Quebec Act, also passed at this time, an enlightened piece of legislation that allowed the French-Canadians to "have, hold, and enjoy the free Exercise of the Religion of the Church of Rome."

Reaction outside New England to these measures was just the opposite of what Lord North and his ministers had so confidently expected. In June, in Philadelphia, a convention attended by some eight thousand people resolved that "the act of parliament for shutting up the port of Boston is unconstitutional, oppressive to the inhabitants of that town, dangerous to the liberties of the British colonies," and that "a congress of deputies from the several colonies in North America is the most probable and proper mode of procuring relief for our suffering brethren." A committee of correspondence was formed to maintain close contact with the other colonies, and deputies were appointed "to attend a general congress."

Similar resolutions were passed two weeks later at a mass meeting in New York, which also urged that the forthcoming continental congress "agree upon a non-importation from Great Britain of all goods, wares, and merchandizes until the act for blocking up the harbour of Boston be repealed." The Resolutions of the Freeholders of Albermarle County, Virginia, drawn up by Thomas Jefferson, who managed to work in a reference to "the common rights of mankind," went a step further and urged non-exportation as well as non-importation and the repeal of all laws prohibiting American manufactures. In August these resolutions were confirmed by the Virginia House of Burgesses, meeting at the Raleigh Tavern in Williamsburg in defiance of the governor, Lord Dunmore, who had formally dissolved them. After confirming the non-importation agreement, "medicines excepted," the self-denying Burgesses also voted that "We will neither ourselves import, nor purchase any slave, or slaves, imported by any person, after the first day of November next, either from Africa, the West Indies, or any other place."

Another resolution ran: "Considering the article of tea as the detestable instrument which laid the foundation of the present sufferings of our distressed friends in the town of Boston, we view it with horror, and therefore resolve that we will not, from this day, either import tea of any kind whatever, nor will we use or suffer even such of it as is now at hand to be used in any of our families."

To Lexington and Concord and Back Again

"Honest Tom" Gage, commander in chief of His Majesty's forces in North America—"a very Good Man" in the opinion of the Patriot merchant, John Rowe—landed in Boston in May 1774, bringing with him a set of instructions from Lord Dartmouth, a royal commission appointing him Governor-in-Chief of His Majesty's Province of Massachusetts Bay, and a copy of the recently passed Boston Port Bill "for discontinuing the loading and unloading of goods and merchandize at the town," with orders to enforce it at once. "His Majesty trusts that no opposition will or can with any effect be made to the carrying the new law into execution," wrote Dartmouth. "Should it happen otherwise, your authority as the first magistrate combined with your command over the King's troops will it is hoped enable you to meet every opposition and fully to preserve the public peace by employing those troops with effect should the madness of the people . . . make it necessary to have recourse to their assistance." However, the king "trusts that such necessity will not occur and commands me to say that it will be your duty to use every endeavour to avoid it, to quiet the minds of the people, to remove their prejudices, and by mild and gentle persuasion to induce such a submission on their part . . . as may give full scope to His Majesty's clemency." As he read these unrealistic and contradictory instructions, Gage must have known that his high-sounding double assignment was likely to be the graveyard of his career.

Nevertheless he soldiered on. The port was closed. "'Tis impossible to describe the Distressed Situation of this Poor Town—not one Topsail Merchantman to be seen," wrote Rowe. "Poor Unhappy Boston! God knows only thy wretched Fate. I see nothing but misery will attend thy Inhabitants." The provincial government was purged "of all its crudities," although threats by the Liberty Boys made many reluctant to serve the new administration. Joshua Loring, for example, "was awaked by a very loud knocking at my door. Immediately I jumped out of bed and threw up the window when I saw five men disguised, their faces blacked, hats flapped and with cutlasses in their hands. I asked them . . . what they wanted. They told me they came to know if I would resign my seat on the Board." Loring refused, but Lieutenant Governor Thomas Oliver was forced to resign from the new council when his house at Cambridge was attacked "by a Mob of 4,000 Men", and "this Mob was not mixed with tag, rag, and Bobtail only; Persons of distinction in the country were in the mass." Afterwards Oliver "was forced to fly to Boston for Protection." This happened in September, by which time the whole of Massachusetts apart from Boston was effectively in the hands of a provincial congress and various committees of correspondence. A month after Gage's arrival, John Hancock and Sam Adams—who had failed to make themselves available for arrest and deportation to England—were among those chosen to go to the continental congress at Philadelphia.

In his talks with the king and his ministers, Gage had urged strong measures, but the army with which he was supposed to overcome "the madness of the people" was composed of a mere eight regiments, all of them under strength and amounting to under three thousand effectives; as he wrote to Dartmouth, "a small force rather encourages resistance than terrifies," whereas "an army twenty thousand strong will in the end save Great Britain both blood and treasure." But this letter crossed one from Dartmouth to him explaining that "the state of this kingdom will not admit of our sending more troops from Great Britain. Considerations of general safety forbid the sending any from our distant garrisons, and though perhaps some might be spared from Ireland, yet the advanced season of the year making it next to impossible for transports to secure a passage to North America, their departure must be postponed until the spring." And in answer to a suggestion by Gage: "The proposition of either raising new corps or augmenting the establishment of the old ones by levies in North America is considered as an experiment too full of hazard to be adopted in the present exigency." Dartmouth did however pass along a suggestion that had been made in London that would "prevent the fatal consequence of having recourse to the sword;" this was to disarm "the inhabitants of the Massachusetts Bay, Connecticut, and Rhode Island." Perhaps feeling embarrassed at having to forward this absurd idea, he added that "whether such a measure can be attempted in the present state of things, you must be the best judge."

Meanwhile, relations between civilians and soldiers in Boston were back to where they had been on the eve of the massacre. In a letter dated August 1, 1774, John Andrews, a merchant, described to his brother-in-law, William Barrel, in Philadelphia, a recent occasion when after dining at the Miss Erskines, "a family noted for their hospitality and kindness to strangers, in admitting all comers to their bed and board," a group of officers had "committed all manner of enormous indecencies by exposing their anteriors as well as their posteriors at the open windows and doors, to the full view of the people, either men or women, that happened to pass by, with a great deal of opprobrious language, which caused a number of boys to gather round the house, at whom they presented pistols, and threatened to fire among 'em." The officers then sallied out into the street "insulting people as they pass'd," overturning an old woman's apple shop, and "running their fists" into the faces of passersby. The next day the selectmen complained to Gage's second in command, Lord Percy (son of the Duke of Northumberland, whose London mansion stood at the top of Craven Street, more or less making him Franklin's neighbor). Percy "treated them very politely and express'd himself much displeas'd with the officers' conduct, and told 'em he would take effectual methods to prevent the like behaviour in future." But in fact there was little Percy or Gage himself could do.

As for the rank and file, many were tempted to change sides. "Am this instant interrupted by a chase of four soldiers after a deserter through the market," wrote John Andrews on August 20. "He proves to belong to the 65th, and left 'em two or three years since. He seems to be a smart, stout fellow, dress'd in a short jacket and long trousers. Am amaz'd he should be so stupid as to appear in so publick a place. They have lugg'd him up to the camp, from whence they will send him to his regiment, where I suppose a thousand lashes at least will be his portion."

But Andrews was wrong. Faced with over two hundred desertions in the past three months, Gage decided to make an example of the "smart, stout fellow."

✴

September 9. Led by a curiosity natural to most men, early this morning I attended the execution of the poor fellow whom I mentioned in one of my former letters to have been taken up in the market for desertion. After the Parson had pray'd with him, and while his grave was digging, he address'd himself to the Soldiers (who were drawn up from all the Regiments around him): he spoke for half an hour very fluently and compos'd, but when he was fix'd to the spot from which he was not to remove but into an awful eternity his spirits were much agitated, and after another exhortation and prayer, which continued about a quarter of an hour, he received the discharge of six muskets from about eight yards distance, and lest that was not sufficient, a fourth stepp'd up and presented his gun close to his head and discharg'd it, which put a period to his life. He was then laid upon the lid of his coffin and expos'd to the view of the whole Army, who were made to march in a slow, solemn step close on one side of his body.

✴

Those redcoats who did not try to desert seem to have done their best to drink themselves to death with cheap rum, supplied wholesale by the townspeople and retailed by the camp followers, all orders to the contrary notwithstanding.

Cooperation with the navy was another problem for Gage, as it was to be for all British generals in America with the exception of Sir William Howe, whose brother, Lord Howe, was the admiral during his command. Personal animosities often sharpened routine inter-service rivalry. When Gage arrived, Admiral Montagu was in command, a man who managed to give offense to almost everyone. "A Porter, a Shoe Black, or Chimney Sweeper would be ashamed of the coarse, low, vulgar dialect of this Sea Officer, tho' a rear Admiral of the Blue," wrote John Adams in his diary. "His continual Language is cursing and damning and God damning— 'My wife's d – -d A – e is so broad that she and I can't sit in a Chariot together'—this is the Nature of the Beast and the common

Language of the Man." The broad-beamed Mrs. Montagu had her failings too. "His lady is very much disliked they say in general. She is very full of her Remarks at the Assembly and Concert. 'Can this Lady afford the Jewels and Dress she wears? —Oh that ever my son should come to dance with a Mantua Maker [a dress-maker]!'"

Montagu's replacement, Admiral Samuel Graves, was hardly an improvement. His wife carried on a public feud with Mrs. Gage and, according to a letter in the *London Chronicle,* of September 1775, "in his own department the Admiral is more hated and despised, if possible, than he is by the army." Meeting him on Milk Street one day, Commissioner Hallowell asked Graves why he had not answered several of his letters. "To this civil question, the Admiral replied in his usual style" and then "returned a blow on the face. Though Mr. Hallowell was unarmed, the Admiral had recourse to his sword, upon which the former rushed upon him, forced it from him, broke it over his knee, and then flung it in Graves's face; after this they went to it with their fists, but were soon parted. The Admiral has come off with a black eye."

It was an article of faith in London that only New England was truly disaffected, but the results of what Gage called the Patriots' campaign "to persuade the other colonies to make the cause of Boston the common cause of America," were discouraging. Not only had a convention in Philadelphia declared that the act of Parliament for shutting up the port of Boston was "unconstitutional, oppressive to the inhabitants of that town, [and] dangerous to the liberties of the British colonies," it had also voted to "set on foot a subscription for the relief of such poor inhabitants of the town of Boston as may be deprived of their means of subsistence."

In Maryland, for "expressly declining, when applied to by some noisy patriots . . . to preach a sermon to recommend the suffering people of Boston to the charity of my parish," the Anglican clergyman, the Rev. Jonathan Boucher, was treated with "open and avowed violence." (He had refused on the grounds that "the true motive was by these means to raise a sum sufficient to purchase arms and ammunition.") As a result "I received letters threatening me with the most dreadful consequences if I did not desist from preaching. All the answer I gave to these threats were in my sermons, in which I declared I could never suffer any human authority to intimidate me from doing what I believed to be my duty to God and his church; and for more than six months I preached, when I did preach, with a pair of loaded pistols lying on the cushion, having given notice that if anyone attempted, what had long been threatened, to drag me out of the pulpit, I should think myself justified in repelling violence with violence."

From Savannah, Governor Sir James Wright wrote to Dartmouth to complain about his colleague to the north, where "the Carolina Sons of Liberty have been suffered to do whatever they pleased without the least mark of disapprobation or attempt to check them." Such weakness by his neighbor made his own position more difficult: "If a man has resolution and integrity enough to stand forth and attempt to do his duty, it's like being set up as a mark to be shot at and raising the resentment of great numbers against him." Everything was going to pot—"nothing but jealousies, rancour and ill blood, law and no law, government and no government, dependence and independence if I may be allowed the expression, and everything unhinged and running into confusion so that in short a man hardly knows what to do or how to act, and it's a most disagreeable state to one who wishes to support law, government, and good order and to discharge his duty with honour and integrity."

From Virginia, a few months later, the governor, Lord Dunmore, wrote that every county "is now arming a company of men whom they call an independent company for the avowed purpose of protecting their committees." As to the royal government, "I can assure your lordship that it is entirely disregarded if not wholly overturned." Dunmore's recommendation was that "these undutiful people should be made to feel the distress and misery of which they have themselves laid the foundation. . . . Their ports should be blocked up and their communication cut off by water even with their neighbouring colonies. . . . The functions of every department of government, which in fact are now entirely obstructed, should be suspended and the governor and all other officers withdrawn. The people, left to themselves and to the confusion that would immediately reign, would I cannot but believe soon become sensible from what source their former happiness flowed and prostrate themselves before the power which they had so lately considered as inimical and treated with contempt."

From New York, Lieutenant Governor Cadwallader Colden was able to report that although "the turbulent factious few who are never easy when the people are quiet and orderly" were now out of power, replaced by the merchant-dominated Committee of 51, yet the situation remained precarious: "The most trifling unforeseen incident may produce the greatest events." Like many other governors, Colden complained that opposition "speeches in Parliament and other inflammatory papers published in London and reprinted in America make the worst impression on the minds of the people."

But everything was worse in Massachusetts where, wrote Gage in September, "the flame of sedition has spread universally throughout the country. . . . Civil government is near its end, the courts of justice expiring one after another." He would do all he could to avoid a "bloody crisis" but "conciliating, moderation, reasoning is over; nothing can be done but by forcible means. The people . . . are numerous, worked up to a fury, and not a Boston rabble but the freeholders and farmers of the country. A check anywhere would be fatal and the first stroke will decide a great deal."

Outside Boston the Liberty Boys and their supporters were busy making life difficult for anyone with Loyalist sympathies. Some of their activities were described by Peter Oliver, Tory author of *Origin & Progress of the American Revolution*.

September 1774. A Mob of 5,000 collected at Worcester, about 50 Miles from Boston, a thousand of whom were armed. It being at the Time when the Court of Common Pleas was about sitting, the Mob made a lane & compelled the Judges, Sheriff & Gentlemen of the

Bar to pass & repass them, Cap in hand, in the most ignominious Manner; & read their Disavowall of holding Courts under the new Acts of Parliament. Brigadier Ruggles's House at Hardwicke, about 70 Miles from Boston, was also plundered of his Guns, & one of his fine Horses poisoned. Mr. Silas Wood, who had signed a paper to disavow the riotous Proceedings of the Times, was dragged by a Mob of 2 or 300 Men about a Mile to a River, in order to drown him; but one of his Children hanging around him with Cries & Tears, he was induced to recant, though even then very reluctantly. The Rev. Mr. Peters, of Hebron in Connecticut, an Episcopalian Clergyman, after having his House broke into by a Mob, & being most barbarously treated in it, was stript of his Canonicals, & carried to one of their Liberty Poles, & afterwards drove from his parish. . . . He was obliged to go to England incognito, having been hunted after, to the Danger of his Life.

Colonel Gilbert was so obnoxious for his Attachment to Government that the Mobs, being sometimes afraid to attack him openly, some of them secretly fired Balls at him in the Woods. And as he was driving a Number of Sheep to his Farm, he was attacked by 30 or 40 of them, who robbed him of part of the Flock, but he beat the Mob off. And this same Col. Gilbert was, some time after, travelling on his Business, when he stopped at an Inn to bait his Horse. Whilst he was in the House, some Person lift up the Saddle from his Horse & put a Piece of a broken Glass Bottle under the Saddle; & when the Colonel mounted, the Pressure run the Glass into the Horse's back, which made him frantick. The Horse threw his Rider, who was so much hurt as not to recover his Senses till he was carried & arrived at his own House, at 3 Miles distance.

A Number of Ladies, at Plimouth, attempted to divert themselves at the publick assembly Room; but not being connected with the rebel Faction, the Committee Men met, and the Mob collected who flung Stones & broke the Windows & Shutters of the Room, endangering the Lives of the Company, who were obliged to break up, & were abused to their Homes.

A Parish Clerk of an Episcopal church at East Haddam in Connecticut, a man of 70 Years of Age, was taken out of his Bed in a cold Night, & beat against his Hearth by Men who held him by his Arms & Legs. He was then laid across his Horse, without his Cloaths, & drove to a considerable Distance in that naked Condition. His Nephew, Dr. Abner Beebe, a Physician, complained of the bad Usage of his Uncle, & spoke very freely in Favor of Government, for which he was assaulted by a Mob, stripped naked, & hot Pitch was poured upon him, which blistered his Skin. He was then carried to an Hog Sty & rubbed over with Hog's Dung. They threw the Hog's Dung in his Face, & rammed some of it down his Throat; & in that Condition exposed to a Company of Women. His House was attacked, his Windows broke, when one of his Children was sick, & a Child went into Distraction upon this Treatment. His Gristmill was broke, & Persons prevented from grinding at it, & from having any Connections with him.

Oliver concludes his account with the note: "All the foregoing Transactions were before the Battle of Lexington, when the rebels say that the War began."

As the situation grew more tense, Gage launched a series of forays out of Boston to seize the gunpowder, artillery, and other supplies belonging to the local towns and their militias. One of these sorties took place on September 1, when a force was sent to the arsenal at Charlestown, where they "arrived early, between one o'clock and day, and waited for Break of day as it was dangerous to enter a powder house with a Lanthern," wrote the Rev. Ezra Stiles, a Congregational minister at Newport, Rhode Island. After seizing 250 barrels of gunpowder and two cannon, the troops left. "This was on Thursday morning. The Thing was done most secretly, the Soldiers were opposed by none, because nobody knew it till they were gone off."

Stiles continued: "The same day, viz. Thursday afternoon, a Report began to be spread in the neighboring Towns, that the Governor had sent a party of Soldiers to Cambridge, who had seized & carried off the Powder; that the people opposed them, a Skirmish ensued, & that the Soldiery had fired upon them & killed six men. Who originated this false story is a secret; but this much is certain that it had propagated itself above forty Miles to as far as Shrewsbury by Midnight on Thursday night, as I was informed by Mr. McNeil of Litchfield, who came from Springfield & lodged at Shrewsbury that night. This Story passed with some mutilations, but under all carrying an account that in Taking the Powder the Soldiery had fired upon the people & *killed six* of them."

An ardent Patriot, Stiles also had a strict regard for the truth. "I have diligently attended to the whole, digested the contradictory accounts, & verified all by conversation with Eye Witnesses." These included Mr. McNeil of Litchfield, who told Stiles that on his way to Boston he had stopped at an inn in Shrewsbury, where

✴

he went to bed without hearing anything. But about midnight or perhaps one o'clock he was suddenly waked up, somebody violently rapping up the Landlord, telling the doleful Story that the Powder was taken, six men killed, & all the people between there & Boston arming & marching down to the Relief of their Brethren at Boston; and within a quarter of an hour he judges fifty men were collected at the Tavern, tho' now deep in Night, equipping themselves & sending off Posts every Way to the neighboring Towns.

In the Morning, being Friday Sept. 2, Mr. McNeil rode forward & passed thro' the whole at the very Time of the Convulsion. He said he never saw such a Scene before—all along were armed Men rushing forward, some on foot, some on horseback, at every house Women & Children making Cartridges, running Bullets, making Wallets, baking Biscuit, crying & bemoaning & at the same time animating their Husbands & Sons to fight for their Liberties, tho' not knowing whether they should ever see them again. I asked whether the men were Cowards or disheartened or appeared to want Courage? No. Whether the tender Distresses of weeping Wives & Children softened, effeminated & overcame the men and set them weeping too? No—nothing of this—but a firm intrepid Ardor, hardy, eager, and courageous Spirit of Enterprise, a Spirit for revenging the Blood of their Brethren & rescue our Liberties .... He thought if anything the women surpassed the Men for Eagerness & Spirit in the Defense of Liberty by Arms. For they had no Thoughts of the Men returning but from Battle, for they all believed the Action commenced between the King's Troops & the Provincials. . . .

By the time the rumor was contradicted, two thousand armed men had gathered at Springfield, another two thousand at Northhampton, and the same number as far away as Bennington. "Even at Albany," wrote Stiles, "the Dutch set off a number of Wagons of Provisions for their Supply. And Mr. Johnson with the Mohawk Indians (forty or fifty) actually set off from the Indian Country beyond Hudson's River in full march for the Relief of Boston." All in all, Stiles estimated that in Connecticut twenty thousand armed men were ready to march, and another forty thousand in Massachusetts and New Hampshire—probably an exaggeration, but vastly outnumbering Gage's three thousand regulars.

The winter of 1774–1775 was to be one of the mildest on record, but the hostile and resentful townspeople and the demoralized and bloodyminded British soldiers were not to know that; and as the days grew shorter, the future seemed bleaker. In mid-November five regiments were still living onboard the transport ships that had brought them, since the Sons of Liberty and local committees would not allow any building materials to be shipped to Boston. For a while the Royal Irish Regiment was quartered in a disused distillery but, as John Andrews reported, had to return to the transports because "the smell of the lees in the cisterns added to their urine has caus'd an infectious distemper among 'em, whereby two or three have dropt dead of a day." There were outbreaks of smallpox among the troops and their families—about one in ten of the soldiers had a wife, legal or otherwise, and many children were born to them. Supply officers complained about the expense, but having a family was considered an incentive not to desert. Among the rest of the troops, however, absenteeism was so high that in late December roll calls were being held every half hour. On Christmas Eve there was another public execution: "There were many intercessions made to the General for his reprieve," wrote Andrews, but Gage "was determin'd to make an example of him. It was debated in a council of officers, but overrul'd, that he should be hung in chains upon the gallows *in terrorem*." Only a few days later, on January 4, 1775, Andrews wrote that "The Discontent of the Soldiers has become so general that they have doubled all the guards and made two regiments lay under arms; as well as that, they have fix'd a field piece in the Centre of the town to be fir'd in case of a mutiny."

Some of the officers did what they could to raise morale and combat the tedium. "The Regiments are frequently practiced at firing with balls at marks. Six rounds per man at each time is usually allotted for this practice," wrote Lt. Frederick Mackenzie, adjutant of the 23rd, the Royal Welch Fusiliers, one of the elite British regiments. "As Our Regiment is quartered on a Wharf which projects into part of the harbour, and there is a very considerable range without any obstruction, we have fixed figures of men as large as life, made of thin boards, on small stages, which are anchored at a proper distance from the end of the Wharf, at which the men fire. Objects afloat, which move up and down with the tide, are frequently pointed out for them to fire at, and Premiums are sometimes given for the best Shots, by which means some of our men have become excellent marksmen."

British troops could still venture out of Boston,

✳

but the people are evidently making every preparation for resistance. They are taking every means to provide themselves with Arms; and are particularly desirous of procuring the Locks of firelocks, which are easily conveyed out of town without being discovered by the Guards.

February 2. Notwithstanding the pains which have been taken to prevent Spirituous liquors from being sold to the Soldiers, Soldiers' wives and others find means to dispose of the New England Rum to them in such quantities, and at so cheap a rate, that numbers of them are intoxicated daily. Some of them have sold Spirits of so pernicious a quality that two men died in one night, affected by it in an extraordinary manner. The townspeople encourage this excessive drinking, as when the Soldiers are in a state of intoxication they are frequently induced to desert.

February 3. It has been customary of late, and approved by the General, for some of the Regiments to go out of town, with their Arms, Accoutrements, and knapsacks, when the weather permits and they are off duty, and march three or four miles into the Country. This practice is conducive to the health of the troops; and may enable the General to send Regiments or Detachments to particular parts of the country without occasioning so much alarm as would otherwise take place. Our Regiment marched out this day towards Cambridge. The people appeared apprehensive that something particular is concealed under these movements; and there are always some persons appointed to watch the motions and direction of the Troops.

February 4. A Soldier of the 4th Regiment who was tried a few days ago for disposing of Arms to the townspeople has been found guilty and sentenced to receive 500 lashes.

March 6. Warm day. Thermometer 54 degrees. This day having been appointed by the Selectmen of Boston for the delivery, according to annual custom, of an Oration in commemoration of the 5th March 1770, on which day some Inhabitants of this town were killed and wounded, in a Riot, by the Military: at 10 o'clock the Old South Meeting was opened for the purpose, and an immense concourse of people assembled therein. As this assemblage was undoubtedly intended to inflame the minds of the people, and the Troops conceived it was a great insult, under the present circumstances, to deliver an Oration on the Occasion, a great number of Officers assembled in the Church and seemed determined to take notice of, and resent, any expressions made use of by the Orator, reflecting on the Military. About 11 o'clock, Doctor Joseph Warren, an Apothecary of Boston came in, and ascended the Pulpit, which was hung with Black Cloth. He was attended by all the most violent fellows in town, particularly Hancock, the Adams's, Church, Cooper, and the rest of the Select Men. Every person was silent, and every countenance seemed to denote that some event of consequence might be expected. The Oration, which, tho' severe on the conduct of the Military, and evidently calculated to excite the resentment of the populace against them, contained nothing so violent as was expected, was delivered without any other interruption than a few hisses from some of the Officers.

As this meeting was called an Adjournment of a former Town meeting, as soon as the Oration was ended, Mr. Samuel Adams came forward from a Pew in which he and the other Selectmen sat, very near the Pulpit, and moved, "that the thanks of the Town should be presented to Doctor Warren for his Elegant and Spirited Oration, and that another Oration should be delivered on the 5th of March next, to commemorate the Bloody Massacre of the 5th of March 1770." On this several Officers began to hiss; others cried out "Oh! Fie! Oh! Fie!" [Shame! Shame!], and a great bustle ensued. As everyone was now in motion, intending to go out, there was a great deal of noise, and the exclamation was mistaken for the cry of Fire! Fire! Numbers immediately called out Fire! Fire! which created a Scene of the greatest confusion imaginable. As there were numbers of Women in the Meeting, their cries increased the confusion, which was further increased by the Drums & fifes of the 43rd Regiment which happened to be passing by from Exercise. Some persons leaped out of the lower windows, and in a short time the Meeting was nearly cleared. As soon as the mistake was discovered, and things grew quiet, the Selectmen proceeded to the choice of some public officers, which being finished, the people dispersed.

March 16. The Provincial Congress having recommended a General Fast on this day throughout the Province, the same was strictly observed by the Inhabitants of this town. All the shops were shut up, and all business suspended.

March 18. A Country man was Stopped at the Lines, going out of town with 19,000 ball Cartridges, which were taken from him. . . . Great numbers of Arms have been carried out of town during the Winter; and if more strict search had been made at the Lines, many of them, and much ammunition, might have been seized.

April 2. A vessel arrived at Salem which sailed from Falmouth in England the 14th February. It appears by the letters and papers brought by her, that a large reinforcement of Ships and Troops may be soon expected to arrive in the Country.

April 18. At 8 this night the Commanding Officers of Regiments were sent for to the Headquarters, and ordered to have their respective Grenadier and Light Infantry Companies on the beach near the Magazine Guard exactly at ten o'clock this night, with one day's provisions in their Havresacks, and without knapsacks. They were directed to order their Companies to parade quietly at their respective Barracks, and to march to the place of Rendezvous in small parties, and if challenged to answer "Patrole." The Companies of our Regiment (the 23rd) marched accordingly, and were the first, complete, at the place of parade; here we found a number of the Men of Wars' and Transports' boats in waiting. . . . Lieut Col Smith of the 10th, who was to have the Command, arrived, and with him Major Pitcairn of the Marines. The boats then put off, and rowed towards Phipps's farm, where having landed the troops they returned for the remainder and landed them at the same place. This was not completed until 12 o'clock. The town was a good deal agitated and alarmed at this Movement.

Thus began the momentous "two-if-by-sea" expedition to Concord via Lexington, dispatched by General Gage in obedience to orders from home. Among the letters brought by the ship that arrived at Salem on April 2 was one from Lord Dartmouth. Gage's earlier reports had convinced the government that the province was now "in open rebellion. The King's dignity and the honour and safety of the empire require that in such a situation force should be repelled by force." Gage's army might be small, but "if put to the test would be able to encounter them [the rebels] with greater probability of success than might be expected from a greater army if the people should be suffered to form themselves upon a more regular plan." Consequently "it is the opinion of the King's servants, in which His Majesty concurs, that the first and essential step to be taken towards re-establishing Government would be to arrest and imprison the principal actors and abettors in the Provincial Congress, whose proceedings appear in every light to be acts of treason . . ." The rebels' arms and ammunition should also be seized. Finally "if the steps taken upon this occasion be accompanied with due precaution and every means be devised to keep the measure secret until the moment of execution, it can hardly fail of success and will perhaps be accomplished without bloodshed."

Gage, whose caution had by now earned him the nickname "The Old Woman" among the more bellicose British officers, could have made excuses: Dartmouth clearly assumed that the Provincial Congress was still at nearby Cambridge rather than at Concord, some twenty miles away; the expedition would require secrecy, but as Mackenzie noted the town was immediately aware that something was afoot; any major excursion was likely to attract a swarm of minutemen, as had happened after the false alarm of the previous September; and the chances of catching such "principal actors and abettors" as Samuel Adams and John Hancock were slender. On the other hand the king clearly expected him to do something, and so, on April 18, Gage issued orders to Lt. Col. Smith:

"Having received intelligence that a quantity of Ammunition, Provision, Artillery, Tents and small Arms, having been collected at Concord, for the Avowed Purpose of raising and supporting a Rebellion against His Majesty, you will march with the corps of Grenadiers and light Infantry, put under your Command, with the utmost expedition and secrecy to Concord, where you will seize and destroy all the Artillery, Ammunition, Provisions, Tents, small Arms and all military Stores whatever. But you will take care that the Soldiers do not plunder the Inhabitants or hurt private property." Gage was specific about the smallest details: "the Powder and Flour must be shook out of the Barrels into the River . . . the Men may put Balls or Lead in their Pockets, throwing them by degrees into Ponds, Ditches, &c., but no Quantity together so that they may be recovered afterwards. If you meet with any brass artillery, you will order their muzzles beat in, so as to render them useless." About the only thing Gage did not specify was what to do if attacked.

Smith was an odd choice to command this force of about seven hundred men, as he was extremely fat and slow-moving, and could never manage to be on time. To preserve the illusion of secrecy, Gage sent out in advance several mounted officers with orders to arrest anyone coming out of Boston to give the alarm. These officers did succeed in capturing Paul Revere, but not the other messengers, and so, while the British troops, after many delays, assembled in the dark near Phipps Farm for the long march to Concord, the whole countryside was being called to arms.

There is no definitive account of exactly what happened soon after dawn on the green at Lexington, but, keenly aware of the importance of public opinion at home and in Great Britain, the Massachusetts Provincial Council immediately afterward appointed a committee, chaired by Dr. Benjamin Church, which in a short while produced *A Narrative of the Excursion & Ravages of the King's Troops,* which began:

"On the nineteenth day of April, one thousand seven hundred and seventy-five, a day to be remembered by all Americans of the present generation, and which ought, and doubtless will, be handed down to ages yet unborn, the troops of Britain, unprovoked, shed the blood of sundry of the loyal American subjects of the British king in the field of Lexington . . ." It was acknowledged that some of these men were armed (as they should have been, since they were all militiamen who had been called out several hours earlier by Captain John Parker on news of the British approach), but

this small party of the inhabitants were so far from being disposed to commit hostilities against the troops of their sovereign that, unless attacked, they were determined to be peaceable spectators of this extraordinary movement. Immediately on the approach of Colonel Smith with the detachment under his command they dispersed; but the detachment, seeming to thirst for blood, wantonly rushed on, and first began the hostile scene by firing on this small party, by which they killed eight men on the spot and wounded several others before any guns were fired upon the troops by our men. Not contented with this effusion of blood, as if malice had occupied their whole souls, they continued the fire, until all of this small party who escaped the dismal carnage were out of the reach of their fire. Colonel Smith, with the detachment, then proceeded to Concord, where a party of this detachment again made the first fire upon some of the inhabitants. . . .

The *Excursion & Ravages* was substantiated by numerous sworn depositions. Elijah Sanderson, for example, did "testify and declare" that as the redcoats approached "I heard one of the regulars, whom I took to be an officer, say, '*Damn them—we will have them!*' and immediately the regulars shouted aloud, run and fired on the Lexington company, which did not fire a gun before the regulars discharged on them . . ." Another witness:

I, John Robbins, being of lawful age, do testify and say, that on the nineteenth instant, the company under the command of Captain John Parker, being drawn up some time before sunrise, on the green or common, and I being in the front rank, there suddenly appeared a number of the king's troops, about a thousand as I thought, at the distance of about sixty or seventy yards from us, huzzaing, and on a quick pace towards us, with three officers in their front on horseback, and on full gallop towards us; the foremost of which cried, *"Throw down your arms, ye villains! Ye rebels!"* Upon which, said company dispersing, the foremost of the three officers ordered their men saying, *"Fire! By God, fire!"* at which moment we received a very heavy and close fire from them; at which instant, being wounded, I fell, and several of our men were shot dead by me. Capt. Parker's men, I believe, had not then fired a gun.

An affidavit signed by two Justices of the Peace added that John Robbins, "being duly cautioned to testify the truth, and nothing but the truth, made solemn oath to the truth of the within deposition . . . he being so maimed and wounded, that he thought he could neither write his name nor make his mark."

Unaware that John Hancock and Sam Adams were right under their noses in Lexington, the British troops continued on to Concord. Here, at the Manse, along with his wife Phebe and a growing family, lived the Reverend William Emerson, minister of the Congregational church. In times of peace Emerson's diary was full of such matters as publicly admonishing Hannah Melvin "for her disorderly Walking," but now he was one of the "flaming preachers," taking for a recent sermon the text from 2 Chronicles, XIII. 12, "Behold, God himself is with us for our Captain and his Priests with sounding Trumpets." (As his congregation would have wished, the sermon was very long and fulminating: "Arise my injured countrymen, and plead even with the Sword, the Firelock and the Bayonet, plead with your Arms, the birthright of Englishmen, the dearly purchased Legacy left you by your never-to-be-forgotten Ancestors; and if God does not help, it will be because your Sins testify against you . . .")

In his diary for April 19, Emerson told how Samuel Prescott had arrived at Concord very early in the morning with news that the regulars were on their way.

Upon this a Number of our Minute Men belonging to the Town, and Acton and Lincoln, with several others that were in Readiness, marched out to meet them, while the alarm Company was preparing to Receive them in the Town. Capt. Minot who commanded them thought it proper to take Possession of the Hill above the Meeting house as the most advantageous Situation.

We then retreated from the Hill near Liberty Pole & took a new Post back of the Town, upon a rising Eminence, where we formed, before we saw the British Troops at the Distance of one quarter of a Mile, glittering in Arms, advancing toward us with the greatest Celerity. Some were for making a Stand, notwithstanding the superiority of their Numbers, but others more prudent thought best to retreat till our Strength should be equal to the Enemy's, by Recruits from neighboring Towns that were continually coming to our Assistance. Accordingly we retreated over the Bridge when the Troops came into the Town.

Unopposed, the British troops occupied the town where they

set fire to several Carriages for the Artillery, destroyed 60 Barrels of flour, rifled several Houses, took possession of the Town house, destroyed 500 pounds of Ball, set a Guard of 100 men at the North Bridge & South, sent up a party to the house of Col. Barrett, where they were in Expectation of finding a quantity of warlike Stores; but these were happily secured just before their arrival, by transportation into the woods and other by-Places.

In the mean Time the Guard set by the Enemy to Secure the Passage at the North Bridge were alarmed by the approach of our People, who had retreated as mentioned before, and were now advancing with Special Orders not to fire upon the Troops, unless fired upon. These orders were so punctually observed that we received the Fire of the Enemy in 3 several and separate Discharges of their Pieces before it was returned by our commanding Officer; the firing then soon became general for several minutes, in which Skirmish two were killed on each Side, and several of the Enemy wounded. It may here be observed by the Way that we were the more careful to prevent beginning a Rupture with the King's Troops as we were then uncertain what had happened at Lexington, & Knew not they had begun the Quarrel there by first firing upon our people and Killing 8 men upon the spot.

The British troops at the bridge rejoined the main force which then "quitted the Town, & retreated by the Way they came. In the mean Time, a Party of our men (150) took the back Way through the great Fields into the East Quarter and had placed 'em to advantage, laying in Ambush behind Walls, Fences, and Buildings, to fire upon the Enemy on their Retreat." (As a clergyman, Emerson did not take part in the fighting that followed, but he did stay with the militia.)

In the meantime, the British troops, who had been up all night and had already marched more than twenty miles, had no choice but to retreat through a countryside whose stone walls provided excellent cover for the growing number of militiamen who surrounded them on all sides. For the honor of his regiment (the 10th), Ensign Lister, aged nineteen, had volunteered to go on the expedition in place of a Lt. Hamilton, "whose illness was suppos'd by everyone to be feign'd." Here is his account of what happened when they left Concord:

The Light Infantry march'd over a Hill above the Town, the Grenadiers through the Town. Immediately as we descended the Hill into the road the Rebels began a brisk fire, but at so great a distance it was without effect; but as they kept marching nearer, when the Grenadiers found them within shot they returned their fire. Just about that time I receiv'd a shot through my Right Elbow joint which effectually disabled that Arm. It then became a general Firing upon us from all quarters, from behind hedges and Walls. We return'd the fire every opportunity, which continued till we arriv'd at Lexington, which from what I could learn is about 9 Miles. We was then met by a Reinforcement of 4 Battalions under Lord Percy to our great joy, our ammunition being then nearly expended.

✳

General Gage had dispatched Lord Percy's relief column almost as an afterthought; without it the main force would very likely have been destroyed or forced to surrender. While they halted to recuperate, Ensign Lister "got Mr. Simes, Surgeon's Mate to the 43rd Regiment, to examine my Arm, when he extracted the Ball, it having gone through the Bone and lodg'd within the Skin. From our long fatiguing March and loss of blood for 9 Miles, want of provisions having not had a Morsel since the day before, I began to grow rather faint." One of the soldiers shared his biscuit and beef with him, another brought him some water from a horse pond in his hat, and he was able to borrow a horse; but "when I had rode about 2 Miles I found the Balls whistled so smartly about my Ears I thought it more prudent to dismount."

Lt. Frederick Mackenzie of the Royal Welch Fusiliers was with Lord Percy's relief force:

✳

During the whole of the march from Lexington, the Rebels kept an incessant irregular fire from all points at the Column, which was the more galling as our flanking parties, which at first were placed at sufficient distances to cover the march of it, were at last, from the different obstructions they occasionally met with, obliged to keep almost close to it. Our men had very few opportunities of getting good shots at the Rebels, as they hardly ever fired but under cover of a Stone wall, from behind a tree, or out of a house; and the moment they had fired they lay down out of sight until they had loaded again, or the Column had passed. In the road indeed in our rear, they were most numerous, and came on pretty close, frequently calling out *"King Hancock forever!"* Many of them were killed in the houses on the road-side from whence they fired; in some of them 7 or 8 men were destroyed. Some houses were forced open in which no person could be discovered, but when the Column had passed, numbers sallied out from some place in which they had lain concealed, fired at the rear Guard, and augmented the numbers which followed us. If we had had time to set fire to those houses, many Rebels must have perished in them, but as night drew on Lord Percy thought it best to continue the march. Many houses were plundered by the Soldiers, notwithstanding the efforts of the Officers to prevent it. I have no doubt this inflamed the Rebels, and made many of them follow us farther than they would otherwise have done. By all accounts some Soldiers who stayed too long in the houses were killed in the very act of plundering by those who lay concealed in them. We brought in about ten prisoners, some of whom were taken in arms. One or two more were killed on the march while prisoners by the fire of their own people.

As soon as the troops had passed Charlestown Neck, the Rebels ceased firing. A Negro (the only one who was observed to fire at the King's troops) was wounded near the houses close to the Neck, out of which the Rebels fired to the last.

According to the meticulous Mackenzie, sixty-eight British soldiers were killed, one hundred and sixty-seven were wounded, and twenty-two were missing; seventeen officers were wounded, two of them fatally. He estimated that by the end of the day the number of rebels was not less than four thousand. Two days later he wrote in his diary: "21 April, 1775. The town is now surrounded by armed Rebels."

As to Ensign Lister, he was able to get on one of the boats ferrying between Charleston and Boston and "proceeded through the town to my Lodgings, where I arriv'd about 9 o'Clock after a March in the whole of about 60 Miles in course of 24 Hours, about 24 Miles after I was Wounded and without a Morsel of Victuals except what I have before mentioned. On my arrival at my Lodgings, Mrs Miller, the mistress of the house, I desired to get me a dish of Tea, which she immediately set about. . . . The Imagination may conceive, though it is beyond the power of Words to express,

the satisfaction I felt from that Tea, notwithstanding I was interrupted with a Thousand Questions."

Atrocity stories were at once put out by both sides. In a letter to
her friend Mrs. Lightbody in England, Anne Hulton described how at
the North Bridge the redcoats had "found two or three of their people
lying in the Agonies of Death, scalp'd & their Noses & ears cut off
& Eyes bored out—which exasperated the Soldiers exceedingly." Soon
she was reporting another story, that at "Kennebec the Committee
there had sentenced a man to be buried alive, for wishing success to
the King's Troops, & that the sentence had been executed upon him."

The buried-alive story had no foundation and soon expired, but
"scalped-while-still-alive" was widely believed, by Ensign Lister among
others. The provincial authorities denounced it as a slander designed to
"dishonor the Massachusetts people and make them appear savage and
barbarous." Zachariah Brown and Thomas Davis swore in an affidavit
"that we buried the dead bodies of the king's troops that were killed
at the north bridge in Concord, on the nineteenth day of April 1775,
where the action first began, and that neither of those persons were
scalped, nor their ears cut off, as has been represented." But as it turned
out there was some truth to the story; many years later the Rev. Emerson's great-granddaughter, Phebe Chamberlin, gave the version that had
been passed down in the family: "The bridge was deserted when a young
fellow of twenty-one from Captain Brown's Company, named Ammi
White, came along, hatchet in hand, and stopped to look at the two
British soldiers. One was not quite dead, and as he stirred, White killed
him with blows to the head."

And of course the Patriots had their own horror stories, many of
them sworn to and notarized:

✳

Hannah Adams, wife of Deacon Joseph Adams, of the second precinct
in Cambridge, testifieth and saith, that on the nineteenth day of April
last past, upon the return of the king's troops from Concord, divers
of them entered our house, by bursting open the doors, and three of

the soldiers broke into the room in which I then was, laid on my bed, being scarcely able to walk from my bed to the fire, not having been to my chamber door from my being delivered in child-birth to that time. One of said soldiers immediately opened my [bed] curtains with his bayonet fixed, pointing the same to my breast. I immediately cried out, "For the Lord's sake do not kill me!" He replied, "Damn you!" One that stood near said, "We will not hurt the woman if she will go out of the house, but we will surely burn it." I immediately arose, threw a blanket over me, went out and crawled into a corn-house near the door, with my infant in my arms, where I remained until they were gone. They immediately set the house on fire, in which I had left five children, and no other person; but the fire was happily extinguished, when the house was in the utmost danger of being utterly consumed.

Benjamin and Rachel Cooper, also of Cambridge, testified that "the king's regular troops under the command of General Gage, upon their return from the blood and slaughter which they had made at Lexington and Concord, fired more than a hundred bullets into the house where we dwelt, through doors, windows, &c. Then a number of them entered the house, where we and two aged gentlemen were, all unarmed. We escaped for our lives into the cellar. The two aged gentlemen were, immediately, most barbarously and inhumanly murdered by them: being stabbed through in many places, their heads mauled, skulls broke, and their brains dashed out on the floor and walls of the house."

Hannah Winthrop, also of Cambridge, where her husband John was professor of mathematics at Harvard, wrote to her friend Mercy Otis Warren to describe "the horrors of that midnight cry, preceding the bloody massacre at Lexington, when we were roused from the benign slumbers of the season by beat of drum and ringing of bells, with the dire alarm that a thousand of the troops of George the Third had gone forth to murder the peaceful inhabitants of the surrounding villages." Seeking safety, she and her husband went to a house a mile out of town, "but what a distressed house did we find it, filled with women whose husbands had gone forth to meet the assailants, seventy or eighty of these (with numberless infant children) weeping and agonizing for the fate of their husbands." After a difficult night, "some nodding in their chairs, some resting their weary limbs on the floor," the Winthrops decided to move on to the town of Anderson, "five of us to be conveyed with one poor tired horse and chaise. Thus we began our pilgrimage, alternately walking and riding, the roads filled with frighted women and children; some in carts with their tattered furniture, others on foot fleeing into the woods. But what added greatly to the horrors of the scene was our passing through the bloody field of Menotomy, which was strewed with the mangled bodies. We met one affectionate father with a cart, looking for his murdered son, and picking up his neighbors who had fallen in battle, in order for their burial."

And then there was this, from the pen of the Tory Peter Oliver:

Many were the instances of the British Soldiers' great Humanity in protecting the aged, the Women & the Children from Injury, notwithstanding the great Provocation they had to a general Slaughter. One among the many was this, viz: a Soldier seeing an old Man with a Musket, who had been in the Battle, much wounded & leaning against a Wall; he went up to him, tore off the lining of his own Coat & bound up his Wounds with it, desiring him to go out of Harm's Way. The Soldier had scarcely turned from him, when the old man fired at his deliverer. Human Passion could not bear such ingratitude, & the Man lost his Life by it.

Also:

There was a remarkable Heroine, who stood at an House Door firing at the King's Troops; there being Men within who loaded Guns for her to fire. She was desired to withdraw, but she answered only by Insults from her Mouth, & by Balls from the Mouths of her Muskets. This brought on her own Death, & the Deaths of those within doors.

From the Charlestown peninsula, the British troops crossed back over to Boston, where they were to remain besieged for nearly a year. From there the wife of one of them wrote home:

Loving Brothers and Sisters: The 19th of April the engagement happened, and my husband was wounded and taken prisoner, but they use him well, and I am striving to get to him, as he is very dangerous [dangerously ill]; but it is almost impossible to get out or in, or to get anything, for we are forced to live on salt provisions entirely, and they are building batteries round the Town, and so are we, for we are expecting them to storm us, and are expecting more troops every day. My husband is now lying in one of their hospitals, at a place called Cambridge, and there are now forty or fifty thousand of them gathered together, and we are not four thousand at most. It is very troublesome times, for we are expecting the town to be burnt down every day, and I believe we are sold; and I hear my husband's leg is broke, and my heart is broke.

BUNKER HILL

Roused in the small hours of April 19 by Paul Revere's pounding on the door of the house where they were staying, John Hancock and Samuel Adams had left Lexington not long before the redcoats arrived. As they hastened away, they heard the sound of gunfire. Adams was delighted. "O, what a glorious morning is this!" he exclaimed. Hancock, slower on the uptake, replied that he thought this was an odd time to comment on the weather. Adams explained: "I mean, what a glorious morning for America."

Next month the second Continental Congress met in Philadelphia. There was much to be done and the delegates were soon hard at work, holding general sessions in the mornings and dividing up into various committees for the rest of the day. John Adams was on the military affairs committee, one of the busiest. "We have been all so assiduous in this exhausting debilitating Climate that Our Lives are more exposed than they would be in Camp," he wrote to Abigail. He suffered from "Smarting Eyes" and even more from "the Whims, the Caprice, the Vanity" of some of the other delegates, and their habit of talking too much. He also mentioned, with perhaps small touches of envy and condescension, that "Colonel Washington appears at Congress in uniform, and by his great experience in military matters is of much service to us."

In June Congress "resolved that a general be appointed to command all the continental forces raised or to be raised for the defense of American liberty," and that "500 dollars a month be allowed for his pay and expenses." Among the candidates were Artemas Ward of Massachusetts, "a fat old gentleman who had been a popular churchwarden"; Charles Lee, tall and spindly, highly regarded for his experience as a former British army officer but lacking a political base and too eccentric (he preferred the company of his dogs to that of people, except when living among the Indians, who aptly named him "Boiling Water"), and too tactless (it was he who had thus described Artemas Ward); Israel Putnam, a pugnacious fighter but at fifty-seven thought to be too old; and the preening John Hancock, who had brought with him a number of fancy uniforms and liked to gallop about town with a mounted escort, sabers drawn. But in fact there was only one serious candidate, and on June 17 Adams wrote to his wife, "I can now inform you that the Congress have made Choice of the modest and virtuous, the amiable, generous and brave George Washington Esqr., to be the General of the American Army." It was Adams who had proposed him, and the vote was unanimous.

As future events were to prove, a better choice could not have been made. Among his many qualifications—his firsthand experience of battle during the French and Indian War, his habit of command, his imposing presence, his fearlessness, his perseverance, his ability to learn from his mistakes—Washington was also an astute politician. He undoubtedly wanted the job but understood that the way to get it was to defer to John Adams, who could then claim that the appointment was due to his own far-sightedness (hence his willingness to be "of much service" to the military affairs committee). The rest of his campaign to win appointment was equally astute: He dressed the part. The uniform that he always wore when attending Congress was surely the same one that he had designed twenty years earlier just after he had been promoted colonel of the Virginia Regiment: "the Coat Blue, faced and cuffed with Scarlet, and Trimmed with Silver; the Waistcoat Scarlet, with a plain Silver lace." The hat was also trimmed with silver lace and the breeches were blue. Thus attired, what need was there to say anything to advance his candidacy?

On accepting the position Washington spoke of the "great distress" he felt "from a consciousness that my abilities and military experience may not be equal to the extensive and important trust. However, as Congress desire it, I will enter upon the momentous duty, and exert every power I possess in their service, and for the support of the glorious cause . . ." Here was another mark of the successful politician: the ability to coin or popularize a memorable phrase. Soon it became the Glorious Cause, with capitals.

Next he had to write a letter explaining things to his wife, Martha, who he usually called Patsy. After breaking the news that he would be leaving immediately for Boston, he tried to set to rest any suspicions she might have that he was fleeing the tedium of domesticity for the excitement and camaraderie of army life. The absurd notion that Washington could not tell a lie was a fabrication dreamed up after his death by the biographer Parson Weems. "You may believe me, my dear Patsy, when I assure you, in the most solemn manner, that so far from seeking this appointment I have used every endeavor in my power to avoid it," he lied, but lied like a gentleman, out of consideration for his wife's feelings, adding that "I should enjoy more real happiness in one month with you at home than I have the most distant prospect of finding abroad [i.e., away from home]." Less tactfully, he then urged her to keep busy in such a way as to produce "a tolerable degree of tranquility; as it must add greatly to my uneasy feelings to hear that you are dissatisfied or complaining"; enclosed a copy of his revised will ("the provision made for you in case of my death will, I hope, be agreeable"), and concluded by assuring her that "I am, with the most unfeigned regard, my dear Patsy, your affectionate, etcetera."

A week later John Adams was again writing to Abigail:

My Dear,

    I have this Morning been out of Town to accompany our Generals Washington, Lee, and Schuyler, a little Way on their Journey to the American Camp before Boston. The Three Generals were all mounted on Horse back, accompanied by Major Mifflin who is gone in the character of Aid de Camp. All the Delegates from the Massachusetts with their Servants and Carriages attended. Many others of the Delegates from the Congress—a large Troop of Light Horse, in their Uniforms. Many Officers of Militia besides in theirs. Musick playing, &c. &c. Such is the Pride and Pomp of War. I, poor Creature, worn out with scribbling for my Bread and my Liberty, low in Spirits and weak in Health, must leave others to wear the Laurells which I have sown; others to eat the Bread which I have earned.—A Common Case.

✷

And so while Washington rode off for his rendezvous with destiny, Adams remained behind to do his committee work and ponder the unfairness of life. Such thoughts must have rankled, for it was not long before his letters were containing snide references to "a certain great man" and complaints about the "superstitious veneration" paid him. Washington was "not a scholar" and was "too illiterate, unlearned, unread for his station and reputation." In fact he, Adams, knew more about military matters because he had read more books about them, especially the classics. But only Abigail seems to have lent a sympathetic ear, and it cannot have helped that while

Washington was soon being routinely referred to as "His Excellency," the title ultimately given the portly Adams—behind his back but probably to his knowledge—was "His Rotundity."

The Provincial Congress of Massachusetts had also been busy. The day after Lexington and Concord, it appealed to the local towns for help in defending "our Wives and our Children from the butchering Hands of an inhuman Soldiery, who . . . will, without the least doubt, take the first Opportunity in their Power to ravage this devoted Country with Fire and Sword. We conjure you, therefore, that you give all Assistance possible in forming an Army. Our all is at Stake. Death and Devastation are the certain Consequences of Delay. Every Moment is infinitely precious; an Hour lost may deluge your Country in Blood," etc. As soon as they were enlisted, troops should be sent to "Headquarters at Cambridge, with that expedition which the vast Importance and instant Urgency of the affair demands."

Among those heeding the call to arms was James Thacher, a young doctor who volunteered to join the medical department, but not without first being subjected to the admonitions of Tory family friends who "assail me with the following powerful arguments: 'Young man, are you sensible you are about to violate your duty to the best of kings, and run headlong into destruction? Be assured that this rebellion will be of short duration. The royal army is all-powerful, and will, in a few months, march through the country and bring all to subjection; for they are experienced in war and expert in discipline. . . . What is your army but an undisciplined rabble? Can they stand against an army of regulars?'" After noting these and other arguments in his *Military Journal*, Thacher commented, "Not a small portion of their reasoning I feel to be just and true." Nevertheless he went ahead and enlisted anyway.

But was the British army really as formidable as Thacher's Loyalist friends made it out to be? Not in the opinion of General Charles Lee, who had served in it for many years before throwing in his lot with the Americans. In a pamphlet designed to refute "the false ter-rors" raised by the Tories, Lee wrote:

Great Britain has, I believe, of infantry at home, comprehending Ireland, and exclusive of the guards [who traditionally stayed at home, since their job was to protect the king] fifteen thousand men. They find the greatest difficulty in keeping the regiments up to anything near their establish-ment: what they are able to procure are of the worst sort. They are com-posed of the most debauched weavers, apprentices, the scum of the Irish Roman Catholics who desert upon every occasion, and a very few Scotch who are not strong enough to carry packs. . . . But, we shall be told, they are still regulars, and regulars have an irresistible advantage. There is, perhaps, more imposition in the term "regular troops" than in any of the jargon which issues from the mouth of a quack doctor. I do not mean to insinuate that a disorderly mob are equal to a trained, disciplined body of men; but I mean that all the essentials necessary to form infantry for real service may be acquired in a few months. I mean that it is very possible for men to be clothed in red, to be expert in all the tricks of the parade, to call themselves regular troops and yet, by attaching themselves principally or solely to the tinsel and show of war, to be totally unfit for real service.

Lee, perhaps deliberately, was underestimating the number of British troops, which was probably closer to 48,000. By European standards this was small. Austria had a standing army of over 100,000, Prussia one of 150,000. The armies of France, whose population was three times that of Great Britain, and of Russia also outnumbered that of Britain, as did the combined fleets of the "Bourbon Alliance" (France and Spain). Moreover, at the outbreak of war the British forces were spread thin. At all times some seven thousand redcoats had to be kept in Ireland to maintain the Anglo-Protestant Ascendancy over the Irish-Catholic majority; another nine to ten thousand were stationed in Scotland in case there was yet another Jacobite uprising; and a substantial number were needed in England to suppress the frequent riots and quell what Lord Barrington called "the very levelling spirit among the people." The British West Indies, represented by a powerful lobbying group in Parliament, had to be garrisoned against slave uprisings and in anticipation of the next war with France. Troops were also stationed in Canada, Louisiana, Gibraltar, Minorca, Senegal, and India. And this was just in times of peace. If there were a war, the time-honored British practice was to hire mercenaries, usually from various German states, though Russia, Holland, and even Morocco were also sometimes approached. In England, regular soldiering was a despised occupation. To provide recruits, magistrates could order "incorrigible rogues" into the army, along with convicted smugglers and "all disorderly persons who could not, upon examination, prove themselves to exercise and industriously follow some lawful trade or employment."

On the other hand, service as an officer was one of the few acceptable careers for members of the upper class, and entry was correspondingly easy. During the social season in Bath, Fanny Burney recorded this story of how one young gentleman switched careers:

Lord Mulgrave's brother Edmund is just entered into the army. "He told me t'other day," said his lordship, "that he did not like the thoughts of being a parson." "Very well," said I, "you are old enough to choose for yourself; what will you be then?"

"Why, a soldier," says he.

"A soldier? Will you so? Why then the best thing you can do is to embark with your brother Henry immediately, for you won't know what to do in a regiment by yourself." Well, no sooner said than done! Henry was just going to the West Indies in Lord Harrington's regiment, and Edmund ordered a chaise, and drove to Portsmouth after him. The whole was settled in half an hour.

In fact, a few further arrangements must have been called for. Lord Mulgrave would need to use his political connections to obtain official approval for Edmund to join this particular regiment, and he would have had to dip into some of the family wealth to buy a commission— the rule of thumb was £100 for every shilling a day in pay. Buying and selling commissions was legal and commonplace. This fairly typical advertisement appeared in an East Anglian newspaper: "To be sold: An Ensigncy in General Cornwallis's Regiment, now lying at Gibraltar. The lowest price is £360. For further particulars enquire of Mr. Shave, Bookseller in Ipswich, of whom may be had the greatest variety of Paperhangings." The higher the rank, and the smarter the regiment, the more the amount of money and influence needed, so that it was not unusual to find a regiment commanded by a titled colonel in his twenties and officered by less privileged lieutenants and captains in their forties and fifties. For the infantry and cavalry, this unfair system actually worked quite well, since when it came time to fight little more was expected of these regiments than to maintain formation, advance upon the enemy when ordered to do so, and stand firm when attacked. Officers in the artillery and engineers, services which required the close study of mathematics, algebra, trigonometry, and other difficult subjects, did not have to buy their commissions but were appointed on merit.

Since much the same system was followed by the other professional European armies any weaknesses canceled each other out, and it was generally assumed that this was the best, indeed the only, way to run an army. But an army that did not follow tradition, where soldiers elected their officers, and whose generals had been farmers (Israel Putnam), horse dealers (Benedict Arnold), or booksellers (Henry Knox), was hardly to be taken seriously. In their letters home, public statements, and doubtless also in their conversations among themselves over drinks, British officers seem to have had nothing but contempt for the American forces. A surgeon in the Royal Navy who was allowed to visit some of the wounded British prisoners in the American camp soon after the Concord fight, wrote that the New England army was "nothing but a drunken, canting, lying, praying, hypocritical rabble, without order, subjection, discipline, or cleanliness; and must fall to pieces of itself in the course of three months." Captain Evelyn informed his cousin, Lord Gower, one of

Lord North's ministers, that New Englanders were "a set of rascals and poltroons . . . upstart vagabonds, the dregs and scorn of the human species." Lord Percy wrote to his father, the Duke of Northumberland, that "to hear them talk, you would imagine they would attack us & demolish us every night; and yet, whenever we appear, they are frightened out of their wits." According to General Murray "the native American is a very effeminate thing, very unfit for and impatient of war." Speaking in the House of Lords, the Earl of Sandwich gave his opinion: "Suppose the colonies do abound in men, what does that signify? They are raw, undisciplined, cowardly men. I wish instead of forty or fifty thousand of these *brave* fellows, they could produce in the field at least two hundred thousand, the more the better, the easier would be the conquest." Furthermore, a friend had told him that the Americans were "egregious cowards." And from the throne, King George III himself declared that "when once these rebels have felt a smart blow, they will submit."

For the most part—at least until the war started to go badly, and to the extent that they paid attention, which was only intermittently— the civilian population chimed in. "Sir," said Dr. Johnson, "they are a race of convicts, and ought to be thankful for anything we allow them short of hanging." Americans, said one British newspaper, were "the scum or off-scouring of all nations . . . a hotchpotch medley of foreign enthusiastic madmen." New Englanders were the worst of the lot, descendants of the so-called Saints who had dodged the English Civil War, "running away like cowards to another world to make their fortunes." Indeed, New England males hardly qualified as men, being "in their own houses too much on the hen-pecked establishment."

Remembering their triumphs in the Seven Years' War, very few people in Britain thought it possible that the present conflict could go wrong. One of them was the radical historian Catharine Sawbridge Macaulay—"the amiable daughter of liberty" to her friends, "the republican virago" to her enemies—who was so greatly respected in America that her multivolume and ultra-Whiggish *History of England* was specifically exempted from the non-importation agreements. Addressing her fellow countrymen, she warned that "either the mother country, by one great exertion, may ruin both herself and America, or the Americans, by a lingering contest, will gain an independency; and in that case, all those advantages which you for some time have enjoyed by our colonies . . . must for ever have an end; and whilst a new, a flourishing, and an extensive empire of freemen is established on the other side of the Atlantic, you, with the loss of all those blessings you have received by the unrivalled state of your commerce, will be left to the bare possession of your foggy islands." (Macaulay did not go unanswered, but for the most part rather than address her arguments, her critics made fun of her appearance—"painted up to the eyes, and looking as rotten as an old Catherine Pear" in the words of John Wilkes— and had great sport at her expense when, as a middle-aged widow, she married a young man of twenty-one. Slurs were also cast upon her historical scholarship; according to Isaac D'Israeli, also an author and Benjamin Disraeli's father, it was her practice when doing research in the British Museum to tear out and destroy any pages or documents that conflicted with her preconceptions.)

In the same paper in which he had written so disparagingly of the British army, General Charles Lee also had encouraging words for the American militia who, "by a simplification of the necessary manoeuvres, may become in a very few months a most formidable infantry. The yeomen of America have, besides, infinite advantages over the peasantry of other countries: they are accustomed from their infancy to firearms, they are expert in the use of them; whereas the lower and middle people of England are, by the tyranny of certain laws, almost as ignorant in the use of a musket as they are of the ancient *catapulta*. The Americans are, likewise, to a man, skillful in the management of the instruments necessary for all military works, such as spades, pickaxes, hatchets, etc. Taking, therefore, all circumstances into consideration, there will be no rashness in affirming that this continent may have, formed for action, in three or four months, an hundred thousand infantry."

Exemplifying Lee's point about the social differences between the two sides was the contrast between becoming an army officer in Ipswich, England, and doing the same in Ipswich, Massachusetts. In the former, according to the advertisement run by Mr. Shave the bookseller, the first step was to come up with the sum of £360. In Massachusetts, men such as Joseph Hodgkins, who later became a captain, began by signing this document:

We whose Names are hereunto subscribed, do voluntarily Inlist our selves, as Minute Men, to be ready for military operation, upon the shortest notice. And we hereby promise & engage, that we will immediately, each of us, provide for & equip himself, with an effective fire arm, Bayonet, Pouch, Knapsack, & Thirty rounds of Cartridges ready made. And that we may obtain the skill of compleat Soldiers, We promise to Convene for exercise in the Art Military, at least twice every week; and oftener if our Officers shall think necessary. And as soon as such a Number shall be Inlisted, as the present Captain, Lieutenant, & Ensign of the Company of Militia shall think necessary, we will proceed to choose such Officers as shall appear to them, & to the Company to be necessary. The Officers to be chosen by a majority of the votes of the Inlisted Company, and when the Officers are duly chosen We hereby promise & engage that we will punctually render all that obedience to them respectively, as is required by the Laws of this Province, or practiced by any well regulated Troops. And if any Officer or Soldier shall neglect to attend the time & place of exercise, he shall forfeit & pay the sum of two shillings Lawful money for the use of the Company, unless he can offer such an excuse to the Officers of the Company as to them shall appear sufficient.

N.B. It is to be understood that when nine Company's of fifty Men each are Inlisted, that then the said Officers of the Minute Company's Proceed to Choose their Field Officers.

By the middle of June, Gage had received reinforcements that did no more than bring his strength up to six thousand men. To compensate for the small number of extra troops (on his visit back to London, Gage had asked for 20,000), the ministry also dispatched three major-generals: Sir William Howe, forty-five, a heavy drinker and gambler, "the most indolent of mortals" in the words of Charles Lee, and "as brave as my sword, but no more of a general than my arse" in the words of the Hessian commander Leopold von Heister; Henry Clinton, in his own words "a shy bitch," with a defensive, querulous personality and a habit of pestering his superiors with advice that often turned out to be right; and the flamboyant "Gentleman Johnny" Burgoyne, who had last seen military service in 1762, when he led a dashing but minor cavalry attack on a town in Portugal. It was Burgoyne who had been in command of the regiment of Light Dragoons when, a few days before his death, George II had attended a demonstration of the shell "charged with fuming combustibles" in Hyde Park.

Meanwhile, across the Charles River in Cambridge, General Artemas Ward—"the churchwarden"—was trying to bring some order into the disparate militias that had rallied to the call from the Provincial Congress and now surrounded Boston. Washington had not yet arrived, and General Putnam, whose legendary past included capturing a wolf in its den with his bare hands and being rescued from Indians just as they were about to burn him alive, was a tough fighter but no staff officer. Even less was he a strategist, but it was on his initiative that a force of a few hundred militiamen commanded by Colonel Prescott took up position on Breed's Hill, an outcropping of Bunker Hill on the Charlestown Peninsula. This was done on the night of June 16, one of the longest days of the year, and in response to a rumor that the British were planning to occupy the same position.

The Americans spent all night and much of the next morning digging in. They were spotted soon after first light by a lookout on the *Lively*, one of the British ships moored nearby, and were soon subjected to a desultory bombardment that did little damage apart from decapitating Asa Pollard, one of the defenders. The firing also served to summon the local population to come and watch what Burgoyne called "one of the greatest scenes of war that can be imagined." Well before the British attack was launched, spectators crowded every window and housetop and steeple in Boston; they also hastened in from neighboring villages and farms, and gathered on the nearby hills. The long slope leading from the water's edge where the British landed up to the American entrenchment on top of Breed's Hill was covered only with grass, against which the red coats and white breeches of the advancing British stood out clearly. All accounts agree that the weather was very hot. Early in the battle the British deliberately set fire to Charlestown by bombarding it from Copp's Hill with heated cannonballs and explosive shells. "The church steeples being of timber were great pyramids of fire above the rest," wrote Burgoyne, and for a while the smoke from the burning town obscured the scene, as did the smoke from the volleys fired by the advancing British, and the continuous fire from the American defenders.

Gage and two of the major generals had decided to take the hill by frontal assault. Clinton advocated a landing on Charlestown Neck, cutting the Americans off from their main force in Cambridge and attacking them from the rear. Had the purpose of the British attack been merely to defeat the Americans, he would have been quite right, but Gage, Howe, and Burgoyne thought they had a chance to crush the entire rebellion with one blow. It would not be enough to give the rebels "a good drubbing." Such terror must be struck into their hearts that never again would they dare take up arms against the king. There was only one way to do this: a bayonet charge. Rather than the slow-loading and inaccurate musket, the preferred weapon of the British army was the bayonet: fourteen inches long, triangular and fluted, burnished to a high sheen, and tapering to a sharp point. "The Bayonet in the Hands of the Valiant is irresistible," said Burgoyne. No one— and certainly not an undisciplined rabble—could stand and face a line of shoulder-to-shoulder redcoats coming steadily at them, their long bayonets glittering brightly in the warm afternoon sunshine.

General Howe was in command of the main assault. The hill was "open and of easy ascent" and in his opinion "would be easily carried." Just as sixteen years earlier he had led the troops in person up to the Heights of Abraham for Wolfe's great victory at Quebec, so now he told his soldiers that he would not ask them "to go a step further than where I go myself at your head." Conspicuous by his height and his gold-braided general's uniform, he was a particular target for the American riflemen but survived, though at one point he was the only officer left standing in his part of the battlefield. (His manservant, Evans, who attended him carrying glasses and a bottle of wine, was wounded when the bottle was shot out of his hands.) While Howe led the British soldiers in an extended line slowly up the grassy slope of Breed's Hill, the bombardment from the floating batteries, men of war, and the cannon on Copp's Hill continued. The noise must have been tremendous—in the words of Burgoyne, "the roar of cannon, mortars and musquetry, the crash of churches, ships upon the stocks, and whole streets falling together in ruin" all contributed to "a picture and a complication of horror and importance."

Only a few hundred Americans were in the redoubt on Breed's Hill; many more were close behind them on the top of Bunker Hill, but decided to remain there during the fight. Among those in the redoubt was militia corporal Amos Farnsworth, of Groton:

✳

As the enemy approached, our men was not only exposed to the attack of a very numerous musketry, but to the heavy fire of the battery on Copps Hill, four or five men of war, several armed boats or floating batteries in Mistick River, and a number of field pieces. Notwithstanding, we within the intrenchment, and at a breast work without, sustained the enemy's attack with great bravery and resolution, killed and wounded great numbers, and repulsed them several times; and after bearing, for about two hours, as severe and heavy a fire as perhaps ever was known, and many having fired away all their ammunition, and having no reinforsement, altho' there was a great boddy of men nigh by, we ware overpowered by numbers and obliged to leave the intrenchment, retreating about sunset to a small distance over Charlestown Neck. N.B. I did not leave the intrenchment untill the enemy got in. I then retreated ten or fifteen rods; then I received a wound in my rite arm, the bawl gowing through a little below my elbow breaking the little shel bone. Another bawl struck my back, taking a piece of skin about as big as a penny. But I got to Cambridge that night.

Also present was Lieutenant Samuel Webb, aged twenty-two, of the Second Connecticut Volunteers, who wrote to his brother from Cambridge very shortly after the battle:

About one o'clock PM we that were at Cambridge heard that the regulars were landing from their Floating Batteries, & the alarm was sounded & we ordered to March directly down to the Fort at Charlestown. Before our Company could possibly get there, the battle had begun in earnest & Cannon & Musket Balls were flying about our Ears like hail & hotter fire you can have no Idea of. . . . On our March down we met many of our worthy friends wounded, sweltering in their Blood, carried on the Shoulders by their fellow Soldiers. Judge you what must be our feelings at this shocking Spectacle! The orders were "Press on! Press on! Our Brothers are suffering and will soon be cut off." We push'd on and came into the field of Battle thro' the Cannonadeing of the Ships. Bombs, Chain Shott, Ring Shot, & Double-headed Shot flew as thick as Hail Stones, but thank heavens, few of our Men suffered by them; but when we mounted the Summit, where the Engagement was, good God how the balls flew! I freely acknowledge I never had such a tremor come over me before. We descended the Hill onto the field of Battle, and began our fire very briskly. The Regulars fell in great plenty, but to do them Justice they kept a grand front and stood their ground nobly; twice before this time they gave way. But not long before we saw numbers mounting the Walls of our Fort, on which our Men in the Fort were ordered to fire and make a swift Retreat. We covered their Retreat by a brisk fire from our small arms. The dead and wounded lay on every side of me; their Groans were piercing indeed, tho' long before this time I believe the fear of Death had quitted almost every Breast. They now had possession of our Fort & four field pieces and by much the Advantage of the Ground, and to tell you the truth, our Reinforcements belonging to this Province, very few of them came into the field, but lay sculking on the opposite side of the hill. Our orders then came to make the best Retreat we could. We set off almost gone with fatigue and ran very fast up the Hill, leaving some of our Dead and Wounded on the field. We retreated over Charlestown Neck, thro' the thickest of the Ships' fire; here some principal Officers fell by Cannon & Bombs. After we had got out of the ships' fire under the covert of a Hill, near another Intrenchment of ours, we again Rallied and lined every part of the Road and fields. Here we were determined to Die or conquer if they ventured over the Neck; but it grew dark and we saw them pitching Tents. We retired to our Intrenchment & lay on our Arms all night, keeping vast Numbers of our Troops out on scouting Parties. They kept up a constant fire from the ships and floating Batteries all Night, but few of them Reach'd us.

Both men complained about the burning of Charlestown—"laid in ashes by the barbarity and wanton cruelty of that infernal villain Thomas Gage" (Corporal Farnsworth), "an everlasting Monument of British Cruelty and Barbarity" (Lt. Webb). Webb also gave the names of four comrades who had been killed and another four who had been wounded. Farnsworth kept the focus on himself: "Oh, the goodness of God in preserving my life althoe thay fell on my right hand and on my left! O, may this act of deliverance of thine, Oh God, lead me never to distrust thee; but may I ever trust in thee and put confidence in no arm of flesh! I was in great pane the first night with my wound."

Because they held the field at the end of the day, it was tacitly agreed by both sides that the British had won. But so heavy were their losses— more than a thousand officers and soldiers killed or wounded out of some two and a half thousand engaged—that, as was often said, a few more such victories would win the war for the Americans. The next day a British "officer of rank" wrote in a letter home: "This victory has cost us very dear indeed, as we have lost some of the best officers in the service, and a great number of private men. Nor do I see that we enjoy one solid benefit in return, or likely to reap from it any one advantage whatever. We have, indeed, learned one melancholy truth, which is that the Americans, if they were equally well commanded, are full as good soldiers as ours; and as it is, are very little inferior to us even in discipline and steadiness of countenance." Another officer concluded his letter: "Our three Generals came over in high spirits, and expected rather to punish a mob than fight with troops that would look them in the face. There is an air of dejection through all our superiors which forebodes no good, and does not look as things ought to do after a victory." And General Gage, in one of his last letters to Lord Dartmouth, after acknowledging that "the number of the killed and wounded is greater than our force can afford to lose," wrote that the colonists were "not the despicable Rabble too many have supposed them to be" and that "their military spirit" was fired by "an uncommon degree of zeal and enthusiasm." In a letter to Lord Barrington, he advised that the army be moved to New York. As to Boston: "I wish this cursed place was burned."

After the battle the British wounded were taken to Boston, "and it was truly a Shocking Sight and Sound to see the Carts loaded with those unfortunate Men, & to hear the piercing Groans of the dying," wrote the Loyalist Peter Oliver. "I was walking in one of the Streets of Boston, & saw a Man advancing towards me, his white Waistcoat, Breeches, & Stockings being very much dyed of a Scarlet Hue. I thus spake to him: 'My friend, are you wounded?' He replied, 'Yes Sir! I have 3 Bullets through me.' He then told me the Places where, one of them being a mortal Wound; he then with a philosophick Calmness began to relate the History of the Battle, & in all Probability would have talked 'till he died, had I not begged him to walk off to the Hospital; which he did, in as sedate a manner as if he had been walking for his Pleasure."

John Randon, a noncommissioned officer of the Royal Welch Fusiliers, dictated this letter to his wife back in England: "Yesterday we had a bloody and obstinate fight, in which many were killed and numbers wounded. I have received two balls, one in my groin, the other near the breast. I am now so weak with the loss of blood that I can hardly dictate these few lines, as the last tribute of my unchangeable love to you. The surgeons inform me that three hours will be the utmost I can survive. Alas, too true was the dire presage that brooded in my mind that we should never meet again on this side an awful eternity."

He then told how, during the voyage to America, he had taken to reading the Bible, and with the help of a proselytizing corporal named Pierce had been converted. It was his hope that his wife would follow his example. "If ever I was dear to you, let me beg of you not to neglect the last advice of your departing husband. It is, that you give yourself up to God, read the Bible and good books, and be often found among them who inquire after Salvation. . . . O endeavour to bring up the dear little ones in the fear of God. Never fix your heart upon the vain and unsubstantial things of the world. . . . More would I say, but life ebbs out apace, my tongue ceases to perform its office; bright angels stand around the gory turf on which I lie, ready to escort me to the arms of my Jesus; bending saints reveal my shining crown, and beckon me away. Yea, methinks my Jesus bids me come. Adieu! Adieu! Dear Love."

Bunker Hill was the bloodiest battle of the war, but its significance did not appear until later. In the opinion of the nineteenth-century statesman Daniel Webster, "It was the first great battle of the Revolution; and not only the first blow, but the blow which determined the contest. It did not, indeed, put an end to the war, but . . . one thing is certain: that after the New England troops had shown themselves able to face and repulse the regulars, it was decided that peace could never be established but upon the basis of the independence of the colonies. When the sun of that day went down, the event of independence was no longer doubtful. In a few days Washington heard of the battle, and he inquired if the militia had stood the fire of the regulars. And when told that they had not only stood that fire, but reserved their own till the enemy was within eight rods, and then poured it in with tremendous effect,—'Then,' exclaimed he, 'the liberties of the country are safe.'"

American losses were estimated at 371 but were harder to calculate than those of the regular British army. One source that helps establish who was at the battle and where they came from is the so-called Coat Rolls, drawn up as a result of a vote by the Provincial Congress on July 5, 1775, "that thirteen thousand coats be provided, as soon as may be, and one thereof given to each noncommissioned officer and soldier in the Massachusetts forces." The coats were valued at one £1 and 5 shillings each. For many months after the battle, the Committee of Clothing received requests such as these:

Haverhill. March 20, 1776. Please to pay to Jonathan Webster one pound and five shillings, it being for a coat allowed to my son John Eaton as bounty by the province, he having never received it; he being killed in the fight at Bunker Hill, signed, John Eaton of Captain James Sawyer's Company.

Pepperell. Sept 30, 1776. To the Gentlemen upon the Committee of Clothing sitting at Watertown, Please to pay to Capt. Edmund Bancroft the money for a uniform coat that my son was entitled to who was a soldier in the year 1775 and lost his life in the battle of Bunker Hill, and you will oblige your humble servant Jeremiah Shattuck.

Hollis. Feb 10, 1776. We do hereby certify that Capt. Reuben Dow is the only proper person to receive the clothing that is due to Peter

Poor, a transient person who enlisted in his company, and last resided in this town and went away in debt. Said Poor was lost in Bunker Hill fight. Signed by 5 Selectmen of Hollis.

Hollis. Feb 10, 1776. A certificate that John Boynton, William Nevens, Shubaell Hobart, Enoch Noyes, Amos Eastman, Abigail Wheet, and Sarah Fisk are the proper heirs of the money due to Jacob Boynton, Phineas Nevens, Isaac Hobart, Nathan Blood, Caleb Eastman, Thomas Wheet, and James Fisk, all of Capt. Dow's company, and all are dead.

The Blockade and Evacuation

Following the battle of Bunker Hill, the Americans encircled the British with a ring of entrenched positions, confining them to Boston and the Charlestown peninsula, but unable to challenge their control of the harbor and access to the sea. On July 3, the twenty-first anniversary of his surrender at Fort Necessity, Washington arrived in Cambridge to take command. Many problems faced him. One of them was the spirit of local independence that led militia units to hold on to their barrels of gunpowder rather than turn them in to the general stores. In one of his first general orders, Washington reminded them that since Congress had voted to take them into its "pay and service," they were "now the troops of the United Provinces of North America," and it was to be hoped "that all distinctions of Colonies will be laid aside." But the New England militiamen remained unconvinced.

Then there was the lack of discipline. From the start of his military career, establishing discipline had been one of Washington's priorities. It was discipline that "makes small numbers formidable, procures success to the weak and esteem to all." Discipline was "the soul of an army." As a Virginian he already had mixed feelings about New Englanders, and closer acquaintance did not improve matters—"an exceeding dirty and nasty people," he called them in a letter to his cousin soon after his arrival; and as a Southern gentleman he deplored their "leveling spirit" as much as any English aristocrat. Indeed, his ideal army would have been an almost exact replica of the British army in which he had once tried so hard to obtain a commission. Orders should be obeyed without question or discussion; everyone should wear a uniform; officers should be appointed, not elected; militiamen should be drilled and regimented until they became what they did not want to be: professional soldiers.

"The Generals Washington and Lee are upon the Lines every Day," wrote the Rev. William Emerson, now an army chaplain, to his wife back in Concord.

✵

New Orders from his Excellency are read to the respective Regiments every Morning after Prayers, the strictest Government is taking Place: great Distinctions made between Officers and Soldiers, everyone is made to know his Place and keep in it, or be immediately triced up and receive . . . 30 or 40 Lashes, according to the Nature of his Crime.

Thousands are at work every Day from 4 to 11 o'clock in the Morning. The Lines are almost extended from Cambridge to Mistick River, so that very soon it will be morally impossible for the Enemy to get between the Works, excepting in one Place, which is supposed to be purposely left unfortified to toll the Enemy out of their Fortress. Who would have thought a twelve month past that all Cambridge and Charlestown would be covered over with American Camps, and cut up into Forts and Entrenchments, & all their Lands, Fields & Orchards laid common, the Horses & other Cattle feeding in the choicest mowing land—whole fields of corn eat down to the Ground. Large parks of well-regulated Locusts [locust trees] cutt down for firewood & other public Uses. This I must say looks a little melancholy—but it is Tory Land the chief of it, and would have done no good to the Public. . . . 'Tis also very diverting to walk among the Camps. They are as different in their form as the Owners are in their Dress, and every tent is a Portraiture of the Temper and Taste of the Person that incamps in it. Some are made of Boards, some of Sailcloth, and some partly of one and partly of another. Others are made of Stone and Turf, and others again of

Brick and others Brush. Some are thrown up in a hurry & look as if they could not help it—mere necessity—others are curiously wrought with doors & windows done with Wreaths and Withes in manner of a Basket. Some are the proper Tents and Markees that look as the regular camp of the Enemy. These are Rhode Islanders, who are furnished with Tent Equipment . . . and everything in the most exact English Taste. However I think that the great Variety of the American Camp is upon the Whole rather a Beauty than a Blemish to the Army.

How Washington would have disagreed with this last sentence! But Emerson's final comment was certainly acceptable: "God is in the midst of us."

Another clergyman (though not yet ordained) who answered the call of God and his country was Daniel Barber of Simsbury, Connecticut, a town that had long been under God's special Providence. On the eve of the Indian uprising known as King Philip's War, a miraculous warning shot from an unknown source had been heard within a radius of fifty miles, sounding the alarm and saving many Protestant lives; and when, in 1768, hailstones "full the bulk of goose-eggs" fell on the town, the damage, according to a report in the local newspaper, was much less than it would have been "had not the hail fell considerably perpendicular." In his memoirs Daniel Barber recalled how on hearing the news of Bunker Hill he had joined the Simsbury militia signing up for five months. His captain was Elihu Humphrey, "a well-bred gentleman" whose "sweetness of disposition secured him the love of all good men"; his lieutenant was Andrew Hilyer, "a handsome sprightly young gentleman"; his three sergeants were Aaron Pinney, "a man of a fierce and fiery countenance"; Jacob Tuller, whose "brow was generally knit together in a forbidding frown"; and Daniel Higley, "who had been a soldier in the old French war, was of a musical turn, and his old war songs made the time pass away to very good account." The Rev. Mr. Pitkin preached a farewell sermon on the text "Play the man for your country, and for the cities of your God; and the Lord do that which seemeth him good," which was well received. "It was tender and pathetic, lively and animating. It was like martial music; while it touched the finer feelings, it roused and animated for the dreadful onset—the shout of war and the cry of victory! During the time of its delivery, abundance of tears were seen to flow, from both old and young, male as well as female."

After the service, the soldiers mingled with their families and sweethearts,

✷

exchanging, as for the last time, the token of their love and the best affections of the heart. In the midst of this mingling scene of sorrow, the drums beat to arms. "Soldiers, take your places!" is the word; the line of march is formed; we add one more wishful, lingering look, while many a silent tear bespeaks the real feeling of the heart.

The word is given. We begin our march with silence, downcast looks, and pensive feelings and reflections. We were now leaving our homes, our friends, and all our pleasant places behind, and which our eyes might never again behold. The most of us had not, at that time, I believe, been twenty miles from home.

After marching awhile, we began to give way to more cheerful and lively feelings. We marched about eight miles that afternoon; at night put up at James Marsh's inn. Here, for the first time, I slept as a soldier on the floor, with a cartridge box for my pillow. At that period, horse wagons being very little in use, an ox team was provided to carry our provision for the way, and a barrel of rum. Our provision was salt pork and peas. Wherever we stopped, a large kettle was hung over the fire, in which the salt meat was put without freshening, and the dry peas without soaking. Cooks and stewards were appointed who took charge of the table department. When all was ready, a stroke on the drum was the signal to begin to eat; and we were generally hungry enough to stand in need of no great urging. While passing through Connecticut, the females were very polite in lending us knives and forks; but, after entering Massachusetts, we were not allowed the like favor, without pledging money or some other kind of security—the people saying that they had lost many of their spoons by the soldiers who had gone before us. Our bread was hard bisquit, in which there was a small quantity of lime, just sufficient to make the mouth sore. They were so hard that the soldiers called them candlestick bottoms.

Now for the first time we traveled on the Lord's day, under arms, and past meeting houses in the time of public worship, with drums and fifes playing martial music; all which was calculated to afford to a New England man some doubts and reflections whether God would be as well pleased with such parade and military performance as if we had stayed home to read our Bibles, or went to meeting to hear the minister. But military discipline and the habits of a soldier soon effected a degree of relaxation in most of us.

After about nine or ten days' marching in company, with our ox team loaded with our salt pork, peas, and candlestick bottoms for bread, and the barrel of rum to cheer our spirits and wash our feet, which began to be very sore by traveling, we came to Roxbury, the place of our destination. There the place of our encampment was already marked out, and a part of our regiment on the spot. For every six soldiers there was a tent provided. The ground it covered was about six or seven feet square. This served for kitchen, parlor, and hall. The green turf, covered with a blanket, was our bed and bedstead. When we turned in for the night, we had to lie perfectly straight, like candles in a box; this was not pleasant to our hip bones and knee joints, which often in the night would wake us, and beg to turn over. Our household utensils, altogether, were an iron pot, a canteen, or wooden bottle holding two quarts, a pail, and a wooden bowl. Each had to do his own washing, and take his turn at the cookery.

Meanwhile, Boston Patriots were moving out of the town. This resulted in a housing shortage in the neighboring countryside. In July Abigail Adams wrote to John complaining of the "abuse and very Ill treatment" she had received at the hands of one Hayden, a farm worker who lived in the adjoining house. Instead of paying rent, Hayden and his two sons worked on the Adams farm; but now both sons had enlisted, leaving Hayden to occupy the whole house by himself. Then Mr. Trott, head of an exiled Boston family that included a pregnant wife and desperate for a place to stay, "applied to me to see if I would not accommodate him with the next house, every other spot in town [Braintree] being full. I sent for Mr. Hayden and handsomely asked him" to find somewhere else to live. "He said he would try, but he took no pains to procure himself a place." Abigail next tried to persuade him to share the house. "He would not tell me whether he would or not, but said I was turning him out of Door to oblige Boston folks, and he could not be stirred up, and if you was at home you would not ask him to go out, but was more of a Gentleman." She tried again, "but he positively tells me he will not, and all the art of Man shall not stir him, even dares me to put any article out of one room into an other. Says Mr. Trott shall not come in—he has got possession and he will keep it. 'What, not have a place to entertain his children in when they come to see him?'" After asking John for "orders what course I shall take," Abigail continued, "it would make your heart ake to see what difficulties and distresses the poor Boston people are driven to. Belcher has two families with him. There are 3 in Vese's house, 2 in Etter's, 2 in Mr. Savil's, 2 in Jonathan Bass's, and yet that obstinate Wretch will not remove his few things into the other part of that house, but live there paying no rent upon the distresses of others. . . . It would be needless to enumerate all his impudence. Let it suffice to say it moved me so much that I had hard work to suppress my temper. . . . I told the old Man I believed I was doing nothing but what I should be justified in. He says well, 'tis a time of war, get him out if I can, but cannon Ball shall not move him."

Abigail also complained about shortages, particularly of goods made in England ("Not one pin is to be purchased for love nor money"), but in Boston itself the shortages were worse. In a letter to his brother-in-law in Philadelphia, John Andrews wrote that "a quarter of lamb when it makes its appearance, which is rarely once in a week, sells for a dollar, weighing only three and a half pounds. . . . Wood not scarcely to be got at twenty-two shillings. Was it not for a trifle of salt provisions that we have, 'twould be impossible for us to live. Pork and beans one day, and beans and pork another, and fish when we can catch it."

Andrews remained in Boston to look after his house and stock of goods since those who left were liable to have their property plundered or confiscated by the British. Timothy Newell, deacon of the Brattle Street Church, also stayed and recorded some of his experiences in *A Journal Kept During the Time that Boston was Shut Up:*

✻

July 14. Last night awoke by the discharge of cannons on the lines. Master James Lovell, Master Leach, John Hunt, have been imprisoned some time past—all they know why it is so is they are charged with free speaking on the public measures.

July 20. Mr. Carpenter was taken up by the night patrole. Upon examination he had swum over to Dorchester and back again, was tried here the next day and sentence of death passed on him and to be executed the next day—his coffin brought into the gaol yard, his halter brought and he dressed as criminals are before execution. Sentence was respited and a few days after was pardoned.

August 1. This morning half past 4 o'clock awoke with cannonade and small arms from Charlestown, which lasted till eleven o'clock after that. Very trying scenes. This day was invited by two gentlemen to dine upon rats. The whole of this day till sunset a constant fire up to Mistic River.

September 1. Almost constant firing from the centinels at each other. New works arise upon the Neck by the Provincials who approach very near.

October 17. Two floating batteries from the Provincials from Cambridge River fired a number of cannon into the camp at the

Common; the shot went thro' houses by the Lamb Tavern, etc. A deserter who came in this morning says one of the cannon split and killed and wounded several. Five or six hats, a waistcoat, and part of a boat came on shore at the bottom of the Common.

October 25. Several nights past the whole army was ordered not to undress. The cannon all loaded with grape-shot from a full apprehension the Provincials would make an attack upon the town. The streets paraded all night by the Light Horse.

October 27. The spacious Old South Meeting House taken possession of by the Light Horse 17th Regiment of Dragoons, commanded by Lieut. Col. Samuel Birch. The pulpit, pews, and seats all cut to pieces and carried off in the most savage manner as can be expressed, and destined for a riding school. The beautiful carved pew with the silk furniture of Deacon Hubbard's was taken down and carried to – -'s house by an officer and made a hog stye.

This desecration of the religiously and politically hallowed Old South Church was done on the orders of General Burgoyne. As well as chopping up the pulpit and pews for use as firewood, "many hundred loads of dirt and gravel were carted in, and spread upon the floor," wrote another witness. "The south door was closed, and a bar was fixed over which the cavalry were taught to leap their horses at full speed. A grog shop was erected in the gallery, where liquor was sold to the soldiery, and consequently produced scenes of riot and debauchery in that holy temple." (This was the gallery where Phillis Wheatley and other slaves used to sit. By this time the Wheatleys had moved out of town, which was fortunate as their house in King Street was struck by a cannonball during the siege.)

Worst off by far were those held in Boston's squalid jail, where political prisoners were crowded in together with common criminals. Among the former was British-born John Leach, a respectable exsailor who had recently founded a school of navigation and was now vaguely accused of "being a spy, and suspected of taking plans." Like

Timothy Newell, he too kept a journal.

From the 2d July to the 17th a complicated scene of oaths, curses, debauchery, and the most horrid blasphemy, committed by the Provost Marshal, his deputy and soldiers who were our guards, soldier prisoners, and sundry soldier women, confined for thefts, etc. We had some of the vilest women for our neighbors; some placed over our heads, and some in rooms on each side of us; they acted such scenes as was shocking to nature, and used language horrible to hear, as if it came from the very suburbs of Hell. When our wives, children, and friends came to see us (which was seldom they were permitted), we seemed to want them gone, notwithstanding we were so desirous of their company, as they were exposed to hear the most abandoned language.

July 7. We are very close confined, having the doors open for air sometimes one hour in 24, and sometimes not at all.

July 17. My son Tileston died, whom I left well in my house; I was not permitted to attend the funeral, notwithstanding my letter to the general this morning requesting the same.

August 9. A poor painter, an inhabitant, was put in the dungeon and very ill used by the Provost and his deputy, Samuel Dyer; then the Provost turned him out and made him get down on his knees in the yard and say, "God bless the King!"

August 15. Close confined, the weather hot. Died, Capt. Walker, a country prisoner from Charlestown. Swearing began at 3 this morning, and held all day: the place seems to be an emblem of Hell. At 9 at night more horrid swearing and blasphemy; the worst man-of-war that ever I knew was nothing to compare with this diabolical place. Poor Mr. Lovell began to droop; he is very weakly. It gives us all great concern, as we were all more afraid of sickness in this dreadful place than anything else, but God wonderfully preserved our healths and spirits. I did not think we could possibly survive such treatment, but our help was from above.

August 17. Today, Phineas Nevers, a Charlestown prisoner, died.

August 19. Close confined; dreadful language from morning to night; Mr. Lovell continues poorly. . . . Doctor Brown complained to Mr. Lovell and me that they had no bread all that day and the day before. He spoke to the Provost, as he had the charge of serving the bread; he replied, they might eat the nail heads and gnaw the plank and be damned.

August 25. Last night, Thomas Forakers, boatbuilder, and his servant John Bouve were brought to gaol on suspicion of concealing a man that swam over from Chelsea, upon false information of a very wicked woman; and this morning the boy, John Bouve (about 16 years of age), was put in irons, in the dungeon, as he had nothing to confess. He was examined by Major Sheriff and Major Rooke and then hand-cuffed and put in the dungeon again. We fed the boy from our room, and encouraged him to keep up his spirits by telling him they were a pack of cowardly scoundrels and dare not hurt the hair of his head. While his irons were putting on, close by our cell door, the Provost said to him, he was a man under sentence of death, and might choose his minister to come and see him, for he was to be hanged in the afternoon. At 5 in the afternoon, finding they could make nothing of him, they took his irons off and put him in a room next to ours, among some soldiers, thieves, etc. The weather very hot and we close confined all day.

Of course, life for the British in Boston was not easy either. In September General Gage was recalled, not exactly in disgrace but clearly not to be congratulated. His American-born wife, widely but improbably suspected of having betrayed his plans for the raid on Concord, went with him, but they soon separated and Gage took up with a clergyman's daughter cryptically referred to by *Town & Country Magazine* as Miss F – -g. His place as commander in chief was taken by Sir William Howe. Orders came from London to abandon Boston and move to New York and Halifax, but Howe did not have enough shipping to comply and so both sides had to sit it out until the spring.

For much of the winter, wrote Peter Oliver, "it seemed to be the principal Employment of both Armies to look at each other with Spy Glasses. . . . Both Armies kept squibbing at each other, but to little Purpose; at one Time a Horse would be knocked in the Head, & at another Time a Man would be killed, or lose a Leg or an Arm; it seemed to be rather in Jest than in Earnest. At some times a Shell would play in the Air like a Sky Rocket, rather in diversion, & there burst without Damage; & now & then another would fall in the Town, & there burst, to the Terror or breaking of a few Panes of Glass." His conclusion was that "the whole Scene was an idle Business."

Morale among the redcoats sagged, as evidenced by these entries in General Howe's *Orderly Book.* "The commanding officer is surprised to find the necessity of repeating orders that long since ought to have been complied with," ran a typical reprimand; soldiers were appearing on duty with their "hair not smooth and badly powdered, several without slings to their firelocks, hats not bound, pouches in a shameful and dirty condition, no frills to their shirts and their linen very dirty, leggings hanging in a slovenly manner about their knees, their arms and accoutrements by no means as clean as they ought to be . . ." It was now almost impossible to desert, and only a few diversions were available: cheap rum, whoring, brawling, vandalism, crime and looting: "The frequent depredations committed by the Soldiers in pulling down fences and houses in defiance of repeated orders has induced the Commander in Chief to direct the Provost to go his rounds attended by the Executioner, with orders to hang up, upon the spot, the first man he shall detect in the fact, without waiting for further proof by trial." Courts-martial were frequent. "For having broken into and robbed the store of Messrs. Coffin, storekeepers, of sundry goods," Privates Owen and Johnston were sentenced to "suffer Death by being hanged by the neck until they are Dead." Also "Thomas Mac-Mahan, private soldier in His Majesty's 43d Regiment of Foot, and Isabella MacMahan, his wife, tried by the above court for receiving sundry stolen goods, knowing them to be such, are found guilty of the crime laid to their charge, and therefore adjudge the said Thomas MacMahan to receive 1,000 lashes on his bare back with a Cat of Nine Tails . . . and the said Isabella MacMahan to receive 100 lashes on her bare back at the Cart's tail, in different portions and the most conspicuous parts of the town, and to be imprisoned three months." At the same court-martial, two privates of the 59th, "for having forcibly entered a dwelling house and stolen from them sundry goods," were sentenced to 800 lashes each; Private Witherspoon of the Marines "for having stolen a piece of linen" was to receive 500 lashes; another private was also to get 500 lashes for mutiny; Private Spillman of the 59th, "for having committed an assault on the person of Mrs. Moore, an inhabitant of the town of Boston, and beating her almost to death," was to receive 1,000 lashes. All these and other floggings, except for Isabella MacMahan's, were "to be inflicted upon them by the drummers of their respective Corps."

For the officers there were a few bright spots. General Howe, who enjoyed a good time, sitting up to all hours at the gaming table with his mistress, Mrs. Loring, at his side, reversed the ban on theatrical performances imposed by General Gage, who thought them too frivolous for the times. This gave rise to a famous anecdote, of which there are many versions; this one is by Lt. Martin Hunter of the Light Infantry:

Plays were acted twice every week by the officers and some of the Boston ladies. Miss Sally Fletcher acted the part of Zara. She was a very pretty girl and did it very well. A farce called The Blockade of Boston written, I believe, by General Burgoyne, was acted. The enemy knew the night it was to be performed and made an attack on the mill at Charlestown at the very hour the farce began. An orderly sergeant that was standing outside the playhouse door heard the firing and immediately ran into the playhouse, got upon the stage, and cried, "Turn out! Turn out! They are hard at it, hammer and tongs." The whole audience thought that the sergeant was acting a part in the farce, and that he did it so well that there was a general clap and such a noise that he could not be heard for a considerable time. When the clapping was over, he again cried, "What the deuce are you all about? If you don't believe me, by Jasus, you need only go to the door, and there you will see and hear both!" If it was the intention of the enemy to put a stop to the farce for that night, they certainly succeeded, as all the officers immediately left the playhouse and joined their regiments.

Soon afterward Mercy Otis Warren, of Plymouth, issued a satire on Burgoyne's farce, which she called *The Blockheads of Boston.* Though never actually performed, it was highly praised by the Patriots, but for reasons that were political rather than literary. (As a writer, Mercy did not really hit her stride until after the war, when she wrote the *History of the Rise, Progress and Termination of the American Revolution.* Until then she was apt to turn out poems with titles such as *Lines Written After a Very Severe Storm Which Cleared Up Extremely Pleasant.*)

Also highly praised at this time was an ode to George Washington on his taking command of the American armies: "Celestial choir! Enthron'd in realms of light,/ Columbia's scenes of glorious toils I write./ While freedom's cause her anxious breast alarms,/ She flashes dreadful in refulgent arms . . ." The general, or one of his staff officers, sent a courteous letter to its author, Phillis Wheatley, thanking her for "the elegant Lines," complimenting her on "her great poetical Talents," extending the invitation that "if you should ever come to Cambridge, or near Head Quarters, I shall be happy to see a person so favoured by the Muses," and signing himself "with great Respect, Your obedient humble servant." (Can the slave-owning Washington have realized that the author was an African—"the Ethiopian poetess"? At any rate, Wheatley never did get to meet him, any more than on her visit to

London she got to be presented to George III. Indeed, her luck was quickly running out: Her kindly owners died, she married a ne'er-do-well, her three children died early, and she ended her days, at the age of only thirty-one, scrubbing the floors in a cheap boardinghouse.)

In January Washington sent a tactful note to John Adams at Braintree: "I am exceedingly desirous of consulting you." The winter was extremely hard, the harbor had frozen, and Washington had come up with a plan to storm the heavily fortified town of Boston by charging across the open ice. A council of war was held in Cambridge to discuss this suicidal idea. "It were to be wished that they would attempt so rash a step," Sir William Howe had said in a letter to London. Fortunately for the American cause, the generals overruled the plan; Adams, though pleased to have been invited, seems not to have given an opinion.

Only at sea was there much going on. Late in the summer, a flotilla commanded by Captain Lindzee, R.N., who had recently married the niece of the Patriot Boston merchant John Rowe, was pursuing a schooner from the West Indies when it managed to get into Gloucester harbor. Lindzee followed, and after anchoring his ship, the *Falcon,* sent in two barges full of armed men to seize the schooner. The militia turned out, fired on the barges, and drove them off. A local paper tells what happened next:

✳

Upon this Lindzee sent the other schooner and a small cutter he had with him, well armed, with orders to fire upon the "damned rebels" wherever they could see them, and that he would in the meantime cannonade. He immediately fired a broadside upon the thickest settlements, and stood with a diabolical pleasure to see what havoc his cannon might make. "Now," said he, "my boys, we will aim at the damned Presbyterian church. Well, my brave fellows! One more shot and the House of God will fall before you." While he was thus venting his hellish rage, and setting himself as it were against heaven, the Almighty was on our side. Not a ball struck or wounded an individual person, although they went through our houses in almost every direction when filled with women and children.

The end of December was a critical time for the American army, for it was then that the enlistments of many of the soldiers expired. There was no law to compel those who wanted to depart to remain; persuasion was the only way. As early as November, Simeon Lyman of Connecticut was noting how those who signed on early for another year "was led down to the colonel's and treated, and . . . they bought 2 bottles of brandy and they drinked it." On December 1 "we was ordered to parade before the general's tent, and General Lee and General Sullivan came out . . . and we was ordered to form a hollow square, and General Lee came in and the first words were 'Men, I do not know what to call you; you are the worst of all creatures,' and flung and curst and swore at us, and said if we would not stay he would order us to go on Bunker Hill and if we would not go he would order the riflemen to fire at us, and they talked they would take our guns and take our names down, and our lieutenants begged of us to stay," but all to little avail as only ten men signed on, all of whom received "a dram." One man tried to persuade his mate not to re-enlist "and the general see him and he catched his gun out of his hands and struck him on the head and ordered him to be put under guard." The next day General Lee posted an order stopping the rations of any soldier who would not agree to stay at least three weeks longer, "and some was mad and said they would not stay the 4 days, and the paper was took down as soon as it was dark, and another put up that General Lee was a fool." On December 9 those who insisted on their right to depart turned in their guns and ammunition; they were then ordered to spend one last night on guard duty on Plowed Hill, but "they all said they would not go, and they did not." Next day "in the morning we was ordered to parade before the general's door, and we was counted off and dismissed, and we went to the lieutenant and he gave us a dram, and then we marched off to Cambridge and I see the brass mortar piece [recently captured from the British], and then we marched to Watertown and then to Waltham and then to Western then to Sudbury. There we stayed all night and I got a good supper and lay in a good bed. We traveled 15 miles and it was wet and sloppy and it rained all night."

Among those who stayed was Joseph Hodgkins, aged thirty-one, of Ipswich, Massachusetts, and by trade a shoemaker, "a very tall man, with strongly marked Roman nose," according to a relative. Following the deaths of his first wife and four of their five children, Hodgkins had married Sarah Perkins and was now the father of a two-year-old daughter, also called Sarah. Formerly a minuteman in a militia company that had elected him as one of their lieutenants, and which had since been incorporated into the Second Essex County Regiment, Hodgkins had been at the Concord fight and at Bunker Hill, which he described as "a very hot engagement," but "God preserved all of us. . . . I had one ball went under my arm and cut a large hole in my coat & a buck shot went through my coat & jacket. But neither of them did me any harm." Despite the pleas of his wife, who wanted him home, Hodgkins was determined to serve what, like Washington, he called "this glorious cause" through to the end. Early in the new year he was stationed on Prospect Hill, outside Boston.

In Camp. January 2, 1776. My Dear, I take this opportunity to write a line or two to inform you that I am in good health at present for which mercy I desire to be thankful & I hope these lines will find you possessed of the mercy. As for news we have none. We have just been to supper on a fine turkey and Capt. Wade is gone to bed & I feel quite dull on account of brother's being gone home, for I miss him a great deal. . . . Our soldiers are very much gone home, but the guards are reduced so I hope the duty will not be over-hard. I have not been on guard yet since I have been here. I must conclude by subscribing as before, Joseph Hodgkins. P.S. I left a bottom of shoe-thread in my old coat pocket which I should be glad of. I should be glad if you would spin some more & send me, for several officers insist on my making them boots. Give my duty to father & mother. Love to all my friends.

✳

Sarah replied:

✳

Ipswich, January 8. Loving Husband, These lines come with my kind regards to you, hoping they will find you in as good health as they leave me and the rest of the family at this time. I received two letters from you since you left home & was glad to hear you were well. I want to hear again, don't miss any opportunity you may have of writing to me since that is all the way we have to converse together. It is much to my grief that it is so. I am a good deal concerned about you on account of the army being so thin for fear the enemy should take the advantage. I hear you have lost one of your company & hope it will be sanctified to you all. A very melancholy providence happened here last Monday night. Mr. Ringe & Spiler as they were coming in from eastward struck upon the bar & were both lost. I have no other news to write so I conclude by subscribing myself your most affectionate companion till death, Sarah Hodgkins. P.S. Father & mother send their love to you & mother is much obliged to you for the present you sent her. Do give my love to Capt. Wade. My pen blots so that I have made a wick of my letter [? – perhaps some tears had fallen on the page] but I trust you won't expose it, so I wish you a good night.

✳

Joseph replied:

✳

In Camp, February 3. My dear, I take this opportunity to inform you that I am well at present & I hope these lines will find you possessed of the same blessings. I received yours of the 28 of January and I rejoice to hear that you & our children are well, and as it gives me great satisfaction to receive letters from you so you may depend on my embracing every opportunity to write to you. I have no news to write. We live in our tent yet, only when we are smoked out, and then we get shelter somewhere else. We live pretty well and our duty is not hard. We go on guard only once in ten days, but we spend a great part of our time in exercising the regiment. I must conclude. Give my duty to my parents and respects to all my friends. So no more at present but remain your loving husband, Joseph Hodgkins.

Sarah replied:

Ipswich, February 11. Loving Husband, Having an opportunity this evening to write a line to you, I gladly embrace it to let you know that we are well, hoping they will find you possessed of the same blessing. I received two letters from you on ordination day after meeting, which was a great comfort to me to hear that you were well. . . . We had a comfortable ordination [of a new minister] but there seems to me to be something wanting—I wanted you at home & that would have crowned all. It is very cold tonight, I hope you will be provided with a comfortable lodging. I think a great deal about you both by night & by day, but I desire to commit you to God, who has hitherto preserved you, & he is able still to preserve you at all times. O my dear, let me beg you to put your trust in him at all times who alone is able to deliver us out of all our troubles, will do it if we trust in him aright. But I must conclude. I remain your most affectionate companion till death, Sarah Hodgkins.

Month after month the letters continued, Joseph always beginning his by saying that he was taking this opportunity to write a few lines, that he was well and hoped that Sarah and the children were also well; Sarah's always full of anxiety for his safety.

At first the American army lacked the heavy artillery needed for a siege, but early in the war Benedict Arnold and Ethan Allen with his Green Mountain Boys (also known as the Bennington Mob) surprised and captured the fortress at Ticonderoga. During the winter Henry Knox, the fat Boston bookseller who by reading up on the subject had taught himself how to be an artilleryman, organized the transport of the fort's great guns, loading them onto strongly built sledges and dragging them over the ice and hard-frozen earth to Boston. Once there, the guns were hauled up at night to fortified positions on Dorchester Heights, from where they commanded not only the town but the British fleet in the harbor. When they opened up, Abigail Adams wrote from Braintree to John that she had been kept awake by "a most terrible and incessant cannonade . . . I could no more sleep than if I had been in the engagement; the rattle of the windows, the jar of the house, the continual roar of twenty-four-pounders, and the bursting of shells . . . I hear that General Howe said upon going upon some Eminence in Town to view our Troops, who had taken Dorchester Hill unperceived by them till sun rise, 'My God, these fellows have done more work in one night than I could make my Army do in three months.'"

Howe had two choices: repeat the pattern of Bunker Hill by crossing the harbor and storming Dorchester Heights, or do what he was already planning to do, and depart. Being the kind of soldier he was, he chose to attack, and his dejected troops were already embarked for the assault when a tremendous storm blew up and the operation was canceled.

"Tis now out of Doubt that General Howe will leave the Town with his Troops &c—which has put the Inhabitants of this Town into great Disorder, Confusion & much Distress," wrote John Rowe in his diary. "The Troops & Inhabitants very busy in Getting all the Goods & Effects on board the Shipping in the Harbour—'tis impossible to describe the Distress of this Unfortunate Town. . . . Nothing but hurry & Confusion. . . . A Great Deal of Firing on both sides this night."

By a tacit or perhaps explicit agreement, Howe agreed not to set fire to the town if allowed to leave unmolested, and Washington ordered a cease-fire while the British and the Loyalists packed up their possessions, along with as many of the possessions of the Patriots as they could lay their hands on. "March 11," wrote John Rowe.

This morning I rose very early & very luckily went to my warehouse—when I came there I found Mr. Crean Brush [a British commissary] with an Order & party from the General who were just going to Break Open the Warehouse, which I prevented by sending for the Keys & Opening the Doors. They took from me to the Value of Twenty Two hundred and Sixty Pounds Sterling, according to the best Calculations I could make, in Linens, Checks, Cloths & Woolens. This Party behaved very Insolently & with Great Rapacity & I am very well Convinced, exceeding their orders to a Great Degree. They stole many things & plundered my Store. Words cannot Describe it. . . . They are making the utmost Speed to get away & carrying Ammunition, Cannon & everything they can away, taking all things they meet with, never asking who is Owner or whose Property—making havock in every house & Destruction of all kinds of Furniture. There never was such Destruction & Outrage committed any day before this. Many other People have suffered the same Fate as we.

March 12. They are hurrying off all their Provisions & destroying & Mangling all Navigation, also large Quantitys of Salt & other things they heave into the Sea & scuttle the stores. The Inhabitants are greatly terrified & alarmed for Fear of Greater Evils when the Troops leave this distressed Place. I got Crean Brush's Receipt for the Goods taken from me but don't expect much Good from it.

Once again, but now for the last time, at least in Boston, drunken British officers went on a rampage, breaking into the house belonging to Mrs. Hooper and "committing Violence & breaking everything left. They broke a Looking Glass over the Chimney which cost

Twenty Guineas—such Barbarous Treatment is too much for the most patient man to bear.

"March 17. St. Patrick's. This morning the Troops evacuated the Town & went on board the Transports at & about Long Wharf. They sailed & got most part of them into King Road. About Noon General Putnam & some Troops came into Town to the Great Joy of the Inhabitants that Remained behind."

For his part, John Rowe's joy must have been tempered by contemplating the worthless receipt for £2,260 left him by Crean Brush, and by the thought that his beloved niece, Sukey, and her two small children had already sailed away on the *Falcon*, "perhaps Forever," with his detestable nephew-in-law, Captain Lindzee, R.N., he who had vented his hellish rage by firing on the church at Gloucester. "God send me Comfort in my Old Age," wrote Rowe.

A bleak scene awaited the victorious Americans as they marched into town. "On crossing the Common we found it very much disfigured with ditches and cellars, which had been dug by the British troops for their accommodation when in camp," recalled a citizen many years later. "To our great regret we saw several large trees lying in the mall, which had been cut down that morning. . . . On passing into the town, it presented an indescribable scene of desolation and gloominess . . . the ruins of many houses which had been taken down for fuel—the dirtiness of the streets—the wretched appearance of the very few inhabitants who had remained during the siege—the contrast between the Sunday we then beheld, compared with those we formerly witnessed when well-dressed people, with cheerful countenances, were going to and returning from church."

"Many Loyalists were left behind," wrote Peter Oliver, who was among those able to get away, "& many who had Families which they were loth should be separated, as there were not Transports for all who would have been willing to have embarked. These were obliged to take their Chances of ill Usage, & some of them felt it severely." But no one was killed or even tarred and feathered, although many Loyalists were banished forever and their property confiscated.

(Oliver himself, after a short stay in Halifax, arrived in London in June 1776, where he wrote in his diary: "Thanks be to Heaven, I am now in a Place where I can be protected from the Harpy Claws of that Rebellion which is now tearing out its own Bowels in America.")

Services of thanksgiving were held everywhere. In Cambridge, where he was still a military chaplain, the Rev. William Emerson preached on the anniversary of Lexington and Concord: "But while I speak I hear, methinks, the alarming Signal that our Enemies were in large Numbers actually upon the March, and even now at Hand! What gratitude is due to Him who gives Strength to the Weak and Courage to the faint-hearted, that we were not seized with a universal Tremor!. . . . No! Though roused from the very depths of Sleep, the Signal inspired us, and the loud-sounding Cannon waked the martial Genius, and called up all the natural Courage and Resolution of freeborn Sons to oppose the daring Foe . . ."

In Boston Dr. James Thacher noted in his diary that Washington had "requested the Rev. Dr. Eliot, at the renewal of the customary Thursday Lecture, to preach a thanksgiving sermon, adapted to the joyful occasion. Accordingly on the 28th, this pious divine preached an appropriate discourse from Isaiah xxxiii. 20 ['Look upon Zion, the city of our solemnities: thine eyes shall see Jerusalem a quiet habitation,'], in the presence of his Excellency and a respectable audience."

In Braintree, on March 31, Abigail Adams sat down to write to John, now back in Philadelphia:

I feel very differently at the approach of spring to what I did a month ago. We knew not then whether we could plant or sow with safety, whether when we had toil'd we could reap the fruits of our own industery, [but now] I feel a *gaieti de Coar* [Boston French for lightheartedness] to which before I was a stranger. I think the Sun looks brighter, the Birds sing more melodiously, and Nature puts on a more chearful countanance . . . . I long to hear that you have declared an independancy—and by the way in the new Code of Laws which I suppose will be necessary for you

to make I desire you would Remember the Ladies, and be more generous to them than your ancestors. Do not put such unlimited power into
the hands of the Husbands. Remember all Men would be tyrants if they
could. If perticuliar care and attention is not paid to the Ladies we are
determined to foment a Rebelion, and will not hold ourselves bound by
any Laws in which we have no voice, or Representation.

John's reply to her "saucy" letter was jocular-dismissive:

As to your extraordinary Code of Laws, I cannot but laugh. We have
been told that our Struggle has loosened the bands of Government
every where, that Children and Apprentices were disobedient—that
schools and Colledges were grown turbulent—that Indians slighted
their Guardians and Negroes grew insolent to their Masters. But your
Letter was the first Intimation that another Tribe more numerous and
powerful than all the rest were grown discontented. . . . Depend upon it,
We know better than to repeal our Masculine systems. Altho they are in
full Force, you know that they are little more than Theory . . . in Practice
you know we are the Subjects. We have only the Name of Masters. . . .

About this time Lt. Joseph Hodgkins was also writing home, and
like John Adams he too was telling his wife something she would not
want to hear. In his case it was that rather than return to Ipswich now
that the siege of Boston was over, he had decided to stay with the
army wherever Washington decided to send it.

Loving Wife,
　　I take this opportunity to write a line or two to let you know that
I am well through the goodness of God & I hope these lines will find
you possessed of the same blessing. I received your letter by Thomas

and I am glad to hear that you are well, & as you informed me that you were full of trouble for fear that I should be called away, I would not have you be uneasy about me, for I am willing to serve my country in the best way & manner that I am capable of; and as our enemy are gone from us I expect we must follow them. It is not certain yet who will stay here but it is generally thought our regiment will march somewhere. I would not be understood that I should choose to march, but as I am engaged in this glorious cause I am willing to go where I am called, with a desire to commit myself & you to the care of him who is able to carry on through all the difficulties that we may be called to. I am sensible that the fatigues of marching will be great, but I hope if we are called to it we shall march with cheerfulness.

General Burgoyne surrenders at Saratoga, October 17, 1777.

CHAPTER THREE

New York and Saratoga

As the British sailed out of Boston harbor, heading northeast for Halifax, hardly a redcoat was to be found in any of the colonies. But, as everyone knew, they would be back; nor was there much doubt about where they would land. Although most Americans lived on farms or in small towns and villages, British military theory held that seizing the cities would inevitably lead to control of the whole country. To be sure, this had not worked in the case of Boston and New England, but just because a strategy had failed once did not mean that it should be abandoned; and capturing towns was one of the things European armies were specially trained to do. So, after taking New York, the British would also occupy Philadelphia and then successfully lay siege to Charleston.

Like all other American towns, New York was tiny when compared with its present-day size, a mere twenty-five thousand or so people squashed into the southern tip of Manhattan, the rest of the island being covered with farms and woodlands; but with its central location on the Atlantic coast, huge harbor that would serve as a base for the Royal Navy, control of the mouth and lower reaches of the Hudson River, and—despite the mobs that had taken to the streets during the Stamp Act riots—generally Loyalist or neutral population, New York was the obvious choice for a British landing. So convenient indeed did the British find the place that they made it their headquarters for the rest of the war; and even when the war was over they were reluctant to go.

MANHATTAN

On the evening of Friday, August 19, 1774, while on their way by coach to Philadelphia for the first Continental Congress, John Adams and his fellow delegates from Massachusetts crossed King's Bridge at the northeast tip of Manhattan, the only bridge connecting the island with the rest of the continent. They lodged at the local inn, "a pretty Place—Uncas [Harlem] River running before the Door and verdant Hills all round. This Place is about fifteen miles from N. York." At ten o'clock next morning, after passing through woods, meadows, and farmland, and taking note of "several very elegant Country Seats," they arrived in the city. As had happened at every other stopping place since leaving Boston, they were welcomed by local leaders and treated as honored guests.

"After Dinner, Mr. McDougal and Mr. Platt came and walked with Us to every Part of the City," wrote Adams in his diary. "We went to the Fort where we saw the Ruins of the magnificent Building, the Governor's House [recently destroyed by a fire]. From the Parade before the Fort you have a fine Prospect of Hudson's River and of the East River, or the Sound, and of the Harbour—of Long Island, beyond the Sound River, and of New Jersey, beyond Hudson's River. The Walk round this Fort is very pleasant, tho' the Fortifications are not strong. Between the Fort and the City is a beautiful Ellipsis of Land, railed in with solid Iron, in the Center of which is a Statue of his Majesty on Horse back, very large, of solid Lead, gilded with Gold, standing on a Pedestal of Marble very high." This ellipsis was Bowling Green, the same spot where the Stamp Act mob had burned the governor's coach. The statue, which had been voted by the Common Council in gratitude for the repeal of that act, represented the king as Marcus Aurelius, the philosopher-emperor.

✯

We then walked up the broad Way, a fine Street, very wide, and in a right Line from one End to the other of the City. In this route we saw the old Church, and the new Church. The new is a very magnificent Building—cost 20,000 Pounds New York Currency. The prison is a large and handsome stone Building. There are two setts of Barracks. We saw the New York Colledge, which is also a Stone building. A new Hospital is building of Stone. We then walked down to the ship Yard, where a Dutch East India Ship is building of 800 Tons burden. Then we walked round thro' another Street which is the Principal Street of Business. Saw the several Marketts. After this we went to the Coffee House, which was full of Gentlemen, read the News Papers &c. Here were introduced to Us Mr. Morine Scott and a Mr. Litchfield, who invited us to Hull's Tavern, where we went and staid till 11 o'Clock. We supped together and had much conversation. . . . The Streets of this Town are vastly more regular and elegant than those in Boston, and the Houses are more grand as well as neat. They are almost all painted—brick buildings and all.

The next day, Sunday, they went to Presbyterian meeting twice and heard two sermons, both delivered "without Notes," an approving comment, since to preach with notes implied a lack of divine inspiration. Then on Monday:

We took Mr. McDougal into our Coach and rode three Miles out of Town to Mr. Morine Scott's to break fast. A very pleasant Ride! Mr. Scott has an elegant Seat there, with Hudson's River just behind his House and a rural Prospect all round him. Mr. Scott, his Lady and his Daughter, and her Husband Mr. Litchfield were dressed to receive Us. We satt in a fine Airy Entry, till called into a front Room to break fast. A more elegant Breakfast I never saw—rich Plate—a very large Silver Coffee Pott, a very large Silver Tea Pott—Napkins of the very finest materials, and toast and bread and butter in great Perfection. After breakfast, a Plate of beautifull Peaches, another of Pairs and another of Plumbs and a Muskmellen were placed on the Table.

The delegates' stay was brief, but despite the warm welcome Adams's parting judgment on New York was severe: "With all the Opulence and Splendor of this City, there is very little good Breeding to be found. We have been treated with an assiduous Respect, but I have not seen one real Gentleman, one well-bred Man since I came to Town. There is no Modesty—No Attention to one another. They talk very loud, very fast, and all together. If they ask you a Question, before you can utter three words of your answer, they will break in upon you again—and talk away."

Though the city was small enough to be visited in a couple of days, there were other places of interest that the delegates did not see: the tenements, low taverns, and grog shops near the docks on the east side. Nor did they visit the Bridewell, a house of correction for vagrants, runaway apprentices, debtors, and other troublemakers. (From a local paper: "*May 7, 1772.* On Saturday last Mr. Montnanny's negro man who had misbehaved, and was a remarkable drunkard, was sent to Bridewell, and underwent the usual discipline of the house for such offenses, viz. a plentiful dose of warm water and salt to operate as an emetic, and of lamp oyl as a purge . . . . Of these he took about 3 quarts of the one, and 2 1/2 spoonfuls of the other, also a gill of New England rum, which operated very powerfully, attended with a violent sickness which obliged him to lye down, and between 8 and 9 at night he was discovered to be dead." Following an autopsy, "the coroner's inquest brought in their verdict that he died of excessive drinking, co-operating with the effects of the medicine he had taken.") Nor would the delegates have visited the Holy Ground, so called because it stood on land belonging to Trinity Church. In the words of Loammi Baldwin, an officer with a New England regiment come to garrison the city, the Holy Ground was inhabited by "bitchfoxly jades, jills, haggs, strums." One of the duties of the officer of the day was to patrol the area with an armed guard, "breaking up knots of men and women fighting, pulling caps, swearing, crying 'Murder!'—Hell's work." Even worse, according to Tom Paine, "the whole race of prostitutes in New York were Tories; and the schemes for supporting the Tory cause in this city . . . were concerted and carried on in common bawdy-houses."

But they were not the only Tories in the city. Alexander Hamilton, who had been a student at King's College, thought that at least half the population of the province were Tories, and during the war well over twenty thousand New Yorkers volunteered to serve in locally raised regiments such as the King's Rangers, the Loyal American Regiment, the Prince of Wales' American Regiment, De Lancey's Brigade, and the Westchester Refugees. Indeed, along with its strategic importance, the fact that so many New Yorkers were Loyalists was an added motive for the British to choose the city for their headquarters once Boston had been evacuated.

In his memoirs, *Travels Through Life*, Dr. Benjamin Rush of Philadelphia gave this analysis of the divide between the Patriots (or Whigs) and Loyalists (or Tories):

✳

It cannot be denied but that private and personal consideration actuated some of those men who took a part in favor of the American Revolution. There were Whigs (1) from a desire of possessing, or at least sharing, in the power of our country. It was said there were Whigs (2) from an expectation that a war with Great Britain would cancel all British debts. There were certainly Whigs (3) from the facility with which the tender [currency] laws enabled debtors to pay their creditors in depreciated money. (4) A few men were Whigs from ancient or hereditary hostility to persons or families who were Tories. But a great majority of the people who took part with their country were Whigs (5) from a sincere and disinterested love to liberty and justice.

Both parties differed as much in their conduct as they did in the motives which actuated them. There were (1) furious Tories who had recourse to violence, and even to arms, to oppose the measures of the Whigs. (2) Writing and talking Tories. (3) Silent but busy Tories in disseminating Tory pamphlets and newspapers and in circulating intelligence. (4) Peaceable and conscientious Tories who patiently submitted to the measures of the governing powers, and who shewed nearly equal kindness to the distressed of both parties during the war.

The Whigs were divided by their conduct into (1) Furious Whigs, who considered the tarring and feathering of a Tory as a greater duty and exploit than the extermination of the British army. These men were generally cowards, and shrunk from danger when called into the field by pretending sickness or some family disaster. (2) Speculating Whigs. These men infested our public councils, as well as the army, and did the country great mischief. A colonel of a regiment informed a friend of mine that he had made a great deal of money by buying poor horses for his waggons, and selling them again for a large profit after he had fattened them at the public expense. (3) Timid Whigs. The hopes of these people rose and fell with every victory and defeat of our armies. (4) Staunch Whigs. These were moderate in their tempers, but firm, inflexible, and persevering in their conduct.

There was, besides these two classes of people, a great number of persons who were neither Whigs nor Tories. They had no fixed principles and accommodated their conduct to their interest, to events, and to their company.

Among the staunch Whigs—firm, inflexible, and persevering—were General Washington, who now shifted his headquarters to New York, and Lt. Joseph Hodgkins of Ipswich, who had marched with cheerfulness from Boston to New London where he and his regiment took ship for the rest of the journey. "Loving Wife," he wrote on April 24, "I take this opportunity to write a few lines to let you know that I am well & I hope these lines will find you and our children & all friends possessed of the same inestimable blessing of health that I enjoy at present through the goodness of God." He found that New York "exceeds all places that ever I saw on many accounts but it is very expensive living here." Soon he was moved to Long Island in expectation of the arrival of the British army and navy. There he was "in a comfortable state of health through the goodness of God though I have had a bad cold, but I have got pretty clear of that, but I have had two bad boils on my right arm, one of

them is not broke yet and it is very painful." He was still homesick—
"My Dear, the thought of being absent from you and my family is
the greatest trouble that I have"—but still put his trust in God: "I
desire to commit you and myself & children to the care of him who
is able to do more and better for us than we are either able to ask or
think, and may we be sensible of God's goodness to us hitherto and
be enabled to put our trust in him for the future. So no more for the
present but I remain your most affectionate companion till death."
In her reply Sarah sympathized about the boils ("They are very troublesome"), reported on the family and neighbors ("I see Sister Hannah yesterday, she told me to give her love to you and tell you they
were well, Brother John's folks are well & send their love"), told of
her own activities ("I have been very busy all day today a-making
you a shirt . . . and Sister Perkins is now a-ironing it"), and gave the
rest of the news, bad as well as good ("I must just tell you that Sally
met with a mishap last Monday, she scalded her arm pretty bad but
it seems in a good way to be well soon. The rest of us are in a comfortable state of health. I want to see you very much. Sometimes I
am almost impatient but considering it is Providence that has parted
us I desire to submit & be as contented as I can be & thankful that
we can hear from one another so often." Finally: "Deacon Potter
died last Saturday and Hannah Fitts the Saturday before, a loud call
to us all to be ready for Death. Oh that we may be prepared for all
events, and if it is the will of God that we are not to meet again in
this world, may we be prepared to meet in a better where we shall
not have the grief of parting any more.")

Soon to join General Washington and Lieutenant Hodgkins
in New York was Private Joseph Plumb Martin, fifteen and a half
years old, "as warm a patriot as the best of them" and anxious "to be
called a defender of my country." Early in 1776 Martin was living
and working on his grandparents' farm in Milford, one of Connecticut's oldest settlements, bought from the Wepawaug Indians in 1639
for "six coats, ten blankets, one kettle, besides a number of hoes,
knives, hatchets, and glasses." Joseph Martin had been sent to live

there as a boy when his father, the Rev. Ebenezer Martin, "an able, but not always a *wise* man," in the words of a family history, had been asked to leave his congregation at Becket because of some unspecified "indiscretions." After also being asked to leave his next congregation because of "unministerial conduct," the Rev. Ebenezer seems to have become an itinerant preacher, and Joseph grew up with his apparently well-to-do grandparents, who gave him an education as well as putting him to work on their farm. Since he later served in the light infantry he was probably above average height; otherwise, all that is known about him is what he reveals in *A Narrative of Some of the Adventures, Dangers and Sufferings of a Revolutionary Soldier*, written many years later. "No alpine wonders thunder through my tale," he warned the reader; rather, it consisted of nothing but "the common transactions of one of the lowest in station in an army, a private soldier." His adventures, dangers, and sufferings began in 1776:

✳

One evening, very early in the spring of this year, I chanced to overhear my grandma'am telling my grandsire that I had threatened to engage on board a man-of-war. I had told her that I would enter on board a privateer then fitting out in our neighborhood. The good old lady thought it a man-of-war, that and privateer being synonymous terms with her. She said she could not bear the thought of my being on board of a man-of-war; my grandsire told her that he supposed I was resolved to go into the service in some way or other and he had rather I would engage in the land service if I must engage in any. This I thought to be a sort of tacit consent for me to go, and I determined to take advantage of it as quick as possible.

Soldiers were at this time enlisting for a year's service. I did not like that; it was too long a time for me at the first trial; I wished only to take a priming before I took upon me the whole coat of paint for a soldier. However, the time soon arrived that gratified all my wishes. In the month of June, this year, orders came out for enlisting men for six months from the twenty-fifth of this month. The troops were styled new levies. They were to go to New York. And notwithstanding I was told that the British army at that place was reinforced by fifteen thousand men, it made no alteration in my mind; I did not care if there had been fifteen times fifteen thousand, I should have gone just as soon as if there had been fifteen hundred. I never spent a thought about numbers; the Americans were invincible in my opinion. If anything affected me, it was a stronger desire to see them.

Well, as I have said, enlisting orders were out. I used frequently to go to the rendezvous, where I saw many of my young associates enlist, had repeated banterings to engage with them, but still when it came "case in hand," I had my misgivings. If I once undertake, thought I, I must stick to it; there will be no receding. Thoughts like these would, at times, almost overset my resolutions.

But mauger all these "doleful ideas," I one evening went off with a full determination to enlist at all hazards. When I arrived at the place of rendezvous, I found a number of young men of my acquaintance there. The old bantering began—come, if you will enlist, I will, says one; you have long been talking about it, says another—come, now is the time. Thinks I to myself I will not be laughed into it or out of it, at any rate; I will act my own pleasure after all. But what did I come here for tonight? Why, to enlist. Then enlist I will. So seating myself at the table, enlisting orders were immediately presented to me; I took up the pen, loaded it with the fatal charge, made several mimic imitations of writing my name, but took especial care not to touch the paper with the pen until an unlucky wight who was leaning over my shoulder gave my hand a stroke, which caused the pen to make a woeful scratch on the paper. "Oh, he has enlisted," said he. "He has made his mark; he is fast enough now." Well, thought I, I may as well go through with the business now as not. So I wrote my name fairly upon the indentures. And now I was a soldier, in name at least, if not in practice; but now I had to go home, after performing this, my heroic action. How shall I be received there? But the report of my adventure had reached there before I did. In the morning when I first saw my grandparents, I felt considerably of the sheepish order. The old gentleman first accosted me with, "Well, you are going a-soldiering then, are you?" I had nothing to answer; I would much rather he had not asked me the question. I saw that the circumstance hurt him and the old lady, too; but it was too late now to repent. The old gentleman proceeded, "I suppose you must be fitted out for the expedition, since it is so." Accordingly, they did "fit me out" in order, with arms and accouterments, clothing, and cake, and cheese in plenty, not forgetting to put my pocket Bible into my knapsack. Good old people! They wished me well, soul and body. I sincerely thank them for their kindness and love to me, from the first time I came to live with them to the last parting hour. I hope, nay, I believe, that their spirits now rest in the realms of bliss. May it be my happy lot to meet them there.

Unlike most rumors, the story that the British at New York were being reinforced by fifteen thousand men greatly underestimated the actual number. Belatedly following General Gage's advice to send a large army to crush the insurrection at one blow, the British government was dispatching some thirty-two thousand soldiers, including several regiments of Hessians, and a powerful fleet commanded by Admiral Lord Howe, brother to army commander Sir William Howe. Some of these troops, including those that had been evacuated from Boston, were coming from Halifax, others from Britain, Ireland, and elsewhere. Since Manhattan and Long Island were held by Washington's army, the British chose Staten Island as a staging area. From there General Howe could cross the Narrows to Long Island and force Washington to engage in a set-piece battle of the traditional kind, which the British were confident of winning. Indeed, the scent of victory was already in the air when, early in July and in advance of the main fleet, ships of the Royal Navy arrived to join those already there, bringing Admiral Lord Howe and his lordship's intelligent, diary-keeping, conscientious, and ultra-Tory secretary, Ambrose Serle.

✴

Friday, July 12th. This Morning, the Sun shining bright, we had a beautiful Prospect of the Coast of New Jersey at about 5 or 6 Miles Distance. The Land was cleared in many Places, and the Woods were interspersed with Houses, which being covered with white Shingles appeared very plainly all along the Shore. We passed Sandy Hook in the Afternoon, and about 6 o'Clock arrived safe off the East Side of Staten Island. The Country on both Sides was highly picturesque and agreeable. Nothing could exceed the Joy that appeared throughout the Fleet and Army upon our Arrival. We were saluted by all the Ships of War in the Harbour, by the Cheers of the Sailors all along the Ships, and by those of the Soldiers on the Shore. A finer Scene could not be exhibited, both of Country, Ships, and Men, all heightened by one of the brightest Days that can be imagined. What added to their Pleasure was that this very Day about Noon the *Phoenix* of 40 Guns & the *Rose* of 20, with three Tenders, forced their Passage up the River in Defiance of all their vaunted Batteries, and got safe above the Town, which will much intercept the Provisions of the Rebels. We heard the Cannonade and saw the Smoke at a Distance.

13th July. The Congress have at length thought it convenient to throw off the Mask. Their Declaration of the 4th of July, while it avows their Right to Independence, is founded upon such Reasons only as prove that Independence to have been their Object from the Beginning. A more impudent, false, and atrocious Proclamation was never fabricated by the Hands of Man. Hitherto, they had thrown all the Blame and Insult upon the Parliament and Ministry: Now, they have the Audacity to calumniate the King and People of Great Britain. 'Tis impossible to read this Paper without Horror at the daring Hypocrisy of these Men, who call GOD to witness the uprightness of their Proceedings, nor without Indignation at the low and scurrilous Pretences by which they attempt to justify themselves.

By a perspective Glass, we have a distinct View of the Rebels' Encampments, of the Town of New York, and of Hudson's River for a considerable Space beyond the Town. The Rebels appeared very numerous, & are supposed to be near 30,000, but from the Mode of raising them, no great matters are to be expected, especially when their loose Discipline is considered.

15th July. Walked in the Evening upon Staten Island. There is something romantic in the wild unbroken Country, which though it does not enchant, gives the Sense a kind of pleasing Melancholy. The Soil is very light & poor, & the Strength of it soon exhausted. It very much resembles the Land on the Edge of Windsor Forest.

20th. I could perceive, several Times in the Day, the Rebels watching the opposite Coast of Long Island, lest any of their People should come over to us. Poor unhappy Men! How are they led astray from the Blessings of a lawful & settled Government into the worst Sort of Tyranny, into Anarchy and Tumult!

Read over Adams's Pamphlet, entitled *Common Sense*. A most flagitious Performance, replete with Sophistry, Impudence & Falsehood; but unhappily calculated to work upon the Fury of the Times, and to induce the full avowal of the Spirit of Independence in the warm & inconsiderate. His Attempt to justify Rebellion by the Bible is infamous beyond Expression.

21st. In some of their papers they are publishing Dr. Price's Book upon Liberty [*Observations on the Nature of Civil Liberty*, by dissenting clergyman the Rev. Richard Price, one of Franklin's London friends] in which he attempts to prove that the British Nation and Government are running into Slavery. Nothing can be a stronger Contradiction to the Fact than this: the Book has never been burnt, nor the author hanged, which would have been the certain Consequence in any State but G. Britain. The Lenity of her Laws, like the mild Temperature of Peru, generates the most monstrous Reptiles, at the same time that it nourishes what is valuable and good. In America . . . a man who should publish such a Pamphlet against an illegal Congress would instantly be deprived of his Life, & his Possessions be confiscated.

9th August. Nothing material occurred this Day, which was extremely warm. In constant Expectation of the Fleet, & still disappointed.

12th. This Morning, as soon as it was light, we were gladdened with the Sight of the grand Fleet in the offing. The Joy of the Navy & Army was almost like that of a Victory . . . .So large a Fleet made a fine Appearance upon entering the Harbor, with the Sails crowded, Colors flying, Guns saluting, and the Soldiers both in the Ships and on the Shore continually shouting. The Rebels (as we perceived by our Glasses) flocked out of their lurking Holes to see a Picture by no means agreeable to them.

13th. The Hessian Generals Heister &c with their officers waited on Lord Howe, and were received in a manner and with an attention that seemed to please them highly. They were well-looking men for the most part. They afterwards made a Visit to Admiral Shuldham, and were saluted with eleven Guns from each of the Ships upon their Departure. A great many Deserters, chiefly Irishmen, came off to the Ships this Day. It appears very evidently that the Rebels are surprized with the appearance of so formidable a Fleet and Army.

14th. This morning early, Sir Peter Parker in the *Bristol*, with the *Experiment* & *Roebuck*, and several Transports, appeared in the offing; and a little after Noon came up & saluted the Admiral. . . . Besides Sloops, Bombs, Fireships, armed Vessels, &c, the whole Fleet consists of about 350 Sail. Such a Fleet was never seen together in America before.

Our Army now consists of about 24,000 men, in a most remarkable State of good Health & in high Spirits. On the other Hand, the Rebels are sickly & die very fast. 'Tis said by some People who came over this morning that not less than 3,000 are upon the Sick List. They give us more & more Accounts of their Cruelties & oppressions, and earnestly pray for a Release from the republican Bondage, under which they so long have groaned without a Remedy.

Serle was not alone in thinking that *Common Sense*, published anonymously early in 1776, had been written by the arch-radical Samuel Adams, and his outrage at its contents would probably have been even greater had he known that its author was an Englishman, Thomas Paine, who had been in America less than a year when he became the great spokesman for independence. Before that Paine had had a mixed career: By trade a lady's corset maker, he had also been an unsuccessful shopkeeper, was twice married, twice divorced, and twice dismissed from the customs and excise service for not doing his job. He had, however, done some polemical writing (advocating higher salaries for customs officers), which caught the eye of Franklin, then still in London, and when Paine, at the age of thirty-six, decided to make a new start in life and settle in Philadelphia, Franklin gave him letters of introduction. *Common Sense*, written in a few months, "burst from the press with an effect which has rarely been produced by types and papers in any age or country," said Dr. Benjamin Rush; Franklin called its effect "prodigious"; Washington commended its "sound doctrine and unanswerable reasoning"; another fan letter concluded: "You must not be too elated and set up when I tell you my belief that you are the only writer in America who can write better than your obliged and obedient servant, T. Jefferson"; and though he was later to revile Paine for turning atheist ("a mongrel between pig and puppy"), at the time John Adams had only the highest praise: "The cannon of Washington was not more formidable to the British than the pen of the author of *Common Sense*." Paine, who donated his royalties to provide clothing for soldiers, not knowing that his publisher would embezzle the money, estimated that the book sold 120,000 copies in three months, a success perhaps due less to his ability to persuade people to change their minds than to his skill in formulating what many people already felt but could not clearly express. And while promising that he would "offer nothing more than simple facts, plain argument, and common sense," Paine also ennobled the Patriot cause, putting the issue of American independence on the highest and grandest level: "The sun never shone on a cause of greater worth. 'Tis not the affair of a city, a county, a province, or a kingdom, but of a continent—of at least one-eighth part of the habitable globe. 'Tis not the concern of a day, a year, or an age; posterity are virtually involved in the contest, and will be more or less affected even to the end of time, by the proceedings now. Now is the seed-time of continental union, faith, and honor."

When it came to demolishing the standard Loyalist arguments, Paine used homely metaphors honed to a sharp edge:

✳

I have heard it asserted by some, that as America hath flourished under her former connection with Great Britain, that the same connection is necessary toward her future happiness, and will always have the same effect. Nothing can be more fallacious than this kind of argument. We may as well assert that because a child has thriven upon milk, that it is never to have meat, or that the first twenty years of our lives is to become a precedent for the next twenty. . . . But Britain is the parent country, say some. Then the more shame upon her conduct. Even brutes do not devour their young, nor savages make war upon their families; wherefore, the assertion, if true, turns to her reproach; but it happens not to be true, or only partly so, and the phrase *parent* or *mother country* hath been jesuitically adopted by the King and his parasites, with a low, papistical design of gaining an unfair bias on the credulous weakness of our minds. [Digs at the Catholics were sure to go down well with his overwhelmingly Protestant readers.] Europe, and not England, is the parent country of America. This new world hath been the asylum for the persecuted lovers of civil and religious liberty from *every part* of Europe. Hither have they fled, not from the tender embraces of a mother, but from the cruelty of the monster; and it is so far true of England, that the same tyranny which drove the first emigrants from home pursues their descendants still.

I challenge the warmest advocate for reconciliation to show a single advantage that this continent can reap by being connected with Great Britain. I repeat the challenge: not a single advantage is derived. Our corn will fetch its price in any market in Europe, and our imported goods must be paid for, buy them where we will. But the injuries and disadvantages we sustain by that connection are without number, and our duty to mankind at large, as well as to ourselves, instructs us to renounce the alliance, because any submission to or dependence on Great Britain tends directly to involve this continent in European wars and quarrels; and sets us at variance with nations who would otherwise seek our friendship, and against whom we have neither anger nor complaint.

In short: "Everything that is right or natural pleads for separation. The blood of the slain, the weeping voice of nature cries, *'tis time to part.'*" Finally:

O ye that love mankind! Ye that dare oppose, not only the tyranny, but the tyrant, stand forth! Every spot of the old world is overrun with oppression. Freedom hath been hunted round the globe. Asia and Africa have long expelled her, Europe regards her like a stranger, and England hath given her warning to depart. O! receive the fugitive, and prepare in time an asylum for mankind.

Having done his duty as a writer, Paine then shouldered a musket and went off to serve as a private in the infantry. A few months later, independence was declared. Writing to Abigail from Philadelphia on July 3, John Adams described the event:

Yesterday the greatest Question was decided, which ever was debated in America, and a greater, perhaps, never was or will be decided among Men. A Resolution was passed without one dissenting Colony "that these united Colonies are, and of Right ought to be free and independent States, and as such, they have, and of Right ought to have full Power to make War, conclude Peace, establish Commerce, and to do all the other Acts and Things which other States may rightfully do." You will see in a few days a Declaration setting forth the Causes which have impell'd us to this mighty Revolution, and the Reasons which will justify it, in the Sight of God and Man.

Later in his letter, Adams reflected on the future:

It may be the Will of Heaven that America should suffer Calamities still more wasting and Distresses yet more dreadfull. If this is to be the Case, it will have this good Effect, at least: it will inspire Us with many Virtues, which We have not, and correct many Errors, Follies, and Vices, which threaten to disturb, dishonour, and destroy Us. The Furnace of Affliction produces Refinement, in States as well as Individuals. And the new Governments we are assuming, in every part, will require a Purification from our vices, and an Augmentation of our virtues. . . .

In her reply from Boston, dated July 21, Abigail described how "last Thursday after hearing a very Good Sermon I went with the Multitude into Kings Street to hear the proclamation of independance read and proclamed." Field artillery and troops were drawn up in the street where six years earlier the massacre had taken place. Colonel Crafts read the Declaration from the balcony of the State House and

great attention was given to every word. As soon as he ended, the cry from the Belcona was God Save our American States and then 3 cheers which rended the air, the Bells rang, the privateers fired, the forts and Batteries, the cannon were discharged, the platoons followed and every face appeard joyfull. Mr. Bowdoin then gave a Sentiment, "Stability and perpetuity to American independence." After dinner the king's arms were taken down from the State House and every vestage of him from every place in which it appeard and burnt in King

Street. Thus ends royall Authority in this State, and all the people shall
say Amen.

A similar scene took place in New York, where the Rev. Philip
Vickers Fithian, an army chaplain, wrote in his diary:

At twelve o'Clock today, at the city Hall, Independency was formally
proclaimed; after which the King's Arms in Canvass was thrown out
of a Window of the Hall among the People & was seized, & torn, &
stamped, & at last burned, with unparalell'd Rage. After this the Arms
cut in Stone in the front of the House were beat out & gathered &
thrown into the fire, amidst repeated Acclamations of the throng.

All over the country, as soon as the Declaration was read, the royal
coat of arms and other insignia were torn down and destroyed, and
portraits of the king were either burnt, turned to face the wall, or hung
upside down. A few "King's Head" inn signs were modified: the red
coat painted blue, the sash eliminated, and the name changed to the
"General Washington." In New York the gilded statue of George III as
Marcus Aurelius at Bowling Green was pulled down, melted, and cast
into musket balls—forty-two thousand of them. (But not the head. In
a footnote to this story, Captain Montresor, of the Royal Engineers,
in a summary of all the services he had performed and for which he
felt he deserved promotion, wrote of his outrage on hearing that "the
Rebels had cut the King's head off the Equestrian Statue . . . and that
they had cut the nose off, clipt the laurels that were wreathed round his
head, and drove a musket Bullet part of the way through his head, and
otherwise disfigured it," and that they had then taken it "to Moore's
tavern, adjoining Fort Washington, on New York Island, in order to
be fixed on a Spike." Since fixing a severed head—even one made
of lead—on a spike and then publicly exposing it was an ignominy

reserved for traitors, Montresor sprang into action, sending one of his men "through the Rebel Camp . . . to steal it from thence, and to bury it, which was effected." After the British had driven the Americans out of New York, the head "was dug up on our arrival, and I rewarded the men, and sent the Head by the Lady Gage to Lord Townshend, in order to convince them at home of the Infamous Disposition of the Ungrateful people of this distressed Country.")

KIP'S BAY

By early June Private Joseph Martin of Milford, Connecticut, had joined his regiment in the city, where he was billeted in a house on Stone Street, so named because it was one of the first streets to be paved with cobblestones. "I was called out every morning at reveille beating, which was at daybreak, to go to our regimental parade in Broad Street, and there practice the manual exercise, which was the most that was known in our levies, if they knew even that."

Expecting that their city would be bombarded, cannonaded, and then stormed by the Royal Navy and British army, about three quarters of its citizens had moved out. Their places were taken by several thousand American soldiers who, for the same reason, set to work with spades and pickaxes, throwing up earthworks, building batteries and redoubts, and digging trenches in the streets, which soon filled with stagnant water.

The British were not idle either. "August 22nd," wrote Ambrose Serle.

※

Early this Morning the English Troops, the Highlanders, & Preston's Light Horse, landed on Long Island. The Disembarkation was effected upon a flat Shore, near Gravesend, without the least Resistance; the inhuman Rebels contenting themselves with burning as much of the People's Corn as they could (tho' the great Rains which fell last night very happily prevented much of their Design), with driving off their Cattle as far as their Time would permit, and doing as much Injury to the Inhabitants, who are generally well disposed, as they possibly could. The Soldiers & Sailors seemed as merry as in Holiday, and regaled themselves with the fine Apples which hung everywhere upon the Trees in great abundance.

(In a footnote, Serle adds: "These are chiefly what are called New-town Pippins, and appear to me to be Descendants of our Broad-nose Pippins, softened by the Soil." Unlike the apples, most Long Islanders of English stock had mutated into "rebels," while those who were "well disposed" came from other countries.)

In a Word, the Disembarkation of about 15,000 Troops, upon a fine Beach, their forming upon an adjacent Plain, a Fleet of above 300 Ships & Vessels with their Sails spread open to dry, the Sun shining clear upon them, the green Hills and Meadows after the Rain, and the calm surface of the Water upon the contiguous Sea and up the Sound, exhibited one of the finest & most picturesque Scenes that the Imagination can fancy or the Eye behold.

To return to Private Martin:

Some time in the latter part of the month of August, I was ordered upon a fatigue party. We had scarcely reached the grand parade when I saw our sergeant major directing his course up Broadway, towards us, in rather an unusual step for him. He soon arrived and informed us and then the commanding officer of the party that he had orders to take off all belonging to our regiment and march us to our quarters, as the regiment was ordered to Long Island, the British having landed in force there. Although this was not unexpected to me, yet it gave me rather a disagreeable feeling, as I was pretty well assured I should have to snuff a little gunpowder. However, I kept my cogitations to myself, went to my quarters, packed up my clothes, and got myself in readiness for the expedition as soon as possible. I then went to the top of the house where I had a full view of that part of the Island; I distinctly saw the smoke of the field artillery, but the distance and the unfavorableness of the wind prevented my hearing their report, at least but faintly. The horrors of battle then presented themselves to my mind in all their hideousness; I must come to it now, thought I. Well, I will endeavor to do my duty as well as I am able and leave the event with Providence. We were soon ordered to our regimental parade, from which, as soon as the regiment was formed, we were marched off for the ferry.

At the lower end of the street were placed several casks of sea-bread, made, I believe, of canel [cinnamon] and peas-meal, nearly hard enough for musket flints; the casks were unheaded and each man was allowed to take as many as he could as he marched by. As my good luck would have it, there was a momentary halt made; I improved the opportunity thus offered me, as every good soldier should upon all important occasions, to get as many of the biscuit as I possibly could; no one said anything to me and I filled my bosom and took as many as I could hold in my hand, a dozen or more in all, and when we arrived at the ferry stairs I stowed them away in my knapsack. We quickly embarked on board the boats. As each boat started, three cheers were given by those on board, which was returned by the numerous spectators who thronged the wharves; they all wished us good luck, apparently; although it was with most of them perhaps nothing more than ceremony.

We soon landed in Brooklyn, upon the Island, marched up the ascent from the ferry to the plain. We now began to meet the wounded men, another sight I was unacquainted with, some with broken arms, some with broken legs, and some with broken heads. The sight of these a little daunted me, and made me think of home, but the sight and thought vanished together. We marched a short distance, when we halted to refresh ourselves. Whether we had any other victuals besides the hard bread I do not remember, but I remember my gnawing at them; they were hard enough to break the teeth of a rat. One of the soldiers complaining of thirst to his officer—"Look at that man," said he, pointing to me, "he is not thirsty, I will warrant it." I felt a little elevated to be styled a man. [Martin was barely sixteen.]

While resting here, which was not more than twenty minutes or half an hour, the American and British were warmly engaged within sight of us. What were the feelings of most or all the young soldiers at this time, I know not, but I know what mine were. But let mine or theirs be what they might, I saw a lieutenant who appeared to have feelings not very enviable; whether he was actuated by fear or the canteen, I cannot determine now. I thought it fear at the time, for he ran around the men of his company, sniveling and blubbering, praying each one if he had aught against him, or if he had injured anyone that they would forgive him, declaring at the same time that he, for his part, forgave them if they had offended him, and I gave him full credit for his assertion; for had he been at the gallows with a halter about his neck, he could not have shown more fear or penitence. A fine soldier you are, thought I, a fine officer, an exemplary man for young soldiers! I would have then suffered anything short of death rather than have made such an exhibition of myself; but as the poet says—Fear does things so like a witch,/'Tis hard to distinguish which is which.

The officers of the new levies wore cockades of different colors to distinguish them from the standing forces, as they were called; the field officers wore red, the captains white, and the subaltern officers green. While we were resting here our lieutenant colonel and major (our colonel not being with us) took their cockades from their hats; being asked the reason, the lieutenant colonel replied that he was willing to risk his life in the cause of his country, but unwilling to stand a particular mark for the enemy to fire at. He was a fine officer and a brave soldier.

We were soon called upon to fall in and proceed. . . . We overtook a small party of the artillery here, dragging a heavy twelve-pounder upon a field carriage, sinking halfway to the naves in the sandy soil. They plead hard for some of us to assist them to get on their piece; our officers, however, paid no attention to their entreaties, but pressed forward towards a creek, where a large party of Americans and British were engaged. By the time we arrived the enemy had driven our men into the creek, or rather millpond (the tide being up), where such as could swim got across; those that could not swim, and could not procure anything to buoy them up, sunk. The British, having several fieldpieces stationed by a brick house, were pouring the canister and grape upon the Americans like a shower of hail. They would doubtless have done them more damage than they did, but for the twelve-pounder mentioned above; the men, having gotten it within sufficient distance to reach them, and opening fire upon them, soon obliged them to shift their quarters. There was in this action a regiment of Maryland troops (volunteers), all young gentlemen. When they came out of the water and mud to us, looking like water rats, it was a truly pitiful sight. Many of them were killed in the pond, and more were drowned. Some of us went into the water after the fall of the tide, and took out a number of corpses and a great many arms that were sunk in the pond and creek.

Our regiment lay on the ground we then occupied the following night. The next day, in the afternoon, we had a considerable tight scratch with about an equal number of the British, which began rather unexpectedly, and a little whimsically. A few of our men (I mean our regiment) went over the creek upon business that usually employed us, that is, in search of something to eat. There was a field of Indian corn at a short distance from the creek, with several cocks of hay about halfway from the creek to the cornfield; the men proposed to get some of the corn, or anything else that was eatable. When they got up with the haycocks, they were fired upon by an equal number of the British, from the cornfield; our people took to the hay, and the others to the fence, where they exchanged a number of shots at each other, neither side inclining to give back. A number, say forty or fifty more of our men, went over and drove the British from the fence; they were by this time reinforced in their turn, and drove us back. The two parties thus kept alternatively reinforcing until we had the most of our regiment in the action. After the officers came to command, the English were soon routed from the place, but we dare not follow them for fear of falling into some snare, as the whole British army was in the vicinity of us; I do not recollect that we had anyone killed outright, but we had several severely wounded, and some, I believe, mortally.

Our regiment was alone, no other troops being near where we were lying. We were upon a rising ground, covered with a young growth of trees; we felled a fence of trees around us to prevent the approach of the enemy's horses. We lay there a day longer. In the latter part of the afternoon there fell a very heavy shower of rain which wet us to the skin and much damaged our ammunition. . . . Just at dusk, I, with one or two others of our company, went off to a barn, about half a mile distant, with intent to get some straw to lodge upon, the ground and leaves being drenched in water, and we as wet as they. It was quite dark in the barn, and while I was fumbling about the floor someone called to me from the top of the mow, inquiring where I was from. I told him. He asked me if we had not had an engagement there, having heard us discharge our guns. I told him. . . . I then heard several others, as it appeared, speaking on the mow. Poor fellows, they had better have been at their posts than skulking in a barn on account of a little wet, for I have not the least doubt that the British had possession of their mortal parts before the noon of the next day.

I could not find any straw, but I found some wheat in the sheaf, standing by the side of the floor; I took a sheaf or two and returned as fast as I could to the regiment. When I arrived the men were all paraded to march off the ground; I left my wheat, seized my musket, and fell in to the ranks. We were strictly enjoined not to speak, or even cough, while upon the march. All orders were given from officer to officer and communicated to the men in whispers. What such secrecy could mean we could not divine. We marched off in the same way that we had come to the island, forming various conjectures among ourselves as to our destination. Some were of opinion that we were to endeavor to get on the flank, or in the rear of the enemy. Others, that we were going up the East River to attack them in that quarter; but none, it seems, knew the right of the matter. We marched on, however, until we arrived at the ferry, where we immediately embarked on board the batteaux and were conveyed safely to New York, where we landed about three o'clock in the morning, nothing against our inclinations.

✳

So much for Private Martin's part in the Battle of Long Island. Though not the disaster it might have been had Howe pressed home his advantage, the battle was a major defeat for Washington. True, his luck stayed with him when a heavy fog came down on the East River and he was able to evacuate his troops from Brooklyn under the noses of the British; it also helped that not a single British warship was patrolling the ferry from Brooklyn. ("General Howe is either our friend, or no general," wrote Israel Putnam. "He had our whole army in his power . . . and yet suffered us to escape without the least interruption.") Still, American losses were heavy. "We lost in the late engagement 54 Killed, all of them of the Light Infantry, and about 140 Wounded, most of them very slightly," wrote Ambrose Serle. "The Rebels lost upwards of 3,400 men, killed, wounded & taken prisoners. Of these last we have so many that we are perplexed where to confine them."

From behind his desk in Philadelphia, where he headed the Board of War, John Adams offered his thoughts on how the war should be conducted. Though busy, he had managed to find time to continue to read extensively on military matters, especially in the classics, and was able to cite precedents from ancient times as needed. In the case of regiments that broke and fled, he recommended that "the good old Roman fashion of Decimation should be introduced. The Legion which ran away had the name of every Man in it put into a Box, and then drawn out, and every tenth Man was put to death. The terror of this Uncertainty, whose Lot it would be to die, restrained the whole in time of danger from indulging their fears." If any officer were guilty of "shameful cowardice . . . I sincerely hope he will be punished with death." And as for generals, though none were mentioned by name, if any displayed "Marks of Negligence, Indolence, Presumption, and Incapacity" or allowed themselves "to be surprized by an Enemy just under his nose, in open day," then they were guilty of "a crime of so capital a nature as to admit neither Alleviation nor

Pardon," and the appropriate punishment, again according to the classics, was to be "nailed to Gibbets alive." In fact, the situation was so alarming that were it not for his health—"a treacherous, shattered Constitution"—Adams was "so vexed, sometimes as almost to make Interest to be a Collonel myself." Instead, "Some time in the month of October, 1776 . . . worn down with continual Application, through all the heats of a Summer in Philadelphia, anxious for the State of my family and desirous of conferring with my Constituents . . . I asked leave of Congress to be absent, which they readily granted."

Having made the mistake of taking on a much better disciplined army, commanded by more experienced generals, in just the kind of battle they were used to, Washington proceeded to blunder again, this time by not immediately evacuating New York. It was a political as much as a strategic decision, for he must have known that despite all the earthworks and trenches, the city was impossible to defend: the Royal Navy controlled the Hudson and East Rivers, and could either pulverize the town with its cannon or starve it into surrender.

As a consequence of this decision, two weeks after the Battle of Long Island, Private Martin and his regiment found themselves stationed several miles north of the city, in the farming country around Turtle Bay, where the fields sloped down to the East River. Their job was to repel any attempted landing by the British, also to guard a warehouse containing a supply of flour; some of this they cooked and ate and some they stole "to exchange with the inhabitants for milk and such small matters as we could get for it." But this easy life did not last long.

One evening while lying here, we heard a heavy cannonade at the city, and before dark saw four of the enemy's ships that had passed the town and were coming up the East River. They anchored just below us [at Kip's Bay]. These ships were the *Roebuck* of forty-four; the *Rose* of thirty-two; and another, the name of which I have forgotten. Half of our regiment was sent off under the command of our major to man something that were called "lines," although they were nothing more than a ditch dug along on the bank of the river with the dirt thrown out towards the water. They stayed in these lines during the night and returned to the camp in the morning unmolested.

The other half of the regiment went the next night under the command of the lieutenant colonel upon the like errand. We arrived at the lines about dark and were ordered to leave our packs in a copse wood under a guard and go into the lines without them. What was the cause of this piece of wise policy I never knew, but I knew the effects of it, which was that I never saw my knapsack from that day to this, nor did any of the rest of our party unless they came across them by accident in our retreat. We "manned the lines" and lay quite as unmolested during the whole night as Samson did the half of his in the city of Gaza. . . . We had a chain of sentinels quite up the river, for four or five miles in length. At an interval of every half hour they passed the watchword to each other, "All is well." I heard the British on board their shipping answer, "We will alter your tune before tomorrow night." And they were as good as their word for once.

It was quite a dark night, and at daybreak the first thing that saluted our eyes was all four ships at anchor with springs upon their cables and within musket shot of us. The *Phoenix* lying a little quartering and her stern towards me, I could read her name as distinctly as though I had been directly under her stern. What is the meaning of all this, thought I, what is coming forward now? They appeared to be very busy on shipboard, but we lay still and showed our good breeding by not interfering with them, as they were strangers, and we knew not but that they were bashful withal. As soon as it was fairly light, we saw their boats coming out of a creek or cove on the Long Island side of the water, filled with British soldiers. When they came to the edge of the tide, they formed their boats in line. They continued to augment their forces from the island until they appeared like a large clover field in full bloom. . . .

We lay very quiet in our ditch waiting their motions, till the sun was an hour or two high. We heard a cannonade at the city, but our attention was drawn toward our own guests. But they being a little dilatory in their operations, I stepped into an old warehouse which stood close by me with the door open inviting me in and sat down upon a stool. The floor was strewed with papers which had in some former period been used in the concerns of the house but were then lying in "woeful confusion." I was very demurely perusing these papers when all of a sudden there came such a peal of thunder from the British shipping that I thought my head would go with the sound. I made a frog's leap for the ditch and lay as still as I possibly could and began to consider which part of my carcass was to go first. The British played their parts well; indeed they had nothing to hinder them. We kept the lines until they were almost leveled upon us, when our officers, seeing we could make no resistance, and no orders coming from any superior officer, and that we must soon be entirely exposed to the rake of their guns, gave the order to leave the lines.

In retreating we had to cross a level, clear spot of ground forty or fifty rods wide, exposed to the whole of the enemy's fire, and they gave it to us in prime order. The grapeshot and langrage [canister shot] flew merrily, which served to quicken our motions. When I had gotten a little out of the reach of their combustibles, I found myself in company with one who was a neighbor of mine when at home and one other man belonging to our regiment. Where the rest of them were I knew not. We went into a house by the highway in which were two women and some small children, all crying most bitterly. We asked the women if they had spirits in the house. They placed a case bottle of rum upon the table and bid us help ourselves. We each of us drank a glass and bidding them good-by betook ourselves to the highway again.

We had not gone far before we saw a party of men, apparently hurrying on in the same direction with ourselves. We endeavored hard to overtake them, but on approaching them we found that they were not of our way of thinking: they were Hessians. We immediately altered our course and took the main road leading to King's Bridge. We had not long been on this road before we saw another party, just ahead of us, whom we knew to be Americans. Just as we overtook these, they were fired upon by a party of British from a cornfield and all was immediately in confusion again. I believe the enemy's party was small, but our people were all militia, and the demons of fear and disorder seemed to take full possession of all and everything on that day. When I came to the spot where the militia were fired upon, the ground was literally covered with arms, knapsacks, staves, coats, hats, and flasks. . . .

We had to advance slowly, for my comrade having been some time unwell was now so overcome by heat, hunger, and fatigue that he became suddenly and violently sick. I took his musket and endeavored to encourage him on. He was, as I before observed, a nigh neighbor of mine when at home and I was loath to leave him behind, although I was anxious to find the main part of the regiment if possible before night, for I thought that that part of it which was not in the lines was in a body somewhere. We soon came in sight of a large party of Americans ahead of us who appeared to have come into this road by some other route. We were within sight of them when they were fired upon by another party of the enemy. They returned but a very few shots and then scampered off as fast as their legs would carry them. When we came to the ground they had occupied, the same display of lumber presented itself as at the other place. We here found a wounded man and some of his comrades endeavoring to get him off. I stopped to assist them in constructing a sort of litter to lay him upon, when my sick companion growing impatient moved on, and as soon as we had placed the wounded man upon the litter, I followed him.

While I was here, one or two of our regiment came up and we went on together. We had proceeded but a short distance, however, before we found our retreat cut off by a party of the enemy stretched across the island. I immediately quitted the road and went into the fields, where there happened to be a small spot of boggy land covered with low bushes and weeds. Into these I ran and, squatting down, concealed myself from their sight. Several of the British came so near to me that I could see the buttons on their clothes. They, however, soon withdrew and left the coast clear for me again. I then came out of my covert and went on, but what had become of my sick comrade or the rest of my companions I knew not. I still kept the sick man's musket. I was unwilling to leave it, for it was his own property and I knew he valued it highly and I had a great esteem for him. I had indeed enough to do to take care of my own concerns; it was exceeding hot weather, and I was faint, having slept but very little the preceding night, nor had I eaten a mouthful of victuals for more than twenty-four hours.

I waddled on as well and as fast as I could, and soon came up with a number of men at a small brook, where they had stopped to drink and rest themselves a few moments. Just as I arrived, a man had lain down to drink at the brook, and as he did not rise very soon, one of the company observed that he would kill himself with drinking, upon which another, touching him without his appearing to notice it, said he had already killed himself, which was the case. Leaving them, I went on again and directly came to a foul place in the road, where the soldiers had taken down the fence to pass into the fields. I passed across the corner of one field and through a gap in a cross fence into another. Here I found a number of men resting under the trees and bushes in the fences. Almost the first I saw, after passing the gap in the fence, was my sick friend. I was exceeding glad to find him, for I had but little hope of ever seeing him again. He was sitting near the fence with his head between his knees. I tapped him upon the shoulder and asked him to get up and go along with me. "No," said he, at the same time regarding me with a most pitiful look, "I must die here." I endeavored to argue the case with him, but all to no purpose; he insisted upon dying there. I told him he should not die there nor anywhere else that day if I could help it, and at length with more persuasions and some force, I succeeded in getting him on his feet again and to moving on.

There happened just at this instant a considerable shower of rain, which wet us all to the skin, being very thinly clad. We, however, continued to move forward, although but slowly. After proceeding about half a mile we came to a place where our people had begun to make a stand. A number, say two or three hundred, had collected here, having been stopped by the artillery officers; they had two or three fieldpieces fixed and fitted for action, in case the British came on, which was momentarily expected. I and my companions (for I had found another of our company when I found my sick man) were stopped here, a sentinel being placed in the road to prevent our going any further. I felt very much chagrined to be thus hindered from proceeding, as I felt confident that our regiment or some considerable part of it was not far ahead, unless they had been more unlucky than I had. I remonstrated with the officer who detained us. I told him that our regiment was just ahead. He asked me how I knew that. I could not tell him, but I told him I had a sick man with me who was wet and would die if exposed all night to the damp and cold air, hoping by this to move his compassion, but it would not do. He was inexorable. I shall not soon forget the answer he gave me when I made the last-mentioned observation respecting the sick man. "Well," said he, "if he dies the country will be rid of one who can do it no good." Pretty fellow! thought I, a very compassionate gentleman! When a man has got his bane in his country's cause, let him die like an old horse or dog, because he can do no more! The only wish I would wish such men would be to let them have exactly the same treatment which they would give to others.

I saw but little chance of escaping from this very humane gentleman by fair means, so I told my two comrades to stick by me and keep together and we would get from them by some means or other during the evening. It was now almost sundown and the air quite chilly after the shower, and we were as wet as water could make us. I was really afraid my sick man would die in earnest. I had not stayed there long after this entertaining dialogue with my obliging friend, the officer, waiting for an opportunity to escape, before one offered. There came to the sentinel I suppose an old acquaintance of his, with a canteen containing some sort of spirits. After drinking himself, he gave it to the sentinel, who took a large pull upon it. They then fell into conversation together, but soon taking a hare from the same hound, it put them into quite "a talkative mood." I kept my eyes upon them and when I thought I saw a chance of getting from them, I gave my companions a wink and we passed by the sentinel without his noticing us at all. A walk of a very few rods concealed us from his view by a turn in the road and some bushes, and thus we escaped from prison, for we thought we were hardly dealt by to be confined by those whom we took to be our friends, after having labored so hard to escape being made prisoners by the common enemy.

We went on a little distance when we overtook another man belonging to our company. He had just been refreshing himself with some bread and dry salt fish and was putting "the fragments" into his knapsack. I longed for a bite, but I felt too bashful to ask him and he was too thoughtless or stingy to offer it. We still proceeded, but had not gone far when we came up with the regiment, resting themselves on the "cold ground" after the fatigues of the day. Our company all appeared to rejoice to see us, thinking we were killed or prisoners. I was sincerely glad to see them, for I was once more among friends or at least acquaintances. Several of the regiment were missing, among whom was our major. He was a fine man and his loss was much regretted by the men of the regiment. We were the last who came up; all the others who were missing were either killed or taken prisoners. And here ends the Kip's Bay affair. . . .

Luckily for Martin and his regiment, General Sir William Howe had once again disregarded the excellent advice so irritatingly offered by his second in command, Sir Henry Clinton. Just as he had done on the eve of Bunker Hill, when he urged landing a force on Charlestown Neck and thus cutting off the Americans' only line of retreat, so on the eve of the present battle Clinton had recommended sending ships up the Harlem River and seizing or destroying King's Bridge, the only route off Manhattan Island other than the ferries. But for reasons known only to himself, Howe wouldn't. Nor did he give orders for the redcoats who landed so successfully at Kip's Bay to move quickly across the island and cut off General Putnam and the large force that had lingered in the city too long. Thanks to a forced march north on a road bordering the Hudson River, Putnam was able to escape.

Though there was some grumbling at these missed opportunities, things had gone so well for them that morale among the British was high as they took possession of New York. "Nothing could equal the Expressions of Joy, shewn by the Inhabitants, upon the arrival of the King's officers among them," wrote Ambrose Serle. "They even carried some of them upon their Shoulders about the Streets, and behaved in all respects, women as well as Men, like overjoyed Bedlamites. One thing is worth remarking; a Woman pulled down the Rebel Standard upon the Fort, and a Woman hoisted up in its Stead His Majesty's Flag, after trampling the other under foot with the most contemptuous Indignation."

But barely a week later, calamity struck. "Yesterday (September 21), there was a terrible fire in New York," reported a Loyalist paper. "It broke out first in the most southerly part of the city, near White Hall, and was discovered between twelve and one o'clock in the morning, the wind blowing very fresh from the south, and the weather exceeding dry. The rebel army having carried off all the bells of the city, the alarm could not be speedily communicated, and very few of the citizens were in town, most of them being driven out by the calamities of war."

Another witness to the fire was Frederick Mackenzie, now a captain and adjutant of the Royal Welch Fusiliers, who had earlier recorded in his diary the events leading up to Lexington and Concord. Mackenzie, who was quartered well out of town, was roused in the night by a sentry, and

✳

on going to the window I observed an immense Column of fire & smoke . . . I dressed myself immediately and ran into town, a distance of two miles, but when I got there the fire had got to such a head there seemed to be no hopes of stopping it, and those who were present did little more than look on and lament the misfortune. As soon as buckets & Water could be got, the Seamen and the troops, assisted by some of the Inhabitants, did what they could to arrest its progress, but the fresh wind, and the combustible nature of the materials of which almost all the houses were built, rendered all their efforts vain.

From a variety of circumstances which occurred, it is beyond doubt that the town was designedly set on fire, either by some of those fellows who concealed themselves in it since the 15th Instant, or by some Villains left behind for the purpose. Some of them were caught by the Soldiers in the very act of setting fire to the inside of empty houses at a distance from the fire; many were detected with matches and combustibles under their Clothes, and combustibles were found in several houses. One villain who abused and cut a woman employed in bringing water to the Engines, and who was found cutting the handles of the fire buckets, was hung up by the heels on the spot by the Seamen. One or two others who were found in houses with fire-brands in their hands were put to death by the enraged Soldiery and thrown into the flames. There is no doubt however that the flames were communicated to several houses by means of burning flakes of the Shingles, which being light, were carried by the wind to some distance and falling on the roofs of houses covered with Shingles (which is most generally the case at New York), and whose Inhabitants were either absent or inattentive, kindled the fire anew. The Trinity Church, a very handsome, ancient building, was perceived to be on fire long before the fire reached the adjacent houses, and as it stood at some distance from any house, little doubt remained that it was set on fire willfully.

During the time the Rebels were in possession of the town, many of them were heard to say they would burn it, sooner than it should become a nest for Tories, and several Inhabitants who were most violently attached to the Rebel cause have been heard to declare that they would set fire to their own houses sooner than they should be occupied by the King's troops.

The appearance of the Trinity Church when completely in flames was a very grand sight, for the Spire being entirely framed of wood and covered with Shingles, a lofty Pyramid of fire appeared, and as soon as the Shingles were burnt away the frame appeared with every separate piece of timber burning, until the principal timbers were burnt through, when the whole fell with a great noise.

⁕

An account in the Loyalist newspaper, *New York Museum,* agrees that the fire was a "preconcerted, deliberate scheme . . . not inferior to the Gunpowder Plot," and there were many stories of arsonists "discovered with large bundles of matches dipped in rosin and brimstone. A New England man, who had a captain's commission under the Continental Congress, and in their service, was seized, having these dreadful implements of ruin. On being searched, the sum of five hundred pounds was found upon him." All in all, four hundred and ninety three houses and many other buildings were destroyed.

Meanwhile, Washington withdrew most of his forces northward into Westchester County, but leaving a large garrison in the fort that he had, perhaps mistakenly, allowed to be named in his honor. Howe followed in due course, taking his troops by water from lower Manhattan and landing them at Throg's Neck; this entailed passing through the narrow passage called Hell-gate, where the waters of the East River and the Sound converged violently, causing whirlpools and "a vast boiling motion." Sharp rocks above and below the water (since dynamited away) compounded the danger. In his memoirs, Sergeant Lamb, also of the Welch Fusiliers, has this:

"The following Anecdote is related of a black Man, the pilot of the *Experiment* of 50 guns, who took her through the passage, to the great astonishment of Lord Howe. At the moment of the greatest danger, Sir James Wallace, the Captain, gave some orders on the quarter-deck which in Mungo's opinion interfered with the duties of his own office. Advancing therefore to Sir James, and gently tapping him on the shoulder, 'Massa,' said he, 'you no speak here!' The Captain felt the full force of the brave fellow's remonstrance; and to the extreme surprise of all those acquainted with the difficulty of navigating a ship through Hell-gate, the Negro carried the *Experiment* safely through. "So highly did his Lordship [Admiral Howe] appreciate the skill and adventurous spirit of the Negro pilot, that he settled on him an annuity of £50 for life." Once his forces were safely landed, General Howe moved north and won another non-decisive victory over Washington at White Plains.

Back in Manhattan Captain Mackenzie was keeping his diary up to date.

22nd Sept. A person named Nathaniel Hales, a Lieutenant in the Rebel Army, and a native of Connecticut, was apprehended as a Spy last night upon Long Island; and having this day made a full and free confession to the Commander in Chief of his being employed by Mr. Washington in that capacity, he was hanged at 11 o'Clock in front of the Park of Artillery. He was about 24 years of age, and had been educated at the College of Newhaven in Connecticut. He behaved with great composure and resolution, saying he thought it the duty of every good officer to obey any orders given him by his Commander in Chief; and desired the Spectators to be at all times prepared to meet death in whatever shape it might appear.

(Like British Major André, who was also to be hanged as a spy, Hale was wearing civilian clothes when arrested, so no one questioned his sentence. Some have doubted whether he did in fact make his famous statement, paraphrased from Addison's play, *Cato*, regretting that he had but one life to lose for his country. Hale spent his last night as the prisoner-guest of Captain Montresor, the man who had saved the severed head of the king's statue from desecration.)

✷

3rd November. General Knyphausen with Six Hessian Battalions which had taken post on the heights near Kingsbridge lately, passed over to this Island yesterday, without a Shot being fired at him, and encamped on the high grounds near Fort Washington. This movement completely cuts off all communication between the Rebel troops on this Island, and those under Gen. Washington.

The first object at present is the reduction of Fort Washington, and thereby the complete possession of this Island: after which Gen. Howe will probably detach a considerable part of the Army to the Southward, where operations may be carried on with advantage during the winter, or else penetrate into Jersey, and endeavor to enlarge the quarters of the Army in a Province abounding with Provisions, fuel, and other necessary supplies. The extension of our quarters will also give the Loyalists an opportunity of declaring themselves, and circumscribe the resources of the Enemy.

A man named Diamond, who says he was Ensign and Adjutant, and acted as Major of brigade in the Rebel Army, deserted yesterday from their advanced post. He says the Rebels remaining on this Island amount to about 2,000 men, who, if they are obliged to abandon their advanced works, are to retire into Fort Washington and defend it to the last extremity, having therein two Months' provisions, many Cannon, and plenty of Ammunition. He says there are great dissensions in the Rebel Army, everybody finding fault with the mode of proceeding, and the inferior officers, even Ensigns, insisting that, in such a cause, every man has a right to assist in Council, and to give his opinion. . . . The people from the Southern Colonies declare they will not go into New England, and the others that they will not march to the Southward. If this account is true in any degree, they must soon go to pieces.

5th Nov. The Rebel Army must suffer greatly as soon as the severe weather sets in for want of proper Clothing, of which they are now in the greatest need. It is a fact that many of the Rebels who were killed in the late affairs were without shoes or Stockings, & several were observed to have only linen drawers on, with a Rifle or Hunting shirt, without any proper shirt or Waistcoat. They are also in great want of blankets. The weather during the former part of the Campaign has been so very favorable that they did not feel the want of those things, but in less than a month they must suffer extremely if not supplied with them. Under all the disadvantages of want of confidence, clothing, and good winter quarters, and constantly harassed by a victorious and incensed Army, it will be astonishing if they keep together 'till Christmas.

※

Ten days later Fort Washington surrendered, the British and Hessian troops "having got close up to the Fort, the Rebels, in the momentary expectation of being Stormed, and finding they were so much crowded in the Fort that they could not possibly defend it, beat their Drums, and soon after sent out to desire terms." They were promised their lives and allowed to keep their baggage, "and about 4 o'Clock they marched out, amounting in all to about 2,300 men. They left their Arms & accoutrements in the Fort, and were sent under the Escort of the 10th & 52nd Regiments to Haerlem."

On November 17 Mackenzie, after looking over the site, entered these reflections in his diary:

※

There would have been no difficulty in Storming it; and if General Howe, after having summoned it the 15th, had not given orders that the troops were only to drive the Rebels into the Fort, there is no doubt they (but especially the Hessians, who were extremely irritated at having lost a good many men in the attack) would have gone on, and taken it by assault. The Carnage would then have been dreadful, for the Rebels were so numerous they had not room to defend themselves with effect, and so frightened they had not the power. Indeed after having rejected the offers made them on the 15th, they had no right to expect the mild treatment they met with: but in this instance, as well as in every other since the commencement of the Rebellion, the British humanity has been conspicuous.

Many are of opinion that if Gen. Howe had treated the Garrison of Fort Washington with the severity which might have been inflicted upon them by the laws of War, it would have struck such a panic through the Continent, as would have prevented the Congress from ever being able to raise another Army. They say we act with too much lenity and humanity towards the Rebels, and that tho' it is praisewor-thy, and might be supposed to be the most likely means of bringing them back to a sense of their duty, yet it will prove bad policy in the end: for they now oppose us as long as they have the power, and when they fall into our hands, instead of being treated as Rebels taken in Arms against their Sovereign, they find they have nothing more to dread than the common sufferings of prisoners of war. Altho' the humanity hitherto shewn to the Rebels has not had the desired effect, I hope it may in the end; and I am of opinion it is right to treat our Enemies as if they might one day become our friends.

BRITISH NEW YORK

Among those taken prisoner at Fort Washington was Alexander Graydon, a junior officer in a silk-stocking Philadelphia militia company, whose mother ran a high-class boardinghouse in that city. Although now a captive, Graydon seems to have had more than his share of good luck: Not only had the fort been allowed to surrender rather than be taken by storm, but the armed guard taking him and other prisoners to the city was soon converted into a protective escort. This happened when the prisoners were "beset by a parcel of soldiers' trulls" who gaped at them and demanded to know, "Which is Washington? Which is Washington?" and crowded so close that "the guard was obliged to exert itself to keep them off. Some of them assailed us with volleys of Billingsgate [foul language]; and Colonel Maxwell, who rode alongside of us

. . . had enough to do to silence one of them, calling out repeatedly: 'Away with that woman! Take her away! Knock her down, the
bitch! Knock her down!'"

On entering the city, the officers were separated from the men
and taken into a church to sign their parole, while a crowd of spectators pressed in to watch. Again, Graydon was lucky:

A portly, well-looking, middle-aged non-commissioned officer of the
42nd Regiment approached me, observing in a low voice that he was sure
he had seen me before: "Was not my name – -?" I answered in the affirmative. "I thought so," said he. "I have often seen you at your mother's
in Philadelphia; and though you were then but a boy, I clearly retrace
your features. As you are probably in want of money, may I beg you to
accept of this?" slipping into my hand a dollar. I objected to taking it,
as I might never have an opportunity of repaying him. "No matter if
you have not," said he. "It is but a trifle, but such as it is, you cannot
oblige me more than by accepting it." I accordingly put it in my pocket,
the confusion and bustle of the scene preventing my taking measures
for ascertaining the means of seeing him again; and having never afterwards met with him, I am still indebted to this amount, together with
the gratitude that is inseparable from it, to this worthy, generous man.

Along with this dollar, Graydon also "knew that I had an
excellent banker in Philadelphia," i.e., his mother, and so took
lodgings near the Holy Ground with a Mrs. Carroll who was
"under the protection of General Robertson, commandant of the
town. . . . She passed for the particular favorite of this gentleman;
and was sufficiently young and buxom to give probability to the
imputation. She played her cards with much address, and bent
her politics, if she had any, to her interest."

His luck still holding, Graydon was able to retrieve the baggage
that he had had with him at Fort Washington, containing not only his

"interesting correspondence" with a young lady in Philadelphia but his best suit of regimentals. His fellow lodgers, also officers on parole, advised him not to wear them outdoors as doing so would invite abuse, but Graydon ignored them, put on his finery, and "sallied forth alone, and walked past the coffee shop, down to the battery. Finding the gateway open, I entered it, and traversing it to its extremity, I strolled back again; almost every sentinel, to my great surprise, I must confess, handling [presenting] his arms to me as I passed."

According to the rules of war as practiced by both sides, captured officers were allowed out on parole, first giving their word of honor not to go beyond certain limits, not to speak ill of their captors, nor try to rejoin their own forces unless officially exchanged. Perhaps this was what Captain Mackenzie had in mind when in his musings on "British humanity" he had commented that "instead of being treated as Rebels taken in arms against their Sovereign," American prisoners "find they have nothing more to dread than the common sufferings of prisoners of war." But had he looked about him within the quite limited confines of the city, it would have been hard not to witness firsthand the "common sufferings" of the ordinary soldier. For that, there is the testimony of Ethan Allen, who with his Green Mountain Boys had captured Fort Ticonderoga in the early days of the war, but had been taken prisoner during the unsuccessful attack on Montreal. As he explained in his autobiographical *A Narration of Colonel Ethan Allen's Captivity,* he had then been sent from Canada to England to be put on public display, but by the winter of 1776 he had been paroled back to America. Here he found that "the private soldiers who were brought to New York were crowded into churches, and environed with slavish Hessian guards," and so harshly treated that they were "dying by hundreds."

✵

I have gone into the churches, and seen sundry of the prisoners in the agonies of death, in consequence of very hunger, and others speechless and near death, biting pieces of [wood] chips; others pleading for God's sake, for something to eat, and at the same time shivering with the cold. Hollow groans saluted my ears, and despair seemed to be imprinted on every of their countenances. The filth of these churches (in consequence of the fluxes) was almost beyond description. The floors were covered with excrements. I have carefully sought to direct my footsteps so as to avoid it, but could not. They would beg for God's sake for one copper, or morsel of bread. I have seen in one of these churches seven dead at the same time, lying among the excrements of their bodies.

It was a common practice with the enemy to convey the dead from these filthy places in carts, to be slightly buried, and I have seen whole gangs of Tories making derision, and exulting over the dead, saying, "There goes another load of damned rebels!" I have observed the British soldiers to be full of their blackguard jokes and vaunting on these occasions, but they appeared to me less malignant than the Tories.

Also in New York at this time was a young Englishman named Nicholas Cresswell. Like Alexander Graydon, he was a parolee, though in his case the parole had been given to a Committee of Safety in Virginia. Strictly speaking, his being in New York meant that Cresswell had broken his word of honor, but his treatment in Virginia had been so harsh that he felt justified in escaping. There could, however, be no question of his enlisting in the British army, much though he would have liked to, and he now had no choice but to return home to Derbyshire. This was a bleak prospect for the normally cheerful Cresswell, for he had come to this country with high hopes of making a quick and easy fortune and was now returning to a narrow life as the son of a gentleman farmer, with nothing to show for his adventure except an interesting diary and a fistful of notes to creditors for money borrowed in his father's name. Staying in New York was not pleasant either. Following the fire and the influx of refugees, rents and other prices had gone way up; he had few friends and nothing to do; and he was dismayed by the condition of "this once flourishing, opulent, and happy city, one third part of it now in ruins."

When the Rebels were driven out of it in September last by the Royal Army, they formed a hellish design, burnt it down to the ground, and then laid the blame upon our troops. They so far succeeded as to burn about one third, the most beautiful and valuable part of the City. If one was to judge from appearances, they would suppose the Rebels had intended to dispute every inch of ground with our troops. In every street they have made ditches and barricades, every little eminence about the town is fortified, but they basely and cowardly deserted them all as soon as ever our people got ashore. Now all these Ditches and fortified places are full of stagnate water, damaged sour Crout and filth of every kind. Noisome vapours arise from the mud left in the docks and slips at low water, and unwholesome smells are occasioned by such a number of people being crowded together in so small a compass almost like herrings in a barrel, most of them very dirty and not a small number sick of some disease, the Itch, Pox, Fever, or Flux, so that altogether there is a complication of stinks enough to drive a person whose sense of smelling was very delicate and his lungs of the finest contexture, into a consumption in the space of twenty-four hours. If any author had an inclination to write a treatise upon stinks and ill smells, he never could meet with more subject matter than in New York.

To economize, Cresswell lived onboard his ship while waiting for it to sail, but was quick to go on shore if invited to a party, as happened when his friend Furneval

came on board and insisted upon me going with him to spend the evening along with some gentlemen of the Navy and Army, at the Hull Tavern, where we stayed till about 12 o'clock. . . . As I went down St. John's Street, I heard something floundering in the ditch. I stopped and by the light of the moon could perceive something like a human being stirred the mud a little. I plunged in and found it to be a man, whom I hauled to the shore quite insensible. I pulled the dirt out of his mouth with my fingers, and in a little time I could perceive him make a noise. I then went to the next sentry, who happened to be a Hessian. I told him the situation of the man below in the Street, but he did not understand English.

After we had sputtered at one another for some time, the Sergeant of the Guard came who could speak English. He very civilly called a light and went with me to the man who by this time could speak, and told us that he had been insulted by a Girl of the Town and had been imprudent enough to treat her rather indelicately. One of her bullies had cut him in several places in the head, knocked him down, and dragged him into the ditch. He desired that we would help him to his lodgings in Queen Street, which the Hessian Sergeant and I did. The bruises he had received and the muddy stinking water he had swallowed made him very ill. I went as soon as we had got him to bed and called Doctor Smith to him, who immediately let him blood. He appears to be a genteel, well-behaved man, returned me thanks in the most polite terms for saving his life.

Another nocturnal adventure began with the note, "Furneval and I went ashore and spent the evening at Hull Tavern" and continues:

In our return to the Boat, coming by some houses that were burnt down, we heard the cries of a Woman. We searched about and soon, to our great surprise, found a poor Woman in labour, and all alone. She told us she was a soldier's widow and begged we would help her to some assistance. We immediately carried her to the house of a Sadler in the Broadway, whom we raised from his pillow and told him the poor woman's situation. But he absolutely refused to let her stay in his house, declaring that he would not keep a lying-in Hospital for our W – s. However with threats, promises, and the poor Woman declaring that it was impossible for her to be removed, he at length consented that she might lay in a back shop he had. We immediately removed her thither and made her a very poor bed of a Bearskin, a Packsheet, and an old blanket. Furneval went with a Negro boy to see for a Midwife, while I stayed with the woman, for fear of the Sadler turning her out of doors. The poor woman cried out lustily and I was confoundedly afraid of the young one coming before the midwife arrived. The Irish rogue of a Sadler nor the unfeeling jade his wife would not come near us, or offer the poor creature the least assistance, tho' she begged for help in the most pitiful tone I ever heard. I was much afraid that I must have been under the disagreeable necessity of trying my skill in the obstetric way, but in the critical minute Furneval arrived with an old drunken woman he had picked up somewhere or other, and she refused to perform the office without we would give her two Dollars. Furneval gave her one and I another. She immediately fell to work. I am sure the pains of labour must be violent for the poor woman roared out most horridly. I think I hear the sound yet in my ears. However, in about ten minutes she produced a girl which was wrapped in the Mother's apron, with the addition of Furneval's handkerchief and mine, for she had not a single rag prepared for the occasion. We then got some wine, rum, Nutmeg Bread &c. to the amount of two Dollars more, and got the good wife a caudle, which she took without much invitation. In about half an hour she was able to sit up in her miserable bed and returned us her thanks for saving her life, as she said, in the most sincere and moving manner. The D – d unnatural B – h of a Sadler's wife never came near us all the time, but lay in bed cursing the poor woman with the most horrid imprecations.

At about 12 o'clock we left her in good spirits considering her situation. When we came away, I gave her one Dollar and a quarter which is the last and all I have in the world. The poor woman is heartily welcome to it and I am happy that I had it in my power to relieve such real distress. Furneval gave her two Dollars and swears he will stand Godfather to the child. I have no intention of doing myself that honour. . . . This is the first birth I have ever been concerned with, and I hope it will be the last time I shall meet with such a complication of distress. She told us a long story about her virtue and sufferings, but she is an Irish woman and I don't believe half of it. I am confoundedly tired with scribbling about the Girl in the Straw, therefore will give over.

For the rest of the war, New York was to remain in the hands of the British. During these years the population grew rapidly, as citizens returned and refugees came in from the outlying districts. Most of these newcomers were Tories, but many neutrals and moderate Patriots also arrived, driven from their homes by the depredations of marauding bands of partisans who sometimes fought the regular troops and sometimes fought each other, but also spent much of their time settling personal scores and plundering civilians. In New York's so-called Neutral Ground, the region between Manhattan Island and the area well to the north that was firmly under American control, these bands were generally known as the Cowboys, who said they were Tories, and the Skinners, who claimed to be Patriots. Similar gangs operated in the contested parts of Long Island, Connecticut, and New Jersey. Along with the turmoil caused by these irregulars, there was also a general breakdown of law and order. Here are some examples from both sides of the conflict:

From the *New York Journal*, September 8, 1777:

We hear from Poughkeepsie that about a week ago seven Tories were committed to jail there, charged with robbing several houses, and putting families in fear. It is said, when taken, they were all painted and dressed like Indian men, but that five of them proved to be women, three of whom are a mother and two daughters. Thus do the infernal designs of the court of Great Britain assimilate to their own character all those who espouse their cause; not only seducing them to become base, treacherous thieves, robbers, murderers, &c., but divesting them of humanity, and converting them into savages and perfect devils in human shape.

✳

From *Gaine's Mercury*, April 14, 1777:

✳

Some days ago, the daughter of Mr. Jonathan Kniffin, of Rye, in Connecticut, was murdered by a party of rebels near or upon Budd's Neck. She was carrying some clothes to her father in company of two men who had the charge of a herd of cattle. They were fired upon by the rebels from behind a stone wall. The poor young woman received a ball in her head, of which she instantly died. The men escaped unhurt. They plundered her dead body of its clothes, cut one of her fingers off almost in order to take a ring, and left the corpse most indecently exposed in the highway. Such are the advocates of this cursed rebellion!

✳

From the *Military Journal* of Dr. James Thacher, on Tory marauders:

✳

November, 1780. Numerous instances have been related of these miscreants subjecting defenseless persons to cruel tortures, to compel them to deliver up their money, or to disclose the places where it has been secreted. It is not uncommon for them to hang a man by his neck till apparently dead, then restore him, and repeat the experiment, and leave him for dead. . . . A peaceable, unresisting Quaker, of considerable respectability, by the name of Quincy, was visited by several of these vile ruffians; they first demanded his money, and after it was delivered, they suspected he had more concealed, and inflicted on him the most savage cruelties in order to extort it from him. They began with what they call scorching, covering his naked body with hot ashes, and repeating the application till the skin was covered with blisters; after this they resorted to the halter, and hung the poor man on a tree by his neck, then took him down, and repeated it a second, and even a third time, and finally left him almost lifeless.

(Thacher also told this story: "It has been noted that a girl walked seven miles in a torrent of rain to see a man hanged, and returned in tears because the criminal was reprieved.")

From *Connecticut Historical Collections*, 1779:

While the [American] troops lay at Reading, two executions took place; one was a soldier, who was shot for desertion—the other was a Mr. Jones, of Ridgefield, a royalist, who was hung as a spy; both suffered on the same day. These executions took place on Gallows Hill, a mile or more from Putnam's headquarters. The scene which took place at the execution of these men is described as shocking and bloody. The man on whom the duty of hangman devolved left the camp, and on the day of execution could not be found. A couple of boys, about twelve years of age, were ordered by Gen. Putnam to perform the duties of the absconding hangman. The gallows was about twenty feet from the ground. Jones was compelled to ascend the ladder, and the rope around his neck was attached to the cross-beam. Gen. Putnam then ordered Jones to jump from the ladder. "No, General Putnam," said Jones. "I am innocent of the crime laid to my charge. I shall not do it." Putnam then ordered the boys before mentioned to turn the ladder over. These boys were deeply affected with the trying scene; they cried and sobbed loudly, and earnestly entreated to be excused from doing any thing on this distressing occasion. Putnam, drawing his sword, ordered them forward, and compelled them at the sword's point to obey his orders.

The soldier that was shot for desertion was but a youth of 16 or 17 years of age. Three balls were shot through his breast; he fell on his face, but immediately turned over on his back; a soldier then advanced, and putting the muzzle of his gun near the convulsive body of the youth, discharged its contents into his forehead. The body was taken up and put into a coffin; the soldiers had fired their pieces so near that they set the boy's clothes on fire, which continued burning. An officer with a drawn sword stood by, while every soldier of the three brigades, who were out on the occasion, was ordered to march by and look at the mangled remains.

From the testimony of Robert Lawrence in *A Brief Narrative of the Ravages of the British and Hessians at Princeton* concerning two British dragoons who "pretended to a Young Woman that they was Searching for Rebels, and had been Informed that some of them were Secreted in the Barn and desired her to go with them and Show them the most Secret Places there, and She (Knowing that no body was there) to convince them Went to the Barn with them to show them that no body was there. And when they had got her there, one of them Laid hold on her, Strangled her to Prevent her crying out while the other villain Ravisht her, and when he had done he Strangled her Again while the other Brute Repeated the horrid crime Upon her again. She is a Farmer's Daughter but her name with her father's must be kept secret to avoid the Reproach above Mentioned," a reference to an earlier statement that "by a Great Defect in Human Nature that is against both Justice and Reason we Despise these poor Innocent Sufferers in this Brutal Crime even as long as they live."

From *Women of the Revolution*, one of the many versions of the notorious case of Mrs. Hannah Caldwell. This occurred later in the war, when British troops from New York mounted a raid on Elizabethtown, New Jersey, landing just before daylight.

When informed of the enemy's approach, the Rev. Mr. Caldwell put his elder children into a baggage wagon and sent them to some of his friends for protection. Three of the younger ones—Josiah Flint, Elias Boudinot, and Maria, an infant about eight months old—remained with their mother in the house. The nurse also remained, and a little girl named Abigail Lennington, a soldier's daughter, whom Mr. Caldwell had taken into the family. Mr. Caldwell had no fears for the safety of his wife and young family, for he believed it impossible that resentment could be extended to a mother watching over her little ones. He had that morning taken an early breakfast, intending to join the force collecting to oppose the enemy. Having in vain endeavored to persuade his wife to go with him, he returned to make a last effort to induce her to change her determination; but she remained firm. She handed him a cup of coffee, which he drank as he sat on horseback. Seeing the gleam of British arms at a distance, he put spurs to the horse, and in a few moments was out of sight.

Mrs. Caldwell herself felt no alarm. She had hid several articles of value in a bucket and let it down into the well; and had filled her pockets with silver and jewelry. She saw that the house was put in order, and then dressed herself with care, that should the enemy enter her dwelling she might, to use her own expression, "receive them as a lady." She then took the infant in her arms, retired to her chamber, the window of which commanded a view of the road, towards which the end of the house stood, and seated herself upon the bed.

The alarm was given that the soldiers were at hand. But she felt confidence that no one could have the heart to do injury to the helpless inmates of her house. Again and again she said, "They will respect a mother." She had just nursed the infant and given it to the nurse, who was in the room. The girl, Abigail, was standing by the window. A soldier left the road, and crossing a space of ground diagonally to reach the house, came to the window of the room, put his gun close to it, and fired. Two balls entered the breast of Mrs. Caldwell; she fell back on the bed, and in a moment expired.

After the murder, Mrs. Caldwell's dress was cut open, and her pockets were rifled by the soldiers. Her remains were conveyed to a house on the other side of the road; the dwelling was then fired and reduced to ashes with all the furniture. The ruthless soldiers went on in their work of destruction, pillaging and setting fire to the houses, piling beds and clothing in the street and destroying them, till the village was laid in waste.

The Patriot press seized upon this story, instantly canonizing the unfortunate victim. "Never did religion produce a more complete triumph than in this virtuous woman," wrote the *Jersey Journal* a few days later. "Defended by every personal charm; protected by a complete collection of the softest and most charming virtues; guarded by a sucking infant and a large family of depending babes; and who, sitting still in her own house, might thereby claim, at least, life from the enemy in whose power she had put hers—yet she falls by the deliberate aim of an instigated soldier! . . ."

But there was a Tory press too, including *Rivington's Gazette*, published in New York, which ran this account by an unnamed British officer:

Whilst the troops were advancing to Connecticut Farms, the rebels fired out of the houses, agreeable to their usual practice, from which circumstance Mrs. Caldwell had the misfortune to be shot by a random ball. What heightens the singularity of this lady's fate is that, upon inquiry, it appears beyond a doubt that the shot was fired by the rebels themselves, as it entered the side of the house from their direction, and lodged in the wall nearest to the troops, when advancing. The manner in which the rebels aggravate this unfortunate affair in their publications is of a piece with their uniform conduct—plausible, but fallacious; nor is it to be wondered at, if a rebellion which originated in falsehood, is prosecuted with deceit. . . . Miserable indeed is the fate of that country which is the theatre of such a quarrel; and accursed is the man, or the set of men, who, from motives of private lucre or inordinate ambition,

have fanned a flame which, if they were willing, they are now, perhaps, unable to extinguish.

✷

As to the Cowboys and the Skinners, whose guerilla warfare,
attacks on civilians, and general brutality devastated the so-called
Neutral Ground, here is an account by Dr. Timothy Dwight, later to
become president of Yale, but at the time an army chaplain, of their
effect on the "unhappy people" of Westchester County:

✷

Often they were actually plundered; and always were liable to this
calamity. They feared everybody whom they saw, and loved nobody
. . . . To every question they gave such an answer as would please the
inquirer; or, if they despaired of pleasing, such an one as would not
provoke him. Fear was, apparently, the only passion by which they
were animated. The power of volition seemed to have deserted them.
They were not civil, but obsequious; not obliging, but subservient
. . . . Both their countenances and their emotions had lost every trace
of animation and of feeling. Their features were smoothed, not into
serenity, but apathy. . . .

Their houses, in the meantime, were in great measure scenes
of desolation. Their furniture was extensively plundered, or broken
to pieces. The walls, floors, and windows were injured both by violence and decay; and they were not repaired, because they had not
the means of repairing them, and because they were exposed to the
repetition of the same injuries. Their cattle were gone. Their enclo-
sures were burnt . . . their fields were covered with a rank growth of
weeds and wild grass. Amid all this appearance of desolation, nothing
struck my own eye more forcibly than the sight of this great road—
the passage from New York to Boston. Where I had heretofore seen
a continual succession of horses and carriages, and life and bustle
lent a sprightliness to all the environing objects, not a single, solitary
traveler was visible from week to week, or from month to month. The

world was motionless and silent. . . . The very tracks of the carriages were grown over and obliterated; and where they were discernible resembled the faint impression of chariot wheels said to be left on the pavement of Herculaneum. . . .

Equally gloomy are these extracts from the diary of Jemima Condict, eighteen, who lived in Pleasantdale, New Jersey, where her father, a farmer, was also a deacon in the Presbyterian Church. The "bloody flux" was dysentery, but many of the deaths she records were probably due to smallpox, which was epidemic throughout the war and probably caused more deaths than the actual fighting. (It has been argued that Washington's wisest decision as commander in chief was to order the inoculation of the Continental Army while in winter quarters.)

Year 1776 July 23, Did that Distressing Disorder the Blody flux Begin to rage in this neighborhood. Rubin Harrison lost his Son Adonijah the 29. He was the 2nd he had lost of that Name. & August the 6th Then Died John Ogdens Child & was buried on the 8th Day.

August the 16th Then Died Jered Freman. He was taken Sick at newyork among the Sogers & was brought home & Died Soon After Isaac Freman also Lost two of his Children with the Same Distemper. John Freman Lost his Child August the 17th.

August the 25 Died Sam Smith's Child.

August the 29th Amos Burrel Lost his Child. The same month Sam Crane Lost one with fits.

August the 30th then Died Timothy Crane with the Same Distemper. The same Day Died Joseph Peirson's Child.

September the 2nd Did Thomas Freman's Daughter Die.

September the 3rd Did John Freman Depart this life.

September the 4th Jonathan Smith Lost his Child. The same Night Jonathan Condict's Daughter Died.

Both few and evil are the Days of man
They Quick away do Pass
Just Like a hands Breath or a Span
All flesh is Like the Grass.

September the 8th Did Jabez William's Child Die. Abel Freman also has lost one of his children & the widow of John Freman has lost one of hers. John Dod lost one about the Same time.

September 1776. We hear News from our army at Montingue & Several of them we hear is Dead. Since there Departure Benjamin Canfield & Steve Morriss, David Luis Died with the Camp Disorder & William Acorn we hear was killed by the injins; Jabez Freman the Son of the Late Diseast John Freman is Dead, also Silas Heady Died up there with Sickness.

When we are at home we think ourselves secure
But at home or abroad we are never shure
When or what our end is to Be
This in veuing others we Dayly may See.

Tuesday the 9th then Died another of Jonathan Condict's Daughters. Enock Beach has Lost three of his Children in About a fortnight.

Tuesday the 10th then Died Joseph William's wife. She has been this many years Confind with Remutism.

Sunday September the 15th then Departed this Life Grandfather Harrison aged Ninety-three years.

Tho he is old, age will not Save
Him nor others from the grave

Sunday the 15 Day Died Jabes Regs & Sunday the 22 they Buried his third Child; two of them a Son & Daughter was In their Prime cut of in full Bloom of Youth; Tuesday the 24th then Died his Wife also.

By the end of the year, Jemima had listed another twenty-six deaths in Pleasantdale. "Well my Dear friends What a time this is!" she concluded. "A Sickly time & a very Dieing time & the People fleeing before their enemies." As to her own family, Jemima later wrote:

My Dear Mother was taken Sick the 25 of October & was so bad that we Did not much Expect her recovery. It was then I thought I Should Bin Deprived of the great Blessing I had so Long undeservedly enjoyd. My Youngist Brother also Lay Very Bad So that we did not Expect him to Live for many Days. Dear father was taken Sik Quick after, but through the Goodness of God they soon recovered; So that we were in Hopes of having health in our habitation. But at Christmas my Sister was taken Sick & was Extreem Bad. She had a Strange Disorder. It lay in her Throat & Stomack. Sometimes she would be So Choack that we never expected She would Come too agin. Another of my Brothers Likewise at the Same time was very Sick; But it has pleased a holy God to show us his Power in Raiseing them to a State of Health.

Meanwhile in New York City, lawlessness was widespread, as witnessed by this notice in the *New York Gazette*:

STOLEN, out of Trinity Church Yard, where she was tied fast with a rope, which appeared to be cut, a milch Goat, with long horns, long hair, and shaggy, of a greyish colour, with some white stripes on her forehead. Whoever will take up said goat, and secure the thief so that he may be brought to justice, shall receive a reward of one guinea, or the Goat only a reward of two dollars by applying to the printer.

    N.B. All masters of vessels are requested if carried on board any of their ships, not to purchase her but to give notice as above.

And finally, shortly before he set sail for England, Nicholas Cresswell had one more adventure:

Wednesday, July 9th, 1777. Drunk tea at Mrs. Bennett's with Major L's Lady and several other ladies. After tea I waited upon Mrs. L to her lodgings. She insisted on me staying to sup and spend the evening with her and I did not need much solicitation to spend an evening with a handsome and polite young lady. After supper and a cheerful glass of good wine, we entered into a very agreeable tête-à-tête and then O! Matrimony, matrimony, thou coverest more female frailties than charity does sins! Nicholas, if ever thou sinned religiously in thy life, it has been this time. This kind, affable, and most obliging lady in public was most rigidly religious. At Mrs. Bennett's she had treated the character of a poor lady in the neighbourhood, who had made a slip and unfortunately been caught in the fact, in a most barbarous and cruel manner. She ran over the Scriptures from Genesis to Revelations. In that strain she continued till after supper and then I soon found she was made of warm flesh and blood. . . .

On Board the Brig, July 10th, 1777. This morning returned to the Ship. Ruminating upon my last night's adventure most of this day; it will not bear reflection.

Friday, July 11th, 1777. A note, or rather billet-doux, from Mrs. L. I am determined to go. It would be ungrateful to refuse so kind an offer. My Shipmates begin to smell a Rat. I am rated by them confoundedly, but let them go on. While I fare well at no expense to myself I care not. Should like her better if she were not so religious.

TRENTON

On December 14, 1776, from his headquarters in New York, General Sir William Howe issued orders that would bring the year's fighting to an end: "The Campaign having closed with the Pursuit of the Enemies' Army near Ninety Miles by Lieut.-Gen. Cornwallis's

Corps, much to the Honour of his Lordship and the Officers and Soldiers under his Command, the Approach of Winter putting a stop to any further Progress, the Troops will immediately march into Quarters."

There was an irony to this British success since Sir William, like his brother the admiral, both members of Parliament, had openly sympathized with the colonists, spoken out against the Coercive Acts, and let it be known that they would refuse to serve in America; but on this last matter they had changed their minds when personally asked to do so by the king (who very probably was also their cousin, the Howes' grandmother having been one of George I's mistresses). "I could not refuse," said Sir William, "without incurring the odious name of backwardness to serve my country in distress." The brothers did, however, ask that they also be appointed peace commissioners, with power to grant pardons and negotiate a settlement, and this was agreed to; indeed, wrote Lord Germain, "it was the King's first wish that his rebellious subjects in America should be brought to a proper sense of their duty without involving them in the calamities of war." Thus armed with the dual authority to wage war and negotiate peace, the Howes followed a halfhearted strategy that failed on both counts, defeating the American army again and again but never decisively, and offering terms of "reconciliation" that were rejected by the Americans as being tantamount to surrender.

In the middle of December came more bad news for the Americans. Charles Lee, the experienced but overrated English-born American general, was captured by a troop of British dragoons led by Colonel the Hon. William Harcourt. Getting wind of the fact that Lee and a small escort were spending the night at an isolated house near Basking Ridge, New Jersey, Harcourt led a swift and stealthy night raid, surprising the sentinels at dawn and surrounding the house before anyone could give the alarm. After ordering his men to smash in the windows and fire several volleys into the house, Harcourt loudly ordered it to be set on fire. Whereupon, according to the Patriot paper, *Freeman's Journal,* the general came down without his hat or outside coat, and said, "I hope you will use me as a gentleman. Let me get my hat and coat." The captain [Harcourt] said, "General Lee, I know you well; I know you are a gentleman; you shall be used as such. I know you too well to suffer you to go for your hat and coat," and ordered him to mount. Upon which they went off, carrying with them the general and a Frenchman, left the baggage, wounded one of the aide-de-camps, and one or two of the guard. There were but thirteen men with the general. He was about four miles from his division, and a mile out of the road.

The enemy showed an ungenerous, nay, boyish triumph after they had got him secure at Brunswick, by making his horse drunk, while they toasted their King until they were in the same condition. A band or two of music played all night to proclaim their joy for this important acquisition. They say we cannot now stand another campaign. Mistaken fools! To think the fate of America depended on one man. They will find ere long that it has no other effect than to urge us on to a noble revenge.

When the news reached England early in March, Harcourt's father, the earl, was warmly greeted by the king at the next royal levee: "Oh, my lord! Your son has behaved with the utmost gallantry. It gives me the utmost pleasure, and I doubt not it does the same to you." Adding, "I shall take care of Colonel Harcourt. Leave his fortune to me."

And in the village of Tring, in Hertfordshire, where the Harcourts had their estate, this poster, signed by the parish clerk, was put up in the marketplace:

This is to give Notis that Thursday next will be held as a day of regoicin in commemoration of the takin of General Lee, when their wil be a sermint preached, and other public demonstrascions of joye, after which will bee an nox roasted whole & everery mark of festivety

& bell ringing imagenable, whith a ball & cock fiting at night in the hassembly room at the black Lyone.

By Christmas the British army had overrun much of Long Island, Westchester County, and New Jersey, and was wrapping things up by establishing outposts along an extensive perimeter, part of which followed the course of the Delaware River. Across this river lay what remained of Washington's army, due to be further reduced on January 1, when many enlistments were to expire. Expecting the redcoats to appear in Philadelphia, Congress had already fled to Baltimore. Although Silas Deane was in Paris negotiating for loans, cannon, ammunition, and uniforms, very little had yet arrived. Paper money was depreciating, winter had already set in, and hopes were low. It was a dark moment indeed. Morale-raisers were badly needed, and once again Thomas Paine rose to the occasion, this time with his pamphlet *The Crisis* and its famously stirring opening lines: "These are the times that try men's souls. The summer soldier and the sunshine patriot will, in this crisis, shrink from the service of his country; but he that stands it NOW, deserves the love and thanks of man and woman. Tyranny, like hell, is not easily conquered; yet we have this consolation with us, that the harder the conflict, the more glorious the triumph."

It was a terrific beginning, and Paine could hardly have been expected to keep it up all the way through, for the pamphlet was actually quite long, but he did get off some memorable hits: "I should suffer the misery of the devils were I to make a whore of my soul by swearing allegiance to one whose character is that of a sottish, stupid, worthless, brutish man" (clearly, King George III). And this: "I love the man that can smile in trouble, that can gather strength from distress, and grow brave by reflection. 'Tis the business of little minds to shrink; but he whose heart is firm, and whose conscience approves his conduct, will pursue his principles unto death" (surely George Washington, among others).

Although Christmas Day was little celebrated in Protestant America, such religious feast-days being suspiciously "Romish," this was not the case in Germany, and it was a fair bet that the thousand or so Hessians stationed at Trenton would make the most of it, including their commander, Colonel Rall, who was well-known to be fond of the bottle. Also, Washington's scouts informed him that the Hessians, overconfident after a long string of successes, had not done much to fortify their position at Trenton. So, by crossing the Delaware on the evening of Christmas Day and then marching through the night, Washington hoped to surprise an ill-prepared and probably hungover enemy with a dawn attack the next day.

It was a gamble that only someone in a desperate situation would have risked: He could easily have been betrayed by a Tory spy; the ice on the Delaware was so heavy that another force that was to make a diversionary attack lower down the river could not get across; night attacks are standing invitations for things to go wrong, even with the most experienced troops, which his certainly were not; and Washington compounded his chances of failure by dividing his forces and having them advance on Trenton by two separate roads, the Pennington road and the river road, hoping they would arrive simultaneously, as if on parade. Yet once again Washington was as lucky as he was bold, and none of the potential disasters happened.

There are many accounts of the battle of Trenton. This one is by John Fitzgerald, a young field officer on Washington's staff. (Fitzgerald probably took hurried notes at the time and wrote them up later, using the dramatic present.)

❋

Christmas, 6 p.m. The regiments have had their evening parade, but instead of returning to their quarters are marching toward the ferry. It is fearfully cold and a snowstorm setting in. The wind is northeast and beats in the faces of the men. It will be a terrible night for the soldiers who have no shoes. Some of them have tied old rags around their feet; others are barefoot, but I have not heard a man complain. They are ready to suffer any hardship and die rather than give up their liberty.

I have just copied the order for marching. Both divisions are to go from the ferry to Bear Tavern, two miles. They will separate there; Washington will accompany Greene's division with a part of the artillery down the Pennington road. Sullivan and the rest of the artillery will take the river road.

Dec. 26, 3 a.m. I am writing in the ferry house. The troops are all over, and the boats have gone back for the artillery. We are three hours behind the set time. Glover's men [Colonel Glover's whaleboatmen from Marblehead] have had a hard time to force the boats through the floating ice with the snow drifting in their faces. I never have seen Washington so determined as he is now. He stands on the bank of the river, wrapped in his cloak, superintending the landing of his troops. He is calm and collected, but very determined. The storm is changing to sleet and cuts like a knife. The last cannon is being landed, and we are ready to mount our horses.

Dec. 26, noon. It was nearly four o'clock [a.m.] when we started. The two divisions divided at Bear Tavern. It was broad daylight when we came to a house where a man was chopping wood. He was very much surprised when he saw us. "Can you tell me where the Hessian picket is?" Washington asked.

The man hesitated, but I said, "You need not be frightened, it is General Washington who asks the question."

His face brightened, and he pointed toward the house of Mr. Howell.

It was just eight o'clock. Looking down the road, I saw a Hessian running out from the house. He yelled in Dutch [Deutsch, i.e., German] and swung his arms. Three or four others came out with their guns. Two of them fired at us, but the bullets whistled over our heads. Some of General Stephen's men rushed forward and captured two. The others took to their heels, running toward Mr. Calhoun's house, where the picket guard was stationed, about twenty men under Captain Altenbockum. They came running out of the house. The captain flourished his sword and tried to form his men. Some of them fired at us, others ran toward the village.

The next moment we heard drums beat and a bugle sound, and then from the west came the boom of a cannon. General Washington's face lighted up instantly, for he knew that it was one of Sullivan's guns.

We could see a great commotion down toward the meeting-house, men running here and there, officers swinging their swords, artillerymen harnessing their horses. Captain Forrest unlimbered his guns. Washington gave the order to advance, and we rushed on to the junction of King and Queen Streets. Forrest wheeled six of his cannon into position to sweep both streets. The riflemen under Colonel Hand, and Scott's and Lawson's battalions, went upon the run through the fields on the left to gain possession of the Princeton road. The Hessians were just ready to open fire with two of their cannon when Captain Washington and Lieutenant [James] Monroe with their men rushed forward and captured them.

We saw Rall coming riding up the street from his headquarters, which were at Stacy Potts' house. We could hear him shouting in Dutch, "My brave soldiers, advance!"

His men were frightened and confused, for our men were firing upon them from fences and houses and they were falling fast. Instead of advancing they ran into an apple orchard. The officers tried to rally them, but our men kept advancing and picking off the officers. It was not long before Rall tumbled from his horse, and his soldiers threw down their guns and gave themselves up as prisoners.

Dec. 26, 3 p.m. I have been talking with Rall's adjutant, Lieutenant Piel. He says that Rall sat down to a grand dinner at the Trenton Tavern Christmas Day, that he drank a great deal of wine and sat up nearly all night playing cards. He had been in bed but a short time when the battle began and was sound asleep. Piel shook him, but found it hard work to wake him up. . . .

"What's the matter?" Rall asked.

Piel informed him that a battle was going on. That seemed to bring him to his senses. He dressed himself, rushed out, and mounted his horse to be mortally wounded a few minutes later.

We have taken nearly one thousand prisoners, six cannon, more than one thousand muskets, twelve drums, and four colors. About forty Hessians were killed or wounded. Our loss is only two killed and three wounded. Two of the latter are Captain Washington and Lieutenant Monroe, who rushed forward very bravely to seize the cannon.

The next day, back in camp, Fitzgerald concluded, "It is a glorious victory. It will rejoice the hearts of our friends everywhere and give new life to our hitherto waning fortunes." Moreover, the victory at Trenton was not merely a fluke, for a few days later Washington scored again, this time defeating British troops commanded by Lord Cornwallis at Princeton.

Following Trenton, Ambrose Serle wrote in his diary that he was "exceedingly concerned on the public Account, as it will tend to revive the drooping Spirits of the Rebels and increase their Force—prolonging a war that I thought might soon end." And the young Englishman Nicholas Cresswell, at that time still on parole in Virginia, wrote in his diary:

Monday, Jan. 6th, 1777. News that Washington had taken 760 Hessian prisoners at Trenton in the Jerseys. Hope it is a lie. Tuesday, Jan. 7th. The news is confirmed. The minds of the people are much altered. A few days ago they had given up the cause for lost. Their late successes have turned the scale and now they are liberty mad again. Their Recruiting parties could not get a man (except he bought him from his master) no longer since than last week, and now the men are coming in by companies. Confound the turncoat scoundrels and the cowardly Hessians together. This has given them new spirits, got them fresh succours and will prolong the War, perhaps for two years. They have recovered their panic and it will not be an easy matter to throw them into that confusion again. Volunteer Companies are collecting in every County on the Continent, and in a few months the rascals will be stronger than ever.

Reenlistments were also up. Back in October Sarah Hodgkins of Ipswich had written to her husband, Joseph, who had survived the Battle of Long Island and the fighting after the Kip's Bay landings: "I hope you will be carried through all you are to meet with in the way of your duty & in God's good time be returned home in safety. I want very much to see you. I hope if we live to see this campaign out we shall have the happiness of living together again. I don't know what you think about staying again but I think it can't be inconsistent with your duty to come home to your family. It will trouble me very much if you should engage again. I don't know but you may think I am too free in expressing my mind & that it would have been time enough when I was asked, but I was afraid I should not have that opportunity, so I hope you will excuse my freedom . . ." Perhaps because he was disgruntled with his rank—he was still only a lieutenant—Joseph assured her that "I have no thoughts of engaging again in the capacity I now sustain, and as for anything better I shall not seek after it, neither do I desire it . . . therefore I hope I shall have the pleasure of facing you & all friends in a few weeks more if nothing extraordinary happens." In early December he wrote that his regiment was moving from Peekskill on the Hudson to Brunswick in New Jersey, "the traveling very bad, but I hope we shall do well. My dear, I am in haste for the Brigade is now marching. I want to see you very much and hope I shall in good time. I did expect to be home by 20 of January if it had not been for this movement." On December 30 he wrote of "the goodness of God which has been great towards me in many instances, especially since I left Peekskill. I cannot express the hardship & fatigue we have undergone on our march from place to place, but I desire to be thankful that I am alive & well & in good spirits at present. I hope God will preserve us & carry us through all difficulties & dangers we have to meet with in the way of duty & give us an opportunity of meeting together again in this world." He then described his part in the Trenton campaign—his unit was to have made a diversionary attack on Mount Holly but was unable to cross the Delaware because of the ice. The rest of his letter is missing; but the vagueness of his expression about "an opportunity of meeting together again" and the fact that the next letter to have survived was written in July from camp in Worcester indicate that he was among the many who reenlisted in the afterglow of Trenton. His next surviving letter was headed "Camp near Saratoga, September 28, 1777."

In the meantime Sir William Howe had to acknowledge that his strategy of achieving reconciliation by repeated demonstrations of British invincibility was doomed. Writing to Lord George Germain, he said, "I do not now see a prospect of terminating the war but by a general action." His brother the admiral seemed to agree. After admitting to his secretary, Ambrose Serle, that "almost all the People of Parts & Spirit were in the Rebellion," Lord Howe concluded that "we must regain Possession of this Country by the Sword." But the Howes had missed their chance, and never again would Washington expose his army to the risk of a major defeat by fully committing it to battle.

A few months later, as his ship was finally about to set sail, Cresswell wrote in his journal: "News that our Army has surprised Washington and taken him prisoner. Afraid it is too good to be authentic." Then this outburst, which must have been a common topic during those evenings with Furneval at Hull's Tavern: "That a Negro-driver should, with a ragged Banditti of undisciplined people, the scum and refuse of all nations on earth, so long keep a British General at bay—nay, even oblige him, with as fine an army of Veteran Soldiers as ever England had on the American continent, to retreat—it is astonishing! It is too much! By Heavens, there must be double-dealing somewhere. General Howe, a man brought up to War from his youth, to be puzzled and plagued for two years together with a Virginia Tobacco planter. O Britain! How thy Laurels tarnish!"

But while the rumor that Washington had been taken prisoner was false, the real news, still on its way to New York, was even more significant. On July 6, 1777, the Anglo-Hessian army advancing south from Canada had with the greatest ease captured the mighty fortress at Ticonderoga, "the Gibraltar of the North." Only a short march now separated the victorious army from Albany. Contact would then be made with the British forces in New York, the colonies would be split in two, New England would be isolated, Washington's army would wither away for lack of supplies, the rebellion would collapse, and untold glory and honors would be heaped on the general who had conceived and executed this triumphant maneuver— "Gentleman Johnny" Burgoyne.

Into the Woods

Pity the poor Hessian as he slogs along in his thick uniform and heavy boots through the forests and swamps that lie between Fort Ticonderoga, now behind him, and Albany, the destination he will never reach. The heat is sweltering, but still he must daily braid his hair, grease it with lard, whiten it with powder or flour, and then cover it with a stiff and heavy hat. The flies and mosquitoes sting his face and hands; there are rattlesnakes in the undergrowth; his shiny buckles and badges invite the attention of the invisible sharpshooters hidden in the surrounding woods. The load he carries—knapsack, haversack, blanket, musket or rifle, bayonet, hatchet, sixty rounds of ammunition, powder flask, provisions, canteen, and share of equipment for the communal tent —weighs well over sixty pounds. Unless he is one of the old-time regulars, his officers, mostly members of the petty nobility, look down on him. "Insolent rabble," in the words of Captain von Ewald. "Mere riffraff." His British allies also despise him, and the locals fear and hate him: "the most savage of the Human Race," according to General Silliman, "for they ravish all Womankind wherever they come with as little Shame as the Cattle." Even the German-speaking immigrants are hostile. "They insult and berate us with the vilest words," wrote Lt.Col von Dincklage while on Long Island, "shouting out their insults in German so loudly that last night we were disturbed in our encampment." Slow-witted though the Hessian was reputed to have been, surely he must sometimes have asked himself, "What on earth am I doing here?"

One answer, and not a very consoling one, was: making money for his prince. Although by and large the British people supported the war, at least so long as it seemed to be going well, few of them actually wanted to fight it; there was no conscription, and press gangs were used only for the navy, since it was hard to desert once a ship had put out to sea but easy enough from a regiment on land. So, early in the war, the king, who took a close interest in military matters, wrote to Empress Catherine of Russia, asking if he could hire twenty thousand of her Cossack soldiers, just back from one of their campaigns against the Turks. This request was turned down, and "not in so genteel a manner as I should have thought might have been expected from Her." (The empress had "thrown out some expressions that may be civil to a Russian Ear but certainly not to more civilized ones.") He was snubbed again when he approached the Dutch, and the proposal to hire troops from Morocco also came to nothing. But when, like George I and George II in earlier wars, he turned to the German princelings, he received a warm welcome. As Elector of Hanover as well as King of England, George was related to many of them, while they, in Burke's words, "snuffed the cadaverous taint of lucrative war." In a series of rental agreements disguised as bilateral treaties of mutual defense, the British contracted with the Landgrave of Hesse-Cassel (George's uncle), the Count of Hesse-Hanau (George's nephew), the Duke of Brunswick and Lüneburg (George's cousin), the Margrave of Anspach-Bayreuth, the Prince of Waldeck, and the Prince of Anhalt- Zerbst to hire a total of almost thirty thousand—29,867 to be exact—mercenaries. Generally known as the

Hessians, they were to receive the same pay and provisions as British soldiers. Their rulers were to receive annual subsidies until two years after the war ended and up-front payments, usually of four guineas per head, and another four pounds, four shillings, and four pence for every soldier killed. Also, "according to custom, three wounded men shall be reckoned as one killed." The bill to the British taxpayer would be well over four and a half million pounds, a bargain according to Lord North, a shameful traffic in the opinion of the opposition minority. Even Frederick the Great of Prussia, certainly no bleeding-heart sentimentalist, declared that these princes were selling their subjects "as one sells cattle to the slaughter house."

The British could afford to pay for the Hessians because they had long ago discovered the magic of a national debt, borrowing from themselves and then repaying the loan with further borrowing. Unlike the French, who also floated loans but kept reneging on them, the British never missed a payment, making "consols" a favorite for anyone with money to invest—even when they were at war with Britain, citizens of Holland and France bought them; so did some Americans. Interest ranged from 3 to 5 percent; prices fluctuated, but much less so than shares in the East India Company. Every so often a fund was established to "sink," or pay off, the debt, but this was too tempting a target, and "raiding the sinking fund" was a common ploy among all parties.

The mercenaries thus hired were not immediately available. Usually the contracting princes had a small army of regulars that could be expanded whenever opportunities such as this arose. Some recruits enlisted voluntarily, drawn by a sense of adventure or by the prospect of getting the same wage as a British soldier, good money by local standards. Others saw it as a free one-way ticket across the Atlantic. Several hundred thousand Germans had already settled in Pennsylvania and elsewhere, and their letters home told of how much their lives had improved in America; but the fare was expensive, and to take free passage as an indentured servant or as a "redemptioner" meant working at least four years for no wages. So why not enlist, embark, disembark, and then desert as soon as possible? For its part, Congress encouraged this way of thinking with a proclamation offering fifty acres of land—a dazzling prospect to a poor German peasant—along with "liberty, safety, and a communion of good laws and mild government, in a country where many of their friends and relations are already happily settled, rather than continue exposed to the toils and dangers of a long and bloody war." The proclamation was printed in German as well as English, and wrapped around complimentary plugs of tobacco for the soldiers to smoke in their clay pipes while they thought matters over.

To the professional officers and regular soldiers, desertion was considered shameful to the regiment and its colors; to the princes it was an insult, a breach of the oath of allegiance that all recruits had been forced to take, and a net loss since the treaties stipulated that a deserter had to be replaced at the prince's own expense. As well as the usual deterrents of flogging, hanging, and the firing squad, men caught trying to desert were made to run the gauntlet, often more than once. (From the diary of Company Surgeon Captain Wasmus: "August 13, 1776: Four of our deserters had to run the gauntlet. Grenadier Heidenbach had to run it eight times, and died eight hours later.") New recruits were closely guarded at all times. There was no such thing as leave; soldiers who left Germany in 1776 served continuously until their return seven years later.

On the whole, recruiters had a hard time meeting their quotas. As in England, complaisant judges would sentence prisoners to military service, but emptying the jails was not enough. Johann Seume, later to become a well-known poet, was a nineteen-year-old student of theology when he was more or less kidnapped on his way home from college and brought to the fortress of Ziegenhain. "Here I found many miserable companions from all parts who were to be sent to America next spring. . . . Nobody at that time was safe from the minions of the slave traders. Persuasion, tricks, fraud and force, everything was legal. Foreigners [i.e., non-Hessians] of all sorts were picked up, imprisoned, and sent off. My university matriculation certificate, my only piece of identification, was torn up. . . . My comrades were another student from Jena, a bankrupt merchant from Vienna, a lace-maker from Hanover, an unemployed postal clerk from Gotha, a monk from Würzburg . . ." Colonel Faucitt of the British army, who traveled around Germany overseeing the recruitment and dispatch of the mercenaries, intervened only when a recruit could not pass muster, rejecting, for example, one man who was sixty-three years old and had a permanent stoop, another who was lame "because one of his legs was some inches shorter than the other," and five who were blind in one eye. One regiment was composed almost entirely of boys, but this was acceptable as they were "stout, bony, and well put together."

The first contingents left early in 1776, headed either for New York to join Sir William Howe's campaign there, or for Canada, where Sir Guy Carleton was planning an invasion from the north. On orders from his ruler, Duke Wilhelm, Captain Georg Pausch of the Hesse-Hanau artillery kept a diary from the day of departure, May 15, 1776. Knowing who his most important reader would be, Pausch did not mince his words: "In obedience to your most gracious orders, assembly was beaten at half past three in the afternoon and the troops gathered on the parade ground with full equipment. Fifteen minutes later, after dressing rank, they marched through the old town and out by the Hospital Gate where they immediately embarked on transports in the most gracious presence of our most gracious officials. As we sailed down the Main River, it pleased our most gracious and best Prince to favor us with his presence on the right bank, thus demonstrating his fatherly concern and love for us and causing the most heartfelt and sincere elevation of spirits among the men so graciously entrusted to me. Here our journey began, with many good wishes and tearful farewells, and here we saw for the last time our most dearly beloved, best Prince and benefactor . . ." On reaching Offenbach, the ships anchored in midstream, to prevent any of the soldiers making their escape. Regiments that had to march overland to their ports of embarkation were escorted by local troops, to protect civilians and prevent desertions.

Writing only for himself, Lieutenant Johann von Bardeleben, of the von Donop Regiment of Hesse-Cassel, described their departure on February 29, 1776: "The regiment marched out of Homburg at ten o'clock this morning. Most of the citizens turned out to give us a most affectionate farewell. Everyone seemed deeply moved, expressions of pain and melancholy were on every face. Large numbers of inconsolable mothers, weeping wives, and crying children followed the regiment. It was a most heart-rending scene and I was greatly affected, but I tried to contain my sorrow within my heart . . ." Soldiers of lower rank were less willing to be reconciled to their fate. The Anspach Regiment mutinied and left their ships, but returned when fired upon by other troops. Grenadiers of the Bayreuth Regiment also mutinied, were also fired upon, and also returned to their ship. In Bamberg, Ridingmaster von Gravenreuth received orders to use his hussars against any recruits who gave trouble.

From ports in Holland, they crossed to England, where they transferred to larger transport ships for the Atlantic crossing. In the eyes of the British, the Navigation Acts were still in force and no foreign merchantmen were allowed into American ports. The ships provided by the profiteering English contractors were not of the best; one of them, the *Juno*, on which Captain Pausch and the Hesse-Hanau artillery embarked, had previously been used for the slave trade. So dirty were the ships that to protect their coats the soldiers wore them inside out. Those headed for Canada were for some reason ordered by the king to take the northernmost—the coldest and stormiest—route. In his diary Lieutenant von Bardeleben writes of violent storms lasting many days and of huge seas, "the waves often breaking over our ship so that the deck was often two or three feet under water." Soldiers confined in their dark and smelly quarters below deck were drenched, and many were injured by the jolting movements of the ship. On another ship a whole row of bunks collapsed during a storm, and the deck-house used for cooking was washed overboard; also "three pigs belonging to the captain broke out of their stall and one of them fell down a hatchway among the soldiers' bunks, squealing in terror until some sailors came with a lantern and a rope which they tied round it, and then hauled it back to its stall." Masts broke and sails were torn to shreds. Captain Pausch wrote in his diary of a near-collision with an iceberg over two hundred feet high. During heavy fogs shots were fired and drums beaten as warnings to prevent ships ramming each other. Von Bardeleben wrote of a "fearsome electric storm with terrible lightning that seemed to encompass fire, water, and ship." The *Benjamin* was nearly destroyed when, while distributing rations, the ship's commissary approached the six-hundred-gallon rum cask with an open-flame lantern and set it ablaze, whereupon "each of our soldiers took his most cherished possession up on deck and gave himself over to God" while also singing Lutheran psalms. Luckily the weather on this occasion was calm and crews from the escorting ships of war rowed across and put the fire out. There were suicides: "May 18, 1777. Officer's servant Peter, servant to Lieutenant von Diemar, lowered himself into the sea from the ship *Myrtle* on a rope at five o'clock in the evening." There were also deaths from sickness: "This morning," wrote Chaplain Waldeck on October 5, "the soldier Teigtmeyer, from Goettingen, died of scurvy. I gave him communion yesterday, but could barely stay with him for an hour, so terrible was the stench." But there were a few bright spots. Many of the soldiers had brought their wives along with them, and on Chaplain Waldeck's ship one of them gave birth to a boy. Waldeck baptized him, an officer stood godfather, and all survived the voyage. A sense of humor also helped: Chaplain Waldeck recorded how they "had all had a hearty laugh" when, just as they were settling down to their evening meal of "soup of burnt oats" and the regimental surgeon "had just sat down next to me, all of a sudden a wave struck the ship and the soup flew out of my bowl onto Herr Surgeon Pfister, covering him from top to bottom, and I was left with the empty bowl in my hands!"

Following the first contingents, new batches of usually unwilling recruits were sent over throughout the war. In the opinion of Captain von Ewald, these newcomers were "the scum of the human race." At first "our regulars were so disgusted that they refused to serve with this rabble, but their resentment grew less when they found that they were accompanied by over sixty 'amazons,' whose company they soon sought out." Von Ewald integrated the newcomers by pairing each with an experienced regular, but finding that they still talked and laughed while on the march, "I had this dregs of humanity severely thrashed with stout canes. Also, several of our more reliable corporals were assigned to this company and given a free hand, and before long discipline was much improved."

Now compare the lot of the Hessians with this recruiting poster for the 16th Light Dragoons, a new regiment that was raised in Northamptonshire, England, during the Seven Years' War: "You will be mounted on the finest horses in the world, with superb clothing and the richest accoutrements; your pay and privileges are equal to two guineas a week; you are everywhere respected; your society is courted; you are admired by the fair, which, together with the chance of getting switched to a buxom widow, or of brushing a rich heiress, renders the situation truly enviable and desirable. Young men out of employment or uncomfortable, 'There is a tide in the affairs of men which, taken at the flood, leads on to fortune.' Nick in instantly and enlist."

Such was warfare as conceived by the handsome and imposing Gentleman Johnny Burgoyne: a light operetta with a happy ending. To be sure, some fighting had to be done, and the 16th Light Dragoons took part in two exciting though minor cavalry actions in Portugal (the sum total of Burgoyne's military experience), and then it was back to England and parades in Hyde Park in the presence of George II. And when the old king died and his grandson cleaned house, so great was Burgoyne's gift for self-promotion, so convincing his impersonation of a professional officer, that before long he was being invited to join the royal party when they went riding and was appointed to a number of lucrative sinecures. Thanks to the influence of his brother-in-law, Lord Derby, he also became a Member of Parliament, like most of the generals who served in America.

Horace Walpole, who didn't like Burgoyne, describing him as "the vapouring Burgoyne . . . a vain, very ambitious man, with a half-understanding that was worse than none," nicknamed him Hurlothrumbo, after a character in a popular burlesque; and surely the theater was where Burgoyne really belonged. As an author he had had some success; one of his plays, *Maid of the Oaks,* was put on by Garrick at the Drury Lane theater. Hannah More, the poet and friend of Mrs. Montagu, went to see it, and though she complained that "the piece is only intended as a vehicle to the scenery," she did allow that there was "some wit and spirit in it." While in America he had written the morale-raising *Blockade of Boston,* performed while that city was besieged. From Boston he had gone to Canada to serve as second in command in Sir Guy Carleton's invasion to the south; and when, because of the onset of winter, that campaign had to be cut off before reaching Ticonderoga, Burgoyne was given leave to return to England. During the voyage he wrote yet another play, although this one was disguised as a work of military strategy: *Thoughts for Conducting the War from the Side of Canada.* He landed at Portsmouth on the afternoon of December 9 and was in the office of his friend Lord Germain by lunchtime the next day.

What the script called for was a three-pronged simultaneous attack. One force would move down Lake Champlain, capture Fort Ticonderoga, and then continue on to Albany; a second force, also starting from Canada, was to land at Fort Oswego on Lake Ontario, move down the valley of the Mohawk River, take Fort Stanwix, and also converge on Albany; and a third would move up the Hudson River from New York, also heading for Albany. The American forces that would have moved northward to meet these invaders would then be surrounded on three sides and crushed. Moreover, by gaining control of the entire length of the Hudson River, New England, that hotbed of rebellion and major source of supply, would be cut off from the other colonies, severed with one slashing blow of the cavalryman's saber.

On the beautifully drawn map spread out before the king, Germain, and Burgoyne (Lord North was not invited), the plan must have looked foolproof; and indeed, who can say that it would not have worked had it been put into execution? But Sir William Howe had ideas of his own for 1777 and wrote to say that he would be heading in the opposite direction, to Philadelphia. Germain approved this plan, on the grounds that it would draw off Washington's army, and if Howe moved swiftly—something he never did—then perhaps he could double back from Philadelphia and head up the Hudson in late summer.

Burgoyne was also informed of Howe's plan, although he later claimed not to have been, but was undeterred. Full of confidence and relishing the starring role he had written for himself, he had already achieved his first major objective, which was to be appointed commander in chief of the Anglo-Hessian army that would head south from Canada. By rights the command should have gone to the experienced and highly competent Sir Guy Carleton, but Germain hated Carleton for taking part in the court-martial that had condemned his craven behavior at the Battle of Minden.

According to Captain Wasmus of the Brunswick troops in Canada, "Our men firmly believe that Spain borders on America . . . and this makes them think they can get from here to Spain, and from Spain to France, and from France to Germany, all on foot." But did the king, Burgoyne, and Germain know all that much more about the region where the proposed campaign was to take place? Lopping off New England was a metaphor rather than a strategy. There were no bridges across the Hudson, only ferries that could be shifted to different crossing places, so if the British were to prevent anyone crossing the river, they would have to build and garrison forts and outposts for its entire length. And anyway, most supplies sent from New England to Washington's army went by fairly small coast-hugging ships that could easily dodge the Royal Navy's patrols. Far more serious was the trio's apparent ignorance of the terrain between the southern end of Lake George and Albany: a short hop on the map, a nightmare slog on the ground.

But all that lay in the future when, after spending an agreeable winter in London and Bath, Burgoyne returned rather late in the spring to take command of his half-British, half-Hessian army. He began with a General Order, issued on June 30, 1777:

The Army embarks tomorrow, to approach the Enemy. We are to contend for the King, and the Constitution of Great Britain, to vindicate Law, and to relieve the oppressed—a cause in which his Majesty's Troops and those of the Princes his Allies will feel equal excitement. The Services required of this particular expedition are critical and conspicuous. During our progress occasions may occur in which nor difficulty, nor labour, nor Life are to be regarded. This Army must not Retreat.

He also issued a high-flown proclamation to the rebels, invoking "considerations of Christianity" and "the mercy of my royal master" in urging them to submit, while also threatening "to let loose the Indians under my command, who number thousands" if they did not give up "the present unnatural revolt."

In fact the Indians numbered only a few hundred rather than thousands, but their reputation for ferocity was expected to chill the hearts of the foe. "When prepared for War they paint themselves with Vermilion & other colours," wrote Lt. Hadden of the British army. "Their dress is a Blanket and Arse Clout, or covering for the Privities; at great War Dances they are sometimes totally Naked, at the end of the Penis the head & Neck of some handsome bird is fasten'd." And in his diary Captain Wasmus wrote, "These savages, particularly the Mohawks, are very warlike and most dangerous. While the Iroquois have their bodies bedecked with beautiful colors and materials, the Mohawks are chestnut brown and go about completely naked. It is their practice to scalp the enemies they take and then to eat them. The other savages with our army always step aside and look away in fear when a Mohawk passes by."

Aware of the damage these allies could do to his and his royal master's reputations for clemency, Burgoyne summoned the chiefs and their warriors to gather around him on the shores of Lake Champlain. After the general had taken his seat in a leafy arbor, his officers sat on tree trunks while "the savages lay down on branches in two rows at the end of the trees, smoking tobacco," wrote Wasmus. A flowery speech of welcome by the oldest chief was interpreted by their titular commander, M. de St. Luc, a Frenchman. Burgoyne replied with a few remarks about the benevolence of the king, the despicable ingratitude of the rebels, and the fidelity, intelligence, and bravery of his audience. "But listen to the will of the common father of us all. He wants to chastise, not destroy the rebels . . . not extirpate them but offer clemency. For this reason it may be permissible that you scalp those whom you have killed in battle and treat them as you are wont. But in the name of my King I forbid you to practice this on any prisoner or wounded; wherefore you shall have a gratuity for every prisoner you bring in. Aged men, women, children, and prisoners must be held sacred from the knife or hatchet, even in time of actual conflict." However, according to the British officer, Lt. Anburey, the Indians were also told that "base lurking assassins, incendiaries, ravagers, and plunderers of the country . . . shall be treated with less reserve." Another loophole: "Should the enemy, on their parts, dare to countenance acts of barbarity towards those who may fall into their hands, it shall be yours also to retaliate."

"After the General had finished his speech," wrote Anburey, "they all of them cried out *Etow! Etow! Etow!* And after remaining some little time in consultation, an old Chief of the Iroquois rose up, and made the following answer: 'I stand up in the name of all the nations present to assure our father that we have listened attentively to his discourse—we receive you as our father, because when you speak we hear the voice of our great father beyond the great lake. We rejoice in the approbation you have expressed of our behavior. We have been tried and tempted by the Bostonians; but we have loved our father, and our hatchets have been sharpened upon our affections . . .'" In conclusion he promised "a constant obedience to all you have ordered," and prayed that the father of heaven would give him "many days and success."

After more shouts of *Etow! Etow!* Burgoyne departed, "highly pleased to find the Indians so tractable." Anburey seems also to have left, but Captain Wasmus remained, at least for a while:

The general having presented them with a barrel of rum, the rest of the day was spent feasting, drinking, singing, and dancing. The savages love strong drink, especially rum, and do not stop drinking until it is all gone; their feasts usually end in bloodshed. Their singing is sometimes harmonious and rhythmical, but sometimes sounds like the howling of wolves. They make their music by beating sticks on a drum which they carry around in a circle, and by blowing on a horn. While dancing they brandish clubs and wooden truncheons, and they have large knives hanging on ribbons round their necks; they keep their heads down and their bodies bent forward, and if anyone laughs at them they become very angry.

But promises to observe European rules of warfare did not last long, and only five days later Wasmus wrote: "On their march from here, the savages lost two men who were shot by rebels hiding in the woods. This so enraged them that they complained to General Burgoyne, asking that they should be allowed to keep the next three rebels taken prisoner. Of these they would roast and eat two, and send the third back to the rebels to tell them what he had seen. The general's answer has not yet been made known."

Wasmus also had good news to record: "Forty-six Americans from the province around Albany, all armed with muskets, have deserted to us. Among them are several whose fathers came over from Germany. They assure us that once we get to Albany everyone will rally to the king's cause."

It was generally agreed on both sides that Fort Ticonderoga, with its massive stone walls and cannon that commanded the lower end of Lake Champlain, was the key strategic point between Montreal and Albany. This had certainly been true in the days when the French ruled Canada and the fort had served as a formidable outpost for their attacks to the south, but in the present conflict it was more a white elephant than the "Gibraltar of America." Benedict Arnold and Ethan Allen with his Green Mountain Boys had easily captured it by a surprise attack early in the war, and the fort was now held by an inadequate garrison of some 2,500 troops under General St. Clair.

Early in July Burgoyne's army drew near the great fort, the Hessians under General von Riedesel advancing down the right bank of Lake Champlain, the redcoats down the left, and a small fleet on the lake itself. On the fourth, a Lt. Twiss was sent ahead to reconnoiter the cone-shaped Mount Defiance, also known as Sugar Hill. After climbing the mountain, eight hundred feet high and steep-sided, Twiss reported that it was within cannon range of the fort. General William Phillips, the expedition's second in command and the officer in charge of the immense train of artillery Burgoyne had brought with him, then went to have a look for himself and pronounced, "Where a goat can go a man can go, and where a man can go he can draw a gun." One day later, four cannon had been hauled to the top of Mount Defiance. Knowing that more would follow, and that he could not return their fire, St. Clair called a council of war and it was unanimously and sensibly decided to evacuate the fort. This they did at night and with great secrecy. Burgoyne pursued them to Skenesboro and Fort Anne, but only at Hubbarton was there much fighting. The fact that he had missed the chance of destroying St. Clair's army was obscured by the glory of taking Fort Ticonderoga.

As the news of the capture of the fort spread, reactions varied. "The patriot armies will never successfully defend a post till they have shot a general who has yielded a fortress uncontested to the enemy," wrote John Adams, from his committee room in Philadelphia.

In London the king burst in on the queen. "I have beat them!" he exclaimed in great excitement, "I have beat all the Americans!"

What a finale that would have made as the curtain came down at the end of Act II of the stage version of *Thoughts for Conducting the War from the Side of Canada.*

BENNINGTON

Having pursued the retreating St. Clair to Skenesboro (now White-hall), Burgoyne decided to press on overland rather than go back to Lake George and continue south by water. One possible reason for this odd decision was that Philip Skene, his political adviser, talked him into it. There was no road between Skenesboro and Fort Edward so the British army would have to build one, and this would greatly increase the value of Skene's extensive landholdings. Another reason may have been that Burgoyne felt obliged to follow the script, even though he had written it himself. By publicly declaring, "This Army must not Retreat," he had committed himself to an unswerving course southward.

It was now mid-July, and soldiers were sometimes fainting from the heat as they headed deeper into the wilderness. "The country between our late encampment at Skenesborough and this place [Fort Edward] was a continuation of woods and creeks, interspersed with deep morasses," wrote Lt. Anburey, "and to add to these natural impediments, the enemy had very industriously augmented them by felling immense trees, and various other modes, that it was with the utmost pains and fatigues we could work our way through them. Exclusive of these, the watery ground and marshes were so numerous that we were under the necessity of constructing no less than forty bridges to pass them, and over one morass there was a bridge of near two miles in length." Because of these conditions, it took the army twenty days to cover twenty-two miles.

As to the roads along the river, so clearly marked on the maps, there was "only one road from Albany for wheel-carriage, and in many places there are deep and wide gullies, where the bridges are broken and must necessarily be repaired. This road is bounded on one side by the river, and on the other by perpendicular ascents, covered with wood, where the enemy . . . in one night could throw impediments in our way that would take nearly the whole day to remove."

Another problem was the length of the British lines of communication and supply. "If you consider," wrote a German officer, "that in these regions the army eats bread baked from flour made in England, and meat that has been salted in England; and that both bread and meat have to be brought to our cooking kettles and mouths across oceans and lakes, down rivers and waterfalls; and that it then has to be carried by porters since we lack horses and carts; then you will understand that keeping the army properly supplied is one of our commanding general's greatest concerns."

But then came some news that was too good not to be true. Some fifty miles to the southeast of Skenesboro lay what Captain Glich called "the obscure village of Bennington, a cluster of poor cottages situated in a wild country between the forks of the Hoosac River." Here, according to reports from Tory spies, or spies who said they were Tories, the rebels had gathered a considerable number of cattle, horses, and wagons, guarded by only a handful of militia. It was also reported that loyalism was high among the locals, who would rally to the royal standard the moment it appeared.

Relations between Burgoyne and General von Riedesel, the Hessian commander, had always been cool, perhaps because Riedesel was a true professional soldier, having been bred to the trade since boyhood when he accompanied his father, also a professional, on his campaigns. Nor did it help when Burgoyne, in violation of military protocol and common courtesy, bypassed Riedesel and directly issued orders to Hessian Colonel Baum to set out with some five hundred men and seize the horses, cattle, and wagons just waiting to be taken. Like General Gage when giving orders for the expedition to Concord, Burgoyne went into great detail, listing which troops Baum was to take, including a number of dismounted dragoons whose thick knee-length riding boots made walking difficult and whose heavy sabers were of little use unless wielded from horseback. The route to be taken was also laid out in detail. Of the thirteen hundred horses that he could expect to capture, some were to be given to the dismounted dragoons, the rest "to be tied together by strings of ten each in order that one man may lead ten horses." The wagons and cattle were to be driven back to the main army, "and you must have a chain of sentinels around your cattle when grazing." Colonel Baum, who like Riedesel had a great deal of battlefield experience, was also told that "you must always take your camps in a good position."

Riedesel, as he later put it, "took the liberty of calling attention to the dangers connected with this undertaking, Bennington being at too great a distance, and the enemy too near it. But the English commander was not a man to be dissuaded by anyone from any project he had determined upon." Very few interpreters were sent along with the German soldiers as they headed out into what Captain Glich called "one prodigious forest, bottomed in swamps and morasses." A few days after Baum had set off, Burgoyne dispatched another, smaller force under the command of Colonel Breymann to support him.

Company Surgeon Captain Wasmus was with the first force, which set out on August 11 accompanied by one hundred Tories, one hundred Mohawks, one hundred Canadians, fifty redcoats, and two small cannons. Next day "we set off at six in the morning and marched up a mountain into the woods. We had barely covered one mile when we turned back, and made our camp a mile behind the place where we camped last night." Two days later there was some skirmishing, and one Tory was shot in the leg. Wasmus bandaged the wound. The same day came news that Colonel St. Leger, who was commanding the British force advancing down the valley of the Mohawk River, had just won a victory, but "without a doubt this news is only being spread to encourage our men." (Wasmus was right; the reverse was the case.) On August 14 they reached a place called Sancoick, deserted like all the other settlements they came to, where "the Savages destroyed the furniture of a beautiful house, including a fine English clock, and stole some

Portuguese dollars and English guineas they found in a chest." They also made contact with the main American force, estimated at nearly two thousand, and drove them back. "Today we learned how they fight: they either lie on the ground or stand behind a tree, load, aim, and fire. They run from one tree to another and then forward." One of the Mohawk leaders was killed in this action and "the Savages were so enraged by this loss that they wanted to depart for Canada at once." The next day "the attack upon our right wing started again." The left was quiet, but "the local inhabitants come and go through our camp, and will surely report to the enemy how weak we are." Also, "the Savages are all lying behind the baggage, dispirited." On August 16, after a quiet morning, it was reported that "the enemy are marching in force against our right wing and plan to encircle us," whereupon the Savages "lay down behind the trees and refused to advance." At half past twelve "a violent volley was discharged against the entrenchment occupied by 35 dragoons, who boldly returned their fire. Our men were able to re-load quickly behind the cover of their entrenchment, but the moment they rose up to take aim, they were shot through the head."

Wasmus set up a dressing station behind a big oak tree near this entrenchment. The Indians crowded in with him until the firing grew heavier, when one of them "emitted a strange, indescribable cry, where-upon they all ran down the mountain to the baggage. The cannon in our entrenchment fell silent because the sergeant and eight men who tended it had all been killed or wounded." Soon

we were completely surrounded. We withdrew as fast as we could while I was still busy dressing wounds. While following the regiment in a great hurry I stumbled over a large fallen tree behind our position. As I got up the enemy came rushing over our entrenchment. Three of them took aim at me and fired. I fell to the ground behind the tree while the bullets whistled terrifyingly over my head. I stayed there lying on the ground until the enemy came up and rather rudely told me to get on my feet. One grabbed my arm and another, saying that he ought to kill me, put the point of his bayonet against my chest and tightened his finger on the trigger of his gun. He asked me whether I was a Britisher or a Hessian. I told him I was a surgeon with the Brunswick army, then shook hands with him and called him friend and brother, for one will do anything when in deep trouble. Fortunately he understood my phrase—"Freund und Bruder"—and lowered his gun. But he took my watch and after holding it to his ear put it in his pocket. After this he made a friendly face and was decent enough to offer me a drink of rum from his wooden flask.

✻

Wasmus was at once put to work tending the American as well as the German wounded, which he did willingly enough.

According to General Stark, who commanded at Bennington (and who reminded Wasmus of a tailor named Müller back home in Wolfen-büttel), the battle was "the hottest I ever saw in my life. It represented one continuous clap of thunder." It also represented a triumph for the two thousand highly motivated but poorly trained and ill-equipped militia-men over Colonel Baum's disciplined troops. Many years later one of those militiamen, David Holbrook, who had been seventeen at the time, put in for a military pension, and in his application recalled an incident that characterized the battle. It occurred when the Hessians took posi-tion in a field, drawn up according to the book in a single line, and Colo-nel Seth Warner was bringing up his Green Mountain Boys to face them.

✻

About the same time, an old man, with an old Queen Anne's iron sword and mounted upon an old black mare, with about ninety robust men following him in files two deep, came up and filed in in front of the company commanded by Captain Parker, in which this declarer [Holbrook] then was. And, just as the old man had got his men to the spot and halted, his mare fell, and he jumped upon a large white oak stump and gave the command. Captain Parker, seeing the old man's company between him and the enemy, ordered his men to file in between their files, which were some distance apart, and which was immediately done, and the battle then became desperate. And immediately this declarer heard a tremendous crash up in the woods at the right wing of the American troops, which was seconded by a yell, the most terrible that he ever heard. Then he heard the voice of Colonel Warner, like thunder, "Fix bayonets! Charge!" Then the old man on the stump cried out, "Charge, boys!" and jumped from the stump and ran towards the enemy. His men, some with, and some without bayonets, followed suit and rushed upon the enemy with all their might, who seeing us coming, took to their heels and were completely routed. As we came up to the enemy's lines, their fieldpieces being charged, a Sergeant Luttington knocked down the man with the port fire and caught hold of the limber and whirled about the piece and fired it at the enemy, and the blaze overtook them before they had got ten rods and mowed down a large number of them. Those of the Americans who had not got too much fatigued pursued and killed and took a number of the enemy.

The son of militia officer Captain Stafford later wrote: "The result of the day's battle is well known. The Hessians and other troops with them suffered a total defeat; and not only were the stores at Bennington protected and saved, and the army of Burgoyne weakened by the loss of a considerable body of troops, but the spirits of the people greatly encouraged, and the hope of final success revived. From that time there was less difficulty in collecting troops; and the recruiting of our army at Bemis's Heights, or Saratoga, as it is often called, was more easily effected."

On August 16 Captain Wasmus wrote in his diary: "The future is alarming. The people here seem to be extremely enraged; none of us can speak their language and we all wonder what will become of us—but we cheered up a bit when we were regaled with a dinner of beef, pork, potatoes, and punch." Two days later he met an American doctor who had been born in Mecklenburg "and had trained with Muncipal Surgeon Fricke in Brunswick. He said his salary amounted to sixty dollars in paper money, and tried to persuade me to accept some. . . . He also regaled us with Madeira wine, and we became high-spirited." On August

19 he was paroled and set off with several others for Boston. On the way "our march went through the parish of Pownal to Williamstown. We were no longer treated as prisoners, but rode and traveled as we pleased. As we passed, people stood in front of their houses looking at us with the same intense curiosity as the people in Germany when the first rhinoceros arrived there. We understood no English but they treated us like friends, spontaneously offering us milk and beer."

Back at headquarters General von Riedesel sat down to write his report to Duke Charles of Brunswick. "Fortune is often fickle, but especially so in war," he began, and then went on, reasonably enough, to lay the entire blame on General Burgoyne.

SARATOGA

Galling though it must have been for General von Riedesel to serve under Burgoyne, his feelings on the subject were mild when compared with those of his wife, Frederika Charlotte Louise von Massow, also born into a military family and daughter of a general who had served under Frederick the Great. A good-looking redhead of strong character and outspoken tongue, known to the Hessian soldiers as "Lady Fritz" or "Red Hazel," she was devoted to her husband, "the best of all men" and was not slow to express her indignation if she thought he was being slighted—even if, to the general's embarrassment, her target on one occasion was the Hereditary Prince of Brunswick himself. (Riedesel acknowledged that the prince had pulled "a knavish trick" and was a man "who cannot exist without intrigue," but he was still the prince and she should mind her tongue.) But though obedient in this and most other matters, she refused to be parted from him for any length of time, and when he was posted to Canada, she was determined to follow. She did agree to stay behind until her current and third pregnancy was completed, but by the time the general landed in Quebec, she was well on her way to London. Here she was presented to the king, who flustered her with a surprise kiss on the cheek ("I became fiery red, it was so sudden"), and to Queen Charlotte, who took a liking to her. She also did some shopping—nothing frivolous, just sensible items such as bouillon cubes "so that the family could always have good soup." ("Portable soup, or solid broth," ran an advertisement in the *London Chronicle*, "made from beef, veal, mutton, and chicken, is found exceedingly useful on various occasions; and has particularly recommended itself to gentlemen on journeys and at sea.") By the time she arrived in Canada, the army had already set out, but the general, as eager to see her as she him, had made arrangements for her to join him immediately at the front. After procuring a light carriage called a calash, she set forth once again, accompanied by her three small daughters, two maids, a cook, and "the faithful Rockel," who had served her father as a forester and was now the family's manservant.

By mid-September the army was in deep trouble. In July Burgoyne had already begun covering himself by writing to Lord Germain that "your lordship will pardon me if I a little lament that my orders do not give me the latitude I ventured to propose in my original project for the campaign. . . . Were I at liberty to march in force immediately to my left, instead of to my right, I should have little doubt of subduing before winter the province where the rebellion originated." Since then the situation had deteriorated. Defeated by Benedict Arnold at Fort Stanwix, St. Leger's army advancing down the Mohawk Valley had been forced to turn back. Howe had gone south to Philadelphia, as he had said he would, and though there was some hope that General Sir Henry Clinton would venture out of New York and move up the Hudson, he had too few troops for anything other than a feint. American forces were moving in behind the Anglo-Hessian army, threatening its already tenuous lines of supply. Slowed down by an artillery train of 138 cannon, far more than he could possibly need, and by an equally cumbersome baggage train that included thirty wagons containing wine, champagne, and clothes for himself and his mistress, Burgoyne's army moved at a crawl. Winter was approaching, and following Bennington volunteers were pouring in to join General Horatio Gates's army, which already outnumbered Burgoyne's and was barring his route to the south.

"During this time my husband was obliged to encamp with the main body of the army while I remained about an hour's march behind," wrote Frederika, who had taken up quarters in a small farmhouse.

✳

Every morning I visited my husband in the camp and often stayed to have lunch with him, or else he would come to my quarters and eat with me. Every day the army was engaged in minor skirmishing of little importance.

On the 7th of October my husband and the entire general staff broke camp; our misfortunes may be said to have begun at that moment. I had just sat down to breakfast with my husband at his quarters. General Frazer, along with Generals Burgoyne and Phillips, were to have dined with me that evening. I saw a good deal of movement among the troops, and my husband told me that there was to be a reconnaissance. On my way home I met many savages in their war dress, armed with guns. When I asked where they were going, they cried out "War! War!"

Feeling greatly distressed, I had scarcely got back to my quarters when I heard skirmishing and firing. This grew steadily heavier, becoming a dreadful, terrifying cannonade which left me more dead than alive. About three in the afternoon, instead of the guests who were to have dined with me, they brought in poor General Frazer on a litter, mortally wounded. Our dining table, which had been set for dinner, was taken away and in its place they fixed up a bed for the general. I sat in a corner of the room trembling. The noise of the firing grew louder all the time. I was constantly tormented by the dreadful thought that they might bring in my husband in the same manner.

The general said to the surgeon, "Do not conceal anything from me. Must I die?"

The bullet had gone through his bowels, just as in the case of Major Harnage; unfortunately, however, the general had eaten a hearty breakfast and his intestines being swollen, the ball had gone through them and not, as in the major's case, in between. Amidst his groans I heard him often exclaim, "Oh, fatal ambition! Poor General

Burgoyne! My poor wife!" Prayers were read to him. He sent a message to General Burgoyne asking to be buried the following day at six in the evening on the top of a hill which was a sort of redoubt.

I did not know which way to turn. The whole entryway and the other rooms were filled with people suffering from camp-sickness, a kind of dysentery. Finally, toward evening, I saw my husband coming. At once I forgot all my sufferings and thanked God for sparing him to me. He ate in great haste behind the house with me and his adjutant. We had been told that we had defeated the enemy, but judging by the gloomy and downcast faces I knew that the opposite was the case. Before my husband left he took me to one side and told me that things might go very badly and that I must be constantly ready to depart.

I could not go to sleep as I had General Frazer and other gentlemen in my room. I was afraid that my children would wake up and cry, and thus disturb the poor dying man, who often apologized for causing so much trouble. About three in the morning they told me he could not last much longer. I wrapped up the children in their bed coverings and went with them into the entryway. At eight o'clock in the morning he died. After they had washed the corpse they wrapped it in a sheet and laid it on a bedstead. We then went back into the room and had this sad sight in front of us the whole day. Wounded officers of my acquaintance kept coming in, and the cannonade resumed. A retreat was spoken of, but no move was made.

About four in the afternoon I watched as a new house that was being built for me went up in flames; the enemy were nearby. We were told that General Burgoyne intended to fulfill General Frazer's last wish and have him buried at six o'clock at the place he had designated. This caused a needless delay, which only added to the army's misfortunes. Precisely at six the corpse was brought out and we watched as all the generals and their retinues went up the hill to take part in the obsequies. The English chaplain, Mr. Brudenel, performed the funeral service. Cannonballs flew constantly around and over them. (Afterwards, the American General Gates was to say that if he had known it was a funeral he would not have allowed any firing.) Many other cannonballs flew by near me, but I had no thoughts for my own danger: my eyes were fixed upon the hill, where I could distinctly see my husband in the midst of the enemy's fire.

Orders had been issued that the army should withdraw after the funeral, and the horses were already harnessed to our calashes. . . . The greatest silence had been enjoined. Fires had been lit in every direction and many tents left standing to deceive the enemy. We traveled through the night. Little Frederika was afraid and often began to cry, and I had to hold a pocket handkerchief over her mouth.

At six in the morning, to everyone's surprise, we halted. General Burgoyne had given orders that the artillery should be drawn up and counted. This alarmed us, as a few more good marches would have brought us to safety. During this delay my husband, who was completely exhausted, came and sat in our calash, which meant that my maidservants had to move out; he slept nearly three hours with his head on my shoulder.

At last the army resumed its march, but we had scarcely gone on for an hour when another halt was made, this time because some of the enemy had been sighted. There were only about two hundred of them, a reconnaissance party, and could easily have been taken by our troops, had General Burgoyne not lost his head. It rained in torrents.

On the 9th we spent the whole day in a pouring rain, ready to march at a moment's notice. The savages had lost their courage, and were seen in all directions going home; the smallest reverse discourages them, especially if there is nothing to plunder. My chambermaid did nothing but curse her situation and tear her hair. When I begged her to compose herself or she would be taken for a savage, she became still more frantic and asked if that would bother me. When I answered "yes," she tore off her bonnet so that her hair hung down over face and exclaimed, "It's all very well for you to talk! You have your husband but we have nothing! We're either going to die here miserably or lose everything we have." To calm her down I promised to make good any losses suffered by her or the other maid, Lena, who was also very frightened but said nothing.

Toward evening we at last came to Saratoga, only half an hour's march from the place where we had spent the whole day. I was soaked by the steady rain, and had to remain wet the entire night as there was nowhere I could change my clothes. I undressed the children in front of a good fire and we lay down on some straw. General Phillips came to visit us and I asked him why we did not continue our retreat; my husband had offered to cover it with his troops and there was still time for the army to get through. "Poor woman, you amaze me!" he replied. "Here you are, wet through, and yet you still want to push ahead in this weather. If only you were our commanding general! He has called a halt because he is tired and wants to spend the night here and give us a supper party." General Burgoyne was particularly fond of indulging himself in this last regard. He spent half the nights singing and drinking, and amusing himself with his mistress, who was the wife of a commissary and shared his love of champagne.

On the 10th, at seven in the morning, I drank some tea by way of refreshment and we hoped that we would at last get on our way once more. To cover our retreat, General Burgoyne ordered that the beautiful houses and mills belonging to General Schuyler should be burned. Then an English officer brought me some excellent broth, which he insisted on sharing with me. After that we set out on our march, but soon halted again. The greatest misery and disorder prevailed in the army. The commissaries had neglected to distribute provisions among the troops. There were cattle enough, but none had been slaughtered. More than thirty officers came to me for relief. I made coffee and tea and divided my food among them; thanks to our cook we were constantly re-supplied. He was an arrant knave but extremely resourceful and at night would often cross small rivers to steal sheep, poultry, and pigs from the country people. For these he charged us a very high price, although we did not realize it at the time.

About two in the afternoon, the firing of cannon and small arms was again heard, and all was alarm and confusion. My husband sent me a message to go at once to a house nearby. I seated myself in the calash with the children, and had only just driven up to the house when I saw on the opposite side of the Hudson River five or six men with guns, aiming at us. Almost involuntarily I threw the children to the floor of the calash and myself over them. At that moment the churls fired, shattering the arm of a poor English soldier behind us, who was already wounded and was also heading for the house. The moment we arrived, a frightful cannonade began, mainly directed at the house where we were sheltering, probably because the enemy, seeing so many people flocking around it, thought it was the generals' headquarters. But alas! It harbored none but wounded soldiers and women. We were finally obliged to take refuge in the cellar, where I lay down on the ground in a corner near the door, my children's heads on my lap. In this manner we passed the entire night. A horrible stench, the cries of the children, and my own anguish prevented me from closing my eyes.

The next morning the cannonade began again, but from a different direction. I urged everyone to leave the cellar while I had it cleaned as otherwise we would all be sick. They agreed, and I at once set many hands to work. This was urgently needed as the women and children, being afraid to venture forth, had soiled the whole cellar. When I was alone I surveyed our place of refuge. It consisted of three fine cellars, well arched. I proposed that the most dangerously wounded officers be brought into one of them; that the women should be in another; and that all the rest should stay in the third, which was nearest the entrance. I had just given the cellars a good sweeping and fumigated them by sprinkling vinegar on burning coals, and people were beginning to take their assigned places, when a new and terrible cannonade once again threw us all into alarm. Many persons who had no right to come in threw themselves against the door. My children were already under the cellar steps and we would all have been crushed if God had not given me the strength to place myself before the door, extend my arms, and prevent them from going in. Had I not done so we would all have been seriously injured.

Eleven cannonballs went through the house and we could plainly hear them rolling over our heads. One poor soldier, whose leg they were about to amputate, having been laid upon a table for this purpose, had the other leg taken off by a cannonball in the very middle of the operation. His comrades all ran off, and when they came back they found him in a corner of the room, where he had rolled in his anguish, scarcely breathing. I was more dead than alive, not because of my own danger but because of my husband's; however, he often sent to see how I was, and to tell me that he was still safe.

The wife of the wounded Major Harnage, who had been shot in the bowels, and Mrs. Reynels, wife of the lieutenant who had shared his broth with the baroness the day before, were among those taking refuge in the cellar. The next day Lt. Reynels was brought in

not yet dead, but a cannonball had taken off his arm close to the shoulder. During the whole night we heard his moans, which resounded fearfully through the vaulted cellars. The poor man died towards morning.

The next day we got things better regulated. Major Harnage, his wife, and Mrs. Reynels made a little room in the corner by hanging curtains from the ceiling. They wanted to fix up another corner for me in the same manner, but I preferred to remain near the door in case of fire. I had some straw brought in and laid my bed on it and slept there with my children, while my maids slept near us.

Our cook saw to our meals but we were short of water. To quench our thirst I was often obliged to drink wine, which I also gave to the children. It was also the only thing my husband could take . . . .He never came into the house at night, but lay outside by the watch-fires;

this alone could have caused his death, as the nights were now damp and cold.

As the shortage of water continued we at last found a soldier's wife who was brave enough to bring us water from the river. No one else dared to do it as the enemy shot at the head of every man who approached the river; but this woman they left alone. Afterwards they told us that they spared her because of her sex.

✳

Many others were also suffering from thirst, among them Lt. Anburey of the British army, which was now pretty much surrounded and greatly outnumbered:

"After the action of the 19th of September, the men continually slept with their accoutrements on, and after the action of the 7th [October], never had a tent to shelter them from the heavy and almost incessant rains." They were

✳

without the refreshment of spirits during this period; and after our arrival at Saratoga, debarred from that very essential to the health and convenience of the troops, water, although close to a fine rivulet, it being at the hazard of life, in the daytime, to get any, from the number of riflemen the enemy had posted in trees; and at night the men were prevented, as they were sure to be taken prisoners if they attempted it. All the water that the army was supplied with was from a very muddy spring, and what they could get out of the holes the cattle made with their feet. By way of luxury, and to render their provisions more palatable, when it rained hard the men used to catch it in their caps, to mix with their flour.

Upon our arrival at Saratoga, three companies of our regiment, one of which was that I belong to, were posted in a small redoubt close to the creek; our situation was by no means capable of making any great defense, but merely to observe if the enemy passed the creek in any force. Had they attempted it, we were to have kept up a fire during their crossing, then to have abandoned our station and joined the main body of the army. This post was a small square redoubt, constructed with logs breast high, and the only shelter afforded to the troops was from those angles which faced the enemy, as the others were so exposed that we had several men killed and wounded in the redoubt by the riflemen, who were posted in trees. We could discern them every morning at daybreak, taking their situations upon the most lofty trees they met with, by which means they commanded some of the interior parts of the redoubt. Our situation was such that a man risked his life if he ventured in the daytime to look over the works; and to convince you how sure these men are of hitting their mark, the soldiers, out of derision, would hoist up a cap upon a stick over the works when instantly there would be one or two shot fired at it, and as many holes through it. I have seen a cap that has been perforated with three balls. We certainly could have dislodged such troublesome neighbours, or prevented their ascending the trees, but we had orders not to fire, as it might bring on a skirmishing attack.

Meanwhile, Baroness von Riedesel remained in her cellar.

One day I undertook the care of Major Plumpfield, adjutant to General Phillips. He had been shot through both cheeks by a small musket ball which had also shattered his teeth and grazed his tongue. The suppurating matter from the wound almost choked him and the only nourishment he could take was a little broth or some other liquid. I gave him one of our bottles of Rhine wine, hoping that its acidity would cleanse the wound. He kept some continually in his mouth, and the effect was so beneficial that he was cured, and I acquired another friend.

In this horrible situation we remained six days. Finally, there was talk of capitulation, as by temporizing for so long our retreat had been cut off. A cessation of hostilities took place and my husband, who was completely exhausted, for the first time in a long while was able to lie down on a proper bed.

On the 17th of October the capitulation was signed. Our generals waited upon the American commander, General Gates, and the troops laid down their arms and surrendered themselves prisoners of war. Now the good woman who had brought us water at the risk of her life received the reward for her services. Everyone threw a whole handful of money into her apron, and she received over twenty guineas. At such a moment, the heart seems to be particularly susceptible to feelings of gratitude.

My husband sent a groom with a message that I should go to him with our children, and once again we took our seats in the dear old calash. As we passed through the American camp I was pleased to see that no one looked at us with scorn. On the contrary, they all greeted us, many showing compassion at the sight of a mother and her small children. I confess I was anxious when I came into the enemy's camp, as the situation was so new to me, but as I approached the tents a noble-looking man came forward, took the children out of the calash, embraced and kissed them, and then, with tears in his eyes, helped me to alight. "You tremble," said he, "but you have nothing to fear." "No," I replied, "for you are so kind, and have been so tender to my children, that it has inspired me with courage."

This was General Schuyler, who took her and the children to his own tent where "he entertained me with excellent smoked tongue, beef-steaks, potatoes, good butter, and bread. Never have I eaten a better meal. I was content, and so was everyone else; but what gladdened me most was that my husband was now out of all danger."

And now, once again, General von Riedesel had to sit down and write to Duke Charles of Brunswick: "Your Serene Highness will understand by the accompanying report, now submitted to you, into what a desolate position our fine maneuvers have placed me and the troops of Your Highness. The reputation I have gained in Germany has been sacrificed to certain individuals, and I consider myself the most unfortunate man on earth . . ."

Fortunately, and quite rightly, neither the duke nor public opinion in Germany blamed Riedesel; rather, as this account of the surrender from the *Brunswick Journal* makes clear, they knew who they had to thank for the calamity:

General Burgoyne did not for a moment lose his sound sleep and good appetite. When he met General Gates, shortly after the signing of the treaty, in the American camp, he not only manifested his usual remarkable serenity and politeness, but had attired himself in full court dress, as if going to attend some gala occasion. He wore costly regimentals bordered with gold, and a hat with streaming plumes. He had bestowed the greatest care on his whole appearance, so that he looked more like a dandy than a warrior. By contrast the American general was dressed in a plain blue coat with few markings of rank.

The two generals approached each other until they were only a few paces apart, when they stopped. The English general doffed his richly decorated hat in an elegant manner, and making a very polite bow, said, "General, fortune of war has made me your prisoner." The American general returned his greeting and said, "You will always find me ready to testify that it was not brought about through any fault of your excellency."

There were at least two reasons why Gates told such a whopper: professional courtesy, and to enhance his own achievement. At any rate, they then adjourned to Gates's tent for a simple meal served on boards laid across barrels.

The drink consisted of cider and rum mixed with water. Burgoyne appeared at this time in excellent humor. He talked a good deal and said many things flattering to the Americans. He also proposed a toast to General Washington, a courtesy that Gates returned by drinking the health of the king of England. Burgoyne ate and drank throughout with the greatest appetite. His behavior under such circumstances caused the German officers who were present great astonishment.

✷

Immediately following the surrender—a word he never used, preferring the term "convention"—Burgoyne began assigning blame: He had been inadequately supported from Canada; the Hessians, thanks to "the strong disposition in the Germans to be prisoners rather than endure hard blows," had let him down badly; and so had Sir William Howe, who had quite unexpectedly taken his army to Philadelphia instead of advancing up the Hudson to Albany. Also, his orders from Lord George Germain were so tightly drawn that he had "no latitude," an excuse for which he had already laid the groundwork. "If our Commander's orders had been general," wrote Lt. Anburey, clearly unaware that Burgoyne himself had been involved in drawing them up, "and not such absolute ones as could not be varied from, he would not have been under the necessity of engaging the King's army in any hazardous attempt, as he might have re-crossed the Hudson's, and changed the war to the defensive."

A few months later, while the rest of his army remained prisoners of war, Burgoyne was allowed to return to England on parole, and the wrangling began. It was to last many years, but Burgoyne was a hard man to keep down, and he not only managed to escape disgrace but within a few years was made commander in chief in Ireland. He also had a big success with his play *The Heiress* (Horace Walpole saw it twice in one day, pronouncing it "the genteelest comedy in the English language"), and, his wife having died, took up with a beautiful young actress, Susan Caulfield, by whom he had four children, all of them raised at the expense of the Derby family.

As an envoi to the general—his final bow—here is an extract from a letter printed in the *London Chronicle* describing a visit he paid to Birmingham in August 1778:

✴

In the afternoon arrived here from Bath, on his way to his seat in Lancashire, attended by two servants only, Lieutenant-General Burgoyne. His arrival was no sooner known than the bells began ringing, and a great number of people assembled before the Swan Inn where the General had stopped. After some little refreshment he proceeded to New-Hall Street, to view Clay's Paper Manufactory there; by which time the spectators were become very numerous, both in the street and at the windows of the houses therein, who all discovered an uncommon propensity to see this unfortunate commander, whose conduct in America had been the subject of universal conversation in the political world. The General, after viewing the manufactory, came to the door and was received with loud acclamations, which he politely returned by bowing; then getting into his carriage he pursued his journey . . . amidst reiterated shouts of the populace.

✴

WINNERS & LOSERS

From the diary of Elijah Fisher of Maine: "Gen. Burgoin and his howl army surrendered themselves Prisoners of Ware and Come to Captelate with our army and Gen. Gates (five thousand seven hundred Prisoners besides the seven hundred toreys that Gen. Gates would not take as prisoners of Ware that the Ingens garded to Canady). . . . By reason of the hardships heat and cold and hard marches broght that Pain on in my side again."

"That pain" was the reason Fisher was in the army rather than out of it. He had enlisted as a militiaman early in 1776, although even then his health was not so good: "July 29th. I was taken sick of the feaver and was sick five or six Weeks and after that I gits better . . . August 29th. I was taken with a stitch of pain in my rite Side (I being very weak). As I grue stronger the pain Increast." After a stay at "the Hospiteble at Newark," which did him no good, his case was brought to the attention of a Mrs. Brown, who "thought it was the gravels in the kitteney and if you took a Quart of ginn and a Tea dish of muster seed and a hand full of horseradish roots and steep them together and take a glass of that Every morning she thought it wode help me. I follow'd her Derections and found Benefit by it." Having survived this kill-or-cure medicine, Fisher had returned home when his time was up, but then reenlisted "with Capt. M. Knapp for three years though I was unwell then, yet he said that as I got my sickness in the army it was no more than Right but I should have my support from the army and that I mite stay at home till I got able to Jine the army and draw my pay all the time." But though a complainer, Fisher was not a malingerer, and in August "having got prity well I Leaves home and sets out for the army." After Saratoga he hoped "that we should go to our own state for winter Quarters, but in lue of that we were sent another way." And so: "Dec. 4th. We Come and jined Gen. Washington's army at Whitemarsh in Pencilvania State. And the Pain in my side Continued to grow Worse."

From Joseph Hodgkins (now a captain), to his wife from Saratoga on October 17, 1777:

My Dear,

These may inform you that I am well, through the goodness of God, and hope these lines will find you and all friends possessed of the same blessing. I must just inform you that this day we have received Gen. Burgoyne and all his army as prisoners of war, and may we all rejoice and give the glory to whom it is due. I have not time to be particular, we are to march immediately.

Ten days later he wrote again from Albany:

※

Loving Wife:

These few lines bring you my most affectionate regards hoping they will find you & our children & friends in as good health as they leave me at this time. Through the goodness of God I am pretty well now. I have had something of the camp disorder & lost most all my flesh but I hope soon to pick up my crumbs again. We have had a very fatiguing campaign, but as we have done the business we came here for, I hope none us of will complain of a little hardship. I wish I could inform you that I thought our fatigue was over for this year, but to the contrary I expect we shall march tomorrow morning down the river towards the Peekskills & I expect we shall be ordered towards Philadelphia to take another winter's campaign in the Jerseys. Soldiers must not complain. . . .

※

From the *Journal of the American War,* by Sergeant Roger Lamb of the British army:

※

During the time of the cessation of arms, while the articles of capitulation were preparing, the soldiers of the two armies often saluted and discoursed with each other from the opposite banks of the river, which at Saratoga is about thirty yards wide, and not very deep. A soldier in the 9th regiment, named Maguire, came down to the bank of the river, with a number of his companions, who engaged in conversation with a party of Americans on the opposite shore. In a short time something was observed very forcibly to strike the mind of Maguire. He suddenly darted like lightning from his companions, and resolutely plunged into the stream. At the very same moment, one of the American soldiers, seized with a similar impulse, resolutely dashed into the water, from the opposite shore. The wondering soldiers on both sides beheld them eagerly swim towards the middle of the river, where they met; they hung on each others' necks and wept; and the loud cries of "My brother! My dear brother!" which accompanied the transaction soon cleared up the mystery to the astonished spectators. They were both brothers, the first had emigrated from this country [Ireland], and the other had entered the army; one was in the British and the other in the American service, totally ignorant until that hour that they were engaged in hostile combat against each other's life.

The British and Hessian wounded were brought into the military hospital in Albany, where, according to Dr. James Thacher, they were treated with the same care and attention as the Americans, and were attended by their own doctors. As a patriot Thacher lamented his country's losses, but as a newly qualified physician, he could not but relish the opportunity to improve his skills:

October 24. Not less than one thousand wounded and sick are now in this city; the Dutch church and several private houses are occupied as hospitals. We have about thirty surgeons and mates; and all are constantly employed. I am obliged to devote the whole of my time, from eight o'clock in the morning to a late hour in the evening, to the care of our patients. Here is a fine field for professional improvement. Amputating limbs, trepanning fractured skulls, and dressing the most formidable wounds, have familiarized my mind to scenes of woe. . . . It is my lot to have twenty wounded men committed to my care by Dr. Potts, our surgeon-general; one of whom, a young man, received a musket ball through his cheeks, cutting its way through the teeth on each side, and the substance of the tongue; his sufferings have been great, but he now begins to articulate tolerably well. Another had the whole side of his face torn off by a cannonball, laying his mouth and throat open to view. A brave soldier received a musket-ball in his forehead; observing that it did not penetrate deep, it was imagined that the ball rebounded and fell out; but after several days, on examination, I detected the ball laying flat on the bone, and spread under the skin, which I removed. No one can doubt but he received his wound while facing the enemy, and it is fortunate for the brave fellow that his skull proved too thick for the ball to penetrate. But, in another instance, a soldier's wound was not so honorable; he received a ball in the bottom of his foot, which could not have happened unless when in the act of running away from the enemy. This poor fellow is held in derision by his comrades, and is made a subject for their wit for having the mark of a coward.

A military escort accompanied the captured army on its march to Boston, but responsibility for keeping order among the troops remained with their own officers, among them Lt. Anburey:

We were two days in crossing the Green Mountains, which are part of the chain of mountains that run through the whole Continent of America, more commonly known by the name of the Allegany Mountains. The roads across them were almost impassable and, to add to the difficulty, when we had got half over there came on a very heavy fall of snow. After this it is impossible to describe the confusion that ensued: carts breaking down, others sticking fast, some oversetting, horses tumbling with their loads of baggage, men cursing, women shrieking, and children squalling! It should seem that I was to encounter every unpleasant duty that can fall to the lot of an officer, for this very day I had the baggage guard; exclusive of being covered with snow, and riding about after the bat-men [orderlies] to keep them together and to assist each other, my attention was directed to a scene which I did not think it possible human nature could have supported, for in the midst of the heavy snowstorm, upon a baggage cart, and nothing to shelter her from the inclemency of the weather but a bit of an old oil-cloth, a soldier's wife was delivered of a child. She and the infant are both well and are now at this place [Cambridge]. It may be said that women who follow a camp are of such a masculine nature they are able to bear all hardships; this woman was quite the reverse, being small and of a very delicate constitution.

Among those watching the captured troops as they passed through Cambridge was Hannah Winthrop, wife to a Harvard professor. On November 11 she wrote to her friend Mercy Otis Warren:

Last Thursday, which was a very stormy day, a large number of British troops came softly through the town via Watertown to Prospect Hill. On Friday we heard the Hessians were to make a procession in the same route. We thought we should have nothing to do with them, but view them as they passed. To be sure, the sight was truly astonishing. I never had the least idea that the Creation produced such a sordid set of creatures in human figure—poor, dirty, emaciated men, great numbers of women, who seemed to be the beasts of burden, having bushel baskets on their backs, by which they were bent double. The contents seemed to be pots and kettles, various sorts of furniture, children peeping through gridirons and other utensils, some very young infants who were born on the road, the women barefoot, clothed in dirty rags. Such effluvia filled the air while they were passing that had they not been smoking all the time, I should have been apprehensive of being contaminated. After a noble-looking [American] advance guard, General Burgoyne headed this terrible group on horseback, the other general also, clothed in blue cloaks. Hessians, Waldeckers, Anspackers, Brunswickers, etc., followed on. The Hessian general [Riedesel] gave us a polite bow as they passed. Not so the British. Their baggage wagons drawn by poor, half-starved horses. But to bring up the rear another fine, noble-looking guard of American brawny victorious yeomanry, who assisted in bringing these sons of slavery to terms.

Ensign Thomas Hughes of the 53rd Regiment, who had been made prisoner when the Americans retook Fort Ticonderoga, had already passed through Boston, where he and some other officers were held for a while on a prison ship. Following several escapes and an outbreak of fever and dysentery, the Commissary of Prisoners agreed to allow the officers to be released on parole, and several of them were sent off to the village of Pepperell. Here, though confined within a radius of one mile, they were free to make their own arrangements. As he records in *Journal by Thos. Hughes for his Amusement, and Designed only for his Perusal by the Time he Attains the Age of 50 if he Lives so Long*, Hughes, who was only eighteen at the time and, like many well-to-do officers, was accompanied by his manservant, made himself comfortable, despite boredom and severe culture shock.

✳

Oct 22nd. Procur'd quarters in a house, in which I have agreed to pay two silver dollars per week for board &c &c. The family are very civil—it consists of Father (who is almost deaf), Mother (a talkative old woman), and two daughters, who are of the order of old maids, confounded ugly, with beards an inch long.

Oct 25th. This town is quite a new settlement and so little clear'd that in some places the houses are a mile distant. We are almost as much out of the world here as if we were in the deserts of Arabia, and the inhabitants as ignorant as the Hottentots. I have been asked how often I have visited Jerusalem and if I did not live close by it, though I told them I lived in England; and then they ask'd if England was not a fine town. What a life am I to lead? I am sick of their absurdities.

Oct 26th. I find that the people here have not the least idea of a gentleman. Our servants are treated just like ourselves, and they are surpris'd to find our men won't eat at the same table with us, to which they are always invited. Two of our gentlemen agreeing with some inhabitants about boarding, the only thing the people objected to was the article of washing. "Oh! If that is the only obstacle," says a Committee man, who went with them, "it is easily remov'd. Send them a tub, and give them a little soap, and they can wash their own clothes."

November 1st. This life being such a one as perhaps I may never see again, I cannot refrain from describing it. We have but one room to eat and sit in, which is in common with all the family, master, mistress, and servant, and what to call it I know not, as it serves for parlour, kitchen, and workroom. About 9 o'clock, Lt. Brown (who lives with me) and myself breakfast, but they all wonder how we can sleep so long. Our breakfast is bread and milk, or boil'd Indian corn with butter and treacle spread over it. This is pretty substantial, and after it we generally walk in the woods, to gather chestnuts or throw stones at squirrels. About 12 o'clock the whole family collects for dinner, which soon after smokes upon the board; and whilst it is cooling, Father shuts his eyes, mutters an unintelligible monstrous long grace, and down we all sit with no other distinction but Brown and me getting pewter plates—whereas the others have wooden platters. Our food is fat salt pork, and sauce (the name they give to roots and greens). . . . The dinners are upon that free and easy mode that neither gentleman or lady use any ceremony—all hands in the dish at once— which gives many pretty opportunities for laughter, as two or three of us often catch hold of the same piece. This meal over, another grace is said, and we all disperse to our different employments, theirs working and ours the best we can find. At nightfall a large fire is made on the hearth, and the kitchen (or whatever it is) receives the whole family, which would present an high scene to an unconcern'd spectator— Mother, Brown, and me around the fire, she knitting and asking us silly questions; our servant at the opposite corner of the chimney from us; at our back two or three women spinning with large noisy wheels, and in the middle of the room sits Father, and one or two apprentice boys shelling Indian corn. We have no candles, but the room is lighted by splinters of pine wood flung into the fire. About 8 o'clock we get bread and milk for supper; a little after Father begins to yawn, upon which we stand up. He says prayers, and we depart to our beds.

Our apartment, or rather the place we lay in, extends over the whole house, and is what is commonly call'd the garret. We have three beds in it—one of which contains Brown and me, in the second sleep our two young ladies, and in the third rest the servant and the apprentice. Our room is not the worse for being a repository of fruit and nuts, and we generally make an attack on the apples before we get up of a morn. If this is the kind of life the poets say so much of, and call Rural Happiness, I wish to my soul that they were here, and I in London.

As it happened, Hughes's stay in Pepperell was cut short as a result of his getting together with other officers on parole for dinner at a tavern; there "we were all very merry, but in the end one or two getting mellow and kicking up a dust, they were sent to prison for talking disrespectfully of the Congress." It was then discovered that the tavern was 150 yards outside the one-mile limit of their parole, for which violation all the officers were sent back to Cambridge.

Lt. Anburey was also paroled, in his case to Mystic, Massachusetts. As he wrote in a letter home, he too had several encounters with the locals, one of which took place in May of the following year:

A few days since, walking out with some officers, we stopped at a house to purchase vegetables; whilst the other officers were bargaining with the woman of the house, I observed an elderly woman sitting by the fire, who was continually eyeing us, and every now and then shedding a tear. Just as we were quitting the house she got up, and bursting into tears said, "Gentlemen, will you let a poor distracted woman speak a word to you before you go?" We, as you must naturally imagine, were all astonished, and upon enquiring what she wanted, with the most poignant grief and sobbing as if her heart was on the point of breaking, asked if any of us knew her son, who was killed at the battle of Hubbarton, a Colonel Francis. Several of us informed her that we had seen him after he was dead. She then enquired about his pocketbook, and if any of his papers were safe, as some related to his estates, and if any of the soldiers had got his watch; if she could but obtain that in remembrance of her dear, dear son, she should be happy. Captain Ferguson, of our regiment, who was of the party, told her, as to the Colonel's papers and pocketbook, he was fearful they were either lost or destroyed; but pulling a watch from his fob, said, "There, good woman, if that can make you happy, take it, and God bless you." We were all much surprised, as unacquainted he had made a purchase of it from a drum-boy. On seeing it, it is impossible to describe the joy and grief that was depicted in her countenance; I never in all my life beheld such a strength of passion; she kissed it, looked unutterable gratitude at Captain Ferguson, then kissed it again. . . . She could only sob her thanks. Our feelings were lifted up to an inexpressible height; we promised to search after the papers, and I believe, at that moment, could have hazarded life itself to procure them.

Two weeks later Anburey had another encounter with an elderly woman:

Some officers who came from the west of England have instituted the diversion of fighting of cocks. For my part, you know, I ever esteeming it a barbarous custom, and a disgrace to our nation, and cannot but say I was a little pleased at a reprimand that some officers met from an old woman to whom they had applied for a couple of fine birds that were in the yard. She enquired if they were to fight or to kill for eating; being told the former, she in a most violent rage exclaimed, "I swear now you shall have neither of them. I swear now I never saw anything so bloodthirsty as you Britonions be. If you can't be fighting and cutting other people's throats, you must be setting two harmless creatures to kill one another. Go along, go! I have heard of your cruel doings in Watertown (the place where the cocks fought), cutting off the feathers, and the poor creature's comb and gills, and putting iron things upon their legs. Go along, I say!" I could not help laughing to see them decamp in haste, as the old woman had worked herself into such a passion that they expected she would have struck them with her crutch, which she lifted up to give the greater energy to her language.

To the dismay of Hannah Winthrop, the smelly Hessians she had seen pass by her house in Cambridge returned to town the next day, and for several months she had to put up with them as neighbors; to her outrage there was even talk of quartering them in the buildings of Harvard College. Things were a little better when it came to the Riedesels, who were assigned one of the town's finest houses; after all, he was a general and a baron and had bowed to her as he rode by, and the baroness had recently become friends with General Schuyler's daughter, who lived nearby. But then again, the Winthrops can hardly have been pleased when the Riedesels invited a large number of Hessian and British officers to a ball and supper party, complete with illuminations and dancing till dawn, to celebrate the king's official birthday on June 4. "Never, I believe, has 'God save the King' been sung with more enthusiasm or good will," wrote the baroness. "All eyes were full of tears, and it seemed as if everyone was proud to have had the spirit to dare to do this in the midst of our enemies."

Soon afterwards Congress decided not to ratify the Saratoga convention, which would have allowed Burgoyne's army to return home, where they would have freed up other troops to be sent to America. Instead the prisoners were ordered to march to new quarters near Charlottesville, Virginia. The general went with them, and the baroness once again followed in a coach with her children and servants. It was to prove a hard winter journey of over six hundred miles.

One day we came to a pretty little place, but our supply wagon had fallen behind and we could barely endure our hunger. Seeing a quantity of butcher's meat in the house where we had stopped, I begged the woman of the house to let me have some. "I have several kinds," she answered. "There's beef, veal, and lamb." My mouth was already watering as I said, "Give me some, I will pay you well for it." But snapping her fingers almost under my nose, she replied, "Not a morsel shall you have! You come over here to kill us and plunder us and destroy our property, but now you are our prisoners and it's our turn to torment you!" In reply I said, "Do but look at these poor children, almost dead with hunger!" but she remained inflexible. Then Caroline, my three-and-a-half-year-old daughter, went up to her, took her by the hand, and said, in English, "Good woman, I am very hungry!" This was too much for the woman, who took Caroline into another room and gave her an egg. "No," said the good little child, "I have two sisters." At this the woman was touched, and gave her three eggs, saying, "I am just as angry as ever, but I can't refuse the child." Then she softened and offered me bread and milk. I made tea for ourselves and she eyed it longingly, for the Americans are very fond of tea but had resolved not to drink it because of the famous duty which caused the war. I offered her a cup, and poured one out for her. This mollified her completely and she asked me to follow her into the kitchen, where I found her husband gnawing at a pig's tail. When his wife came back from the cellar with a basket of potatoes, which I was delighted to see, he offered her his tit-bit. She chewed it for a while then gave it back to him and he resumed his gnawing. I watched this remarkable display of mutual feeding with astonishment and disgust, but mistaking my expression for one of hunger and envy, the husband held the well-chewed tail out to me. What should I do? If I refused I would hurt his feelings and probably also lose the potatoes. So I took it, pretended to eat it, and then quietly threw it into the fire. We were now on very good terms. They gave me potatoes and some excellent butter, and we made a good supper. Afterwards they provided us with three pretty rooms with good beds where we spent the night.

Following his capture at Bennington, Captain Wasmus, the Brunswick company surgeon, was to spend several years on parole in Massachusetts, mostly at Brimfield, where he boarded with a family called Hitchcock and soon became an accepted member of the community. He learned English, resumed the practice of medicine, and also found time to keep a voluminous diary in which he recorded his observations on New England customs, particularly this:

When a young man sees a young woman he likes, he goes to her house and asks for her company at night. They then spend the whole night sitting together, or lying on the bed, but without taking off their underclothes. They call this "bundling." The parents have no say in the matter, nor do they pay much attention; the young woman is free to bundle if she likes the young man. Nor are there any hard feelings if, after several months, one of them tells the other, "Our characters and temperaments are too different for us ever to be happy together. It's best to part." And that's that.

You would expect that this freedom would result in fornication, but it is very rare for the young woman to become pregnant; however, if she does, the young man has to marry her or leave the area. Before she gives birth the young woman swears an oath that the person she names is the father of her child, and the young man is then sentenced to marry her—unless he can afford to buy her off, and she is willing to take his money.

As a doctor Wasmus seems to have been popular, perhaps because he was easygoing about his fees. In 1781, Ebenezer Washborn, the impoverished but grateful husband of a patient suffering from ulcerated legs whom Wasmus had cured for a token fee, dedicated a poem "to the respected Doctor Wasmus in Commemoration of Favours received by his obliged Friend and obedient Servant, who groans under the Pressure of a Burden of Benefits." (Part of the poem ran:

"Directed by his friendly Heart/ He play'd the Skillful Surgeon's Part/ And cur'd the raging Ulcers Smart . . .")

But in the summer of 1781 came news that he had been exchanged, and he was ordered to rejoin his regiment in Canada before returning to Germany. Though tempted to remain "in this fortunate country among these good people; never will I have such good fortune again," he nevertheless made up his mind to go. On July 24, he wrote in his diary:

Wherever I go these days people refuse to believe that I am going to leave since I have more patients than any other doctor in New England. But there is no way that I can remain here. If I did, I would be posted as a deserter. What a shock that would be to my wife and children, to hear that I had become a deserter! No, my friends, I have to leave you. I am obliged to return by the most solemn and unbreakable commitments. . . . The sweet thought of once again embracing my beloved wife and greeting my friends in Germany is enlivening my soul. What warmth I am feeling in my heart even while I write this! I will see you all again—Providence will grant me this happiness.

What happened when he returned home will be told later. In the meantime, to complete the dismal story, of Wasmus and the other Hessians, here are some extracts from the diary he kept after rejoining his regiment in Canada:

January 6, 1782: Terrible snowstorms. We were once again snowed into our barracks and for a period of twelve hours nobody could come in or go out. A tunnel was dug through the snow. January 18. This morning Sergeant Major Reinemund, perhaps tired of the comforts of life here, fell through a hole in the ice on the St. Lawrence River where water was drawn, and was drowned. There is no news here. In winter Canada is cut off from the rest of the world. February 1. Today a deserter by the name of Müller was frostbitten and I had to amputate all five toes on his right foot. When he has recovered he will be hanged, so why not execute him right away? April 3. One of our jaegers was taken to the hospital; he had tried to shoot himself but missed his aim. May 8. I was ordered to be present when three deserters were sentenced to death. They were Müller from the Specht Regiment, who had lost all five toes on one foot, Schulze from the Riedesel Regiment, and the porter Scott, a watchmaker. May 24. Today the jaeger who tried to shoot himself ran a gauntlet of 200 men 8 times. May 28. Another soldier from the Riedesel Regiment has been brought in after deserting. As he is a Catholic, the priest from the Anhalt-Zerbst Regiment has been assigned to him. June 11. At 3 o'clock this morning the garrison was called to arms and the capital court-martial convened at the main guardhouse. At 5, the offenders were taken to the place where they were to be hanged. When they had entered the area, a sealed order was opened and read aloud by Lt. Col von Barner. It was from General von Riedesel and ordered that two of the men were to be shot, but none hanged. The four men were ordered to cast lots on a drumhead. The outcome was that Schulze and Weber were shot, while the two cripples, Scott with his crooked arm and Müller who had lost all five toes on his right foot, were condemned to serve as slaves on a frigate.

The Catholic Chaplain Braunsdorf of the Anhalt-Zerbst contingent also kept a record, known as a church book, listing births, marriages, and deaths, mostly the latter, many of them suicides:

Gottfried Wegener, of Captain Gogel's Company, hanged himself in the barracks at Quebec on July 5, 1779. Born at Potsdam, he was of the Evangelical faith and a rope-maker by trade. He was 22 years old. He was buried privately outside the churchyard by the regimental servants.

Friedrich Wendt shot himself with his own weapon in the garden of his billet in the parish of St. Pierre, Quebec, on February 17. He had quietly loaded his weapon and said he was going bird shooting but then shot himself in the garden. He was born at Erlangen and was 25 years old.

Johann August Heyne, servant of Chaplain Braunsdorf, hanged himself in the chaplain's quarters in Becancour parish. He became melancholy during the three-week absence of his master and while in this mood hanged himself. He was born in Zerbst, was of the Evangelical faith, and 22 years old.

Christian Hoffmann shot himself with his own weapon in the living room of his quarters at Trois Rivières on April 17. As he was never melancholy, the reason is unclear. He was a corporal in Captain Picquet's Grenadier company. Born at Eulenberg in Saxony, he was of the Evangelical faith, a shoemaker by trade, and 26 years old.

Carl Friedrich Meyne died in an unknown manner on October 28 at Trois Rivières. He had been with Captain von Wietersheim and was returning to his quarters in Becancour. There are many deep valleys between the two places and he apparently fell down one of the hillsides, rolled into the St. Lawrence River, and drowned. He was known to be fond of drinking and was probably drunk. He was born in Schoennebeck, of the Evangelical faith, and his age was unknown.

Heinrich Schiede froze to death on March 12, 1783, in River Ouelle parish in the district of Quebec. From all indications his death was deliberate. He had wandered into a field where there was a pile of hay, stripped off his winter clothing, sat down on the hay, and awaited death. He was a private in Captain Picquet's Grenadier company. Born in Lauterbach in Hesse-Darmstadt, he was of the Reformed faith and 35 years old.

Chaplain Braunsdorf also recorded this:

Adam Apfel died November 28, 1781, in the St. Croix parish hospital in the district of Quebec, after running the gauntlet. As a corporal he had led a group of privates into stealing. On one occasion they broke into a merchant's shop at night and stole bolts of silk, cotton, and linen, as much as they could carry. Because he was the leader and had led his comrades into wrongdoing, he was sentenced to hang, but the sentence was then reduced to running a gauntlet of 200 men 36 times on three consecutive days, twelve times each day. This was carried out, and as a result he died three days later. He was a member of Captain Gogel's company. Born at Muehlhausen, he was of the Evangelical faith, a cooper by trade, and 24 years old.

Lt. Anburey also spent a winter in Canada, stationed next to a Hessian regiment with whom the British shared a hospital. In his diary he observed that when the ground froze so hard as to make it impossible to dig a grave, the Canadians kept the body until spring in "some private chamber," but that "in our general hospital there is a long room appropriated for that purpose." One winter's day, with nothing else to do, Anburey decided to visit the place.

The superintendent of this room, an apothecary, being a man possessed of whimsical ideas and a turn for the ludicrous, had placed the dead bodies of these poor Germans in various postures, some kneeling with books in their hands, others sitting down with pipes in their mouths, many standing erect against the wall, and as they have their cloaths on you scarcely at first imagine they are dead; but upon nearer approach, what with their long mustaches, which are put in form, and their ghastly countenance, you cannot picture to yourself any thing so horrible, yet at the same time so laughable and ridiculous.

Hessians prisoners of war captured at Trenton, December 26, 1776.

CHAPTER FOUR

Pennsylvania and the Frontier

Along with the great victory at Saratoga, often considered the turning point of the war since it encouraged the French to enter into an open military alliance with the Americans, the years 1777–78 also witnessed what has since become one of the best known episodes of the war—Valley Forge—and also one of the least known—Sullivan's Expedition. For this allocation of fame to have taken place, a good deal of historical editing has been necessary: To exalt Valley Forge, the graft and incompetence of those responsible for supplying the American army have been played down, as has the unequal sharing of the suffering—while the common soldiers had to stay in camp shivering and starving, many of their officers were allowed to go home on extended leave. As to Sullivan's campaign of "total destruction and devastation" against the Iroquois, since there was no way in which the brutalities committed by both sides could be romanticized into a legend, it has largely, but wrongly, been forgotten.

Even more forgotten have been the excitements and miseries of the ordinary men and women whose lives were thrown into turmoil by the war: anxious housewives worried about their children and husbands, unmilitary clergymen who suddenly found themselves regimental chaplains; young women flirting excitedly with officers who dashed up to their doorways, lingered awhile, and then dashed away again; runaway boys who found themselves in more trouble than they had bargained for; civilian Patriots whose fortunes rose as those of the Loyalists fell, and vice versa, and then vice versa again.

Pennsylvania on the Eve

While in Philadelphia for the Continental Congress, John Adams had kept up his diary:

Tuesday, August 30, 1774. Walked a little about Town. Visited the Markett, the State house, the Carpenters Hall where the Congress is to Sit, &c—then call'd at Mr. Mifflins—a grand, spacious, and elegant House. . . . The Regularity and Elegance of this City are very striking. It is situated upon a Neck of Land, about two Miles wide between the River De la Ware and the River Schuilkill. The Streets are all exactly straight and parallel to the River. Front Street is near the River, then 2d street, 3d, 4th, 5th, 6th, 7th, 8th, 9th. The cross Streets which intersect these are all equally wide, straight, and parallel to each other, and are named from forrest and fruit Trees—Pear Street, Apple Street, Walnut Street, Chestnut Street, &c.

Dr. Shippen, a leading citizen, took Adams and other recently arrived delegates to visit the hospital. "We saw, in the lower Rooms under Ground, the Cells of the Lunaticks, a Number of them, some furious, some merry, some Melancholly, and among the rest John Ingram, whom I once saved at Taunton Court from being whipped and sold for Horse stealing. We then went into the Sick Rooms which are very long, large Walks with rows of Beds on each side, and the lame and sick upon them—a dreadful Scene of human Wretchedness."

The next week, after Congress had opened, he was among those invited to dinner by one of the Quaker elite. "Wednesday, Sept. 7. Dined with Mr. Miers Fisher, a young Quaker and a Lawyer. . . . This plain Friend, and his plain, tho' pretty Wife, with her Thee's and Thou's, had provided us the most Costly Entertainment—Ducks, Hams, Chickens, Beef, Pigg, Tarts, Creams, Custards, Gellies, Fools, Trifles, floating Islands, Beer, Porters, Punch, Wine &c . . ." The next day he dined at Mr. Powell's: "A most sinfull Feast again! Every Thing which could delight the Eye or allure the Taste, Curds and Creams, Jellies, Sweet meats of various sorts, 20 sorts of Tarts, fools, Trifles, floating Islands, whippd Sillabubs, &c. &c. . . . At Evening we climbed up the Steeple of Christ Church, with Mr. Reed, from whence we had a clear and full View of the whole City and of Delaware River."

The next Sunday "Dined at Mr. Willings, who is a Judge of the Supream Court here, with the Gentlemen from Virginia, Maryland, and New York. A most splendid Feast again—Turtle and every thing else." Afterwards "we drank Coffee, and then Reed, Cushing, and I strolled to the Moravian Evening Lecture where we heard soft, sweet Music and a dutchified English Prayer and Preachment." On another occasion he attended "the Romish Chappell" where he found that "the Scenery and Musick is so calculated to take in Mankind that I wonder the Reformation ever succeeded—the Paintings, the Bells, the Candles, the Gold and Silver—Our Saviour on the Cross, over the Altar, at full Length, and all his Wounds a-bleeding. The Chanting is exquisitely soft and sweet." He also visited "the Bettering House, a large building—very clean, neat, and convenient for the Poor" and a few days later "Dined with Dr. Morgan, an ingenious Physician and an honest Patriot. He shewed us some curious paintings upon Silk which he brought from Italy which are Singular in this Country, and some Bones of an Animal of enormous Size, found upon the Banks of the River Ohio."

Late in October, mistakenly thinking that "it is not very likely that I shall ever see this Part of the World again," Adams left "the peacefull, the elegant, the hospitable and polite city of Philadelphia" and went home. But although there had been much that he could approve, the city failed the ultimate test: "Philadelphia with all its Trade, and Wealth, and Regularity is not Boston. The Morals of our People are much better. . . . Our Language is better, our Persons are handsomer, our Spirit is greater, our Laws are wiser, our Religion is superiour, our Education is better. We exceed them in every Thing, but in a Markett, and in charitable public foundations."

Philadelphia was now the largest city in America and the main port of entry for the immigrants who continued to pour in even after the war had started. It was also efficiently run. Its wide sidewalks and broad, well-paved streets were kept clean by being regularly sluiced down with water from the public waterworks. Its disorderly houses were tucked away between Third Street and Race in an area known as Hell-Town. At night oil-burning lamps encased in glass globes lit the streets. The city was also renowned for being home to America's most famous citizen and philanthropist, Ben Franklin (now absent in London), the man whose invention of the lightning conductor had prompted the Rev. Ezra Stiles to hail him as the "Electric Philosopher." The fate of the house at the corner of Chestnut and Seventh Streets, belonging to John Dickinson and rented during the war to the French ambassador, demonstrated just how valuable this invention could be. "In one of those dreadful storms of thunder with which America is so frequently visited in the summer months, this house, though lower than the State House [Independence Hall], and that of his neighbor, Mrs. Allen, was struck by lightning, and a French officer, sitting alone in one of the rooms, burnt to death; the lightning had set fire to his clothes, and thrown him into a fainting fit, during which part of his body was miserably scorched, and his private parts reduced to ashes, so that he survived but a few hours. But the principal ravage was in a chamber containing an iron bedstead, in which the Ambassador himself slept, by way of security from the bugs; in that room, large blocks of marble were rent in pieces, and torn from the chimney-piece. . . . It may be proper to add that this was the only house in the neighborhood *unprovided with an electrical apparatus.*" (This story was told by George Greive in a footnote to his 1787 translation of the Marquis of Chastellux's *Travels in North America.*)

After founding his colony as a "Holy Experiment" where people of all faiths could live together, William Penn had actively recruited in the Protestant regions of Germany, which ever since had continued to be a major source of immigration. By the time of the

Revolution the so-called Dutch made up about half the population of Pennsylvania, enough to enable them to hold on to their
old ways. This was particularly so with the sects known as Pietists,
whose utopian way of life and deep-seated pacifism put them at
odds with almost everyone else. Lt. Anburey, who had been captured with Burgoyne's army but had since been exchanged, was
in Lancaster just before Christmas 1778, from where he wrote a
letter to a friend back in England:

✷

The diversity of religions, nations, and languages here is astonishing, at the same time the harmony they live in no less edifying. . . .
Among the numerous sects of religion with which this province
abounds—for there are Churchmen [Anglicans], Quakers, Calvinists,
Lutherans, Catholics, Methodists, Menists [Mennonites], Moravians,
Independents, Anabaptists—there is a sect which perhaps you never
heard of called the Dumplers [also known as Dunkers, Dunkards,
Tunkers, Taufers, and Donkelaards, all referring to their practice of
triple immersion when administering baptism]. This sect took its
origin from a German who, weary of the world, retired to a very
solitary place about fifty miles from Philadelphia in order to give up
his whole time to contemplation. Several of his countrymen came
to visit him in his retreat, and by his pious, simple, and peaceable
manners many were induced to settle near him; and in a short time
adapting his modes they formed a little colony which they named
Euphrates [Ephrata].

Their little city is built in the form of a triangle, and bordered
with mulberry and apple trees, very regularly planted. In the center of
the town is a large orchard, and between the orchard and the ranges
of trees that are planted round the borders are their houses, which are
built of wood and three stories high. In these every Dumpler is left to
enjoy his meditations without disturbance.

They have women of their community who live separate from the
men; they seldom see each other but at places of worship, and never

have meetings of any kind but for public business. Their whole life is spent in labor, prayer, and sleep. Twice every day and night they are summoned from their cells to attend divine service. As to their religion, in some measure it resembles the Quakers, for every individual, if he thinks himself inspired, has a right to preach. The subjects they chiefly discourse upon are humility, temperance, charity, and other Christian virtues.

Religion among the Dumplers has the same effect philosophy had upon the Stoics, rendering them insensible to every kind of insult. They are more passive and disinterested than the Quakers, for they will suffer themselves to be cheated, robbed, and abused, without the least idea of retaliation, or even complaint.

Their dress is very simple and plain, consisting of a long white gown, from whence hangs a hood to serve the purposes of a hat, a coarse shirt, thick shoes, and very wide breeches somewhat resembling those the Turks wear. The men wear their beards to a great length, some I saw were down to the waist. At the first sight of them I could not help comparing them to our old ancient bards, the Druids, from their reverential appearance. The women are dressed similar to the men, excepting the breeches.

Their life is very abstemious, and eating no meats, not that they deem it unlawful but more conformable to the spirit of Christianity, which they argue has an aversion to blood; and upon these grounds they subsist only on vegetables and the produce of the earth.

They follow with great cheerfulness their various branches of business, in some one of which every individual partakes, and the produce of their labor is deposited in one common stock, to supply the necessities of every individual; and by this union of industry they have not only established agriculture and manufactures sufficient to support this little society, but superfluities for the purpose of exchange for European commodities.

Though the two sexes live separate they do not renounce matrimony, but those who are disposed to it leave the city and settle in the country on a tract of land which the Dumplers have purchased for that purpose. The couple are supported at the public expense, which they repay with the produce of their labor, and their children are sent to Germany for education. Without this wise policy the Dumplers would be little better than Monks, and in process of time annihilated.

Although there are so many sects, and such a difference of religious opinions in this province, it is surprising the harmony which subsists among them; they consider themselves as children of the same father and live like brethren because they have the liberty of thinking like men. To this pleasing harmony in a great measure is to be attributed the rapid and flourishing state of Pennsylvania above all the other provinces. Would to heaven that harmony was equally as prevalent all over the globe!

And there was yet another Pennsylvania, far removed from the prosperous city and the peaceable communes. This was the frontier, which had now advanced from the shoreline, which was where it had been when the first settlers arrived, to several hundred miles inland. Like the backcountry regions of the other colonies, the frontier was an undefined area many miles wide and constantly moving west, with few roads and little law and order. It was inhabited by a dwindling number of Indians and a growing number of runaway slaves, indentured servants who had fled their masters, escaped criminals, traders, and fur-trappers. The fastest growing segment of the population was newly arrived immigrants, generally from the British Isles—small tenants driven out by rack-renting landlords, artisans who had lost their jobs to industrialization, religious dissenters tired of discrimination, and young men who could not get a start in life. For these people the journey across the Atlantic and then, usually on foot, into the backcountry was a one-way affair, their new life a struggle for survival. Few could have had any tender feelings toward the Indians whose land they were taking or toward the country they had been forced to leave.

Early in the summer of 1775, having recently graduated from the College of New Jersey (Princeton), Philip Vickers Fithian found himself dispatched to the Pennsylvania-Virginia backcountry to complete his training as a Presbyterian minister by serving for twelve months as an itinerant preacher. This was a big change from the life he had led the previous year, which he had spent in great comfort as resident tutor to the children of the Virginia aristocrat, Colonel Carter, of Nomini Hall. When his time with them was up, the Carters had warmly urged him to stay. There were hints that a plain but well-connected young lady would welcome his attentions, and that as her spouse he would be accepted as a member of Virginia society. But Fithian remained true to the girl he had left behind in New Jersey and to his calling as a minister. So instead of being waited on hand and foot by household slaves, he found himself in the remote backwoods, bringing the Word of God to the rough-living settlers, lodging with whichever family would put him up, and living on whatever his random congregations put in the plate. The region was already in the grip of war fever, and Fithian, who would later become an army chaplain, had volunteered for the militia, but finding it hard to master the drill had dropped out, cheerfully reproaching himself for being "a lubberly unteachable Oaff." When not traveling or preparing his sermons, he spent much of his time daydreaming about his fiancée, Elizabeth, addressing her in his journal sometimes as Eliza or Betsey, sometimes with more fanciful literary names such as Laura or Belinda.

✳

Tuesday, June 6, 1775. The Drum beats, & the Inhabitants of this Village [Stevensburg] muster each morning at five o'clock—I am all this Morning in my chamber studying; dull, heavy, thick Weather—After Dinner, with Capt. Holmes & Capt. Hunter I rode to Winchester—the Court was sitting—Mars, the great God of Battle, is now honoured in every Part of this spacious Colony, but here every Presence is warlike, every Sound is martial! Drums beating, Fifes & Bag-Pipes playing, & only sonorous & heroic Tunes—Every Man has a hunting-Shirt, which is the Uniform of each Company. Almost all have a Cockade, & Bucks-Tail in their Hats, to represent that they are hardy, resolute, & invincible Natives of the Woods of America—

Thursday, June 8. A fine, warm damp growing Season—We see many every Day travelling out & in to & from Carolina, some on Foot with Packs; some on Horseback, & some in large covered Waggons. The Road here is much frequented, & the Country for an hundred & fifty miles farther West, thick inhabited.

Monday, June 12. A Report came to Town this Day pretty well confirm'd that in the upper Part of Augusta, some few Days ago was committed a base Murder—A Gentleman travelling towards Carolina was assaulted, & stabbed in many Places in the Breast, & afterwards robbed of Cash about £110. Soon after the Murder while the unhappy Victim was yet bleeding but quite dead, two Gentlemen from the Northward came up, saw the dead Body, perceived it to have been just injured, & looking about, at some Distance, they discovered a Person washing his Hands & Clothes in a Brook; they seized him. At first he denied the Fact; but when he was bound & threatened, he owned that he destroyed the Man, & robbed him of his Money, which was upwards of an hundred Pounds! They then carried the dead Body & the Murderer back to a Tavern kept by a Widow Woman at a small Distance & desired her to take the Charge of all, & carry on the Prosecution, as he there acknowledged before Witnesses that he was the Murderer; the Woman, however, obstinately refused, in every Respect. They then asked for a Rope, called several as Witnesses of his Acknowledgement of the Murder, took him out from the House, & without the Formality of a legal trial, hung him dead themselves. After having thus secured him they left the murdered Body, the Money, & an Account of their Procedure with the Widow, & proceeded on their Journey!

Tuesday, June 13. Cloudy, damp, & warm. Spent a good Share of the Day reading Addison's admirable Evidences for the Christian

Religion—Many Servants & Negroes are daily running off. One was brought into Town this Day with a huge iron Collar on his Neck, a large, long, very heavy Chain on his Feet; & the poor victim was on his Way to a Scene of Usage little inferior to Papal Purgatory!

Saturday, June 17. I arrived in Martinsburg a little before Evening—Mr. Hunter just arrived from Jersey—Laura is in health! Kind Father of all Good, go on & guard, through this calamitous State, that dear girl. He tells me that the Negroes have, in Pittsgrove, murdered one Mr. Sherry, & many are in this Conspiracy—Here Slaves are running off daily—Servants skulking about, and pilfering—Horses & many other things stolen weekly— Riots on many Occasions in most parts of the Continent—And in every Place much Anxiety & Debt, & almost no Attention to Business. Mr. Hunter brings word that the Bloody-Flux is already very bad in Maryland.

Thursday, June 29. I rode up the West-Branch Sesquihannah 2 Miles to Mr. Andrew Gibson's. In the Way I crossed the River twice over a fine rich Island, shaded with lofty, smooth Beech-Trees. On one of these I carved my Name; & near it I carved the Name of my fair Friend—There as the beautiful Trees grow, let our Love & Friendship also increase in Magnitude & Serenity. After Dinner, with two of Mr. Gibson's, I went down the River for Exercise & Diversion, in a small Boat. The River is perfectly transparent, so clear that you may see in its deepest Parts the smallest Fish. All the bottom is one, undivided, solid rock. Evening came the Philadelphia Papers—All things yet look dark & unsettled.

Wednesday, July 19. Two Waggons, with Goods, Cattle, Women, Tools &c, went through Town to Day from East-Jersey, on their Way to Fishing Creek up this River, where they are to settle; rapid, most rapid, is the growth of this Country. [At Sunbury] As we were returning, in our slim Canoes, I could not help thinking over with myself how often the Savage Tribes, while they were in Possession of these inchanting Wilds, have floated over this very Spot. My Heart feels for the wandering Natives. I make no Doubt but Multitudes of them, when they were forced away, left these long-possessed & delightsome

Banks with swimming Eyes. It is not a Trifle, I suppose, that can make an Indian weep; but these were pleasant Places.

Saturday, July 22. Unseasonably cool & in the morning foggy. I slept late. Indeed I have a bad Habit brought on by too much indulgence of lying til' six & seven. One thing here I don't like—In almost all these rural Cots I am under the Necessity of sleeping in the same Room with the Family. It seems indelicate, at least new, to strip, surrounded by different Ages & Sexes, & rise in the Morning, in the Blaze of Day, with the eyes of at least one blinking Irish Female searching out Subjects for Remark.

Monday, July 24. Yesterday, & this morning we breakfasted on Tea. It is boil'd in a common Dinner-Pot, of ten or fifteen Gallons, & from thence poured out in Tin Cups. We have with it boil'd Potatoes, & Huckleberry-Pye— All in Love, Peace, & good Welcome. Again I had near been all over bemeasled with the Fleas— Fleas biting! —Bugs crawling! —On a hard Board, surrounded with a snoring Family! If America was now embosom'd in Peace, I should think myself in singular & deep Distress. But when I recollect how many are dying by the Sword, by Famine & Disease, I adopt that Sentiment of Scripture "Why should a living Man complain?"

On August 6, when in Penn's Valley, another trial:

Just at my Bed's Head is a Window under which stands a Table—here I laid my clean Linnen finished last night by Mrs. Potter. The Night has been very stormy; when I waked this Morning I found a large Dog had jumped in through an open Light of the Window & had softly bedded himself, dripping with Water & Mud, among my clean, new-washed Clothes! At first I felt enraged; I bore it however with a Sabbath-Day's Moderation.

At another time he works himself into a state worrying about what will happen to his "expected Felicity with Eliza" as the years go by:

Will any of the Qualities which have so deeply smitten me retain the Power of pleasing when she will have lost her Beauty, & be furrowed by Age? When I picture her, in Fancy, & place her before me at the Age of sixty, conflicting with the Infirmities of Age, added to those which already belong to her feeble Sex, would my Heart have such warm Emotions towards her as I feel now? Shall I love Eliza with the same Ardour . . . when I view her sitting in the Corner, over a slow-burning Fire, in a low Chair, bended downwards with Years, resting her hoary, withered Head upon the hollow of her shaking Hand, & with the other Hand poorly supporting a Pipe in her Toothless Mouth. . . . Should I clasp my Arms with the same Transport round that Death-like, Rib-encircled Waist? . . . Short indeed is the Empire of Beauty! What then, I ask, is the Security for my Happiness with Eliza?

But soon he is taking a much more optimistic view of his and his country's future:

Stanton, January, 1776. I saw a Person this Day who has just arrived, in three Weeks, from Transylvania [Kentucky]. What he declares, I am told by many from his established Veracity, may not be doubted. He is himself so highly pleased with the Situation, Soil, & Terms of Settlement there, that he is determined to remove with his Family & moveable Effects next Summer . . . I am in a perplexing Dilemma, whether I ought not to determine also that it shall be, remote & wild as it is, the Habitation of me & my lovely Betsey—

Friday Evening, by Request, I attended Mr. Trumble's Singing School. Several have made large Improvements. It is beautiful to behold the Progress of Civilization. It is westward. A few Years ago this very

Settlement was the habitation of Cruelty emphatically; now Men civi-lized & religious, by legal Purchase too, are the more useful Inhabitants.

The March of Commerce & Improvement to the westward is so rapid, that soon, perhaps before the present Century is quite filled up, we shall have Towns overlooking the Banks of the Pacifick Ocean!

✻

THE GOD OF BATTLE

To go back now to the dark days of early December 1776, when the depleted American army has sought safety by crossing to the south side of the Delaware River. Congress has packed up and fled to Baltimore already; soldiers whose time is out, are making their way home on foot along the wintry roads; the florid Sir William Howe and his mistress, Mrs. Loring, are looking forward to a bright social season in New York; Lord Cornwallis is about to embark for a long leave in England; Washington is mulling over plans to reverse the tide of defeat; and the civilians in the area are leading lives burdened with danger and anxiety.

One of these civilians was Margaret Morris, a middle-aged Quaker widow with four children and very little money, but a large house on the banks of the river in Burlington, a town that changed hands several times during that winter. To make ends meet Margaret ran a shop and also practiced some medicine, her father having been a doctor. Her journal, "parts of it written in a serious, others in a waggish mood," was composed "after the family were abed, and I sat up to keep guard over my fences, etc, while the soldiers were next door, for fear they should pull them down [for firewood]." Sometimes the soldiers were redcoats, sometimes Hessians, and sometimes they were the crews of American gunboats, called galleys or gondolas, which sailed up and down the Dela-ware, blazing away at any house they thought might hold enemy troops.

✻

December 12, 1776. This morning a galley, with a great many men and a number of troops, came ashore at our wharf. I ordered the children to keep within doors, and went myself down to the shore, and asked what they were going to do. They said to fire the town if the [British] Regulars entered. I told them I hoped they would not set fire to my house. "Which is your house, and who are you?" I told them I was a widow, with only children in the house, and they called to others and bid them mark that house, there was a widow and children and no men in it. "But," said they, "it is a mercy we did not fire on it last night, thinking there were Hessians or Tories in it. But a hair of your head shall not be hurt by us." See how Providence looks on us! Then they offered to move my valuable goods over the river, but I pointed to the children at the door, and said, "See, there is all my treasure. Those children are mine."

But while it was true that there were no Hessians in the house, Margaret was in fact sheltering a Tory, the Rev. Jonathan Odell, a well-known pamphleteer and old family friend. A small secret chamber—the "auger hole" —had been contrived in the attic, its entry hidden behind some removable shelves. In case of need, warning to hide would be given by ringing a bell in the attic that was activated by wires that ran down to a bell-pull just inside the front door.

Four days later, while several American gunboats were moored in the river near her house, there was "a very terrible account" that thousands of Hessians were coming into the town

& now actually to be seen on Gallows Hill. My incautious Son catch'd up a Spy Glass & was running to the Mill to look at them. I told him it would be liable to misconstruction, but he prevail'd on me to let him gratify his curiosity, & he went, but return'd much dissatisfy'd, for no troops could he see. As he came back poor Dick [another son] took the glass & resting it against a tree, took a view of the fleet—both of these was observ'd by the people on board, who suspected it was an Enemy that was watching their Motions. They mann'd a boat & sent her on

Shore—a loud knocking at my door brought me to it—I was a little flutter'd & kept locking and unlocking it that I might get my ruffled face a little compos'd. At last I open'd it, & half a dozen Men all Arm'd demanded the keys of the empty House [next door]. I asked what they wanted there, they said to search for a D – -d Tory who had been spying at them from the Mill—the name of a Tory so near my own door seriously alarm'd me—for a poor refugee [Dr. Odell] dignify'd by that Name had claim'd the shelter of my roof & was at that very time conceal'd, like a thief, in an Auger hole. I rung the bell violently, the signal agreed on, if they came to Search—& when I thought he had crept into the hole I put on a very simple look & cry'd out, "Bless me! I hope you are not Hessians! Say, good men, are you the Hessians?" "Do we look like Hessians?" ask'd one of them rudely. "Indeed, I don't know." "Did you never see a Hessian?" "No, never in my life, but they are Men, and you are Men, and may be Hessians for anything I know—but I'll go with you into Colonel Coxe's house, tho' indeed it was my Son at the Mill, he is but a Boy and meant no harm, he wanted to see the Troops." So I march'd at the head of them, open'd the door, & search'd every place—but we could not find the Tory. Strange! Where could he be? We return'd, they greatly disappointed, I pleas'd to think my house was not Suspected. The Captain, a smart little fellow named Shippen, said he wish'd he could see the Spy Glass—SD [her sister, Sarah Dillwyn] produced it & very civilly desir'd his acceptance of it, which I was sorry for, as I often amus'd myself in looking thro' it. They left us & search'd the two next houses—but no Tory could they find.

December 27th. A letter from Gen. Read to his Brother inform-ing him that Washington had had an engagement with the Regulars [at Trenton] on the 25th [in fact the 26th] early in the Morning, taking them by surprise, kill'd fifty, & took 900 prisoners. The loss on our side not known, or if known not suffer'd to be publick. It seems this heavy loss to the Regulars was owing to the prevailing custom among the Hessians of getting drunk on the eve of that great day which brought peace on Earth & good Will to Men—but oh, how unlike Christians is the Manner in which they Celebrate it! Can we call ourselves Christians while we act so Contrary to our Master's rule—he set the example which we profess to follow, & here is a recent instance that we only profess it. Instead of good will, envy & hatred seem to be the ruling passions in the breasts of thousands. This evening the 27th about 3,000 of the Pennsylvania Militia, & other troops, landed in the Neck & march'd into Town with Artillery, Baggage &c, & were quarter'd on the inhabitants. . . . An Officer spent the Evening with us, & appear'd to be in high spirits, & talk'd of engaging the English as a very trifling affair—Nothing so easy as to drive them over the North River &c—not considering that there is a God of Battle, as well as a God of Peace, who may have given them the late advantage in order to draw them out to meet the Chastisement that is reserv'd for them.

But where was the God of Battle? Having just favored Washington with his turnaround victories at Trenton and Princeton, perhaps he had gone to London and was now looking over the shoulder of General Burgoyne as he, the king, and Lord Germain pored over the map of North America and traced the line of march that would win the war at a stroke. Or maybe he was in New York, where Sir William Howe was desultorily working out his own plan, one that would take him south to Philadelphia, so that instead of advancing toward each other, both British armies would be heading in the same direction.

Making Philadelphia his target was a change of plan for Howe, who had at first intended to campaign to the north. One reason for this change was that, like the king, he was convinced that most Americans were Loyalists at heart but intimidated by the rebels. Let the king's standard but appear at the head of the royal army, and the liberated people would flock to it—particularly in Pennsylvania, where, in the words of Joseph Galloway, they would find "friends thicker than woods." Another reason was the belief that the war could be won by occupying the enemy's principal cities, true enough in Europe but not in America, where most people lived on farms or in villages. Perhaps also, in the very back of his mind, Howe foresaw what might happen were he to advance on Albany: Threatened with an attack from the rear, the American army, instead of encircling and throttling Burgoyne's Anglo-Hessian army, would have had to break off and redeploy. And if that happened, was it not possible that Burgoyne, no longer surrounded, would be able to push his way through those last few miles and then burst out of the woods, bands playing, champagne corks popping, his plumed hat crowning the hero of the war? Was that what Sir William really wanted?

Finally there were the reports coming into headquarters in New York about how weak Washington's army was, despite his recent victories. One such report was recorded by Admiral Lord Howe's secretary, Ambrose Serle:

Saturday, May 17th, 1777. Two men came in from Pennsylvania & Jersey, one of whom was on Thursday in Washington's Lines. He says, that his whole Force does not exceed 7,000 men, the principal Part of which is at Bound-brook & Morris Town; that he is acquainted with a maid-servant in Washington's family who has told him that she has frequently caught him in Tears about the House, and that, when he is alone, he appears constantly dejected and unhappy; that the Succors from the Southward have been but small; that the Rebels themselves think it impractical to keep Philadelphia . . . that the Country in general is groaning under the present Tyranny and Oppression, and longing for a speedy deliverance.

Having decided on Philadelphia, the dilatory Howe settled on the longest possible route for getting there. Instead of marching across New Jersey, he embarked his troops on his brother's ships and then, instead of sailing to the Delaware Bay, he had the fleet go all the way down to the Chesapeake Bay and then all the way up to the Head of Elk. There they disembarked and headed for Philadelphia, plundering as they went. The journey had taken nearly seven weeks but did at least succeed in perplexing Washington, who flatteringly supposed that it was part of some deep and subtle strategy: "Howe's in a manner abandoning General Burgoyne is so unaccountable a matter that till I am sure it is so, I cannot help casting my eyes continually behind me." Washington's intelligence service was much superior to that of the British—there were no reports of maidservants finding a dejected Sir William Howe in floods of tears—but could not penetrate the logic of overall British strategy because there was no such thing.

Unlike New York, where the streets had been dug up to make trenches and redoubts erected at almost every corner, no attempt was made to fortify Philadelphia once it was known that Howe was on his way. A few radicals wanted to deprive him of the city by burning it down, the pacifist Quakers favored nonresistance, and a number of Patriots prepared for defense. Among these were some Germans of Reading, who had already formed what was called the Old Man's Company. According to a Philadelphia paper, the company "consists of about eighty Germans, of the age of forty and upwards. Many of them have been in the military service in Germany. The person who, at their first assembling, led them to the field, is ninety-seven years of age; has been forty years in the service, and in seventeen pitched battles; and the drummer is eighty-four. In lieu of a cockade they wear in their hats a black crape, as expressive of their sorrow for the mournful events which have occasioned them, at their late time of life, to take arms against our brethren, in order to preserve that liberty which they left their native Country to enjoy."

Another active Patriot was Alexander Graydon, later to be taken prisoner at Fort Washington, but at present still a member of a socially elite unit known to its members as The Greens and to others as The Silk Stocking Company. In his memoirs Graydon was emphatic that they took their duties and training seriously and only when they had made themselves into "a truly respectable militia corps" did they allow themselves to ease off.

When it had attained some adroitness in the exercises, we met but once a day. This was in the afternoon, and the place of the rendezvous the house of the captain [John Cadwalader], where capacious demi-johns of Madeira were constantly set out in the yard where we formed, for our refreshment before marching out to exercise. The ample fortune of Mr. Cadwalader had enabled him to fill his cellars with the choicest liquors; and it must be admitted that he dealt them out with the most gentlemanly liberality.

Perhaps this liberality with the demi-johns of Madeira had something to do with an incident that occurred when Graydon and his friend Captain Biddle set out to improve their skill with the pistol. Having

posted ourselves in a situation thought convenient and safe, we marked our target on a board fence, in a cross street, between Arch and Race Streets. We had fired several times, and were loading again, when a man suddenly coming upon us, out of breath, pale as ashes, without his hat and his hair standing on end, exclaimed that we had killed his child! This information, as may be supposed, put a stop to our amusement; and we immediately accompanied him to his house, with feelings not to be envied. When we arrived, however, we found matters not so bad as had been anticipated. The child was crying in its mother's arms: it had been struck in the body, but the force of the blow had been broken by a loose, linsey petticoat. The ball had passed through a pane of glass; and from the appearance of the hole corresponding to its size without diverging cracks, it must have had considerable force, though discharged at a distance greater than we thought our pistols would carry. By expressions of concern for the accident and the accompaniment of a few dollars, our transgression was overlooked, and all perturbation composed.

Following a vote by Congress to raise continental battalions in every state, Graydon applied for a commission to the Pennsylvania Committee of Safety, of which his uncle was a member, and in January 1776, he was appointed captain in a regiment commanded by John Cadwalader's younger brother, Lambert. As yet the unit existed only on paper, so the next step was to go recruiting. In Europe, this was a job for sergeants and corporals, but in America "to see the persons who were to command them, and above all the captain, was deemed of vast importance by those inclining to enlist." Though feeling that this kind of duty was beneath him, Graydon set forth and after a while arrived at Frankford:

A number of fellows at the tavern, at which my party rendezvoused, indicated a desire to enlist, but although they drank freely of our liquor, they still held off. I soon perceived that the object was to amuse themselves at our expense, and that if there might be one or two among them really disposed to engage, the others would prevent them. One fellow in particular, who had made the greatest show of taking the bounty, presuming on the weakness of our party, consisting only of a drummer, corporal, my second lieutenant, and myself, began to grow insolent, and manifested an intention to begin a quarrel, in the issue of which he no doubt calculated on giving us a drubbing. . . . At length the arrogance of the principal ruffian rose to such a height that he squared himself for battle and advanced towards me in an attitude of defiance. I put him by, with an admonition to be quiet, though with a secret determination that if he repeated the insult to begin the war, whatever might be the consequence. The occasion soon presented itself; when taking excellent aim, I struck him with my utmost force between the eyes and sent him staggering to the other end of the room. Then instantly drawing our hangers [swords], and receiving the manful cooperation of the corporal and the drummer, we were fortunate enough to put a stop to any farther hostilities. It was some time before the fellow I had struck recovered from the blow, but when he did, he was quite an altered man. He was as submissive as could be wished, begging my pardon for what he had done, and although he would not enlist, he hired himself to me for a few weeks as a fifer, in which capacity he had acted in the militia; and during the time he was in this employ, he bore the effects of his insolence, in a pair of black eyes. This incident would be little worthy of relating did it not serve in some degree to correct the error of those who seem to conceive the year 1776 to have been a season of almost universal patriotic enthusiasm.

While the British army slowly approached Philadelphia from the south, there was also a good deal of military activity to the north of the city. On June 11, Margaret Morris, the Quaker widow of Burlington, wrote in her journal:

Certain intelligence arriv'd express that the English are at Bound brook—the Americans at Morris town. 13th. Early this Morning the Soldiers beat to March from Bristol, & in the course of the day several boats full of Soldiers, with the Pennsylvania Militia, sail'd up the River. 14th. Before day light this Morning, the Alarm guns at Prince town, Trenton, Borden town, & Bristol were fired, & Answer'd by those below. About 9 oClock the Gondolas & Barges began to appear in Sight, and from that time to 9 at Night there have gone up the River five or six Gondolas—Several flat Bottom boats are also gone to Bristol. There is a report of a Battle today, which seems probable, as we have heard much fireing above. . . .

On July 4, despite the impending invasion, the citizens of Philadelphia celebrated the first anniversary of Independence "with demonstrations of joy and festivity," according to the *Pennsylvania Journal.* "All the armed ships and galleys in the river were drawn up before the city, dressed in the gayest manner, with the colors of the United

States and streamers displayed. At one o'clock, the yards being properly manned, they began the celebration of the day by a discharge of thirteen cannon from each of the ships, and one from each of the thirteen galleys, in honor of the thirteen United States. . . . The Hessian band of music, taken in Trenton the twenty-sixth of December last, attended and heightened the festivity with some fine performances suited to the joyous occasion." After a formal dinner there were numerous toasts, "all breathing Independence and a generous love of liberty," a military parade and review, bell-ringing and "a grand exhibition of fireworks. . . . Thus may the fourth of July, that glorious and ever memorable day, be celebrated through America by the sons of freedom, from age to age, till time shall be no more. Amen and amen."

John Adams was doubtless among the guests at the dinner, but his job of presiding over the Board of War and Ordnance was so demanding that he had given up keeping his diary. He was in "drooping health," dismayed at the loss of Ticonderoga, and greatly worried about Abigail, who was nearing the end of another pregnancy, Adams having gone back "to confer with his constituents" the previous fall. Then came a letter from Dr. Thaxter in Braintree, to say that "the day before Yesterday Mrs. Adams was delivered of a daughter. It grieves me to add, Sir, that it was still born. It was an exceeding fine looking child." A few days later Abigail wrote that "tho' my sufferings were great, thanks be to Heaven I have been supported through, and would silently submit to its dispensations in the loss of a sweet daughter; it appeared to be a very fine Babe, and as it never opened its Eyes in this world it look'd as tho' they were only closed for sleep."

In September, four days after the American army had been defeated but not destroyed at Brandywine, Adams resumed his diary:

✳

Sept 15. We live in critical Moments! . . . This City is the Stake for which the Game is play'd. I think there is a Chance of saving it, although the Probability is against Us. Mr. Howe I conjecture is waiting for his Ships to come into the Delaware. Will W. attack him? I hope so—and God grant him Success.

Sept 16. No newspaper this Morning. Mr. Dunlap [the printer] has moved or packed up his Types. . . . The City seems to be asleep, or dead, and the whole State scarce alive. . . . The Prospect is chilling on every side. Gloomy, dark, melancholly, and dispiriting. When and where will the light spring up? Shall we have good News from Europe? Shall we hear of a Blow struck by Gates? . . . It is said that Howe has marked his Course, from [Head of] Elk with Depredation. His Troops have plunder'd Henroosts, dairy Rooms, the furniture of Houses, and all the Cattle of the Country. The Inhabitants, most of whom are Quakers, are angry and disappointed, because they were promised the Security of their Property.

Sept 18. The violent N.E. Storm which began the Day before Yesterday continues. We are yet in Philadelphia, that Mass of Cowardice and Toryism. . . .

Sept 19. At 3 this Morning was waked by Mr. Lovell, and told that the members of Congress were gone, some of them, a little after Midnight. That there was a letter from Mr. Hamilton, Aid de Camp to the General, informing that the Enemy were in Possession of the Ford and the Boats, and had it in their Power to be in Philadelphia before Morning, and that if Congress was not removed they had not a Moment to lose. Mr. Merchant and myself arose, sent for our Horses, and after collecting our Things, rode off after the others.

Many families had already left Philadelphia, among them the Wisters, prosperous wine merchants whose large house on Market Street had been used by Benjamin Franklin for his first experiment with lightning rods. The Wisters were Quakers of German descent, though Mrs. Wister was Welsh. There were eight children, of whom Sarah—Sally—was barely sixteen at this time. Formerly a pupil at

Anthony Benezet's renowned Quaker Girls' School in Philadelphia, Sally was also skilled at needlework and was described as having auburn hair and ringlets. Since early in the year she and her family had been living at Gwynedd in the countryside not far from the city with some relatives called Foulke, who had two large farmhouses quite close to each other, a good deal of land, and a nearby mill. Since it had now become almost impossible to send letters to her friends back in Philadelphia, Sally kept a journal for them to read later.

✹

Yesterday which was the 24th September two Virginia officers call'd at our house and inform'd us that the British Army had crossed the Schuylkill. Presently after another person stop'd and confirm'd what they had said and that Genl Washington and Army were near Pottsgrove. Well, thee may be sure we were sufficiently scar'd! However, the road was very still till evening about seven o'clock we heard a great noise. To the door we all went, a large number of Waggons with about three hundred of the Philadelphia Militia. They beg'd for drink and several push'd into the house. One of those that enter'd was a little tipsy and had a mind to be saucy. I then thought it time for me to retreat, so figure me (mightily scar'd as not having presence of mind enough to face so many of the Military) running in one door and out another, all in a shake of fear. But after a while, seeing the officers appear gentlemanly and the soldiers civil, I call'd reason to my aid. My fears were in some measure dispell'd tho' my teeth rattled and my hands shook like an aspin leaf. They did not offer to take their quarters with us, so with many blessings and as many adieus they march'd off.

Fourth day, 25th Sept. This day till 12 o'clock the road was mighty quiet when Hobson Jones came riding along like a madman. He made a stop at our door and said the British were at Skippac road, that we should soon see the light horse and a party of Hessians actually turn'd into our lane. My Dadda and Mamma gave it the credit it deserv'd, for he does not keep strictly to the truth in all respects, but the delicate chicken-hearted Liddy [a cousin] and me were wretchedly scar'd. We cou'd say nothing but "Oh what shall we do? What will become of us?" These questions only augmented the terror we were in. Well, this fright went off, we seen no light horse or Hessians.

Fifth day, 26th Sept. We were unusually silent all the morning. No passengers came by the house except to the Mill & we don't place much dependence on Mill news. About 12 o'clock our cousin Jesse heard that Gen. Howe's Army had moved down towards Philadelphia. Then, my dear, our hopes & fears were engag'd for you. However, my advice is summon up all your resolution, call Fortitude to your aid, don't suffer your spirits to sink. My dear, there's nothing like courage—'tis what I stand in need of myself, but unfortunately have little of it in my composition. I was standing in the kitchen about 12 when somebody came to me in a hurry screaming, "Sally! Sally! Here are the light horse!" This was by far the greatest fear I had endur'd—fear tack'd wings to my feet, I was at the house in a moment. At the porch I stopt and it really was the light horse. I ran immediately to the western door where the family were assembled, anxiously waiting for the event. They rode up to the door and halted, enquir'd if we had horses to sell. He was answered negatively. "Have not you, sir"—to my father—"two black horses?" "Yes, but have no mind to dispose of them." My terror had by this time nearly subsided. The officer and men behav'd perfectly civil, the first drank two glasses of wine, rode away bidding his men follow, which after adieus in number they did. The officer was Lieutenant L. Lindsay of Bland's Regiment, Lee's troops. The men to our great joy were Americans and but four in all. What made us imagine them British, they wore blue and red, which with us is not common. . . .

Oct 19th, second day. Now for new and uncommon scenes! As I was laying in bed and ruminating on past and present events, and thinking how happy I shou'd be if I cou'd see you, Liddy come running into the room and said there was the greatest drumming, fifing, and rattling of Waggons that ever she had heard. What to make of this we were at a loss. We dress'd and downstairs in a hurry—our wonder ceased—the British had left Germantown and our Army were marching to take possession. It was the general opinion we would evacuate the capitol. Sister Betsy, myself, and G.E. went about a half mile from home where we cou'd see the army pass. Thee will stare at my going, but no impropriety in my opine, or I would not have gone. We made no great stay but return'd with excellent appetites for our breakfast. Several officers call'd to get some refreshment, but none of consequence till the afternoon. Cousin Prissa and myself were sitting at the door, I in a green skirt, dark short gown, &c. Two genteel men of the military order rode up to the door—"Your servant, ladies" &c, —ask'd if they could have quarters for General Smallwood. Aunt Foulke thought she cou'd accommodate them as well as most of her neighbours said they cou'd. One of the officers dismounted and wrote "Smallwood's Quarters" over the door, which secur'd us from straggling soldiers. After this he mounted his steed and rode away. When we were alone our dress and lips were put in order for conquest, and the hopes of adventures gave brightness to each before-passive countenance. Thee must be told of a Dr. Gould who by accident had made an acquaintance with my father, a sensible, conversible man, a Carolinian, and had come to bid us adieu on his going to that State. Daddy had prevail'd upon him to stay a day or two with us. In the evening his Generalship come with six attendants, which compos'd his family [staff], a large guard of soldiers, a number of horses and baggage Waggons. The yard and house was in confusion, and glitter'd with military equipments. Gould was intimate with Smallwood and had gone into [cousin] Jesse's to see him while he was there. There was great running up and down stairs, so I had an opportunity of seeing and being seen, the former the most agreeable, to be sure. One person in particular attracted my notice. He appear'd cross and reserv'd, but thee shall see how agreeably disappointed I was. Dr. Gould ushered the gentlemen into our parlour and introduc'd them—Genl. Smallwood, Capt. Furnival, Major Stodard, Mr. Prig, Capt. Finlay, and Mr Clagan, Col Wood, and Col Line—these last two did not come with the Gen'l, they are Virginians and both indispos'd. The Genl and suite are Marylanders. Be assured I did not stay long with so many men but secur'd a good retreat, heart safe so far. Some sup'd with us, others at Jesse's. They retired about ten in good order. How new is our situation! I feel in good spirits tho' surrounded by an Army, the house full of officers, yard alive with soldiers—very peaceable sort of men tho', they eat like other folks, talk like them, and behave themselves with elegance, so I will not be afraid of them, that I won't. Adieu—I am going to my chamber to dream I suppose of bayonets and swords, sashes, guns, and epaulets.

Meanwhile, Margaret Morris was also having her encounters with the soldiery:

Some of the Gondola Men & their Wives being Sick, & no Doctor in Town to apply to, they were told that Mrs. M [herself] was a Skillful woman & kept Medicines to give to the poor—& notwithstanding their late attempt to Shoot my poor boy they Ventured to come to me, & in a very humble manner begg'd me to come and do something for them. At first I thought they might have a design to put a trick on me & get me aboard of their Gondolas & then pillage my house, as they had done to some others—but on asking where the sick folks were, was told they were lodged in the Governor's house, so I went to see them. There was several, both men and women, very ill with a fever, some said the Camp or putrid fever. They were broke out in blotches, & on close examination it appear'd to be the itch fever—I treated them according to art, & they all got well. I thought I had received all my pay when they thankfully acknowledged my kindness—but lo!— in a Short time afterwards a very rough ill-looking Man came to the door & ask'd for me. When I went to him he drew me aside, & ask'd if I had any friends in Philadelphia. The question alarm'd me, supposing there was some mischief meditated against that poor City. However I calmly said, "I have an Antient Father, some sisters and other near friends there." "Well," said the man, "do you wish to hear from them?

Or to send anything by way of refreshment to them? If you do, I will take charge of it, and bring you back anything you may send for." I was very much surprised—& thought to be sure he only wanted to get provisions to take to the Gondolas—when he told me his Wife was one of those I had given Medicines to, & this was the only Thing he could do to pay me for my kindness. My heart leap'd with Joy, & I set about preparing something for my dear absent friends—a Quarter of Beef— some Veal—fowls—& flour—were soon put up, & about Midnight the man call'd & took them aboard his boat. He left them at R. Hopkins at the point, from whence my beloved friends took them to town. And 2 nights after, a loud knocking at our front door greatly alarm'd us. Opening the Chamber Window we heard a man's voice saying, "Come down softly & open the door—but bring no light." There was something Mysterious in such a call, & we concluded to go down & set the Candle in the kitchen. When we got to the front door we ask'd, "Who are you?" The man reply'd, "A friend—open quickly." So the door was open'd, & who should it be but our honest Gondola Man with a letter, a bushel of Salt, A Jug of Molasses, a bag of Rice, some tea, Coffee & Sugar, & some Cloth for a Coat for my poor boys—all sent by my kind Sisters. How did our hearts & eyes overflow with love to them & thanks to our heavenly Father for such seasonable Supplys—May we never forget it! Being now so rich, we thought it our duty to hand out a little to the poor around us, who were mourning for want of Salt. So we divided the bushel—and gave a pint to every poor person that came for it, & had great plenty for our own use—indeed it seem'd as if our little Store encreas'd by distributing of it, like the bread broken by our Saviour to the Multitude, which when he had blessed it was so Marvelously Multiplied.

THE BRITISH ARRIVE

Late in 1776 Pennsylvania adopted a new constitution, framed by the radicals and containing few checks and balances or guarantees of civil liberties. Habeas corpus was suspended, people could be arrested on mere suspicion, loyalty oaths were administered to all males over twenty-one, and anyone who refused the oath could be banished without appeal. Many of these laws were aimed at the Quakers, whose religion did not allow them to take oaths or engage in warfare. It was useless for them to appeal to Congress, since that body had already passed a resolution declaring it "certain and notorious that those persons [Quakers] are with rancor and bitterness disaffected to the American cause."

Early in September 1777, as the British drew near, the Philadelphia Committee of Safety ordered the arrest and banishment of a number of these embittered disafectees, among them Henry Drinker. A successful shipper and importer, Drinker was married to Elizabeth Sandwith, also a Quaker. They had three daughters, two sons, and a substantial house on Front Street. Rather than leave the city, like the Wisters, Elizabeth remained to look after the family's property, and also because one of their boys was sick. These extracts from her diary begin the day after the Battle of Brandywine.

�֍

Sept 12. A part of Washington's army has been routed, and have been seen coming into Town in great numbers, the slain is said to be very numerous. Hundreds of their muskets laying in the road—which those that made off have thrown down.

Sept 15. Carriages are constantly passing, and the inhabitants going away. Last night I heard of several friends having lost their Horses—taken from the stables—for which reason I ordered our Horse and Cow to be put in the washhouse, where they at present remain. I have heard from 2 or 3 persons to day that the Church Bells are being taken down; the Bridge over the Schuylkill taken up, and the Ropes across the Ferry cut.

Sept 19. Jenny [a maid] awoke me this morning about 7 o'clock with the news that the English were near; we find that most of our neighbors, and almost all the town, have been up since one o'clock in the morning. Congress, Council, &c are flown; Boats, Carriages going off all night. Town in great confusion.

Sept 20. The Town has been very quiet all this day. It is said that Washington's army has crossed the Ford, and are at present on this side. Some expect a battle hourly, as the English are on the opposite side. The shipping all ordered up the River the next tide, on pain of being burnt, should Howe's vessels approach. The inhabitants continue going out—some are returning.

Sept 21. First day. This evening our little sick son received a letter from his dear Father, which is well worth the store he sets by it; he has ordered it to be put in his Pocket-book until he learns to read.

Sept 23. Went to meeting. It is our monthly meeting, where my dear was missed and thought of by many. Wm. Brown appeared in Testimony, recommending Faith and Patience.

Sept 24. Sister and H.D. Jr. sat up last night till 2 o'clock, as did many others in the city; cannon placed in some of the streets—the Gondelows along the wharf. The sign (over the way) of G. Washington, taken down this afternoon. There is talk of the city being set on fire.

Sept 25. Things seem very quiet and still, and if we come off so, we shall have great cause of thankfulness. Numbers met at the State House since nine o'clock to form themselves into different companies to watch the city; all things appear peaceable at present, the watchmen crying the hour without molestation.

Sept 26. Well! Here are the English in earnest! About two or three thousand came in through Second Street, without opposition or interruption—no plundering on the one side or the other.

Sept 27. About 9 o'clock this morning the *Province* and *Delaware* Frigates, with several Gondelows, came up the River with a design to fire on the Town. They were attacked by a Battery which the English have erected at the lower end of the town. The engagement lasted half an hour, when many shots were exchanged. The people in general, especially downwards, exceedingly alarmed. The Cook on board the *Delaware*, 'tis said, had his head shot off, another of the men wounded. She ran aground and by some means took fire, which occasioned her to strike her colors. The English immediately boarded her—the others sheared off. Part of this scene we were spectators of from the little window in our loft.

Sept 29. Some officers are going about this day numbering the Houses with chalk on the doors. A number of citizens taken up and imprisoned.

Oct 1. Several fire rafts which were sent down the River in order to annoy the Fleet ran ashore and were burnt.

Oct 3. Sister and the girls went to meeting. 'Tis reported to day that Gates has beaten Burgoyne, also that Burgoyne has beaten Gates; which is the truth we know not—perhaps neither.

Oct 4. This has been a sorrowful day at Philadelphia, and much more so at Germantown and thereabouts. It was reported in the forenoon that 1,000 of the English were slain, but Chalkley James who lodges here to night, as Henry is out on guard, tells us that he has been as far as B. Chew's place, and could not learn of more than 30 of the English being killed, tho' a great number were wounded and brought into the City. He counted 18 of the Americans lying dead in the lane from the Road to Chew's House. Washington is said to be wounded in the thigh. Friends, and others in the Jerseys, and indeed almost all around the country, are suffering deeply. 'Tis now past 12 o'clock, and all in the House except myself are I believe asleep. The watchman has cried the hour, and all seems quiet. Fine starlight.

Oct 6. The heaviest firing that I think I ever heard was this evening, for upwards of two hours. It is thought to be the English troops engaged with the Mud-Island Battery. An officer called this afternoon to ask if we could take in a sick and wounded Captain. I put him off by saying that as my Husband was from me, I should be pleased if he could provide some other convenient place. Two of the Presbyterian meeting Houses are made Hospitals of, for the wounded soldiers, of which there are great numbers.

Oct 9. Firing last night, and heavy firing this morning. Cloudy all day, and rain the greatest part.

Mud Island was home to Fort Mifflin, built many years earlier under the supervision of Captain John Montresor of the Royal Engineers and now a dilapidated mishmash of stone walls, wooden palisades, trenches, embankments, barracks, and gun batteries. The ground was so low that but for the dikes it would have been flooded when the tide rose, and the mud was so soft that shells coming in at a high trajectory buried themselves so deep that they could not be heard when they exploded. Since they could not hold Philadelphia without controlling the Delaware, the British had no choice but to lay siege to Fort Mifflin. The Royal Navy would bombard it, while the honor of storming it was assigned to the Hessians. The fort was at first undermanned and could easily have been taken by a surprise attack, but Colonel Count von Donop, going by the book, began the proceedings by formally summoning it to surrender, thus giving the Americans time to strengthen their defenses. These included the so-called *chevaux de frise,* wooden frames bristling with sharp metal spikes, long used in European wars to fend off a cavalry charge or fill a gap in a defensive position, but now cunningly submerged just below the surface of the Delaware, all set to rip out the bottom of an advancing man-of-war. By the time the British appeared, about a dozen of these were in place. Also helping in the defense of Mud Island was Joseph Martin of the Connecticut infantry, who had survived the Kip's Bay landings in New York the previous year, and several other engagements since then.

The first attempt the British made against the place after I entered it was by the *Augusta,* a sixty-four-gun ship. While maneuvering one dark night she got on the *chevaux de frise* which had been sunk in the channel of the river. As soon as she was discovered in the morning we plied her so well with hot shot that she was soon in flames. Boats were sent from the shipping below to her assistance, but our shot proving too hot for them, they were obliged to leave her to her fate. In an hour or two she blew up with an explosion which seemed to shake the earth to its center, leaving a volume of smoke like a thundercloud, which, as the air was calm, remained an hour or two. A twenty-gun ship which had come to the assistance of the *Augusta* in her distress shared her fate soon after.

Our batteries were nothing more than old spars and timber laid up in parallel lines and filled with mud and dirt. The British batteries in the course of the day would nearly level our works, and we were, like the beaver, obliged to repair our dams in the night. During the whole night, at intervals of a quarter or half an hour, the enemy would let off all their pieces, and although we had sentinels to watch them and at every flash of their guns to cry, "A shot!" upon hearing which everyone endeavored to take care of himself, yet they would ever and anon, in spite of all our precautions, cut up some of us.

The engineer in the fort was a French officer by the name of Fleury, the same who struck the British flag at the storming of Stony Point. He was a very austere man and kept us constantly employed day and night; there was no chance of escaping his vigilance.

Between the stone walls and the palisadoes was a kind of yard or pen, at the southern end of which was a narrow entrance not more than eight or ten feet wide, with a ditch about four feet wide in the middle, extending the whole length of the pen. Here, on the eastern side of the wall, was the only place in the fort that anyone could be in any degree of safety. Into this place we used to gather the splinters broken off the palisadoes by the enemy's shot and make a little fire, just enough to keep from suffering. We would watch an opportunity to escape from the vigilance of Colonel Fleury, and run into this place for a minute or two's respite from fatigue and cold. When the engineer found that the workmen had begun to grow scarce, he would come to the entrance and call us out. He had always his cane in his hand, and woe betided him he could get a stroke at. At his approach I always jumped over the ditch and ran down the other side, so that he could not reach me, but he often noticed me and as often threatened me, but threatening was all, he could never get a stroke at me, and I cared but little for his threats.

It was utterly impossible to lie down to get any rest or sleep on account of the mud, if the enemy's shot would have suffered us to do so. Sometimes some of the men, when overcome with fatigue and want of sleep, would slip away into the barracks to catch a nap of sleep, but it seldom happened that they all came out again alive. I was in this place a fortnight and can say in sincerity that I never lay down to sleep a minute in all that time.

The British knew the situation of the place as well as we did. And as their point-blank shot would not reach us behind the wall, they would throw elevated grapeshot from their mortar, and when the sentries had cried, "A shot!" and the soldiers, seeing no shot arrive, had become careless, the grapeshot would come down like a shower of hail about our ears.

We continued here, suffering cold, hunger, and other miseries, till the fourteenth day of November. On that day, at the dawn, we discovered six ships of the line, all sixty-fours, a frigate of thirty-six guns, and a galley in a line just below the *chevaux de frise*; a twenty-four-gun ship (being an old ship cut down), her guns said to be all brass twenty-four-pounders, and a sloop of six guns in company with her, both within pistol shot of the fort, on the western side. We immediately opened our batteries upon them, but they appeared to take very little notice of us. We heated some shot, but by mistake twenty-four-pound shot were heated instead of eighteen, which was the caliber of the guns in that part of the fort. The enemy soon began their firing upon us and there was music indeed. The soldiers were all ordered to take their places at the palisadoes, which they were ordered to defend to the last extremity, as it was expected the British would land under the fire of their cannon and attempt to storm the fort. The cannonade was severe, as well it might be, six sixty-four-gun ships, a thirty-six-gun frigate, a twenty-four-gun ship, a galley, and a sloop of six guns, together with six batteries of six guns each and a bomb battery of three mortars, all playing at once upon our poor little fort, if fort it might be called.

Some of our officers endeavored to ascertain how many guns were fired in a minute by the enemy, but it was impossible, the fire was incessant. In the height of the cannonade it was desirable to hoist a signal flag for some of our galleys that were lying above us to come down to our assistance. The officers inquired who would undertake it. As none appeared willing for some time, I was about to offer my services. I considered it no more exposure of my life than it was to remain where I was. The flagstaff was of easy ascent, being an old ship's mast, having shrouds to the ground, and the roundtop still remaining. While I was still hesitating, a sergeant of the artillery offered himself. He accordingly ascended to the round top, pulled down the flag to affix the signal flag to the halyard, upon which the enemy, thinking we had struck, ceased firing in every direction and cheered. "Up with the flag!" was the cry of our officers in every part of the fort. The flags were accordingly hoisted, and the firing was immediately renewed. The sergeant then came down and had not gone half a rod from the foot of the staff when he was cut in two by a cannon shot. He was killed! Had I been at the same business I might have been killed, but it might have been otherwise ordered by Divine Providence, we might have both lived. I am not predestinarian enough to determine it. The enemy's shot cut us up. I saw five artillerists belonging to one gun cut down by a single shot, and I saw men who were stooping to be protected by the works, but not stooping low enough, split like fish to be broiled.

The cannonade continued, directed mostly at the fort, till the dusk of the evening. As soon as it was dark we began to make preparations for evacuating the fort and endeavoring to escape to the Jersey shore. When the firing had in some measure subsided and I could look about me, I found the fort exhibited a picture of desolation. The whole area of the fort was as completely ploughed as a field. The buildings of every kind were hanging in broken fragments, and the guns all dismounted, and how many of the garrison sent to the world of spirits I knew not. If ever destruction was complete, it was here. The surviving part of the garrison were now drawn off and such of the stores as could conveniently be taken away were carried to the Jersey shore.

I happened to be left with a party of seventy or eighty men to destroy and burn all that was left of the place. I was in the northwest battery just after dark when the enemy were hauling their shipping on that side higher up to a more commanding position. They were so nigh that I could hear distinctly what they said on board the sloop. One expression of theirs I well remember: "We will give it to the d – -d rebels in the morning." The thought that then occupied my mind I as well remember: "The d – -d rebels will show you a trick which the devil never will—they will go off and leave you." After the troops had left the fort and were embarking at the wharf, I went to the waterside to find one of my messmates to whom I had lent my canteen in the morning, as there were three or four hogsheads of rum in the fort, the heads of which we were about to knock in, and I was desirous to save a trifle of their contents. There being nothing to eat I thought I might have something to drink. I found him, indeed, but lying in a long line of dead men who had been brought out of the fort to be conveyed to the main, to have the last honors conferred upon them which it was in our power to give. Poor young man! He was the most intimate associate I had in the army, but he was gone, with many more as deserving as himself.

I returned directly back into the fort to my party and proceeded to set fire to everything that would burn, and then repaired immediately to the wharf where three batteaux were waiting to convey us across the river. And now came on another trial. Before we could embark, the buildings in the fort were completely in flames, and they threw such a light upon the water that we were plainly seen by the British as though it had been broad day. Almost their whole fire was directed at us. Sometimes our boat seemed to be almost thrown out of the water, and at length a shot took the sternpost out of the rear boat. We had then to stop and take the men from the crippled boat into the other two, and now the shot and water flew merrily, but by the assistance of a kind Providence we escaped without any further injury and landed, a little after midnight, on the Jersey shore.

We marched a little back into some pitch-pine woods, where we found the rest of the troops that had arrived before us. They had made up some comfortable fires and were enjoying the warmth, and that was all the comfort they had to partake of, except rest, for victuals was out of the question. I wrapped myself up in my blanket and lay down upon the leaves and soon fell asleep and continued so till past noon, when I awoke from the first sound sleep I had had for a fortnight.

Soon after taking Fort Mifflin, the British sent forces up the Delaware. One of the places they visited was Burlington, where Margaret Morris and her family were still living in their house on the bank of the river.

One Morning, having left my Chamber at an earlier hour than usual, & casting my eyes towards the river, was Surpriz'd to see some hundreds of boats all filled with British Soldiers—The boats were order'd up the river to Borden Town to burn all the Gondolas— The last boat we saw was a small one, with only 3 men & the rowers in it—they were not Soldiers. When they came opposite to the town Wharf they stop't rowing & pull'd off their hats, & bowed to the people on the Wharf. We heard afterwards it was our poor Refugee [Dr. Jonathan Odell], Dr S. Burling, & J. Stansbury who intended to have come on Shore & paid us a Visit—but so many people appearing on the Wharf & Street, they thought it safest to take to their Oars & follow the fleet. One large Vessel with Cannon was in the fleet, & when they returned were order'd to fire if they saw Soldiers on the Wharfs or about the Streets. . . .

It was First day morning & all the family but myself gone to meeting & I was laying on the bed, and hearing a large gun look'd out of the Window & saw the large ship so close to our landing that I thought they were coming ashore —when behold, they fired 2 or 3 of their great guns, which shook the House & went through the walls of our next door neighbor, who was a Captain in the rebel Army. I still kept at the window unapprehensive of danger—& seeing two men on the Deck, talking & pointing to my house, one of them said, "In that house lives a woman to whom I am indebted for my life. She sheltered me when I was driven from my own home." This I was afterwards told by a person who heard it—it is needless to add that it was our poor Refugee who made the above acknowledgment.

Meanwhile, Sally Wister had been passing judgement on the American officers who had taken up quarters with her relatives in Gwynedd. General Smallwood: "Tall, portly, well-made, a truly martial air, the behaviour and manner of a gentleman." Colonel Wood: "Tall and genteel, an agreable countenance and deportment." Colonel Line "is not married so lett me not to be too warm in his praise lest you suspect. He is monstrous tall, & brown, but has a certain something in his face and conversation very agreable." Captain Furnival: "The handsomest face I ever seen, a very fine person, fine light hair and a great deal of it adds to the beauty of his face." Major Stodard: "I at first thought the major cross and proud, but I was mistaken. He is about nineteen, nephew to the General and acts as Major of brigade to him. . . . He is large in his person, manly, and an engaging countenance and address." Captain Finley "is wretched ugly, but he went away last night."

Fourth day, Oct 21st. I just now met the major, very reserv'd, nothing but "Good morning," or "Your servant, madam." I have heard strange things of the major—worth a fortune of thirty thousand pounds independent of anybody. The major moreover is vastly bashful, so much so he can hardly look at the ladies.

Fifthday, sixthday, and seventhday pass'd. The General still here, the major still bashful.

Secondday, 26th October. A very rainy morning, so like to prove the officers in the house all day. Afternoon the general and officers drank tea with us and stay'd part of the evening. After supper I went into aunt's where sat the General, Col. Line, and Major Stodard. So Liddy and me seated ourselves at the table in order to read a verse book. The Major was holding a candle for the General who was reading a newspaper. He look'd at us, turn'd away his eyes, look'd again, put the candlestick down, up he jumpt, out of the door he went. "Well!" said I to Liddy. "He will join us when he comes in." Presently he return'd and seated himself at the table. "Pray, ladies, is there any songs in that book?" "Yes, many." "Can't you favor me with a sight of it?" "No, major, 'tis a borrow'd book." "Miss Sally, can't you sing?" "No." (Thee may be sure I told the truth there.) Liddy, saucy girl, told him I cou'd. He beg'd and I deny'd, for my voice is not much better than the voice of a raven. We talk'd and laugh'd for an hour. He is very clever, amiable, and polite. He has the softest voice, never pronounces the R at all. . . .

Seventhday, Oct 31st. A most charming day. I walk'd to the door, receiv'd the salutation of the morn from Stodard and other officers. As often as I go to the door so often have I seen the major. We chat passingly, as, "A fine day, Miss Sally!" "Yes, very fine, major." Seventhday night another very charming conversation with the young Marylander. He seems possest of very amiable manners, sensible and agreable—he has by his unexceptionable deportment engag'd my esteem.

Firstday morn. For all I do not mention Col. Wood as often as he deserves it, it is not that we are not sociable—we are very much so, and he is often at our house, dines or drinks tea with us every day. Liddy and I had a kind of adventure with him this morn. We were in his chamber chatting about our little affairs, and no idea of being interrupted. We were standing up—each an arm on a chest of drawers—the door bang'd open—Col. Wood was in the room. We started, the colour flew into our faces and crimson'd us over. Tears flew into my eyes. It was very silly, but his coming was so abrupt. He was between us and the door. "Ladies, do not be scar'd! I only want something from my portmanteau. I beg you not to be disturb'd." We ran by him like two partridges into mamma's room, threw ourselves into chairs and reproach'd each other for being so foolish as to blush and look so silly. I was very much vex'd at myself. So was Liddy. The Colonel laughed at us and it blew over.

The General, Colonels Wood, Line, Guest, Crawford, Majors Stodard and Letherberry ["a lawyer, a sensible young fellow and will never swing for want of tongue"] din'd with us today. After dinner Liddy, Betsy, and thy smart journaliser put on their bonnets, determin'd to take a walk. We left the house. I naturally look'd back, when behold, the two majors seem'd debating whether to follow us or not. Liddy said, "We shall have their attendance," but I did not think so. They open'd the gate and came fast after us. They overtook us about ten pole [fifty yards] from home and beg'd leave to attend us. No fear of a refusal. They enquir'd where we were going. "To neighbour Roberts. We will introduce you to his daughters, you us to Genl Stevens." The affair was concluded and we shortened the way with lively conversation. Our intentions of going to Roberts was frustrated, as the rain that had fall'n had rais'd Wisahicken too high to attempt crossing it on foot. We alter'd the plan of our ramble, left the road and walk'd near two miles thro' the woods. . . . 'Tis nonsense to pretend to recount all that was said, my memory is not so obliging, but it is sufficient that nothing happened during our little excursion but what was very agreable and intirely consistent with the strictest rules of politeness & decorum. I was vex'd a little at tearing my muslin petticoat. I had on my white whim [head scarf], quite as nice as a first day in town. We return'd home safe.

Secondday morn, November 1st. Today the Militia marches and the General and officers leave us. High ho! I am very sorry, for when you have been with agreable people 'tis impossible not to feel regret when they bid you adieu, perhaps for ever. When they leave us we shall be immur'd in solitude. The major looks dull. Secondday noon, about two o'clock, the General and major come to bid us adieu. With daddy and mammy they shook hands very friendly, to us they bow'd politely. Our hearts were full. I thought the major was affected. "Good-bye, Miss Sally"—spoken very low. He walk'd hastily and mounted his horse. They promis'd to visit us soon. We stood at the door to take a last look, all of us very sober. The major turn'd his horse's head and rode back, dismounted—"I have forgot my pistols"—pass'd us and run upstairs. He came swiftly back, as if wishing through inclination to stay, but duty compell'd to go. He remounted his horse—"Farewell, ladies, till I see you again!"—canter'd away. We look'd at him till the turn in the road hid him from our sight. "Amiable major!" "Clever fellow!" "Good young man!" was echo'd from one to the other. I wonder whether we shall ever see him again.

Three weeks later Elizabeth Drinker, wife to the imprisoned Quaker merchant Henry Drinker, was writing in her diary:

Nov 21. I was awakened this morning before 5 o'clock by the loud firing of cannon—my Head aching very badly. All our family were up but little Molly, and a fire was made in the Parlor more than an hour before day. All our neighbors were also up, and I believe most in Town. The Americans had set their whole Fleet on fire, except one small vessel, and several of the Gondelows, which passed by the city in the night. Billy counted 8 different vessels on fire at once, in sight; one lay near the Jersey shore opposite our House; we heard the explosions of 4 of them when they blew up, which shook our windows greatly. We had a fair sight of the blazing Fleet from our upper windows.

Nov 22. Firing again this morning, cannon and small arms. An American Schooner burnt in our river this morning by the English, nearly opposite our House. An Earthquake was felt this morning, between 7 and 8 o'clock. These are tremendous times indeed!

Nov 25. We were very much affrighted this evening, before 9 o'clock. Jenny happened to go into the Yard—where she saw a man with Ann [Ann Kelly, an indentured servant]. She came in and whispered to Sister, who immediately went out, and discovered a young officer with Ann. Sister held the candle up to his Face, and asked him who he was. His answer was—"What's that to you?" The gate was locked, and he followed Ann and sister into the kitchen—where he swore he had mistaken the House; but we could not get him out. Chalkley James who happened to be here came into the kitchen and asked him what business he had there. He damned him, and said, "What's that to you?" shook his sword, which he held in his Hand, and seemed to threaten, when Chalkley, with great resolution, twisted it out of his Hands, and collared him. Sister took the sword from Chalkley, and locked it up in the drawer in the parlor—all his outcry was for his sword. He swore he would not stir a foot until he had it. I then sent in for Joshua Howell, when he [the officer] declared that he knew we were peaceable people, and that he gave up his sword on that account, out of pure good nature, which he had said to us before. He told Chalkley in the kitchen that he would be the death of him tomorrow. Joshua got him to the door, and then gave him his sword, expecting he would go off, but he continued swearing there. Joshua left him, and went to call Abel James; in the meantime the impudent Fellow came in again, swearing in the Entry, with the sword in his hand. Sister had locked Chalkley up in the middle room, and we shut ourselves in the parlor—where he knocked, desiring entrance. Our poor, dear children were never so frightened before—to have an enraged, drunken man—as I believe he was—with a sword in his hand, swearing about the House. After going two or three times up and down the Entry, desiring we would let him in to drink a Glass of Wine with us, he went to the end of the alley—when Harry locked the Front door on him. He knocked and desired to come in, when J. Howell and A. James, whom Joshua had gone for, came to him. They had some talk with him, and he went off, as I supposed. I had all the back doors bolted; the Gate and Front door locked; when in about ten minutes after, Harry came out of the kitchen and told us he was there. I then locked the parlor door, and would not let Chalkley out. Harry ran into Howells for Joshua, who did not come for some time after the Fellow was gone, and Ann with him. He came over the Fence, and they went out the same way. 'Tis now near one o'clock in the morning, and I have not yet recovered from the fright. Ann called him Captain Tape, or John Tape.

Nov 26. No news to day from Ann and her Gallant. I have not yet got over last night's fright, but have been in a flutter all day.

Nov 27. The Aurora Borealis, or Northern Light, appeared greater tonight than ever I remember to have seen it before.

Nov 28. The *Vigilant*, man-of-war, and a number of other vessels came up to day.

Dec 2. Our saucy Ann came while I was at meeting, desiring to know what I would take for her time [i.e., the rest of her indenture], and she would bring me the money in a minute. Sister told her she did not know, but that she had heard me talk of putting her in the Work-House. She replied, "If you talk so, you shall neither have me nor the money." Sister then ordered her to come again at 12 o'clock, but she has not been here since.

Dec 4. Ann Kelly called this morning to know what I would take for her time. Sister told her £20; she did not see me, I being again out.

Dec 9. I took a walk after dinner to Bartram's shop in Market Street. Nothing will pass at this time (unless with a Few) but Gold and Silver, which is hard upon those who have a quantity of the old paper money by them. These are sad times for thieving and plundering; 'tis hardly safe to leave the door open a minute. A number of Friends to Government about the country have lately been plundered and ill-used by the British Troops. Things wear a very gloomy aspect at this present time.

But not so gloomy as the prospects facing Henry Yeager, fourteen, a drummer boy in a Pennsylvania militia regiment that had evacuated the city when the British arrived. Along with his friend George Lechler, Henry had thought it safe to sneak back into town to visit their families. Not until many years later, when applying for a pension, did Henry get a chance to tell what happened next. (His application, a formal document, was probably dictated, which is why he is referred to in the third person as "the declarant.")

They had been at home in Philadelphia but a few days when they were both arrested by British authority and taken to General Howe's quarters in Second Street below Spruce, opposite Little Dock Street. Declarant was accompanied by his mother, and when they arrived at the general's quarters, a Major Bedford asked her if declarant was her son, and being answered affirmatively, he remarked that declarant would be hanged. Declarant was put in a guardhouse at the corner of Second and Little Dock Streets. Lechler was confined separately in another in Little Dock Street.

The next day they were taken to the house at the northwest corner of Second and Spruce Streets for trial. Declarant was taken before the judges first. He was charged with having brought letters from the American army, and he was asked if it was true. He answered in the negative. He was asked if he belonged to the rebel army. He answered that he belonged to Washington's army. He was then charged with having come to the city as a spy and was asked if such was not the fact. He answered no, but that he came to see his parents. He was examined for a length of time upon similar matters without eliciting more than is herein stated. After a short conference, one of the judges asked him his name, and, upon declarant giving it, the former said to him, "You are to be hanged by the neck until you are dead, dead, dead." Declarant was then conducted from the room. In the entry or hall, he met Lechler, who inquired what had taken place, and declarant informed him that he was to be hanged. Lechler was then conducted before the judges, and declarant was afterwards informed by him that similar proceedings occurred, and a like sentence pronounced on him.

They were then both taken to the Walnut Street prison. Soon after they had been there, Provost Marshal Cunningham, in the hearing of declarant, directed the "spies" to be brought before him. Declarant and Lechler were accordingly conducted to him, when he said to them, "I'll give you half an hour and no longer," and ordered them to be confined in separate dungeons. At the expiration of the half hour (to declarant a very short one), they were again taken before Provost Marshal Cunningham, who ordered a Negro to bring two halters. The marshal asked who was the oldest. Lechler answered that he was the youngest. The marshal then directed that all the other prisoners should quit the yard and the gates be closed. He directed the Negro to place one halter on Lechler's neck, and the other on claimant's, to back both against the gate, and to draw the ropes through the top of it, which was done. At this moment, a man came in and gave a paper to the marshal, who read it and then ordered the ropes to be loosed from the gate and wound round the prisoners' bodies. Declarant and Lechler were then ordered to their dungeons, where they were taken. The next morning they were brought to the marshal's room, when the ropes were taken off them and they put into the yard among the other prisoners. After this, declarant remained in prison eight weeks and three days before he was released.

Before the war "Bloody Bill" Cunningham had been a riding instructor in New York where he had been roughed up by some Liberty Boys for proposing a toast to the king, and ever since, as provost-marshal in Boston and Philadelphia (and later in New York), he was insatiable in his thirst to settle scores. But it seems improbable that Yeager and Lechler were really to be hanged. More likely Cunningham and the others were just having a bit of fun, justifiable in their eyes as an attempt to bring the boys to their senses. The result was foreseeable: as soon as he was released Yeager hastened back to the American lines where he reenlisted, not as a drummer boy but as a gunner in an artillery regiment. How he must have longed for the day when he would have the provost-marshal in his sights! But that was not to be. Nor did he get a pension—his application was denied on the grounds that at the time he enlisted he was under sixteen, the official minimum age.

Meanwhile war was coming closer to Sally Wister and her family in Gwynedd, outside Philadelphia:

December 5th, sixth day. Oh gracious, Debby, I am all alive with fear! The English have come out to attack (as we imagine) our army—they are on Chestnut Hill, our army three miles this side. What will become of us? Only six mile distant—we are in hourly expectation of an engagement. I fear we shall be in the midst of it. Heaven defend us from so dreadful a sight! The battle of Germantown and the horrors of that day are recent in my mind. It will be sufficiently dreadful if we are only in hearing of the firing.

Seventh day, December 6th. No firing this morn. I hope for one more quiet day. Seventh day, noon. I was much alarm'd just now, sitting in the parlour indulging melancholy reflections, when somebody burst open the door, "Sally, here's Major Stodard!" I jump'd. Our conjectures were various concerning his coming. The poor fellow, from great fatigue and want of rest together with being expos'd to the night air, had caught cold, which brought on a fever. He could scarcely walk and I went into aunt's to see him. I was surpriz'd—instead of the lively, alert, blooming Stodard who was on his feet the instant we enter'd, he look'd pale, thin, and dejected, too weak to rise and bow. "And how are you, Miss Sally?" "How does thee do, major?" I seated myself near him, inquir'd the course of his indisposition, ask'd for the general, receiv'd his compliments. Not willing to fatigue him with too much chat I told him adieu. Tonight Aunt Hannah Foulke administer'd something, Jesse assisted him to his chamber. He had not lain down five minutes before he was fast asleep.

First day morn, December 7th. I tripp'd into aunt's, there sat the major rather more like himself. How natural it was to see him. "Good morning, Miss Sally." "Good morrow, major. How does thee do today?" Major: "I feel quite recover'd, Sally." "Well, I fancy this indisposition has sav'd thy head this time." Major: "No, ma'am, for if I hear a firing I shall soon be with them." That was heroic! About eleven I dress'd myself—silk and cotton gown, it is made without an apron. I feel quite awkwardish and prefer the girlish dress.

First day afternoon. A Mr. Seaton and Stodard drank tea with us. He and me had a little private chat after tea. In the eve Seaton went into aunt's, mamma went to see Prissa who is poorly, pappa withdrew to talk to some strangers. Liddy just then came in so we engag'd in an agreeable conversation. I begg'd him to come and give us a circumstantial account of the battle if there shou'd be one. "I certainly will, ma'am, if I am favour'd with life." Liddy unluckily took it into her head to blunder out something about a person being in the kitchen who had come from the army. Stodard, ever anxious to hear, jump'd up. "Goodnight to you, ladies," was the word, and he disappear'd. . . . "Liddy, thee hussy! What business had thee to mention a word of the army? Thee sees it sent him off. Thy evil genius prevail'd and we all feel the effects of it." "Lord bless me," said Liddy. "I had not thought of his going or for ten thousand worlds I wou'd not spoke. But we cannot recall the past." Well we laugh'd and chatted at a noisy rate till a summons for

Liddy parted us. I sat negligently on my chair, thought brought on thought, and I got so low spirited that I cou'd hardly speak—the dread of an engagement, our dreadful situation if a battle shou'd ensue . . . and yet I did not feel half so frightened as I expected to be. 'Tis amazing how we get reconcil'd to such things. Six months ago the bare idea of being within ten, aye twenty miles of a battle wou'd almost distracted me and now tho' two such large armies are within six miles of us, we can be cheerful and converse calmly of it.

[The next day] in the afternoon we distinctly heard platoon firing. Everybody was at the door, I in the horrors. The armies were as we judg'd engag'd. Very composedly, says the major to our servant, "Will you be kind enough to saddle my horse? I shall go." Accordingly the horse was taken from the hospitable quiet barn to plunge into the thickest ranks of war. Cruel change! Seaton insisted to the major that the armies were still nothing but skirmishing with the flanking parties—"Don't go." We happen'd (us girls I mean) to be standing in the kitchen. The major passing through in a hurry and I forsooth discover'd a strong partiality by saying "Oh major, thee is not going?" He turn'd round. "Yes I am, Miss Sally," bow'd and went into the road. We all pitied him . . . I don't think we shall see him again.

VALLEY FORGE

On December 20,1777, Sally Wister wrote in her journal: "General Washington's army have gone into winter quarters at the Valley Forge. We shall not see many of the military now. We shall be very intimate with solitude, I am afraid."

For the American soldiers huddled in their makeshift huts on the exposed slopes of Valley Forge, solitude was one of the few problems they did not have to face. "Poor food—hard lodging—Cold Weather—fatigue—Nasty Cloaths—Nasty Cookery," wrote Albigence Waldo, a young army surgeon of delicate health and sensitive temperament from Pomfret, Connecticut.

"Why are we sent here to starve and freeze? What sweet Felicities have I left at home—a charming wife—pretty children—Good Beds—good food—good cookery—all agreeable—all harmonious. Here all Confusion—smoke & Cold—hunger & filthyness—A pox on my bad luck! . . . I am Sick—discontented—Vomit half my time—smoak'd out of my senses." As for the ordinary soldier, "his bare feet are seen thro' his worn out Shoes, his legs nearly naked from the tatter'd remains of an only pair of stockings, his Breeches not sufficient to cover his nakedness, his Shirt hanging in Strings, his hair dishevell'd, his face meagre; his whole appearance pictures a person forsaken & discouraged."

"What our soldiers have suffered this winter is beyond expression," wrote Joseph Hodgkins to his wife, Sarah, back home in Ipswich. "One half has been barefoot & almost naked all winter, the other half very badly on it for clothes of all sorts, & to complete our misery very short on it for provision. Not long since our brigade drew but an half day's allowance of meat in eight days. But these difficulties the men bore with a degree of fortitude becoming soldiers."

For some, even getting to Valley Forge had been a hardship. Private Elijah Fisher of Maine, still with a pain in his side, had been sent there with his regiment directly after Saratoga:

The howl army had orders to march at sunset and about Dark it did begun to storm, the wind being at the N.E., and the Artillery went before and Cut up the roads and the snow Come about our shoes and then set in to rain, and with all which made it very teges [tedious], and I was so unwell and such a pain frequented my side which made it very teges to bear. At twelve at night we come into a wood and had order to bild ourselves shelters to brake off the storm and make ourselves as Comforteble as we could, but jest as we got a shelter bilt and a good fire and Dried some of our Cloths and begun to have things a little Comforteble, though but poor at the best, thare come orders to march and leave all we had taken so much pains for. So we marches to the Gulfe-mills and bilt us Camps till the baggage Come up.

Strategically, Valley Forge was a good choice for winter quarters, and there was plenty of wood for building huts, but the open valley offered little protection against the harsh winter weather. Foragers from the British army had already picked the area clean, and the American supply services were plagued by incompetence and corruption. Washington's decision to remain in camp with his army was good for morale, and so was Sir William Howe's decision to stay put in Philadelphia. Indeed the only member of the British army to appear in Valley Forge during the entire winter was "a fine sporting dog," which wandered into American headquarters, evidently lost but with the name of its owner, General Howe, engraved on its collar. A French officer, the Chevalier de Pontgibaud, sent it back under a flag of truce and in return "received from Sir William a very warm letter of thanks for this act of courtesy." Such social niceties mattered a great deal to the officers and gentlemen of the European armies, but not very much to the ordinary American soldiers as they hunched together round the smoky fires in their uninsulated huts and made do on a diet of "fire cake"—thin cakes of flour cooked over hot stones—washed down by cold water.

"December 21, 1777," wrote Albigence Waldo.

Sent a letter to my Wife. Heartily wish myself at home, my Skin & eyes almost spoil'd with continual smoke. A general cry thro' the Camp this Evening among the Soldiers, "No meat! No Meat!"—the distant vales Echo'd back the melancholly sound—"No Meat! No Meat!" Immitating the noise of Crows & Owls also made a part of the confused Musick. What have you for your Dinners, boys? "Nothing but fire Cake & Water, Sir." At night, "Gentlemen, the supper is ready." What is your Supper, Lads? "Fire Cake & Water, sir."

Dec. 22. Lay excessive Cold & uncomfortable last night—my eyes are started out from their Orbits like a Rabbit's eyes, occasion'd by a great Cold & Smoke. What have you got for Breakfast, Lads? "Fire Cake & Water, Sir." The Lord send that our Commissary of Purchases may live on Fire Cake & Water, 'till their glutted Gutts are turned to paste-board.

Our Division are under Marching orders this morning. I am ashamed to say it, but I am tempted to steal Fowls if I could find them, or even a whole Hog, for I feel as if I could eat one. But the impoverish'd Country about us affords but little matter to employ a Thief. At 12 of the Clock at Night, Providence sent us a little Mutton, with which we immediately had some Broth made, & a fine Stomach for same. Ye who eat Pumkin Pie and Roast Turkies, and yet Curse fortune for using you ill, Curse her no more, lest she reduce your Allowance of her favours to a bit of Fire Cake & a draught of Cold Water, & in Cold Weather too.

Dec 23. This evening an excellent Player on the Violin, in that soft kind of Musick which is so finely adapted to stir up the tender passions, while he was playing in the next Tent to mine these kind of soft Airs, it immediately called up in remembrance all the endearing expressions, the Tender Sentiments, the sympathetic friendship that has given so much satisfaction and sensible pleasure to me from the first time I gained the heart & affections of the tenderest of the Fair. A thousand agreeable little incidents which have Occurr'd since our happy connection . . . were now recall'd to my mind, and filled me with these tender emotions, and Agreeable Reflections, which cannot be described, and which in spite of my Philosophy forced out the sympathetic tear. I wish'd to have the Musick Cease, and yet dreaded its ceasing, lest I should lose sight of these dear Ideas, which gave me pain and pleasure at the same instant. Ah Heavens! Why is it that our harder fate so often deprives us of the enjoyment of what we most wish to enjoy this side of thy brighter realms?

Although there were no major actions during the winter, scouting and foraging parties often skirmished. One such incident was described by John McCasland, a Pennsylvania militiaman:

On one occasion, sixteen of us were ranging about hunting Hessians, and we suspected Hessians to be at a large and handsome mansion house in Bucks County, Pennsylvania, about sixteen miles from Philadelphia. We approached near the house and discovered a large Hessian standing in the yard with his gun, as a sentinel we supposed, and by a unanimous vote of the company present it was agreed on that Major McCorman or myself, who were good marksmen, would shoot him (McCorman was then a private). We cast lots, and it fell to my lot to shoot the Hessian. I did not like to shoot a man down in cold blood . . . and I concluded to break his thigh. I shot with a rifle and aimed at his hip. He had a large iron tobacco box in his breeches pocket, and I hit the box, the ball glanced, and it entered his thigh. . . . He fell and then rose. We scaled the yard fence and surrounded the house. They saw their situation and were evidently disposed to surrender. They could not speak English and we could not understand their language. At length one of the Hessians came out of the cellar with a large bottle of rum and advanced with it at arm's length as a flag of truce. The family had abandoned the house, and the Hessians had possession. They were twelve in number. We took them prisoners and carried them to Valley Forge and delivered them up to General Washington.

Making military decisions by majority vote and by casting lots were practices that would soon come to an end, thanks largely to the stout and formidable Friedrich Wilhelm Ludolf Gerhard Augustin, Baron von Steuben. (The title was a recent gift from a German princeling; the "von" had been self-conferred by his grandfather.) Born in 1730 in Magdeburg, where his father was a military engineer, Steuben had joined the officer corps of the Prussian army at the age of seventeen, had served throughout the Seven Years' War, and become a well-regarded staff officer and aide-de-camp to Frederick the Great; but promotion was slow and he never rose above the rank of captain. When peace came, he served various other German rulers, usually with a higher rank but never for very long. In the summer of 1777, he was once again looking for a job when he was advised to go to Paris and call on Benjamin Franklin, who recognized in Steuben an experienced staff officer who could be of great help in training and organizing the American army. In his letter of recommendation to George Washington, Franklin helped matters along by upgrading the baron's rank from captain to lieutenant general, adding that "he goes to America with a true zeal for our cause." More importantly, at least from the diplomatic point of view, "he is recommended to us by two of the best judges in military merit in this country, Messrs. les comtes de Vergennes [chief minister] and de St. Germain [minister of war]." Beaumarchais, the playwright turned businessman who had set up the front corporation Hortalez & Cie to funnel French aid to the Americans, also sent a letter of recommendation. Steuben, he wrote, "has not left the side of Frederick the Great for the past twenty-two years, and is generally considered excellently qualified to assist Mr. de Washington, for whom the baron has the greatest esteem." Moreover Hortalez & Cie was ready to pick up all Steuben's expenses, so that when he presented himself before Congress he could offer to serve as an unpaid volunteer. This went down well, and Steuben arrived at Valley Forge on February 23, 1778.

Washington was at first guarded, for the European officers who had come to join his army had been a mixed blessing. Lafayette was welcome for his military skill and personal charm, and also as a well-placed advocate for the American cause on his visits back to France, but apart from him and a few others, "I do most devoutly wish that we had not a single foreigner among us." Perhaps when he said this Washington was thinking of Tronson du Coudray, an expert artillerist but conceited and arrogant, who on the basis of promises made to him by Silas Deane in Paris expected to be put in command of the

Continental Army's artillery, much to the indignation of Generals Knox, Sullivan, and Greene, who threatened to resign. The turmoil ended when, in what Lafayette described as "perhaps a fortunate accident," du Coudray was drowned in the Schuylkill. According to John Adams, "he rode into the Ferry Boat, and rode out at the other End, into the river, and was drowned. His horse took fright." Adams did not speculate why his horse took fright, but his very terseness makes one wonder whether some fellow passenger on the ferry— perhaps a friend of Knox, Sullivan, or Greene—standing nearby, and observing how the haughty du Coudray had not dismounted, which was the usual thing to do on a ferryboat, and happening to have a penknife or some other sharp object, and being close to the horse's flank. . . . At any rate, as Adams noted: "This Dispensation will save us much Altercation."

Unlike du Coudray, Steuben must have had an exceptionally engaging personality, for not only was the commander in chief soon won over but so were all the other ranks. Privately, he was appalled by the condition in which he found the American army, much of it due to their having "imitated the English administration, which is certainly the most imperfect in Europe." In letters to his friend Baron von Frank, he filled page after page with an account of what was wrong, starting with the great variety in terms of enlistment:

The eternal ebb and flow of men engaged for three, six, and nine months, coming and going every day, made it impossible to have a regiment or company at full strength. . . . Sometimes a regiment was stronger than a brigade. I have seen a regiment of thirty men, and a company of one corporal! . . . A general would have thought himself lucky to find a third of the men ready for action whom he found on paper. . . . The arms at Valley Forge were in a horrible condition, covered with rust, half of them without bayonets, many of them incapable of firing a single shot. . . . Muskets, carbines, fowling-pieces, and rifles were often found in the same company. . . . Officers wore coats of every color and make. At a grand parade at Valley Forge I saw officers mounting guard wearing a sort of dressing-gown made of an old blanket or woolen bed-cover. . . . Each colonel had his own system of drill, one according to the English style, another according to the French or Prussian style. They were uniform only in their way of marching, which was in single file, like the Indians. . . . The officers did not remain with the troops when the army was in camp, but lived in houses, often several miles away. In winter, they nearly all went home, and there were often not more than four officers with a regiment. . . . It would be an endless task to enumerate the abuses which nearly ruined the army.

Following his appointment as inspector general Steuben selected a small number of officers to assist him and set to work, rising like an old soldier at five every morning. "I commenced operations by drafting one hundred and twenty men from the line, whom I formed into a guard and made this guard my military school. I drilled them myself twice a day; and to remove that English prejudice shared by some officers, that to drill a recruit was a sergeant's duty and beneath the dignity of an officer, I often took the musket myself to show the men the manual exercise I wanted them to learn." This method was successful. "To see a gentleman dignified with a lieutenant general's commission from the great Prussian monarch condescend with a grace peculiar to himself to take under his direction a squad of ten or twelve men in the capacity of a drill sergeant, commands the admiration of both officers and men," wrote Colonel Alexander Scammell. The one hundred and twenty men of the hand-picked guard set the example, which was then extended throughout the army, transforming it into a disciplined force that, as the summer campaign was to show, could meet the British on equal terms.

To Steuben, the well-being of the ordinary soldier was vital. In his drill book, *Regulations for the Order and Discipline of the Troops of the United States,* he had this to say under the heading "Instructions for the Captains":

A captain cannot be too careful of the company the state has committed to his charge. He must pay the greatest attention to the health of his men, their discipline, arms, accoutrements, ammunition, clothes, and necessaries. His first object should be to gain the love of his men by treating them with every possible kindness and humanity, enquiring into their complaints, and when well-founded seeing them redressed. He should know every man of his company by name and character. He should often visit those who are sick, speak tenderly to them, see that the public provision, whether of medicine or diet, is duly administered, and procure them besides such comforts and conveniences as are in his power. The attachment that arises from this kind of attention to the sick and wounded is almost inconceivable; it will moreover be the means of preserving the lives of many valuable men.

Dr. James Thacher was present one day when the baron inspected his brigade, first

passing in front with a scrutinizing eye; after which he took into his hands the muskets and accoutrements of every soldier, examining them with particular accuracy and precision, applauding or condemning according to the condition in which he found them. He required that the muskets and bayonets should exhibit the brightest polish; not a spot of rust, or defect in any part, could elude his vigilance. He inquired also into the conduct of the officers toward the men, censuring every fault and applauding every meritorious action. . . . He appears to be about fifty years of age, and is venerable and dignified in his deportment, rich and elegant in dress, having a yellow medal of gold and diamonds designating the order of Fidelity suspended at his breast. He is held in universal respect, and considered as a valuable acquisition to our country. . . . The continental army has improved with great rapidity under his inspection and review.

Remarkably, the baron did all this while still barely able to speak English. According to Captain Benjamin Walker, one of his American aides, when drilling his demonstration squad, if "some movement or maneuver was not performed to his mind he began to swear in German, then in French, and then in both languages together. When he had exhausted his artillery of foreign oaths, he would call to his aides, 'My dear Walker and my dear Duponceau, come and swear for me in English. These fellows won't do what I bid them.' A good-natured smile then went through the ranks and at last the maneuver or the movement was properly performed." Writing to a friend back in Europe, Steuben summarized the key to his success: "The spirit of this nation is very different to that of the Prussians, Austrians, or French. You say to your soldier, 'Do this!' and he does it. But I am obliged to say, 'This is the reason why you should do this'—and then he does it."

Valley Forge soon became a legend, and as often happens with legends, there were those eager to improve on the original. Prominent among these was the Rev. Mason L. Weems—"Parson Weems"— author of uplifting books such as *God's Revenge Against Adultery, The Drunkard's Looking Glass,* and, most famously, *The Life and Memorable Actions of George Washington.* It was Weems who concocted the story of the cherry tree and the immortal lines "I can't tell a lie, Pa! You know I can't tell a lie! I *did* cut it with my hatchet." Although Weems introduced the anecdote by firmly stating it was "too true to be doubted," he also made it clear that his "chief purpose" as an author was "to entice the young mind to the affectionate love of virtue." And so, when later in the biography he posed the question,

"What was it that raised Washington to such height of glory?" it was not surprising that he should answer: "His great talents, *constantly guided and guarded by religion!*" As proof he then offered the story of Isaac Potts, the Quaker:

In the winter of '77, while Washington with the American army lay encamped at Valley Forge, a certain good old Friend, of the respectable family and name of Potts, if I mistake not, had occasion to pass through the woods near headquarters. Treading his way along the venerable grove, suddenly he heard the sound of a human voice, which as he advanced increased on his ear, and at length became like the voice of one speaking much in earnest. As he approached the spot with a cautious step, whom should he behold, in a dark natural bower of ancient oaks, but the commander in chief of the American armies on his knees at prayer! Motionless with surprise, Friend Potts continued on the place till the general, having ended his devotions, arose, and with a countenance of angel serenity, retired to headquarters. Friend Potts then went home, and on entering his parlor called out to his wife, "Sarah, my dear! Sarah! All's well! All's well! George Washington will yet prevail!"

"What's the matter, Isaac?" replied she. "Thee seems moved."

"Well, if I seem moved, 'tis no more than what I am. I have this day seen what I never expected. Thee knows that I ever thought the sword and the gospel utterly inconsistent; and that no man could be a soldier and a Christian at the same time. But George Washington has this day convinced me of my mistake."

He then related what he had seen, and concluded with this prophetical remark: "If George Washington be not a man of God, I am greatly deceived—and still more shall I be deceived if God do not, through him, work out a great salvation for America."

By April things were looking up. The weather got warmer, campaigning would soon begin, and the newly disciplined army looked forward to taking on the British. From Paris Franklin reported that, encouraged by the American victory at Saratoga, the French had at last signed a treaty "of alliance for mutual defense" which "guarantees to the United States their liberties, sovereignty and independence, absolute and unlimited . . ." War between France and England was now almost certain. Word of the treaty had already been secretly reported to Lord North, who warned the king that they could expect their coasts to be raided and "a body of French Troops to land under the American Banner in the North of Ireland & by the bait of Independency to engage that part of the Kingdom in rebellion. . . . The turbulent disposition of Irish Presbyterians who are almost to a man favourers of the American Cause" would add to the danger, while "the utmost that can be expected from the Papists would be neutrality."

During the winter Joseph Hodgkins had applied for leave, but though he was now a captain, he had been outranked by another officer who also wanted to return home. So he was still at Valley Forge on April 17, 1778.

Loving Wife,

These lines bring you my most affectionate regards hoping they will find you & our children & all friends in as good health as they leave me at this time through the goodness of God. I am very well now but since I wrote last to you I have been a good deal troubled with the rheumatism but through mercy it is left me & I feel hearty. But I am very uneasy in mind about you for I am certain that you have long looked for me & I am afraid will suffer for the necessaries of life, for I am informed that things are as dear with you as they are here & if that is the case I wish you would let me know & if you do suffer I am determined to come home and suffer with you. I believe you think I don't care much about you as I do not send anything home but my dear you are always in my heart & in my thoughts. . . . I have nothing more to write only I must repeat my earnest desire of seeing you as soon as I possibly can & now commending you & myself & children to the care of kind Providence, hoping he will preserve us while absent & in his good time give us an opportunity of meeting together again, which is the hearty desire of him who is your most affectionate & loving companion till death,

  Joseph Hodgkins

Since mails were slow, Joseph's letter would have crossed this one from Sarah, dated Ipswich, April 26, 1778.

My Dear,

  These lines come with my most affectionate regards to you, hoping they will find you in good health as they leave me & the rest of my family at this time through the goodness of God. But I am very full of trouble on account of your not coming home. I received your letter of the 22 February by Mr. Horten. He told me you was inoculated for the smallpox a day or two before he came away. You wrote me word you should come home as soon as you could but did not set any time when. I concluded you would come as soon as you got well, if you lived to get well, and I never heard a word from you since till about ten days ago, which you must think gave me great uneasiness, fearing how it was with you. Nat Treadwell wrote a few lines home which they received about ten days ago & he was so kind as to send word that you had had the smallpox & was got well which I was rejoiced to hear & it gave me new courage to look for you but I have looked for you till I know not how to look any longer. . . . When I began I thought I would write but a few lines & began upon a small piece of paper, but it is my old friend & I don't know how to leave off & some is wrong end upwards & some right. If it was not that I have some hope of your coming home yet I believe I should write a volume. I can't express what I feel but I forbear. Disappointments are allotted for me. So committing you to the care of kind Providence I once more subscribe myself your most affectionate companion till death,

Sarah Hodgkins

PS. Brother Perkins & sister send their love to you. Sister Chapman is got to bed of a fine son. I have got a sweet babe almost six months old, but have got no father for it. . . .

THE BRITISH DEPART

While the ultimately victorious Americans shivered and hungered in Valley Forge, the confident British were having a good time in Philadelphia. "The greater part of the citizens who had left gradually returned to their homes," wrote Captain von Ewald of the Hessian jaegers. "The city came back to life; trade and commerce began to flourish once again; citizen and soldier got on well together. We had balls, concerts, assemblies, and gambling clubs. At one club the bank was a thousand guineas, and more than once I have seen fifty thousand dollars change hands in an evening. Some won a fortune, others were ruined and had to leave the army because of their debts; some even shot themselves. A guinea was the smallest wager. Everyone from the Commanding General to the youngest ensign were to be found gathered round the table."

Among those gracing the balls and assemblies was Becky Franks, the pretty and lively daughter of the merchant David Franks, who was driving a profitable business supplying the British army. In a letter to her friend Anne Harrison Paca of Wye Island, Maryland, Becky urged her to come to Philadelphia and join in the "rakeing."

You can have no idea of the life of continued amusement I live in. I can scarce have a moment to myself—I have stole this while everybody is retired to dress for dinner. I am but just come from under Mr. J. Black's hands, and most elegantly am I dressed for a ball this evening at Smith's, where we have one every Thursday. You would not know the room 'tis so much improv'd. . . . I spent Tuesday evening at Sir Wm. Howe's where we had a concert and a Dance. I asked his leave to send you a Handkerchief to show the fashions. He very politely gave me permission to send anything you wanted. . . . I want to get a pair of Buckles for your brother, Joe. If I can't, tell him, to be in fashion, he must get a pair of Harness ones.

As to her dress for that evening, it

is more ridiculous and pretty than anything that ever I saw—great quantity of different coloured feathers on the head at a time, besides a thousand other things; the hair dress'd very high. . . . No loss for partners, even I am engaged to seven different gentlemen, for you must know 'tis a fix'd rule never to dance but two dances at a time with the same person. Oh, how I wish Mr. P. wou'd let you come in for a week or two! Tell him I'll answer for your being let to return. I know you are as fond of a gay life as myself. You'd have an opportunity of rakeing as much as you choose, either at Plays, Balls, Concerts, or Assemblys. I've been but three evenings alone since we mov'd to town. . . . Two or three more of your old acquaintances are in town such as Prideaux and Jock De Lancy. . . . All your Philadelphia friends well, and desire their loves; mine to all in Maryland. . . . I must go finish dressing as I'm engaged out to tea, God bless you, B.F.

P.S. I send some of the most fashionable ribbon and gauze. . . .

(As might have been expected, the middle-aged Mr. Paca, a lawyer, delegate to Congress and signer of the Declaration of Independence, made his wife stay at home.)

To most Loyalists it was an article of faith that the British were there to stay. But others were not so sure, as Captain von Ewald discovered when "partly out of curiosity and partly hoping to hear something edifying," he went to one of the Friends' meeting houses. As he entered everyone had their heads bent down

and a holy silence prevailed over all. I made my steps as silently as my boots, spurs, and big saber permitted, and stood as still as an oak for half an hour. Just as I was about to leave, an aged woman suddenly arose and asked the congregation to grant her its attention, because the Holy Spirit had inspired her with the following admonition:

"My warning is directed to my sex. In these frightful times, which we have deserved through our sins—when our whole region is swarming with all sorts of foreign peoples—I hear very bad things about our women and their daughters. They are said to be exchanging visits with these soldiers. I know that some have made so light of their shame that they stroll about with these people in broad daylight! I beseech you, mothers and fathers, put an end to these depravities. Remember that these people have a wandering foot, and that you cannot prosecute them under our laws if your daughters go too far with them. Bear in mind—and it will be to your own disgrace—that you will be responsible for what they leave behind. Think! No good will come of it."

The matron sat down. A devout silence prevailed for a while, and then the congregation left the place of worship. I went back to my quarters, my curiosity satisfied, but feeling little edified.

That other Quaker lady, Elizabeth Drinker, also had her worries. Her husband was still under detention in Lancaster for refusing to swear allegiance to the Patriot cause; her servant, Ann Kelly, had still not made amends for breaking her indenture by running off with an

English officer; crime in the city was on the increase; and so was the likelihood of having some unwelcome British or Hessian officer billeted on a household composed only of women and children.

✳

December 14. We were a little frightened about 11 o'clock by seeing 2 fellows peeping into Becky Jones's yard, and climbing on top of her Gate. Watch barked, and Harry went into the yard. They went off. It causes me to recollect last night, at about one o'clock, I heard a noise against our fence; the Dog barked violently. I awoke Jenny, who looked out of the window, and saw 2 men in the alley, who went out of sight. I often feel afraid to go to Bed.

Dec 15. Last night about 11 o'clock, as we were going to Bed, we saw 2 soldiers in the alley, standing by the Fence. We went downstairs again, and into the yard. We asked Harry aloud if John and Tom were yet in bed? Harry answered, "Yes." Sister ordered him to untie the Dog and then come in. While we were contriving in this manner down stairs, Jenny saw them from my room window move off with a large bundle which she took to be a Bed. After we had been in Bed about an hour we heard a great noise in the alley. Jenny, Sister, and the children ran to the window, and saw the Baker next door running up the alley in his shirt, with only a little red Jacket on; the rest of his Family were with him. We did not discover the cause of the uproar until this morning, when we found the Baker had been robbed of some of his wife's clothes—which we suppose was the bundle the fellows went off with some time before.

Dec 18. An officer who calls himself Major Crammond called this afternoon to look for Quarters. I plead off; he would have persuaded me that it was a necessary protection at these times, to have one in the House. He said that I must consider of it, and that he would call in a day or two. I desired to be excused, and after some more talk we parted. He behaved with much politeness, which has not been the case at many other places. I have just finished a letter to my dearest. 'Tis now past 12 o'clock, and Watch has put me in a flutter by his violent barking, as if someone was in the alley, which I believe was the case. Hail since night.

Dec 19. E. Story called this evening; he says he thinks he shall be able to get us, whose Husbands are gone from us, clear of the military gentlemen. He says they are much chagrined at the difficulty they find in getting quarters, and the cool reception they have met with, or something to that effect; that several young Noblemen are at this time obliged to sleep at Taverns, on board Ships, or in the Redoubts, for which I think they may, in great measure, thank themselves. We are told this evening that Owen Jones's family has been very ill-used indeed by an officer who wanted to quarter himself, with many others, upon them. He drew his sword; used very abusive language, and had the Front door split in pieces. Mary Eddy has some with her who, they say, will not suffer her to use her own Front door, but oblige her and her Family to go up and down the alley. Molly Foulke has been affronted, and so have many others. We have come off, as yet, wonderfully well. My resolution and fortitude have failed me much of late; my dear Henry's absence, and the renewed fears on his account, and thoughts of our dear children, and my health but very middling—all together—it seems, at times, hard to bear up against.

Dec 21. First day. Mary Eddy called this afternoon in much affliction. She wanted Sister or myself to go to Abel James with her, and to desire him to accompany her to some Head officer, to make complaint of the insolence of one who has quartered himself upon her with a woman he calls his wife—but many think otherwise. He has insulted her, and behaved very abusively. Abel advised her to go to Galloway [Joseph Galloway, now the city's civilian leader].

Dec 23. Sister and the 4 children went to meeting this morning. Sister met Ann [Kelly] in the street, who promised to pay for her time.

Dec 24. This is Christmas Eve, and the few Troops that are left in this city I fear are frolicking.

Dec 29. Very clear and cold. Major Crammond was here this morning. We have at last agreed on his coming to take up his abode with us—I hope it will be no great inconvenience. He came again this evening, with a servant, to look at the Stable, and stayed to tea.

Dec 31. J. Crammond, who has now become one of our Family, appears to be a thoughtful, sober young man; his servant also, sober and orderly; which is a great favor to us. Robert Veree came towards evening; he and J.C. supped with us.

Jan 1, 1778. Crammond has 3 Horses, 3 Cows, 2 Sheep, and 2 Turkeys with several Fowls in our stable. He has also 3 servants—2 white Men and one Negro boy called Damon. The servants are here all day, but away at night. He has 3 Hessians, who take their turns to wait upon him as messengers, or orderly men, as they call them—so that we have enough of such sort of company.

Jan 4. First day. I forgot to mention yesterday that I had a conference with the officer who took away Ann. I stopped him as he passed the door, and after desiring him to stand still till a noisy waggon which was going by had passed, I then addressed him: "If thee has no sense of Religion or Virtue, I should think that what you Soldiers call Honor would have dictated to thee what was thy duty after thy behavior some time ago in this House." "Who, me?" "Yes, I know thee very well; I have, as yet, been careful of exposing thee, but if thee don't very soon pay me for my Servant's time; as there are officers quartered among numbers of my acquaintances, I will tell all that I meet with." He stuttered and said, "I haint got your servant." "I don't care who has her, it was thee who stole her." "Well," said he a little impudently, "if you'll come up to my quarters up Town—." I told him, if he did not bring the money, or send it soon, he would hear further from me. "Well, well, well," said he—and away he went, seemingly confused.

Jan 5. J.C. had 11 or 12 officers to dine with him to day. They made very little noise and went away timeously. Most of our acquaintance seem to be much taken with our Major; I hope he will continue to deserve their good opinion. He tells us this evening that a cessation of arms is concluded upon. Everything that I hear, as it makes for the continued confinement or deliverance of my dearest Henry, has its effect upon my spirits.

Jan 10. I went this morning to Hannah Pemberton's; found her smoking her pipe, with 2 officers—one of whom is quartered there. After they had gone, Hannah and myself were comparing notes, and reading our last letters. We are neither of us so happy in our expectations as some others. I left Hannah near 1 o'clock, and as I was returning I met Susanna Jones and Richard Wister talking together. I stopped, and heard him say that he had just parted with Billy Lewis, who told him that Andrew Robinson was come from Lancaster this morning, and that our dear Friends were actually discharged. I have heard the same report, several times, since morning, and I know not what ails me that I cannot believe such good news. So much has, however, laid hold upon me, that I shall be grievously disappointed if it should fall through. A letter from my dearest confirming it would rejoice my Heart.

Happily, the Richard Wister/ Billy Lewis/ Andrew Robinson rumor proved true; the Quaker prisoners had indeed been released and Elizabeth's husband Henry was on his way home. So now there were plenty of men to protect the Drinker household: Henry, Major Crammond, his three servants, and three Hessian orderlies.

In February, news arrived of the treaty of alliance with the French. "This fatal treaty is at length executed," wrote the Loyalist Samuel Curwen, living in exile in England. "The *coup de grace* given to British glory—its sun is set—alas, how fallen! How short-sighted is human wisdom, how weak is human power at best! The roar of the British lion will no more be heard; the French cock may now crow and strut undisturbed." On March 8 he noted that "stocks have fallen to 59 ½ which has produced an almost universal panic . . ." March 20: "Heard the dreaded sound, war declared against France! It is reported the House of Lords is almost in tumult, and that they implore the King to drive from his service his ministers, and take Lords Chatham [William Pitt the Elder], Camden, and Shelburne." July 13, referring to the ill-omened incident at the coronation ceremony: "The prophetic falling off of the best jewel in our king's crown is now accomplished by the loss of America . . ."

But at the top nothing changed. Not for a moment did the king waver. "Firmness is the Characteristick of an Englishman," he told Lord North, who had hinted that the country's dire situation was largely due to "the obstinate perseverance in the American War" and once again asked to be allowed to resign. "Lord North's diffidence of himself is grounded upon seven years' experience," he wrote, "and will for ever render it fatal to his Majesty to continue him at the head of affairs. In short, peace with America and a change of Ministry are the only steps which can save this country." But the king wouldn't hear of it. He would "never consent to the Independency of America," and Lord North could not "desert at this hour." For the rest it was politics as usual. Germain and Sandwich clung to office; the majority of the Members of Parliament still supported the ministry, whether from conviction, routine, or gratitude for benefits conferred; as for the rest of the country, a war against the French was as popular as ever.

There were, however, major changes in strategy. "The contest in America," wrote Lord Amherst to Admiral Howe, was now "a secondary consideration. Our principal object must be distressing France." The expanded war also gave the ministry political cover for recalling Sir William Howe without alienating his influential friends, and replacing him with Sir Henry Clinton. (This was another piece of good news for the Americans, since Clinton, though in different ways and for different reasons, was an even worse commander in chief than Howe. Later in the war Alexander Hamilton strongly opposed a plan to kidnap Sir Henry while he was taking his afternoon nap in a pavilion in the garden of his house in New York, arguing that if the plan succeeded, "it would be our misfortune, since the British government could not find another commander so incompetent to send in his place.") Also, eight thousand troops, more than a quarter of the British army in America, were to be detached and sent to the West Indies, where the French already had a force of nine thousand. New York would be the center of operations for a primarily defensive war in America, and Philadelphia would be evacuated.

By now many in the British army were convinced that the Howes had never really tried to win the war. "The two Howe brothers belong to the Opposition Party—therefore no more need be said," wrote Captain von Ewald. According to another officer, Charles Steuart, "The Howes would have rather lost America than subdued it under the present administration." Even some Americans wondered about them: "General Howe is either our friend, or no general," wrote Israel Putnam after Washington's evacuation of Brooklyn following the Battle of Long Island. "He had our whole army in his power . . . and yet suffered us to escape without the least interruption." Nevertheless, on the eve of his departure Sir William was given the kind of triumphal celebration that Burgoyne might have dreamed up for himself after winning the war.

"May 18th. This afternoon was exhibited a strange kind of Entertainment, which the Projectors styled a *Meschianza* or Medley, consisting of Tilts & Tournaments, in Honor of the General upon his Departure," wrote Ambrose Serle in his diary. "It cost a great Sum of money. Our Enemies will dwell upon the Folly & Extravagance of it with Pleasure."

The Meschianza was the brainchild of Major John André, later to be captured and hanged as a spy in the aftermath of Benedict Arnold's treason. The theme was medieval, with jousting, tournaments, and fancy costumes—the bill for silks and other fine materials alone came to more than £12,000. Officers wearing suits of armor divided into two groups: the Knights of the Blended Rose, who chose Miss Auchmuty as their Queen of Beauty, and the Knights of the Burning Mountain, who chose Becky Franks. To prepare for her part, Miss Franks wore a "polonaise dress which formed a flowing robe, and was open in front to the waist. The sash, six inches wide, was filled with spangles, as was the veil, which was edged with silver lace. The head-dress was towering . . . and was filled with a profusion of pearls and jewels." The tournament took place in an open square surrounded by pavilions and raised seats. After much flourishing of trumpets and throwing down of gauntlets, the opposing knights attacked each other with lances and swords until "at length the two

Chiefs, spurring forward into the centre, engaged furiously in single combat, till the Marshal of the Field rushed in between the Chiefs, and declared that the Fair Damsels of the Blended Rose and Burning Mountain were perfectly satisfied with the proofs of love and the signal feats of valour given by their respective Knights; and commanded them, as they prized the future favours of their Mistresses, that they would desist from further combat."

Other features of the Meschianza included a procession through a triumphal arch; music played by several military bands; "tea, lemonade, and other cooling liquors" served in a spacious hall; a ballroom with "festoons of flowers in their natural colours . . . heightened by eighty-five mirrors decked with rose-pink silk ribands"; an elaborate dinner served by black slaves wearing "oriental dresses, with silver collars and bracelets"; toasts to the King, the Queen, the Royal Family, the Army and Navy, "with their respective Commanders, the Knights and their Ladies, the Ladies in general," each toast being "followed by a flourish of music"; and dancing until ten "when the windows were thrown open and a magnificent bouquet of rockets began the fire-works." As this display drew to an end "the triumphal arch was illuminated midst an uninterrupted flight of rockets and bursting balloons. The military trophies on each side assumed a variety of transparent colours. The shell and flaming heart on the wings sent forth Chinese fountains, succeeded by fire-pots. Fame appeared at the top, spangled with stars, and from her trumpet blowing the following device in letters of light, *Tes lauriers sont immortels.*" (All these quotations come from a long and highly favorable review of the occasion that appeared in the London *Annual Register* and was written by the show's producer and director, Major André.)

Three days later, Ambrose Serle wrote in his diary:

✳

May 21st. Very uneasy this morning on the information by Mr. Galloway of a Conversation which passed between Genl. H. and one of the first Magistrates (Schumacher) in this City, who waited to take

Leave of him. Upon representing the Uneasiness which prevailed among the loyal Subjects on Account of the Rebels, the Genl. advised him "to make his peace with the States, who, he supposed, would not treat them harshly; for that it was probable, on Account of the French War, the Troops would be withdrawn." This was soon circulated about the Town, & filled our Friends with melancholy on the Apprehension of being speedily deserted; now a Rope was (as it were) about their necks, & all their Property subject to Confiscation.

May 22nd. A Confirmation of the sad Intelligence of yesterday was communicated to Mr. Galloway by Sir Wm. Erskine from Sir. Wm. Howe & Sir H. Clinton. It filled my poor Friend, as might be expected, with Horror & melancholy on the View of his deplorable Situation; exposed to the Rage of his bitter Enemies, deprived of a fortune of about £70,000, and now left to wander like Cain upon the Earth without Home, & without Property. Many others are involved in the like dismal Case for the same Reason—attachment to their King & Country, & opposition to a Set of daring Rebels, who might soon be crushed by vigorous Exertions—I now look upon the Contest as at an end. No man can be expected to declare for us when he cannot be assured of a Fortnight's Protection. Every man, on the contrary, whatever might have been his primary Inclinations, will find it his Interest to oppose & drive us out of the Country. I endeavored to console, as well as to advise my Friend. I felt for & with him. Nothing remains for him but to attempt Reconciliation with (what I may now venture to call) the United States of America.

Captain von Ewald and his Hessian jaegers left Philadelphia with the main army:

June 4th. For several days all trade and pleasurable activities have been suspended while the loyalist families pack up and flee the city before the wrath of Congress. The streets are crowded with wagons loaded with personal effects on their way to the ships that have been provided for these unfortunates. Some fifteen hundred families, it is said, are abandoning the city and all their property. Those opposed to us are openly rejoicing, their only regret being that our hard money will leave with us.

The Drinkers' lodger, who had gone in a very short while from "an officer who calls himself Major Crammond" to the "thoughtful, sober young man . . . who has now become one of our Family," to "J.C." or "Our Major," remained with them until near the end of the evacuation. "He was very dull at taking leave" and departed very early in the morning of June 9. "Sister and self stayed at the Door until the two Regiments, which quartered up Town, had passed. J.C. bid us adieu as they went by, and we saw no more of them. A fine, moonlight morning."

June 18. Last night it was said there were 9,000 of the British Troops left in Town; 11,000 in the Jerseys. This morning when we arose there was not one Red-Coat to be seen in town, and the encampment in the Jerseys also vanished. Col. Gordon and some others had not been gone a quarter of an hour before the American Light-Horse entered the city—not many of them, but they were in and out all day. . . . The few that came in to-day had drawn swords in their Hands; they galloped about the streets in a great hurry. Many were much frightened at their appearance.

July 2. The Congress came in to day; firing of Cannon on the occasion.

July 4. A great fuss this evening, it being the Anniversary of Independence; firing of Guns, Sky-Rockets &c. Candles were too scarce and dear to have an illumination. . . . A very high Head-dress was exhibited thro' the streets this afternoon, on a very dirty Woman, with a mob after her, with Drums &c., by way of ridiculing that very foolish fashion.

Many Tories left Philadelphia with the British, among them Joseph Galloway, who had been singled out for an act of attainder by the Pennsylvania assembly. Before going on to London, he and his daughter Betsy went to New York, as did Becky Franks, who continued her "rakeing" until she met and married Henry Johnson ("a wrong-headed blockhead," in the opinion of Lord Cornwallis, but a colonel and later a general in the British army, very rich, and a baronet). However Galloway's wife, the heiress Grace Growden, stayed behind, claiming that the large house on Market Street and all its contents belonged to her and not to her husband, and were exempt from confiscation. But this view was rejected by the courts and the Executive Council, and on August 20, 1778, Elizabeth Drinker wrote in her diary: "Grace Galloway turned out of her house this forenoon."

The man responsible for executing the order against the high-born Mrs. Galloway was Charles Willson Peale, a former leather worker and clock maker, best known as a portrait painter, and now also the city's agent for confiscated estates: "a disagreeable business," he called it, but one that also provided lucrative opportunities for buying in and then re-selling some of the condemned properties. Helping him were Colonel Will, Mr. Smith, and some local tradesmen. Among those coming to Mrs. Galloway's assistance were a neighbor, Mrs. Craig, some female servants, and a friend called Lewis. John Dickinson had given her legal advice, and another lawyer advised her to stay in her house "and if they made a forcible entry he wou'd bring an action against them."

Confident in the justice of her cause, Mrs. Galloway prepared to resist:

✳

Thursday, August 20th. Lewis sent me word that I must shut my doors & windows & if they wou'd come to let them make a forcible entry. Accordingly I did so & a little after 10 o'clock they Knocked Violently at the door three times. The third time I sent Nurse & call'd out myself to tell them I was in possession of my own House & wou'd keep so & they shou'd gain No admittance. Hereupon which they went round in the yard & try'd every door but cou'd None Open. Then they went to the Kitchen door & with a scrubbing brush which they broke to pieces they forced that open—we Women standing in the entry in the Dark. They made repeated strokes at the door & I think was 8 or 10 Minutes before they got it open. When they came in I had the windows open'd. They look'd very Mad. There was Peale, Smith, the hatter, & a Col. Will, a pewterer in Second Street. I spoke first & told them I was Used ill & show'd them the Opinion of the lawyers. Peale read it but they all despised it & Peale said he had studied the Law & knew they did it right. I told them Nothing but force shou'd get me out of my House. Smith said they knew how to manage that & that they would throw my clothes in the street. . . .

While Mrs. Galloway and Mr. Smith argued, Peale went through the house, locking things up and checking to see that nothing had been removed. He then went to the nearby house recently taken over by General Benedict Arnold, now governor of the city, and arranged for the loan of his coach (the "chariot") to transport Mrs. Galloway in safety and comfort from her house to Mrs Craig's.

Peale then went upstairs & brought down my Work Bag & 2 bonnets & put them on the side table. . . . Mrs. Craig asked for my Bed [bedding] but they wou'd let me Have Nothing & as I told them acted entirely from Malice. After we had been in the Entry some time, Smith & Will went away & Peale said the Chariot was ready, but he would not hasten me. I told him I was at home & in My own House & nothing but force shou'd drive me out of it. He said it was not the first time he had taken a Lady by the Hand—an insolent wretch! . . . At last he beckoned for the Chariot, for the General wou'd not let it come till I wanted it & as the Chariot drew up Peale fetched My Bonnets & gave one to me the other to Mrs. Craig, then with greatest air said, "Come, Mrs. Galloway, give me your hand." I answer'd, "Indeed I will not! Nor will I go out of my house but by force." He then took hold of my arm & I rose & he took me to the door. I then took hold on one side & Looked round & said "Pray take Notice I do not leave my house of My own accord or with my own inclination, but by force; and Nothing but force shou'd have made me give up possession." Peale said with a sneer, "Very well, madam," and when he had led me down the step I said, "Now, Mr. Peale, let go my arm. I want not your assistance." He said he cou'd help me to the Carriage. I told him I cou'd go without—"And you, Mr. Peale, are the last man on earth I wou'd wish to be Obliged to." Mrs. Craig then step'd into the Carriage & we drove to her house, where we din'd.

With the departure of the high-living British, republican virtue of the kind approved by Sam Adams became the fashion. "Tell those Philadelphia ladies who attended Howe's assemblies and *levées*," sneered General Anthony Wayne, who had helped save the day at the Battle of Monmouth Court House, "that the heavenly, sweet, pretty red-coats, the accomplished gentlemen of the Guards and Grenadiers, have been humbled on the plains of Monmouth. The Knights of the *Blended Roses* and the *Burning Mount* have resigned their laurels to rebel officers, who will lay them at the feet of those virtuous daughters of America who cheerfully gave up ease and affluence in a city, for liberty and peace of mind in a cottage."

In the opinion of an anonymous letter-writer to the *Pennsylvania Packet*, the city should be purged of its "internal enemies" and "bosom-vipers" —the Tories. "Whenever I meet one in the street, or at the Coffee-house, my blood boils within me. Their guilt is equalled only by their impudence. They strut, and seem to bid defiance to every one. In every place and in every company they spread their damnable doctrines and then laugh at the pusillanimity of those who let them go unpunished. . . . Awake, America, to a sense of your danger! No time is to be lost—instantly banish every Tory from among you. Let these walls, let America be sacred to freemen. Drive far from you every baneful wretch who wishes to see you fettered with the chains of tyranny. Send them where they may enjoy their beloved slavery in perfection. Send them to the island of Britain, there let them drink the cup of slavery and eat the bread of bitterness all the days of their existence . . ." And there was a great deal more.

Two years after the British had left, the polished and diplomatic Marquis de Chastellux, an English-speaking French officer serving with General Rochambeau's expeditionary force, came to Philadelphia. Balls were still being given but "all the Tory ladies have been publicly banned" and apparently those were the pretty ones. Only a Miss Vining caught the attention of the marquis and that was because of her "extraordinary mode of dressing her hair" and because her dress was colored red, white, and blue. Those who did not want to dance could play cards, but gambling was not allowed.

A manager, or master of ceremonies, presides over these methodical entertainments. Each gentleman and lady is presented with a folded paper stating who is to partner whom; no changes are allowed. The dances, like the toasts we drink at table, all have a distinctly patriotic theme. One is called "The Success of the Campaign,"another "Burgoyne's Defeat," and a third "Clinton's Retreat." Colonel Mitchell, a squat, fat little man of fifty, an excellent judge of horses and until recently the contractor for supplying wagons and carriages to the French and American armies, was the master of ceremonies. He has a reputation for exercising his office with great strictness. Once, when a young lady in a square dance forgot her turn because she was chatting with a friend, he came up to her and called out loudly, "Come, come! Watch what you are doing! Do you think you are here to enjoy yourself?"

In obedience to his orders from London, Sir Henry Clinton returned to New York not by sea but by marching across New Jersey. Morale among his troops was low and the summer weather was exceptionally hot. Of course, it was hot for the Americans too, but their spirits were high, they were welcomed wherever they went, and, thanks to Baron von Steuben, they were now much better trained, although still poorly uniformed and equipped. Clinton did not expect that Washington would allow his return to New York to become a military promenade, and he was right.

Having survived the siege of Fort Mifflin on Mud Island and other engagements, Private Joseph Martin of Connecticut was now with a light infantry unit assigned to harass the retreating British. They set out on June 24.

> Our detachment marched in the afternoon and towards night we passed through Princeton. Some of the patriotic inhabitants of the town had brought out to the end of the street we passed through some casks of ready-made toddy. It was dealt out to the men as they passed by, which caused the detachment to move slowly at this place. The young ladies of the town, and perhaps of the vicinity, had collected and were sitting on the stoops and at the windows to see the noble exhibition of a thousand half-starved and three-quarters naked soldiers pass in review before them. I chanced to be on the wing of a platoon next to the houses, as they were chiefly on one side of the street, and had a good chance to notice the ladies, and I declare that I never before nor since saw more beauty, considering their number, than I saw at that time. . . .
>
> We passed through Princeton and encamped on the open fields for the night, the canopy of heaven for our tent. Early next morning we marched again and came up with the rear of the British army. We followed them several days, arriving upon their camping ground within an hour after their departure from it. We had ample opportunity to see the devastations they made in their rout; cattle killed and lying about the fields and pastures, some just in the position they were in when shot down, others with a small spot of skin taken off

their hind quarters and a mess of steak taken out; household furniture hacked and broken to pieces; wells filled up and mechanics' and farmers' tools destroyed. It was in the height of the season of cherries; the innocent industrious creatures could not climb the trees for the fruit, but universally cut them down. Such conduct did not give the Americans any more agreeable feelings toward them than they entertained before.

It was extremely hot weather, and the sandy plains of that part of New Jersey did not cool the air to any great degree, but we still kept close to the rear of the British army. Deserters were almost hourly coming over to us, but of stragglers we took only a few.

That night they

turned into a new ploughed field, and I laid down between two furrows and slept as sweet as though I had laid upon a bed of down.

The next morning, as soon as the enemy began their march, we were again in motion and came to their last night's encamping ground just after sunrise. Here we halted an hour or two, as we often had to do, to give the enemy time to advance, our orders being not to attack them unless in self-defense. We were marching on as usual, when, about ten or eleven o'clock, we were ordered to halt and then to face right-about. As this order was given by the officers in rather a different way than usual, we began to think something was out of joint somewhere, but what or where our united wisdom could not explain. The general opinion of the soldiers was that some part of the enemy had by some means got into our rear. We, however, retraced our steps till we came to our last night's encamping ground, when we left the route of the enemy and went off a few miles to a place called Englishtown. It was uncommonly hot weather and we put up booths to protect us from the heat of the sun, which was almost insupportable.

Next day

⚜

we were early in the morning mustered out and ordered to leave all our baggage under the care of a guard (our baggage was trifling), taking only our blankets and provisions (our provisions were less), and prepare for immediate march and action.

The officer who commanded the platoon that I belonged to was a captain, belonging to the Rhode Island troops, and a fine brave man he was; he feared nobody nor nothing. When we were paraded—"Now," said he to us, "you have been wishing for some days past to come up with the British. You have been wanting to fight—now you shall have fighting enough before night." The men did not need much haranguing to raise their courage, for when the officers came to order the sick and lame to stay behind as guards, they were forced to exercise their authority to the full extent before they could make even the invalids stay behind; and when some of their arms were about to be exchanged with those who were going into the field, they would not part with them. "If their arms went," they said, "they would go with them at all events."

After all things were put in order, we marched, but halted a few minutes in the village, where we were joined by a few other troops, and then proceeded on. We now heard a few reports of cannon ahead. We went in a road running through a deep narrow valley, which was for a considerable way covered with thick wood; we were some time in passing this defile. While in the wood we heard a volley or two of musketry, and upon inquiry we found it to be a party of our troops who had fired upon a party of British horse, but there was no fear of horse in the place in which we then were.

It was ten or eleven o'clock before we got through these woods and came into the open fields. The first cleared land we came to was an Indian cornfield, surrounded on the east, west, and north sides by thick tall trees. The sun shining full upon the field, the soil of which was sandy, the mouth of a heated oven seemed to me to be but a trifle hotter than this ploughed field; it was almost impossible to breathe. We had to fall back again as soon as we could, into the woods. By the time we had got under the shade of the trees and had taken breath, of which we had been almost deprived, we received orders to retreat, as all the left wing of the army, that part being under the command of General Lee, were retreating. Grating as this order was to our feelings, we were obliged to comply.

We had not retreated far before we came to a defile, a muddy, sloughy brook. While the artillery were passing this place, we sat down by the roadside. In a few minutes the Commander in Chief and suite crossed the road just where we were sitting. I heard him ask our officers, "By whose order the troops were retreating?" And being answered, "By General Lee's," he said something, but as he was moving forward all the time this was passing, he was too far off for me to hear it distinctly. Those that were nearer to him said that his words were "D – -n him." Whether he did thus express himself or not I do not know. It was certainly very unlike him, but he seemed at the instant to be in a great passion; his looks if not his words seemed to indicate as much. After passing us, he rode on to the plain field and took an observation of the advancing enemy. He remained there some time upon his old English charger, while the shot from the British artillery were rending up the earth all around him. After he had taken a view of the enemy, he returned and ordered the two Connecticut brigades to make a stand at a fence, in order to keep the enemy in check while the artillery and other troops crossed the before-mentioned defile. When we had secured our retreat, the artillery formed a line of pieces upon a long piece of elevated ground. Our detachment formed directly in front of the artillery, as a covering party, so far below on the declivity of the hill that the pieces could play over our heads. And here we waited the approach of the enemy, should he see fit to attack us.

By this time the British had come in contact with the New England forces at the fence, when a sharp conflict ensued. These troops maintained their ground, till the whole force of the enemy that could be brought to bear had charged upon them through the fence; and after being overpowered by numbers and the platoon officers had given orders for their several platoons to leave the fence, they had to force them to retreat, so eager were they to be revenged on the invaders of their country and rights.

As soon as the troops had left this ground the British planted their cannon upon the place and began a violent attack upon the artillery and our detachment, but neither could be routed. The cannonade continued for some time without intermission, when the British pieces being mostly disabled, they reluctantly crawled back from the height which they had occupied and hid themselves from our sight.

Before the cannonade had commenced, a part of the right wing of the British army had advanced across a low meadow and brook and occupied an orchard on our left. The weather was almost too hot to live in, and the British troops in the orchard were forced by the heat to shelter themselves from it under the trees. We had a four-pounder on the left of our pieces which kept a constant fire upon the enemy during the whole contest. After the British artillery had fallen back and the cannonade had almost ceased in this quarter, and our detachment had an opportunity to look about us, Colonel Cilly of the New Hampshire Line, passed along in front of our line, inquiring for General Varnum's men, who were the Connecticut and Rhode Island men belonging to our command. We answered, "Here we are!" He did not hear us in his hurry, but passed on. In a few minutes he returned, making the same inquiry. We again answered, "Here we are!" "Ah!" said he. "You are the boys I want to assist in driving those rascals from yon orchard."

We were immediately ordered from our old detachment and joined another, the whole composing a corps of about five hundred men. We instantly marched towards the enemy's right wing, which was in the orchard, and kept ourselves concealed from them as long as possible by keeping behind bushes. When we could no longer keep ourselves concealed, we marched into the open fields and formed our line. The British immediately formed and began to retreat to the main body of their army. Colonel Cilly, finding that we were not likely to overtake the enemy before they reached the main body of the army, on account of the fences and other obstructions, ordered three or four platoons from the right of our corps to pursue and attack them, and thus keep them in play till the rest of the detachment could come up. I was in this party; we pursued without order. As I passed through the orchard I saw a number of the enemy lying under the trees, killed by our fieldpiece, mentioned before. We overtook the enemy just as they were entering upon the meadow, which was rather bushy. When within about five rods of the rear of the retreating foe, I could distinguish everything about them. They were retreating in line, though in some disorder. I singled out a man and took my aim directly between his shoulders. (They were divested of their packs.) He was a good mark, being a broad-shouldered fellow. What became of him I know not; the fire and smoke hid him from my sight. One thing I know, that is, I took as deliberate aim at him as ever I did at any game in my life. But after all, I hope I did not kill him, although I intended to at the time.

By this time our whole party had arrived, and the British had obtained a position that suited them, as I suppose, for they returned our fire in good earnest, and we played the second part of the same tune. They occupied a much higher piece of ground than we did, and had a small piece of artillery, which the soldiers called a grasshopper. We had no artillery with us. The first shot they gave us from this piece cut off the thigh bone of a captain, just above the knee, and the whole heel of a private in the rear of him. We gave it to poor Sawney (for they were Scotch troops) so hot that he was forced to fall back and leave the ground they occupied. When our commander saw them retreating and nearly joined with their main body, he shouted, "Come, my boys! Reload your pieces and we will give them a set-off." We did so, and gave them the parting salute, and the firing on both sides ceased. We then laid ourselves down under the fences and bushes to take breath, for we had need of it. I presume everyone has heard of the heat of that day, but none can realize it that did not feel it. Fighting is hot work in cool weather, how much more so in such weather as it was on the twenty-eighth of June, 1778.

Afterward Washington sought out General Lee and confronted him about ordering his troops to retreat in the middle of the battle.

A quarrel followed during which Washington, who as Jefferson was to say could be "most tremendous in his wrath," used what Lee complained were some "very singular expressions." ("You damned poltroon!" was said to be one of them.) Washington's version was that "what I recollect to have said was dictated by duty and warranted by the occasion." But General Charles Scott, who was there, reported that Washington "swore like an angel from heaven. Yes, sir," Scott added approvingly, "he swore till the leaves shook on the trees."

But that was not what most people, Joseph Martin included, wanted to hear about the hero who had come to embody the Glorious Cause. Far more acceptable was the portrait of "this truly great and good man" written by Dr. James Thacher some time after the battle when Washington paid a surprise visit to the military hospital at Peekskill:

The personal appearance of our Commander in Chief is that of the perfect gentleman and accomplished warrior. He is remarkably tall, full six feet, erect and well-proportioned. The strength and proportion of his joints and muscles appear to be commensurate with the preeminent powers of his mind. The serenity of his countenance, and majestic gracefulness of his deportment, impart a strong impression of that dignity and grandeur which are his peculiar characteristics, and no one can stand in his presence without feeling the ascendancy of his mind, and associating with his countenance the idea of wisdom, philanthropy, magnanimity, and patriotism. There is a fine symmetry in the features of his face, indicative of a benign and dignified spirit. . . . His uniform dress is a blue coat, with two brilliant epaulettes, buff colored under clothes, and a three cornered hat, with a black cockade. He is constantly equipped with an elegant small sword, boots, and spurs, in readiness to mount his noble charger. There is not in the present age, perhaps, another man so eminently qualified to discharge the arduous duties of the exalted station he is called to sustain, amidst difficulties which to others would appear insurmountable, nor could any man have more at command the veneration and regard of the officers and soldiers of our army, even after defeat and misfortune. This is the illustrious chief, whom a kind Providence has decreed as the instrument to conduct our country to peace and to Independence.

Indeed, an almost magical aura had come to surround Washington. Such was the "superstitious veneration," to use John Adams's phrase, with which he was regarded that his mere presence was sometimes enough to leave people spellbound. That at any rate is what happened to Mrs. Crafts, whose story was told in *Women of the Revolution*. The source was Mrs. Martha Wilson, whose house Washington and his staff often visited in 1780.

One Mrs. Crafts, a native of Germany, who had emigrated and settled in New Jersey, through the industry of herself and husband had become the owner of a fine farm near Hackettstown, and was in comfortable and easy circumstances. She was an excellent neighbor, and though an ardent Tory, was universally respected for her many kind and good qualities. On the morning of General Washington's departure, Mrs. Wilson's house was surrounded by a throng of persons eager to obtain a glance at him. In this state of things, Mrs. Crafts, Tory as she was, repaired to the spot and sent a message to Mrs. Wilson in her parlor, requesting from her the privilege of seeing the General. A reply was sent, saying that General Washington was at that time surrounded by a crowd of officers; but if Mrs. Crafts would station herself in the hall till he passed through, her desire would be gratified. She accordingly took her post there, and patiently waited his appearance. When, at length, she obtained a full view of his majestic form and noble countenance, raising both hands, she burst into tears, uttering in her native tongue an exclamation expressive of intense astonishment and emotion! Mrs. Crafts never afterwards ranked herself on the Tory side. "The august and commanding presence of the Father of his Country," as Mrs. Wilson remarks, "having alone inspired her with such profound veneration for the man as to produce an abiding respect for the cause of which he was leader."

William Burnett also had his encounter with Washington, which he recounted long after the war when making his application for a pension. In 1780, at the age of fourteen, Burnett, an illiterate and dim-witted Virginia farmboy, had run off to enlist in the army, thinking it would be "a frolic." Too young and timid to fight, he was put to work as a wagon driver where he had a few memorable adventures—on one occasion hearing "a noise like the clashing of arms in an old field, he left his wagon and run to see, and saw the British and Americans fight; they were all horsemen, and he was so scared that he caught hold of a pine and trembled so that he shook the bush mightily,"—but most of his memories were vague. "He does not now recollect whether he ever was out of the state of Virginia and North Carolina or not, but thinks his services was confined to them two states or nearly so. He recollects of hauling a load of provisions to the mouth of Queens Creek, where there was a number of soldiers stationed. Recollects passing by with the wagon a mountain called Kings Mountain, as they told him." But Burnett also had this treasured memory: "Also recollects of seeing General Washington twice on the road with his life guard with him and will never forget while he retains his memory the polite bow that the general made to the poor wagoners as he passed them."

In the spring of 1781, Washington visited Count Rochambeau and the French army at Newport, Rhode Island, to discuss strategy and to be introduced to his allies. Almost all the officers were aristocrats and professional soldiers, as far removed as could be from William Burnett and Mrs. Crafts, but they too were deeply impressed. Count de Fersen: "Handsome and majestic—he looks the hero." Commissary Claude Blanchard: "A truly great man." Count Mathieu Dumas: "The hero of liberty." Baron de Closen: "Clearly a great man." The Marquis de Chastellux: "The greatest and the best of men."

And yet apart from Chastellux not one of the French officers could speak English. Nor did Mrs. Crafts or William Burnett ever exchange a word with him. It was as Mrs. Wilson had said: "The august and commanding presence of the Father of his Country" was in itself enough to inspire "profound veneration for the man" and "abiding respect for the cause of which he was leader."

SULLIVAN'S EXPEDITION

All this time another war was going on, one that had begun over 150 years earlier when Powhatan's Indians had massacred 350 English settlers—men, women, and children—at Jamestown, Virginia, and was to continue off and on for another hundred years after the Revolution, ending only when nearly two hundred Sioux—men, women, and children—were massacred by the American army at Wounded Knee, South Dakota. Although this conflict had little to do with the issue of independence, it could have been exploited by the British, but their attempts to do so were sporadic and usually ineffective. Burgoyne had tried to recruit a large force of native warriors, but the few hundred who did turn up soon scented defeat and departed, though not before handing the Americans a propaganda coup by murdering and scalping a young white woman named Jenny McCrea, "a young lady lovely to the sight, of virtuous character and amiable disposition," in the words of General Horatio Gates, who had never met her but knew how to pour it on. (Gates also professed outrage and astonishment that Burgoyne, "in whom the fine Gentleman is united with the Soldier and the Scholar, should hire the savages of America to scalp Europeans . . .")

Much as white people in the South lived in dread of a slave rebellion, so the nightmare for settlers on the frontier was that the Indians would set aside their rivalries and unite in a concerted attack; but even so great a leader as Pontiac, who led the uprising of 1763, was unable to hold them together for any length of time. So although there was continual fighting with the Indians, much of it consisted of inconsequential skirmishes, such as this incident described by David Welch of Rutland, Vermont. In 1777, when he was seventeen, Welch had enlisted for three years in a local line regiment but was soon assigned to a company of rangers. Presumably because of his skills as a woodsman and his qualities of courage and personal initiative, he was often "placed in detachments separate from his regiment and frequently separate from the main body of his company." One such detachment took place in the summer of the following year when he and five others were sent on a scouting party "to range the wood north of Rutland about twenty-five miles to see if we could discover any approach of the enemy, either Tories, British, or Indians." On the second day they decided to split up and keep about two hundred yards apart

for the double purpose of making as small a trail or track as possible and the better to explore that part of the country in which we had reason to apprehend we might meet the enemy.

It fell to my lot to be placed the most westerly man of our party as we marched northward. In this way of marching, about the middle of the day, I had, as I afterwards found, become separated upward of half a mile from my companions, when I discovered through a thicket of hemlock brush the appearance of a smoke evidently indicating the fact of there being a fire. We were then in a wilderness some fifteen miles beyond our then most frontier garrisons. Immediately on making this discovery, I crept with the utmost caution toward the spot from whence the smoke rose. Presently I saw through the bush two Indians sitting by a smoke that appeared to have been kindled to keep off the mosquitoes. I instantly laid myself flat down, keeping my eye upon the spot to see if there were more than the two. In a few moments I became impressed with the belief that there were but the two. I was not more than eight rods [about forty-five yards] distant from them.

After much hesitation as to what might be most proper, I finally came to the conclusion that my companions were proceeding on and might perhaps soon be surprised, as there might be more Indians within a short distance. I drew my gun, and whilst lying thus flat on the ground, I took deliberate aim at one of the Indians and shot him dead. The other Indian instantly sprung upon his feet, seizing his gun, and started to run. Without reflecting upon the consequence, I immediately run after him, having my gun unloaded. The Indian made but a few leaps after I started before he turned and fired upon me, but his fire missed as I supposed by several feet. He then dropped his gun and came at me with his tomahawk. I encountered him with my empty gun. The first blow which he aimed with his tomahawk I warded off with my gun, and in doing it I was so fortunate as to hook the deadly weapon from him. It fell upon the ground rather behind me. I was then encouraged and sprung to get the tomahawk, in which effort I succeeded. Whilst I was yet bent in picking up the tomahawk, the Indian, who had drawn his knife, gave me a cut, giving me a deep but short wound upon my right leg a little above my knee. He then aimed a second stroke at me with the same weapon. This blow I warded off with my left hand, in doing which I received a wound between the thumb and the forefinger. About the same instant, with the tomahawk I hit him a blow on the head which brought him to the ground, and with another blow after he had fallen I made sure he was beyond doing me any further harm.

I immediately secured the guns of the two dead Indians and had the three, including my own, ready charged before my companions, who had heard the fire, came up. The corporal, after seeing what was done, ordered our immediate retreat, which we did toward Rutland Fort, where we arrived the next day some time in the afternoon, bringing with us the guns of the two dead Indians and their tomahawks and knives.

Since they had so much more at stake, the Americans tried harder than the British to enlist the aid of the people they were steadily dispossessing. "I always love Indians and have hunted a great deal with them," wrote Ethan Allen to the "Councillors at Caughnawaga" soon after he and his Green Mountain Boys had captured Fort Ticonderoga in the spring of 1775. "I know how to shoot and ambush just like Indians and want your warriors to come and see me and help me fight Regulars. You know they stand all along close together, rank and file, and my men fight so as Indians do, and I want your warriors to join with me and my warriors like brothers and ambush the Regulars."

That same spring the Provincial Congress of Massachusetts made an approach to the Stockbridge Indians, descendants of the once-powerful Narragansetts and Pequods, now placidly settled in the western part of that state where they lived under the protection of the local minister. Since this was not their fight the Stockbridge Indians were reluctant to be drawn in, and were fortunate enough to have had in Solomon Ahhaunnauwaumut a chief sachem who turned out to be a first-rate diplomat. Summoned to Concord by the Provincial Congress, Chief Solomon showed himself master of every trick in the book: flatter your listeners without their realizing it, rewrite the past in such a way as to predetermine the future, pretend to be confused about issues that are in fact quite clear, ask for advice that you do not need, make promises that are too vague to be kept, and offer to use your good offices to persuade someone else to do whatever it is that you do not want to do yourself. Finally, couch all this in the kind of colorful pidgin English his listeners would expect from a simple-minded savage. As follows:

✳

Brothers! We have heard you speak by your letter—we thank you for it—we now make answer. You remember when you first came over the great waters, I was great and you was little, very small. I then took you in for a friend, and kept you under my arms, so that no one might injure you. Since that time we have ever been true friends. There has never been any quarrel between us. But now our conditions are changed. You are become great and tall. You reach to the clouds. You are seen all around the world, and I am become small, very little. I am not so high as your heel. Now you take care of me, and I look to you for protection.

Brothers! I am sorry to hear of this great quarrel between you and Old England. It appears that blood must soon be shed to end this quarrel. We never till this day understood the foundation of this quarrel between you and the country you came from.

Brothers! Whenever I see your blood running, you will soon find me about to revenge my brother's blood. Although I am low and very small, I will grip hold of your enemy's heel, that he cannot run so fast and so light as if he had nothing at his heels.

Brothers! You know that I am not so wise as you are, therefore I ask your advice in what I am now going to say. I have been thinking, before you come to action, to take a run to the westward, and feel the mind of my Indian brethren, the Six Nations, and know how they stand—whether they are on your side or for your enemies. If I find they are against you, I will try to turn their minds. . . . I think I can do more service this way than by marching off to Boston, and staying there.

Ahhaunnauwaumut was right when he implied that the people who really mattered were not the Stockbridge Indians but the Six Nations of the Iroquois Confederacy. Of these, the Oneidas soon sent a message to Governor Trumbull of Connecticut that they did not want to be involved. The quarrel was "unnatural," they said. "You are two brothers of one blood. We are unwilling to join on either side in such a contest, for we bear an equal affection to both Old and New England. Should the great king of England apply to us for aid, we shall deny him; if the Colonies apply, we shall refuse . . . . We are for peace."

Since many of the tribes still felt loyal to the English, who had often recruited them in their wars against the French, the Continental

Congress soon realized that the most they could hope for was neutrality. "This is a family quarrel between us and Old England," ran one of their messages. "You Indians are not concerned in it. We do not wish you to take up the hatchet against the King's troops. We desire you to remain at home, and not join on either side, but keep the hatchet buried deep."

But while many of the Iroquois had adopted a fairly "civilized" way of life, living in houses and towns, planting orchards of fruit trees and raising annual crops, governing themselves by consensus, they must have known that even if they remained neutral in the current war they would eventually be done in by the white man and what he brought with him: rum, smallpox, measles, unscrupulous trading practices, one-sided treaties, and the steady encroachment of racially prejudiced settlers in whose eyes they were, and always would be, "savages." And in truth, in their heart of hearts, many Iroquois men do seem to have hankered for the good old days when, like English gentlemen, they could spend their days hunting, shooting, and fishing, their evenings drinking and gambling, rushing off to fight if there was a war but first taking great care to dress properly for the occasion: cocked hats, lace frills, and brightly colored coats with gold trim for British officers, elaborately painted war masks, sculpted hairdos, and necklaces of bear's claws for the Indian warriors.

And so when British commissioners invited the Six Nations to a meeting at Oswego, all talk of neutrality was soon forgotten. Stirred by reminders of earlier wars when they were comrades in arms and lured by promises that the king's rum would be "as plenty as the water in Lake Ontario," they dug up the hatchet. "As soon as the treaty was finished, the Commissioners made a present to each Indian of a suit of clothes, a brass kettle, a scalping knife, a quantity of powder and lead, a piece of gold, and promised a bounty on every scalp that should be brought in. Thus richly clad and equipped, they returned home, after an absence of about two weeks, full of the fire of war." (The quotation is from the narrative of Mary Jemison, who will appear again later. The sole survivor of a family of Irish immigrants massacred on the Pennsylvania frontier in 1758 when she was a small child, Mary had been adopted by the Senecas and later married a famous warrior called Hiokatoo—Big Lance—and had eight children. At one point she had a chance of returning to the white world but refused because of worries about how her children would be treated. Many years later her story was written up by Dr. James Seaver, of upstate New York, who rephrased it to conform to current literary convention.)

Meanwhile, two of the Six Nations, the Oneidas and Tuscaroras, remained neutral, and in December 1777, received a message of congratulation from Congress ("believe us who never deceive") for having "kept fast hold of the ancient covenant chain, and preserved it free from rust and decay, and bright as silver." As a reward, "while the sun and the moon continue to give light to the world, we shall love and respect you. As our trusty friends, we shall protect you, and shall at all times consider your welfare as our own." The other four, the Cayugas, Senecas, Onondagas, and Mohawks, were reprimanded for listening to the British emissaries and warned of the consequences. In all other parts of the country, "our Indian brethren" had seen the light:

The Cherokees, like some of you, were prevailed upon to strike our people. We carried the war into their country, and fought them. They saw their error, they repented, and we forgave them. The United States are kind and merciful, and wish for peace with all the world. We have, therefore, renewed our ancient covenant chain with their nation. The Shawanese and Delawares give us daily proofs of their good disposition and their attachment to us, and are ready to assist us against all our enemies. The Chickasaws are among the number of our faithful friends. And the Choctaws, though remote from us, have refused to listen to the persuasions of our enemies, rejected all their offers of corruption, and continue peaceable. The Creeks are also our steady friends. Oboylaco, their great chief, and the rest of the sachems and warriors, as the strongest mark of their sincere friendship, have presented the great council with an eagle's tail and rattle trap. They have desired that these tokens might be shown to the Six Nations and their allies, to convince them that the Creeks are at peace with the United States.

Fine words, but unpersuasive because unaccompanied by presents. To the Indians parsimony was almost as contemptible as cowardice; treaty negotiations that did not conclude with breaking out the rum, handing round the blankets, and opening up the crates of brand-new muskets and shiny-bladed scalping knives were meaningless. As Sir Guy Johnson, one of the crown's agents, put it in a speech to the Six Nations: "Are they able to give you anything more than a piece of bread and a glass of rum? Are you willing to go with them, and suffer them to make horses and oxen of you, to put you to the wheelbarrows, and to bring us all into slavery?" That was more like it; and after appealing to their pride, Johnson followed up with a lavish distribution of gifts shipped in from the agency's main warehouse in Montreal.

Moreover the Mohawks now had an outstanding leader, Thayendanegea—"Two sticks of wood bound together" (but also translatable as "He places two bets")—more generally known as Joseph Brant, whose sister Molly was the common-law wife of Sir William Johnson, the British superintendent of Indian affairs in the Mohawk Valley. Brant, who had long been an anglophile, was a man of parts. Before taking up the hatchet, he had assisted the Anglican missionary, the Rev. Dr. Stewart, in translating the Psalms and revising the Mohawk version of the Book of Common Prayer. In 1776 he had visited London, staying at an inn called The Swan with Two Necks and, like Phillis Wheatley, the "Ethiopian poetess," causing a minor sensation in society. He met Boswell, had his portrait painted by Romney, was written up in the *London Magazine,* and was presented, wearing full Mohawk regalia, to the king, to whom he promised to raise three thousand warriors.

Also planning on giving the Americans a hard time was Colonel John Butler, director of Tory activities at Niagara, who intended to "break up the back settlements," particularly those in the Wyoming Valley, scene of the Pennamite Wars between Pennsylvania and Connecticut. About five thousand white people now lived there in various settlements, among them Lackawanna, Exeter, Kingston, and Wilkes-Barre, but bitter feelings lingered, especially among the settlers who had been driven out during the wars between the two colonies. Over a thousand of these dispossessed exiles joined Butler's expedition, along with some Tory renegades, many of them disguised as Indians. Some three hundred real Indians under their own chiefs were also recruited, as well as a small number of regulars.

In late June 1778, the expedition reached Tioga (present-day Athens), where they built rafts on which they floated down the Susquehanna River, entering the Wyoming Valley from the north and quickly capturing two small forts. In response, the Patriot Col. Zebulon Butler, cousin of the Tory John Butler, gathered about sixty continental soldiers and three hundred militiamen at Fort Forty, but a surprise sortie turned into a disaster when he was ambushed by a much larger force, only seventy of his men surviving. The *New York Journal*, a Patriot newspaper, basing its story on accounts given by survivors, told what happened next:

Saturday morning, July 4. The enemy sent one hundred and ninety-six scalps into Fort Kingston, which they invested on the land side, and kept up a continual fire upon it. Colonel Nathan Dennison went with a flag to Exeter Fort, to know of Colonel John Butler what terms he would grant on surrender. Butler answered, the Hatchet! Colonel Dennison returned to Fort Kingston, which he defended till Sunday morning, when his men being nearly all killed or wounded, he could hold out no longer, and was obliged to surrender at discretion. The enemy took away some of the unhappy prisoners, and shutting up the rest in houses, set fire to them, and they were all consumed together. These infernals then crossed the river to Fort Wilkesbarre, which in a few minutes surrendered at discretion. About seventy of the men, who had listed in the continental service to defend the frontiers, they inhumanly butchered, with every circumstance of horrid cruelty; and then shutting up the rest, with the women and children in the houses, they set fire to them, and they all perished together in the flames.

After burning all the buildings in the fort, they proceeded to the destruction of every building and improvement (except what belonged to some Tories) that came within their reach, on all these flourishing settlements, which they have rendered a scene of desolation and horror. . . . When these miscreants had destroyed the other improvements, they proceeded to destroy the crops on the ground, letting in the cattle and horses to the corn, and cutting up as much as they could of what was left. Great numbers of the cattle they shot and destroyed, and cutting out the tongues of many others, left them to perish in misery.

The course of these truly diabolical proceedings was marked by many particular acts of distinguished enormity, among which were the following, viz.:

The Captains James Bedlock, Robert Duryee, and Samuel Ransom, being made prisoners by the enemy, they stripped Captain Bedlock, tied him to a tree, and stuck him full of sharp splinters of pine knots, then piling a heap of pine knots round him, they set all on fire, put Duryee and Ransom into the fire, and held them down with pitchforks.

Thomas Hill with his own hands killed his own mother, his father-in-law, his sisters and their families. Partial Terry, the son of a man who bore a very respectable character, had several times sent his father word that he hoped to wash his hands in his heart's blood. Agreeable to such a horrid declaration, the monster, with his own hand, murdered his father, mother, brother, and sisters, stripped off their scalps, and cut off his father's head.

The story also mentioned that "these wretches, after completing their horrid business at Wyoming, are going or gone to Cherry Valley." About three hundred settlers were killed at Wyoming; thirty-two others, including sixteen soldiers, at Cherry Valley.

That the fight at Wyoming was indeed bloody is confirmed by the testimony of one of the Indians who took part, the Seneca warrior later known to the whites as Governor Blacksnake and a nephew of Chief Cornplanter, whose dictum was "War is war, death is the death, a fight is a hard business." Here, dictated late in life, is Blacksnake's account of what he did at Wyoming:

As for myself what I done during the actions of this battle—I started when all the rest started from, but I did not see the rest of them for some time after I got into among the village. The first man I came to him I fire at him and kill 'em. But in the next one I just took the butt end of my gun overhead, down he went, mind him no more about it, expected him dead. But the third one I took him the same way, thought I may take his scalp. As I drawed my knife to his head and looking back and saw this the same man that I butt him over just come at me, and drawed his gun and pointed to me and was so near too. I sprang and he fire the gun at me. But just as he fire there was the Indian behind him, I give the war whoop, just touch my clothes with his ball, never draw no blood out of me. I had me knife in hand, I just drawed upon his throat and cut it, down he go the second time. I says to myself now I guess he stay down, and off again for another one. I run, I saw a couple of Indians wounded and they are not able to go on. I run on farther and tell to other Indians to go back and take care of the Indian, and did so. I went to another street, there was some more for me to do. I just then took my tomahawk and struck one and two, another, and so on. Don't mind anything about crying women and children and men, some just dying, some fighting and all. There was not many guns fired that fight and did not last a great while. I did not know how many I kill, only I kill some, many. . . .

Concluding its account, the *New York Journal* wrote: "It is hoped speedy and effectual methods will be taken to punish and extirpate these monsters in human shape from the face of the earth."

Luckily for the Americans, nothing much was going on in the war with the British, and Washington was able to provide enough troops for a major punitive campaign. Equally luckily General Horatio Gates turned down the offer of command, which was then accepted by General John Sullivan. In his letter of instructions, Washington ordered the "total destruction and devastation" of the Iroquois settlements; they were to be "not merely overrun but destroyed." Sullivan was also to capture "as many prisoners of every age and sex as possible" to be held as hostages. In short, collective punishment, such an outrage when imposed on the citizens of Boston following the Tea Party; nor did it matter that the man most responsible for the massacres was Colonel John Butler, and not Thayendanegea (Joseph Brant), or that the majority of the raiders were not Iroquois but white Tories. No one seems to have expressed any surprise at these orders, least of all the Indians themselves.

It took a while to organize the expedition, but in July of 1779 Washington could write to Lafayette that Sullivan "has already marched to the Susquehanna with about 4,000 Men, all Continental Soldiers, and I trust will destroy their Settlements and extirpate them from the Country."

Sullivan's army was at first divided into several parts. One, under his command, set out from Easton and moved up the Susquehanna to Tioga; another, under General George Clinton, advanced up the Mohawk Valley to Canajoharie before joining Sullivan at Tioga, which was the place of rendezvous for other columns. Once united, the army set out to devastate the Indian country.

Among those marching with George Clinton's force was Lt. Erkuries Beatty, of the 4th Pennsylvania Regiment, twenty years old and already a veteran of several battles: Long Island, White Plains, Brandywine, Germantown, where he was badly wounded, and Monmouth. His unusual first name may have been a corruption of Hercules.

✳

Saturday, August 14. Went over a high hill and got to Onoquagua at 3 oClock where we encamped on very pretty ground. This town was one of the neatest of the Indian towns on the Susquehanna. It was built on each side of the River with good Log houses with Stone Chimneys and glass windows. It likewise had a Church & burying ground and a great number of apple trees and we likewise saw the Ruins of an Old Fort which formerly was here many years ago. The Indians abandoned this town when they heard of our Detachment coming to destroy it. They had but just left it when we came in but we did not catch any of them but burnt their Town to ashes and the Detachment returned.

August 15. Marched today 22 Miles and burnt several Indian houses on the road.

Thursday 19th. Marched this morning 7 oClock. Went 2 Miles when we burnt 7 or 8 houses on the East side of the River. 4 Miles further at Chuggnuts we fell in with Genl. Poor's army who was ready to march. They had Burnt this Settlement which lies on the East side of the River, about 20 houses.

Friday 20th. Raind a little last night and Successively all this day. Therefore did not move. Went a party down to Owego town which lies one mile lower down and burnt it, consisted of about 20 houses.

Sunday 22nd. Arrived at Tioga 11 oClock where we found Genl. Hand's Brigade encamped one Mile above the mouth of the Tioga where they was building 4 Block houses. The other troops was encamped on the point which was Genl. Poor's & Maxwell's Brigades. We encamped on the Right of the whole. On our coming in to camp we was saluted by 13 Pieces of Cannon which was returned by our two little pieces. On the River we found Genl. Hand's Brigade under arms with a Band of Musick which played beautiful as we passed by them. We encamped on a very pretty piece of ground and Spent the Remainder of the day in seeing our friends in the different Regts.

Thursday 26th. Marched off about 11 oClock, leaving all our heavy baggage & women at the Garrison. Carried on pack horses 27 Day provision. Likewise went with us 7 Pieces of Ordinance with three Ammunition Waggons. Four boats came up the River.

Saturday 28th. Very heavy Dew this morning. Did not move to day till 2 oClock occasioned by our Ammunition Waggons breaking yesterday & had to mend them before we started. A few of our Volunteers went across the river to burn a house. They was fired on by 6 or 7 Indians. They immediately recrossed the river in a fright without even returning a Shot.

Sunday 29th. Marched this morning 9 oClock, went about 3 Mile when we found the enemy strongly Entrenched with Logs, Dirt, brush &c. The firing imidiately begun in front with the Rifle Corp & the Indians made great halooing. Orders was given then for the troops to form in line of battle which was done. Genl. Hand's brigade in front but none of the troops advanced as we discovered the main body of the enemy was here and had their front secured by a large Morass & brook, their right by the river, & on their left partly in the rear was a very large hill. Their lines extended upwards of a Mile. The firing was kept up very briskly by the Rifle men & a company who was sent to reinforce them. Likewise the Indians returned the fire very brisk with many shouts for about 2 hours while a disposition was made for to attack them. Genl. Clinton's & Poor's brigades was sent off round their left flank to take possession of the hill in the enemy's rear and extend their line intirely round them if Possible. After they had gone about half an hour Genl. Hand's brigade advanced in a line of battle with all our Artillery in the Centre within about 300 Yards of the enemy's works but in full View of them. A very heavy cannonade began & throwing of Shells. The enemy returned the fire very brisk for about half an hour when the Enemy retreated up the hill in a great Disorder & as they got near the top received a very heavy fire from Genl. Poor's brigade. The enemy then took round Genl. Poor's right flank by the river which Genl. Poor had not guarded as he had not time to, therefore they made their escape, leaving a number of their dead behind them. As soon as the enemy left their works, Genl. Hand's brigade pursued them up the hill as far as Genl. Poor was when we made a halt. The rifle men pursued them about one mile farther and made a Negro prisoner, likewise saw some of their wounded going up the river in Canoes. They fired on them but they all made their Escape, wounded and all. The Army then returned down the hill & encamped about 2 Mile above the Enemy's works, our loss about 40 killed & wounded among which is three Officers one of which is since Dead. Their loss cannot be ascertained as they all carry their dead & wounded off.

Monday 30th. Went up the River about 2 Miles then took up a large branch of the River one Mile. Burnt 5 houses and destroyed all the corn in our way. Our Brigade destroyed about 150 Acres of the best corn that ever I saw (some of the Stalks grew 16 feet high) besides great Quantities of Beans, Potatoes, Pumpkins, Cucumbers, Squashes & Watermellons, and the Enemy looking at us from the hills but did not fire on us.

Sunday Sept 5th. Very fine day but did not march till 10 oClock as we was 2 or 3 Mile in front of the Army & all our Pack horses did not come till this morning. Marched to Kandaia 2 or 3 Mile, Destroying two houses and 2 corn fields on our March.

Monday 6th. This morning went very early round to see the Situation of the place. The houses was chiefly all pulled down for firewood. The Appletrees which is a good number & very old was either cut down or killed, likewise the peach trees.

Tuesday 7th. [At Kandasago.] This is the Chief town in the Seneca Nation. . . . There is about 70 or 80 houses in it and built very Compact and the chief of the houses very good. It was dark when we came in and the men began immediately to pull down the houses for firewood. I believe the Indians had left it several Days as there was not much appearance of their being here lately. On the first entrance of our Brigade a young Child I believe about 3 year old found running about the houses which one of our Officers pickt up and found it to be a White Child but it was so much tann'd & smoaked that we could hardly Distinguish it from an Indian Child and was Exceeding poor, scarcely able to walk. It could talk no English, nothing but Indian & I believe but little of that. The Officer took great care of it and Cloathed it as it was naked when he found it & could give no Account of itself, only said, "His mamy was gone." The men got very little plunder.

Friday 10th. Marched this morning 6 oClock. Each Brigade was ordered to leave a small Detachment behind to bring our Straggled horses & cattle. We marched thro a very low swamp chiefly timbered with Maple & beach about 5 Mile when we came to upland, pretty good part of it no trees on but great quantities of Wild Grapes growing. 3 Mile farther we came to a small lake called Kanandaqua which is I believe about 5 Mile long & one wide, runs N & S. We crossed over the outlett which was about 3 foot deep & about 20 Yards wide. Soon after we came to Kanandaqua town, which I believe the Enemy had just left as the fire was yet burning. We halted here about an hour & burnt the houses which was about 25 and very Compact & Neatly built. But no good water near it.

Sunday 12th. Thunder last Night and Rain and this morning it Raind till 10 oClock when it cleared up and the Army marched at 11. Today I heard there was another town & Corn Destroyed on Kanandaqua lake nearly as big as Kandaqua and 2 or 3 Miles from it. On this day's march a party of the Enemy kept just ahead of us as we could Discover their tracks very fresh and the water muddy where they had crossed.

Monday 13th. March this morning about 6 oClock and a very heavy Dew on the Grass and the morning very Cold. In about one Miles marching came to Adjutse town lying near a small lake a little to the Northward consisting of 10 or 15 Houses; here we halted, made fires & drew 3 Days' beef. After a little time fatigue parties was sent out to collect the Corn in houses to burn. About 10 oClock we heard a few Guns firing in front. The troops was imediately formed and marched over the Inlett of the Lake, a very bad morass & Creek and a large hill on the opposite side where we found the Indians who was formed on this hill, had fired on the Surveyor & his party & had mortally wounded one of his men. The Rifle Men Rushed up the hill & the Enemy made their Escape soon as possible, leaving behind them their Packs, Hatts &c which the Rifle Men got. Our Brigade marched up to the top of the hill and formed the line of battle where we halted till the Army would get over. Here one of our men came in wounded who informed us that Lt. Boyd with his party 18 Riflemen & 8 Musquet men of our Regt. who was sent last night to reconoiter the next town was intirely cut to pieces. . . . We found 4 or 5 of our men on the ground Dead & scalped and it is supposed that Lt. Boyd was made prisoner. After the Army had got over the creek we marched on to Cossawauloughly town 7 Miles.

Tuesday 14th. The whole Army was under arms this morning an hour before Day & remained so till sunrise. About 12 oClock we marched, crossed over the branch of the Jinasee River, and came upon a very beautiful flat of great extent growing up with wild Grass higher in some places than our heads. We marched on this flat 2 Mile and crossed the Jinasee River which is about as big as the Tyago but very Crooked. Left the flats and marched thro the woods 3 Mile and arrived at Chenesee Town, which is the largest we have yet seen; it lies in a Crook of the River on extraordinary good land, about 70 houses very compact and very well built and about the same number of out houses in Cornfields &c. On entering the town we found the body of Lt. Boyd and another Rifle Man in a most terrible mangled condition. They was both stripped naked and their heads Cut off and the flesh of Lt. Boyd's head was entirely taken off and his eyes punched out. The other man's head was not there. They was stabbed I suppose in about 40 different places in the body with a spear and great gashes cut in their flesh with knifes, and Lt. Boyd's Privates was nearly cut off & hanging down, his finger and Toe nails was bruised off and the Dogs had eat part of their Shoulders away, likewise a knife was sticking in Lt. Boyd's body. They was imediately buried with the honour of war.

Wensday 15th. The whole Army went out this morning 6 oClock to destroy corn and was out till 12 oClock. There was here the greatest quantity of corn & beans of any of the towns. Some of it we husked and threw in the river, the rest we Carried to the houses & burned. The whole we totally destroyed. About 10 oClock we received orders to begin our march home which we did, leaving the town in flames.

Ten days later, on their return to Tioga, the army celebrated its success along with the news that Spain was now also at war with Great Britain. "The General ordered a Feu De Joy to be fired by the army this afternoon at 5 oClock and likewise he ordered to be delivered to the Officers of each Brigade one of the best oxen there was & 5 Gallons of Spirits." In the evening the officers "assembled at a large bower made for that purpose illuminated with 13 pine knot fires round and each officer attended with his bread, knife, and plate and sat on the ground." Thirteen toasts were drunk, including one to "the memory of Lt. Boyd and the Brave soldiers under his command who was unhumanly massacred" and concluding with "May the enemies of America be Metamorphised in Pack horses and sent on a Western Expedition." After that "there was two or three Indian Dances led down by Genl. Hand and performed by the rest middling well, then each officer returned to their Quarters after kicking up a Small Dust of Striking tents &c." Next day: "Did not feel very well this morning after my frolick."

On October 17, in his general orders issued at West Point, Washington formally congratulated Sullivan and his troops on carrying out "the just and necessary punishment" of the Indians for their "unparalleled and innumerable cruelties, their deafness to all remonstrances and their perseverance in the most horrid acts of barbarism." Forty towns had been burned to the ground, their crops had been entirely destroyed, and "their whole country has been overrun and laid waste." Moreover "the whole of this has been done with the loss of less than forty men on our part."

Indian losses were unknown but surely many more than forty; and large numbers were to die of starvation during the following winter. But not Mary Jemison and her children. While her husband, Hiokatoo, retreated with the other warriors to British-held Niagara, she focused on survival. (As noted earlier, her account comes to us courtesy of her well-intentioned but genteel ghostwriter, Dr. Seaver.)

✳

The weather by this time had become cold and stormy; and as we were destitute of houses and food too, I immediately resolved to take my children and look out for myself, without delay. With this intention I took two of my little ones on my back, bade the other three follow, and the same night arrived on the Gardow Flats, where I have ever since resided.

At that time, two Negroes, who had run away from their masters some time before, were the only inhabitants of those flats. They lived in a small cabin and had planted and raised a large field of corn, which they had not yet harvested. As they were in want of help to secure their crop, I hired to them to husk corn till the whole was harvested.

I have laughed a thousand times to myself when I have thought of the good old Negro who hired me, who fearing that I should get taken or injured by the Indians, stood by me constantly when I was husking, with a loaded gun in his hand, in order to keep off the enemy, and thereby lost as much labor of his own as he received from me, by paying good wages. I, however, was not displeased with his attention; for I knew that I should need all the corn I could earn, even if I should husk the whole. I husked enough for them to gain for myself, at every tenth string, one hundred strings of ears, which were equal to twenty-five bushels of shelled corn. This seasonable supply made my family comfortable for samp [corn mush] and cakes through the succeeding winter, which was the most severe that I have witnessed since my remembrance. The snow fell about five feet deep, and remained so for a long time, and the weather was extremely cold; so much so indeed, that almost all the game upon which the Indians depended for subsistence, perished. . . . When the snow melted in the spring, deer were found dead upon the ground in vast numbers; and other animals of every description perished from the cold also, and were found dead, in multitudes. Many of our people barely escaped with their lives, and some actually died of hunger and freezing."

French troops land at Newport, Rhode Island, July 1780.

CHAPTER FIVE

At Sea and Overseas

By 1780 what had begun as a skirmish between redcoats and militia-men on the green at Lexington had grown into a war fought around the world: as far south as Honduras, as far east as the Philippines, on the west coast of Africa, and in the North Sea. For the Americans this was of course nothing but good news, since it meant that the attention and resources of the British were now largely diverted elsewhere. And there were reports from England of other encouraging developments: Lord North, the prime minister, was teetering on the verge of nervous collapse; in Parliament and among the general public, support for a war against fellow Protestants with strong ties of blood and trade was dwindling; there were very real threats of invasion by a combined French and Spanish fleet; and the worst outbreak of violence in the history of London, the Gordon Riots, reduced parts of the city to a smoldering rubble.

Meanwhile Benjamin Franklin, who had so enjoyed his residence in London, had found an even more congenial city: Paris. Revered by modish *philosophes* who enthused over the cause of the noble American savage; adored by society ladies who competed for the chance to flirt with him; and trusted and respected by the Comte de Vergennes, the king's chief minister, for whom the rebel colonists were a handy stick with which to thrash the perfidious English—small wonder that in his last years, though spent in great comfort and high esteem in Philadelphia, Franklin was to write of Paris that "all my pleasantest dreams are laid in that city."

THE RUNAWAY

Ebenezer Fox was twelve years old when, discontented with his lot in life, he decided to run away to sea. His troubles had begun five years earlier when his father, a poor tailor of Roxbury with a large family, had sent him to live with and work for a local farmer—a common practice, but one that Ebenezer resented. "I imagined that I suffered many privations and endured much hardship," he wrote many years later, explaining how in his mind his personal grievances had become conflated with those of the colonists. "I, and other boys situated similarly to myself, thought we had wrongs to be redressed, rights to be maintained . . . I thought that I was doing myself great injustice by remaining in bondage when I ought to go free." Soon he and a friend, John Kelley, "came to the sage conclusion that we were living in a state of servitude that ought to be scorned by the sons of freemen" and agreed to head for Providence, Rhode Island, "where we expected to find employment as sailors on board some vessel."

They set off at night, on April 18, 1775, the eve of Lexington and Concord, and as the two boys headed out of Roxbury, they encountered "people out in all directions to hear the news from town." That night they slept on the ground under a stone wall and the next morning reached Walpole, where "we stopped at a tavern and called for a bowl of bread and milk, the price of which was three pence; but the kind-hearted landlord refused to take any compensation." At another tavern a crowd had collected "and being seen coming from the direction of Boston, we were again assailed with more questions than we knew how to answer consistently with our safety. The tavern-keeper excited our apprehension by abruptly asking us whither we were going?

'To seek our fortunes,' we replied.

'You have taken hard times for it,' and he advised us to return home."

This advice was repeated by his aunt when they arrived in Providence, where she was housekeeper to a merchant. By the time Ebenezer looked her up, he had lost contact with Kelley; they had gone their separate ways to look for jobs but neglected to arrange a rendezvous and never saw each other again. The kindly aunt, after feeding him "an abundance of good things to which I had been some days a stranger," and seeing through his evasive answers to her questions, urged him to go home, but "this I obstinately refused, and finding it useless to remonstrate with me any more she dropped the subject after warning me of many evils which might ensue if I persisted in my undertaking."

A few days later he was hired as cabin boy by Captain Joseph Manchester at a wage of twenty-one shillings a month. The ship was a smuggler, running in duty-free molasses from Cap François, in French-held Haiti.

✻

After a pleasant voyage of about fourteen days, we arrived at our destined port. . . . We carried out staves and hoops in a state of preparation to be converted into hogsheads, and I worked at coopering till we were ready to receive our cargo. Having filled the hogsheads with molasses, which was apparently all our cargo, we set sail, and afterwards took on board a quantity of coffee, a prohibited article, which was conveyed to us by vessels employed for that purpose.

Our loading being thus completed, we directed our course for Providence, and after a passage of about fifteen days we arrived at Stonington, Connecticut. During our absence from home, the Revolutionary War had commenced, and we found that the British had begun their depredations upon our commerce and maritime towns.

We left Stonington in the night, entertaining the hope that, with a favorable wind, we might get into Providence without being discovered by the British cruisers, which we knew were cruising somewhere between Newport and Providence. If the breeze had continued favorable, we should have effected our object; but unfortunately the wind subsided a little before daylight, and in the morning we found ourselves close by the enemy, consisting of two ships of war and a small vessel called a tender between them and the land. The American commander, Commodore Whipple, with a naval force greatly inferior to the British, was seen by us higher up the bay, out of reach of the enemy, making signals for us to press all sail and approach. But unluckily we were ignorant of the meaning of the signals, and did not know whether they came from a friend or an enemy. As the cruisers were to the windward of us, we tacked one way and the other, hoping that we should be able to beat up the bay; but finding that the tender was about to intercept our progress in one direction while the cruisers approached us in the other, and no chance of escape appearing, we bore away and ran our vessel ashore.

Preparations were hastily made for leaving the vessel, our captain having given permission to all who were disposed to run the risk to make their escape. The mate and crew jumped overboard and swam for the shore, where they all arrived safe, although fired upon by the British tender. Captain Manchester, supposing that I should be unable to reach the shore by swimming, kindly advised me to remain on board with him and be taken prisoner.

I hesitated a short time about taking his advice, but finally concluded to run the risk of being drowned; and with nothing on but a shirt and a pair of trousers, I plunged into the sea and swam for the shore, where I arrived without injury, but nearly exhausted with fatigue and fear, not a little augmented by the sound of the bullets that whistled around my head while in the water. In dread of pursuit, I ran into a cornfield, and finding my wet clothes an encumbrance, I stripped them off and ran with all speed through the field.

At a little distance in front of me I could discover a number of men, whom I soon found to be our ship's crew, who had landed before me. My appearance among them in a state of entire nakedness excited not a little mirth. "Holloa, my boy!" exclaimed one of them. "You cut a pretty figure! Not from the garden of Eden, I can swear for it, for you have not even an apron of fig-leaves to cover you with. You were not born to be drowned, I see, though you may live to be hanged." But after a few jests at my expense, the mate took off one of the two shirts with which he had taken the precaution to provide himself before he left the vessel, and gave it to me. This garment answered all the purposes of a covering, as it effectually covered my person from my shoulders to my feet. After traveling about half a mile, we came to a house where the good woman, taking pity on my grotesque and unique condition, gave me a decent suit of clothes.

I immediately proceeded to Providence, where I arrived the same day, and lost no time before visiting my good aunt, although I had great doubts and fears of the reception I should meet with. She was glad to see me again, but did not lose the opportunity of giving me a long lecture upon the folly of my conduct in leaving home; and appealed to my candor to acknowledge the justice of her reproof, by comparing my present condition with what it formerly was. The anxiety and distress of my parents, too, were described to me in all the eloquence of female affection, as an additional inducement to return to them. The misfortunes I had thus far experienced, she alleged, I ought to consider as judgments against any more attempts to be separated from my friends: and concluded with advising me, in the kindest manner, to return home.

Naturally, such excellent advice, coming from such a warm-hearted and motherly figure, was listened to but disregarded; and within a week Ebenezer was once again onboard a smuggler, headed for Cap François. (More of his adventures will appear later.)

CROSSING THE ATLANTIC

Three years later another American boy also went to sea, though under very different circumstances. This was John Quincy Adams, future president but now eleven years old, who was accompanying his father, also a future president and now forty-three years old, across the Atlantic to France, where he (John Adams) was to replace Silas Deane as one of the three American commissioners to the French court. Until recently Adams had headed the Board of War, but in November 1777, while Washington was encamping his army at Valley Forge, Adams decided to leave Congress and return to his law practice. As he wrote in his autobiography, "after four years of drudgery and Sacrifice," he felt that he had given enough; indeed, "no Man ever did so much Business for so little profit." Also, his "children were growing up without my care in their Education," and his "finances were in a very loose condition." In fact, "I was losing a fortune every year by my Absence. Young Gentlemen who had been clerks in my Office . . . were growing rich, for the Prize Causes and other Controversies had made the profession of a Barrister more lucrative than it had ever been before."

But he had barely begun work on one of these "Prize Causes" —a lawyer's dream, the case which concerned a ship seized by a privateer was to go on for another eighteen years—when word came that he had been appointed by Congress to replace Silas Deane as one of the "Plenipotentiaries to the King of France" and thereby share in the glory of putting his name to the crucial treaty of alliance that was now in the works. "I could scarcely believe the news to be true," Adams assured his readers. "As I had never solicited such an Appointment, nor intimated to anyone the smallest inclination for it, the News was altogether unexpected."

The letter from the president of Congress also informed him that the frigate *Boston* was being fitted out to carry him to France as soon as possible. But first, Adams had to decide whether to accept.

✳

The dangers of the Seas and the Sufferings of a Winter passage, although I had no experience of either, had little Weight with me. The British Men of War were a more serious Consideration. The news of my Appointment I had no doubt were known in Rhode Island where a part of the British Navy and Army then lay. . . . I had every reason to expect that ships would be ordered to intercept the *Boston*. . . . Intelligence would be secretly sent. . . . The Consequence of a Capture would be a Lodging in New Gate [prison in London] . . . . Their Act of Parliament would authorize them to try me in England for Treason, and proceed to execution too. . . . My Family consisting of a dearly loved Wife and four young Children, excited sentiments of tenderness. . . . And my Want of qualifications for the Office was by no means forgotten.

✷

All this and more he brushed aside. "My Country was in deep distress . . ." the position had been "committed to me without my Solicitation . . . my Wife who had always encouraged and animated me in all antecedent dangers and perplexities did not fail me," and so, "after much Agitation of mind . . . I resolved to devote my family and my Life to the Cause, accepted the Appointment, and made preparation for the Voyage."

The *Boston* was not made ready until February 13, 1778, when Captain Samuel Tucker came to the Adams home in Braintree to fetch his distinguished passenger. After saying farewell to his adoring wife and three of his children, but accompanied by John Quincy, Adams walked to a point called Moon Head where the *Boston*'s barge awaited them. En route they were waylaid by Mrs. Spear, an Adams cousin, "much afflicted with hysterical complaints, often a little disarranged in her imagination. At this time she was somewhat flighty and accosted me in an alarming manner. 'Mr. Adams, you are going to embark under very threatening Signs. The Heavens frown, the Clouds roll, the hollow Winds howl, the Waves of the Sea roar upon the Beach . . .'" Adams tried to laugh it off, but it seems that she knew what she was talking about, as Adams recorded in his autobiography:

✷

Feb 14. 1778. A fine morning, the Wind at North West. At Daybreak orders were given for the Ship to unmoor. My Lodging had been a Cott with a double Mattress, a good Bolster, my own Sheets, and Blankets enough. My little Son with me. We lay comfortably and slept well though there was a violent gale of Wind in the Night.

Feb 17. I set a Lesson to my Son in Chambaud's French Grammar and asked the favour of Dr. Noel ["a French gentleman, Surgeon of the

Ship"] to shew him the precise critical pronunciation of all the French Words, Syllables, and Letters, which the Dr. very politely undertook to do. [For some reason Adams did not also ask Dr. Noel for lessons for himself, but persisted in studying alone from a grammar book, and learning very little.]

Feb 18. We had a fine Wind for twenty-four hours; but the constant rolling and rocking of the Ship last night made Us all Sick. Half the Sailors were so. I was seized with it in the afternoon.

Feb 19. The Mal de Mer seems to be the Effect of Agitation. The vapours and exhalations from the Sea; the Smoke of Seacoal [used for cooking], the Smell of stagnant, putrid Water, the Odour of the Ship where the Sailors sleep, or any other offensive Odour will increase the Qualminess, but of themselves, without the violent Agitation, they will not produce it.

✳

That same day they espied three large ships, and the rumor ran among the crew that they were "three fine rich English Merchantmen, or perhaps transports, and would make fat Prizes." However, on closer inspection they turned out to be British frigates, and "no man had an Appetite for fighting three frigates at once." The *Boston* changed course and night came on; but in the morning one of the frigates (which was probably copper-bottomed) was still in sight, and gave chase.

✳

Feb 20. I sat in the Cabin at the Windows in the Stern and saw the Enemy gaining upon Us very fast, she appearing to have a Breeze of Wind, while we had none. Our officers were of Opinion she had Oars out or some other machinery to accelerate her course. Our Powder, Cartridge, and Balls were placed by the Guns and every thing ready to begin the Action. Although it was calm on the Surface of the Sea where we lay, the Heavens had been gradually overspread with very thick black clouds and the Wind began to spring up, our

Ship began to move, the night came on and it was soon dark. We lost sight of the Enemy who did not appear to me to be very ardent to overtake Us. But the Wind increased to a Hurricane. The Ship laboured under the Weight of her Guns which were all out ready for Use, she shuddered and shivered like a Man in an Ague, she darted from Side to Side and pitched forward with such Velocity that it was a very dangerous Operation to get the Guns into their places. If by any Accident or want of Skill or care one of those heavy Cannon had got loose, it would have rolled with the Vessel and infallibly gone through the Side. All hands were called, and with much difficulty the Guns were all got in and secured. As it was impossible to sleep upon deck or in the Cabin, one of the Lieutenants came to me and begged me to go down to his Berth below. But such was the Agitation of the Vessel that instead of sleeping it was with the utmost difficulty that my little Son and I could hold ourselves in bed with both our hands, and bracing ourselves against the boards, planks, and timbers with our feet. In this Situation, all of a sudden, we heard a tremendous Report. Whether the British Frigate had overtaken Us, and fired upon Us, or whether our own Guns had been discharged We could not conjecture, but immediately an Officer came down to Us and told Us that the Ship had been struck with lightning and the Noise we had heard was a Crash of Thunder: that four Men had been struck down by it upon deck, one of them wounded by a Scortch upon his Shoulder as large as a Crown. (This man languished and died in a few Weeks.) That the Mainmast was struck and it was feared, damaged, but to what degree could not yet be ascertained. In the midst of all this terror and confusion, I heard a Cry that the [gun-]Powder room was open. Cartridges, Powder horns, if not some casks of Powder had been left rather carelessly in various parts of the Ship, near the Guns. If a Spark of the lightning had struck any of these, the Consequences might have been disagreeable enough, but if it had reached the Powder room, it would have made an End of the Business. The Men were alarmed at the danger to the Powder room, and Sailors and Marines scampered away with their Lanthorns in such a hurry that I apprehended more danger to the Powder room from their candles than from the Lightning, but instantly I heard the Voice of an Officer: "Be cool! No Confusion! Come back with all your Lanthorns. I will go with mine and secure the Powder room." I was as much pleased to perceive the immediate Obedience of the Men, as to hear the Voice of the Officer. He soon returned and proclaimed that he had secured the Powder room and all was safe.

Next morning the British frigate was nowhere to be seen, but the storm raged on for several days. The ship was in the Gulf Stream and

the Wind blowing against the current, not directly, but in various Angles, produced a tumbling sea, vast mountains sometimes dashing against each other, and sometimes piling up one on another like Pelion on Ossa, and not unfrequently breaking on the Ship threatened to bury Us all at once in the deep. The Sails were all hauled down but a foresail under which We hoped to scudd, but a sudden Gust of Wind rent it in an instant from the bottom to the top, and We were left with bare poles entirely at the Mercy of Wind and Water. The Noises were such that We could not hear each other speak at any distance. The Shrouds and every other rope in the Ship exposed to the Wind became a Chord of a very harsh Musick. Their Vibrations produced a constant and hideous howl, of itself enough to deafen Us; added to this the howl and Whistle of the Winds and incessant roar of the Ocean all in boiling rage and fury, white as Snow with foam through the whole Extent of the horizon; and to compleat the whole, a Sound more alarming I found to our Officers than all the rest, a constant Cracking night and day from a thousand places in all parts of the Ship, excited very serious Apprehension of the Starting of the Butts.

Fortunately, the butts did not start, that is, the planks did not come apart; the storm abated, and Adams could write of John Quincy that

✳

the child's Behaviour gave me a Satisfaction that I cannot express. Fully sensible of our Danger, he was constantly endeavouring to bear up under it with a manly courage and patience, very attentive to me, and his thoughts always running in a serious Strain.

Feb 27. A calm. As soft and warm as Summer.

March 1. It was discovered that our Mainmast was sprung in two Places; one beneath the Main deck, where, if the Mast had wholly failed in the late Storm it must have torn up the Main deck, and the Ship must have foundered. This was one among many instances in which it had already appeared that our Safety had not depended on ourselves.

✳

The fair weather continued, the ship made good speed, and Adams settled down to improve his French by reading a bilingual edition of Molière's plays. But they were not there yet:

✳

March 10. We espied a Sail and gave her chase. We soon came up with her, but as we had borne directly down upon her, she had not seen our Broadside and knew not our force. She was a Letter of Mark [a privateer] with fourteen Guns, eight Nines and six Sixes. She suddenly turned and fired a broadside into Us, but did Us no other damage than by cutting some of our rigging, piercing some of our Sails, and sending one of her Shot through our Mizzen Yard. I happened to be standing in the gangway between the Quarter Deck and the Main Deck . . . so that the Balls flew directly over my head. We upon this Salutation turned our broadside towards her. As soon as she saw this she struck her colours. Our Sailors were all in a rage to sink her for daring to fire. But Captain Tucker very promptly and prudently ordered his Officers not to fire, for he wanted the Egg without breaking the Shell. . . . The prize was the ship *Martha*, Captain McIntosh, from London to New York, loaded with a Cargo of great Value. The Captain told us that seventy thousand Guineas had been insured upon her at Lloyds, and that she was worth Eighty thousand.

Then came some bad luck. Because they were now near the coast of France they encountered many other ships, among them a brig from Marseilles, and

Mr. Barron, our first Lieutenant, attempting to fire a Gun as a Signal to the Brig, the Cannon burst, and tore in pieces the right leg of this worthy officer so that the Surgeon was obliged to amputate it, a little below the Knee. I was present at this afflicting Scene and, together with Captain Tucker, held Mr. Barron in our Arms, while the doctor put on the Turnequett and cutt off the Limb.

March 27. On Wednesday Evening Mr. Barron died, and yesterday was committed to the Deep, from the Quarter Deck. He was laid in a chest made for the purpose by the Carpenter; about a Dozen twelve pound Shot were put in with him and then nailed up. The Fragment of the Gun which destroyed him was lashed on the Chest, and the whole launched overboard, through one of the Ports, in presence of all the Ship's company. . . .

Two days later, early in the morning, they saw land.

About four o'clock we cryed "France! France!". . . . In the Afternoon we had an entire calm and Mr. Goss played on his Violin and the Sailors danced, which seemed to have a happy effect on their Spirits and put them in good humour. Numbers of small Birds from the

Shore came along today, some of which alighted on our Rigging, Yards, &c.

March 30. This day has been fortunate and happy. . . . Our Pilot had brought Us safely into the River of Garonne, and we had run up with the Wind and Tide as far as Pouliac, when we anchored for the night. . . . The River was very beautiful: on both sides of it the plantations were pleasant. On the South Side especially we saw Horses, Oxen, Cows, and great Flocks of Sheep grazing. The Husbandmen ploughing and Women half a dozen in a drove with their hoes. The Churches, Convents, Gentlemen's Seats, and the Villages appeared to me, simple Inhabitant of the American Wilderness, very magnificent.

But then, even before the *Boston* docked at Bordeaux, a message was delivered to Adams on board that "Dr. Franklin has been received by the King in great pomp and that a Treaty is concluded . . ." Wonderful news for the American cause, a turning point in the course of the war, but negotiated entirely without him. A bitter pill indeed, and a harbinger of what was to come: with little of importance to do, and always overshadowed by the hugely popular Franklin, Adams was in for a long period of frustration and mortification. This began even before he left Bordeaux, when he discovered to his chagrin that the warm welcome given him there was due to the mistaken belief that he was his cousin Samuel Adams, generally supposed in France to be the author of *Common Sense*. And when it was "settled that he was not the famous Adams," he wrote of himself in his diary, "the Consequence was plain— he was some Man that nobody had ever heard of before—and therefore a Man of no Consequence—a Cypher."

AMERICANS IN PARIS

Much of the credit for negotiating the treaty with France is usually given to Franklin, whose skill as a diplomat and great personal prestige were certainly helpful; but in fact even before the Declaration of Independence, plans were afoot in France to help their enemy's enemy. As early as February 1776, Caron de Beaumarchais, a businessman as well as playwright (*The Marriage of Figaro, The Barber of Seville*) had come up with a scheme that would keep the pot boiling in America but without involving France in a war.

In a memorandum addressed "To the King only," and endorsed by Vergennes, the chief minister, Beaumarchais explained how he would start by setting up a front company called Rodrigue Hortalez & Cie, to be funded by a government loan of a million *livres,* about $200,000. Half would be sent across the Atlantic in gold to shore up the paper currency Congress was already busy printing, and half would be used as collateral to raise further money from private investors. The result would be dazzling, because "by multiplying this money by its increase, a single million enhanced by being again put in circulation produces the same results in favor of the Americans as if your Majesty had actually paid out nine millions." Even better, "every million spent by your Majesty to enable the Americans to defend their soil will cost the English one hundred million if they persevere in going two thousand leagues from home to attack them. In other words, to sacrifice a million in order to occasion a loss of one hundred million to the English is precisely the same thing as advancing a million to gain ninety-nine million. It is impossible, Sire, that you could ever find another opportunity to make a less expensive or greater profit." In return for the half million in gold, the Americans would ship large quantities of tobacco, which Hortalez & Cie would sell at a high price. Money would also be spent on gunpowder, but not at the current market price of 20 to 30 *sous* a pound; instead the powder would be bought from the royal arsenals at 4 to 6 *sous* a pound and "the firm of Hortalez will then contract with the Americans to ship the powder to them at a price of 20 *sous* a pound." Mortars and cannon would also come from the royal arsenals, which had a large surplus, the French army having recently switched to a new and improved type of artillery. Without going into further details, "enough has been stated to demonstrate to your Majesty that the returns in this enterprise, when properly considered in accordance with the basic principles of commerce, should grow by circulation not by a mere multiple of two—as 1, 2, 4, 8 and so on—but by a multiple of three, as in 1, 3, 9, 27 etc. For if the first million produces three million, these three million when used for further operations will, according to the same theory, produce nine million; and these nine million will produce twenty-seven million, and so on, as I think I have sufficiently demonstrated."

One other point: "This assistance will serve not so much to end the war between America and England as to sustain and keep it going to the detriment of the English, our natural and determined enemies." This chimed with official thinking. "At present, the government's policy should be to draw out the struggle for as long as possible," wrote an official in the Ministry of War in April 1778. "By protracting the conflict between America and Britain we will have an opportunity of strengthening relations between our nation and the Americans, gradually accustoming them to our manufactures, our tastes, and our ways of doing business. The aid we give them will do much to eradicate the anti-French feeling now so prevalent among Americans as a result of their having been so long under the influence of the British." Many Americans understood this policy. "The primary motive of France for the assistance which she gave us was obviously to enfeeble a hated and powerful rival by breaking in pieces the British Empire," Alexander Hamilton wrote later. "He must be a fool who can be credulous enough to believe that a despotic court aided a popular revolution from regard to liberty or friendship to the principles of such a revolution."

Franklin also had no illusions on this score but he had the tact and good sense not to say so. He and Vergennes understood each other, but for public consumption "the old Conjuror," as Adams called him, waved his magic wand and summoned up a warm and fuzzy glow of goodwill that shrouded the hard realities of business and politics with an aura of benevolent philanthropy. Also, by playing on French preconceptions about America, which were based almost entirely on literary theory rather than actual observation, Franklin conjured up a vision of a pristine new world arising in the west, an unspoiled paradise where man in the state of nature could fulfill whatever expectations the *philosophes* might have dreamed up on his behalf. And then too there was his own carefully crafted persona: the simple clothes, the owlish glasses, the frontiersman's fur hat and *Poor Richard's* cracker-barrel nuggets of practical wisdom. No wonder the *beau monde* loved him.

John Adams also claimed to believe in the simple life. Corresponding with Mercy Otis Warren about what form of government the newly independent country should adopt, he said he preferred a republic, but warned that "such a Government is only to be supported by pure Religion or Austere Morals. Public Virtue cannot exist in a Nation without private, and public Virtue is the only Foundation of Republics." This being so, it is not surprising that having at last arrived in Paris he found almost nothing to commend. "I am wearied to death with gazing wherever I go at a Profusion of unmeaning Wealth and magnificence. . . . Gold, Marble, Silk, Velvet, Silver, Ivory, and Alabaster make up the Shew everywhere." Time was frittered away: "Every fashionable House at least has a Billiard Table, a Backgammon Table, a Chess Board, a Chequer Board, Cards, &c." True, the present king, Louis XVI, did not have a mistress (indeed it took him several years to consummate his marriage), but Marie Antoinette was known to wield excessive influence. Even his official visit to Versailles did not go well. "The Count [Vergennes] went up to the King, and informed him that Mr. Adams was present to be presented to his Majesty. The King turned round and looked upon me and smiled. 'Is that Mr. Adams?' said his Majesty [in French]. Being answered in the affirmative by the count, he began to talk to me, and with such rapidity that I could not distinguish one Syllable nor understand one Word . . ." Vergennes then "went up to him and very respectfully said, 'Mr. Adams will not answer your Majesty, for he neither speaks nor understands our language yet . . .'" This was a disappointment, especially for the king, as Adams felt certain that he had "a great inclination to have a Dialogue with me."

But it was his relationship with Franklin that embittered his time in France. Despite his affectations of simplicity, Franklin enjoyed Paris even more than he had enjoyed London. Comfortably lodged in Passy in a large house whose cellar held over a thousand bottles of wine; the darling of the literary salons; flirted with by pretty women; barely able to go to the theater without the audience rising to their feet to applaud him; author of the popular *Le Bonhomme Richard* (the French version of *The Way to Wealth*); liked and trusted by Vergennes and prime signatory of the all-important treaty of alliance—how could Adams contain himself?

"The Life of Dr. Franklin was a Scene of continual dissipation," he later wrote.

✳

I could never obtain the favour of his Company in the Morning before Breakfast which would have been the most convenient time to read over the Letters and papers, deliberate on their contents and decide upon the Substance of the Answers. It was late when he breakfasted, and as soon as Breakfast was over, a crowd of Carriages came to his Levee, or if you like the term better to his Lodgings, with all Sorts of People; some Philosophers, Academicians and Economists . . . but by far the greater part were Women and Children, come to have the honour to see the great Franklin, and to have the pleasure of telling Stories about his Simplicity, his bald head and scattering strait hairs, among their Acquaintances. These Visitors occupied all the time, commonly, till it was time to dress and go to Dinner. He was invited to dine abroad every day and never declined unless when We had invited Company to dine with Us. I was always invited with him, till I found it necessary to send Apologies that I might have some time to study the French Language and do the Business of the mission. Mr. Franklin kept a large horn-book always in his

pocket in which he minuted down all his invitations to dinner, and
Mr. Lee [another commissioner and Adams's friend] said it was the
only thing in which he was punctual. . . . Often when I had drawn
the Papers and had them fairly copied for Signature, and Mr. Lee
and I had signed them, I was frequently obliged to wait several days
before I could obtain the signature of Dr. Franklin to them. He
went accordingly to his Invitation to his Dinner and after that went
sometimes to the Play, sometimes to the Philosophers, but most
commonly to visit those ladies who were complaisant enough to
depart from custom in France so far as to procure Setts of Tea Geer,
as it is called, and make Tea for him. Some of these ladies I knew,
as Madam Helvétius, Madam Brillon, Madam Chaumont, Madam
LeRoy &c. and others whom I never knew and never enquired for.
After Tea the Evening was spent in hearing the Ladies sing and play
upon their Piano Fortes and other instruments of Musick, and in
various Games as Cards, Chess, Backgammon &c.

After that it was home to bed, often as late as midnight. "This
course of Life contributed to his health and Longevity. He was now
between Seventy and Eighty and I had so much respect and compassion for his Age that I should have been happy to have done all
the business, or rather the Drudgery, if I could have been favoured
with a few moments in a day to receive his Advice concerning the
manner in which it ought to be done. But this condescension was
not attainable."

This comes from the autobiography, written many years later
when Adams had had a chance to calm down; but despite the
"respect and compassion" that he then professed to feel for Franklin, his day-to-day diary trembles with indignation at the old man's
"Outrages to Morality and Decorum," his sloth, his fondness for
champagne, the way he allowed Madame Brillon to sit on his lap in
public, his shameless attempts to get the widowed Madame Helvétius to share his bed, either as mistress or as wife, the scandalous

life of that lady herself—friend of the atheist Voltaire, owner of eighteen angora cats that she dressed in fur-lined brocaded satin cloaks and fed on roast partridge served on fine china dishes placed on the sofas and chairs in her drawing room, the handsome young priests who seemed to be always in residence. "'Oh *Mores!*' Said I to myself, what Absurdities, Inconsistencies, Distractions, and Horrors would these Manners introduce into our Republican Government in America!"

In the meantime French aid had been flowing across the Atlantic. As early as December 1776, Silas Deane had reported to John Jay that "by General Coudray I send 30,000 fusils [muskets], 200 pieces of brass cannon, 30 mortars, 4,000 tents and clothing for 30,000 men, with 200 tons of gunpowder, lead, balls, &c, &c . . ." But Deane, who got "a clear commission of five percent on the original costs" and had very likely padded this inventory, was only a minor figure in the supply business. Rather it was Beaumarchais who drove things forward. This he did with great success, despite a fondness for the kind of theatrical stratagem that worked well enough in his plays, where an exchange of cloaks between a master and his servant fooled everyone. Thus instead of simply landing his cargo of military supplies at the Cap François entrepot in Haiti, where it would be collected by American ships, Captain de Montaut was ordered to arrange to have his ship seized by American privateers, who would then carry her off to their home port. "The captain will then protest loudly and lodge a formal protest with Congress. Congress will disavow the brutal privateer and order the ship to be released, while also apologizing for the insult to the French flag. And while all this is going on you will land the military supplies and take on a cargo of tobacco which you will bring back to me here." Et voilà! But there were other problems: what, for example, should be done about the surplus brass cannon from the royal arsenals that had been stamped with the arms of France? Suppose one of them should fall into the hands of the English—wouldn't that give the game away? Should artificers try to drill out the stamped insignia? Or would that weaken the cannon?

Apart from Franklin, who always claimed that he had no secrets and therefore no need for secrecy, members of the American mission also tried to be security-conscious, writing letters in elaborate codes that must have taken hours to decipher; but such precautions were quite unnecessary since the British always knew exactly what they were up to. This was because the longtime secretary to the mission, Dr. Edward Bancroft, was a British spy. So well did Bancroft cover his tracks that this was not discovered until a hundred years later—when it also emerged that he was a double spy, betraying the British as well as the Americans, though since he was born in Massachusetts, he was more of a traitor to the Americans than to the British. He did it for the money, £1,000 a year, which he then used to speculate on the London stock market on the basis of inside information, for example selling British government bonds short on advance news of Burgoyne's surrender. Bancroft did his work with a flair that would have appealed to Beaumarchais, writing his messages in invisible ink and then putting them in sealed bottles, which he dropped off every Tuesday evening in a hollow tree in the gardens of the Tuileries. The French secret police, who knew everything, must have known about this; and so no doubt did Vergennes too. Franklin liked and trusted Bancroft. John Adams did not distrust him but did dislike him, mainly because Bancroft often drank too much Burgundy and this "would set his tongue a-running at a most licentious rate at Table and after dinner, as gave me great pain. The Bible and the Christian Religion were his most frequent Subjects of Invective and ridicule . . ." (But it was Bancroft, who later went to live in London, who had the last word. Long after the war, in 1787, Adams published his *Defense of the Constitutions of Government of the United States,* "my Confession of political Faith." In May a review appeared in the London publication *Monthly Review.* The opening sentence ran: "We have not met with a greater disappointment in the course of our literary labours than we have experienced with respect to the work before us . . ." and things did not get any better after that. The review was anonymous, and Abigail, flying to her husband's defense, ascribed it to "that poor envy-ridden, contemptible, Ignorant, self-conceited Wretch Silas Deane." But her husband knew who he had to thank.)

After a few months in Paris, Adams wrote to Congress with the sensible suggestion that the American mission needed only one man, not three. But who should that man be? Not Arthur Lee, though a political ally. Not Franklin: "He is too old, too indolent and dissipated." So who—*who*? But Vergennes, getting wind of what was up (perhaps thanks to Bancroft's bottle), also sent a message to Congress saying that if it valued the French alliance, Franklin was to stay. And so, victim of his own stratagem, in the spring of 1779, a little more than a year after his epic crossing, Adams departed. "The Pleasure of returning home is very great," he told his diary, though it was "a Mortification" to leave France now that, after a year and a half of study, he had "acquired enough of the Language to understand a Conversation as it runs at a Table at Dinner . . ."

Yet another mortification was in store. Having arrived at the port of Nantes in early March, he then had to wait more than two months for a ship. Clearly, someone was trying "to prevent me from going home, lest I should tell some dangerous truths. . . . Does the old Conjuror dread my Voice in Congress? He has some Reason, for he has often heard it there, a Terror to evil doers."

COASTAL ACTIVITIES

In July 1777, after being stationed in Boston and New York, Captain Mackenzie of the Royal Welch Fusiliers found himself in British-occupied Rhode Island Bay, where the weather was hot, there was little to do, and morale was low.

✳

5ᵗʰ July. A Soldier of the 43ʳᵈ was drowned this Evening. It is imagined he did it willfully, as a paper was found in his Cloathes on the
shore, indicating such a design . . . 6ᵗʰ July. Fine weather. Wind
South. A soldier of the 43ʳᵈ Regt shot himself last night in the rear
of the Camp. The discovery of a Connection he had with a married
woman of the same Regiment appears to have been the cause of this
rash action. I cannot help observing here that a Soldier of the 22ⁿᵈ
Regiment shot himself through the body (of which he languished
about 12 days) and that another soldier of the 43ʳᵈ cut himself with
a Razor across the wrists, since we have been encamped. Several
Soldiers have also deserted, some of them men of good Characters
who were not suspected of such an act. I am inclined to believe
that many of these things proceed from our having remained so
long in a State of inactivity. . . . If we were to undertake little enterprizes against the Enemy, in which we could run no risque, it would
employ the minds of the Soldiery, give them something to do and
talk of, fit them for the undertaking and execution of those of a
more arduous nature, and would at the same time teach the young
Soldiers and give them confidence.

✳

In fact "little enterprizes against the enemy," such as bombarding
and launching amphibious raids on coastal towns, were already official policy. As early as January 1776, the London *Morning Chronicle*
had carried this letter from an officer on the *Otter*, a British sloop of
war. "I have the pleasure to assure you that the rebel town of Norfolk
is in ashes. It is glorious to see the blaze of the town and shipping. . . .
We are now proceeding on this business, and will burn every port on
the sea shore."

By the summer of 1779 it was Connecticut's turn. "The province
of Connecticut," wrote Sergeant Lamb of the Royal Welch Fusiliers,
"was the great source from whence the Americans recruited their
armies and supplied them with provisions. It had, from its situation,

hitherto sustained little of that rage of war which most of the other provinces had endured. The British commander [Sir Henry Clinton], to convince the inhabitants that their province was not inaccessible, and that it was to our lenity and forbearance they were indebted, planned an expedition against it. It formed also part of the general's plan to compel Washington to quit his strong situation on the North [Hudson] River, and descend into the country, for the defense of the sea coast."

Ezra Stiles, now President of Yale College, tells what happened next.

About eleven o'clock Monday Morning July 5th the Fleet of about 38 or 40 sail, under Command of Sir George Collyer, anchored off West Haven. Alarm Guns were fired and Lt. Col. Sabin of the Militia ordered to beat to Arms. A Lethargy seemed to have seized the inhabitants, who would believe the Fleet would pass by in the Morning. However some of us set about putting up & removing Furniture. But all was Confusion. At daylight we descryed the Fleet, and with a Telescope on the Top of the Tower of the College Steeple we plainly saw the Boats putting off from the Shipping for Shore at five o'clock in the morning, or a little after sunrise. All then knew our Fate. Perhaps one Third of the Adult male Inhabitants flew to Arms & went out to meet them; a quarter removed out of Town, doing nothing, and the rest remained unmoved, partly Tories, partly timid Whigs. Sundry of the Tories armed & went forth. About 90 or an hundred Men finally stayed in Town.

Stiles sent off his four daughters "on foot for Carmel. I sent the College Record & a Quantity of College papers 3 Miles off by my youngest son. I sent off a horse Load of Bags of Cloaths another way. Then sent Isaac with a Carriage to overtake his Sisters. And then my oldest son Ezra went off towards West Bridge, and was in all the actions of both the days on both sides of the Harbour."

Also taking part in the defense of New Haven was the Rev. Dr. Napthali Daggett, professor of divinity at Yale College, aged fifty-two. Shortly after the event, Daggett made this sworn statement:

✴

On Monday morning, the 5th inst. [July], the town of New Haven was justly alarmed with very threatening appearances of a speedy invasion from the Enemy. Numbers went armed to oppose them. I, among others, took the station assigned to me on Milford Hill, but was soon directed to quit and retire further north, as the motions of the Enemy required. Having gone as far as I supposed was sufficient, I turned down the hill to gain a little covert of bushes which I had in my eye; but to my great surprise, I saw the Enemy much nearer than I expected, their advanced guards being little more than 20 rods distant, plain open ground between us. They instantly fired upon me, which they continued till I had run a dozen rods, discharging not less than 15 or 20 balls at me alone; however, through the preserving Providence of God, I escaped them all unhurt, and gained a little covert at which I aimed, which concealed me from their view, while I could plainly see them thro' the weeds and bushes advancing towards me within about 12 rods. I singled out one of them, took aim, and fired upon him; I loaded my musket again, but determined not to discharge it any more; and as I saw I could not escape from them, I determined to surrender myself a prisoner. I begged for Quarter, and that they would spare my life. They drew near to me, I think only two in number, one on my right hand, the other on my left; the fury of infernals glowing in their faces, they called me a damned old Rebel and swore they would kill me instantly. They demanded, "What did I fire on us for?" I replied, "Because it is the exercise of war." Then one made a pass at me with his bayonet, as if he designed to thrust it thro' my body. With my hand I tossed it up from its direction and sprung in so near to him that he could not hurt me with his bayonet. I still continued pleading and begging for my life, with the utmost importunity, using every argument in my power to mollify them, and induce them to desist from their murderous purpose. One of them gave me four gashes on my head with the edge of his bayonet, to the skull bone, which caused a painful effusion of blood. The other gave me three light pricks with the point of his bayonet on the trunk of my body, but they were no more than skin deep. But what is a thousand times worse than all that has been related, is the blows and bruises they gave with the heavy barrels of their guns on my Bowels, by which I was knocked down once, or more, and almost deprived of life; by which bruises I have been almost confined to my bed ever since. These scenes might take up about two minutes of time. They seemed to desist a little from their design of murder, after which they stript me of my shoe and knee buckles, and also my stock buckle. Their avarice further led them to rob me of my pocket handkerchief and a little old tobacco box. They then bade me march towards the main body, which was about twelve rods distant, where some officers soon inquired of me who I was. I gave them my name, station, and Character, and begged their protection, that I might not be any more abused or hurt by the soldiers. They promised me their protection, but I was robbed of my shoes and was committed to one of the most unfeeling savages that ever breathed. They then drove me with the main body, a hasty march of five miles or more. I was insulted in the most shocking manner by the ruffian soldiers, many of which came at me with fixed bayonets and swore that they would kill me on the spot. They damned me, those that took me because they spared my life. Thus amidst a thousand insults my infernal driver hurried me along faster than my strength would admit in the extreme heat of the day, weakened as I was by my wounds and the loss of blood, which at a moderate computation could not be less than one quart. And when I failed in some degree, thro' faintness, he would strike me on the back with a heavy walking staff and kick me behind with his foot. At length, by the supporting power of God, I arrived at the green in New Haven. But my life was almost spent, the world around me several times appearing dark as midnight. I obtained leave of an officer to be carried into Widow Lyman's and laid upon a bed, where I lay the rest of the day and succeeding night, in such acute and excruciating pain as I never felt before.

"On Tuesday Morning," wrote Ezra Stiles, "upon their crossing over the ferry, the Enemy displayed their Vengeance by setting fire to Houses, Barns & Stores in East Haven." They also burned large parts of New Haven, but not the college. On Wednesday they moved on to Fairfield, where they "laid in ashes all the Town except perhaps a dozen Buildings & even these were set fire to but extinguished by our people—and among the rest not only the Meeting House & State House, but the Episcopal Church were laid in ashes by a member of the Society for Propagating the Gospel." The next target was Norwalk, which they also burned, including the meeting house and Episcopal church "with this blasphemous & heaven-daring Expression at setting fire to the latter, 'Now, God Almighty, come & defend your own House!'"

Other accounts from local papers of British atrocities include these:

One Kennedy, a noted Tory who rejoiced in their coming, they plundered of his buckles &c, and on his expressing some resentment, immediately stabbed him to death. A very old man of the name of English (whose daughter was busy in providing for their entertainment), on expression of reproof, uttered in the most gentle, inoffensive manner, they murdered by running through the body several times with bayonets; and as he lay on his back bleeding on the floor in the agonies of death, his daughter coming in, exclaimed, "Oh! How could you murder my poor old father so cruelly?" One of them asking, "Is he your father?" to which she answered, "Oh! Yes, he is my father," the inhuman villain immediately stood and stamped on his breast, and then upon his face, crushing down his nose.

One Tuttle (a man who on some late very great losses and misfortunes, occasioned by his having espoused the cause of the British tyrant, had lost his senses and been in a state of distraction, not having spoken a word for above six weeks before the time), being met by some of the British cut-throats, they asked him a question, and making no answer, they stabbed with a bayonet, which some person of the town seeing, told them the man was crazy, and had not spoken a word these six weeks. "Damn him," replied the murderer. "It is time he should be made to speak," and forcing the bayonet into his mouth, thrust it into his tongue, drew it out, and cut it off.

There was also the story of the women who, relying on "the politeness and generosity" of the British invaders, had stayed in town. "To these they behaved with worse than savage cruelty, and though most, if not all of them, were reputed of Tory principle, yet very few, if any, of the young women, nor not all of the old, or even the Negroes, escaped violation—some in the presence of their husbands, and others by great numbers successively. Some of these unhappy victims they carried off with them in their ships."

Lies! All lies! "Gross misrepresentation to render the British name odious to humanity," wrote Sergeant Lamb of the Fusiliers. To be sure, there had been some unintended and regrettable incidents— "in such excursions many scenes occur at which the feeling heart must revolt. But if persons whose residences unfortunately become the seat of war will not govern themselves prudently, whom have they to blame except themselves for all the disastrous consequences that may ensue?" For example, at New Haven, "notwithstanding the opposition of the inhabitants, and their even firing from the windows after the troops were in possession of the town, such was the British humanity that, instead of indiscriminate death, which by the laws of war they were liable to, the town was saved from damage, and private houses, as much as possible, exempted from plunder by placing sentinels before them, many of whom (such is American gratitude) were actually wounded at their posts!" And when the troops re-embarked, "New Haven was left in a far better situation than many less offending places have experienced in all countries during war."

Lamb also managed to convince himself that rather than harden the American will to resist, the raids were a big success. Intelligence was soon received by Sir Henry Clinton that the inhabitants of Connecticut "were highly dissatisfied both with Congress and General Washington. In particular they loudly complained of the latter, in permitting the destruction of so many towns on the sea-coast, and remaining fixed, if not inattentive, in his strong position on North River; and further, Sir Henry had been secretly and positively informed that many were hesitating, from these circumstances, about withdrawing their support from Congress and making terms with the parent country."

The Rev. Dr. Napthali Daggett died the following year, "choaked up with blood," probably the result of the "blows and bruises" the British soldiers had given him with "the heavy barrels of their guns." According to another account of what happened to him that day, the British would almost certainly have finished him off but for the intervention of their guide, a Tory called Chandler who had formerly been one of his pupils at Yale. Just before he was taken off to Widow Lyman's, Daggett was asked whether, if released, he would again take up arms against the British? To which he answered, "I rather believe I shall, if I get an opportunity."

THE RAIDER

But now, thanks to their new allies, the Americans were able to return the compliment in the matter of paying visits to coastal towns. French ports could be used as bases, French ships could be borrowed, and French troops could provide landing parties. "It is certain that the coasts of England and Scotland are extremely open and defenseless," wrote Franklin to Lafayette in March 1779. "There are also many rich towns near the sea, which four or five thousand men, landing unexpectedly, might easily surprise and destroy, or exact from them a heavy contribution, taking a part in ready money and hostages for the rest."

"Ready money" —that had an appealing ring to it. One reason why America's navy was so small was that sailors generally preferred to serve on privateers, where if they were lucky their share of the prize money could add up to a very nice nest egg; and so successful were they that by mid-1778 Lloyds of London was charging an insurance premium of eleven percent of the value of a cargo going to New York if the ship were sailing under convoy, and double that rate if traveling alone. Towns near the sea could also be profitable targets. During the Seven Years' War, the Royal Navy had extorted so huge a sum from the citizens of Havana in return for not destroying their city that the British admiral and general each got over £120,000, while the ordinary seaman got £3, 14 shillings and 9 pence.

With such examples in mind, small wonder that Franklin's enthusiasm grew as his letter progressed. "I should suppose, for example, that two millions sterling, or forty-eight millions of *livres*, might be demanded of Bristol for the town and shipping; twelve millions of *livres* for Bath; forty-eight millions for Liverpool; six millions from Lancaster; and twelve million from Whitehaven . . ."—already he's up to 126 million *livres*—and "on the east side there are the towns of New Castle, Scarborough, Lynn . . ."

Lafayette, who was back in France for a while, was to command the land forces, and the naval commander was to be the man now known as John Paul Jones. Like Thomas Paine, also a former British subject, Jones had had a mixed career before hitching his star to the Revolution and finding the glory and plunder that were his great ambitions in life. Born plain John Paul, the son of a Scottish gardener, and apprenticed at age twelve to a ship owner in Whitehaven (worth twelve million *livres*), he had spent some years on a slave ship that shuttled between Guinea and Jamaica. Disliking what he called "that abominable trade," he then served on a merchantman trading between Scotland and the West Indies, rising rapidly to the rank of captain. But there had been unfortunate incidents along the way. A ship's carpenter had died as the result of a flogging, and in Tobago a crew member had expired with the captain's sword through his body—according to John Paul the victim was a mutinous and violent troublemaker whom he was holding at bay with his sword, when the fellow suddenly rushed forward and impaled himself.

It was to put all this behind him that John Paul had settled in Virginia and added Jones to his name, just as the former Thomas Pain on coming to America had added an "e" to his. When the war started, he at once sided with the Americans, drawing his sword, as he put it, "only upon principles of Philanthropy and in support of the dignity of Human Nature." By 1776 he was captain of the *Providence*; two years later, as commander of the *Ranger*, he raided his home town of Whitehaven, burned some ships, seized the Selkirk family silver but missed the person of the earl himself—Jones had hoped to exchange him for captured American sailors—took several other prizes, threw panic into the coastal regions of Britain, and sailed into Brest a hero. (But not to everyone. In a statement of grievances the warrant and petty officers of the *Ranger* complained that "his government [was] arbitrary, his Temper & Treatment insufferable, for the most trivial matters threatening to shoot the Person or Persons whom he, in sallies of Passion, chooses to call Ignorant or disobedient . . .")

On shore, Jones was unimpressive. He was short, thin, "bookish," and round-shouldered, and his voice, according to John Adams, who met him several times in Nantes, was "soft and still and small." But in battle he had "a visage fierce and warlike." Thomas Berry, who served on the *Bonhomme Richard*, wrote that during the fight Jones "was dressed in a short jacket and long trousers, with about twelve charged pistols slung in a belt around his middle, and a cutlass in his hand." Berry, by the way, was one of the many English seamen serving on the *Bonhomme Richard*. Although all the officers were American, more than half the crew of 207 were from other countries: fifty-nine were British, twenty-nine came from Portugal, twenty-one from Ireland, seven from Sweden, four from Scotland, and two from the East Indies.

For the joint expedition with Lafayette, his command was to be a former East Indiaman that had been converted into a ship of war and renamed the *Bonhomme Richard*, in honor of Franklin. But by the time he sailed from L'Orient in August 1779, plans had changed; there would be no land force and Jones was to do no more than sail his flotilla clockwise round the British Isles, taking ships and laying the coastal towns under "heavy contribution" if he could.

The first part went well, and by the time he met up with the *Serapis* he had taken seventeen British merchant ships. But his attempt to extort £200,000 from Leith, the port of Edinburgh, failed when a local clergyman, the Rev. Mr. Shirra of Kirkaldy, summoned his congregation to the beach where they prayed aloud for deliverance. "Now dear Lord, dinna ye think it a shame for ye to send this vile pirate to rob our folk o' Kirkaldy, for ye ken they're puir enow already, and hae nothing to spare. The way the wind blaws he'll be here in a jiffie, and wha kens what he may do? The puir weemen are maist frightened out o' their wits, and the bairns skirling after them . . . I hae been lang a faithful servant to ye, Laird; but gin ye dinna turn the wind about, and blaw the scoundrel out of our gate, I'll nae stir a foot, but will just sit here till the tide comes. So take your will of it!" Whereupon—no surprise here—a mighty rushing wind arose and Jones was driven out to sea. "I prayed," the Rev. Mr. Shirra later acknowledged, "but the Lord sent the wind."

From Leith, Jones sailed south and by September 21 was off Flamborough Head, a high promontory on the Yorkshire coast. Early the next morning he saw coming toward him a fleet of merchant ships escorted by a man-of-war. This turned out to be the Baltic Fleet, bringing naval supplies for British dockyards. The man-of-war was the *Serapis*, pronounced to rhyme with "rapist" and named after an Egyptian god of healing. It was commanded by Captain Pearson, had more guns than the *Bonhomme Richard*, and was accompanied by a smaller fighting ship, the *Countess of Scarborough*. Jones also was accompanied by other, smaller fighting ships, including the *Pallas*, which took on the *Countess of Scarborough*, and the *Alliance*, commanded by a demented Frenchman, Captain Landais, who for the most part sat the battle out, except when deliberately firing broadsides at his ally, the *Bonhomme Richard*.

The battle of Flamborough Head did not begin until the evening of September 23, when Captain Pearson, having parked the Baltic Fleet safely close in to the shore, dutifully went out to meet the enemy. It was a clear evening, the sea was calm and the harvest moon was full. Hundreds of spectators from nearby farms and villages gathered on the shore and on the heights of Flamborough Head—just as the citizens of Boston had once crowded their rooftops and upper windows to watch the redcoats advance up Bunker Hill.

It was seven o'clock when, on being hailed by the *Serapis*, the *Bonhomme Richard* "answered him by firing a whole broadside," wrote Jones. "The battle being thus begun, was continued with unremitting fury. As I had to deal with an enemy of greatly superior force, I was under the necessity of closing with him, to prevent the advantage which he had over me in point of manoeuvre." Once the two ships had closed,

the enemy's bowsprit came over the *Bonhomme Richard*'s poop by the mizzen-mast, and I made both ships fast together in that situation, which, by the action of the wind on the enemy's sails, forced her stern close to the *Bonhomme Richard*'s bow, so that the ships lay alongside each other, the yards being all entangled, and the cannon of each ship touching the opponent's. When this position took place, it was eight o'clock, previous to which the *Bonhomme Richard* had received sundry eighteen-pound shots below the water, and leaked very much. My battery of twelve-pounders . . . was entirely silenced and abandoned. As to the six old eighteen-pounders that formed the battery of the lower gun-deck, they did no service whatever, except firing eight shot in all. Two out of three of them burst at the first fire, and killed all the men who were stationed to manage them.

It was at about this point in the battle that, according to Lt. Richard Dale (and, it must be said, no one else), the following famous exchange took place:

"We had remained in this situation [grappled together] but a few minutes when we were again hailed by the *Serapis*, 'Has your ship struck?' To which Captain Jones answered, 'I have not yet begun to fight!'" (Jones' own version, in his memoirs, runs: "The English Commodore asked me if I demanded quarters, and I having answered him in the most determined negative, they renewed the battle with double fury.")

Also present at the battle was Nathaniel Fanning, a midshipman who was posted to "the top," that is, one of the platforms high up the masts from which American and French riflemen could throw grenades and shoot down on the enemy ship. The *Serapis* also had men in her top, but by now they were all dead; however, that ship had a covered deck which protected her gun crews, who continued to blast away point blank, while the *Bonhomme Richard* did the same. This had been going on for about three hours, by Fanning's estimate, when what he calls "the following farcical piece" occurred:

✺

It seems that a report was at this time circulated among our crew between deck, and was credited among them, that Captain Jones and all his principal officers were slain, the gunners were now the commanders of our ship, that the ship had four or five feet of water in her hold, and that she was then sinking. They therefore advised the gunner to go up on deck, together with the carpenter and master-at-arms, and beg of the enemy quarters, in order, as they said, to save their lives. These three men, being thus delegated, mounted the quarter-deck, and bawled out as loud as they could, "Quarters! Quarters! For God's sake, quarters! Our ship is sinking!" and immediately got up on the ship's poop with a view of hauling down our colors. . . .

The three poltroons, finding the ensign and ensign-staff gone, they proceeded upon the quarter-deck, and were in the act of hauling down our pennant, still bawling for "Quarters!" when I heard our commodore say in a loud voice, "What d – -d rascals are them? Shoot them! Kill them!" He was on the forecastle when these fellows first made their appearance upon the quarter-deck where he had just discharged his pistols at some of the enemy. The carpenter and the master-at-arms, hearing Jones's voice, skulked below, and the gunner was attempting to do the same when Jones threw both of his pistols at his head, one of which struck him in the head, fractured his skull, and knocked him down at the foot of the gangway ladder, where he lay till the battle was over.

The masts and rigging of both ships now caught fire—what a sight that must have been for the spectators on Flamborough Head as the flames lit up the night sky and were reflected on the calm waters of the sea! Fighting was suspended until the fires were doused, when once again Jones was invited to surrender. "Ay, ay," he replied according to Fanning. "We'll do that when we can fight no longer, but we shall see yours come down the first . . ." The battle was then renewed "with redoubled vigor with what cannon we could manage, hand grenadoes, stink pots, etc., but principally, towards the closing scene, with lances and boarding pikes. With these the combatants killed each other through the ships' port holes, which were pretty large."

Just after midnight, the battle came to a sudden end. According to Lt. Dale, the "powder-monkeys on the *Serapis*" —boys whose job it was to bring the canvas bags of gunpowder from the magazine up to the gun deck—"finding no officer to receive the eighteen-pound cartridges . . . threw them on the main deck, and went for more. These cartridges being scattered along the deck, and numbers of them broken, it so happened that some of the hand grenades thrown from the main-yard of the *Bonhomme Richard*, which was direct over the main hatch of the *Serapis*, fell upon this powder, and produced a most awful explosion. The effect was tremendous; more than twenty of the enemy were blown to pieces, and many stood with only the collars of their shirts upon their bodies. In less than an hour afterwards the flag of England, which had been nailed to the mast of the *Serapis*, was struck by Captain Pearson's own hand, as none of his people would venture aloft on this duty."

Dale was then ordered by Jones to go over to the *Serapis* and invite Captain Pearson to step onboard the *Bonhomme Richard*. Once there, Pearson handed over his sword in surrender. Jones, though fond of the grand gesture, did not return it; but he did say, according to Midshipman Fanning, "Sir, you have fought like a hero, and I make no doubt that your sovereign will reward you in a most ample manner for it." After a few more mutually complimentary remarks, "the two captains now withdrew into the cabin and there drank a glass or two of wine together."

Since the *Bonhomme Richard* had five feet of water in the hold and was once again on fire, the flames now nearing the powder magazine, the two captains probably did not linger over their wine; and though the fire was once again put out, the damage had been so great that "it was impossible to prevent the good old ship from sinking," and the decision was made to abandon her. "The water was then up to the lower deck," wrote Jones, "and a little after ten I saw, with inexpressible grief, the last glimpse of the *Bonhomme Richard*."

As a reward for his victory Jones became a hero in America and France; but as a result of maneuvering by better-connected American naval officers and their friends in Congress, he was never given another important command—no doubt to the relief of the Royal Navy and the residents of Britain's coastal towns.

The *Serapis* also came to a disappointing end. Though badly damaged, she was taken over by the French navy, refitted and sent out to fight the British in the Indian Ocean. One night en route, having put in to Madagascar, an officer decided that the time had come to broach a barrel of brandy. Since it was dark in the hold, he ordered a sailor to bring a lamp so that he could see what he was doing. Somehow the sailor managed to drop the lamp into the open barrel, the brandy caught fire, and the ship was destroyed.

THE MOTHER COUNTRY REVISITED

And what of the man at the helm of the British ship of state? "As for me," he assured Lord North, as things went from bad to worse, "I thank Heaven my Resolution rises with difficulties, and I put the strongest reliance in the protection of the Almighty, the justice of my Cause, and the purity of My own intentions. These are such props that nothing can shake and I am resolved to show I can save my Country." The National Debt may have soared but we must avoid "weighing such events in the Scale of a Tradesman behind his Counter." To be sure, "the times are certainly hazardous, but that ought to rouze the Spirit of Every Englishman to support me, who have no wish but . . . to do my Duty, and to shew by firmness in difficulties, that I am not unworthy of the Station into which it has pleased Providence to call me." The "just and unprovoked" war in America must continue. Should the Americans become independent then "the West Indies must follow them . . . Ireland would soon follow the same plan and be a separate state," and "then this Island would be reduced to itself, and soon would be a poor Island indeed." (Just what Catharine Macaulay, the "Republican Virago," had predicted before the war.) Never would he "suffer his dominions to be dismembered . . . I will rather risk my Crown than do what I think personally disgraceful, and whilst I have no wish but for the good and prosperity of my Country it is impossible that the nation shall not stand by me. If they will not, they shall have another King."

Long gone was the "fine pleasant-looking young man" once so admired by Lady Susan Fox-Strangways with his "look of happiness & good humour that pleas'd everyone." Now well into his middle age, he was "tall, square over the shoulders, large ugly mouth, talks a great deal, and shows his teeth too much," according to the American Loyalist exile Samuel Curwen, who saw him at evening prayers in Windsor Chapel in 1781. "His countenance," Curwen added, was "heavy and lifeless, with white eyebrows." Already there had been episodes of the madness that would later overwhelm him.

Though generally sane, George was certainly becoming eccentric. At Windsor he liked to wander about alone, visiting the local bookshop or, to the dismay of their occupants, strolling into the cottages and farmhouses of his tenants who he would then engage in awkward conversations, thrusting his pop-eyed, bright red face close up to theirs and barking out unanswerable exclamations such as "What? What?" and "Eh? Eh?" When he left he would leave a tip, usually a penny. Fanny Burney, the novelist and lady-in-waiting to the queen, once had this literary conversation with him:

"Was there ever," cried he, "such stuff as great part of Shakespeare? Only one must not say so! But what think you?—What? Is there not sad stuff? What? What?"

"Yes, indeed, I think so, sir, though mixed with such excellences that—"

"O!" cried he, laughing good-humouredly, "I know it is not to be said! But it's true! Only it's Shakespeare, and nobody dares abuse him."

As for Queen Charlotte, still addicted to snuff and still more at ease in German than in English, Curwen described her as being "of middle size and bulk" and "though far removed from beautiful she has an open placid aspect, mouth large, foot splay." Two more years were to pass before she gave birth to the last of their fifteen children, but already two had died and the oldest, the Prince of Wales, who had been raised under a regimen of Spartan strictness, was causing his parents grief by following a course of scandalous self-indulgence and extravagance. On his very first visit to the theater, to see *The Winter's Tale* at Drury Lane, he had fallen head over heels in love with Mrs. Robinson, the beautiful actress-cum-courtesan who played the role of Perdita. But unlike his father when similarly smitten with Lady Sarah Lennox, the young prince began an open affair—so open that

Mrs. Robinson had his coat of arms (three ostrich feathers) painted on the side of her coach. He also wrote her letters which were not the less compromising for being signed "Florizel" and which, when their affair ended, had to be bought back for £5,000, "an enormous sum," as the king acknowledged when approving payment from the government's Special Services account.

Lord North was also sighted by the churchgoing Samuel Curwen, this time while on his way to Whitehall Chapel when "who should cross me but a large clumsy gentleman with a blue ribbon across his breast. . . . He is rather above the common height, and bulk greatly exceeding; large legs, walks heavily, manner clumsy; very large featured, thick lips, wide mouth, high forehead, large nose, eyes not lively . . ." The burden of defending policies not of his making and clearly not working, the attacks often "most violent and personal" that he had to endure in the House of Commons, worries about family finances, the death of an adored son, his bloated body—all were taking their toll. Again and again he begged the king to allow him to resign, on various occasions writing that "his former incapacity is so much aggravated by his present distress of mind that he will soon be totally unfit for the performance of any ministerial duty . . . his spirits, strength, memory, judgment & abilities sensibly & considerably impair'd . . . his frailties both of mind & body much less equal to his situation than they were this twelvemonth . . . my ancient indolence is much increased . . . my memory grievously impaired. . . . I feel myself losing every day the good opinion of the House of Commons . . . the ruin and disgrace of the Country must be the consequence of my remaining in the Cabinet where I never could, nor can, decide between different opinions." In short, "If your Majesty does not allow me to retire, you and this country are ruined."

Perhaps most piteous was this note, dated only "Sunday afternoon," about his struggles with a dispatch box that had just arrived at Downing Street from the king: "Lord North has the honour of acquainting his Majesty that either from the newness of the Box, or the badness of Ld. North's key, he cannot open the Box. That Mr. Robinson [his secretary] is out of Town, & no Locksmith to be met with, as it is a holiday. Lord North hopes it will not be troublesome or impertinent in him to request for a moment the use of his Majesty's key."

But though the king was willing to lend his key, he would not allow Lord North to resign. "No man has a right to talk of leaving me at this hour," and "the day of trial is not the honourable one to desert me."

The other chief ministers also remained. Already disliked for his arrogance and more recently, with some help from General Burgoyne, blamed for the Saratoga disaster, Lord George Germain refused to resign unless promised a peerage that, unlike the courtesy title he bore as the son of a duke, would allow him to sit in the House of Lords in his own right. Any other way of quitting would make it appear that his conduct of the war in America had not been a success. Members could impeach him if they wanted to, but he would not be "brow-beaten" out of office. "The noble Lord said, 'Impeach me then; why do we not impeach him?'" replied George Byng, of the Opposition. "Let the noble Lord look round him, and he will see the reasons why he is not impeached. He will see a band of hired men ready to support him, or any minister who will pay them, against all the consequences of the American war. Give us an honest Parliament, and then let us see if the noble Lord would desire to find his security in impeachment."

Lord Sandwich also had no plans to leave. In 1779 the Earl of Bristol, one of the admirals who, like Lord Howe, "hated and despised" Sandwich, had introduced a resolution to remove him from office. Shortly afterward, Martha Reay, Sandwich's middle-aged mistress and mother of nine of his children, was assassinated by a love-crazed clergyman half her age, the Rev. James Hackman, who shot her at close range as she emerged from the Covent Garden Theatre where she had just seen a performance of *Love in a Village*. Sandwich, who to use the current expression had taken her "under his protection" when she was a thirteen-year-old apprentice to a dressmaker, was truly upset by her death, but it could not have happened at a better time, for it was in large part thanks to the sympathy aroused by his loss that the motion to remove him was defeated 78 to 39. Also, or so he later claimed, Sandwich did have some successes. When first appointed, he had taken over a navy that was "greatly out of repair . . . and a total despondency in the Navy Office." But "the First Lord of the Admiralty [i.e., himself] was not of a disposition to join with these melancholy ideas." He had broken the "combination among the Timber Growers and Timber Merchants" who hoarded their wares and jacked up their prices; he had forced the East India Company to stop competing with the Royal Navy by its "vast and unnecessary profusion of shipbuilding;" he had pushed through a program of copper-bottoming more than three hundred ships, making them faster and more formidable; and he had introduced into the shipyards a system of "Task Work," i.e., piecework, rather than "Day Work," which paid a flat rate of two shillings and one penny for a twelve-hour day. And when "the men laid down their tools and quitted their work," he "set them at defiance" and left them "to shift for themselves for two or three months, till they were starved again into the Dockyards."

Mrs. Montagu, related by marriage to Lord Sandwich, also knew how to handle her workers in times of national crisis. "You ask me if my black Regiment under ground would not oppose Invaders," she wrote to her friend Mrs. Carter while on a visit to her coal mines during the invasion scare of 1779. "I have no doubt they would make as stout resistance as any unarmed men. They desired last summer that I would send them a stand of Arms, but I begged to be excused. . . . There is no question but amongst us we could furnish a number of very fine fellows, stout of heart and limb for the defence of our Coast; but as the Coal trade will, I hope, long outlive the War, it would be dangerous to teach them the military discipline, and have arms which they might on improper occasions seize upon."

For three years running, a rebellion was expected in Ireland and an invasion in England. On August 23, 1779, while on a visit to

Somerset, the Rev. James Woodforde wrote in his diary: "A Mr. Cambridge and his two sisters from Richmond called at Mr. Wickham's in a Chaise this afternoon, being just returned from Plymouth, he informed us that Plymouth and Exeter were in great consternation about the French and Spanish Fleets who were on Wednesday last about 5 leagues from Plymouth, they saw them very plain from the Hill near Plymouth. . . . Mr. Cambridge saw an engagement between one of our Ships by name the *Ardent* of 50 Guns, Capt. Boteler, and 3 of the Enemy's and she was obliged to strike to them after an engagement of 4 Hours and half. It happened on Tuesday last— Sir Charles Hardy not to be found—a general engagement is daily expected between the Fleets . . ."

Fortunately for Admiral Hardy, who was outnumbered 64 to 38, the combined French and Spanish fleets were unable to coordinate their movements and there was no "general engagement." Even more fortunately for him there were such virulent outbreaks of typhus, smallpox, and scurvy among the twenty thousand troops they were bringing as an invasion force that they had to return to port. But they would try again the next year.

The expected rebellion in Ireland was also postponed, but there was plenty of other bad news. "I have been looking out for the Loss of the Eastern Wing of the great British Eagle in Bengal, as well as the lopping off of the Western Wing in America," wrote Ezra Stiles as early as 1777, a prophecy that Hyder Ali and his son, Tipu Sahib, rulers of Mysore, were doing their best to fulfill, with help from the French. Much of this warfare was carried on by the East India Company's own armed forces, but help was needed from the regular army and navy, which were already overextended. As well as the campaigns in America, there was fighting in the Caribbean and expeditions were sent to Mindanao, the Celebes, Nicaragua, Honduras, and Senegal. Gibraltar and Minorca were besieged. In 1780 the Dutch declared war against the British, and it looked as if Russia would soon do the same.

But the news from home was the worst of all—the Gordon Riots of June 1780, the worst outbreak of violence in London's history. Led by the fanatical Lord George Gordon, the riots were occasioned by modest amendments to the laws that barred Catholics from the professions, suspending, for example, the requirement that army officers swear an oath of allegiance to the Church of England. Like the Stamp Act, the law was passed easily and with little debate. But England was now under threat of invasion by its traditional enemies, the "treacherous French" and the "cruel Spaniards," and anti-Catholic feelings ran high, fueled by reports of treachery and sabotage: Advance parties of Jesuit priests were reported to be hiding in secret tunnels near the river, Benedictine monks had been discovered poisoning the flour in south London, black-clad members of the Inquisition would accompany the invaders, bringing with them the rack, the thumbscrew, and faggots for burning Protestant martyrs at the stake. . . . All over the country Protestant Associations drew up petitions deploring "the progress of that soul-deceiving and all-enslaving superstition, Popery." In London a mass meeting, said to number forty thousand, was held at St. George's Fields, site of the massacre of 1768. From there the crowd headed across Westminster Bridge for Parliament to present their petitions. "And now their insolence began," wrote Samuel Curwen. Members of both houses "received marks of their indignant rage; some were stopped and threatened, otherwise abused and assaulted, pulled out of their carriages, and glad to get off without hats, wigs, with lacerated garments and flesh-wounds . . ."

Another eyewitness to the growing violence was Dr. Johnson, who wrote his account in a letter to his friend, Mrs. Thrale, then in Bath:

❋

At night the outrages began by the demolishing the Mass-house near Lincoln's Inn. . . . On Tuesday night they pulled down Fielding's house (the public office in Bow Street), and burnt his goods in the street. They had gutted, on Monday, Sir George Savile's house, but the building was saved. On Tuesday evening, leaving Fielding's ruins, they went to Newgate to demand their companions, who had been seized for demolishing the chapel. The keeper could not release them but by the mayor's permission, which he went to ask. At his return he found all the prisoners released, and Newgate in a blaze.

They then went to Bloomsbury, and fixed upon Lord Mansfield's house, which they partly pulled down; and, as for his goods, they totally burnt them. They went to Caen Wood (his lordship's country seat); but a guard was there before them. They plundered several Papists, and burnt a Mass-house, and some dwelling-houses in Moorfields the same night.

On Wednesday I walked with Dr. Scott to look at Newgate, and found it in ruins, with the fire yet glowing. As I went by, the Protestants were plundering the Sessions House at the Old Bailey. . . . At night they set fire to the Fleet [prison] and the King's Bench, and I know not how many other places; and one might see the glare of the conflagration fill the sky from many parts. The sight was dreadful. . . . Such a time of terror you would have been happy in not seeing.

The king said in Council "That the magistrates had not done their duty, but that he would do his own," and a proclamation was published, directing us to keep our servants within doors, as the peace was now to be preserved by force.

And so indeed it was. "When the regiments of militia, which had been ordered from a distance by forced marches, entered London, they kept up an incessant fire upon the lawless mob, until they were everywhere dispersed," ran an account in the Newgate Calendar. "The boats in which the robbers were carrying off the money plundered from the toll-houses of Blackfriars Bridge were sunk by the fire of a party of the North Hampshire militia, who also threw several of the rioters over the balustrades into the river Thames, where they perished. A proclamation was issued, and a reward of five hundred pounds was offered for the discovery and conviction of the person or persons who demolished the houses and chapels of the foreign ambassadors; and military law was established."

Estimates of the number of rioters killed by the soldiers ranged from a hundred to a thousand. Better score was kept of those who were brought to trial: 194, of whom 59 were convicted. According to the Newgate Calendar, "among those tried and convicted were several women and boys; but not one individual of the smallest respectability or good fame: Negroes, Jews, Gypsies, and vagabonds of every description—the very refuse of society." Some examples:

Richard Roberts and William Lawrence, mere lads in appearance, hardly seventeen years of age, convicted of pulling down the house of Sir John Fielding. They were hanged in Bow Street (i.e., at the scene of their crime).

William M'Donald, a cripple, who had lost an arm and had formerly been a soldier, hanged on Tower Hill for destroying the house of J. Lebarty, a publican, in St. Catharine's Lane, near thereto.

George Bawton, a poor drunken cobbler, who meeting Mr. Richard Stone, in High Street, Holborn, stopped him, saying, "Pray remember the Protestant religion." Mr. Stone offered twopence, but the cobbler damned him, and swore he would have sixpence, which was complied with; and for this, in times like those, he was justly hanged.

John Gray, Charles Kent, and Letitia Holland, hanged in Bloomsbury Square for being parties to setting fire to the mansion of Lord Chief Justice Mansfield.

Mary Roberts and Charlotte Gardener, the latter a Negress, hanged on Tower Hill for assisting to demolish the house of J. Lebarty, as before mentioned.

Lord George Gordon got off, thanks to his rank and to family influence. Not long afterwards he gave up the Protestant cause and when next heard of he "was discovered in a Jewish garb at Birmingham, with a long beard; and having undergone circumcision, he had firmly embraced the faith of the unbelievers."

Concluding his letter to Mrs. Thrale, Dr. Johnson wrote, "There has been, indeed, an universal panic, from which the king was the first that recovered. Without the concurrence or assistance of his ministers, or even the assistance of the civil magistrates, he put the soldiers in motion, and saved the town from calamities such a rabble's government must naturally produce." The king did more than just put the soldiers in motion. After telling the dithering Privy Council that "There shall be one that I can answer for, that will do his duty," he announced that he was ready to lead the troops himself. "I am persuaded," said a captain in the Horse Guards, "that the King does not know what fear is."

The Gordon Riots did more than greatly enhance the king's prestige; they were also taken as a warning of what would happen if the present system of government were changed. In a letter to her friend Mr. Smelt, Mrs. Montagu—who must surely have known that the lightning conductor had been invented by Franklin, but probably not that as a boy in Boston he had been a tallow chandler—explained that "His Lordship [Gordon] has wonderfully purged all the ill humours of his fellow subjects, and I hope in a great degree cured the epidemical democratick madness. . . . We are coming to our right senses, and begin to understand that our mild government is preferable to anarchy, and that it is better to be subject to our anointed Sovereign than to 10,000 greasy Tallow chandlers, Butchers, etc. I consider Lord George as a State electric conductor; the gathering storm which threatened our strongest, noblest, most Venerable edifices, has by him been brought down and sunk into the earth before it bursts on our heads . . ."

The Volunteer

In June 1780, just as the Gordon Riots were getting going, Ebenezer Fox was onboard an American warship cruising the waters off

Newfoundland in a heavy fog. Following his earlier adventures, which began when he ran away to sea at the age of twelve, Fox had settled down in Boston as an apprentice to Mr. John Bosson, barber and wig maker;, but he was still barely seventeen, and "a spirit of roving once more got possession of me."

Our coast was lined with British cruisers, which had almost annihilated our commerce; and the state of Massachusetts judged it expedient to build a government vessel, rated as a twenty-gun ship named the *Protector*, commanded by Captain John Foster Williams. She was to be fitted for service as soon as possible, to protect our commerce and to annoy the enemy. A rendezvous was established for recruits at the head of Hancock's wharf, where the national flag, then bearing thirteen stripes and stars, was hoisted. All means were resorted to, which ingenuity could devise, to induce men to enlist. A recruiting officer, bearing a flag and attended by a band of martial music, paraded the streets, to excite a thirst for glory and a spirit of military ambition. . . . He was a jovial, good-natured fellow, of ready wit and much broad humor. Crowds followed in his wake when he marched the streets; and he occasionally stopped at the corners to harangue the multitude in order to excite their patriotism and zeal for the cause of liberty. When he espied any large boys among the idle crowd around him, he would attract their attention by singing in a comical manner the following doggerel:

> All you that have bad masters,
> And cannot get your due;
> Come, come, my brave boys,
> And join with our ship's crew.

A shout and a huzza would follow, and some would join in the ranks. My excitable feelings were roused; I repaired to the rendezvous, signed the ship's papers, mounted a cockade, and was in my own estimate already more than half a sailor.

Once the crew was complete, the *Protector*—named in honor of Oliver Cromwell, the man who had sent King Charles I to the block—put to sea and headed for the banks of Newfoundland,

✼

where we cruised for nearly eight weeks, most of the time in a dense fog, without meeting with friend or foe.

On the morning of June 9th, 1780, the fog began to clear away; and the man at the masthead gave notice that he saw a ship to the westward of us. As the fog cleared up, we perceived her to be a large ship under English colors to the windward, standing athwart our starboard bow. Our relative position gave us an opportunity to escape, but our valiant captain did not see fit to avail himself of it.

As she came down upon us, she appeared as large as a seventy-four; and we were not deceived respecting her size, for it afterwards proved that she was an old East-Indiaman, of eleven hundred tons burden, fitted out as a letter-of-marque for the West India trade, mounted with thirty-two guns, and furnished with a complement of one hundred and fifty men. She was called the *Admiral Duff*, commanded by Richard Strang, from St. Christopher and St. Eustatia, laden with sugar and tobacco, and bound for London.

Our captain ordered English colors to be hoisted, and the ship to be cleared for action. The shrill pipe of the boatswain summoned all hands to their duty. The bedding and hammocks of the sailors were brought up from between decks; the bedding placed in the hammocks, and lashed up in the nettings; our courses hauled up; the topgallant sails clewed down; and every preparation was made which a skilful officer could suggest, or active sailors perform.

The enemy approached till within musket shot of us. The two ships were so near to each other that we could distinguish the officers from the men; and I particularly noticed the captain, on the gangway, a noble-looking man, having a large gold-laced cocked hat on his head, and a speaking trumpet in his hand. Lieutenant Little possessed a powerful voice, and he was directed to hail the enemy; at the same time the quarter-master was ordered to stand ready to haul down the English flag and to hoist up the American. Our lieutenant took his station on the after part of the starboard gangway, and elevating the trumpet, exclaimed, "Hallo! Whence come you?" "From Jamaica, bound for London," was the answer. "What is the ship's name?" inquired the lieutenant. "The *Admiral Duff*," was the reply.

The English captain then thought it his turn to interrogate, and asked the name of our ship. Lieutenant Little, in order to gain time, put the trumpet to his ear, pretending not to hear the question. During the short interval thus gained, Captain Williams called upon the gunner to ascertain how many guns could be brought to bear upon he enemy. "Five," was the answer. "Then fire, and shift the colors," were the orders. The cannons poured forth their deadly contents, and with the first flash the American flag took the place of the British ensign at our masthead.

The compliment was returned in the form of a full broadside, and the action commenced. I was stationed on the edge of the quarter-deck, to sponge and load a six-pounder: This position gave me a fine opportunity to see the whole action. Broadsides were exchanged with great rapidity for nearly an hour; our fire, as we afterwards ascertained, produced a terrible slaughter among the enemy, while our loss was as yet trifling.

I happened to be looking for a moment towards the main deck, when a large shot came through our ship's side and killed Mr. Benjamin Scollay, a very promising young man, who was, I think, a midshipman. At this moment a shot from one of our marines killed the man at the wheel of the enemy's ship, and his place not being immediately supplied, she was brought alongside of us in such a manner as to bring her bowsprit directly across our forecastle. Not knowing the cause of this movement, we supposed it to be the intentions of the enemy to board us. Our boarders were ordered to be ready with their pikes to resist any such attempt, while our guns on the main deck were sending death and destruction among the crew of the enemy. Their principal object now seemed to be to get liberated from us, and by cutting away some of the rigging they were soon clear, and at the distance of a pistol shot.

The action was then renewed with additional fury; broadside for broadside continued with unabated vigor; at times so near to each other that the muzzles of our guns came almost in contact, then again at such a distance as to allow of taking deliberate aim. The contest was obstinately continued by the enemy, although we could perceive that great havoc was made among them and that it was with much difficulty that their men were compelled to remain at their quarters.

While Captain Williams was walking the quarter-deck, which he did during the whole action, a shot from the enemy struck the speaking trumpet from his hand, and sent it a considerable distance from him. He picked it up with great calmness of manner, and resumed his walk, without appearing to have been at all disturbed by the circumstance.

The action had now lasted about an hour and a half, and the fire from the enemy began to slacken, when we suddenly discovered that all the sails on her mainmast were enveloped in a blaze. The fire spread with amazing rapidity, and, running down the after-rigging, it soon communicated with the magazine, when her whole stern was blown off, and her valuable cargo emptied into the sea.

Our enemy's ship was now a complete wreck, though she still floated, and the survivors were endeavoring to save themselves in the only boat that had escaped the general destruction. The humanity of our captain urged him to make all possible exertion to save the miserable wounded and burnt wretches who were struggling for their lives in the water. Our boats had been much exposed to his fire, as they were placed in spars between the fore and main masts during the action, and had suffered considerable damage. The carpenters were ordered to repair them with the utmost expedition, and we got them out in season to take up fifty-five men, the greater part of whom had been wounded by our shot, or burned when the powder magazine exploded. These men exhibited a spectacle truly heart-rending to behold. Their limbs were mutilated by all manner of wounds, while some were burned to such a degree that the skin was nearly flayed from their bodies. . . .

Several of them suffered amputation of their limbs, while the wounds of the others were treated in a skilful manner, and every attention was paid to them which our circumstances would allow. Five of them died of their wounds and were committed to their watery graves.

Following the battle, Captain Williams decided to return to Boston for repairs to his ship. On the way he put into Penobscot Bay, where he landed the sick and wounded, leaving them in the care of a prosperous farmer who had several buildings that could house them and the surgeon's mate who was to look after them. While this was going on, particular care was taken by the ship's officers to see that none of the crew raided the property of the helpful farmer, but:

A copper-colored fellow, half Indian and half Negro, had seen a fatted calf in the farmer's barn, which he coveted to such a degree as to induce him to make a desperate attempt to make it a prize. The graceless rascal found another of the crew, whose appetite for veal overcame what little moral sense he possessed, ready to second him in the undertaking.

Late at night, after all hands had retired, Cramps, for that was the name of the principal adventurer, took a boat, went on shore, secured the calf, and returned to the ship without discovery. He came with great caution under the ship's bows, and hailed his fellow worker in iniquity, whom he expected to find ready with a rope to hoist the calf on board.

It so happened that, just at this time, our first lieutenant, Mr. Little, had occasion to come on deck, and the fellow who had been watching for the arrival of Cramps dodged out of sight and secreted himself. Cramps, mistaking the lieutenant for his coadjutor, hailed him in a low tone, requesting him to lower a rope as quick as possible. The lieutenant, suspecting some mischief, did as he was directed.

Cramps soon fixed a noose round the calf's neck and then cried out, "Now haul away, blast your eyes! My back is almost broke with carrying the creature so far down to the boat." The lieutenant obeyed, and a strong pull on his part, with some boosting by Cramps in the rear, soon brought the animal upon deck. Cramps immediately followed his prize and found, to his no small consternation, not only the calf but himself in the powerful grasp of the lieutenant. The calf was alive and uninjured, although Cramps had carried him a considerable distance from the barn to the boat, and came very near choking him when hoisting him up the side of the ship.

The calf enjoyed more comfortable quarters that night than his captor, for the latter was handcuffed and secured below for further punishment the next day. In the morning, the calf and the culprit were sent on shore and, when landed, Cramps was ordered to shoulder the calf and march to the farmer, confess, and ask his forgiveness; and then to return on board with the consolation that he should receive fifty lashes for his fault, and the assurance that he should be hung at the yard-arm if he was detected in such an undertaking again.

The result of this expedition proved Cramps to be the greater calf of the two. The fifty lashes were remitted at the solicitation of the kind-hearted farmer.

After repairs in Boston, the *Protector* set out once again. Winter was now coming on so, after a brief and fruitless cruise to the Grand Banks, it was decided to head for the West Indies, where the climate was warmer and the prospects of prize money better. On arrival, they put into Martinique for water, then steered for Dominica.

The next morning we espied an English sloop sailing to leeward of us close under the land. We gave chase, and soon came up with her. Our captain sent an officer and some men on board, and took possession of her. We then bore away with our prize for St. Juan in the island of Porto Rico, where our captain disposed of the sloop and cargo, part of which consisted of fourteen Negroes, who were sold to the Spaniards.

We then continued our cruise; and in a few days fell in with an English schooner, which we took, putting some men and a prize-master on board, ordering her for Boston, where she arrived in safety. After cruising for some time and not falling in with anything, our captain concluded to leave the West India seas and steer for the southern coast of the United States. We arrived off the bar of Charleston, South Carolina; and in the course of a few days fell in with a ship called the *Polly*, a letter-of-marque, of twenty guns, bound for London. We gave chase late in the afternoon and, as it soon grew dark, lost sight of her.

A thunderstorm came on, and all hands were watching for her; and by the flashes of the lightning we at length discovered her, standing in a different direction from what we had at first seen her pursuing. We accordingly shifted our course, and crowded sail in pursuit. By the aid of the lightning, we kept in her course, and soon came up with her.

"What ship is that, and where from?" roared our lieutenant through his trumpet, in a voice that bore no slight resemblance to the thunder which rolled above our heads.

"The ship *Polly*, from Charleston, bound to London," was the reply. The lightning, flashing upon her colors, showed that they were English, while the enemy had the same means of seeing the American flag flying at our masthead. We were completely prepared for action; the matches were lighted; the lanterns burning fore and aft; and all anxiously waiting for the commands of the officers. One shot was fired, and our captain ordered the enemy to "Haul down his colors, or he would blow him out of the water."

The appearance of our ship being formidable, our captain's demand was instantly complied with. Our boat was lowered, and a prize-master and crew put on board, who took possession of the sloop, and she was ordered for Boston.

From Charleston they headed north, capturing two more ships en route, and had just decided to return to Boston when their luck ran out: Two powerful and fast-sailing British frigates, the *May-Day* and the *Roebuck,* caught sight of the *Protector,* gave pursuit, and as soon as they had come up with her "sent an eighteen-pound shot over our quarter-deck. We were then ordered to strike our colors, or a broadside would be sent to enforce compliance with the demand. To attempt resistance against a force so much our superior would have been unjustifiable; and the flag of thirteen stars and stripes, under which we had sailed with much satisfaction and success, was reluctantly pulled down."

Up the River & Along the Sound

From the journal of Dr. James Thacher, now stationed at the military hospital near West Point on the Hudson River:

July 28, 1778. We are just informed of a new order of fanatics who have recently introduced themselves into our country, pretending to be a religious sect; but, if reports be true, they are a disgrace both to religion and human nature. They are called Shaking Quakers, or dancing Quakers, though they have no affinity either in principle or character to the established order of Quakers. Their leader is a female by the name of Ann Lee, niece of General Lee of our army. She is lately from England and has brought over with her a few followers, and has had the address to seduce several individuals of our country to her party. She is known by the appellation of Mother Ann, and pretends to have received a revelation from heaven. The method which they practice under the idea of religious worship is so obviously impious as to exceed the bounds of credibility; but we have the particulars from eyewitnesses, who have been admitted to their midnight orgies. They spend whole nights in their revels and exhibit the most unbecoming scenes, violating all rules of propriety and decency. Both sexes, nearly divested of clothing, fall to dancing in extravagant postures, and frequently whirl themselves round on one leg with inconceivable rapidity, till they fall apparently lifeless on the floor. . . . No imagination can form an adequate idea of the extravagant conduct of these infatuated people—a burlesque on all moral and religious principle.

✷

Down on the coast at New Haven, the Rev. Ezra Stiles was equally concerned by the activities of Jemima Wilkinson, a young woman who went about on horseback "dressed like a Man in a long Habit or Vestment coming up round the neck & tied there with a Ribbon," and followed by twelve disciples on foot. "Her eyes black and remarkably brilliant," ran another description, "her hair black and waving in beautiful ringlets upon her neck and shoulders." However, she was "not genteel in person" and "her first address to strangers is usually in a grum, masculine, authoritative tone of voice."

"When I was at Narragansett Sept. 24, 1779," continued Stiles,

✷

I heard much about Jemima, who calls herself the Public Universal Friend. She is now aged 21 & more, and came forth about 3 years ago, or 1776. After a Series of Weakness, Infirmity & Sickness she says she died & is no more Jemima Wilkinson, but upon her Restoration, which was sudden, the person of Jesus Christ came forth & now appears in her body, with all the miraculous Powers of the Messiah. She preached a while against Sin, War & fighting—with liberty went into Newport where, hearing the British asperse the Rebels, she told them publickly in the streets that those they called Rebels were not so great rebels as those profane persons were; for the one were rebels only against an Earthly King, they against the great King of Heaven. Coming out of Newport, she goes about preaching & warning all, declaring if they reject the Truth they will incur everlasting Damnation.

✷

Another diary entry by Stiles: "Lately at Dighton Jemima began the miracle of healing the sick, a woman long confined to her bed by

Infirmities. A company gathered—Jemima raised the Woman (who had great faith in her) from her bed & led her across the room. . . . But when the Miracle had proceeded thus far, Mrs. Dagget, a noisy religionist, began a warm dispute with Jemima & she left the Miracle unfinished and poor Mrs – -'s Limbs are as fixt as ever & she returned to her Confinement in bed."

At first Stiles was not sure what to make of the Public Universal Friend or of the reports that came in about Mother Ann Lee who, far from being related to the aristocratic General Charles Lee, was the daughter of an English blacksmith and had worked as a velvet cutter in a textile mill before God told her, in a vision, to come to America with her small band of Shaking Quakers. (God also told her that sex was to be shunned since it was the root of all evil—so much for the lurid tales reported by Dr. Thacher—and that at the Second Coming, due to happen soon, the Messiah would be a woman.) As a pacifist, Ann drew the attention of New York's Committee for Detecting and Defeating Conspiracies which ordered her arrest for "dissuading the friends to the American cause from taking up arms in the defense of their Liberties." But the arrest was unpopular, and after being held without trial for five months, she was released.

"It is remarkable that there should be two Women deceiving the public at the same time with two such different monstrous & sacrilegious Systems," wrote Stiles, but perhaps "these things may be wisely ordered in Providence to convince people of comparing all things with the sure word of Prophecy." But then, after further thought, it came to him that rather than being part of the divine plan, they were secret agents, Mother Ann in particular, "sent over into America by Ministerial Connexions, to excite Confusion & religious Disturbance and propagate principles against fighting & resisting Great Britain; and also to cover themselves with this cloud of religious Dust while they are acting as Spies among us & procuring & faithfully transmitting political Intelligence to the Enemy . . ."

Spies! And here in his innocence young Dr. Thacher had been naively supposing that the Shaking Quakers were up to nothing worse than midnight orgies! Next time, he would not be so easily deceived—and as it happened, there *was* a next time, for the young doctor was on the spot for the war's most notorious act of treason: General Benedict Arnold's attempt to betray the fortress at West Point to the British. When the plot was exposed following the arrest of Major John André, his British contact, Arnold had hastily fled to the *Vulture,* which was waiting for André in the Hudson River, and sailed away to New York, abandoning his young wife, Peggy Shippen, a famous beauty, member of one of Philadelphia's leading families, and, as was pretty obvious at the time and has since been confirmed, fully complicit in her husband's treachery. But now Peggy was in a tough spot. Not only had she been left on her own with her small baby, but George Washington and Alexander Hamilton had just arrived at West Point, and questions were bound to be asked.

"In about an hour and a half after Arnold had absconded," wrote James Thacher,

✸

Dr. Eustis, who had charge of the hospital in the vicinity, was called to the assistance of Mrs. Arnold, whose situation was alarming. He found her at the head of the stair-case, in great dishabille [i.e., half undressed], her hair disheveled, knowing no one, and frantic in the arms of her maid and Arnold's two aides, struggling to liberate herself from them. She was carried back to her chamber and fell into convulsions, which lasted several hours. In a lucid interval, she inquired of the doctor if General Washington was in the house, expressing a wish to see him. Believing that she intended to say something which would explain the secret of Arnold's unaccountable absence, he [Dr. Eustis] hastened below, gave notice of her request, and conducted the general to her chamber, who remained no longer than to hear her deny that he was General Washington, and to witness the return of her distraction.

✸

("That is not General Washington!" she exclaimed, according to Colonel Varick. "That is the man who was a-going to assist Colonel

Varick in killing my child!" Also: "General Arnold will never return!" she exclaimed. "He is gone forever, *there, there, there!*"—pointing at the ceiling—"the spirits have carried him up there—they have put hot irons in his head!")

Alexander Hamilton, a youth of twenty-three, swallowed the performance whole. "It was the most affecting scene I was ever witness to," he wrote in a letter to his fiancée, Elizabeth Schuyler. "She for a considerable time entirely lost her senses. . . . One moment she raved; another she melted into tears; sometimes she pressed her infant to her bosom and lamented its fate. . . . All the sweetness of beauty, all the loveliness of innocence, all the tenderness of a wife, and all the fondness of a mother showed themselves in her appearance and her conduct. We have every reason to believe she was entirely unacquainted with the plan . . ." Later in the letter he mentions that he visited Peggy the next morning when "she received us in bed, with every circumstance that could interest our sympathy"—doubtless a perfectly innocent statement, although other witnesses mention how the attractive Peggy had run through the halls almost naked and how her nightclothes kept parting when she was "in a frenzy."

It is hard to believe that Washington, a man of the world with a fondness for amateur theatricals, was taken in, but perhaps he saw an easy way out of a difficult situation. It was bad enough that a man he trusted had turned traitor. Then had come news that on his arrest Major André had been wearing civilian clothes rather than his uniform, which meant that he would have to be tried and executed as a spy. André was an extremely popular figure and the adjutant-general of the British army, and Washington must have known that he would receive many appeals for clemency, which he would have to turn down. It was all going to be extremely disagreeable. But by going along with the fiction that Peggy Arnold was mad, he could rid himself of at least one problem. And so, as Thacher noted, "Mrs. Arnold was permitted to go unmolested to her husband at New York"—where she soon made a miraculous recovery.

In New York the Arnolds doubtless crossed paths with the Riedesels who, after a long but comfortable parole in Virginia, where they had become friendly with their neighbors, the Jeffersons, had recently been exchanged and were now on their way to Canada, where the general was to take command of the Hessian forces. Along with the trusty Rockel and their small children, the Riedesel party included three Negro servants who had been taken from their owner because he was a rebel. Since then a royal proclamation had restored confiscated property to all those who "returned to duty" and took an oath of allegiance to the king. And so, "just as we were on the eve of embarking, we met with a great vexation," wrote the baroness.

✳

Our faithful Negroes—a man, his wife, and a young kinswoman—were reclaimed by their original owner on the grounds that he had once again become a loyal subject of the king. At the very moment that the signal was being given for our ship to leave, he arrived with an order that they should be handed over to him. As they had served us faithfully, and the man was a bad master who had treated them shockingly, great were the shrieks and lamentations of these poor people. The young maiden, Phillis by name, fainted, and when she recovered threw herself at my feet, embracing them so tightly with her clasped hands that she had to be forcibly pulled away. My husband offered to buy her, but when the owner saw how much we wanted to keep her he demanded thirty guineas, which was more than my husband wanted to pay. Had this not happened at the very moment of our departure we would probably have been able to keep her, but all we could do now was make them a gift of the clothing and the bedding we had provided them for the voyage. Such generosity, however, only served to affect them still more, and Phillis cried out, "If I live, I will come to you again, even to the end of the earth!" Later, this excellent young woman actually begged some other people who were going to Canada to take her with them and bring her to me, promising, "My good lady will be very glad to pay for my passage." She was quite right, but no one wanted to take the responsibility. My husband again tried to buy her, but he had only enough money on hand for this one purchase, and the owner now refused to sell Phillis separately, insisting that we buy all three. This was more than we could afford, so we had to refuse. Later on, however, we regretted that we had not made the sacrifice, as we found that female domestic servants in Canada were as stupid as they were clumsy.

As the Riedesels sailed up the Sound, with Loyalist-dominated Long Island on their right and Patriot-dominated Connecticut on their left, their ship must have intersected the course taken by a boat-load of Tories who, like Benedict Arnold, were taking advantage of wartime opportunities to enrich themselves. Arnold got £10,000 up front, with the promise of more to come, and the villains in the following story, taken from Barber's *Connecticut Historical Collections,* didn't do so badly either.

Mr. Dayton, who belonged to Long Island, was, on account of his attachment to the American cause, obliged to leave that island, and bring his effects with him to Bethany [on the Connecticut coast]. A number of men, some of his neighbors, were obliged to leave the island for the same cause, and brought a considerable quantity of money with them, and for a while resided in Mr. Dayton's house. With these facts the robbers appear to have become acquainted. At the time of the robbery, Mr. Dayton was absent on business at Boston, and the men who had been staying in the house had left the day before, so that there was no one in the house but his wife, Mrs. Phebe Dayton, three small children, and two colored servant children. About midnight, while they were all asleep, the window of the bedroom where Mrs. Dayton was sleeping was burst in at once; seven armed men rushed in, passed through the room, and immediately rushed into the chambers, expecting (it is supposed) to find the men who had left the day before. While they were upstairs, Mrs. Dayton went to the front part of the house, raised the window, and endeavored to alarm the neighbors. Mr. Hawley, the minister of the parish, and Dr. Hooker, the physician of the place, both lived within 20 rods distance, both had lights in their houses at the time, and both heard the alarm, but did not know from whence it proceeded. The robbers, hearing Mrs. Dayton, came down, and tearing a sheet into strips, tied her hands behind her, made her sit in a chair, and placed her infant, (about six months old) in her lap, while one of the robbers, placing the muzzle of his gun near her head, kept her in this position for about two hours, while the house was thoroughly ransacked from top to bottom. They found about 450 pounds in gold and silver, which belonged to Mr. Dayton, besides other valuable articles; what they could not conveniently carry off they wantonly destroyed, breaking in pieces all the crockery, furniture, &c. The whole amount of property carried off and destroyed, including bonds, notes, &c, amounted to five thousand pounds.

The robbers left the house about 2 o'clock, and went to a place in Middlebury, called Gunn-town, where they were secreted in a cellar by a family who were friendly to the British cause. While they were on their way to Gunn-town they met a young man by the name of Chauncey Judd, of Waterbury, on a bridge, who had been to see the young lady he afterwards married. Fearing he might discover them, they took him along with them. In the cellar kitchen where they were all secreted, there was a well. Into this they talked of putting Mr. Judd; but the old lady of the house begged they would not think of it, as it would spoil the water. They stayed in this house a number of days; afterwards they went to Oxford, where they were secreted for several days longer in a barn; from there they went to Stratford, took a whale boat, and crossed over to Long Island.

The Prisoner

When it became clear that the *Protector* was about to be captured by the British, her cabin steward, Ebenezer Fox, did the sensible thing. "Being unwilling that the stores, especially of crackers, cheese, and porter, should fall a prey to the appetite of the enemy, and not knowing when we should have an opportunity of enjoying such luxury again, I invited about a dozen of my friends into the store room where we exerted ourselves to diminish the quantity of this part of the prize. . . . The porter made us cheerful if not happy, and having eaten and drank to our satisfaction, we shook hands as friends soon to part, uncertain when we should meet again, and returned on deck."

After their capture the crew was transferred to the *Roebuck*, which then sailed for New York, anchoring off Sandy Hook. Here "preparations were made to examine prisoners to ascertain what part of them were Englishmen; or rather who among them would carry the appearance of able-bodied seamen. We were called up from the hold; ordered to the larboard side of the quarter-deck; thence marched in single file past a number of British officers on the starboard side; after that to the gangway, and down again into the hold. The object of thus moving in procession before the officers was to give them an opportunity to select such as they chose, to serve on board their ships. With fear and trembling we passed through this examination. Whenever a healthy, athletic-looking man passed by, he was hailed and accused of being an Englishman. In vain would his comrades attest to the fact of his being a native-born American; tell the place of his birth and the circumstances of his youth . . . it was all to no purpose. Sailors they wanted, and have them they would, if they set law and gospel at defiance."

About a third of the *Protector's* crew was thus conscripted into the Royal Navy. "The remainder of us were put on board of a wood coaster, to be conveyed on board the noted prison ship called the *Jersey*. . . . We proceeded slowly up the river towards our much-dreaded place of confinement, and at doubling a point we came in sight of the gloomy-looking hulk of the old *Jersey*, aptly named by the sailors 'The hell afloat.'"

The former seventy-four-gun man-of-war was

✷

moored with chain cables at the Wallabout, a lonely and unfrequented place on the shore of Long Island. Her external appearance was forbidding and gloomy. She was dismantled; her only spars were the bowsprit;

a derrick, that looked like a gallows, for hoisting supplies onboard; and also a flagstaff at the stern. Portholes were closed and secured. Two tiers of holes were cut through her sides, about two feet square and about ten feet apart, strongly guarded by a grating of iron bars.

After being detained in the boats alongside a little while, we were ordered to ascend to the upper deck of the prison ship. Here our names were registered, and the capacity in which we had served previous to our capture. Each of us was permitted to retain whatever clothing and bedding we had brought, after having been examined to ascertain that they contained no weapons nor money; and then we were directed to pass through a strong door, on the starboard side, down a ladder leading to the main hatchway.

I now found myself in a loathsome prison, among a collection of the most wretched and disgusting-looking objects that I ever beheld in human form. Here was a motley crew, covered with rags and filth; visages pallid with disease, emaciated with hunger and anxiety, and retaining hardly a trace of their original appearance. . . . Here, thought I, must I linger out the morning of my life, in tedious days and sleepless nights, enduring a weary and degrading captivity, till death shall terminate my sufferings.

The prisoners were divided into messes of six men each. The food was adequate in quantity but most of it was bad: "the bread was moldy and filled with worms," the pork had "the appearance of variegated fancy soap," the peas were "as indigestible as grapeshot . . . the flour and oatmeal were often sour," the beef looked like "dark mahogany." And the way the food was prepared made it even worse.

Cooking for the prisoners was done in a great copper vessel, that contained between two and three hogsheads of water set in a brick work. The form of it was square, and it was divided into two compartments by a partition. In one of these the peas and oatmeal were boiled; this was done in fresh water. In the other the meat was boiled, in salt water taken up from alongside the ship.

The *Jersey* from her size and lying near the shore was imbedded in the mud; and I do not recollect seeing her afloat during the whole time I was a prisoner. All the filth that accumulated among upwards of a thousand men was daily thrown overboard, and would remain there till carried away by the tide. The impurity of the water may be easily conceived; and in this water our meat was boiled.

It will be recollected too that the water was salt, which caused the inside of the copper to become corroded to such a degree that it was lined with a coat of verdigris. Meat thus cooked must in some degree be poisoned; and the effects were manifest in the cadaverous countenances of the emaciated beings who had remained on board for any length of time.

The prisoners were confined in the two main decks below. The lowest dungeon was inhabited by those prisoners who were foreigners, and whose treatment was more severe than that of the Americans. The inhabitants of this lower region were the most miserable and disgusting-looking objects that can be conceived. Daily washing with salt water, together with their extreme emaciation, caused their skin to appear like dried parchment. Many of them remained unwashed for weeks; their hair long and matted, and filled with vermin; their beards never cut, excepting occasionally with a pair of shears. . . . Their clothes were mere rags, secured to their bodies in every way that ingenuity could devise. Many of these men had been in this lamentable condition for two years, part of the time on board other prison-ships; and having given up all hope of being exchanged, had become resigned to their situation.

In the morning, the prisoners were permitted to ascend to the upper deck, to spend the day, till ordered below at sunset. A certain number, who were for the time called the "Working Party," performed in rotation the duty of bringing up the hammocks and bedding for airing, likewise the sick and infirm, and the bodies of those who had died during the night: of these there were generally a number every morning. After these services, it was their duty to wash the decks. Our beds and clothing were allowed to remain on deck till we were ordered below for the night; this was of considerable benefit, as it gave some of the vermin an opportunity to migrate from the quarters they inhabited.

About two hours before sunset, orders were given to the prisoners to carry all their things below, but we were permitted to remain above till we retired for the night into our unhealthy and crowded dungeons. At sunset, our ears were saluted with the insulting and hateful sound from our keepers, of "Down, rebels, down," and we were hurried below, the hatchways fastened over us, and we were left to pass the night amid the accumulated horrors of sighs and groans, of foul vapor, a nauseous and putrid atmosphere and almost suffocating heat.

Naturally, the thoughts of many prisoners turned to escape, but although there was only a small guard onboard and the ship was moored close to land, the neighboring area of Long Island was occupied by the British army and most of its inhabitants were Tories. Still, it was worth a try, and Fox and the other members of his mess soon came up with a plan that hinged on the "round house," a small and seldom-used toilet built under the forecastle, for the use of officers only. Although there was a lock on the door, some prisoners had picked it and no one had noticed.

At sunset, when the usual cry from the officer of the guard, "Down, rebels, down," was heard, instead of following the multitude down the hatchway, our mess, consisting of six, all Americans, succeeded in getting into the round house, excepting one. The round house was found too small to contain more than five; and the sixth man, whose name, I think, was Putnam, of Boston, concealed himself under a large tub, that happened to be lying near the place of our confinement. The situation of the five, as closely packed in the round house as we could stand and breathe, was so uncomfortable as to make us very desirous of vacating it as soon as possible.

We remained thus cooped up, hardly daring to breathe, for fear that we should be heard by the guard. The prisoners were all below, and no noise was heard above, save the tramp of the guard as he paced the deck.

It was customary, after the prisoners were secured below, for the ship's mate every night to search above: this however was considered a mere form, and the duty was very imperfectly executed. While we were anxiously waiting for the completion of this service, an event transpired that we had little anticipated, and which led to our detection.

One of the prisoners, an Irishman, made his arrangements to escape the same evening, and had not communicated with anyone on the subject, excepting a countryman of his, whom he persuaded to bury him up in the coal-hole, near the forecastle. Whether his friend covered him faithfully or not, or whether the Irishman thought that if he could not see anybody, nobody could see him; or whether, feeling uncomfortable in his position, he turned over to relieve himself, I know not; but when the mate looked into the coal-hole he espied something rather whiter than coal, which he soon ascertained to be the Irishman's shoulder. This discovery made the officer suspicious, and induced him to make a more thorough search than usual. We heard the uproar that followed the discovery, and the threats of the mate that he "would search every hole and corner." He soon arrived at the round house, and we heard him ask a soldier for the key. Our hopes and expectations were a little raised when we heard the soldier reply "there is no need of searching this place, for the door is kept constantly locked." But the mate was not to be diverted from his purpose, and ordered the soldier to get the key.

During the absence of the soldier, we had a little time to reflect upon the dangers of our situation; crowded together in a space so small as not to admit of motion, with no other protection than the thickness of a board; guarded on the outside by about a dozen soldiers armed with cutlasses; and the mate, considerably drunk, with a pistol in each hand, threatening to fire through, our feelings may be more easily conceived than described. There was but little time for deliberation; something must be immediately done.

In a whispering consultation of a few moments, we concluded that the safest course we could pursue would be to break out with all the violence we could exercise, overcome every obstacle, and reach the quarter-deck. By this time, the soldier had arrived with the key, and upon applying it, the door was found to be unlocked. We now heard our last summons from the mate, with imprecations too horrid to repeat, and threatening us with instant destruction if we did not immediately come out.

To remain any longer where we were would have been certain death to some of us; we therefore carried our hastily-formed plan into operation. The door opened outwards, and, forming ourselves into a solid body, we burst open the door, rushed out pell-mell, and making a brisk use of our fists knocked the guard heels over head in all directions, at the same time running with all speed for the quarter-deck. As I rushed out, being in the rear, I received a wound from a cutlass on my side, the scar of which remains to this day.

As nearly all the guard were prostrated by our unexpected sally, we arrived at our destined place without being pursued by anything but curses and threats. The mate exercised his authority to protect us from the rage of the soldiers [a task in which he was assisted by the captain's mistress (presumably an American)] whom the noise had brought upon deck, and whose sympathy was excited when she saw we were about to be murdered. She placed herself between us and the enraged guard, and made such an outcry as to bring the captain up, who ordered the guard to take their station at a certain distance and watch us narrowly. We were all put in irons, our feet being fastened to a long bar, a guard placed over us, and in this manner we were left to spend the night.

With disappointed expectations, we passed a dreary night. A cold fog followed by rain came on, to which we were exposed without any blankets or covering to protect us from the inclemency of the weather. Our sufferings of mind and body during that horrible night exceeded any that I have ever experienced. . . .

As for Putnam, who had hidden under the tub, "he was not suffered to remain long in suspense. A soldier lifted up the tub and, seeing the poor prisoner, thrust his bayonet into his body just above his hip, and then drove him to the quarter-deck to take his station in irons among us. The blood flowed profusely from his wound and he was soon after sent on board of the hospital ship, and we never heard anything respecting him afterwards."

OPPOSITE NUMBERS

While Ebenezer Fox languished onboard the *Jersey*, another British ship, the *Prince George* of ninety-eight guns, also docked in the East River, but downstream and on the Manhattan side. Among those onboard were Admiral Digby and a ruddy-faced midshipman who had asked his mess-mates to call him William Guelph but who as everyone knew was in fact Prince William Henry, later Duke of Clarence, fifteen years old, third son of King George III, and the first and only member of the royal family ever to have set foot in America. As a going-away present, the king had given him a Bible, urging him to read it regularly. Also on board was Midshipman the Rev. Henry Majendie, whose unlikely task was to tutor the young prince in the classics.

William, who would later become King William IV, the "Sailor King," was warmly received by the British forces and New York's Tories. "It is impossible to express the satisfaction felt by persons of all ranks from the ease, affability, and condescension shown by this most pleasing, manly youth, when he appears abroad amongst the happy and approved loyal subjects of the good and gracious king, our best and firmest friend, the Majesty of England, his Royal Highness' sincerely beloved father," wrote the Tory editor, James Rivington (but this was September 1781, and Rivington, who could not only write but also read the writing on the wall, was already in contact with Benjamin Tallmadge, head of Washington's secret service, with the result that *The Royal Gazette,* instead of going out of business, eventually became *Rivington's New York Gazette and Universal Advertiser*).

The governor and council were no less fulsome: "Your presence animates every loyal breast," they assured him in a formal address. "The glow in our own persuades us you are formed to win every heart. A rebellion that grew upon prejudice should sink at the approach of so fair a representation of the royal virtues. . . . Every man of spirit will be proud to fight in the cause for which you expose your life."

The prince was keen to get into the fighting. He had already been in action at the siege of Gibraltar and on his return to London had been toasted as "the intrepid boy"—when his parents took him to the theater, the cheering, hat-throwing, and handkerchief-waving had gone on for a quarter of an hour before the curtain could go up on Act I, Scene I of *The Tempest.* ("On a Ship at Sea. A Storm, with Thunder and Lightning. Enter a Shipmaster and a Boatswain" etc. etc.) But he arrived too late for the Battle of Chesapeake Capes and so, after wintering in New York, where he much enjoyed the ice-skating, he sailed with Admiral Rodney for the West Indies, where he took part in the Battle of the Saints, a smashing victory over the French but too late to affect the outcome of the American war. "A very fine youth, and bids fair to be a very shining Character in the profession," reported Captain Feilding. "His Activity & Attention to his Duty is much to be admired; he keeps a very strict watch, and is the first Aloft when any thing is going forward. Weather makes no difference to him." In fact so active was Prince William that he was injured in a fall and had to spend the following winter recuperating in Kingston, Jamaica, where he became the darling of planter society and where he once again came within hailing distance of that other young warrior, Ebenezer Fox. This is how that came about:

After other failed attempts to escape, it became clear to Ebenezer that he could either go on moldering away in a rotting prison hulk until he died of sickness or starvation, or he could sign on with one of the recruiting officers who often visited the *Jersey* with promises that anyone who joined the British army would not be required to fight against his own countrymen. One day

a recruiting officer came on board to enlist men for the 88th Regiment, to be stationed at Kingston, in the island of Jamaica. We had just been trying to satisfy our hunger upon a piece of beef, which was so tough that no teeth could make an impression on it, when the officer descended between decks and represented to us the immense improvement that we should experience in our condition if we were in his Majesty's service: an abundance of good food, comfortable clothing, service easy, and in the finest climate in the world, were temptations too great to be resisted by a set of miserable, half-starved, and almost naked wretches as we were.

The recruiting officer presented his papers for our signature. We stared at each other, and felt that we were about to do a deed of which we were ashamed, and which we might regret. Again we heard the tempting offers, and again the assurance that we should not be called upon to fight against our government or country; and, with the hope that we should find an opportunity to desert, of which it was our firm intention to avail ourselves when offered—with such hopes, expectations, and motives, we signed the papers, and became soldiers in his Majesty's service.

The British, of course, expected that their new recruits would try to desert and kept close guard on them until they arrived in Jamaica. Here they had nothing much to do other than drill, prepare to resist an attack by the French, and help hold the slaves in subjection, but the thought of escape never left them. One idea was to get onboard one of the British merchant ships in the harbor. Because their sailors were so often stolen by Royal Navy press-gangs, merchant ships were always short-handed and their captains would welcome able-bodied replacements, no questions asked; but this plan was betrayed. Soon afterwards, thanks to his apprenticeship to Mr. Bosson, wig maker and barber of Boston, Fox was "promoted to the high station of hairdresser and shaver for the officers," and as a result enjoyed many privileges. "But although my duties were light and I experienced much kind treatment, I still felt myself in a state of servitude—a prisoner, as it were, among the enemies of my country . . . I was willing to incur any hazard to obtain my liberty, and to breathe once more the air of freedom." True to his word, he and six others did manage to escape, and after a harsh and perilous cross-country journey over the island, they seized a small sailing boat, threw its crew into the sea (after first ascertaining that they could all swim), and landed in Cuba. There a friendly captain gave them free passage on a ship bound for Haiti; and on their arrival there, "with gratitude to the captain for his kindness, and to God for his mercies, we went on board of the American frigate *Flora*, of thirty-two guns, commanded by Henry Johnson, esq. of Boston." Captain Johnson, who was en route for France, was also short of men and offered to take them on at a wage of ten dollars a month. The others declined but Fox accepted. He liked the thought of visiting France, and even more he liked the prospect of earning some prize-money and of engaging the enemy— "an opportunity to pay off some old scores, which I fancied were then their due."

But first, one more adventure:

✦

There were lying in the port of Cap-François while we were there several Spanish and French ships of war, in want of men, waiting until they could obtain their complement, with the intention of sailing in quest of the British fleet. The Sunday previous to our sailing, I with several of the crew obtained permission to go on shore. . . . While we were enjoying ourselves over a bottle of good wine at a public house, a large press-gang of Frenchmen suddenly entered, and seizing upon all of us hurried us off into their boat; and notwithstanding our protestations against this outrage upon Americans, conveyed us on board of a French seventy-four. We immediately made known to the captain that we belonged to the *Flora*, and demanded to be released. But he showed no disposition to comply with our demands, saying that he was in want of hands and that we should receive as good pay and treatment on board of his ship as in our own.

This was poor consolation for us. It was provoking as well as distressing to be thus imprisoned as it were in the sight of our own ship; but having no communication with her, we could not give any information of our situation. We were aware that the combined fleet was to sail in days; and although we had no objection to fighting our old enemy, the British, we yet had some choice as it respected the company we fought in, and had but little desire to obey the orders of French officers, or to mingle our blood with that of their crew.

Of our impressed party, consisting of four or five, not one could swim except myself. We conferred together and came to the conclusion that the only chance we had for escape consisted in my attempting to swim in the night to the *Flora*, which lay about a quarter of a mile from the seventy-four. I had no fear of not being able to swim that distance; the only danger I apprehended was from the sharks, which were very abundant in those waters.

I agreed with my companions that this appeared to be the only practicable method of escape; and after some urging on their part, and some flattery of the honor I should gain by the achievement, I concluded to undertake it that night. Late at night I went on deck, accompanied by one of my friends, and finding the sentinel asleep we went forward, and divesting myself of my jacket but keeping on my hat, shirt, and trousers I slid down by the cable quietly into the water, and struck out for the *Flora*.

Of all the dangers to which I had been exposed in the course of my adventures, I consider this the greatest. The horror of mind I experienced whilst swimming is indescribable. My agitation was so great that I wonder that I did not sink through fear of being devoured. I imagined a shark at my feet every time I threw them out. I exerted myself with so much vigor that in a very short time I was alongside of the *Flora*, but in so exhausted a state that I could hardly raise myself over the side of the boat, which floated alongside of the ship. I threw myself into the bottom, from which I was scarcely able to move for some time.

After I had recovered a sufficient degree of strength, I ascended the side of the ship, and finding no one on deck, I lay down in my wet clothes, and putting my hat under my head slept soundly all night. When I awoke in the morning, I found that I was unable to move in consequence of my clothes adhering to the pitch, which the heat of the climate caused to ooze from the seams in the deck. By using considerable exertion, and rolling one way and the other, I at length liberated myself from my confinement, and stood erect once more on the deck of an American ship.

✳

The British surrender at Yorktown, Virginia, October 20, 1781.

CHAPTER SIX

The South and Yorktown

For its final throes the war moved south. This had long been the battleground for yet another conflict—that of white owners against black slaves—fought on one side with armed force and draconian laws and on the other with passive resistance and the occasional violent but unsuccessful insurrection. Since 1775 the South had also been the scene of a bitter civil war between Patriots and Loyalists, intermittent and inconclusive but flaring up angrily with the arrival of the regular British army in South Carolina early in 1780. After taking and garrisoning Charleston this army would then set forth in a generally northern direction with no specific strategy other than to show the flag, encourage the Loyalists and give battle to the Americans whenever the occasion offered, sometimes winning, sometimes losing, but always diminishing in numbers. After a year and a half of this, their commander, Lord Cornwallis, decided to take a break and await reinforcements, and that a good place to do this would be Yorktown.

As disasters go, the British surrender to a combined American and French force was not, in military terms, so very terrible—no worse than Saratoga, from which they had recovered. But from a political point of view it was the end. As usual in those days, the British were willing enough to go on fighting the French, but the will to continue the war against their American cousins was gone.

SOUTHERNERS

In the war of words that preceded and accompanied the actual war, the British made great sport of those who claimed freedom for themselves but denied it to others. "How is that we hear the loudest yelps for liberty among the drivers of Negroes?" asked Dr. Johnson in his thunderbolt pamphlet, *Taxation No Tyranny*. A fair question, and one to which Americans had various answers:

→ Agree. "I wish most sincerely there was not a Slave in the province," wrote Abigail Adams early in the war. "It always appear'd a most iniquitous scheme to me—fight ourselfs for what we are daily robbing and plundering from those who have as good a right to freedom as we have." But apart from a small though growing number of Quakers, few others shared this opinion.

→ Stop being a driver of Negroes. The Virginia aristocrat, Robert Carter of Nomini Hall, freed nearly five hundred of his slaves during his lifetime; and in the final draft of his will, George Washington made provision for his slaves to be freed on his death. But these were exceptions. More typical were Thomas Jefferson, who talked loftily but clung to his property, and Patrick "Give me Liberty or give me Death" Henry, who agreed that slavery was "repugnant to humanity" but acknowledged that "I am drawn along by the general inconvenience of living without them."

→ Blame others. Among the "assemblage of horrors" that Jefferson included in his draft of the Declaration of Independence was the "piratical warfare" that "the *Christian* king of Great Britain" had waged against "a distant people who never offended him, captivating & carrying them into slavery in another hemisphere." However, to please the southern states this section was omitted. And then there was Henry Laurens, Patriot merchant of Charleston and future president of the Continental Congress: "You know, my Dear Sir," he wrote to his son John in August 1776, "I abhor Slavery. I was born in a Country where Slavery had been established by British Kings & Parliaments. . . . Not less than £20,000 Sterling would all my Negroes produce if sold at public Auction to-morrow. I am not the man who enslaved them, they are indebted to English Men for that favour."

→ Quote the Bible. Did not the Good Book say, "Servants, be obedient to your masters?" (And slaves certainly counted as servants.) And where did God, or Jesus, or the Apostles, or anyone else in authority say a single word condemning slavery? If slavery was against the Divine Will, why had it been allowed to flourish in all ages and in all countries? And while on the subject of the Bible, never forget that, as Phillis Wheatley had put it in her poem ("'Twas Mercy brought me from my Pagan land,/ Taught my benighted soul to understand/ That there's a God, that there's a Saviour too . . ."), to bring pagan Africans to a Christian country was in fact doing them a big favor.

→ Then there was the humanitarian argument. Just look, for example, at the history of Georgia. Founded by well-meaning English philanthropists, Georgia was to be a charity colony where debtors and other "miserable wretches, lately relieved out of jail" could make a fresh start in life as hardworking settlers on land that would be given to them virtually free. Irish Catholics, German Protestants, and even criminals spared the gallows were also welcome, but no Africans. This was because, as General Oglethorpe, the moving spirit in establishing the colony, put it, using the words "slave" and "Negro" interchangeably, "Wherever Negroes are, though never so few, the white men grow idle." But it was not long before petitions from discontented Georgians were on their way to London complaining of the inhumanity of the no-slavery rule. The summers were hot and long, one petition explained, "and vast perspiration occasions such an expense of spirits that no Englishman can work in the field without endangering his life, and summer is the time when all the field work is done. How shocking must it be even to a person of the least humanity to see his own countrymen, perhaps his own townsmen, labouring in the corn or rice field, broiling in the sun, pale and fainting under the excessive heat, and instances there have been of their dying on the spot! How terrible must such a sight be to any man who has the least grain of compassion within him! How must it make his heart flow with sorrow to see the misery of his fellow creatures!" But let the reader of the petition "turn his eyes 'round to the Negroes in the same fields. There he will see the reverse. He will see the utmost vigours exerted in every act. They go through their work with pleasure. They welcome the rising sun with their songs and when in his meridian their spirits are at the highest. They are far more happy here than in their own country. There they are abject slaves, their lives and whatever else they have are every hour in the hands of some petty tyrant. Here, it is true, they are property of particular men but their lives are in no danger. They are sure of being fed and clothed, it being their masters' interest to take the utmost care of them . . ."

→ Finally, the economic argument. "There is a great deal of difference between the expense of white servants and of Negroes," ran another of the Georgia petitions, "for Negroes can endure this climate almost without any clothes, only a cap, jacket, and pair of trousers made of some coarse woollen stuff in the winter and one pair of shoes; whereas white men must be clothed as Europeans and proportionable to the season all the year throughout. And then as to their diet, the charge of maintaining Negroes is much less than of white men, for the first live in good plight and health upon salt, Indian corn and potatoes which they raise themselves with no expense to the master but the seed, and have nothing to drink but water; whereas white men must be fed with flesh meat, bread, and other victuals suitable to the European diet which they have been used to and bred up with from their infancy, and must likewise have beer or other strong liquors in due quantities for their drink, otherwise they turn feeble and languid and are not capable to perform their work."

In 1770 Lieutenant Governor William Bull sent to Lord Hillsborough a long and optimistic report on South Carolina. "Agriculture is in a very prosperous state. . . . The introducing rice hath proved a very fortunate circumstance to this province as it is a grain which yields the most plentiful harvest when the ground is overflowed with water. . . . Many large swamps, otherwise useless and affording inaccessible shelter for deserting slaves and wild beasts, have been drained and cultivated. . . . The amount of our indigo is about five hundred thousand pounds weight a year." Hemp, flour, and tobacco were also doing well. As to the Indians "the trade of the Cherokees is not very beneficial. This nation commands the attention of government more upon political than commercial considerations, as they form a barrier against powerful incursions of Indians of the Ohio and Illinois tribes and as a counterbalance against the Creeks in case of a war with them. I cannot quit the Indians without mentioning an observation that has often raised my wonder: that in this province, settled in 1670, then swarming with tribes of Indians, there remains now, except the few Catawbas, nothing of them but their names within three hundred miles of our sea coast."

Some other facts and figures:

The number of negroes returned in last tax is seventy-five thousand one hundred and seventy-eight. The number of dwelling-houses in town [Charleston] taken this summer was one thousand two hundred and ninety-two, and the white inhabitants five thousand and thirty, and the black five thousand and eight hundred and thirty-one, employed as domestic servants and mechanics [workmen]. . . . Our commerce keeps equal pace with our agriculture in improvement. . . . We employ near five hundred sail of vessels to carry off the superfluous produce and import supplies for the wants of the province. Though by the annual importation of three or four thousand negroes the balance of trade may be against us, yet we cannot be considered in debt as the negroes remain part of our stock and are the means of increasing our riches.

As to security,

Our militia is now increased to about ten thousand men, divided into ten regiments. . . . In great danger the militia is to be reinforced with a number of trusty negroes (and we have many such) not exceeding one third of the corps they are to join. To observe good order among the slaves one-fourth of the militia must be left at home. . . . The interior quiet of the province is provided for by small patrols drawn every two months from each company who do duty by riding along roads and among negro-houses in all districts in every parish once a week or as occasion requires.

Also:

There is a particular system of laws adapted to the condition of slaves called our Negro Act, passed in 1740, calculated to punish offending and to protect abused slaves. The jurisdiction is lodged in two justices and five freeholders in capital, and one justice and three free-holders in inferior cases. The expense of these trials is defrayed by the public, and in order to discourage men from screening their criminal slaves from justice a certain sum equal to the value of a new negro is allowed to the master where his slave is executed. The royal humanity has often recommended to governors that a white man who murders a negro should be punished with death. It is so in all the English colonies north of Maryland where the number of negroes is small. But in Maryland, Virginia, and all southern colonies and islands it has been thought dangerous to the public safety to put them on a footing of equality in that respect with their masters, as it might tempt slaves to make resistance and deter masters and managers from inflicting punishment with an exemplary severity, though ever so necessary.

By the happy temperament of justice and mercy in our Negro Acts and the general humanity of the masters, the state of slavery is as comfortable in this province as such a state can be; not but there are monsters of cruelty sometimes appear, who are punished and abhorred. To the mildness of law and prudent conduct of masters and patrols I attribute our not having had an insurrection since the year 1739. . . .

Insurrections were hard to organize and execute in what, from the slave's point of view, was a police state, but individual acts of resistances were widespread. Of these the most common was depriving the owner of his property by running away, especially from masters who were "monsters of cruelty"—and who may have been abhorred but were almost never punished. Many of the runaways were recaptured, but not David George, who after the war served as a Baptist minister in Nova Scotia and then in Sierra Leone. During a stopover in England, he told his story to two fellow Baptists, who then arranged for its publication. This is how he begins:

I was born in Essex County, Virginia, about fifty or sixty miles from Williamsburg, on Nottaway River, of parents who were brought from Africa but who had not the fear of God before their eyes. The first work I did was fetching water and carding of cotton. Afterwards I was sent into the field to work about the Indian corn and tobacco till I was about nineteen years old. My father's name was John and my mother's name Judith. I had four brothers and four sisters who, with myself, were all born in slavery. Our master's name was Chapel—a very bad man to the Negroes. My older sister was called Patty. I have seen her several times so whipped that her back has been all corruption, as though it would rot. My brother Dick ran away but they caught him and brought him home, and as they were going to tie him up he broke away again, and they hunted him with horses and dogs till they took him up, and they hung him up in a cherry tree in the yard by his two hands, quite naked except his breeches, with his feet about half a yard from the ground. They tied his legs close together and put a pole between them, at one end of which one of the owner's sons sat to keep him down, and another son at the other. After he had received five hundred lashes or more they washed his back with salt water and whipped it in, as well as rubbed it in with a rag, and then directly set him to work in pulling off the suckers of tobacco. I also have been whipped many times on my naked skin, and sometimes till the blood has run down over my waistband. But the greatest grief I then had was to see them whip my mother, and to hear her on her knees begging for mercy. She was master's cook, and if they only thought she might do anything better than she did, instead of speaking to her as to a servant, they would strip her directly and cut away. I believe she was on her deathbed when I got off, but I have never heard since. Master's rough and cruel usage was the reason for my running away. . . .

In his indictment of George III, Jefferson had also complained that, even as he wrote, the king was "now exciting those very people to rise in arms among us, and to purchase that liberty of which he has deprived them, by murdering the people on whom he has also obtruded them . . ." And it was certainly true that in November 1775, Lord Dunmore, the last royal governor of Virginia, "being compelled by my duty to this most disagreeable but now absolutely necessary step," had issued a proclamation that not only declared martial law but went on to "farther declare all indented servants, Negroes, or others appertaining to rebels, *free*, that are able and willing to bear arms, they joining his Majesty's troops as soon as may be, for the more speedily reducing this colony to a proper sense of their duty to his Majesty's crown and dignity . . ."

Reporting back to London, Dunmore wrote that "there are already between two and three hundred come in, and those I form into corps as fast as they come in, giving them white officers and non-commissioners in proportion." The new unit was called "Lord Dunmore's Ethiopian Regiment," and bore the insignia "Liberty to Slaves." Along with the all-white Queen's Own Loyal Regiment that he had also recently recruited, "I make no doubt of getting men enough to reduce this colony to a proper sense of their duty." But the two new regiments were routed at the battle of Great Bridge in December of 1775, after which Dunmore withdrew himself and his forces to the safety of some British warships, where most of the "Ethiopians" died of smallpox.

But though its military results were feeble, the proclamation did more "to work an eternal separation between Great Britain and the Colonies than any other expedient which could possibly have been thought of," wrote Edward Rutledge. And in a letter to a London newspaper a Philadelphian wrote, "Hell itself could not have vomitted anything more black than his design of emancipating our slaves . . . . We know not how far the contagion may spread. The flame runs like wildfire through the slaves, who are more than two for one white in the Southern Colonies. The subject of their nocturnal revels, instead of music and dancing, is now turned upon their liberty. I know not whence these troubles may lead us." Meeting at Williamsburg in January 1776, the Virginia Convention passed a resolution warning—or rather, reminding—slaves who "take up arms against the good people of this colony" that they faced punishment by death, "without benefit of clergy," but promising that all those "who have taken this unlawful and wicked step may return in safety to their duty" and receive a full pardon, provided they surrendered at once.

As was pointed out in a letter to the *Virginia Gazette*, Dunmore's Proclamation offered freedom only to those who actually enlisted in his regiment.

✳

The aged, the infirm, the women and children are still to remain the property of their masters, of masters who will be provoked to severity should part of their slaves desert them. . . . But should there be any amongst the negroes weak enough to believe that Lord Dunmore intends to do them a kindness, and wicked enough to provoke the fury of the Americans against their defenseless fathers and mothers, their wives, their women and children, let them only consider . . . what must be their fate should the English prove conquerors in this dispute. If we can judge of the future from the past, it will not be much mended. Long have the Americans, moved by compassion, and actuated by sound policy, endeavoured to stop the progress of slavery. Our Assemblies have repeatedly passed acts laying heavy duties upon imported negroes, by which they meant altogether to prevent the horrid traffick; but their humane intentions have been as often frustrated by the cruelty and covetousness of a set of English merchants, who prevailed upon the king to repeal our kind and merciful acts, little indeed to the credit of his humanity. Can it then be supposed that the Negroes will be better used by the English, who have always encouraged and upheld this slavery, than by their present masters, who pity their condition, who wish in general to make it as easy and comfortable as possible, and who would willingly, were it in their power, or were they permitted, not only prevent any more Negroes from losing their freedom, but restore it to such as have already unhappily lost it?

✳

(There was some truth in this. The London government had indeed vetoed a Virginia law imposing an import tax on slaves, but the motive for the law was not compassion but the high birth rate among slaves already there; the surplus crop could be profitably sold to other colonies—but not if undercut by cheap imports.)

Throughout the war the generals and politicians struggled with the question of whether blacks should be recruited into the Continental Army; at first they were allowed to serve, then they were expelled, and then, as it got harder and harder to find whites willing to enlist, they were allowed in again. Also, different states followed different policies. In Rhode Island slaves who were willing to enlist were bought from their masters and promised their freedom at the end of the war; but owners in the South were no more willing to arm their slaves than was Mrs. Montagu to see her "black regiment" of coal miners with weapons in their hands. But there was a third way, as set forth in South Carolina's Act to Procure Recruits and Prevent Desertion: "As an encouragement to those who are willing to serve their country in the defense of her rights and liberties," the law provided that "every able-bodied [white] recruit between the ages of sixteen and forty-five years . . . shall be entitled to and shall receive for each and every year's service, the bounty of one sound Negro between the age of ten years and forty . . ." If the recruit were killed, his heirs would receive the bounty. Deserters got nothing. Slaves to pay the bounty were to come from estates confiscated from Loyalists.

Like many another slave owner, Henry Laurens was convinced that he was a good master and in return was looked up to with loyalty and affection: "My Negroes there [in Georgia] are strongly attached to me, so are all mine in this Country [South Carolina]." He may have been right, but it seems unlikely. A different view of matters was expressed by the Hessians. Though used to brutal treatment, many were shocked by what they saw in South Carolina. "The field Negroes, who till the soil, are often treated worse than an ox in Europe," wrote Quartermaster Carl Bauer. "They go about almost naked, with scarcely an old rag to cover their private parts. Their living quarters are miserable huts made of logs piled one top of another, without any fireplace or hearth. For food they get a quart of corn or rice a day. Their punishment is harsh and inhuman; for a simple act of disobedience they are pulled up with their hands tied together and most cruelly flogged on the naked back. If a master kills a slave, nobody pays much attention. If a Negro should but raise his hand to a white person he is put to death." And Lieutenant Wiederholt: "The Negroes are kept from all knowledge of the Word of God and made to believe that they are of a lower race of mankind, meant only to be slaves. The barbaric way they are treated is a disgrace to all mankind. I was horrified by what I saw."

CHARLESTON

The Hessians, along with a large British force, were in South Carolina to execute yet another winning strategy devised in London by Lord George Germain and King George III. Writing to General Sir Henry Clinton in March 1778, Germain had explained that because of the well-established fact that the South was teeming with Loyalists, the region would be easy to conquer. If even a small force were to land at Cape Fear "and make an impression on North Carolina, it is not doubted that large numbers of the inhabitants would flock to the King's standard, and that His Majesty's Government would be restored." The same would happen in the neighboring colonies. "The conquest of these provinces is considered by the King as an object of great importance in the scale of the war, and their possession might be easily maintained, and thereby a very valuable branch of commerce [tobacco] would be restored to this country and the rebels deprived of a principal resource for the support of their foreign credit, and of paying for the supplies they stand in need of." Diversionary attacks should be made into Virginia and Maryland, which would be easy enough as "the great number of deep inlets and navigable rivers in these provinces expose them in a peculiar manner to naval attacks, and must require a large force to be kept on foot for their protection, and disable them from giving any assistance to the Carolinas." Finally: "Should the success we may reasonably hope for attend these enterprizes, it might not be too much to expect that all America to the south of the Susquehanna would return to their allegiance, and in the case of so happy an event, the northern provinces might be left to their own feelings and distress to bring them back to their duty . . ."

A year and a half later, Clinton, bold in advice but cautious in command, embarked for Charleston. This would not be the first time the British were to attack it. That had been early in 1776, a humiliating fiasco when several of Admiral Sir Peter Parker's ships ran aground and were savaged by the guns on Sullivan's Island, commanded by then Colonel Moultrie. The next attempt was made in 1779 shortly after the British had taken Savannah. While Moultrie and General Lincoln went down to Georgia to counterattack, a British force came north and demanded Charleston's immediate surrender. Fearful that the British presence would encourage an uprising by the town's slaves, who outnumbered the white inhabitants, the council was all set to cave in when news suddenly came that Lincoln and Moultrie were on their way back, whereupon the British departed. So this was the third try, and Clinton, who had been in command of the land forces on the first attempt and still smarted from the humiliating memory, was determined that this time there would be no mistakes.

The Americans were of course expecting them.

"The enemy have worked with untiring effort on the fortification of the city," wrote the Hessian Captain Hinrichs.

One trench, one battery after another, was thrown up, springing like mushrooms from the soil. From the point of the city along the Ashley River alone I counted twenty-two gun embrasures. The inhabitants have been moving from their houses on this side of the city to the eastern side because several days ago, when our six-gun battery on Fenwick's Point opened fire on the enemy's ships in the mouth of the Ashley, they found that we could easily throw heated shot into the city. Since we landed their garrison has been reinforced by six hundred men from North Carolina. Their regular troops amount to three thousand men; the rest are militia, Negroes, and inhabitants of the city, as well as about one hundred French.

✵

According to *The Women of the American Revolution*, Mrs. Rebecca Motte, the wealthy and matronly mother-in-law of General Pinckney, had also been doing her bit.

✵

When an attack upon Charleston was apprehended, and every man able to render service was summoned to aid in throwing up entrenchments for the defense of the city, Mrs. Motte, who had lost her husband at an early period of the war, and had no son to perform his duty to the country, dispatched a messenger to her plantation, and ordered down to Charleston every male slave capable of work. Providing each, at her own expense, with proper implements and a soldier's rations, she placed them at the disposal of the officer in command. The value of this unexpected aid was enhanced by the spirit which prompted the offer.

✵

Laying siege to a town was a standard procedure of European warfare, and the British and Hessian engineers knew just what to do. First, the town was summoned to surrender, but, as expected, the summons was refused and the siege officially began. "We opened the first parallel with three redoubts the night of April 1–2," wrote Captain Hinrichs, who was a great one for details. "Every redoubt required sixteen mantelets, which were carried by 400 workmen who were accompanied by another 100 with tools. Thus each face required 125 workmen, with whom were one field officer and five captains, which made a total of 500 men per redoubt and a grand total of 1,500 workmen for the night." April 3: "Toward noon the enemy opened a masked battery of two brass 18-pounders in the demi-bastion to the right of the city gate but did no damage. Toward evening they opened two 12-pounders in the advanced work of their left wing, which raked the road and No.3. This night the trench was continued to the left of No.5 in an oblique line, where a battery (No.6) was begun for the nine cannon with masked embrasures. No.2 was finished, and farther to the right, towards the Ashley, a new redoubt (No.1) was begun. The latter lay nearer the enemy than the others and was separated from the first parallel (No.3) by a bog . . ."

And so it went on for almost six weeks. As well as mantelets, demi-bastions and redoubts, siege-work also featured banquettes, fascines, barbettes, barbettes, hornworks, half-moons, abatis, glacis, traverses, saps, and redans. The gunnery included enfilading fire, flanking shot, ricochet fire, reverse fire, hot fire, and cold fire. As a conscientious and brave professional officer, Hinrichs seems to have relished every moment of it, but for most others, including those who were besieged, it must have been a tedious business.

On May 8, with the besiegers' trenches now up next to the town's defensive ditch and with the British fleet in control of the harbor, Charleston was once again summoned to surrender. Two hours were allowed for the offer to be considered. Some of the terms were immediately accepted and the time was extended, but then, quite unexpectedly, wrote Hinrichs, "the enemy rang all the bells in the city and after shouting 'Hurray!' three times opened a furious cannonade which they kept up until dark. Most of the fire went wide, and it is my opinion that the entire garrison were drunk." The fire was returned and fighting went on until May 11, when "a flag of truce came out of the town; but our fire was so fierce that we did not see them coming, and they had to withdraw. At two in the afternoon the enemy hoisted a large white flag on the hornwork [an outwork consisting of two demi-bastions connected by a wall] and sent out a second flag, offering capitulation of the city on the terms we had proposed.

"May 12: At two o'clock our commanders rode into the city accompanied by many staff officers and adjutants. They were followed by two grenadier companies, the 7th British, commanded by Lt. Col. Hope, and the Hessian guard commanded by Lt. Col. von

Linsing, each with a battery of fieldpieces. Then came the King's flag. At the city's gate our generals were received by Maj. Gen. Lincoln on horseback and Maj. Gen. Moultrie on foot, who surrendered the city. As the British grenadiers came through the gate, our oboists played 'God Save the King.'"

Once he had had a chance to look around, Hinrichs liked Charleston: "No other American city can compare with it in the beauty of its houses and the splendor and taste displayed in them." Methodical as ever, he counted the number of houses and came up with a total of 1,020 "built along broad unpaved streets intersecting one another at right angles, each house having a garden and standing twenty to one hundred paces from each other." Of the streets, Broad Street was the finest: "It is one hundred feet wide and one thousand, one hundred and twenty feet long, and extends from the Cooper to the Ashley, dividing the city into two parts. The principal street is King Street, eighty feet wide and three thousand, seven hundred and thirty feet long." He also took note of a statue of William Pitt, erected to honor his role in the repeal of the Stamp Act. The statue was eight feet high, the pedestal ten; the right hand had once held a stone replica of the Magna Carta, but during the siege it "had been knocked off by a stray cannonball."

The worst damage did not occur until after the surrender, when the American militia were paraded and ordered to lay down their arms. General Moultrie watched them do so. "When the British received their arms, they put them in wagons and carried them to a store-house where we had deposited our fixed ammunition (about 4,000 pounds); and although they were informed by some of our officers that the arms were loaded . . . yet, in taking them out of the wagons they threw them so carelessly into the store that some at last set fire to the powder, which blew up the whole guard of fifty men, and many others that were standing by; their carcasses, legs, and arms were seen in the air, and scattered over several parts of the town. One man was dashed with violence against the steeple of the new independent church, which was at a great distance from the explosion, and left the marks of his body there for several days. The houses in the town received a great shock, and the window sashes rocked as if they would tumble out of the frames."

According to another Hessian, Captain von Ewald, a fire following the explosion "destroyed six houses, including a brothel and the poorhouse. Over two hundred persons lost their lives in the disaster.... During the years that I have been a soldier, I have witnessed many a sad spectacle of war, but never such a horrible one as this. Some twenty charred and wounded people were dug out of the debris. Others had been blown against a neighboring church and were so mutilated that they no longer looked like human beings. Many others were half dead, suffering from burns and writhing like worms on the ground. Parts of human bodies were scattered about here and there. A battlefield could not have looked worse. Five thousand muskets and the swords of the captured officers melted in the heat of the explosion, flying up into the air and killing and wounding many at a considerable distance."

The Harum-Scarum Boys

"Dear Godfather," wrote Baikia Harvey, aged sixteen, in a letter written early in the war and not long after he had arrived in South Carolina from his birthplace in the Orkney Islands, "tell all my country people not to come hear, for the Americans will kill them like deer in the woods & they will never see them. They can lie on their backs & load & fire & every time they draw sight at anything they are sure to kill or criple, & they run in the woods like horses. I seed the Liberty Boys take between two & three hundred Torrys and one Liberty man would take & drive four or five before him just as the shepards do the sheep in our country, & they have taken all their arms from them and putt the head men in gaile so that they will never be able to make head against them any more."

For his part, however, Baikia would stay where he was, despite the danger: America was a "good poor man's country," and he had recently been hired by a merchant named Hammond and "he & his lady uses me vere well & gives me cloaths & I ride with my master & loves them both." But he wanted no part of the fighting, least of all against American riflemen who "can kill the bigness of a dollar betwixt two & three hundred yards distance."

Between the siege of Charleston and the British surrender at York-town, two very different kinds of warfare were fought: one by the regular American and British armies, with set-piece battles whose outcome favored one side or the other (Camden, Cowpens, Guilford Court House) and an irregular, uncoordinated, inconclusive guerrilla war of partisan raids and skirmishes, often fought with great brutality. Both parties "raised their inveteracy to so great a height that they carried on the war with savage cruelty," wrote General Moultrie. "Although they had been friends, neighbors, and brothers, they had no feelings of humanity left. When the British party prevailed after the surrender of Charleston . . . some of the most abandoned characters came from their hiding places, called themselves king's men, and committed the most violent acts of cruelty and injustice." Later, when "the injured and exasperated Whigs" got the upper hand, "sweet revenge comes now to seek her vengeance." To sum up: "The conduct of those two parties was a disgrace to human nature."

Among those fighting on the American side were Daniel Collins of York County, South Carolina, and at least one (James) of the twenty children that he had fathered on his two wives. A school-teacher in winter and a farmer in the summer, and at all times a strict sabbatarian, Daniel Collins had emigrated from Ireland as a young man and after a stint in Philadelphia had settled in the back country. His son James, the narrator, who described himself as "a wayfaring man," had been briefly apprenticed to a tailor, a shoemaker, and a weaver; but he disliked all three trades and was much happier when Captain Moffitt took him on as a scout for the local militia. Unsuspected because he was still not much more than a boy, James gathered information about the activities of the local Tories, but so far had done no actual fighting. This, however, was soon to change.

✳

So soon as Charleston fell, there was a proclamation for all to come forward, submit, and take protection; peace and pardon should be granted. In order to expedite the business, there were officers sent out in various directions, with guards or companies of men, to receive the submission of the people. Vast numbers flocked in and submitted; some through fear, some through willingness, and others, perhaps, through a hope that all things would settle down and war cease. But not so; there was some conditions annexed that some of the patriots of the day could not submit to and therefore determined to hold out a little longer.

Among the officers sent out on this occasion there was one Lord Hook, who came up and stationed himself at or near Fishing Creek at some distance below where we lived. His proclamation came out and a day was appointed to deliver his speeches. Almost all the men of families attended. He got up, harangued the people in a very rough and insulting manner and submitted his propositions for their acceptance. Some bowed to his scepter, but far the greater part returned home without submitting.

Not many miles distant from where this Lord Hook had made his stand, there was a set of ironworks called Billy Hill's Ironworks, which were very profitable both to the proprietor and all the country around. Lord Hook, provoked at the non-compliance of the people, determined to take vengeance; and to that end mustered his forces, charged on the ironworks, killed several men, set the works on fire, and reduced them to ashes.

I must here relate the expression of my father when he returned home from Lord Hook's exhibition. My stepmother asked him thus: "Well, Daniel, what news?" My father replied: "Nothing very

481

pleasant. I have come home determined to take my gun and when I lay it down, I lay down my life with it." Then turning to me said: "My son, you may prepare for the worst; the thing is fairly at issue. We must submit and become slaves, or fight. For my part I am determined—to-morrow I will go and join Moffitt."

Moffitt, while these things were transpiring, had been engaged in raising volunteers, to be all mounted and ready at a minute's warning, to be called "Minute Men." He had already raised about seventy men. A nomination of officers had taken place, and he was unanimously chosen colonel of the troops. Accordingly, next day we shouldered our guns and went to Moffitt. The gun that I had taken was what was called a blue-barrel shotgun. When we presented ourselves, "Well," said the colonel to my father, "Daniel, I suppose you intend to fight." My father said he had come to that conclusion. "Well, James," he said to me, "we shall have plenty for you to do, and two or three more such, if they could all have as good luck as you. We will try to take care of you and not let the Tories catch you."

In a few days there was a meeting of several officers, and it was determined to attack Lord Hook and take vengeance for the burning of the ironworks. The time and place was appointed for a rendezvous, several parties united in the plan, we met, mounted on horseback, and advanced towards his lordship, early in the morning.

Not long after sunrise we came in sight of their headquarters, which were in a log building. In the rear of the building was a large peach orchard; at some distance behind the peach orchard we all dismounted and tied our horses; we then proceeded on foot through the orchard, thinking the peach trees would be a good safeguard against the charge of the horsemen. We had not proceeded far until the sentinels discovered us—fired on us and fled. The troops were soon mounted and paraded. This, I confess, was a very imposing sight, at least to me, for I had never seen a troop of British horse before, and thought they differed vastly in appearance from us— poor hunting-shirt fellows. The leader drew his sword, mounted his horse, and began to storm and rave, and advanced on us; but we kept close to the peach orchard. When they had got pretty near the peach trees, their leader called out, "Disperse, you damned rebels, or I will put every man of you to the sword!" Our rifle balls began to whistle among them, and in a few minutes my Lord Hook was shot off his horse and fell at full length; his sword flew out of his hand as he fell and lay at some distance, and both lay till some of his men gathered about him and around him two or three times. At length one halted and pointed his sword downward, seemed to pause a moment, then raising his sword wheeled off and all started at full gallop. We then moved on to the house without opposition, but all had disappeared. In the yard sat two good-looking fellows bleeding pretty freely, their horses standing at no great distance; one of whom was shot through the thigh.

Before the body of Hook was examined, two claimed the honor of killing him; both showed their guns and named the part of his body they had taken aim at, and both claimed the sword. One presented a large rifle, the other a very small one. The person having the small gun cried, "I shot him! I shot him! I shot two balls which entered under the ear." When Hook was examined, the two small balls were found to have passed through the place as described. We then bound up the wounds of the two men, took three swords, three brace of pistols, some powder and lead, perhaps my Lord Hook's watch, and but little else, and departed, every man for his own place.

Later in his memoirs Collins described how his unit operated.

We were a set of men acting entirely on our own footing, without the promise or expectation of any pay. There was nothing furnished us from the public; we furnished our own clothes, composed of coarse materials, and all home spun; our over-dress was a hunting shirt, of what was called linsey woolsey, well belted around us. We furnished our own horses, saddles, bridles, guns, swords, butcher knives, and our own spurs; we got our powder and lead as we could, and often had to apply to the old women of the country for their old pewter dishes and spoons to supply the place of lead; and if we had lead sufficient to make balls half lead and the other pewter we felt well supplied. Swords at first were scarce, but we had several good black-smiths among us; besides, there were several in the country. If we got hold of a piece of good steel, we would keep it; and likewise go to all the sawmills and take all the old whipsaws we could find, set three or four smiths to work in one shop, and take the steel we had to another. In this way we soon had a pretty good supply of swords and butcher knives. . . . We carried no camp equipage, no cooking utensils, nor any thing to encumber us; we depended on what chance or kind providence might cast in our way, and were always ready to decamp in a short time, so that we were what might be called the harum-scarum boys—the ranting squad.

Fighting grew much fiercer after the Battle—also called the Massacre—of Waxhaws, which took place in May 1780, on the border between South and North Carolina, when a force from Virginia commanded by Colonel Buford, belatedly on its way to reinforce the Charleston garrison, was intercepted by Colonel Banastre Tarleton. Known to the British from the color of his uniform as the "Green Dragoon," and to the Americans as "Bloody Tarleton," the young cavalry colonel was certainly ruthless but also bold and enterprising, with a string of successes to his name, amorous as well as military. Most of the officers and troopers of his command, the Loyal Legion, were American Tories.

According to Robert Brownsfield, an American who was present at Waxhaws, Buford, surrounded and overwhelmed, and

perceiving that further resistance was hopeless, ordered a flag to be hoisted and the arms to be grounded, expecting the usual treatment sanctioned by civilized warfare. This, however, made no part of Tarleton's creed. His ostensible pretext for the relentless barbarity that ensued was that his horse was killed under him just as the flag was raised. He affected to believe that this was done afterwards, and imputed it to treachery on the part of Buford; but, in reality, a safe opportunity was presented to gratify that thirst for blood which marked his character at every conjuncture that promised probable impunity to himself. Ensign Cruit, who advanced the flag, was instantly cut down. Viewing this as an earnest of what they were to expect, a resumption of their arms was attempted, to sell their lives as dearly as possible; but before this was fully effected, Tarleton with his cruel myrmidons was in the midst of them, when commenced a scene of indiscriminate carnage never surpassed by the ruthless atrocities of the most barbarous savages. The demand for quarter, seldom refused to a vanquished foe, was at once found to be in vain; not a man was spared, and it was the concurrent testimony of all the survivors that for fifteen minutes after every man was prostrate they went over the ground plunging their bayonets into every one that exhibited any signs of life, and in some instances, where several had fallen one over the other, these monsters were seen to throw off on the point of the bayonet the uppermost, to come at those beneath.

Such incidents inevitably led to reprisals, and the reprisals to counter-reprisals, and so on and on and on. Moses Hall of the North Carolina infantry recalled an event that took place early in 1781:

The evening after our battle with the Tories, we having a considerable number of prisoners, I recollect a scene which made a lasting impression upon my mind. I was invited by some of my comrades to go and see some of the prisoners. We went to where six were standing together. Some discussion taking place, I heard some of our men cry out, "Remember Buford!" and the prisoners were immediately hewed to pieces with broadswords. At first I bore the scene without any emotion, but upon a moment's reflection I felt such horror as I never did before nor have since, and, returning to my quarters and throwing myself upon my blanket, I contemplated the cruelties of war until overcome and unmanned by a distressing gloom from which I was not relieved until commencing our march next morning. Before day, by moonlight, I came to Tarleton's camp, which he had just abandoned, leaving lively rail fires. Being on the left of the road as we marched along, I discovered lying upon the ground something with the appearance of a man. Upon approaching him he proved to be a youth about sixteen who, having come out to view the British through curiosity, for fear he might give information to our troops, they had run him through with a bayonet and left him for dead. Though able to speak, he was mortally wounded. The sight of this unoffending boy, butchered rather than be encumbered with him on the march, I assume, relieved me of my distressful feelings for the slaughter of the Tories, and I desired nothing so much as the opportunity of participating in their destruction.

Levi Smith also had a story to tell. A Loyalist merchant of Amelia Township, he had been put in command of the Tory militia in nearby Fort Motte, on the Congaree River. In May 1781, the fort, named after a large house and plantation belonging to Mrs. Rebecca Motte, was captured by General Marion, whose cavalry commander was Colonel "Light-Horse Harry" Lee. After a brief parole, Smith and the other Tory officers taken prisoner were confined in a local mill-house. (The "Little Lee" who figures in Smith's story was a cadet serving under Col. Lee. There were also two Coopers: Lt. Cooper, who had guarded Smith when first captured, and Samuel Cooper, probably a relative of the lieutenant, who was being held prisoner by the British in Charleston and awaiting exchange. Mrs. Motte's gate must have included a cross-beam as well as tall side-posts.)

✵

A little after sunset Colonel Lee sent Little Lee to the mill-house for Lieut. Fulker of the militia with orders to carry him to the fort and hang him on the gate of Mrs. Motte's fence. This unfortunate young man, who did not exceed nineteen years of age, was accused of being the cause of the death of a Mrs. Tate on Poplar Creek, who was turned out of her house when in the small-pox, by which she catched cold and died. . . . Fulker utterly denied his being the cause of her death and begged he might be brought to trial to make his innocence appear, but that was refused him and Little Lee told him it was in vain to expect mercy. He was accordingly carried to the gate where he was stripped naked and hanged without a trial or even a hearing in his own defense. When he was dead and cut down, Col. Lee sent the same messenger for John Jackson, a private militia man, and ordered him to prepare for death, accusing him of having carried expresses for the King's troops and having killed in action one of General Sumter's men. The poor man begged to be brought to trial, but to no purpose. He was hurried off, stripped, and tied up about dark, and left hanging all night on the gate. As soon as Jackson was cut down, Hugh Maskelly was sent for and ordered to prepare for death. Maskelly was immediately stripped of his clothes, and had an old dirty shirt tied round him, and was then turned off, as the others had been, without the slightest trial or hearing.

All this while I had no suspicion that I was doomed to the same fate . . . I expected to be sent to Charleston along with the regular officers on parole, there to remain until exchanged. These agreeable ideas did not last long. A sergeant and two privates of the Continentals came to the quarter guard and asked if one Levi Smith was among the prisoners. I immediately came forward and avowed myself; but I leave you to guess the horror and astonishment with which I was seized when they told me that they had orders from Col. Lee to carry me to Mrs. Motte's gate and hang me. I replied it was impossible; it could not be; but the sergeant answered that he would show me his authority, and produced a written order in these words: "Bring Levi Smith from the quarter guard and hang him."

487

I now found that I had not a moment to spare. I therefore begged
one of the quarter guard to run to my house and desire my wife and
children to meet me at the gallows and take their last farewell. The
fellow instantly went off and I was delivered to the sergeant. When
we began to ascend the hill on which the fort stood, my new guard
desired me to strip, declaring they would have my clothes. I very readily pulled off my coat, but this did not satisfy them; they declared
they would have my shirt also. I begged them not to treat me with so
much indignity but wait till I was dead, but they swore they would
have it then and wounded me slightly in two places with a bayonet,
upon which I pulled it off and delivered it to them. I now walked to
the gallows having no other clothes on but a pair of trousers. . . . Being
arrived, I found Maskelly had just been turned off and my wife and
children coming up. They were instantly ordered away by a Captain
Smith of the Continentals who desired them not to come within a
hundred yards of the spot.

An officer now rode up who I took to be Col. Lee. I asked him if
it was lawful to hang a man without a trial and received for answer that
I had got all the trial I need expect to get; that I had acted as a Justice
of the Peace and Militia Officer under the Crown, that I was an enemy
to the United States, and that I had been the cause of Mrs. M'Cord's
house at the ferry being burnt—a transaction of which I knew nothing
until two hours after the house was burned. I found that all protestations of my innocence were vain and that no appeal could be made
to the Laws of Nations. I heard one of the Continental officers say to
another, "It is a shame to take the life of any man without a trial. This
man, let him be the devil or what he will, ought to have had a trial."

I was now made ready for execution. The old dirty shirt was
taken from Maskelly's body and wrapped round mine and my arms
were pinioned. A number of indecent jokes were passed on Maskelly's
naked body, and as he did not appear to be quite dead, some of the
soldiers pulled down his feet to dispatch him quickly, the reason of
which was that no rope could be got to hang me by and they were
obliged to wait for Maskelly's being dead to get his halter for that

purpose. In the meantime, as they did not use a cart and the gate was pretty low, inquiry was made for a tall horse to mount me on. Maskelly was now ordered to be cut down and I had nearly taken farewell of the world, when a sudden noise turned my attention to the outside of the crowd, where I perceived Gen. Marion on horseback with his sword drawn. He asked in a passion what they were doing there. The soldiers answered, "We are hanging them people, sir." He then asked them who ordered them to hang any person. They replied, "Colonel Lee." "I will let you know, damn you," replied Marion, "that I command here and not Colonel Lee. Do you know that if you hang this man Lord Rawdon will hang a good man in his place—that he will hang Sam Cooper who is to be exchanged for him?"

The general then ordered me to be returned to the quarter guard and I found that I was indebted for my life to Lieut. Cooper, who, being apprehensive of what the consequences might be to Samuel Cooper, instantly went in quest of Gen. Marion, who arrived barely in time to save my life; but his interjection must have been too late if a spare rope could have been found for me when I came to the gallows.

�֍

The Ladies

Mrs. Rebecca Motte, whose house had been turned into a fort and front gate into a gibbet, was the same lady who had lent her slaves to work on the defenses of Charleston, supplying them "at her own expense" with rations and tools. In his *Memoirs of the War in the Southern Department of the United States,* "Light Horse Harry" Lee, the father of Robert E. Lee and the villain of Levi Smith's story, told of another occasion when "this amiable lady" displayed her patriotic spirit. This was when her newly built country house on the Congaree River, strategically located near the main route between Charleston and Camden, was seized and occupied by an enemy force of nearly two hundred men, commanded by Captain McPherson of the British army.

While her mansion was being built, Mrs. Motte had taken up residence in a nearby farmhouse, and was once again living there when Col. Lee and General Marion arrived to assess the situation. Rather than mount a direct assault, they concluded that "burning the house must force their surrender" and that the way to do this was to shoot arrows tipped "with missive combustible matter" at the newly shingled roof, which the "rays of the scorching sun" had prepared "for the projected conflagration."

"This measure was reluctantly adopted," wrote Lee, "for the destruction of private property was repugnant to the principles which swayed the two commandants and upon this occasion was peculiarly distressing. The devoted house was a large, pleasant edifice, intended for the summer residence of the respectable owner, whose deceased husband had been a firm patriot, and whose only marriageable daughter was the wife of Major Pinckney, an officer in the South Carolina line." Nevertheless "the obligations of duty were imperative: the house must burn," and it fell to Col. Lee to break the news.

With a smile of complacency this exemplary lady listened to the embarrassed officer, and gave instant relief to his agitated feelings by declaring that she was gratified with the opportunity of contributing to the good of her country, and that she should view the approaching scene with delight. Shortly after, seeing accidentally the bow and arrows which had been prepared, she sent for the lieutenant-colonel, and presenting him with a bow and its apparatus imported from India, she requested his substitution of these, as probably better adapted for the object than those we had provided.

In no time at all the house was aflame and Captain McPherson hung out the white flag. Since McPherson had been twice summoned to surrender and had twice refused, Lee felt that "he had subjected himself to punishment by his idle waste of his antagonist's time" but "not a drop of blood was shed nor any part of the enemy's baggage taken." Not only that, but "McPherson and his officers accompanied their captors to Mrs. Motte's, and partook with them of a sumptuous dinner; soothing in the sweets of social intercourse the ire which the preceding conflict had engendered. The deportment and demeanor of Mrs. Motte gave a zest to the pleasures of the table. She did its honors with that unaffected politeness which ever excites esteem mingled with admiration, conversing with ease, vivacity, and good sense . . ." (As to Levi Smith's story of nearly being hanged, Lee acknowledged in his memoirs that among the Loyalist prisoners who were handed over to Brigadier General Marion—and not to himself—"was a Mr. Smith," a "very obnoxious" person "who had been charged with burning the houses of his neighbors friendly to their country. . . . His punishment was loudly demanded by many of the militia serving under the brigadier; but the humanity of Marion could not be overcome" and Smith was at all times kept safe and sound.)

Another southern lady who had much to endure was Eliza Wilkinson. Like the middle-aged Rebecca Motte, she was a widow, but young and pretty and not, it seems, greatly bereaved—in the words of Elizabeth Ellet, editor of *The Women of the American Revolution,* she was "beautiful, with fascinating manners, quick at repartee, and full of cheerfulness and good humor." Her house on Yonge's Island, thirty miles south of Charleston, was separated from the mainland by a small creek and approached from the road by a long avenue hedged on either side with rose bushes. There was a gate where the avenue met the road.

Eliza, who told her story in a series of letters written in a "clear and feminine" hand, had at first refused to believe "the terrible accounts of the actions of the British troops at the northward; but (fool that I was) I thought they must be exaggerated, for I could not believe that a nation so famed for humanity, and many other virtues, should, in so short a time, divest themselves of even the least trace of what they once were."

Unfortunately for her, Yonge's Island was often the scene of military activity. In the spring of 1780, "upwards of sixty dreaded redcoats passed our gate. . . . A Negro wench was their informer, and also their conductor," but they did not actually come up to the house. Not long afterward they were visited by the local militia and Patriot irregulars, responding to news that "the Negroes were very unruly, and doing great mischief; so they rode from plantation to plantation, in order to quell them in time." Next came the Tory irregulars.

✳

The second of June, two men rode up to the house; one had a green leaf, the other a red string in his hat; this made me suspect them as spies (for we heard M'Girth's men wore such things in their hats). They were very particular in their inquiries "if there were any men in the house?" (Foolish fellows! If there were, they would not have had time to have asked us this question.) "If any had been there?" "No." "Did any go from here this morning?" Impertinents! thought I. Do you think we are bound to answer to all your interrogations? But I must not say so. "Well," says one, "do you know Colonel M'Girth will be along here presently with two hundred men? You may expect him in an hour or two." Ah! thought I—I'd far rather (if I must see one) see old Beelzebub; but here are some of his imps—the forerunners of his approach. "Why," said my friend, Miss Samuells, "if Colonel M'Girth should come, I hope he won't act ungenteelly, as he'll find none but helpless women here, who never injured him!" "Oh!" says one, "he'll only take your clothes and Negroes from you." After a little farther chat, they rode off, leaving us in a most cruel situation, starting at every noise we heard, and dreading the enemy's approach.

Well, now comes the day of terror—the 3d of June. (I shall never love the anniversary of that day.) In the morning, fifteen or sixteen horsemen rode up to the house; we were greatly terrified, thinking them the enemy, but from their behavior were agreeably deceived, and found them friends. They sat a while on their horses, talking to us; and then rode off, except two, who tarried a minute or two longer, and then followed the rest, who had nearly reached the gate. One of the said two must needs jump a ditch—to show his activity, I suppose; for he might as well, and better, have gone in the road. However, he got a sad fall; we saw him, and sent a boy to tell him, if he was hurt, to come up to the house and we would endeavor to do something for him. He and his companion accordingly came up; he look'd very pale, and bled much; his gun somehow in the fall had given him a bad wound behind the ear, from whence the blood flowed down his neck and bosom plentifully; we were greatly alarmed on seeing him in this situation, and had gathered round him, some with one thing, some with another, in order to give him assistance. We were very busy examining the wound when a Negro girl ran in, exclaiming, "Oh! The king's people are coming! It must be them, for they are all in red!" Upon this cry, the two men that were with us snatched up their guns, mounted their horses, and made off; but had not got many yards from the house before the enemy discharged a pistol at them. Terrified almost to death as I was, I was still anxious for my friends' safety; I tremblingly flew to the window to see if the shot had proved fatal; when, seeing them both safe, "Thank heaven," said I, "they've got off without hurt!"

I'd hardly utter'd this when I heard the horses of the inhuman Britons coming in such a furious manner that they seemed to tear up the earth, and the riders at the same time bellowing out the most horrid curses imaginable—oaths and imprecations that chilled my whole frame. Surely, thought I, such horrid language denotes nothing less than death! But I'd no time for thought—they were up to the house—entered with drawn swords and pistols in their hands; indeed, they rushed in, in the most furious manner, crying out, "Where're these women rebels?" (Pretty language to ladies from the once famed Britons!) That was the first salutation. The moment they spied us, off went our caps. . . . And for what, think you? Why, only to get a paltry stone and wax pin, which kept them on our heads; at the same time uttering the most abusive language imaginable, and making as if they'd hew us to pieces with their swords. But it's not in my power to describe the scene; it was terrible to the last degree; and, what augmented it, they had several armed Negroes with them, who threatened and abused us greatly. They then began to plunder the house of every thing they thought valuable or worth taking; our trunks were split to pieces, and each mean, pitiful wretch crammed his bosom with the contents, which were our apparel, &c. &c. &c.

I ventured to speak to the inhuman monster who had my clothes. I represented to him the times were such we could not replace what they'd taken from us, and begged him to spare me only a suit or two; but I got nothing but a hearty curse for my pains; nay, so far was his callous heart from relenting that, casting his eyes towards my shoes, "I want them buckles," said he, and immediately knelt at my feet to take them out; which, while he was busy about, a brother villain, whose enormous mouth extended from ear to ear, bawled out, "Shares there, I say! Shares!" So they divided my buckles between them.

The other wretches were employed in the same manner; they took my sister's ear-rings from her ears; hers, and Miss Samuells's buckles; they demanded her ring from her finger; she pleaded for it, told them it was her wedding ring, and begged they'd let her keep it; but they still demanded it, and, presenting a pistol at her, swore if she did not deliver it immediately, they'd fire. She gave it to them and, after bundling up all their booty, they mounted their horses. But such despicable figures! Each wretch's bosom stuffed so full they appeared to be all afflicted with some dropsical disorder. Had a party of rebels (as they called us) appeared, we should soon have seen their circumference lessen.

They took care to tell us, when they were going away, that they had favored us a great deal—that we might thank our stars it was no worse. But I had forgot to tell you that, upon their first entering the house, one of them gave my arm such a violent grasp that he left the print of his thumb and three fingers in black and blue, which was to be seen very plainly for several days after. . . . To be brief: after a few words more, they rode off, and glad was I. "Good riddance of bad rubbish," and indeed such rubbish was I never in company with before. One of them was an officer too! —a sergeant or some such, for he had the badge of honor on his shoulders! After they were gone I began to be sensible of the danger I'd been in, and the thoughts of the vile men seemed worse (if possible) than their presence; for they came so suddenly up to the house that I'd no time for thought; and while they stayed I seemed in amaze! Quite stupid! I cannot describe it. But when they were gone, and I had time to consider, I trembled so with terror that I could not support myself. I went into the room, threw myself on the bed, and gave way to a violent burst of grief, which seemed to be some relief to my full-swollen heart.

There is a postscript to this story. Soon afterward a troop of American soldiers arrived at the Wilkinson house, bringing with them some prisoners, among them one of M'Girth's men who had been shot in the arm. Miss Samuells at once began to take care of him, but when she needed a bandage, "we could find no rag to dress his wounds, every thing in the house being thrown in such confusion by the plunderers. But (see the native tenderness of an American!) Miss Samuells took from her neck the only remaining handkerchief the Britons had left her, and with it bound up his arm! Blush, O Britons, and be confounded! . . ."

Another heroine of the partisan warfare was Nancy Hart, of Wilkes County, Georgia, whose story was also told in *The Women of the American Revolution*. Far removed from Eliza Wilkinson in looks and social status, Nancy Hart was "vulgar and illiterate . . . ignorant of all the conventional civilities of life . . . cross-eyed, with a broad angular mouth—ungainly in figure, rude in speech, and awkward in manners," but also "hospitable and valorous . . . having a woman's heart for her friends and that of a tigress for the enemies of her country." Her home, which she shared with her husband (whom she called "a poor stick" because he was not active in the Patriot cause) and their young daughter, Sukey, was a single-room cabin on the edge of a swamp near Broad River and close to a stream since named "Warwoman's Creek" in her honor—and for good reason. (Her story was written up a few years later by Elizabeth Ellet, who added a few literary flourishes to the firsthand material she collected from interviews.)

On the occasion of an excursion from the British camp at Augusta, a party of loyalists penetrated into the interior; and having savagely massacred Colonel Dooly in bed in his own house, proceeded up the country with the design of perpetrating further atrocities. On their way, a detachment of five from the party diverged to the east and crossed Broad River to examine the neighborhood and pay a visit to their old acquaintance Nancy Hart. When they arrived at her cabin, they unceremoniously entered it, although receiving from her no welcome but a scowl. . . . They contented themselves with ordering her to prepare them something to eat. She replied that she never fed traitors and king's men if she could help it—the villains having put it out of her power to feed even her own family and friends by stealing and killing all her poultry and pigs, "except that one old gobbler you see in the yard." "Well, and that you shall cook for us," said one who appeared to be a leader of the party; and raising his musket he shot down the turkey, which another of them brought into the house and handed to Mrs. Hart to be cleaned and cooked without delay. She stormed and swore awhile—for Nancy occasionally swore—but seeming at last to make a merit of necessity, began with alacrity the arrangements for cooking, assisted by her daughter, a little girl ten or twelve years old, and sometimes by one of the party, with whom she seemed in a tolerably good humor—now and then exchanging rude jests with him. The Tories, pleased with her freedom, invited her to partake of the liquor they had brought with them—an invitation that was accepted with jocose thanks.

The spring—of which every settlement has one close by—was just at the edge of the swamp; and a short distance within the swamp was hid among the trees a high snag-topped stump, on which was placed a conch-shell. This rude trumpet was used by the family to convey information, by variations in its notes, to Mr. Hart or his neighbors who might be at work in a field, or "clearing," just beyond the swamp—to let them know that the "Britishers" or Tories were about, that the master was wanted at the cabin, or that he was to keep close, or "make tracks" for another swamp. Pending the operation of cooking the turkey, Nancy had sent her daughter Sukey to the spring for water, with directions to blow the conch for her father in such a way as should inform him there were Tories in the cabin, and that he was to "keep close" with his three neighbors who were with him until he should again hear the conch.

The party had become merry over their jug, and sat down to feast upon the slaughtered gobbler. They had cautiously stacked their arms where they were in view and within reach; and Mrs. Hart, assiduous in her attentions upon the table and to her guests, occasionally passed between the men and their muskets. Water was called for; and our heroine having contrived that there should be none in the cabin, Sukey was a second time dispatched to the spring, with instructions to blow such a signal on the conch as should call up Mr. Hart and his neighbors immediately. Meanwhile Nancy had managed, by slipping out one of the pieces of pine which form a "chinking" between the logs of a cabin, to open a space through which she was able to pass to the outside two of the five guns. She was detected in the act of putting out the third. The whole party sprang to their feet when, quick as thought, Nancy brought the piece she held to her shoulder, declaring she would kill the first man who approached her. All were terror-struck; for Nancy's obliquity of sight [i.e., her being cross-eyed] caused each to imagine himself her destined victim. At length one of them made a movement to advance upon her; and true to her threat, she fired, and shot him dead! Seizing another musket, she leveled it instantly, keeping the others at bay.

By this time Sukey had returned from the spring, and taking up the remaining gun, she carried it out of the house, saying to her mother, "Daddy and them will soon be here." This information much increased the alarm of the Tories, who perceived the importance of recovering their arms immediately; but each one hesitated, in the confident belief that Mrs. Hart had one eye at least on him for a mark. They proposed a general rush. No time was to be lost by the bold woman—she fired again, and brought down another of the enemy. Sukey had another musket in readiness, which her mother took, and posting herself in the doorway called upon the party to surrender "their d – -d Tory carcasses to a Whig woman." They agreed to surrender, and proposed to "shake hands upon the strength of it." But the victor, unwilling to trust their word, kept them in their places for a few minutes, till her husband and his neighbors came up to the door. They were about to shoot down the Tories, but Mrs. Hart stopped them, saying they had surrendered to her; and her spirit being up to boiling heat, she swore that "shooting was too good for them." This hint was enough; the dead man was dragged out of the house; and the wounded Tory and the others were bound, taken out beyond the bars, and hung! The tree upon which they were suspended was shown in 1828 by one who lived in those bloody times, and who also pointed out the spot once occupied by Mrs. Hart's cabin; accompanying the mention of her name with the emphatic remark: "Poor Nancy! She was a honey of patriot—but the devil of a wife!"

LOYALISTS

Just because he was commander in chief of the British army did not mean that General Sir Henry Clinton felt in any way responsible for the outcome of the war. "None of the misfortunes of the very unfortunate campaign of 1781 can, with the smallest degree of justice, be imputed to me," he wrote in his memoirs, published less than two years after Yorktown. And it was true that he could hardly be held accountable for the disastrous battle of King's Mountain, fought on October 7, 1780, on the border between South and North Carolina—"the first link of a chain of evils that followed each other in regular succession until they at last ended in the total loss of America." Young James Collins, viewing the same event from the opposite perspective, agreed: "After the result of the battle was known, we seemed to gather strength, for many that before lay neutral, through fear or some other cause, shouldered their guns and fell in the ranks, some of them making good soldiers."

Among the reasons why Clinton felt blameless was that following his success at Charleston, he had returned to New York, leaving Lord Cornwallis in command in the south; so he was not the man on the spot. Also, because the orders he gave Cornwallis were contradictory, whatever the earl did was bound to be in some way disobedient—and Cornwallis himself, first-rate on the battlefield but a poor strategist, already had a habit of picking and choosing which orders to obey. On the other hand it was Clinton who appointed Major Patrick Ferguson of the 71st Highlanders to be Inspector of the Militia in the Southern Provinces, with responsibility for recruiting and commanding a force of Loyalists.

Within a few months the energetic Ferguson had raised about four thousand troops, but these dribbled away as he headed north out of their home districts, and by late September the number was down to about one thousand. Meanwhile the Patriot militia that was coming after him had grown to some sixteen hundred, many of them "over-mountain" men from Tennessee. Finding himself outnumbered, Ferguson decided to make a stand at what seemed an impregnable position: the flat, rocky, and treeless summit of King's Mountain, whose steep slopes were heavily wooded and strewn with boulders. The ensuing battle was notable for the fact that of the approximately 2,600 men engaged on both sides, only one, Ferguson himself, was British. Everyone else was American.

Ferguson was famous in the British army for having invented the first successful breech-loading rifle. Unlike the musket, which was effective enough when fired in volleys at close range, but was so inaccurate that the order to fire did not even include the word "aim" (it was "Load—Present—Fire!"), Ferguson's rifle was accurate at two hundred and fifty yards, could be reloaded four times in a minute, and worked even when wet. Although he gave a demonstration to the king himself at Windsor early in the war, the weapon was swallowed up by military bureaucracy and never adopted. Ferguson was also said to be the best shot in the British Army. At the battle of Brandywine he had George Washington squarely in his sights but did not shoot because "it was not pleasant to fire at the back of an unoffending individual who was acquitting himself very coolly of his duty." Later in that battle Ferguson himself was wounded and his right arm crippled, but he soldiered on regardless.

Yet despite these military virtues, Ferguson was a poor tactician and too rash to be suited for independent command. Though outnumbered he decided against joining forces with Cornwallis, only seventy miles away, and the site he chose for taking his stand could not have been more favorable to the enemy: The rocks and trees on the mountainsides provided cover for the advancing Americans while the flat and open top provided none for the defenders; and the slopes were so steep that it was hard to fire down them. Moreover Ferguson, already conspicuous because of his crippled arm, made himself even more so by wearing a checkered shirt over his uniform, and American sharpshooters had no gentlemanly inhibitions about picking off enemy officers.

James Collins, who had taken part in the skirmish when Lord Hook was killed, was with the lightly equipped militia tracking Ferguson:

The pursuing army had not a single baggage wagon or any kind of camp equipage; every one ate what he could get, and slept in his own blanket, sometimes eating raw turnips and often resorting to a little parched corn.

On Friday evening we came to the river [Broad River], with the full expectation of meeting them, and being attacked in the crossing. We passed over, but no enemy appeared. The enemy had moved on, I think about nine miles, and made a stand on a place called King's Mountain, and determined to give battle. We had encamped for the night on the ground the enemy had left. On Saturday morning, October 7th, 1780, we were paraded and harangued in a short manner on the prospect before us. The sky was overcast with clouds, and at times a light mist of rain falling; our provisions were scanty, and hungry men are apt to be fractious; each one felt his situation; the last stake was up and the severity of the game must be played; everything was at stake—life, liberty, property, and even the fate of wife, children, and friends seemed to depend on the issue; death or victory was the only way to escape suffering.

Near two o'clock in the afternoon we came in sight of the enemy, who seemed to be fully prepared to give battle at all risks. When we came up, we halted, and formed in order of battle. Shelby happened to be in command that day as every colonel took command day about. The men were disposed of in three divisions—the right was commanded by Cleveland and Sevier, the left by Campbell and Williams, and the center by Shelby and Hamright. The enemy was posted on a high, steep, and rugged ridge, or spur of the mountain, very difficult of access, with a small stream of water running on each side. Along each stream was a narrow strip of flat ground. The plan was to surround the mountain and attack them on all sides, if possible. In order to do this, the left had to march under the fire of the enemy to gain the position assigned to them, on the stream on the right of the enemy, while the right was to take possession of the other stream; in doing this they were not exposed, the cliff being so steep as to cover them completely. Each leader made a short speech in his own way to his men, desiring every coward to be off immediately. Here I confess I would willingly have been excused, for my feelings were not the most pleasant—this may be attributed to my youth, not being quite seventeen years of age—but I could not well swallow the appellation of coward. I looked around; every man's countenance seemed to change; well, thought I, fate is fate, every man's fate is before him and he has to run it out, which I am inclined to think yet.

I was commanded this day by Major Chronicle and Capt. Watson. We were soon in motion, every man throwing four or five balls in his mouth to prevent thirst, also to be in readiness to reload quick. The shot of the enemy now began to pass over us like hail; the first shock was quickly over, and for my own part I was soon in a profuse sweat. My lot happened to be in the center, where the severest part of the battle was fought. We soon attempted to climb the hill, but were fiercely charged upon and forced to fall back to our first position; we tried a second time, but met the same fate; the fight then seemed to become more furious. Their leader, Ferguson, came in full view within rifle shot, as if to encourage his men, who by this time were falling very fast. He soon disappeared. We took to the hill a third time; the enemy gave way; when we had gotten near the top some of our leaders roared out, "Hurrah, my brave fellows! Advance! They are crying for quarter!" By this time the right and left had gained the top of the cliff; the enemy was completely hemmed in on all sides, and no chance of escaping—besides, their leader had fallen. They soon threw down their arms and surrendered.

After the fight was over, the situation of the poor Tories appeared to be really pitiable; the dead lay in heaps on all sides, while the groans of the wounded were heard in every direction. I could not help turning away from the scene before me with horror, and though exulting in victory, could not refrain from shedding tears—"Great God!" said I. "Is this the fate of mortals, or was it for this cause that man was brought into the world?"

On examining the dead body of their great chief, it appeared that almost fifty rifles must have been leveled at him at the same time; seven rifle balls had passed through his body, both of his arms were broken, and his hat and clothing were literally shot to pieces. Their great elevation above us had proved their ruin; they overshot us altogether, scarce touching a man, except those on horseback, while every rifle from below seemed to have the desired effect. In this conflict I had fired my rifle six times, while others had perhaps fired nine or ten. I had by this time learned to shoot a rifle pretty well, was not a bad hand in the second class, and had come to this conclusion: never to retreat alone, shoot without an object, or lay down my gun until the last extremity; for, thought I, a gun, though empty, might keep an enemy at bay. Whether I effected anything or not is unknown to me. My first shot I ever doubted, for I really had a shake on me at the time; but that soon passed over, and I took the precaution to conceal myself as well as I could behind a tree or rock, of which there were plenty, and take as good aim as possible.

Next morning, which was Sunday, the scene became really distressing; the wives and children of the poor Tories came in, in great numbers. Their husbands, fathers, and brothers lay dead in heaps, while others lay wounded or dying—a melancholy sight indeed!—while numbers of the survivors were doomed to abide the sentence of a court-martial, and several were actually hanged.

We proceeded to bury the dead, but it was badly done; they were thrown into convenient piles and covered with old logs, the bark of old trees, and rocks; yet not so as to secure them from becoming a prey to the beasts of the forest or the vultures of the air; and the wolves became so plenty that it was dangerous for anyone to be out at night for several miles around. Also, the hogs in the neighborhood gathered in to the place to devour the flesh of men, inasmuch as numbers chose to live on little meat rather than eat their hogs, though they were fat. Half of the dogs in the country were said to be mad, and were put to death. . . .

In the evening there was a distribution made of the plunder, and we were dismissed. My father and myself drew two fine horses, two guns, and some articles of clothing, with a share of powder and lead. Every man repaired to his tent or home. It seemed like a calm after a heavy storm had passed over, and for a short time every man could visit his home or his neighbor without being afraid.

The defeat at King's Mountain was a serious blow to British efforts to recruit Tories; but even in times of victory, these had never gone much beyond trying to enlist them as second-class soldiers in provincial regiments or local militias. Issues of pay, rank, bounties, promotion, and their relations with regular troops were never settled, while the attitude of regular army officers seems not to have changed much since the days when young George Washington had bristled at their condescension. Moreover Loyalist troops were generally used as auxiliaries, dependent on the continued presence of the Regulars, and who knew how long they would be around? In February 1781, Captain von Ewald of the Hessian jaegers, who was serving under Benedict Arnold during his diversionary campaign in Virginia, had something to say on the subject:

February 21, 1781. General Arnold has summoned a large provincial assembly in Princess Anne County to urge the inhabitants to take a new oath of allegiance to the King. Colonel Simcoe marched with his rangers and jaegers to Kemp's Landing to protect the people assembled there. More than four hundred adults of both sexes took the oath after being assured that the King was determined to protect his loyal subjects so long as the war should last. General Arnold then assured them that he would sacrifice his life and blood for them. While taking the oath several people made a wry face, as if swallowing something nasty.

Shortly before we left on the morning of the 23rd I had breakfast with one of the richest and most prominent residents of the area, a man named Walker, with whom I had this conversation. I said, "Why don't you raise a battalion for the defense of this region? As the county's leading citizen you could do great things by setting an example for your neighbors. Where you lead others will follow. You would be provided with weapons and uniforms, and your soldiers would be well paid."

He replied: "First I have to see if the army really intends to stay here. You have already been in this area twice before. General Leslie gave me exactly the same assurances last autumn, and where is he now? In Carolina! Who knows where you will be this autumn? And suppose the French were to join forces with the Americans—they'd carry everything before them. What would happen to the loyalists then? We would be ruined."

I said: "How can you call yourselves friends of the King if you won't risk anything for his cause? Look at the way the rebels behave: they abandon wife, child, house, and home, leaving everything at our mercy. They fight passionately without shoes or clothes, gladly enduring hunger and all the hardships of war. But you loyalists won't do a thing! All you want is to be protected by us and live in peace at home, while we do all the fighting for you."

At this point a jaeger arrived with the message that the rangers were about to march, so I took my leave and rode off. But when I had cooled down I realized that this man who had no desire to fight would have been a fool to have taken my advice. He possessed a great fortune, his property being worth at least £50,000 sterling, and his wife was one of the most charming blondes that I have ever seen in my life!

Many Americans who were neither what Dr. Rush had called "furious Whigs" nor "furious Tories" became serial swearers of oaths of allegiance, depending on who happened to have the upper hand at that particular time and place. "Notwithstanding what Mr. Tryon says of the Numbers of friends to Government in this country," wrote Captain Bowater from New York, to his patron, Lord Denbigh, earlier in the war, "I should be very sorry to trust any one of them out of my sight. They swallow the Oaths of Allegiance to the King, and Congress, alternately, with as much ease as your Lordship does poached Eggs."

The beautiful widow Eliza Wilkinson was also ready to come to terms of sorts with the other side when, after her unpleasant experiences at Yonge's Island, she went to stay for a while in Charleston. The general attitude of the citizens of that town towards their occupiers was "sullen, silent, and thoughtful," wrote a British officer, while fashion seems to have been dictated by Republican Virtue.

The assemblies which the officers have opened, in hopes to give an air of gayety and cheerfulness to themselves and the inhabitants, are but dull and gloomy meetings; the men play at cards, indeed, to avoid talking, but the women are seldom or never to be persuaded to dance. Even in their dresses the females seem to bid us defiance; the gay toys which are imported here they despise; they wear their own homespun manufactures, and take care to have in their breasts knots, and even on their shoes something that resembles their flag of the thirteen stripes. An officer told Lord Cornwallis not long ago that he believed if we had destroyed all the men in North America, we should have enough to do to conquer the women. I am heartily tired of this country, and wish myself at home.

But not all British officers were so easily discouraged, nor did all the young ladies go about in drab homespun: "One day Kitty and I were going to take a walk on the Bay to get something we needed," wrote Eliza Wilkinson.

Just as we had got our hats on, up ran one of the Billets [a British officer billeted in their house] into the dining room, where we were— "Your servant, ladies." "Your servant, sir." "Going out, ladies?" "Only to take a little walk." He immediately turned about and ran downstairs, I guessed for what.

"Kitty, Kitty, let us hurry off, child! He is gone for his hat and sword as sure as you are alive, and means to accompany us." We immediately caught up our silk gowns to keep them from rustling, and flew down stairs as light as we could, to avoid being heard. Out of the street door we went, and I believe ran near two hundred yards, and then walked very fast. Looking behind, we saw him at some distance, walking at a great rate. We hurried down another street, and went in a half-run until we came to Bedon's Alley, and turning that, we walked on leisurely to rest ourselves. It was near an hour after, being in a store on Broad Street [one hundred feet wide and one thousand one hundred and twenty feet long, according to Captain Hinrichs] that we saw him pass, in company with five or six other officers, with one of whom he was hooking arms. Kitty spied him out and pointing at him and looking at me, we ran behind the door to hide ourselves; but he got a glimpse of us before we could do so, and quitting his companions, came immediately into the store, and seemed quite transported to find us. Foolish fellow! I could not help pitying him for his good nature, and behaving *mighty civil* to him. Had he been one of your impudent, blustering red-coats, who think nothing bad enough they can say of the *rebels*, I should have discarded him that moment, and driven him from my presence; but he accosted us so smilingly, and with such an air of diffidence that I could not find in my heart one spark of ill-nature towards him. So I smiled too, and away we walked.

He offered me his hand, or arm rather, to lean on. "Excuse me, sir," said I. "I will support myself, if you please." "No, madam. The pavements are very uneven—you may get a fall. Do accept my arm." "Pardon me. I cannot." "Come, you do not know what your condescension may do—I will turn rebel!" "Will you?" said I, laughing. "Turn rebel first, and then offer your arm."

We stopped in another store, where were several British officers. After asking for articles which I wanted, I saw a broad roll of ribbon, which appeared to be of black and white stripes. [Black and white symbolized the alliance with France.] "Go," said I to the officer that was with us, "and reckon the stripes of that ribbon. See if they are thirteen!" (With an emphasis I spoke the word—and he went too!)

"Yes, they are thirteen, upon my word, madam."

"Do hand it me." He did so. I took it and found that it was narrow black ribbon, carefully wound round a broad white. I returned it to its place on the shelf.

"Madam," said the merchant, "you can buy the black and white too, and tack them in stripes."

"By no means, sir. I would not have them slightly tacked, but firmly united." The above-mentioned officers sat on the counter kicking their heels. How they gaped at me when I said this! But the merchant laughed heartily.

THE ALLIES

A dozen years before he first set foot on American soil as one of the senior officers in Rochambeau's expeditionary force, Armand Louis de Gontaut, Duc de Lauzun (and also Duc de Biron), had found the "kind of life that suits me best." This was "to be under fire all day, and then to sup with my mistress at night." The fire on that occasion had come from Corsican soldiers led by Count Paoli, who were defending their island from the French invaders, and the mistress was eighteen-year-old Madame Chandon, "a gift of the gods." True, the jealousy of her much older husband, the island's governor, "was somewhat disturbing to my happiness" but nothing serious. Since then Lauzun's list of conquests had grown to include Lady Sarah Bunbury "with her dazzling white bosom and the freshness of a rose," (before her marriage she had been Lady Sarah Lennox, with whom the youthful George III had been infatuated); Madame du Barry, "called the Angel, because of her heavenly countenance" (and soon to be mistress to Louis XV); Miss Paddock, a young English courtesan who kept him company at Calais where his regiment was stationed pending the invasion of her country; Madame Dillon and Princess Czartoryska, ornaments of the *beau monde*; and, or so it was rumored, Queen Marie Antoinette herself. But here the story is not quite clear. What had happened was that the insatiable Empress Catherine II of Russia, hearing of Lauzun's reputation, had written inviting him to take command of some newly raised Cossack regiments. The position would be "among the highest in my empire," and other benefits were hinted at. Lauzun, who was ambitious to shine in the higher reaches of diplomacy and politics, wanted to accept, confident that he could negotiate a Franco-Russian alliance, or at least an *entente cordiale*; but Vergennes, the foreign minister, was opposed on grounds of policy, and the queen wanted him nearby: "Do not forsake me, I beg of you!" she had cried during a "private encounter" at Versailles.

Her eyes filled with tears. Touched to the bottom of my heart I threw myself at her feet, exclaiming: "Oh that I could repay such kindness with my life!" She gave me her hand, I kissed it many times with ardor. . . . She bent over me with great tenderness; she was in my arms when I rose, I pressed her to my heart, which was throbbing violently; she blushed; but I could see no anger in her eyes. "Well!" she went on, drawing back a little, "am I to obtain nothing?" "Do you think so?" I retorted hotly. "Am I my own master? Are you not everything to me? It is you alone whom I wish to serve. You are my Queen, the Queen of France!" Her eyes seemed to be asking me to give her yet another title. I was tempted to enjoy the good fortune which appeared to be offered me. Two reasons restrained me: I have never cared to owe the surrender of a woman to a moment of which she might afterwards repent, and I could not have borne the thought that Madame Czartoryska might suppose herself sacrificed to my ambition.

Another consideration was that "the King's Ministers were zealously collecting evidence to have me sent to the Bastille"—evidence that might have included the way Marie Antoinette was soon parading about wearing in her hair a single white plume that had been plucked from Lauzun's helmet, and exclaiming, "Never have I felt more splendidly ornamented!"

But Lauzun was restless. Since the Corsican campaign he had seen little military action. He had commanded the recent expedition against British-held Senegal, but that was a sideshow, and he had looked forward to the projected invasion of England—nothing personal: Lauzun was an anglophile, and had been the first to introduce English-style horse-racing into France—so when the invasion was cancelled he asked for permission to join Rochambeau's army and, perhaps not unexpectedly, the king gave him leave to depart. On their arrival in Rhode Island, he and his legion were stationed some distance from the rest, at Lebanon, to acquire horses for his troops and to serve as an outpost in case of a land attack by the British. It was also possible that the diplomatic "Papa" Rochambeau felt that the irresistible duke would be too much of a good thing for the straitlaced citizens of Newport.

Though numbering only a few thousand, the French army was well equipped and supported by a naval force. They had also brought a supply of "presents for the Savages which will revive their love for us—red vermilion, striped woolen blankets, silver bracelets, medals with the portrait of the King, tomahawks, scalping knives, ammunition, and long rifles." In August twenty Oneidas, Tuscaroras, and Caghnawagas came to Newport

to offer us their alliance. They were taken to see the General, to whom they made the following address through a Canadian interpreter: "O my Father, whom we have chosen of our own free will to lead us in war, we promise you every assistance. We should have been pleased if some of our neighboring tribes [i.e., the Iroquois] had not gone over to the enemy, but the English have such good rum! Besides, they give us gunpowder to go hunting. They are very bad when you resist them, but that is how they have often deceived us and lured us over to their side."

M. de Rochambeau replied that the King thanked them and would not let them lack for strong drink. Then he gave them a medal bearing the arms of France, along with swords, shirts, blankets, and red paint. They seemed well satisfied and hastened to try on their new clothes. As soon as they got to their quarters they combed the red paint into their hair and daubed it all over their shirts and blankets, since it is their custom to redden their faces as well as their hair and the rest of their bodies.

That evening the narrator of this account, Jean-Baptiste de Verger, an eighteen-year-old "gentleman cadet" in the Royal Deux-Ponts Regiment, went to visit them and found them

listening intently to one of their comrades who was beating a small drum in a very monotonous fashion. He seemed quite entranced by the noise he was making. They abandoned their music in order to examine my epaulet and one of them asked for my sword-knot, explaining by signs that he would hang it from his nose as an ornament. But just then a watch-chain worn by one of my companions struck their fancy, and they left me to go and ask him for it.

The next day M. de Rochambeau paraded his army before these savages, but nothing pleased them so much as our pioneers with their axes. We drilled, then fired our muskets to the accompaniment of cannon fire, which alarmed them greatly. That evening they all gathered in a large room to dance, and we were admitted. They marched in, two by two, their chief at their head, singing a war song. Each held two small pieces of wood which he struck together as an accompaniment. When they got ready to dance half of them remained standing and the rest, having removed their animal skins to reveal very well-proportioned bodies that were oiled and daubed with red paint, began to dance with swords in their hands. Meanwhile their comrades intoned a very monotonous chant, accompanying themselves with the little sticks and jumping in strict rhythm. They danced with great strength and agility, assuming various postures that represented a man in combat and breaking out from time to time into war-cries or dirges so piercing and violent that they filled one with terror.

With them was a German from near Mannheim, who lived in their country. We asked him if he had no desire to return to his native land. He replied that he would be very loath to leave a country where he was his own master and to part from these good people to return to a place where he would be little more than a slave.

Following this visit, Rochambeau fortified Newport against a possible raid by the British fleet and then turned his attention to maintaining the health and morale of his troops during the coming months when they would be cooped up with little to do. "At the beginning of winter," wrote Louis Alexandre Berthier, an officer in the engineers who would later become one of Napoleon's marshals,

Count de Rochambeau had a large hall built in Newport where all the officers could assemble. There were tables where one could play commerce [a popular card game], he himself setting the example of playing for small stakes. Everyone, including the young officers, would come here every day, which prevented them from frequenting low places where they would ruin themselves through debauchery, as happens all too often when young officers have nothing to do. Our general also hosted a series of delightful balls and dances, presiding over them like the head of one large family.

Unlike so many of the British, who came to America ready to despise what they found, Berthier and other Frenchmen were full of enthusiasm for the new world. For example, two years earlier Captain Bowater, in a letter to Lord Denbigh, had complained that Rhode Islanders were "a Levelling, underbred, Artful Race of people. . . . For instance, as to leveling, I met a man of very good property a few days ago, who had a Complaint to make, and I Refer'd him to Lord Percy. I heard him enquire at his Lordship's door for Mr. Percy. Thinking him Ignorant I stept up & told him again Lord Percy, he Replied to me, he knew no Lord but the Lord Jehovah. Thus it is throughout America and a sad set of Presbyterian rascals they are . . ." And here is Berthier on the same subject:

Newport is well settled with honest simple families who are content to live on what they produce. They are of exceptionally pure descent. All the women are good-looking and have fresh complexions, which they owe to the upright, regular, and sober nature of their lives, and to the climate, which is very healthy. Because it never occurs to them that a man might try to seduce them, the girls here are extraordinarily free in their conduct. Parents often leave young people alone together who then embrace, but nothing more. . . . But once a young woman is married, she becomes as reserved as she was once forward. As a married woman, she devotes herself entirely to her husband, her home, and her children—not at all the way things are in France!

When we first arrived, and found all the young ladies welcoming us with such freedom, we of course attributed it to our personal charms and were delighted to find such easily accessible prospects before us. When all of a sudden we found an insurmountable barrier in front of us, we felt complete fools. And if a few of our officers got beyond that barrier it was only by resorting to the despicable ruse of making false promises, a method of seduction entirely unknown before our arrival. As to the married women, there was not a single instance of one of them being seduced. . . .

When we left [in May 1781] our departure was universally regretted. Every officer had become like a member of the family where he was billeted, and even the most extreme of the Tories had become friendly with the French. This too was the result of the wise and benevolent conduct of Count de Rochambeau and of the excellent discipline he maintained among his army.

In the spring they had another visitor when Washington arrived at Newport by ferry. He was welcomed with military pomp and genuine warmth; the fleet was decked with flags and the ships fired a thirteen-gun salute. "All our senior officers had assembled on the dock," wrote Berthier.

As he stepped ashore he was greeted by the entire general staff while our cannon fired the salute for a Marshal of France. All our troops were under arms and drawn up in full parade on either side of the road leading from the dock to General Washington's quarters. After receiving him at the head of the senior regiment, Count de Rochambeau and his staff preceded the general as he passed through our army, being saluted by the senior officers at the head of each division. The nobility of his bearing and appearance, expressive of all the virtues, inspired everyone with the affection and respect due to a man of his character, increasing, if that were possible, the high opinion we already had of his exceptional merit.

After dining with Count de Rochambeau, he took an evening walk through the town, where there was a general illumination, with candles in every window. Crowds of people pressed ahead in front of him carrying flaming torches and exhibiting signs of the most sincere joy. One house, belonging to some Tories who did not illuminate, had its windows smashed by stones thrown by the crowd. . . .

This was the second time Washington and Rochambeau had met—the first had been at Hartford in September 1780, just before Benedict Arnold's treason—and there was to be a third meeting, at Wethersfield, in May. It was on these occasions that Washington made the favorable impressions mentioned earlier: "The greatest and best of men" (the Marquis de Chastellux); "Handsome and majestic, he looks the hero" (the Count de Fersen); "The hero of liberty" (Count Mathieu Dumas); "A great man" (Baron von Closen). On Washington's departure, Closen, an Alsatian, added, "He bears with him the regrets, affection, respect, and veneration of our entire army."

The purpose of Washington's visit had been to agree with Rochambeau on a strategy for the coming campaign. One choice would be to concentrate on Virginia where two British forces were then active, one under the command of the renegade Benedict Arnold that was ravaging the countryside, putting Governor Jefferson to precipitate flight and cowing the Patriots; the other being the army under Cornwallis that for the last year had been zigzagging its way northward from Charleston, generally victorious in battle but constantly losing men who could not be replaced.

The other option was to attack New York, scene of Washington's defeats in 1776 and now headquarters of the British army and the Royal Navy. This was the choice Washington greatly preferred and the one to which Rochambeau tentatively agreed. It would be hard to attack the island without naval support, but news had just arrived that Admiral de Grasse was leaving Brest and heading across the Atlantic with a large fleet, and though his main mission was to repulse British attacks on French possessions in the West Indies, he had written to the French ambassador, the Chevalier de la Luzerne, to say that, circumstances permitting, he would be willing to assist in North America and could bring with him twenty-eight ships of war and about 3,300 more soldiers.

And so, in the spring of 1781, "to the regrets of the whole town, especially the women," as Berthier said, the French left Newport and set off by an inland route to rendezvous with the American army on the Hudson River north of New York. The Duc de Lauzun, glad to see the last of Lebanon—"a few huts dispersed in the immense forest" that he compared to Siberia—protected the left flank of the main force by taking a route closer to the coast, his troops now well-mounted on American horses procured during the winter. Very few members of the Lauzun Legion were French; most were Irish, Poles, or Germans. Indeed, only two-thirds at most of Rochambeau's army were French; one entire regiment, the Royal Deux-Ponts, recruited in Alsace, was also and more accurately known by its German name, Zweibrücken. But these soldiers were volunteers, not mercenaries. While on the march they crossed paths with the Rhode Island Regiment, also volunteers, "strong, robust men who made a very good appearance," wrote the Marquis de Chastellux. "The most neatly dressed, the best under arms, and the most precise in its maneuvers," in the opinion of the Baron von Closen, who added, "Three quarters of this regiment consists of Negroes."

It was springtime when the French set out from Newport; their spirits were high, and they must have made a fine show as they marched along the country roads past farms and through small towns. Wherever they went, the locals turned out to gape and applaud, as well they might, for unlike the American troops who had to make do with their scruffy, patched-up clothes and worn-out equipment, the French soldiers were beautifully dressed in white uniforms with trimmings that varied from regiment to regiment: crimson lapels and pink collars for the Bourbonnais; rose-colored lapels, sky-blue collars, and yellow buttons for the Soissonnais; green lapels and yellow buttons for the Saintonge. The officers, all mounted, were bedecked with silver lace and gold trimmings. There was no looting, and each regiment had its own band. "Whenever we halted thousands of curious Americans came into our camps and were immediately made to feel welcome," wrote the Abbé Robin, an army chaplain. "Our bands played for them, and they loved to listen to the music. Officers and soldiers, American men and women, all would join in the dancing. It was a feast of equality, the first fruits of an alliance that must surely endure between our two nations."

On their arrival in the area north of New York, the French were warmly greeted by their American allies, among them James Thacher, the doctor and diarist, and now a surgeon with Colonel Scammell's regiment of light infantry stationed at King's Bridge, at the northeast tip of Manhattan Island and scene of some recent skirmishing.

July 13. Notwithstanding the active bustle which attends our present situation, I received an invitation, with a number of officers of our regiment, to dine with a party of French officers in their camp. We were politely received under an elegant marquee. Our entertainment consisted of excellent soup, roast-beef, &c., served in French style [that is, one course after another, rather than all at the same time, which was the American style]. The gentlemen appear desirous of cultivating an acquaintance with our officers, but being ignorant of each others' language, we can enjoy but little conversation.

Thacher added that "during their march from Newport to join our army their course has been marked with the most exemplary order and regularity, committing no depredations, but conducting towards the inhabitants on their route with great civility and propriety. This conduct must have a happy tendency to eradicate from the minds of the Americans their ancient prejudices against the French people. They punctually paid their expenses in hard money, which made them acceptable guests wherever they passed."

And not only did the French pay for everything in hard cash, they were also acting as paymasters for the American army. A little later in the summer, when de Grasse sailed up from the West Indies, he brought with him 800,000 *livres* in silver that he had raised among the French and Spanish planters and merchants there. Claude Blanchard, Rochambeau's chief commissary, took charge of the money and stored it in an abandoned house near Williamsburg that he was using as his headquarters. Then, "having spent much of the previous night on my feet," he went to bed early. "I threw myself on my bed. As I lay there, exhausted and overcome with worries, the floor of the room next to mine collapsed with a tremendous crash. That was the room where I had put the 800,000 *livres* in silver; the floor was too weak to bear the weight. Fortunately we were on the ground floor and the cellar beneath was not very deep. My servant, who was sleeping in the same room, also fell into the cellar, but was not hurt."

A few days later Blanchard also noted in his diary that on the other side of the world the French had recaptured Pondicherry, lost to the British in the previous war, and were now besieging Madras.

Among those benefiting from this infusion of hard cash—"the first that could be called money which we had received as wages since the year '76"—was Joseph Plumb Martin, formerly of the Connecticut infantry, who had been at the Battle of Brooklyn Heights, the Kip's

Bay landing, the retreat out of New York, and the siege of Mud Island outside Philadelphia. Although by now he had been in the army for five years, he was yet to reach his twenty-first birthday; however, having transferred to the Sappers and Miners, he had risen to the rank of sergeant. The last two years had been fairly quiet for him, but his view of events remained largely personal and he was still always hungry—he gives more space in his memoirs to the story of how a cow ate a shad he was about to cook ("and the last I saw of it was the tail of the fish sticking out of the side of her mouth") than he does to Arnold's treason and the execution of Major André ("Poor man! He had better have stayed where he was better acquainted.") In May of 1781 the Miners and Sappers were sent down to Morrisania, at the junction of the Harlem River and the East River, where they took a position opposite a British redoubt.

The next morning we were joined by the French army from Rhode Island. Between us and the British redoubt there was a large deep gully. Our officers gave leave to as many as chose, of our men, to go over the gully and skirmish with the small parties of horsemen and footmen that kept patrolling from the redoubt to the gully, watching that none of us took shelter there to annoy them. Accordingly, a number of us kept disturbing their tranquillity all day. Sometimes only four or five of us, sometimes ten or twelve; sometimes we would drive them into the redoubt, when they would reinforce and sally out and drive us all over the gully. We kept up this sport till late in the afternoon, when myself and two others of our noncommissioned officers went down near the creek that makes the island upon which New York is situated. The two other men that were with me stopped under an apple tree that stood in a small gully. I saw four or five British horsemen on their horses a considerable distance from me, on the island. When they saw me they hallooed to me, calling me "a white-livered son of a b – h." (I was dressed in a white hunting shirt, or was without my coat, the latter, I think, as it was warm, and I wore a white underdress.) We then became quite sociable; they advised me to come over to their side and they would give me roast turkeys. I told them that they must wait till we left the coast clear, ere they could get into the country to steal them, as they used to do. They then said they would give me pork and 'lasses; and then inquired what execution some cannon had done, just before fired from the island, if they had not killed and wounded some of our men, and if we did not want help, as our surgeons were a pack of ignoramuses. I told them in reply that they had done no other execution with their guns than wounding a dog (which was the case), and as they and their surgeons were of the same species of animals, I supposed the poor wounded dog would account it a particular favor to have some of his own kind to assist him.

While we were carrying on this very polite conversation, I observed at a house on the island, in a different direction from the horsemen, a large number of men, but as they appeared to be a motley group, I did not pay them much attention. Just as I was finishing the last sentence of my conversation with the horsemen, happening to cast my eyes towards the house (and very providentially, too), I saw the flash of a gun. I instinctively dropped, as quick as a loon could dive, when the ball passed directly over me and lodged in the tree under which my comrades were standing. They saw the upper part of my gun drop as I fell, and said, "They have killed him." But they were mistaken. The people at the house set up a shouting, thinking they had done the job for one poor Yankee, but they were mistaken too, for I immediately rose up, and slapping my backsides to them, slowly moved off.

BAGGING THE FOX

"I am very anxious to receive Your Excellency's commands, being as yet totally in the dark as to the intended operations of the summer," wrote Cornwallis to Clinton in early April 1781. However, "I cannot help expressing my wishes that the Chesapeake region may become the seat of war, even (if necessary) at the expense of abandoning New York . . ." Strategically, this seemed like a reasonable suggestion, and no more than a suggestion, but Sir Henry wasn't fooled. He knew he was surrounded by enemies: the Americans, who kept outnumbering him; the French; "that rancorous Minister" Lord George Germain who had sided with Sir Peter Parker in blaming him for the failure of the 1776 attack on Charleston; seventy-year-old Admiral Arbuthnot of the Royal Navy, "full of deceit and artifice"; and now, worst of all, "very artful and designing," Cornwallis himself, whose "behaviour to me has been at all times so jesuitical that I am upon my guard with him all summer long."

In May Clinton received another letter from Cornwallis, again urging an offensive campaign in Virginia but insisting "that I neither wish nor expect to have the command of it." Indeed, "few things would give me greater pleasure than being relieved by your presence from a situation of so much anxiety and responsibility"—lines that can have served only to deepen Clinton's suspicions of a scheme to entrap him. Cornwallis also mentioned his immediate plans: "I shall now proceed to dislodge La Fayette from Richmond. . . . From thence I purpose to move to the Neck at Williamsburgh, which is represented as healthy and where some subsistence may be procured, and keep myself unengaged from operations which might interfere with your plan for the campaign, until I have the satisfaction of hearing from you. . . . At present I am inclined to think well of York." By York he meant Yorktown, a good choice for a temporary base since it could easily be supplied by sea.

Another possible British strategy was outlined by Captain Frederick Mackenzie of the Royal Welch Fusiliers, still stationed in New York:

If the troops now embarked in Virginia were immediately brought here, and as soon as they arrived the Commander in Chief was to move with all the force he could collect against Washington's Army, it would be productive of the best consequence. 12 or 14,000 men, which might be collected for this purpose, would certainly overturn all that are now collected against us. . . . A Victory over the Rebel Army at this juncture would put it out of the power of Congress to collect another of any consequence.

Washington's plan for an attack on New York had to be called off when French naval officers, who disliked the idea, claimed that the channel through the sand bar at the mouth of the harbor was at most times too shallow for their ships, whose draught was three to four feet deeper than that of British ships. Also the channel was so narrow and winding that only one ship could enter at a time, making them easy targets for the British warships already in the harbor. So, although Admiral de Grasse sent a message that he would be willing to bring his fleet up from the West Indies even before the hurricane season made operations there difficult, some other objective would have to be chosen.

On August 14, Washington wrote in his diary: "Matters having now come to a crisis and a decisive plan to be determined on, I was obliged . . . to give up all idea of attacking New York; and instead thereof to remove the French Troops, and a detachment from the American Army, to the Head of Elk, to be transported to Virginia for the purpose of co-operating with the force from the West Indies."

This change of plan was kept secret for as long as possible. "General Washington and Count Rochambeau have crossed the North River [i.e., the Hudson]," wrote Dr. Thacher in his journal,

and it is supposed for the purpose of reconnoitering the enemies' posts from the Jersey shore. A field for an extensive encampment has been marked out on the Jersey side, and a number of ovens have been erected and fuel provided for the purpose of baking bread for the army. From these combined circumstances we are led to conclude that a part of our besieging army is to occupy that ground. But General Washington possesses a capacious mind, full of resources, and he resolves and matures his great plans and designs under an impenetrable veil of secrecy. . . .

And indeed the ovens for baking bread and the fields of encampment soon turned out to be a ruse to deceive the enemy, and Thacher found himself marching briskly toward Philadelphia and points south with the rest of the American and French armies. "Wagons have been prepared to carry the soldiers' packs, that they may press forward with greater facility. . . . It is now rumored that a French fleet may soon be expected to arrive in Chesapeake Bay." While on the march, their flank was exposed to attack by a British sortie from New York, but then and later Clinton did little except hold councils of war at which nothing was decided, or at which it was decided to do nothing. Already preparing his defense, he also wrote memoranda of who said what, and why they were wrong and why he was right. "The inactivity of the royal army in New York is truly unaccountable," wrote Thacher. "They might without risking a great deal harass our army on its march, and subject it to irreparable injury."

On September 1 Thacher and Scammell's light infantry crossed the Delaware.

September 2nd. In the afternoon, marched through the city of Philadelphia. The streets being extremely dirty and the weather warm and dry, we raised a dust like a smothering snowstorm, blinding our eyes and covering our bodies with it; this was not a little mortifying, as the ladies were viewing us from the open windows of every house as we passed through this splendid city. . . . In the rear of every brigade were several field pieces, accompanied by ammunition carriages. The soldiers marched in slow and solemn step, regulated by the drum and fife. In the rear followed a great number of wagons loaded with tents, provisions, and other baggage, such as a few soldiers' wives and children; though a very small number of these are allowed to encumber us on this occasion. The day following, the French troops marched through the city, dressed in complete uniform of white broadcloth, faced with green, and besides the drum and fife they were furnished with a complete band of music, which operates like enchantment.

"The arrival of the French army at Philadelphia was more like a triumphal march than merely passing through the place," wrote the military chaplain, Abbé Robin.

The day after our arrival the Soissonnais Regiment, which had encamped in a large open space next to the Schuylkill River, publicly exercised their fire arms. At least twenty thousand people came to watch, and the vast number of carriages, remarkable for their lightness and elegance, added luster to the occasion. It was a fine sunny day, and the campsite was charmingly situated. The soldierly appearance of the troops, and the skill, speed, and precision with which they performed their drills and exercises astonished and delighted the audience. . . . The President of Congress, the Honorable Thomas M'Kean, Esquire, in a suit of black velvet, honored this review with his presence.

Also,

M. le Chevalier de la Luzerne [the French ambassador] welcomed his countrymen with the dignity and grace to be expected of one who represents our great monarch, and also with the informality and warmth

of a private citizen. After the review, he invited all the officers to dine
with him. Hardly were we seated at table when an express arrived.
Alarmed, every guest at once fell silent. All eyes were on the Chevalier
de la Luzerne, everyone trying to guess what the message could be.
Then: "Thirty-six ships of the line, commanded by Monsieur le
Comte de Grasse, have arrived in Chesapeake Bay. Three thousand
men have landed, and have made contact with the Marquis de La
Fayette.". . . . The news soon spread throughout the city and cries of
joy were heard from every quarter. Some merry fellows climbed up on
scaffoldings and delivered funeral orations for Cornwallis. . . . People
ran in crowds to the residence of Ambassador de la Luzerne, crying
out, "Long live King Louis the Sixteenth!"

In his journal the Baron von Closen also noted that the Soissonnais Regiment "with its rose-colored lapels and facings, and
grenadiers caps with large red and white plumes, greatly impressed
the fair sex." However, there was a problem with the Deux-Ponts,
or Zweibrücken, Regiment, whose soldiers "found many relatives
among the Philadelphia Germans, who came to visit them in camp.
This led us to double our guard against desertion, as there are many
who would be glad to seek their fortune in this country." But on a
more positive note: "The merchants of Philadelphia profited greatly
from the army's passing through; everyone stocked up."

Sergeant Joseph Martin of the Sappers and Miners remained in
Philadelphia for several days,

proving and packing off shells, shot, and other military stores. . . .
When we had finished our business at Philadelphia, we (the Miners)
left the city. A part of our men, with myself, went down the Delaware
in a schooner which had her hold nearly full of gunpowder. We
passed Mud Island, where I had experienced such hardship in Nov.
'77. It had quite a different appearance to what it had then, much

like a fine, fair, warm, and sunny day succeeding a cold, dark, stormy night. Just after passing Mud Island, in the afternoon, we had a smart thundershower. I did not feel very agreeably, I confess, during its continuance, with such a quantity of powder under my feet. I was not quite sure that a stroke of electric fluid might not compel me to leave the vessel sooner than I wished—but no accident happened, and we proceeded down the river to the mouth of Christiana Creek, up which we were bound.

Also en route to Yorktown was Sarah Osborn, the young wife of Aaron Osborn, formerly a blacksmith in Albany and now a commissary sergeant with the Third New York Regiment, commanded by Colonel van Schaick. His company commander was Captain Gregg, who had a "bare spot on his head where he had been scalped by the Indians. Captain Gregg had turns of being shattered in his mind and at such times would frequently say to the deponent, 'Sarah, did you ever see where I was scalped?' showing his head at the same time." Sarah—"the deponent"—did not tell her story until she was eighty-one, when she applied for a pension as a veteran's widow. While with the army, she often did washing, sewing, and cooking for the soldiers, and traveled sometimes on horseback, sometimes in a wagon.

She and the Third New York Regiment were encamped by the Schuylkill when some "Quaker ladies who came round urged deponent to stay, but her husband said, 'No, he could not leave her behind.' Accordingly, next day they continued their march from day to day till they arrived at Baltimore." Here they embarked on a boat and sailed down the Chesapeake. "They continued sail until they had got up the James River as far as the tide would carry them, about twelve miles from the mouth, and then landed, and the tide being spent, they had a fine time catching sea lobsters, which they ate." From there they went on to their encampment about one mile from Yorktown.

Deponent's attention was arrested by the appearance of a large plain between them and Yorktown and an entrenchment thrown up. She also saw a number of dead Negroes lying round their encampment, whom she understood the British had driven out of the town and left to starve, or were first starved and then thrown out. Deponent took her stand just back of the American tents, say about a mile from the town, and busied herself washing, mending, and cooking for the soldiers, in which she was assisted by the other females; some men washed their own clothing.

For most northerners the Yorktown campaign was their first and only visit to the South. "How vastly different is this part of the world from the ideas I used to have of it!" wrote Josiah Atkins, a pious and thoughtful blacksmith from Waterbury, Connecticut, who was serving as a doctor's assistant in the Continental Army.

Instead of a plain clear'd country (as I used to think it), I find it cover'd with vast lonely woods. Sometimes 'tis 10, 15, or 20 miles between houses, & they say we have a place to pass that is 30. This day we pass Gen. Washington's plantation, which is of large extent. Some men in these parts, they tell me, own 30,000 acres of land for their patrimony, & many have two or three hundred Negroes to work on it as slaves. Alas! That persons who pretend to stand for the rights of mankind, for the liberties of society, can delight in oppression, & that even of the worst kind!. . . . What pray is this but the strikingly inconsistent character pointed out by the Apostle, *While they promise them liberty, they themselves are the servants of corruption!*

Josiah also had a hard time coping with Virginia's wood ticks, which were "exceeding many & exceeding troublesome." There was also "a most venomous spider" and "a small creature that afflicts us far worse than the wood-ticks, yea, though they are the smallest living things I ever saw. Indeed I think they wou'd hardly be discerned were it not for their colour, which is scarlet red. They go thro' one's clothes, creep into the pores of the skin, where they cause it to swell to the degree of a bee sting, & are exceeding itching, smarting & sometimes dangerous. They have a shell like a tortoise; the inhabitants call them gigar & they comparatively are as thick as the dust of the earth."

The farther south he went, the worse things were. When near Williamsburg he wrote:

Here I must take notice of some villainy. Within these days past, I have marched by 18 or 20 Negroes that lay dead by the way-side, putrefying with the smallpox. How such a thing came about appears to be thus: the Negroes here being much disaffected (arising from their harsh treatment), flock'd in great numbers to Cornwallis, as soon as he came into these parts. This artful general takes a number of them (several hundreds), inoculates them, & just as they all are growing sick, he sends them out into the country where our troops had to pass & repass. These poor creatures, having no care taken of them, many crawl'd into the bushes about & died, where they lie infecting the air around with intolerable stench & great danger.

Other alleged British atrocities, according to Karl Gustaf Tornquist, a Swede serving with the French navy, included the murder of a pregnant woman, stabbed to death by redcoats' bayonets, "and on the canopy of her bed was written, 'Thou shalt never give birth to a rebel.' And in another room five severed heads were arranged on a shelf in a cupboard, in place of plaster-cast figures which lay broken to pieces on the floor."

But there was no question that the British had a problem with runaway slaves. Captain von Ewald, who had been with the army since it left Charleston, explained:

As it advanced, the army had increasingly come to look like a wandering Arabian or Tartar horde. Lord Cornwallis had allowed junior officers to provide themselves with two horses and one Negro servant, captains were allowed four horses and two Negroes, and so on. Even among our jaegers and rangers some officers had four to six horses, three or four Negro servants, and often a Negress or two as cook or mistress. The wives of ordinary soldiers were mounted on horseback and had a couple of Negro servants, who were also mounted. Noncommissioned officers had two horses and a Negro, and even ordinary soldiers had a Negro to carry their bundles and provisions.

In addition, following the baggage train, came a straggling mass of another four thousand or more Negroes of both sexes and of every age. Wherever they went the place was picked clean, like a field attacked by a swarm of locusts. Adding to the unmilitary appearance of this motley horde was the way the Negroes were dressed. Before leaving many of them had plundered the wardrobes of their masters and mistresses and were now wearing bits and pieces of their loot. One Negro, for example, was just about naked except for a pair of silk breeches, another wore a finely colored coat, a third had on a silk waistcoat without sleeves, a fourth wore only an elegant shirt, a fifth had on a fine clergyman's hat, a sixth was entirely naked except for a white wig. The Negresses also were variously tricked out in silk skirts, dresses with long trains, jackets, laced bodices, silk corsets, and a variety of hats and bonnets.

So long as the army was on the move, the Negro servants were useful; but once it had taken position in Yorktown, they were a burden. "On the day that we were first attacked by the enemy, all our black friends, who had been freed by us and taken away so that they could not work in their masters' fields, and who had served us well by digging entrenchments, were driven out of our camp and towards the enemy," wrote Ewald. "They trembled with fear at the prospect of having to go back to their former owners. When I went out on night patrol I encountered many of these unhappy people who were desperate from hunger and were trapped between the lines, exposed to the fire from both sides."

In the meantime, everything depended on the actions of the French and British fleets.

"At our first halt after Philadelphia," wrote the Duc de Lauzun," General Washington heard that M. de Grasse had anchored in Chesapeake Bay with more than thirty ships of the line and had there landed M. de Saint-Simon with 3,000 men of the land forces. I have never seen a man more overcome with great and sincere joy than was General Washington. We heard at the same time that Lord Cornwallis had received orders from Sir Henry Clinton to fortify himself at Yorktown until relief came to him there." Soon came news that "the English fleet having appeared outside Chesapeake Bay, M. de Grasse had gone out to give battle, and had not yet returned."

According to Frederick Mackenzie,

Should Admiral Digby arrive at this Critical period we shall be fully equal to the French; and we have every reason to hope that should a general engagement take place between the fleets, the abilities and courage of our Officers and men, and their ardour to distinguish themselves under the eyes of The King's Son in so important a battle, on which it may be said the Sovereignty of the Seas and the fate of America depends, will ensure us that Victory over our Ancient & perfidious Enemy, which the justness of our cause so well deserves.

But Admiral Digby and Prince William Henry did not arrive in time, and command of the British fleet remained with Clinton's friend and kindred spirit, Admiral Thomas Graves, who earlier in his career had been court-martialed and reprimanded for failing to attack the enemy. No such charge could have ever been brought against his opponent, the Comte de Grasse. After five days of inconclusive fighting, the Battle of the Chesapeake Capes, one of history's decisive actions, came to an end when Graves decided to return to New York to refit. "Three days later," wrote Lauzun, "one our corvettes came to inform us that M. de Grasse, having defeated the English and captured two frigates, had returned to anchor in the Bay."

But the encirclement of Cornwallis at Yorktown was not quite complete, as Lauzun explained after another meeting. "General Washington told me that, as Lord Cornwallis had sent all his cavalry and a considerable body of troops to Gloucester, opposite Yorktown, he was afraid lest he might be seeking to withdraw in that direction, and therefore was having him watched by a corps of three thousand militiamen under the Continental officer, Brigadier-General Weedon, a good enough soldier, but one who hated war, in which he had never wished to engage." Before the war Weedon had been a tavernkeeper, and was known to his soldiers as "Joe Gourd." Lauzun's mission, as he saw it, was to put some backbone into this wretched amateur and cut off Cornwallis's only possible line of retreat.

I went with my regiment to join General Weedon's corps. His method of blockading Gloucester was original; he was more than fifteen miles from the enemy's outposts, was frightened to death, and dared not send out a patrol as much as half a mile from his camp. He was the best fellow in the world, and his one desire was not to interfere in anything. I suggested to him that we should move closer to Gloucester, and should go the next day to make a reconnaissance near the English outposts; he agreed, and we set out with fifty of my hussars. When we were still six or seven miles from the enemy, he said to me that he thought it useless and very dangerous to go any further, and that we should see no better. I pressed him so hard that he dared not refuse to accompany me. I drove back the enemy's outposts and approached near enough to form an accurate idea of his position. My general was in despair; he told me that he would never go out with me again; that he did not wish to throw away his life.

I made M. de Rochambeau a report of what I had seen; I told him that we could not rely on the American militia, and that it was essential he should send me at least two additional battalions of French infantry. I had no artillery, no rations, no powder. I asked him for them. He at once sent artillery and eight hundred of the men stationed on board the fleet and under the command of M. de Choisy, who outranked General Weedon as well as myself.

M. de Choisy is a good and gallant man, absurdly violent, constantly in a rage, always making scenes with everyone, and entirely devoid of common sense. He began by finding fault with General Weedon and all the militia, told them that they were cowards, and in five minutes had them almost as frightened of himself as of the English, which is certainly saying a good deal. He decided to move the next day and occupy the ground I had reconnoitered. General Weedon preferred to join him a day later, and remained behind with about six hundred men of his division.

Just as we were entering the plain of Gloucester, some dragoons of the State of Virginia came in a great panic to tell us that they had seen some English dragoons in the open, and, for fear of accidents, had ridden away hell for leather, without examining them further. I rode forward to find out more about them. I caught sight of a fine-looking woman at the door of a little house upon the high road; I went to question her; she told me that Colonel Tarleton had just that moment left her house; that she did not know how many troops had come out of Gloucester; that Colonel Tarleton was most anxious "to shake hands with the French duke." I assured her that I had come there on purpose to give him that satisfaction. She expressed her sympathy, thinking, I suppose from her own experience, that it was impossible to resist Tarleton.

I had not gone a hundred yards from the house when I heard my advance guards firing their pistols. I advanced at a gallop to find a terrain suitable for battle. As I approached I saw that the English cavalry

outnumbered mine three to one; I charged them without drawing
rein; our lines met; Tarleton caught sight of me, and came towards
me with raised pistol. We were about to fight a duel between our lines
when his horse was overthrown by one of his dragoons pursued by
one of my lancers. I dashed upon him to take him prisoner; a troop of
English dragoons thrust themselves between us and covered his retreat;
his horse remained in my hands. He charged me a second time, without breaking my line. I charged him a third time, routed part of his
cavalry, and pursued him as far as the earthworks of Gloucester. He
lost one officer and fifty men, and I took a good number of prisoners.

Having thus shown the Americans how to fight, Lauzun
remained at Gloucester, cutting off the only British line of retreat
and leaving the two main armies to face each other on the Yorktown side of the river.

This was not the first confrontation between Washington and Cornwallis. That had occurred much earlier in the war, when Cornwallis had led the counterattack just after the Battle of Trenton. At the
end of a long day's marching, skirmishing, and maneuvering, he was
confident that he had the rebel force safely cornered, but rather than
launch an attack that evening, he decided to take his time, airily
declaring, like a master of hounds, that "he would bag the fox in the
morning." All night long the British could see the American camp-
fires burning brightly, but when morning came the fox was gone—
after slipping away under cover of darkness, Washington then circled
round behind the British and hit them hard at Princeton.

And now, nearly five years later, as he sat in his headquarters at
Yorktown, weakly defended by hastily built earthworks, his escape
route cut off, his supplies limited, many of his troops sick, hemmed
in at sea by the French fleet and outnumbered on land by more than

two to one, Cornwallis must surely have looked back on that missed opportunity and asked himself the awkward question: Who now was the master of hounds, who the fox?

YORKTOWN
From the *Military Journal* of Dr. James Thacher:

❋

Camp, before Yorktown, September 28th. 1781. The French troops have arrived and encamped on our left. Yorktown is situated on the south bank of the river, about fifteen miles from its entrance into Chesapeake Bay. In this little village, Lord Cornwallis, with about seven thousand troops, has taken his station, and is endeavoring to fortify himself against the impending danger of our combined operations. His communication by water is entirely cut off by the French ships of war stationed at the mouth of the river, preventing both his escape and receiving succor from Sir Henry Clinton at New York. The allied army is about twelve thousand strong, exclusive of the militia under Governor Nelson. The Americans form the right and the French the left wing of the combined forces, each extending to the borders of the river, by which the besiegers form a half circle round the town. His Excellency General Washington commands in person, and is assisted by Major General Lincoln, Baron Steuben, the Marquis de la Fayette, General Knox, &c. The French troops are commanded by General the Count Rochambeau, a brave and experienced officer, having under him a number of officers of distinguished character. Unbounded confidence is reposed in our illustrious commanders, the spirit of emulation and military ardor universally prevail, and we are sanguine in our expectations that a surrender of the royal army must be his Lordship's fate.

Sept. 29th. A cannonade commenced yesterday from the town, by which one man received a wound, and I assisted in amputating his leg.

30th. We were agreeably surprised this morning to find that the enemy had, during the preceding night, abandoned three or four of their redoubts, and retired within the town, leaving a considerable extent of commanding ground which might have cost us much labor and many lives to obtain by force. Our light infantry and a party of French were ordered to advance and take possession of the abandoned ground, and to serve as a covering party to our troops who are employed in throwing up breast works. Considerable cannonading from the besieged in the course of the day, and four militia men were wounded by a single shot, one of whom died soon after.

October 1st and 2nd. Our troops have been engaged in throwing up two redoubts in the night time; on discovery, the enemy commenced a furious cannonade, but it does not deter our men from going on vigorously with their work. Heavy cannon and mortars are continually arriving, and the greatest preparations are made to prosecute the siege.

3rd and 4th. A considerable cannonading from the enemy, one shot killed three men and mortally wounded another. While the Reverend Mr. Evans, our chaplain, was standing near the Commander in Chief, a shot struck the ground so near as to cover his hat with sand. Being much agitated, he took off his hat and said, "See here, General!" "Mr. Evans," replied his Excellency, with his usual composure, "you had better carry that home and show it to your wife and children.". . . . The enemy from the want of forage are killing off their horses in great numbers; six or seven hundred of these valuable animals have been killed, and their carcasses are almost continually floating down the river.

7th. A large detachment of the allied army, under command of Major General Lincoln, were ordered out last evening for the purpose of opening entrenchments near the enemy's lines. This business was conducted with great silence and secrecy, and we were favored by Providence with a night of extreme darkness, and were not discovered before daylight. The working party carried on their shoulders fascines and entrenching tools, while a large part of the detachment was armed with the implements of death. Horses drawing cannon and ordnance, and wagons loaded with bags filled with sand for constructing breast works, followed in the rear. . . . Our troops were indefatigable in their labors during the night and before daylight they had nearly completed the first parallel line of nearly two miles in extent, besides laying a foundation for two redoubts within six hundred yards of the enemy's lines.

Sergeant Joseph Martin was among those preparing the entrenchments. So far, things had gone well for the Sappers and Miners. Although they had "encountered our old associate, Hunger," they were soon encamped near a large wood where "there was a plenty of shoats, fat and plump, weighing generally from fifty to a hundred pounds apiece. We soon found some of them and as no owner appeared to be at hand and the hogs not understanding our inquiries . . ." Thus fortified, they were ready

to assist the engineers in laying out the works. It was a very dark and rainy night. However, we repaired to the place and began by following the engineers and laying laths of pine wood end-to-end upon the line marked out by the officers for the trenches. We had not proceeded far in the business before the engineers ordered us to desist and remain where we were and be sure not to straggle a foot from the spot while they were absent from us. In a few minutes after their departure, there came a man alone to us, having on a surtout [overcoat], as we conjectured, it being exceeding dark, and inquired for the engineers. . . . The stranger inquired what troops we were, talked familiarly with us a few minutes, when, being informed which way the officers had gone, he went off in the same direction . . . . In a short time the engineers returned and the aforementioned stranger with them. They discoursed together some time when, by the officers often calling him "Your Excellency," we discovered that it was General Washington. Had we dared, we might have cautioned him for exposing himself too carelessly to danger at such a time, and doubtless he would have taken it in good part if we had. But nothing ill happened to either him or ourselves.

Washington indeed seems to have been everywhere. More than fifty years later, in her pension application, "deponent" Sarah Osborn, wife of Sergeant Osborn of the Third New York Regiment, recalled that while in the American camp "she heard the roar of the artillery for a number of days," and that when "the Americans threw up entrenchments it was a misty, foggy night, rather wet but not rainy." Later that night she went up to the front line herself. Her "husband was there, throwing up entrenchments, and deponent cooked and carried in beef, and bread, and coffee (in a gallon pot) to the soldiers in the entrenchment. On one occasion when deponent was thus employed carrying provisions, she met General Washington, who asked her if she 'was not afraid of the cannonballs?'"

She replied that she was not, and that "it would not do for the men to fight and starve too."

Having fired the first shot of the Seven Years' War, in the Jumonville Affair of 1754, it was but fitting that Washington should round things out by firing the first shot of the bombardment that officially opened the last battle of the Revolutionary War. Dr. Thacher was present at the occasion:

October 8th and 9th. Two or three of our batteries being now prepared to open on the town, his Excellency General Washington put the match to the first gun, and a furious discharge of cannon and mortars immediately followed. . . . From the 10th to the 15th, a tremendous and incessant firing from the American and French batteries is kept up, and the enemy return the fire, but with little effect. A red-hot shell from the French battery set fire to the *Charon*, a British 44-gun ship, and two or three smaller vessels at anchor in the river, which were consumed in the night. From the bank of the river, I had a fine view of this splendid conflagration. The ships were enwrapped in a torrent of fire, which spreading with vivid brightness among the combustible rigging, and running with amazing rapidity to the tops of the several masts, while all around was thunder and lightning from our numerous cannon and mortars, and in the darkness of night, presented one of the most sublime and magnificent spectacles which can be imagined. Some of our shells, overreaching the town, are seen to fall into the river, and bursting, throw up columns of water like the spouting of the monsters of the deep. We have now made further approaches to the town by throwing up a second parallel line, and batteries within about three hundred yards. . . .

Being in the trenches every other night and day, I have a fine opportunity of witnessing the sublime and stupendous scene which is continually exhibiting. The bomb-shells from the besiegers and the besieged are incessantly crossing each others' path in the air. They are clearly visible in the form of a black ball during the day, but in the night they appear like fiery meteors with blazing tails, most beautifully brilliant, ascending majestically from the mortar to a certain altitude, and gradually descending to the spot where they are destined to execute their work of destruction. It is astonishing with what accuracy an experienced gunner will make his calculations, that a shell shall fall within a few feet of a given point, and burst at the precise time, though at a great distance. When a shell falls, it whirls round, burrows, and excavates the earth to a considerable extent, and bursting, makes dreadful havoc around. I have more than once witnessed fragments of the mangled bodies and limbs of the British soldiers thrown into the air by the bursting of our shells; and by one from the enemy, Captain White, of the Seventh Massachusetts Regiment, and one soldier, were killed, and another wounded near where I was standing. About twelve or fourteen men have been killed or wounded within twenty-four hours; I attended at the hospital, amputated a man's arm, and assisted in dressing a number of wounds.

The enemy having two redoubts about three hundred yards in front of their principal works, which enfiladed our entrenchment and impeded our approaches, it was resolved to take possession of them by assault. The one on the left of the British garrison, bordering on the banks of the river, was assigned to our brigade of light infantry, under the command of the Marquis de la Fayette. The advance corps was led on by the intrepid Colonel Hamilton, who had commanded a regiment of light infantry during the campaign, and assisted by Colonel Gimat. The assault commenced at eight o'clock in the evening, and the assailants bravely entered the fort with the point of the bayonet without firing a single gun.

The other redoubt was to prove harder to take, and once again, although there were well over fifteen thousand American and French soldiers at the siege, Joseph Martin found himself singled out for special duty.

One afternoon, I, with the rest of our corps that had been on duty in the trenches the night but one before, were ordered to the lines. I mistrusted something extraordinary, serious or comical, was going forward, but what I could not easily conjecture.

We arrived at the trenches a little before sunset. I saw several officers fixing bayonets on long staves. I then concluded we were about to make a general assault upon the enemy's works, but before dark I was informed of the whole plan, which was to storm the redoubts, the one by the Americans and the other by the French. The Sappers and Miners were furnished with axes and were to proceed in front and cut a passage for the troops through the abatis, which are composed of the tops of trees, the small branches cut off with a slanting stroke which renders them as sharp as spikes. These trees are then laid at a small distance from the trench or ditch, pointing outwards, and the butts fastened to the ground in such a manner that they cannot be removed by those on the outside of them. It is almost impossible to get through them. Through these we were to cut a passage before we or the other assailants could enter.

At dark the detachment was formed and advanced beyond the trenches and lay down on the ground to await the signal for advancing to the attack, which was to be three shells from a certain battery near where we were lying. All the batteries in our line were silent, and we lay anxiously waiting for the signal. The two brilliant planets, Jupiter and Venus, were in close contact in the western hemisphere, the same direction that the signal was to be made in. When I happened to cast my eyes to that quarter, which was often, and I caught a glance of them, I was ready to spring on my feet, thinking they were the signal for starting. Our watchword was "Rochambeau," the commander of the French forces' name, a good watchword, for being pronounced Ro-sham-bow, it sounded, when pronounced quick, like Rush-on-boys.

We had not lain here long before the expected signal was given, for us and the French, who were to storm the other redoubt, by the three shells with their fiery trains mounting the air in quick succession. The word "Up! Up!" was then reiterated through the detachment. We immediately moved silently on toward the redoubt we were to attack, with unloaded muskets. Just as we arrived at the abatis, the enemy discovered us and directly opened a sharp fire upon us. We were now at a place where many of our large shells had burst in the ground, making holes sufficient to bury an ox in. The men, having their eyes fixed upon what was transacting before them, were every now and then falling into these holes. I thought the British were killing us off at a great rate. At length, one of the holes happening to pick me up, I found out the mystery of the huge slaughter.

As soon as the firing began, our people began to cry, "The fort's our own!" and it was "Rush on, boys!" The Sappers and Miners soon cleared a passage for the infantry, who entered it rapidly. Our Miners were ordered not to enter the fort, but there was no stopping them. "We will go," said they. "Then go to the d – -l," said the commanding officer of our corps, "if you will." I could not pass at the entrance we had made, it was so crowded. I therefore forced a passage at a place where I saw our shot had cut away some of the abatis; several others entered at the same place. While passing, a man at my side received a ball in his head and fell under my feet, crying out bitterly. While crossing the trench, the enemy threw hand grenades (small shells) into it. They were so thick that I at first thought them cartridge papers on fire, but was soon undeceived by their cracking. As I mounted the breastwork, I met an old associate hitching himself down into the trench. I knew him by the light of the enemy's musketry, it was so vivid.

The fort was taken and all quiet in a very short time. Immediately after the firing ceased, I went out to see what had become of my wounded friend and the other that fell in the passage. They were both dead. In the heat of the action I saw a British soldier jump over the walls of the fort next the river and go down the bank, which was almost perpendicular and twenty or thirty feet high. When he came to the beach he made off for the town, and if he did not make good use of his legs I never saw a man that did.

Though mainly occupied in cooking meals and bringing them up to her husband and other soldiers in the front line, Sarah Osborn also worked as a servant in the officers' mess, earning some extra money and probably also gaining access to their provisions. "They dug entrenchments nearer and nearer to Yorktown every night," she deponed. Then came the day when

the enemy fired very heavy till about nine o'clock next morning, then stopped, and the drums from the enemy beat excessively. Deponent was a little way off in Colonel van Shaick's or the officers' marquee and a number of officers were present, among whom was Captain Gregg, who, on account of infirmities, did not go out much to do duty.

The drums continued beating, and all at once the officers hurrahed and swung their hats, and deponent asked them, "What is the matter now?"

One of them replied, "Are not you soldier enough to know what it means?"

Deponent replied, "No."

They then replied, "The British have surrendered!"

Deponent, having provisions ready, carried the same down to the entrenchments that morning, and four of the soldiers whom she was in the habit of cooking for ate their breakfasts.

✻

From James Thacher's *Military Journal*:

✻

October 17th. Lord Cornwallis, at length realizing the extreme hazard of his deplorable situation, and finding it in vain any longer to resist, has this forenoon come to the humiliating expedient of sending out a flag, requesting a cessation of hostilities for twenty-four hours, that commissioners may be appointed to prepare and adjust the terms of capitulation.

Oct 18th. At an early hour this forenoon General Washington communicated to Lord Cornwallis the general basis of the terms of capitulation, which he deemed admissible, and allowed two hours for his reply. Commissioners were soon after appointed to prepare the particular terms of agreement . . . and being confirmed by the commanders of both armies, the royal troops are to march out tomorrow and surrender their arms.

Oct 19th. This is to us a most glorious day, but to the English one of bitter chagrin and disappointment. . . . At about twelve o'clock, the combined army was arranged and drawn up in two lines extending more than a mile in length. The Americans were drawn up in a line on the right side of the road, and the French occupied the left. At the head of the former the great American commander, mounted on his noble courser, took his station, attended by his aides. At the head of the latter was posted the excellent Count Rochambeau and his suite. The French troops, in complete uniform, displayed a martial and noble appearance, their band of music, of which the timbrel formed a part, is a delightful novelty, and produced, while marching to the ground, a most enchanting effect. The Americans though not all in uniform nor their dress so neat, yet exhibited an erect, soldierly air, and every countenance beamed with satisfaction and joy. The concourse of spectators from the country was prodigious, in point of numbers probably equal to the military, but universal silence and order prevailed.

It was about two o'clock when the captive army advanced through the line formed for their reception. Every eye was prepared to gaze on Lord Cornwallis, the object of peculiar interest and solicitude, but he disappointed our anxious expectations; pretending indisposition, he made General O'Hara his substitute as the leader of his army. This officer was followed by the conquered troops in a slow and solemn step, with shouldered arms, colors cased and drums beating a British march. Having arrived at the head of the line, General O'Hara, elegantly mounted, advanced to his Excellency the Commander in Chief, taking off his hat, and apologized for the non-appearance of Lord Cornwallis. With his usual dignity and politeness his Excellency pointed to Major General Lincoln for directions, by whom the British army was conducted into a spacious field, where it was intended they should ground their arms. The royal troops, while marching through the line formed by the allied army, exhibited a decent and neat appearance, as respects arms and clothing, for their commander opened his store and directed every soldier to be furnished with a new suit complete, prior to the capitulation. But in their line of march we remarked a disorderly and unsoldierly conduct, their step was irregular, and their ranks frequently broken. But it was in the field when they came to the last act of the drama, that the spirit and pride of the British soldier was put to the severest test, here their mortification could not be concealed. Some of the platoon officers appeared to be extremely chagrined when giving the word "Ground arms," and I am a witness that they performed this duty in a very unofficer-like manner, and that many of the soldiers manifested a sullen temper, throwing their arms on the pile with violence, as if determined to render them useless. This irregularity, however, was checked by the authority of General Lincoln. After having grounded their arms and divested themselves of their accoutrements, the captive troops were conducted back to Yorktown and guarded by our troops till they could be removed to the place of their destination.

Thacher adds: "We are not to be surprised that the pride of the British officers is humbled on this occasion, as they have always entertained an exalted opinion of their own military prowess, and affected to view the Americans as a contemptible, undisciplined rabble."

In the opinion of Joseph Martin, who paraded with the rest of the victorious army, "the British did not make so good an appearance as the German forces, but there was certainly some allowance to be made in their favor. The English felt their honor wounded, the Germans did not greatly care whose hands they were in. The British paid the Americans, seemingly, but little attention as they passed them, but they eyed the French with considerable malice depicted in their countenances."

Sarah Osborn also watched the British surrender, and remembered how they "marched out beating and playing a melancholy tune, their drums covered with black handkerchiefs and their fifes with black ribbon," and that General O'Hara was a "large portly man, full face, and the tears rolled down his cheeks as he passed along." Later on she saw Cornwallis—"a man of diminutive appearance and having cross eyes"—and then,

on going into town, she noticed two dead Negroes lying by the market house. She had the curiosity to go into a large building that stood nearby, and there she noticed the cupboards smashed to pieces and china dishes and other ware strewed around upon the floor, and among the rest a pewter cover to a hot basin that had a handle on it. She picked it up, supposing it to belong to the British, but the governor [Thomas Nelson, who owned the house] came in and claimed it as his, but said he would have the name of giving it away as it was the last one of twelve that he could see, and accordingly presented it to deponent, and she afterwards brought it home with her to Orange County and sold it for old pewter, which she has a hundred times regretted.

For a decisive battle, the number of casualties was small. "The loss on the part of the French during the siege was fifty killed and one hundred and twenty-seven wounded," wrote Thacher. "Americans: twenty-seven killed and seventy-three wounded. Cornwallis's account of his loss during the siege is one hundred and sixty-three [killed], three hundred and twenty-six wounded, and seventy missing, probably deserted, total five hundred and twenty-two. The whole numbers surrendered by capitulation, seven thousand two hundred and forty-seven. The amount of artillery and military stores, provisions, &c, is very considerable." Also: "From the military chest we received two thousand one hundred and thirteen pounds, six shillings sterling."

The honor of carrying the great news back to France was assigned to the Duc de Lauzun. He was reluctant to accept—the gentleman-to-gentleman parties at which the French officers would wine and dine and swap stories with their captured British counterparts were just about to begin, nor was it at all certain that the fighting was over—but the diplomatic Rochambeau, aware of the outspoken duke's opinions on American valor, told him that as he had been foremost in battle so he should be the first to announce the victory. That settled it, and Lauzun boarded the frigate *Surveillante,* which crossed the Atlantic in a mere twenty-two days. From Brest he hastened to Versailles, where "my news gave the King the greatest joy." Foreign minister Vergennes informed Franklin, the word soon spread, and it was from France rather than America that the news—now become very bad news—reached London. Lord George Germain was the first to be told; it was late at night, but he set off at once in a hackney carriage to pick up two other cabinet members, Lord Stormont and Chancellor Thurlow. All three were then driven to Downing Street, arriving there in the small hours. When told the news, Lord North flung open his arms and took it "as he would have taken a ball in the chest," exclaiming, "Oh God! It is all over!" Almost everyone agreed with this assessment, with one notable exception. "I have no doubt," said King George III, "that when Men are a little recovered of the shock felt by the bad news they will find the necessity of carrying on the War."

The last word belongs not to Lord North or George III but to William Burdett, the dim-witted farmboy who had run off to war thinking it would be "a frolic" and who, while serving as a wagon driver, had once passed Washington on the road and would never forget "the polite bow that the general made to the poor wagoners as he passed them." Burdett had one other treasured memory. This was of the day in the late fall of 1781 when, having volunteered for the militia, he was guarding some British prisoners at Prince Edward Courthouse and "an officer rode up on a panting horse with a cocked hat on and ordered the guards to form a square with the prisoners in the inside, and then news of the surrender of Lord Cornwallis was read, and remembers that the officer threw his cocked hat up in the air, and almost every American present done the same, and the words 'America is ours!' seemed to almost rend the air, such was the joy at that time."

British troops prepare to leave New York, April 1783.

CHAPTER SEVEN

Aftermath

And finally here are brief accounts of what happened in later life to some of the people we have come to know in the course of this history:

This was the second time that Sergeant Roger Lamb of the Royal Welch Fusiliers had been taken prisoner. The first had been at Saratoga, almost exactly four years earlier. After escaping he had taken part in the New Haven raid and then had fought throughout the southern campaign, saving Cornwallis's life at the battle of Guildford Courthouse and admiring the way this "beloved officer" while on campaign had always "fared like a common soldier," dining on turnips or roughly ground corn, and sleeping on the ground without even "the distinction of a tent." Now, although suffering from camp fever, Lamb was once again determined to escape. His destination was British-held New York, several hundred miles distant, a journey he would have to make on foot and in weather that had turned cold and rainy. After changing into the uniform of a private soldier to make himself less conspicuous, he eluded the French and American sentries who were doing a slack job of guarding the prisoners and set off

on the great road which led to Fredericktown in Maryland.

I immediately struck into the woods, to avoid the picquet guard which I knew was posted on it. Night approaching, and finding myself very weak, I made every exertion to extricate myself from the wood. Before it was completely dark, I perceived a few houses and went into one of them. I entreated the inhabitants to let me remain there all night; this they refused in the most peremptory terms, and immediately turned me out of doors, threatening that if I did not instantly depart they would take me back a prisoner to Gloucester Point. I went away with a very sorrowful heart, and after remaining some time in the woods, scarcely able to determine what course to take, the weather being very severe and cold, and finding myself become very weak, I made a desperate effort, and went into a house where there was a woman surrounded by a number of children. I asked her the favor of remaining in her house for the night. She looked at me very sternly and said, "How can you expect such a favor from me, or any of the Americans, seeing you came from England with an intent to destroy our country?" As I stood talking with her, her husband came in. He seemed to be a humane man, and said, "It would be very hard indeed to turn you out of my door such a severe evening as this. I will permit you to remain here this night." He then desired his wife to get a little straw, and make me a bed near the fireplace. After supper I lay down; and not being disturbed by the roaring of cannon and the alarm of war, which had been my portion for many months before, I slept soundly, and awaked in the morning greatly refreshed. I gave the children some trifling presents, with which they and their parents seemed much gratified, and left them with the warmest emotions of thankfulness. . . .

During this day (the 29th of November) I marched very hard on the main road, without encountering any interruption; this arose from its being the route our troops had taken, the inhabitants thinking that I had not been able to keep up with the party, had lagged behind, and was endeavouring to overtake them. In the evening I came to a large building, when a gentleman accosted me, observing: "There are a great many of your men in this house, who are determined to remain in the country. They have hired themselves to different gentlemen. You had better join with them. You shall be well used, and in a short time you may become a citizen of America."

Upon my entering the house I found there were above forty British soldiers who had hired themselves to different gentlemen about the country. Early on the next morning, their masters came with horses, &c. and took them away. I was strongly importuned to go with them; but my mind revolted at the thought. When I was preparing to leave the house, the gentleman said to me, "You had better remain with me. I am told you can write a good hand, and understand accounts. I will build a school-house for you, and make you as comfortable as I can."

I felt my whole frame agitated at the proposal, and notwithstanding the weather was stormy and severe, and that I was very unwell, I immediately left his house with indignation. This dishonorable practice of enticing British soldiers to become settlers was but too common during the greater part of the American war. When a prisoner with them [after Saratoga] I was often strongly solicited, and promised many rewards, if I would desert and remain in the country. But I was determined to die rather than serve any state hostile to Great Britain.

Soon afterward Lamb met up with some other escaped soldiers, and together they eventually reached New York. After the war he returned to his native Ireland, where he became a schoolmaster and wrote *An Original and Authentic Journal of Occurrences During the Late American War from its Commencement to the Year 1783,* and a follow-up volume, *Memoir of His Own Life,* both of which sold very well.

That other sergeant, Joseph Plumb Martin, of the Sappers and Miners, also wrote his memoirs, which he entitled *A Narrative of Some of the Adventures, Dangers and Sufferings of a Revolutionary Soldier;* the book was published anonymously and brought its author little in the way of money or fame. Martin had remained in the army until the peace treaty, then after a stint as a school-teacher, he had settled down as a farmer in a small town near the Penobscot River and married a local girl called Lucy Clew-ley. Though he was at various times a justice of the peace and a selectman, he never prospered. In 1797, as a bounty for his military service, he was given a grant of one hundred acres in Ohio, but like most other veterans he sold it to a speculator. In 1818, when he was fifty-nine, Congress passed a bill making provision for veterans in need, and he applied. "I have no real nor personal estate, nor any income whatever, my necessary bedding and wearing apparel excepted, except two cows, six sheep, one pig. I am a laborer, but by reason of age and infirmity I am unable to work. My wife is sickly and rheumatic. I have five children, viz: Joseph, aged nineteen, an idiot from birth; Thomas and Nathan, twins, fifteen; James Sullivan, eight; Susan, six." His total property was independently valued at fifty-two dollars. In response to his application he was given a pension of eight dollars a month which, along with occasional work as a laborer and steady work as the town clerk, enabled him to get by.

In spite of these setbacks, Martin seems to have enjoyed life; he was good company and well-liked, had time to read widely in history and the classics, sketched wild birds, and composed the occasional hymn for church dedication ceremonies. He died in 1850 at the age of ninety. A few years later the town erected a gravestone at public expense with the epitaph: "A Soldier of the Revolution."

A long life also awaited Ebenezer Fox, whose many adventures had begun when he first ran away to sea at the age of twelve on the eve of Lexington and Concord, and who was last heard of when, having escaped from a French man-of-war in Cap François, Haiti, he "stood erect once more on the deck of an American ship." That ship, the *Flora,* a privateer, soon set sail for France and, while crossing the Atlantic, captured a brig from Liverpool, which was taken to Boston and sold. Fox's share of the prize money was thirty dollars; to his chagrin, a much larger and more valuable prize was soon re-captured by the British. By the time the *Flora* arrived at Bordeaux, the war was winding down, privateering was at an end, and Fox eventually had to join the crew of an American merchant-ship that was bound for home, "where I hoped to enjoy the sweets of liberty."

Our voyage was a pleasant one, and nothing uncommon occurred till we arrived on the American coast, when we fell in with six or eight British ships, bound to England. Their decks were covered with the well-known "red coats" who had survived the attempt to conquer our country. As our flag of stripes and stars was conspicuously displayed, they knew that we were "Yankees," with whom they showed no desire to continue an acquaintance. Our captain hailed them to know "whence they were from, and whither bound?" but no answer was returned. Again he repeated his question; but his Yankee curiosity was not gratified. He once more put his trumpet to his mouth, and roared with a voice like thunder, "Go and be—! We neither love nor fear you."

After a joyful reunion with his family, Ebenezer returned to complete his term with Mr. Bosson, the hairdresser and wig maker to whom he had been apprenticed, and who, as his master, was entitled to, and did actually claim, Fox's thirty dollars in prize money. "I remained with him till I was twenty-one years of age, when I established myself in business in my native place [Roxbury], where I have continued to this day. I commenced business in the practice of the trade I had learned; but after a few years I relinquished it and opened a store for the sale of crockery, glass, and hard-ware, in which business I continued until the year 1837, when, finding my infirmities, especially my deafness, increasing, I thought it time to quit all active employment, and to ride at anchor the remainder of my days."

Private Elijah Fisher of Maine, who often suffered from a "a stitch of pain in my side" and had enlisted for three years in January 1777 on the grounds that "as I got my sickness in the army it was no more than Right but I should have my support from the army," also served on a privateer but was captured, imprisoned on the *Jersey*, and not released until the spring of 1783. He then went to the area around Boston where he did odd jobs, but nothing went right, perhaps because he was convinced that his employers were always trying to cheat him. Part of his account of one altercation runs:

he said how much have you Received of me. I said two months Pay, which was twenty Dollars, then he takes a paper out of his pocket and said that he agreed with me the first of May last for six months for Nine Dollars a month. I said it was true we Did agree for six months but it was for ten Dollars a month, which is sixty Dollars, he says it was but for Nine Dollars in his Book. I said it was for ten Dollars in mine, he said that it was but Nine Dollars and he should not give me no more then that. I told him that I would have what I agreed for if I had anything, which was for ten Dollars a month. He said how have you the empedence to look me in the faice and tell such a lye. I told him that I was not afraid to Look him or any other man in the faice in a good cause and that I told no Lyes but the truth, asking his parding and what we agreed too. . . .

On May 14, 1783, Elijah mentions another reason why he had difficulty finding work: He had just taken the ferry from Charleston to Boston and "there was so meny that Come from the army and from sea that had no homes that would work for little or nothing but their vitels, that I Could not find any Employment . . ."

Two days later he wrote in his journal:

I Com Down by the markett and sits Down all alone allmost Descureged and begun to think over how that I had ben in the army, what ill success I had met with there and allso how I was ronged by them I worked for at home, and lost all last winter and now that I could not get into any besness, and no home, which you may well think how I felt. But then Come into my mind that there ware thousands in wors sircumstances then I was, and having food and rament be with these Content, and that I had nothing to reflect on myself and I to do my endever and leave the event to Provedance, and after that I felt as contented as need to be.

George Washington also returned to civilian life. Dr. James Thacher, who had joined the army outside Boston at just about the same time as the commander in chief, recorded the event in one of the last entries in his journal:

November 25, 1783. The British army evacuated New York, and the American troops under General Knox took possession of the city. Soon after, General Washington and Governor [George] Clinton, with their suite, made their public entry into the city on horseback. . . . On Monday the governor gave an elegant entertainment to the French ambassador, the Chevalier de la Luzerne. General Washington, the principal officers of New York State and of the army, and upwards of a hundred gentlemen were present. Magnificent fireworks, infinitely exceeding everything of the kind before seen in the United States, were exhibited at the Bowling Green in Broadway, on the evening of Tuesday, in celebration of the definitive treaty of peace. They commenced by a dove descending with the olive branch, and setting fire to a marron [rockets] battery. On Tuesday noon, December 4th, the principal officers of the army assembled at Fraunces' Tavern to take a final leave of their much-loved commander in chief. Soon after, his Excellency entered the room. His emotions were too strong to be concealed. Filling a glass, he turned to them and said, "With a heart full of love and gratitude, I now take leave of you. I most devoutly wish that your latter days may be as prosperous and happy as your former ones have been glorious and honorable." Having drunk, he added, "I cannot come to each of you to take my leave, but shall be obliged to you, if each of you will come and take me by the hand." General Knox, being nearest, turned to him. Incapable of utterance, Washington, in tears, grasped his hand, embraced and kissed him. In the same affectionate manner he took leave of each succeeding officer. In every eye was the tear of dignified sensibility; and not a word was articulated to interrupt the eloquent silence and tenderness of the scene. Leaving the room, he passed through the corps of light infantry, and walked to White Hall, where a barge waited to convey him to Paulus' Hook. The whole company followed in mute and solemn procession, with dejected countenances, testifying feelings of delicious melancholy which no language can describe. Having entered the barge, he turned to the company and waving his hat, bid them a silent adieu. They paid him the same affectionate compliment, and after the barge had left them, returned in the same solemn manner to the place where they had assembled.

Skeptics had predicted that, like Oliver Cromwell and other generals who had triumphed in a civil war, Washington would make himself the country's dictator; but after leaving New York his next stop was Annapolis, where Congress met in a special session.

After Thomas Mifflin, the presiding officer, had informed him that "the United States in Congress assembled were prepared to receive his communications," Washington delivered a brief message which concluded: "Having now finished the work assigned to me, I retire from the great theatre of action; and bidding an affectionate farewell to this august body, under whose orders I have long acted, I here offer my commission, and take my leave of all the employments of public life."

That, of course, was not to be, and Washington really had no choice but to serve two terms as the country's president. Nor could he do anything to stem the billowing clouds of purple oratory. "O Washington! How I love thy name!" exclaimed the Rev. Ezra Stiles in an election sermon. "Thy fame is of sweeter perfume than the Arabian spices in the gardens of Persia. A Baron de Steuben shall waft its fragrance to the monarch of Prussia, a Marquis de Lafayette shall waft it to a far greater monarch, and diffuse thy renown throughout Europe. Listening angels shall catch the odor, waft it to heaven, and perfume the universe!"

Worse was to come once he was dead. In 1808, the Rev. Mason L. Weems, who had recently taken to calling himself "Formerly Rector of Mount Vernon Parish," brought out the sixth and "greatly improved" edition of *The Life of General Washington; with Curious Anecdotes, Equally Honourable to Himself and Exemplary to his Young Countrymen.* Among the stories that had not appeared in the earlier editions, or indeed anywhere else, was that of the Quaker, Isaac Potts, coming upon Washington on his knees in the snow at Valley Forge; and this account of the great pains taken by Mr. Washington to inspire his son

✳

with an *early love of truth.* "Truth, George," said he, "is the loveliest quality of youth. I would ride fifty miles, my son, to see the little boy whose heart is so honest, and his lips so pure, that we may depend on every word he says. O how lovely does such a child appear in the eyes of everybody! His parents doat on him; his relations glory in him; they are constantly praising him to their children, whom they beg to imitate him . . . ! But, Oh! how different, George, is the case with the boy who is so given to lying that nobody can believe a word he says! He is looked on with aversion wherever he goes, and parents dread to see him come among their children. Oh, George! my son! rather than see you come to this pass, dear as you are to my heart, gladly would I assist to nail you up in your little coffin and follow you to your grave. Hard, indeed, would it be to me to give up my son, whose little feet are always so ready to run about with me, and whose fondly looking eyes and sweet prattle make so large a part of my happiness: but still I would give him up, rather than see him a common liar."

"Pa," said George very seriously, "do I ever tell lies?"

"No, George, I thank God you do not, my son; and I rejoice in the hope that you never will . . ."

After this comes the famous story, "too true to be doubted," which begins when George, then six years old, is given a hatchet and ends

when looking at his father with the sweet face of youth brightened with the inexpressible charm of all-conquering truth, he bravely cried out, "I can't tell a lie, Pa; you know I can't tell a lie! I did cut it with my hatchet!" —"Run to my arms, you dearest boy!" cried his father in transports; "run to my arms! Glad am I, George, that you killed my tree; for you have paid me for it a thousand fold. Such an act of heroism in my son is more worth than a thousand trees, though blossomed with silver and their fruits of purest gold . . ."

On leaving the army Dr. James Thacher went to live in Plymouth, Massachusetts, where he became the town's leading physician; he also wrote two volumes of local history as well as books on medicine, agriculture (*The Management of Bees, The American Orchardist*), and the supernatural (*Demonology, Ghosts and Apparitions*). Mercy Otis Warren and her husband, James, were neighbors until they acquired the large house and estate at Milton that had been confiscated from the exiled former royal governor, Thomas Hutchinson. ("It has not always happened in like manner that the forfeited seats of the wicked have been filled with men of virtue," wrote Arthur Lee in congratulation. "But in this corrupt world it is sufficient that we have some examples of it for our consolation.") Soon after the war Mercy welcomed her fellow historian Catharine Macaulay, the "amiable daughter of liberty," who with her young husband was visiting America. Though on the higher plane there was a meeting of minds, Mercy did have to admit to John Adams that she found her guest "a little too prolix in conversation." (This was before her falling-out with Adams, who, on reading her *History of the Rise, Progress and Termination of the American Revolution,* was scalded to find that, though highly praised, he was also spoken of as one whose "prejudices were sometimes too strong for his sagacity and judgment" and who suffered from "pride of talents and much ambition." Adams, who had earlier put Mercy on notice that "I have long contemplated in many very solemn hours the Injustice, Ingratitude, and Abuse experienced by myself," responded with letters which she described as "marked with passion, absurdity, and inconsistency." In the end the quarrel was patched up, and the two exchanged locks of hair, but Adams never forgave her: "History," he wrote, "is not the province of the Ladies.")

Sarah "the deponent" Osborn, who had brought hot meals up to her husband in the trenches in front of Yorktown, lived to a great age. Interviewed for an 1854 article in the *American Phrenological*

Journal, she claimed to be 109 although, on the basis of her 1837 pension application, she was a mere 98. In his book, *Influence of the Revolution upon the Human Body,* Dr. Benjamin Rush had listed some of the medical benefits that wars could bring, especially to women, for "when either love, jealousy, grief, or even devotion wholly engross the female mind, they seldom fail to cure or suspend hysterical complaints." Dr. Rush also noted that the growth of "the population of the United States was more rapid from births during the war than it had ever been," and included "several children born of parents who had lived many years together without issue." Among these wartime children was Sarah's daughter, Phebe, who was still alive at the time of the pension deposition. Phebe's birth had been followed a year and a half later by that of Aaron Osborn Jr., who "had fits and was crazy, and became a town charge, and finally died at the age of about thirty."

Other trials awaited Sarah:

About three months after the birth of her last child, she last saw her said husband, who then left her at New Windsor and never returned. He had been absent at intervals before this from deponent, and at one time deponent understood he was married again to a girl by the name of Polly Sloat, above Newburgh about fifteen or sixteen miles. Deponent got a horse and rode up to inquire into the truth of the story. She arrived at the girl's father's and there found her said husband, and Polly Sloat, and her parents. Deponent was kindly treated by the inmates of the house but ascertained for a truth that her husband was married to said girl. After remaining overnight, deponent determined to return home and abandon her said husband forever.

Aaron later left Polly and tried to make up to Sarah, but she refused "under a firm belief that her husband would conduct no better, and her said husband the same night absconded with two others, crossed the river at Newburgh, and she never saw him afterwards." She did, however, hear that he had married yet again, and this encouraged her to remarry too, to another veteran, John Benjamin of Blooming Grove, Orange County, New York. Like Joseph Martin, Aaron Osborn was awarded a grant of land for his military service, but he too sold it to a speculator, and "about twenty years ago, deponent heard that her said husband Osborn died up the Mohawk, and she has no reason to believe the contrary." Also, "deponent was informed more than forty years ago, and believes, that said Polly Sloat, Osborn's second wife above mentioned, died dead drunk, the liquor running out of her mouth after she was dead. Osborn's third wife she knows nothing about."

Sarah's second husband, John Benjamin, had also died by the time of her deposition, but there was a happy ending of sorts to her story: Although her own services counted for nothing, it was decided that because both her husbands had been veterans, she should receive a double pension.

As to some of the other ladies of the Revolution—for Margaret Morris of Burlington and Elizabeth Drinker of Philadelphia, life seemed to have returned to normal, but a complete change was in store for Sally Wister. Although the bashful Major Stodard never did return, news that there was a house full of pretty young girls at Gwynedd must have spread through the American camp, for plenty of other officers found reason to stop by, among them a dashing captain from Virginia named Alexander Spottiswood Dandridge, who flirted with her extravagantly but ended up marrying someone else. When the British left Philadelphia, the Wisters returned to the city but then went to live with Sally's grandfather at his large house, called Grumblethorpe, in Germantown. Here soon afterward she had a sudden and total religious conversion, and for the rest of her fairly short life she filled her diary with nothing but pious meditations, prayers, and accounts of good works.

Ann Lee, founder of The United Society of Believers in Christ's Second Appearing—the Shakers—survived her wartime persecution at the hands of the Commissioners for Detecting Conspiracies, which accused her of spying and pacifism. After a proselytizing postwar tour through New England, during which she urged simplicity, frugality, and piety—"put your hands to work, and give your hearts to God"—she won many converts, who, after she died in 1784, remained in communication with her spirit while awaiting her return as the female Messiah.

Jemima Wilkinson, the tall, dark-eyed, and good-looking Public Universal Friend, also continued her ministry but faced such persecution from the orthodox churches that in 1790 she moved to Seneca Lake, in western New York, where she acquired a large tract of land and established a religious colony called Jerusalem. She got on well with the local Indians, who called her Squaw Shinnewanagistagwe (Great Woman Preacher). A few of her followers resented the fact that she did not live in the colony but in a large and comfortable private house some distance away, and also objected to her habit of taking their possessions on the grounds that "The Friend hath need of these things." But until the day she died (in 1819) her grip on her followers never slackened, not even in the aftermath of her announcement that she intended to imitate one of Jesus' better-known miracles. For this purpose a platform

※

was built on the banks of the Seneca Lake, at Rappleyea's ferry, ten miles south of Dresden. At the appointed time, having approached within a few hundred yards of the lake shore, she alighted from an elegant carriage, the road being strewed by her followers with white handkerchiefs. She walked to the platform, and having announced her intention of walking across the lake on the water, she stepped ankle deep into the clear element, when suddenly pausing, she addressed the multitude, inquiring whether or not they had faith that she could pass over, for if otherwise she could not; and on receiving an affirmative answer returned to her carriage, declaring that as they believed in her power it was unnecessary to display it. (From John Barber's *Historical Collections of the State of New York.*)

Abigail Adams also took to the water, but in a more conventional way. After a lengthy separation from "the Dear long-absent partner of my Heart," she was at long last able to fulfil her earlier wish to visit the mother country, though by now with a rather more critical attitude. On Sunday, June 20, 1784, accompanied by her daughter Nabby, she went onboard the *Active,* bound for England, where she was to join her husband, now minister to the Court of St. James. Like John on his voyage to France in 1777, she had to endure a terrible crossing—the food was so awful that "I have been obliged to turn cook myself and have made two puddings, the only thing I have seen fit to eat," and the weather so rough that "when in bed I was obliged to hold fast by the sides till my hands and wrists aked to keep in. Only conceive a great cradle rocking with amaizing force from side to side, whilst a continual creek from every part of the Ship responded to the Roll. Not a wink of sleep to be had, bottles, mugs, plates, every thing crashing to peices. . . . I am more and more of the mind that a Lady ought not to go to sea. It is impossible to preserve that Decency and Cleanliness which ought to be an inherint principal in every female." After celebrating "the Anniversary of our Glorious Independence" at sea—"While the Nations of Europe are enveloped in Luxery and dissipation, and a universal venality prevails throughout Britain, may the new empire, Gracious Heaven, become the Guardian and protector of Religion and Liberty, of universal Benevolence and Phylanthropy"—they at last arrived at Deal, in Kent. Here she, Nabby, and some other passengers took a coach for London, stopping en route at Canterbury, which she did not like, seemingly on religious principles. "Canterburry is a larger town than Boston, it contains a Number of old Gothick Cathedrals, which are all of Stone very heavy, with but few windows which are grated with large Bars of Iron, and look more like jails for criminals than places design'd for worship of the deity. One would suppose from the manner in which they are Gaurded that they apprehend devotion would be Stolen. They have a most gloomy appearance and realy made me shudder."

From there it was on to Chatham,

where we stopped at a very elegant inn to dine. As soon as you drive into the yard you have at these places as many footmen round you as you have Carriages, who with their politest airs take down the Step of your Carriage, assist you out, inquire if you want fresh horses or carriages; will supply you directly, Sir, is the answer. A well-dresst hostess steps forward, making a Lady-like appearance and wishes your commands; if you desire a chamber, the Chamber maid attends; you request dinner, say in half an hour, the Bill of Fare is directly brought, you mark what you wish to have, and suppose it to be a variety of fish, fowl, meat, all of which we had, up to eight different dishes; besides vegetables. The moment the time you stated is out, you will have your dinner upon the table in as elegant a Stile as at any Gentleman's table, with your powdered waiters, and the master or Mistress always brings the first dish upon table themselves.

But if the excellent inn and the gloomy gothic cathedral more or less balanced each other out as representative examples of the British way of life, what happened next firmly tipped the scales in America's favor.

From Chatham we proceeded on our way as fast as possible wishing to pass Black Heath before dark. Upon this road, a Gentleman alone in a post chaise passed us, and very soon a coach before us stopped, and there was a hue and cry, "A Robbery! A Robbery!" The Man in the chaise was the person robbed and this in open day with carriages constantly passing.

We were not a little allarmed and every one were concealing their money. Every place we past, and every post chaise we met were crying out "A robbery!" Where the thing is so common I was surprized to see such an allarm. The Robber was pursued and taken in about two miles, and we saw the poor wretch gastly and horible, brought along on foot, his horse rode by a person who took him; who also had his pistol. He looked like a youth of 20 only, attempted to lift his hat, and looked Dispair. You can form some Idea of my feelings when they told him "Aya! You have but a short time. The assise set next Month, and then, my Lad, you Swing." Tho every robber may deserve Death yet to exult over the wretched is what our Country is not accustomed to. Long may it be free of such villainies and long may it preserve a commiseration for the wretched!

And here is what happened to some of the men of the Revolution:

Charles Lee, who had been Washington's right-hand man until his questionable conduct at the Battle of Monmouth Courthouse, died in 1782 "in a small dirty room in a Philadelphia tavern, called the Conestoga Wagon." An eccentric to the last, Lee died virtually alone, as always preferring the company of his dogs to that of humans. In his will he wrote that "I desire most earnestly that I may not be buried in any church or church yard, or within a mile of any Presbyterian or Anabaptist Meeting House, for since I have resided in this country, I have kept so much bad company while living, that I do not choose to continue it when dead."

Thomas Paine also came to an unconventional end. "The times that tried men's souls are over," he had written in the April 1783 issue of *The Crisis*, "and the greatest and completest revolution the world ever knew is gloriously and happily accomplished." That being so, Paine moved on and was soon taking an active part in the French Revolution. In 1802 he returned to America, expecting to be honored for his earlier services but instead was reviled as the atheistic author of *The Age of Reason*. Few attended his funeral in New Rochelle when he finally managed to drink himself to death in 1809, but ten years later the English radical William Cobbett, who was visiting this country, decided to dig him up and ship him back to England for a more fitting burial. Unfortunately, although the body is known to have reached Liverpool, it was lost somewhere between there and London, and has never been found.

Major John André, hanged for his part in Benedict Arnold's treason, was also dug up and shipped home, in his case without mishap. He was reburied in Westminster Abbey, where a monument in his honor had already been erected.

Honorable reburial was also in store for another native-born Englishman, although he had to wait for more than a hundred years. Only then did President Theodore Roosevelt rouse himself at the thought that John Paul Jones, the greatest hero of the American navy, was lying in an obscure grave in the Protestant cemetery in Paris. Never one to do things by halves, Roosevelt dispatched a squadron of four cruisers to escort the body back to America, where it was re-interred with great pomp and ceremony in a marble tomb in the Naval Academy at Annapolis.

After spending two years on parole following his capture at Charleston, General William Moultrie was released in a prisoner exchange—"a whole brigade of American officers" in return for the overpriced General Burgoyne. From Philadelphia Moultrie made his way south to visit his friend General Greene, on the Ashley River, a route that took him through an area devastated by years of guerilla warfare—"the most dull, melancholy, dreary ride that anyone could possibly take, of about one hundred miles through the woods of that country, which I had been accustomed to see abound with live-stock and wild fowl of every kind. . . . Not the vestiges of horses, cattle, hogs, or deer &c. was to be found . . . no living creature was to be seen, except now and then a few camp scavengers [turkey buzzards], picking the bones of some unfortunate fellows who had been shot or cut down, and left in the woods above ground."

Although already accompanied by a troop of volunteer dragoons, Moultrie

made a circuitous route to General Marion's camp, then on Santee River, to get an escort, which he gave me, of twenty infantry and twenty cavalry. Those, with the volunteers that attended me from Georgetown, made us pretty strong. On my way from General Marion's to General Greene's camp, my plantation was in the direct road, where I called and stayed a night. On my entering the place, as soon as the Negroes discovered that I was of the party, there was immediately a general alarm, and an outcry through the plantation that "Massa was come! Massa was come!" and they were running from every part with great joy to see me. I stood in the piazza to receive them. They gazed at me with astonishment, and every one came and took me by the hand, saying, "God bless you, massa! We glad for see you, massa!" and every now and then some one or other would come out with a "Ky!" And the old Africans joined in a war song in their own language of "Welcome the warrior home." It was an affecting meeting between the slaves and their master. The tears stole from my eyes and ran down my cheeks. A number of gentlemen that were with me could not help being affected by the scene. . . . I then possessed about two hundred slaves, and not one of them left me during the war, although they had had great offers, nay, some were carried down to work on the British lines, yet they always contrived to make their escapes and return home.

Moultrie's sincerity is no doubt genuine, but the joy of his slaves? But then, what would *you* have done if after a long absence massa suddenly turned up with "an escort of twenty infantry and twenty cavalry" along with the dragoon "volunteers from Georgetown" and "a number of gentlemen," all undoubtedly well armed? Tell him what was on your mind? Or tell him what he wanted to hear?

At any rate, from his plantation Moultrie continued on for "that happy day when we marched into Charlestown with the American troops. It was a proud day to me, and I felt myself much elated at seeing the balconies, the doors, and windows crowded with the patriotic fair, the aged citizens and others, congratulating us on our return home, saying, 'God bless you, gentlemen! You are welcome home, gentlemen!' Both citizens and soldiers shed mutual tears of joy."

By then of course the British had evacuated Charleston, taking several thousand Negroes with them; but it would be a mistake to suppose that these were the lucky ones. Most were going because they were the property of Loyalists planning to re-settle in Florida or the West Indies; others had been recruited into British regiments to serve in the continuing war against France and Spain; and others were loot. "The prospects of gain from the sale of plundered Negroes," wrote Moultrie, "were too seducing to be resisted by the officers, privates, and followers of the British army. On their departure from Charlestown, upwards of eight hundred slaves, who had been employed in the engineer department, were shipped off for the West Indies." According to Moultrie, this was done on the orders of Colonel Moncrieff of the Royal Engineers, who then sold the slaves for his own profit. True or not, their fate in the West Indies was worse than if they had remained in America. So brutal was the treatment of slaves there that about one in ten died every year. Many were suicides. William Hickey, the man-about-town who had been an eyewitness to the St. George's Fields Massacre of 1768 and since then had traveled much of the world, happened to be in Jamaica at about this time and described the practice known as "dirt eating," which was apparently quite common. "It is no less singular that the miserable Africans employed to cultivate our West India Islands were driven by despair, more especially from harsh and cruel treatment, to destroy themselves by eating the earth, a small quantity of which they swallow daily. This gradually reduces them, finally causing death as certainly as the most potent poison. I saw several so weak and ill from this practice they could scarcely drag one leg after the other, with countenances inexpressibly melancholy and ghastly." On one estate alone "upwards of two hundred of the unhappy men . . . had thus destroyed themselves, to the enormous loss of six thousand pounds."

After Yorktown most of the French troops were sent to the West Indies and Central America to continue the war against "notre éternel et tyrannique ennemi," to use La Fayette's phrase. The British won a major naval victory at the Battle of the Saints, but by late 1782 both parties were ready to call it quits, at least for the time being.

Among those who then returned home was the "gentleman-cadet" Jean-Baptiste de Verger of the Royal Deux-Ponts (Zweibrücken) Regiment, who wrote that "the first thing that struck me on my arrival in Brest was finding myself surrounded by beggars asking for alms, something I never saw in America." The Alsatian Baron von Closen wrote more cheerfully of the "beautiful breeze" that carried his ship into the same harbor "whose entire bank was lined with men and women making signs of joy to us and cheering loudly, while our ship fired her guns in salute and the shore batteries responded." As soon as he set foot on land, along with the Comte de Deux-Ponts and the Comte de Fersen, "our first purchase was six bunches of delicious cherries bought from a pretty fruit-seller which we devoured as we walked along." To add to his pleasure von Closen's pockets were full of *louis d'or* that he had won gambling during the voyage. With six months' leave in which to spend it all, he began by buying "a good carriage large enough to accommodate—in front, behind, and on top—my servants (one white, and my superb and faithful Negro, Peter), three monkeys, four parrots, and six parakeets. After hiring post-horses I left that evening with this noisy and unruly display, like a merchant arriving from Smyrna . . ." In Paris the Rochambeau family insisted that he stay with them. The general presented him at court where the Minister of War promised him a colonelcy as soon as he provided proof that this nobility was sufficiently ancient to warrant being included "in the prerogatives of rank and distinctions." He also received a letter from his fiancée that she "was waiting for me impatiently *and with open arms!*" So it was on to Zweibrücken as soon as possible, to "my beautiful betrothed, my divine Doris [von Fürstenwärther] who had had the constancy to keep her heart and hand for me during the four years of my absence in America"—despite offers from much wealthier suitors—and with her "to fly gaily into the arms of Hymen."

Three years later Rochambeau, then living in Calais, again played host, this time to Lord Cornwallis, who was on his way out to India where he had been appointed Governor General and Commander in Chief. Nobody—apart from Sir Henry Clinton—had blamed Cornwallis for the defeat at Yorktown, least of all the king. In India he would have another opportunity to put down a rebellion, this one led by the insurgent prince, Tipu Sahib, and this time he would be successful. The dinner at Calais apparently went well, although as Rochambeau wrote to Washington in his fractured English, "As you may believe, I could not drink with him your health in toast."

Once the French Revolution had swept away the barriers facing officers whose nobility did not stretch back several generations, a great military career awaited Alexandre Berthier, whose father had been a cartographer and grandfather a wheelwright. An outstanding staff officer, he became Napoleon's right hand, was made Minister of War, Marshal of France, and a prince twice over—Prince de Neuchâtel and Prince de Wagram. But when Napoleon returned from Elba for the Hundred Days, Berthier did not rally to him, and two weeks before the battle of Waterloo, tormented by guilt, he threw himself out of a high window in the royal castle of Bamberg. The only decoration he was wearing at the time of his death was the ribbon of the Order of the Cincinnati. "He told me once," said his aide-de-camp, "that of all the honors and decorations he had been awarded during his career, the one he was proudest of was the small eagle of that Order."

By then the Duc de Lauzun was no more. On his return to France, bringing the news of Yorktown, he had picked up where he left off: Madame de Coigny "was more charming than ever . . . it was impossible not to yield to the irresistible attraction that drew me to her . . . I also met Mrs. Robinson . . . I was an object to excite her fancy, a man who had brought home great tidings, who came from the war, who had already suffered greatly and would suffer still more. She felt that she could not do too much for him; and so I enjoyed Perdita—but I did not conceal my success from Madame de Coigny . . ."

Lauzun had at first welcomed the French Revolution and had even fought against the royalist uprising in the Vendée, but during the Reign of Terror he was too obvious a target for "revolutionary justice." Accused of treason, he was sentenced to the guillotine, a verdict he is said to have received "with a smile." When the executioner came to fetch him, Lauzun was just sitting down to a dish of oysters. "Citizen," he said, "allow me to finish." Then offering the man a drink, he said, "Have some wine. A man in your trade needs to keep up his courage."

Of the 29,867 German mercenaries sent to America, 7,754 died, some as military casualties, most from sickness and suicide. The number of deserters and of those given permission to remain was not so precisely tabulated, but was between five and seven thousand. Among those staying was an officer named Kuster, who had served under Burgoyne and whose descendant, George Armstrong Custer, seems to have inherited that general's flamboyant style along with his instinct for military disaster. Among those returning were Captain Hinrichs, Captain von Ewald, who later became a general in the Danish army during the Napoleonic Wars, and Captain (now Major) Pausch, of the Hesse-Hanau artillery, who had been ordered by his prince to keep a diary and was now also writing directly to that personage: "The order to return is the most enjoyable order we have ever received and we now write with the most comforting and most hopeful joy that we may again see the most gracious face of our most gracious and best Prince, and be permitted to kiss the hem of Your Highness' robes in the most humble obedience . . ."

On their way home the Riedesels and their four children, the youngest a three-year-old named America, stopped off in London. Six years earlier the baroness had spent the winter there and become friendly with the queen, so it was not long before

her Majesty's first lady-in-waiting, Lady Howard, sent word that we were to be received by the Queen. Since my court dress was not ready, and I had nothing to wear but a plain simple angloise, I sent my apologies in advance, and repeated them when we had the honor of being presented to their Majesties. But the Queen, who received us most graciously, as did the King, replied in the friendliest way, "When we are happy to see people, we pay no attention to what they are wearing." They were surrounded by all their daughters, the Princesses. They, the Queen, the lady-in-waiting and I sat in a half-circle before the fireplace, while my husband stood with the King in front of the fire, talking about America in German, which the King spoke extremely well. Tea and cakes were passed around. I sat between the Queen and one of the Princesses and was plied with questions. The Queen very graciously said to me, "I have followed all your movements and have often asked after you. It was always a satisfaction to hear that you were in good health, not discouraged, and beloved by everyone." I happened to have a dreadful cough at the time and Princess Sophia herself went to fetch some black-currant jelly, which she recommended as a particularly good remedy, insisting that I accept the full jar. At nine the Prince of Wales came in. His sisters ran to him and he embraced them and danced around with them. Indeed the royal family had such a gift of banishing all feelings of restraint that it felt like being in a happy family circle among people of one's own kind. We stayed until ten o'clock.

Company Surgeon Wasmus took a more direct route home: From Canada his regiment sailed to Holland and from there marched across north Germany, on the way parading through the medieval city of Lüneburg, where a crowd turned out to cheer the returning soldiers and gawk at the black drummer boys recruited in America. On October 8 "we marched to Weddel, where we witnessed moving scenes of father and son, wife and husband, meeting each other with tears of joy." Next day they reached their final destination, Wolfenbüttel.

The closer we came, the more people crowded around us. Everyone called to friends or relatives, and wherever I looked I saw friendly people waving at me, some of them calling my name. Many had changed so greatly in these last eight years that I did not recognize them. I found my wife and children in good health; the children had grown so much during the last eight years and looked so different that I would never have recognized them. When I left, my son had been ten and my daughter eight. The various moving scenes that I witnessed cannot be described. Strict orders were issued that everyone in our corps was to remain in Wolfenbüttel and no one was to go on to Braunschweig.

So much for "the sweet thought of once again embracing my beloved wife" that had been one of Wasmus's reasons for deciding not to remain in Massachusetts! Soon after entering this chilly account of his family reunion, Wasmus gave up keeping a diary altogether. His last entry ran: "Lord, you who have helped me bear the morning and midday of my life, let the evening now approaching with rapid steps be fairer and calmer than the day. And when it comes, keep me in your Holy Care. Amen."

But perhaps his wife had her reasons for giving him such a cool welcome, and perhaps her husband's earlier interest in the New England custom of bundling, described so carefully in his diary, had not been entirely folkloric. At any rate, in the Brimfield, Massachusetts, register of births there is this entry: "Wasmus, Demas, son of Sarah Hitchcock, May 23, 1779." No father is listed, but Wasmus was hardly a common name in New England, while Demas is mentioned in the Bible as a companion to Luke, "the beloved physician." The Hitchcocks were the family with whom Wasmus lodged for a while. And the dates fit.

Also in London at the same time as the Riedesels were Benedict and Peggy Arnold. Though cold-shouldered by some, the Arnolds were taken up by society: A friend of Sir Henry Clinton described Peggy as having "an ease in her behaviour which astonished everybody, and novelty made everybody desirous of being presented to them. He played at high whist with the Duchess of Bedford, and 'twas observed how little of the *mauvaise honte* he had about him. Indeed it was the same at St. James's, for they both seemed quite at home when they were presented."

Banastre Tarleton, the "Green Dragoon," also spent much of his time gambling for high stakes. On one occasion, in a club called the Cocoa Tree, Lord Malden wagered a thousand guineas that he (Tarleton) would not be able to seduce Perdita Robinson, now back in London from France, where she had been visiting with the Duc de Lauzun. Rising to the challenge of once again "crossing swords with the French duke," even if only metaphorically, Banastre accepted the bet: "Aye, win her—and jilt her too!" he boasted, though in fact after winning her he kept the affair going off and on for fifteen years. Tarleton also stood for Parliament, presenting himself to the voters as "that Hero who fought your Battles midst Clouds of Smoke and Streams of Blood," and once elected took the lead in defending the slave trade, calling abolition "a dangerous interference with trade" and a "violent aggression upon property." He later made an advantageous marriage with the daughter of an English duke, was promoted to the rank of general, was knighted in 1820, and did not die until he was nearly eighty.

Lord George Germain also had a soft landing. Refusing to lower his terms, he clung to office until late December 1781, when the king at last agreed to grant him a peerage in his own right. As Lord Sackville, he then took his seat in the House of Lords, and "no one," as he then put it, "can say he is disgraced."

Following the news of Yorktown, the king had urged Lord North not "to despond on difficulties" but to buck up and "see how to get out of them." They should "adopt a Plan and abide by it" and then, "with the assistance of Parliament, I do not doubt, if measures are well concerted, a good end may yet be made to this War." But the purchased majorities in the House of Commons were melting away, and in March 1782 "Lord North has the honour of informing His Majesty" that this House had passed a motion declaring that anyone "who should advise, or in any way attempt to prosecute an offensive War in America for the purpose of reducing the Colonies to obedience by force" should be considered an enemy of his country.

Now it was the king's turn to despond. In a draft of a message he explained that

the sudden change of Sentiment of one Branch of the Legislature has totally incapacitated Him from either conducting the War with effect, or from Obtaining any Peace but on conditions which would prove destructive to the Commerce as well as essential Rights of the British Nation. His Majesty therefore with much sorrow finds He can be of no further Utility to His Native Country which drives Him to the painful step of quitting it for ever. In consequence of which Intention His Majesty resigns the Crown of Great Britain and the Dominions appertaining thereto to His Dearly Beloved Son and lawful Successor, George Prince of Wales.

But the message was never more than a draft; every personal pronoun was still capitalized; the Prince of Wales was not ready to take over; and, on further reflection, there was no reason why he should pay for the mistakes of others. "I cannot conclude without mentioning how sensibly I feel the dismemberment of America," he wrote to Lord Shelburne, "and that I should be miserable indeed if I did not feel that no blame on that account can be laid at My door." Another consoling thought about America: "Knavery seems to be so much the striking feature of its inhabitants that it may not in the end be an evil that they become aliens to this Kingdom."

But once again he had second thoughts and was soon wishing the Americans well. "My prayers to Almighty God," he told Parliament, were that they would soon realize "how essential monarchy is to the enjoyment of constitutional liberty," adding that "religion, language, interest, affection, may and I hope will yet prove a bond of permanent union between the two countries."

And here, four years after Yorktown, at a royal levée, came reconciliation itself, personified in the form of a short and roly-poly figure dressed in black silk breeches, silk stockings, and buckled shoes, with a white powdered wig above his ruddy face, a small ceremonial sword at his side, and bowing thee times as he advanced: none other than His Rotundity, John Adams, come to present himself as his country's first ambassador to the Court of St. James's.

"The appointment of a minister from the United States to Your Majesty's Court will form an epoch in the history of England and America," he informed the king. Then, his voice, as he later acknowledged, occasionally breaking into a quaver because he was so nervous, he launched into this long but well-rehearsed sentence:

✳

I think myself more fortunate than all my fellow-citizens in having the distinguished honor to be the first to stand in your Majesty's royal presence in a diplomatic character; and I shall esteem myself the happiest of men if I can be instrumental in recommending my country more and more to your Majesty's royal benevolence, and of restoring an entire esteem, confidence and affection, or, in other words, the old good nature and the old good humor between people who, though separated by an ocean, and under different governments, have the same language, similar religion, and kindred blood.

The king, who as Adams reported to John Jay, "listened to every word I said and seemed much affected," made a brief reply, concluding, "I will be very frank with you. I was the last to consent to separation; but the separation having been made, and having become inevitable, I have always said, as I say now, that I would be the first to meet the friendship of the United States as an independent power."

With that behind them, George tacitly invited Adams to join in a little friendly French-bashing: "There is an opinion among some people that you are not the most attached of all your countrymen to the manners of France," he said with a smile. But Adams, apparently unable not to be pompous, plonked him. "I must avow to your Majesty, I have no attachment but to my own country." "An honest man will never have any other," replied the king, who then bowed, indicating that the interview was over.

As always in his travels, Adams was an alert and interested observer, even if he still had only one standard of comparison. Thus in July 1786, after walking along the Edgware Road in what was then outer London, he wrote in his diary how he had seen "on the Side of the Way several heaps of Manure, an hundred Loads perhaps in each heap. I have carefully examined them and found them composed of Straw, and dung from the Stables and Streets of London, mud, clay, or Marl, dug of the Ditch. . . . This may be good manure, but it is not equal to mine, which I composed in similar heaps upon my own Farm, of Horse Dung from Brackett's Stable in Boston, marsh Mud from the sea shore, and Street Dust from the Plain at the Foot of Pen's Hill . . ."

"At length we are at peace, God be praised, and long, very long, may it continue," wrote Benjamin Franklin from Paris in January 1783 to his friend Polly Hewson, daughter of his former landlady in London, Mrs. Stevenson. "All wars are follies, and very mischievous ones. When will mankind be convinced of this, and agree to settle differences by arbitration? Were they to do it even by the cast of a die, it would be better than by fighting and destroying each other."

Final agreement on the terms of the peace treaty was slow to achieve, especially after Henry Laurens joined the American negotiators and started insisting on the full return of slaves who had joined the British; but by mid-September Franklin could write to Josiah Quincy that "the definitive treaty was signed the 3rd instant. We are now friends with England and with all mankind. May we never see another war, for in my opinion *there never was a good war or a bad peace.*"

His diplomatic mission now over, Franklin wrote to Congress submitting his resignation. For a while he toyed with the idea of staying on as a private citizen. "The French are an amiable people to live with. They love me, and I love them. Yet I do not feel myself at home, and I wish to die in my own country." And so, in July 1785, he left his house in Passy and set off for Le Havre. Hearing that he suffered from kidney stones and gout, which made traveling in a jolting coach hard to endure, Marie Antoinette lent him a pair of royal mules "which walk steadily and easily" and the Duc de Coigny provided a special litter that was slung between the mules. As a parting gift the king gave him a miniature portrait of himself set with a hundred diamonds. The Minister of Marine offered a frigate, but this was declined. "A very great concourse of the people of Passy came to see him depart," wrote his grandson Benny Bache. "A mournful silence reigned around him, and was only interrupted by a few sobs." Madame Brillon was so upset that she had to stay indoors. "My heart will regret him for ever," she wrote. Madame Helvétius sent a letter urging him to come back "to me and all my friends who love you so much and to whom you leave such long regrets."

While crossing the Atlantic for the fourth time, Franklin as usual kept himself busy working either on scientific studies or on practical ideas that would improve the lives of ordinary people: observations on the Gulf Stream and the temperature of the water at various depths, a paper on why chimneys smoke and what to do about it, a design for another stove, notes on the use of watertight compartments to prevent ships from sinking, a more efficient way to rig small sailing vessels. On September 14 he wrote in his journal, "With the flood in the morning came a light breeze, which brought us above Gloucester Point, in full view of dear Philadelphia! . . . My son-in-law came with a boat for us; we landed at Market Street wharf, where we were received by a crowd of people with huzzas, and accompanied with acclamations quite to my door. Found my family well. God be praised and thanked for all his mercies." And then before long it was back to work on papers about lead poisoning, correspondence with Noah Webster about simplifying spelling, and the presidency of The Pennsylvania Society for Promoting the Abolition of Slavery.

Franklin has often been called the first American, and like most Americans who have been to Paris, he left a piece of his heart there. In October 1788, not long before he died, he replied to a letter from his friend Madame Lavoisier:

✳

It is true, as you observe, that I enjoy here every thing that a reasonable mind can desire—a sufficiency of income, a comfortable habitation of my own building, having all the conveniences I could imagine; a dutiful and affectionate daughter to nurse and take care of me, a number of promising grandchildren, some old friends still remaining to converse with, and more respect, distinction, and public honours than I can possibly merit. These are the blessings of God, and depend on his continued goodness; yet all do not make me forget Paris, and the nine years' happiness I enjoyed there, in the sweet society of a people whose conversation is instructive, whose manners are highly pleasing, and who, above all the nations of the world, have, in the greatest perfection, the art of making themselves beloved by strangers. And now, even in my sleep, I find that the scenes of all my pleasantest dreams are laid in that city. . . .

✺

By early June 1825, Washington was long dead, buried, and resurrected as the perfect hero the country wanted him to have been. John Adams and Thomas Jefferson were both still alive, though scheduled to die the following year, on the very same day, July 4. Louis XVI and Marie Antoinette had been guillotined, and George III, blind, deaf, and mad, had died in 1820 at the age of eighty-two. John Quincy Adams had recently become president and the fiftieth anniversary of the Battle of Bunker Hill was coming up.

Naturally, there was to be a big celebration, including a parade through Boston and a ceremony of dedication at the site of the battle-field monument. Daniel Webster, the great orator of the age—"The God-like Daniel"—was to give a speech. The Marquis de Lafayette—"The Hero of Two Worlds"—had been invited, as had surviving veterans of the battle. Among these was the Ipswich shoemaker and former minuteman Joseph Hodgkins, who had marched cheerfully from one battle to another and written home so punctually to Sarah, his "Loving Wife." Though now eighty-two years old, Hodgkins was still "in good health through the goodness of God" and spry enough to refuse the offer of a coach ride to Boston, choosing instead to ride there on his own horse.

Only the site of the battlefield monument was to be dedicated, as work had not yet started on the granite structure itself. Combining thrift with patriotism, the General Court had recently passed a law "that the Bunker Hill Monument Association shall be entitled to have the stone, of which the intended monument may be constructed, hammered and prepared to be used at the state prison at Charlestown, and the proper officers of the prison are hereby authorized and required to cause the same stone to be hammered and prepared accordingly." The cost of such hammering "shall never exceed in value the sum of ten thousand dollars." Two cannon, known as the Hancock and Adams, were also donated "to adorn the intended monument, and to be preserved as the earliest reliques of the revolutionary struggle," and five acres of land were to be measured off, appraised, and purchased "at their just value."

The great day itself was described in her usual exclamatory style by Mrs. Anna Royall, one of the country's first professional travel writers, in her book *Sketches of History, Life and Manners in the United States.*

✳

I was likewise present at the celebration of the battle of Bunker Hill; the greatest procession probably that ever took place in the history of America. . . . From a window in School-street, I viewed the procession from beginning to end. I should be at a loss to say with which part I was most pleased; the whole was grand beyond conception. The music of all New England was there, and all the Masons, which are numerous in those states; the bands were divided, and every lodge by itself, each leaving a small vacancy, with a splendid banner on which was the number and name of the lodge, and the state to which it belonged. The Knights all in black, with lofty black plumes waving in their hats, their black pointed aprons, Gen. Lafayette in an open carriage, the soldiers of the Revolution in open carriages (a venerable band) drove by young gentlemen of the first distinction in the city. It was a moving scene! But while our ecstasy was wrought up to the highest pitch, a dear old man, dressed in an old coat, and an old hat, passed under us. He was sitting in the front of the carriage, with his right hand extended, and in his hand he held an old continental shot bag, with the same bullets in it which he used in the battle of Bunker Hill. He gently waved it backwards and forwards from one side to the other, so that the people on each side might have a chance to see it; and continued to do so throughout the procession. The coat he had on, and the hat, were likewise those he wore in the battle. We saw distinctly several bullet holes in each—the solemn motion of the carriage! The effect cannot be described! Gen. Lafayette, and even the Knights, all glorious as they shone, shrunk into nothing beside this war-worn soldier! It transported us fifty years back, and we in imagination were fighting the battle of Bunker Hill. The sacred relic he bore in his hand seemed endued with speech; its effect, like an electric shock, flew through the lines, and held each heart in fond delusion. Not a word was uttered for several minutes! Till, "Did you see that?" whispered one to the other, whilst every cheek was wet! The music was ravishing, the Masons looked divine, and the Knights Templar like supernatural beings! The whole was not only grand, it was sublime! But our language is too poor for such occasions. The procession was about an hour and half passing through the street, and supposed to consist of eighty thousand persons, while we were favored throughout with one of the most brilliant suns.

The scene then shifted to the site of the future monument, where the principal speaker was Daniel Webster. Like most orators of his age, he spoke at great length and in a soaring, florid style much appreciated by his listeners. In the course of his speech, he turned toward the group of aged veterans who were gathered there, and addressed them thus:

Venerable men! You have come down to us from a former generation. Heaven has bounteously lengthened out your lives that you might behold this joyous day. You are now where you stood, fifty years ago this very hour, shoulder to shoulder, in the strife of your country. Behold, how altered! The same heavens are indeed over your heads; the same ocean rolls at your feet; but all else, how changed! You hear now no roar of hostile cannon, you see no mixed volumes of smoke and flame rising from burning Charlestown. The ground strewed with the dead and the dying; the impetuous charge; the steady and successful repulse; the loud call to repeated assault; the summoning of all that is manly to repeated resistance; a thousand bosoms freely and fearlessly bared in an instant to whatever of terror there may be in war and death; all these you have witnessed, but you witness them no more. All is peace. The heights of yonder metropolis, its towers and roofs, which you then saw filled with wives and children and country-men in distress and terror, and looking with unutterable emotions for the issue of the combat, have presented you to-day with the sight of its whole happy population, come out to welcome and greet you with an universal jubilee. . . . All is peace; and God has granted you this sight of your country's happiness ere you slumber in the grave forever. He has allowed you to behold and partake the reward of your patriotic toils; and he has allowed us, your sons and countrymen, to meet you here, and in the name of the present generation, in the name of your country, in the name of liberty, to thank you!

A Brief Outline of the Revolutionary War

May 28, 1754. Colonel Washington of Virginia, twenty-two, attacks a party of French and Indians near Fort Duquesne (Pittsburgh), setting off the French and Indian War.

July 1755. General Braddock defeated at Monongahela River.

May 1756. Britain declares war on France. Almost all Europe is soon involved in the Seven Years' War. After early reverses, the British, under the dynamic leadership of William Pitt the Elder, are victorious and drive the French out of Canada.

October 1760. George III, young and popular, comes to the throne, determined to rule as well as reign; Pitt is dismissed, the war ends in 1763 with the Treaty of Paris, but Anglo-French rivalry continues. To help pay off its huge National Debt, the London government tightens customs collection in the colonies, then introduces the Stamp Act (March 1765). Widespread resistance in all colonies, British goods boycotted, the Stamp Act Congress meets in New York. The act is repealed (March 1766); calm returns.

June 1767. London again tries to tax the colonies without their consent by imposing import duties on tea, glass, paint, etc. (the Townshend Revenue Act); colonies again refuse to import British goods.

June 1768. Boston mob attacks British customs officers who had seized John Hancock's sloop *Liberty* on suspicion of smuggling; two regiments sent to Boston to keep order. Growing friction between redcoats and townspeople.

March 5, 1770. The Boston Massacre. John Adams defends the soldiers at their trial; gets them off. Most Townshend Duties repealed; non-importation movement ends; calm again returns.

April 1773. Parliament passes the Tea Act; widespread resistance.

December 16, 1773. The Boston Tea Party. Prime Minister Lord North claims this is treason; Coercive (or Intolerable) Acts close the port of Boston and put Massachusetts under more direct British rule.

September 1774. Colonies convene First Continental Congress in Philadelphia. Militias drill.

April 19, 1775. British General Gage sends troops to Concord to arrest John Hancock and Sam Adams and seize military supplies. At Lexington redcoats are confronted by a company of minutemen; first shots of the war. On return to Boston the British are besieged.

June 17, 1775. Battle of Bunker Hill; British take the hill but lose over 1,000 troops. Stalemate follows; American army now commanded by George Washington.

January 10, 1776. Thomas Paine publishes *Common Sense*, advocating independence.

March 1776. General Sir William Howe evacuates Boston, sails for Halifax to re-group.

March–June 1776. Washington moves to New York expecting a British attack; France begins to supply money and weapons; British attack on Charleston, South Carolina, fails; American attempt to invade Canada also fails; British assemble large fleet and army at Staten Island, New York.

July 4, 1776. Declaration of Independence.

August 27, 1776. Americans defeated at Battle of Long Island, withdraw to Manhattan.

September 15, 1776. British land at Kip's Bay on east side of Manhattan; Washington retreats to Harlem Heights.

September 21, 1776. Fire destroys much of New York.

September 26, 1776. Benjamin Franklin appointed commissioner to negotiate alliance with France.

October 28, 1776. Battle of White Plains; Washington again retreats.

November 16, 1776. British take Fort Washington, on Manhattan, then take Fort Lee, New Jersey.

November–December 1776. Washington retreats across New Jersey, pursued by Lord Cornwallis; crosses the Delaware River into Pennsylvania.

December 12, 1776. Congress abandons Philadelphia for Baltimore.

December 26, 1776. Washington re-crosses the Delaware, scores historic victory against Hessians at Trenton.

January 3, 1777. Another victory for Washington at Princeton.

July 1777. Americans abandon Fort Ticonderoga on Lake Champlain as General Burgoyne's army approaches from Canada. August 16, large detachment of Hessians defeated at Bennington, Vermont. September, British getting bogged down. October, move to Saratoga; surrounded and outnumbered. October 17, entire army surrenders.

July 1777. General Sir William Howe leaves New York and heads south for Philadelphia by sea. August 25, arrives at Head of Elk. September 11, defeats Washington's army at Brandywine Creek. Congress flees, the British occupy Philadelphia. October 4, Washington's counterattack at Germantown fails. November 20, Americans abandon Fort Mercer, on Mud Island in the Delaware River. The British settle into Philadelphia for the winter, Washington encamps at nearby Valley Forge; joined by the Marquis de Lafayette and Baron von Steuben.

February 6, 1778. France signs alliance with the United States; war with Britain looms.

May 8, 1778. Sir Henry Clinton takes over as British commander in chief; evacuates Philadelphia. June 28, Washington mauls retreating British at Monmouth Court House, New Jersey; British return to New York, their headquarters for the rest of the war.

July 3, 1778. Loyalists and Indian allies attack settlers in Wyoming Valley, Pennsylvania, and Cherry Valley, New York. Punitive expedition under General John Sullivan destroys many Indian settlements (May–November 1779).

June 21, 1779. Spain declares war on Britain; combined Franco-Spanish fleet threatens invasion.

September 23, 1779. John Paul Jones in *Bonhomme Richard* defeats *Serapis* off Flamborough Head, England.

September–October 1779. French fleet and American troops besiege Savannah; repulsed.

January 1780. Southern campaign begins; Sir Henry Clinton lays siege to Charleston; succeeds. May 29, British Colonel Tarleton defeats Americans at Waxhaws.

July 11, 1780. Count Rochambeau and 5,000 French troops land at Newport, Rhode Island.

August 16, 1780. Lord Cornwallis defeats Horatio Gates at Battle of Camden.

September 25, 1780. Benedict Arnold's treason revealed.

October 7, 1780. Southern militia victorious at King's Mountain, South Carolina.

March 15, 1781. Cornwallis victorious at Guilford Courthouse moves north to Virginia.

May 1781. Washington and Rochambeau agree to attack New York.

August 1781. Cornwallis takes up position at Yorktown, Virginia. Washington abandons plan to attack New York, heads south.

August 30, 1781. De Grasse and French fleet arrive off Yorktown, blockade Cornwallis.

September 5–10, 1781. Protracted sea battle between British and French off Chesapeake Capes; British fleet withdraws to New York. Cornwallis surrounded by land and sea.

September 28, 1781. Siege begins.

October 19, 1781. British capitulate. The war is now effectively over.

For those who would like to read more about the people, places, and events covered in this book, here is a partial list of the sources that I have found most helpful. It is divided into three parts: secondary works of general interest, listed alphabetically by author; works consisting entirely or largely of original material that has been quoted throughout, also listed alphabetically by author; and chapter-by-chapter lists of sources for people, places, and events, generally listed as they make their first appearance.

Secondary works of general interest:

The Ideological Origins of the American Revolution by Bernard Bailyn (Cambridge: Harvard University Press, 1967); *Encyclopedia of the American Revolution* by Mark Mayo Boatner (New York: David McKay, 1974); *The Women of '76* by Sally Smith Booth (New York: Hastings House, 1973); *Cities in Revolt* by Carl Bridenbaugh (New York: Alfred A. Knopf, 1955); *Women in the American Revolution* by Paul Engle (Chicago: Follett Publishing Co., 1976); *Almost a Miracle* by John Ferling (New York, Oxford: Oxford University Press, 2007); *The Coming of the Revolution* by Lawrence Gipson (New York: Harper Torchbooks, 1962); *A Restless People: Americans in Rebellion* by Oscar and Lilian Handlin (New York: Doubleday, 1982); *Growth of the American Revolution, 1766–1775* by Bernard Knollenberg (New York: The Free Press, 1975); *The War for America* by Piers Mackesy (Cambridge: Harvard University Press, 1964); *From Resistance to Revolution* by Pauline Maier (New York: Alfred A. Knopf, 1972); *The Wind from America* by Claude Manceron (New York: Alfred A. Knopf, 1978); *The Glorious Cause* by Robert Middlekauf (New York, Oxford: Oxford University Press, 1982); *Origins of the*

American Revolution by John C. Miller (Boston: Little, Brown & Co., 1943); *The Story of the Continental Army* by Lynn Montross (New York: Barnes & Noble, 1967); *George III and the American Revolution* by Frank A. Mumby (New York: Kraus Reprint Co., 1970); *The Cousins' Wars* by Kevin Phillips (New York: Basic Books, 1999); *The American Revolution: A People's History* by Ray Raphael (New York: The New Press, 2001); *A New Age Now Begins,* two volumes, by Page Smith (New York: McGraw-Hill, 1976); *The Negro in the American Revolution* by Benjamin Quarles (New York: W.W. Norton, 1961); *Connecticut's Black Soldiers 1775–1783* by David O. White (Chester, Connecticut: Pequot Press, 1973).

Works largely or entirely composed of original material that has been quoted throughout:

The Lost War: Letters from British Officers during the American Revolution edited by Marion Balderston and David Syrett (New York: Horizon Press, 1975); *Connecticut Historical Collections* by John Warner Barber (New Haven: Durrie & Peck, 1838); *Historical Collections of the State of New York* by John W. Barber and Henry Howe (New York: S. Tuttle, 1841); *Reminiscences of an American Loyalist 1738–1789* by Jonathan Boucher (Boston: Houghton Mifflin, 1925); *Journal, or Historical Recollections of the American Events During the Revolutionary War* by Elias Boudinot (Philadelphia: Frederick Bourquin, 1894); *The Loyalists in Revolutionary America* by Robert Calhoon (New York: Harcourt Brace Jovanovich, 1965); *Unchained Voices: An Anthology of Black Authors in the English-speaking World of the 18th Century* by Victor Carretta (Lexington, Ky: University Press of Kentucky, 1996); *Documents of American History* edited by Henry Steele Commager (New York: Appleton-Century-Crofts, 1958); *The Spirit of 'Seventy-Six* edited by Henry Steele Commager and Richard B. Morris (New York: Harper & Row, 1958); *The Autobiography of Benjamin Rush, (His "Travels Through Life" Together with his Commonplace Book),* edited by George W. Corner (Princeton, N.J.: Princeton University

Press, 1948); *The Price of Loyalty: Tory Writings from the Revolutionary Era* edited by Catherine Crary (New York: McGraw-Hill Book Co., 1973); *The Revolution Remembered: Eyewitness Accounts of the War of Independence* edited by John C. Dann (Chicago: The University of Chicago Press, 1980); *Documents of the American Revolution*, twelve volumes, edited by K.G. Davies (Shannon: Irish University Press, 1976); *The Literary Diary of Ezra Stiles* edited by Franklin Bowditch Dexter (New York: Charles Scribner's Sons, 1901); *American Rebels*, by Richard Dorson (New York: Pantheon, 1953); *Letters from America* by William Eddis (Cambridge: Harvard University Press, 1969); *The Royal Commission on the Losses and Services of American Loyalists* edited by Hugh Edward Egerton (New York: Arno Press and *The New York Times*, 1969); *The Women of the American Revolution* by Elizabeth F. Ellet (New York: Haskell House Publishers, 1969); *American Archives, Fourth and Fifth Series* edited by Matthew St. Clair Clarke and Peter Force (Washington: Matthew St. Clair Clarke and Peter Force, 1837); *Documentary History of the American Revolution*, two volumes, by Robert W. Gibbes (New York: D. Appleton, 1855); *Colonies to Nation, a Documentary History of the American Revolution* edited by Jack P. Greene (New York: W.W. Norton, 1967); *Fragments of Revolutionary History* by Gaillard Hunt (Brooklyn, N.Y.: The Historical Printing Club, 1892); *Tracts of the American Revolution* edited by Merrill Jensen (Indianapolis: Bobbs-Merrill, 1966); *The American Revolutionaries, A History in their Own Words* edited by Milton Meltzer (New York: Thomas Y. Crowell, 1987); *Diary of the American Revolution*, two volumes, edited by Frank Moore (New York: Charles Scribner, 1860); *The American Revolution* by Richard B. Morris (Columbia, S.C.: University of South Carolina Press, 1971); *Chronicles of the American Revolution* originally compiled by Hezekiah Niles, edited by Alden T. Vaughan (New York: Grosset & Dunlap, 1965); *Narratives of the American Revolution* by Hugh Rankin (Chicago: The Lakeside Press, 1976); *Rebels and Redcoats* by George F. Scheer and Hugh Rankin (New York: World Publishing Co., 1957); *The Wealth of Nations* by Adam Smith (New York: Prometheus Books, 1991);

Memoir of Lieut. Col. Tench Tilghman by Tench Tilghman (Albany: J.Munsell, 1876); *The Literary History of the American Revolution* by Moses Coit Tyler (New York: Barnes & Noble, 1941); *History of the Rise, Progress and Termination of the American Revolution* by Mercy Otis Warren (Indianapolis: Liberty Fund, 1989); *Letters on the American Revolution* edited by Margaret W. Willard (Port Washington, N.Y.: Kennikat Press, 1925).

Chapter One

Books about life in eighteenth-century London and England include Mary Dorothy George's *London Life in the Eighteenth Century* (New York: Capricorn Books, 1965); Thomas Gray's *Correspondence of Thomas Gray,* edited by Paget Toynbee and Leonard Whibley (Oxford: The Clarendon Press, 1971); Derek Jarrett's *England in the Age of Hogarth* (New York: Viking Press, 1974); Dorothy Marshall's *Dr. Johnson's London* (New York: John Wiley & Sons, 1968); Richard Schwartz's *Daily Life in Johnson's London* (Madison: University of Wisconsin Press, 1983); A.S. Turberville's *Johnson's England* (Oxford: Oxford University Press, 1933); Arthur Young's *A Six Months' Tour through the North of England* (New York: Augustus M. Kelly, 1967); and *The Newgate Calendar, or Malefactors' Bloody Register* (New York: G.P. Putnam's Sons, 1932).

For Benjamin Franklin my principal sources were: *Autobiography* (New York: Dover Publications, 1996); H.W. Brands' *The First American* (New York: Anchor Books, 2002); the multivolume *Papers of Benjamin Franklin* edited by Leonard W. Labaree (New Haven: Yale University Press, 1959–present); Claude-Anne Lopez's *Mon Cher Papa: Franklin and the Ladies of Paris* (New Haven: Yale University Press, 1966); Edmund S. Morgan's *Benjamin Franklin* (New Haven: Yale University Press, 2002); Carl Van Doren's *Benjamin Franklin* (New York: Viking Press, 1938); and Gordon Wood's *The Americanization of Benjamin Franklin* (New York: The Penguin Press, 2004).

Most of James Boswell's adventures appear in *Boswell's London Journal 1762–1763* edited by Frederick A. Pottle (New York:

McGraw-Hill Book Co., 1950); for Casanova's adventures see his *Memoirs* (New York: The Modern Library, 1929).

For John Adams see the multivolume *Papers of John Adams* (Cambridge: Belknap Press, Harvard University Press, 1977–present); also the four-volume *Diary and Autobiography of John Adams* edited by L.H. Butterfield (New York: Atheneum, 1964). Many of the letters between Abigail and John Adams appear in *The Book of Abigail and John, 1762–1784* edited by L.H. Butterfield, Marc Friedlander, and Mary-Jo Kline (Cambridge: Harvard University Press, 1975). Biographies include *Dearest Friend, A Life of Abigail Adams* by Lynne Withey (New York: The Free Press, 1981); and two works both titled *John Adams*, one by Page Smith (New York: Doubleday, 1962); the other by David McCullough (New York: Simon & Schuster, 2001).

For George Washington see *George Washington: Writings* (New York: The Library of America, 1997); *George Washington* by John R. Alden (Baton Rouge: Louisiana State University Press, 1984); *George Washington*, four volumes, by James Thomas Flexner (Boston: Little, Brown & Co, 1965–1972); *An Imperfect God*, by Henry Wiencek (New York: Farrar, Straus and Giroux, 2003); *The Life of George Washington* by Mason L. Weems, ninth edition, edited by Marcus Cunliffe (Cambridge: The Belknap Press of Harvard University Press, 1962).

For King George III see *The Correspondence of King George III, 1760–1783*, six volumes, edited by Sir John Fortescue (London: Frank Cass, 1967); *George III, Lord North and the People* by Herbert Butterfield (New York: Russell & Russell, 1968); *George III and the Historians* by Herbert Butterfield (New York: Macmillan Co., 1959); *George III* by Christopher Hibbert (New York: Basic Books, 1998); *Wilkes and Liberty* by George Rudé (Oxford: Clarendon Press, 1965).

Other sources include: anonymous, *Grievances of the American Colonies Candidly Examined* (London: J.Almon, 1766); Edmund Burke's *Speeches and Letters on American Affairs* (London: J. M.

Dent, 1908); Lord Hervey's *Memoirs* (London: Macmillan, 1963); Sir Nathaniel Wraxall's *Historical Memoirs of My Own Time* (London: Kegan, Paul Trench, Trubner & Co, 1904); Horace Walpole's four-volume *Memoirs of the Reign of King George III* edited by Derek Jarrett (New Haven: Yale University Press, 2000); Samuel Curwen's *The Journal and Letters of Samuel Curwen* (New York: Da Capo Press,1970); Thomas Gray's *Correspondence*, edited by Paget Toynbee (Oxford: Oxford University Press, 1915); also his *Selected Letters* edited by Joseph Wood Krutch (New York: Farrar, Strauss, 1952); James Boswell's *Life of Johnson* (Oxford: Oxford University Press, 1904); Thomas Paine's *Collected Writings* (New York: The Library of America, 1995); Catharine Macaulay's *An Address to the People of England, Ireland, and Scotland, etc.* is included in *English Defenders of American Freedom* compiled by Paul Smith (Washington, D.C.: The Library of Congress, 1972); see also Bridget Hill's *The Republican Virago* (Oxford: Oxford University Press, 1992); Edward Gibbon's *Autobiography* (New York: Meridian Books, 1961); William Hickey's *Memoirs of William Hickey* edited by Alfred Spencer, (New York: Alfred A.Knopf, 1923); Captain Montresor's *The Montresor Journals* edited by G. Scull (New York: Collections of the New York Historical Society for the Year 1881). For Mrs. Montagu see *"Queen of the Blues," Her Letters and Friendships from 1762 to 1800* edited by Reginald Blunt (Boston: Houghton Mifflin, 1923); for Lord George Germain see *Lord George Germain* by Alan Valentine (Oxford: Oxford University Press, 1962) and for Lord North see *Lord North,* also by Alan Valentine (Norman: University of Oklahoma Press, 1967).

Chapter Two

Books about eighteenth-century Boston and New England include Oliver M. Dickerson's *Boston Under Military Rule as Revealed in A Journal of the Times* (Boston: Mt. Vernon Press, 1936); Esther Forbes's *Paul Revere and the World He Lived In* (Boston: Houghton Mifflin, 1942); Robert A. Gross's *The Minutemen and Their World*

(New York: Hill & Wang, 1976); Dr. Alexander Hamilton's *Itinerarium* is included in *Colonial American Travel Narratives* (New York: Penguin Classics, 1994); Howard Mumford Jones and Bessie Zaban Jones, editors, *The Many Voices of Boston* (Boston: Atlantic Monthly Press, 1975); Clifford K. Shipton's *New England Life in the Eighteenth Century* (Cambridge: Harvard University Press, 1963); Walter M. Whitehill's *Boston, A Topographical History* (Cambridge: Harvard University Press, 1959); Hiller Zobel's *The Boston Massacre* (New York: W.W. Norton, 1970).

Original American sources include Anna Green Winslow's *Diary of Anna Green Winslow, a Boston School Girl* (Boston: Houghton Mifflin, 1894); G. Herbert Renfro's *Life and Works of Phillis Wheatley* (Salem, New Hampshire: Ayer Co, 1993); *Letters and Diary of John Rowe, Boston Merchant* edited by Anne Rowe Cunningham (Boston: W.B. Clarke Co., 1903); *Recollections of Samuel Breck* (Philadelphia: Porter & Coates, 1877); Peter Oliver's *Origin and Progress of the American Rebellion* (Stanford: Stanford University Press, 1961); James Thacher's *Military Journal During the American Revolutionary War* (Boston: Cotton & Barnard, 1827); *Letters of John Andrews, Esq, of Boston, 1772–1776* (Cambridge: John Wilson & Sons, 1866); Rev. William Emerson's *Diaries and Letters of William Emerson* (privately printed by Amelia Forbes Emerson, 1972). For the Hodgkins letters see *This Glorious Cause* by Herbert T. Wade and Robert Lively (Princeton, N.J.: Princeton University Press, 1958).

For the British see Anne Hulton's *Letters of a Loyalist Lady* (Cambridge: Harvard University Press, 1927); John Barker's *The British in Boston, Being the Diary of Lieutenant John Barker* (Cambridge: Harvard University Press, 1924); John R. Alden's *General Gage in America* (Baton Rouge: Louisiana State University Press,1948); Ira Gruber's *The Howe Brothers and the American Revolution* (New York: Atheneum, 1972); *General Howe's Orderly Book* (New York: New York Historical Society, Vol. XVI, 1883); *The Papers of Cadwallader Colden* (New York: New York Historical Society, Vols. IX–X,

1876–7); Frederick Mackenzie's *Diary* (Cambridge: Harvard University Press,1930); Ensign Lister's *Concord Fight* (Cambridge: Harvard University Press, 1931); Fanny Burney's *Diary and Letters of Madame D'Arblay* (London: Macmillan & Co., 1904); W.G. Evelyn's *Memoirs and Letters of Captain W. Glanville Evelyn of the 4th Regiment* (New York: *The New York Times*, 1974); F. J. Hudleston's *Gentleman Johnny Burgoyne* (Indianapolis: Bobbs-Merrill, 1927); Richard J. Hargrove Jr.'s *General John Burgoyne* (Newark: University of Delaware Press, 1983); James Lunt's *John Burgoyne of Saratoga* (New York: Harcourt Brace Jovanovich, 1975).

Other topics: Bernard Bailyn's *The Ordeal of Thomas Hutchinson* (Cambridge: Harvard University Press, 1974); Benjamin W. Labaree's *The Boston Tea Party* (New York, Oxford: Oxford University Press, 1964); David Hackett Fischer's *Paul Revere's Ride* (New York, Oxford: Oxford University Press, 1994); anonymous, *The Lexington-Concord Battle Road* (Concord, Massachusetts: Concord Chamber of Commerce, no date); anonymous, *A Narrative of the Excursion and Ravages of the King's Troops* (Worcester, Massachusetts: Provincial Congress, 1775); anonymous, *The Nineteenth of April 1775: A Collection of First Hand Accounts* (Lincoln, Massachusetts: Sawtells of Somerset, 1968); Richard M. Ketchum's *Decisive Day: The Battle for Bunker Hill* (New York: Doubleday, 1962).

Chapter Three
Books about New York include Edwin Burrows' and Mike Wallace's *Gotham* (New York, Oxford: Oxford University Press, 1999); Robert A. East and Jacob Judd, editors, *The Loyalist Americans, a Focus on Greater New York* (Tarrytown, N.Y.: Sleepy Hollow Restorations, 1975); Barnet Schechter's *The Battle for New York* (New York: Walker & Co., 2002); Samuel Tallmadge's *Orderly Books for the Fourth New York Regiment* and *Diaries* edited by Almon W. Lauber (New York: University of the State of New York, 1932); Joseph Plumb Martin's *A Narrative of Some of the Adventures, Dangers and Sufferings of a Revolutionary Soldier* (New York: *The New*

York Times and Arno Press, 1962); Ambrose Serle's *The American Journal of Ambrose Serle, Secretary to Lord Howe, 1776–1778*, edited by Edward H. Tatum Jr. (San Marino, California: The Huntington Library, 1940); Philip Vickers Fithian's *Journal, 1775–1776*, edited by Robert Albion and Leonidas Dodson (Princeton, N.J.: Princeton University Press, 1934).

For the campaigns of 1776 see: Roger Lamb's *An Original and Authentic Journal of Occurrences During the Late American War from Its Commencement to the Year 1783* (Dublin: Wilkinson & Courtney, 1809) and *Memoir of His Own Life* (Dublin: J. Jones, 1811); Alexander Graydon's *Memoirs of His Own Times, with Reminiscences of the Men and Events of the Revolution* edited by John Stockton Littell (New York: *The New York Times* and Arno Press, 1969); Nicholas Cresswell's *The Journal of Nicholas Cresswell 1774–1777* (New York: The Dial Press, 1924); Varnum Lansing Collins, editor, *A Brief Narrative of the Ravages of the British and Hessians at Princeton in 1776–1777* (Princeton. N.J.: Princeton University Library, 1906); Timothy Dwight's *Travels in New England and New York* (New Haven: Timothy Dwight, 1821); Jemima Condict's *Jemima Condict, Her Book* (Newark, N.J.: The Carteret Book Club, 1930); David Hackett Fischer's *Washington's Crossing* (Oxford: Oxford University Press, 2004). John Fitzgerald's story appears in *Rebels and Redcoats* by George F. Scheer and Hugh Rankin (see above).

For the Hessians see: Rodney Atwood's *The Hessians* (Cambridge, U.K.: Cambridge University Press, 1980); Lieut. von Bardeleben's *The Diary of Lieut. von Bardeleben and other von Donop Regiment Documents* translated and edited by Bruce Burgoyne (Bowie, MD: Heritage Books, 1998); Carl Leopold von Baurmeister's *Revolution in America: Confidential Letters and Journals 1776–1784 of Adjutant General Major Baurmeister* translated and edited by Bernhard A. Uhlendorf (New Brunswick, N.J.: Rutgers University Press, 1957); also *Letters from Major Baurmeister to Colonel von Jungkenn 1777–1778*, edited by Bernhard A. Uhlendorf and Edna Vosper (Philadelphia: The Historical

Society of Pennsylvania, 1937); Bruce Burgoyne's *Enemy Views: The American Revolutionary War as Recorded by the Hessian Participants* (Bowie, MD: Heritage Books, 1996); Johann Ewald's *Diary of the American War,* translated and edited by Joseph P. Tustin (New Haven: Yale University Press, 1979); Ernst Kipping's *The Hessian View of America 1776–1783* (Monmouth Beach, N.J.: Philip Freneau Press, 1971); Ray Pettengill's *Letters from America 1776–1779* translated by Ray W. Pettengill (Cambridge: Houghton Mifflin, 1924); Johann Ernst Prechtel's *A Hessian Officer's Diary of the American Revolution* translated and edited by Bruce Burgoyne (Bowie, MD: Heritage Books, 1994); General Riedesel's *Memoirs, and Letters and Journals of Major General Riedesel* translated by William L. Stone (Albany: J. Munsell, 1868); Baroness von Riedesel's *Journal* translated by William L. Stone, edited by Hugh Rankin (Chicago: The Lakeside Press, 1976); Johann Gottfried Seume's *My Life* translated by Margaret Woelfel (William and Mary Quarterly, 3rd Series, Vol.V., 1948); William L. Stone, editor, *Letters of Brunswick and Hessian Officers During the American Revolution* (New York: Da Capo Press, 1970); J. F. Wasmus's *An Eyewitness Account of the American Revolution and New England Life: The Journal of J. F. Wasmus, German Company Surgeon, 1776–1783* translated by Helga Doblin, edited by Mary C. Lynn (New York: Greenwood Press, 1990).

Other accounts include Thomas Anburey's *Travels Through the Interior Parts of America in a Series of Letters* (London: William Lane, 1789); Lieut. James Hadden's *Hadden's Journal and Orderly Books* edited by Horatio Rogers (Boston: Gregg Press, 1972); Thomas Hughes' *A Journal, for his Amusement and Designed only for his Perusal by the Time he Attains the Age of 50 if He Lives so Long* (Cambridge, U.K.: Cambridge University Press, 1942); Elijah Fisher's *Journal While in the War for Independence and Continued Two Years After He Came to Maine* (Augusta, Maine: Badger and Manley, 1880). For Hannah Winthrop see *Warren-Adams Letters* (Boston: The Massachusetts Historical Society, 1925).

Chapter Four

Books about the war in Pennsylvania include Philip Vickers Fithian's *Journal 1775–1776 Written on the Virginia-Pennsylvania Frontier and in the Army Around New York,* edited by Franklin Bowditch Dexter (Princeton, N.J.: Princeton University Press, 1934); Margaret Morris' *Private Journal Kept During the Revolutionary War* edited by John W. Jackson (Philadelphia: George S. MacManus & Co, 1949); *The Journal and Occasional Writings of Sarah Wister* edited by Kathryn Zabelle Derounian (Rutherford, Madison, Teaneck: Fairleigh Dickinson University Press, 1987); *Extracts from the Journal of Elizabeth Drinker from 1759 to 1807* edited by Henry Biddle (Philadelphia: J.B. Lippincott, 1889); *Diary of Albigence Waldo* edited by Hugh Rankin (Chicago: The Lakeside Press, 1976); Friedrich Kapp's *The Life of Frederick William von Steuben* (Gansevoort, N.Y.: Corner House Historical Publications, 1999); for Becky Franks see Jacob Rader Marcus's *Early American Jewry: The Jews of Pennsylvania* (Philadelphia: Jewish Publication Society of America, 1953); William B.Willcox's *Portrait of a General: Sir Henry Clinton in the War of Independence* (New York: Alfred A. Knopf, 1964); Charles Willson Peale's *The Selected Papers of Charles Willson Peale and his Family* edited by Lillian B. Miller (New Haven: Yale University Press, 1983); for Mrs. Galloway see "Diary of Grace Galloway," Werner ed. (Penna. Mag. Hist. Biog., vol LV, pp 40–53); the Marquis de Chastellux's *Travels in North America in the Years 1780, 1781 and 1782* (Chapel Hill: University of North Carolina Press, 1963).

For Sullivan's Expedition see Barbara Graymont's *The Iroquois in the American Revolution* (Syracuse: Syracuse University Press, 1972); *Chainbreaker: The Revolutionary War Memoirs of Governor Blacksnake* edited by Thomas Abler (Lincoln: University of Nebraska Press, 1989); *A Narrative of the Life of Mary Jemison* by James E. Seaver (Norman: University of Oklahoma Press, 1992); William L. Stone's *The Life of Joseph Brant-Thayendanegea* (New York: Alexander V. Blake, 1838); *Journals of the Military Expedition of Major General*

John Sullivan Against the Six Nations of Indians in 1779 (Glendale, N.Y.: Benchmark Publishing Co., 1970).

Chapter Five

For Ebenezer Fox see *The Revolutionary Adventures of Ebenezer Fox of Roxbury, Massachusetts* (Chicago: The Lakeside Press, 1976); for Beaumarchais see *Les Français Sous les Trois Étoiles* by André Lasseraye (Paris, France: Désiré Janvier, 1935); see also *The Deane Papers* (New York: Collections of the New York Historical Society 1886, 1887 & 1889); for Alexander Hamilton see Ron Chernow's *Alexander Hamilton* (New York: Penguin Press, 2004); for John Paul Jones see *Memoirs of Rear-Admiral Paul Jones* (New York: Da Capo Press, 1972) and Samuel Eliot Morison's *John Paul Jones* (Boston: Little, Brown,1959); for Parson Woodforde see *James Woodforde: Diary of a Country Parson* (London: Humphrey Milford, Oxford University Press,1981); for more on the *Jersey* see Albert Greene's *Recollections of the Jersey Prison Ship, taken and prepared for publication from the original manuscript of the late Captain Thomas Dring, of Providence, R.I.* (Providence, R.I.: H. H. Brown, 1829).

Chapter Six

For the South in general see William Bartram's *Travels Through North and South Carolina, Georgia, East and West Florida* (New York: Dover Publications, 1955); Thomas Jefferson's *Notes on the State of Virginia* (New York: Penguin Classics, 1999); Janet Schaw's *Journal of a Lady of Quality* (New Haven: Yale University Press, 1934); Charles Woodmason's *The Carolina Backcountry on the Eve of the Revolution* (Chapel Hill: The University of North Carolina Press, 1953).

For the campaign in the South see Robert D. Bass's *The Green Dragoon: The Lives of Banastre Tarleton and Mary Robinson* (New York: Henry Holt and Co., 1957); Walter Hart Blumenthal's *Women Camp Followers of the American Revolution* (New York: Arno Press, 1974); James Collins's *A Revolutionary Soldier* (Clinton, La: Feliciana Democrat, 1859); Henry Lee's *Memoirs of the War in the Southern*

Department of the United States (New York: Arno Press, 1969); Gregory Massey's *John Laurens and the American Revolution* (Columbia: University of South Carolina Press, 2000); William Moultrie's *Memoirs of the American Revolution* (New York: David Longworth, 1902); Bernhard A.Uhlendorf's *The Siege of Charleston: Diaries and Letters of Hessian Officers from the von Jungkenn Papers in the William L. Clements Library* (Ann Arbor: University of Michigan Press, 1938); Franklin and Mary Wickwire's *Cornwallis: The American Adventure* (Boston: Houghton Mifflin, 1970); Eliza Wilkinson's *Letters of Eliza Wilkinson* (New York: Arno Press, 1969).

For the French see Alexandre Berthier's *Journal de la Campagne d'Amérique* (Easton, PA: The American Friends of Lafayette, 1952); Claude Blanchard's *The Journal of Claude Blanchard* translated by William Duane (New York: Arno Press, 1969); Ludwig von Closen's *The Revolutionary Journal of Baron Ludwig von Closen 1780–1783* translated by Evelyn A. Acomb (Chapel Hill: University of North Carolina Press, 1958); Marquis de Lafayette's *The Letters of Lafayette to Washington 1777–1791* edited by Louis Gottschalk (New York: privately printed, 1944); *Memoirs of the Duc de Lauzun,* translated by C.K. Scott Moncrieff (London: George Rutledge & Sons, 1928); Howard C. Rice. and Anne S.K. Brown's *Rochambeau's Army* (Princeton, N.J.: Princeton University Press, 1972); Karl Gustaf Tornquist's *The Naval Campaigns of Count de Grasse During the American Revolution* translated by Amandus Johnson (Philadelphia: Swedish Colonial Society, 1942); Arnold Whitridge's *Rochambeau* (New York: Macmillan, 1965).

Chapter Seven

For the 1826 celebration in Boston see Mrs. Royall's *Sketches of History, Life and Manners in the United States, by a Traveler* (New Haven: Printed for the Author, 1826); for the Bunker Hill Monument and for Daniel Webster's oration see *A Memorial of the American Patriots Who Fell at the Battle of Bunker June 17, 1775* (Boston: Printed by Order of the City Council, 1889).

INDEX